A Twentieth-Century
Musical Chronicle

A TWENTIETH-CENTURY MUSICAL CHRONICLE

Events 1900–1988

Compiled by
CHARLES J. HALL

Music Reference Collection, Number 20

GREENWOOD PRESS
New York • Westport, Connecticut • London

Library of Congress Cataloging-in-Publication Data

Hall, Charles J.
   A twentieth-century musical chronicle : events, 1900-1988 /
compiled by Charles J. Hall.
      p.   cm.—(Music reference collection, ISSN 0736-7740 ; no.
20)
   Includes bibliographies and index.
   ISBN 0-313-26577-1 (lib. bdg. : alk. paper)
   1. Music—20th century—Chronology.   I. Title.   II. Title: 20th-
century musical chronicle.   III. Series.
ML197.H15   1989
780'.9'.04—dc20   89-2138

British Library Cataloguing in Publication Data is available.

Library of Congress Catalog Card Number: 89-2138
ISBN: 0-313-26577-1
ISSN: 0736-7740

First published in 1989

Greenwood Press, Inc.
88 Post Road West, Westport, Connecticut 06881

Printed in the United States of America

The paper used in this book complies with the
Permanent Paper Standard issued by the National
Information Standards Organization (Z39.48-1984).

10 9 8 7 6 5 4 3 2 1

Contents

Preface

A Twentieth Century Musical Chronicle is the first of three volumes chronicling musical history since 1750. This project originated as program notes for a radio show broadcast in Michigan in the mid-70s in which musical selections of a given year were accompanied by commentary on contemporaneous events. The resulting books present musical events year-by-year in the context of political, social, and cultural history. Emphasis is on "art" music, but some highlights in popular genres are included. Information has been gathered from myriad sources--recognized authorities, magazines, newspapers and, when possible, directly from those who create musical history or their agents. Where different sources yield conflicting information about musical events, the author has chosen for the most part to accept the authority of the *New Grove Dictionary of Music and Musicians*.

Each year begins with selected World Events and Cultural Highlights. Musical Events follow, divided into nine sections: A. Births, B. Deaths, C. Debuts, D. New Positions, E. Prizes and Honors, F. Biographical Highlights, G. Institutional Openings, H. Musical Literature, and I. Musical Compositions. Category C. covers three types of debuts: original debuts (with location); a U.S. debut, when different (also with location), and the Met debut for singers and conductors. Other debuts, such as those in Paris, Vienna or Covent Garden, may be found under F. Biographical Highlights. The dates given for compositions under Category I are actual completion dates rather than premieres; however, it is not always possible to make the distinction. A detailed index provides access from the name or term to the year and category letter.

A word of acknowledgment should be given to those who helped and gave encouragement, to the many students who pored over the tomes in search of obscure items and pounded the typewriter keys, and to my wife who patiently put up with me in the hectic days of getting all the resources together; and a special word of thanks is due Allyn Craig, without whose computer expertise I could not have survived.

Charles J. Hall
B.M., M.M., Ph.D.

Abbreviations

COUNTRIES

Am	United States	Fin	Finland	Pan	Panama
Arm	Armenia	Fr	France	Peru	Peru
Arg	Argentina	Ger	Germany	Phil	Philippines
Aus	Austria	Gr	Greece	Pol	Poland
Aust	Australia	Hol	Holland	Por	Portugal
Azer	Azerbaijan	Hun	Hungary	P.R.	Puerto Rico
Bel	Belgium	Ind	India	Rom	Romania
Boh	Bohemia	Ir	Ireland	Rus	Russia (USSR)
Bol	Bolivia	Iran	Iran	Scot	Scotland
Br	Great Britain	Is	Israel	Serb	Serbia
Bra	Brazil	It	Italy	S.Af.	South Africa
Bul	Bulgaria	Jp	Japan	Sp	Spain
Can	Canada	Kor	Korea	Swe	Sweden
Chi	China	Lat	Latvia	Swi	Switzerland
Chil	Chile	Leb	Lebanon	Tai	Taiwan
Cub	Cuba	Lith	Lithuania	Tur	Turkey
Cz	Czechoslovakia	Man	Manchuria	Urg	Uruguay
Den	Denmark	Mex	Mexico	Ven	Venezuela
Egypt	Egypt	Nor	Norway	Yug	Yugoslavia
Est	Estonia	N.Z.	New Zealand		

PROFESSIONS

acous	acoustics	fl.m	flute maker	pat	patron of arts
act	actor, actress	folk	folk music	ped	pedagogue
alto	contralto	gui	guitar	perc	percussion
arr	arranger	harm	harmonica	pop	popular artist
au	author	hn	horn virtuoso	pn	piano
bal	ballet	hp	harp	pt	poet
band	band	hp.m	harp maker	pub	publisher
bar	baritone	hps	harpsichord	rec	recorder
bn	bassoon	hum	humorist	rel	religion
bs	bass	hymn	hymn writer	sax	saxophone
cas	castrato	imp	impresario	scul	sculptor
cb	contrabass	ind	industrialist	sing	singer
cd	conductor	inv	inventor	sop	soprano
cel	cello	lib	librettist	ten	tenor
clar	clarinet	mez	mezzosoprano	the	theory
cm	composer	m.ed	music educator	tpt	trumpet
cri	music critic	mus	musicology or	vn	violin
c.ten	countertenor		music history	vla	viola
ed	educator	ob	oboe	voc	vocalist
film	film music	org	organ	ww.m	woodwind maker
fl	flute	org.m	organ maker		

The above abbreviations are found primarily in the Births and Deaths of each year. The country given in each case is the country of birth, except in rare cases where the parents are residing temporarily in another country.

THE CHRONICLE,
1900–1988

1900

World Events:
The U.S. census shows a population of 76,212,000 in 45 states, an increase of 21% in ten years; by Congressional action, Hawaii becomes a U.S. territory; William McKinley is re-elected President; Carrie Nation begins her hatchet crusade against liquor. Internationally, the Boxer Rebellion comes to an end in China with help from the U.S. and other western powers; in Europe, Victor Emanuel III becomes king of Italy; the Paris Universal Exposition draws world-wide crowds; Ibn Saud forms the Kingdom of Saudi Arabia; British Labor Party formed; the first rigid dirigible flight is made by Count Zeppelin in Germany.

Cultural Highlights:
Doves Press, a private printing press, is founded at Hammersmith; the Wallace Collection at Hartford House in London opens to the public. Deaths in the field of art include American artist Frederick Church, German artist Wilhelm Liebl, French sculptor Jean Falguière and British art critic John Ruskin; the world of literature loses Russian novelist Dmitri Grigorovich, American novelist Stephen Crane and poet Richard Hovey, Irish novelist Oscar Wilde and poet William Lariminie, British novelist Richard Blackmore and poet Richard Dixon; Born are American authors Taylor Caldwell, Margaret Mitchell and Thomas Wolfe, British novelist James Hilton, Greek poet George Seferis, Austrian author Hermann Reutter, Canadian poet Robert Finch and German novelist Anna Seghers; births in the art field include French artist Yves Tanguy and American sculptor Louise Nevelson. Other highlights include:

Art: Pierre Bonnard, *Man and Woman*; Émile Bourdelle, *Head of Apollo*; Thomas Eakins, *The Thinker*; Henri Matisse, *Notre Dame*; Pablo Picasso, *Le Moulin de la Galette*; Auguste Rodin, *The Gates of Hell*; John S. Sargent, *Wyndham Sisters*; Henri Toulouse-Latrec, *La Modiste*; John Twachtman, *Frozen Brook*; Édouard Vuillard, *Waiting*.

Literature: Frank Baum, *The Wonderful Wizard of Oz*; Anton Chekhov, *Uncle Vanya*; Joseph Conrad, *Lord Jim*; Theodore Dreiser, *Sister Carrie*; Sigmund Freud, *Interpretation of Dreams*; Jack London, *Son of the Wolf*; George Bernard Shaw, *Caesar and Cleopatra*; Booth Tarkington, *Monsieur Beaucaire*; William Yeats, *The Shadowy Waters*.

MUSICAL EVENTS

A. Births:

Jan 26	Karl Ristenpart (Ger-cd)	Jun 26	Richard Crooks (Am-ten)
Mar 2	Kurt Weill (Ger-cm)	Jul 8	George Antheil (Am-cm)
Mar 6	Gina Cigna (It-sop)	Jul 26	Jacques Février (Fr-pn)
Mar 21	Paul Kletzki (Pol-cd)	Aug 10	Alexander Mossolov (Rus-cm)
Apr 14	Salvatore Baccaloni (It-bs)	Aug 23	Ernst Krenek (Ger-cm)
Apr 26	Joseph Fuchs (Am-vn)	Oct 19	Erna Berger (Ger-sop)
May 5	Hans Schmidt-Isserstedt (Ger-cd)	Nov 7	Efrem Kurtz (Ger-cd)
		Nov 14	Aaron Copland (Am-cm)
May 22	Vina Bovy (Bel-sop)	Nov 25	Tibor Serly (Hun-vn-cd)
Jun 9	Fred Waring (Am-cd)	Dec 13	Jonel Perlea (Cz-cd)
Jun 15	Otto Luening (Am-cm)	Dec 25	Gladys Swarthout (Am-sop)
Jun 22	Jennie Tourel (Am-mez)		

B. Deaths:

Jan 3	Edwin G. Monk (Br-org)	May 25	Giuseppe del Puente (It-bar)
Feb 3	Ottokar Nováček (Hun-vn)	May 28	George Grove (Br-mus)
Mar 6	Karl Bechstein (Ger-pn.m)	Jul 4	Charles Adams (Am-ten)
Mar 10	Johann Hartman (Den-cm)	Aug 11	Franz Betz (Ger-bar)
Mar 19	Charles L. Hanon (Fr-pn)	Oct 15	Zdenek Fibich (Cz-cm)
Apr 21	Heinrich Vogl (Ger-ten)	Nov 22	Arthur Sullivan (Br-cm)
May 13	Hermann Levi (Ger-cd)	Dec 8	Henry Russell (Br-ten)

C. Debuts:

Met ---Theodor Bertram (bar), Lynn Blair (sop), Robert Blass (bs), Arturo Borin (bar), Isabelle Bouton (mez), Carrie Bridewell (mez), Hans Breuer (ten), Eleonora de Cisneros (alto), Philippe Fion (cd), Fritz Friedrichs (bar), Johanna Gadski (sop), Charles Gilibert (bs), Louise Homer (alto), Marcel Journet (bs), Aristide Masiero (ten), Fritzi Scheff (sop), Ernst von Schuch (cd), Milka Ternina (sop), Minnie Tracy (sop)

U.S. --Harold Bauer (Boston), Ossip Gabrilowitsch (N.Y.), Edwin Lemare (tour)

Other -Pasquale Amato (Naples), Jane Bathori (Nantes), Paul Bender (Breslau), Arthur Bodanski (Vienna), Lina Cavalieri (San Carlo), Povla Frijsh (Paris), Mary Garden (Paris), Blanche Marchesi (Prague), Friedrich Plaschke (Dresden), Joseph Schwarz (Linz), Tullio Serafin (Ferrara), Clarence Whitehill (Paris)

D. New Positions:

Conductors: Frederick Cowen (London PO), Ferdinand Löwe (Vienna SO), Fritz Scheel (Philadelphia Orchestra)

Educational: Granville Bantock (music director, Birmingham Institute), Rudolf Ganz (piano, Chicago Musical College), Samuel de Lange (director, Stuttgart Conservatory), Charles H. Parry (professor, Oxford)

Others: Wilhelm Altmann (Royal Library, Berlin), Charles Ives (organ, Central Presbyterian Church, N.Y.), John J. McClellan (organ, Mormon Tabernacle), Henry Newbolt (editor, *Monthly Review*), Louis Vierne (organ, Notre Dame)

E. Prizes and Honors:

Prizes: Alexander Goedicke (Rubinstein), Paul M. Lanowski and Florent Schmitt (Prix de Rome)

Honors: Gustav Charpentier (Legion of Honor), Edward Elgar (honorary doctorate, Cambridge)

F. Biographical Highlights:

Béla Bartók's schooling is interrupted by a severe bout of pneumonia; Arnold Bax enters the Royal Academy of Music in London; Ernst Bloch studies with Knorr at the Hoch Conservatory in Frankfurt; Nadia Boulanger enters Paris Conservatory; Enrico Caruso makes his La Scala début; Manuel de Falla's family loses a fortune and moves to Madrid; Zoltán Kodály enters Budapest University but studies composition with Koessler at the Conservatory; Nicolai Medtner graduates from the Moscow Conservatory with a gold medal; Wallingford Riegger and family move to New York where he begins serious music study at the Institute of Musical Art; Artur Schnabel moves to Berlin; Leo Slezak and Edyth Walker make their Covent Garden débuts; Moritz Steiner donates his instrument collection to Yale University; Edgard Varèse begins music study with Bolzoni in Turin; Ermanno Wolf-Ferrari decides to return to Munich where he is appreciated.

G. Institutional Openings:

Performing Groups: Cherniavsky Trio, Dallas SO, Honolulu SO, Filharmoniska Sällskapet (Stockholm Choir), Huddersfield Chamber Music Society, Philadelphia Orchestra, Vienna SO

Festivals: Bethlehem Bach Festival (Pennsylvania)

Educational: Paderewski Foundation (N.Y.), Seminar für Schulgesang (Berlin)

Other: Cahiers de la Quinzaine, Casa Dotesio (Unión Musical Española) Publishing Co. (Spain), Melville Clark Piano Co., Hall of Fame for Great Americans, "His Master's Voice" (patent by Emil Berliner), King Cole Chamber Music Club (London), Leedy Manufacturing Co. (Indianapolis), People's Symphony Concerts (N.Y.), Society of Classical Concerts (Barcelona), Symphony Hall (Boston), Tonal Art Club (London Musician's Club), *Weiner Konzerthausgesellschaft*

H. Musical Literature:
Abrányi, Kornél, *Hungarian Music in the 19th Century*
Baker, Theodore, *Baker's Biographical Dictionary of Musicians*
Eitner, Robert, *Biographisch-Bibliographisches Quellen-Lexicon der Musiker...I*
Galli, Amintore, *Estetica della musica*
Hanslick, Eduard, *Aus Neuer und Neuster Zeit*
Hughes, Rupert, *Contemporary American Composers*
d'Indy, Vincent, *Cours de Composition Musicale I*
MacPherson, Stewart, *Practical Counterpoint*
Riemann, Hugo, *Musikalische Rückblick--Die Elemente der Musikalischen Aesthetic*
Specht, Richard, *Kritisches Skizzenbuch*

I. Musical Compositions:
Arensky, Anton, *Egyptian Nights* (ballet)
Chadwick, George, *Judith* (opera)
Charpentier, Gustave, *Louise* (opera)
Coleridge-Taylor, Samuel, *Hiawatha's Departure* (cantata)
Converse, Frederick, *Festival of Pan* (orchestra)
Cui, Cesar, *Mam'zelle Fifi* (opera)
Drigo, Riccardo, *Les Millions d'Arlequin* (ballet)
Dvorák, Antonin, *Russalka, Op. 114* (opera)
Elgar, Edward, *The Dream of Gerontius, Op. 38* (oratorio)
Fauré, Gabriel, *Prométhée, Op. 82* (opera)
Fibich, Zdenek, *The Fall of Arkun* (opera)
Foerster, Josef B., *My Youth, Opus 44* (symphonic poem)
Glazunov, Alexander, *Ruses d'Amour* (ballet)
Glière, Reinhold, *Symphony No. 1, Op. 8*
Grieg, Edvard, *10 Songs, Op. 69, 70*
Herbert, Victor, *The Viceroy* (cantata)
               Episodes Amoureuses (orchestra)
Ippolitov-Ivanov, Mikhail, *Asya* (opera)
Lecocq, Charles, *La Belle au Bois Dormant* (operetta)
Leoncavallo, Ruggiero, *Zaza* (opera)
               Requiem for King Umberto I
MacDowell, Edward, *Piano Sonata No. 3, Op. 57, "Norse"*
MacKenzie, Alexander, *The Cricket on the Hearth* (opera)
Mahler, Gustave, *Symphony No. 4* (with soprano)
Mascagni, Pietro, *Requiem in Memory of King Umberto I*
Massenet, Jules, *Phèdre* (incidental music)
Paderewski, Ignace Jan, *Manru* (opera)
Paine, John Knowles, *Azara* (opera)
Puccini, Giacomo, *Tosca* (opera)
Rimsky-Korsakov, Nicolai, *Tsar Saltan* (opera)
Scriabin, Alexander, *Symphony No. 1, Op. 26j*
Strauss, Richard, *15 Songs, Op. 46, 47, 48*
Suk, Josef, *Pohádka, Opus 16* (orchestra)
Sullivan, Arthur, *The Rose of Persia* (opera)
Vaughan-Williams, Ralph, *Bucolic Suite* (orchestra)
Wolf-Ferrari, Ermano, *Cenerentola* (opera)

1901

World Events:

In the U.S., Theodore Roosevelt becomes President No. 26 when President McKinley is assassinated by anarchist Leon Czolgosz; former president Benjamin Harrison dies; New York issues the first known auto licenses; the Hay-Pauncefote Treaty opens the way for a U.S.-built Panama Canal. Internationally, Queen Victoria dies and Edward VII becomes British monarch; the Commonwealth of Australia is formed; the Phillipines seeks to form its own democratic system of government as a U.S. protectorate; Guglielmo Marconi sends the first transatlantic wireless message.

Cultural Highlights:

The American School of Playwriting opens in New York while the Nobel Prize for Literature goes to the French author René Sully Prudhomme. Deaths in the field of art include Swiss artist Arnold Böcklin, Swedish artist Johann A. Malmström, French artists Jean Charles Cazin and Henri Toulouse-Latrec; in the literary field, British authors Walter Besant and Robert Buchanan. Births include the French artist Jean Dubuffet, American sculptor Richmond Barthé and artist Philip Evergood, Italian sculptor Marino Marini and Scotch artist Joseph Paton; the literary field loses German novelist Heinrich Hauser and Italian poet Salvatore Quasimodo. Other highlights include:

Art: Maurice Denis, *Homage à Cézanne*; Paul Gauguin, *The Gold in their Bodies*; William Glackens, *Hammerstein's Roof Garden*; Aristide Maillol, *Seated Woman*; Maurice Prendergast, *Central Park*; Pierre Renoir, *Flowers in a Vase*; Everett Shinn, *Early Morning, Paris*; Henri Toulouse-Latrec, *Opera Messalina*; Maurice Vlaminck, *The Dock at Bougival*.

Literature: *The Bible: American Revised*; Anton Chekhov, *The Three Sisters*; Hamlin Garland, *Her Mountain Lover*; Thomas Hardy, *Poems of the Past and Present*; Thomas Mann, *Buddenbrooks*; Frank Norris, *The Octopus*; Rudyard Kipling, *Kim*; August Strindberg, *The Dance of Death*; Booker T. Washington, *Up from Slavery*.

MUSICAL EVENTS

A. Births:

Jan 7	John Brownlee (Aust-bar)	Jul 14	Gerald Finzi (Br-cm)
Feb 2	Jascha Heifetz (Rus-vn)	Jul 16	Fritz Mahler (Ger-cd)
Feb 16	Tomáz Alcaide (Por-ten)	Jul 31	Alexander Schreiner (Am-org)
Mar 15	Colin McPhee (Am-cm)	Aug 14	Franz Konwitschny (Ger-cd)
Mar 16	Marta Krásová (Cz-alto)	Aug 28	John Corigliano (Am-vn)
Mar 22	Oliver Strunk (Am-mus)	Aug 28	Paul Henry Lang (Am-cri)
May 7	Marcel Poot (Bel-cm)	Sep 3	Edward van Beinum (Hol-cd)
May 17	Werner Egk (Ger-cm)	Nov 1	H.H. Stuckenschmidt (Ger-cri)
May 17	Max Lorenz (Ger-ten)	Nov 21	Giacomo Vaghi (It-bs)
May 23	Edmund Rubbra (Br-cm)	Nov 25	Adele Kern (Ger-sop)
Jun 16	Conrad Beck (Swi-cm)	Nov 25	Tibor Serly (Hun-cm)
Jun 24	Harry Partch (Am-cm)	Dec 5	Grace Moore (Am-sop)
Jun 29	Nelson Eddy (Am-bar)	Dec 22	André Kostelanetz (Am-cd)
Jul 3	Ruth Crawford (Am-cm)	Dec 26	Victor Hely-Hutchinson (Br-cm)

B. Deaths:

Jan 11	Vasily Kalinnikov (Rus-cm)	May 1	Georg Vierling (Ger-org)
Jan 27	Giuseppe Verdi (It-cm)	Jul 19	Alfredo Piatti (It-cel)
Feb 17	Ethelbert Nevin (Am-cm)	Sep 3	Karl F. Chrysander (Aus-mus)
Mar 8	Pierre Benoît (Bel-cm)	Sep 6	Johann G. Leitert (Ger-pn)
Mar 31	John Stainer (Br-org-cm)	Sep 28	Adelaide Borghi (It-mez)
Apr 3	Richard d'Oyly Carte (Br-imp)	Nov 25	Josef Rheinberger (Ger-org)

C. Débuts:
Met ---Lucienne Bréval (sop), Maurice Declery (bar), Marguerite MacIntyre (sop), Marguerite Marylli (sop), Marie Mattfield (mez), Albert Quesnel (ten), Albert Reiss (ten)

U.S. --Florence Austin (N.Y.), E. Azalia Hackley (Denver)

Other -Richard Buhlig (Berlin), Julia Culp (Magdeburg), Geraldine Farrar (Berlin), Rita Fornia (Hamburg), Mieczyslaw Horszowski (Warsaw), Serge Koussevitsky (Moscow), Frieda Langendorff (Strassbourg), Margarete Matzenauer (Strassbourg), Maria Philippi (Paris), Tina Poli-Randaccio (Bergamo), Karl Seydel (Altenburg), Leo Slezak (Vienna), Laurent Swolfs (Antwerp), Hermann Weil (Freiburg).

D. New Positions:
Conductors: Charles V. Stanford (Leeds Festival), Bruno Walter (assistant to Mahler, Vienna)

Educational: Frederick Converse (composition, Harvard), Willem Kes (director, Moscow Music School), Emil von Sauer (piano, Vienna Conservatory)

Others: Hugh Allen (organ, New College, Oxford), Claude Debussy (music critic, *La Revue Blanche*), Lawrence Gilman (music critic, *Harper's Weekly*), Richard Terry (organ, Westminster Cathedral)

E. Prizes and Honors:
Prizes: André Caplet (Prix de Rome), Henry Hadley (Paderewski), Fernand Leborne (Chartier)

Honors: Carl Nielsen (annual state pension), Charles V. Stanford (knighted), Joseph Suk (Czech Academy of Sciences)

F. Biographical Highlights:
Ernst Bloch begins studying private lessons with Ludwig Thuille in Munich; Ferruccio Busoni teaches piano in Weimar for a year; Feodor Chaliapin makes his first appearance outside Russia as Mephistopheles in Boito's opera at La Scala; Emmy Destinn makes her Bayreuth debut as Senta; Gustav Holst marries Isobel Harrison; Lilli Lehmann begins her long association with the Salzburg Festivals; Max Reger decides to leave Weiden and makes Munich the center of his concert tours; Arnold Schoenberg marries Alexander Zemlinsky's sister, Mathilde; Leo Slezak is called by Mahler to Vienna where he begins a long and active career; Johan Svendsen marries his second wife Juliette Hasse; Karol Szymanowski goes to Warsaw for music study with Moskowski.

G. Institutional Openings:
Performing Groups: Choral Arts Society of Boston, Czech PO, Glasgow Orpheus Choir, Liverpool Welsh Choral Union, Moscow Symphonic Chapel, Poznán Musical Society, Slovene Philharmonia (Ljubljana), Société des Instruments Anciens Casadesus, Verein der Musikfreunde (Kiel), Warsaw PO

Educational: Academia Granados (Barcelona)

Other: Bechstein (Wigmore) Hall (London), C.C. Birchard Co. (Boston), Brook Mays Music (Dallas), *Church Music Review*; George G. Harrap and Co., Ltd. (London); *Musical Record and Review*, *Die Musik*, *Revue d'Histoire et de Critique Musicale*, Skinner Organ Co. (Dorchester, Mass.), Universal Edition (Vienna), Wa-Wan Press (Boston)

H. Musical Literature:
Apthorp, William F., *Opera, Past and Present*
Banister, Henry C., *The Art of Modulating*
Clarke, Hugh A., *Highways and By-ways of Music*
Dreves, Guido M., *Psalteria Rhythmica*
Dubois, Théodore, *Traité de Contrepoint et de Fugue*
Elson, Arthur, *A Critical History of Opera*

Galli, Amintore, *Storia e teoria del sistemes musicale*
Gédalge, André, *Traité de la Fugue*
Krüger, Felix, *Über das Bewusstein de Konsonanz*
Mantuani, Josef, *Über den Beginn des Notendrucks*

I. Musical Compositions:
Bond, Carrie Jacobs, *I Love You Truly* (song)
Coleridge-Taylor, Samuel, *Toussaint l'Ouverture* (orchestra)
            The Blind Girl of Castel Cuille (opera)
Converse, Frederick, *Endymion's Narrative* (orchestra)
Cui, Cesar, *Matteo Falcone* (opera)
Debussy, Claude, *Pour le Piano*
Delius, Frederick, *A Village Romeo and Juliet* (opera)
Elgar, Edward, *Pomp and Circumstance Marches 1 and 2*
            Cockaigne Overture, Opus 40
Enescu, Georges, *Romanian Rhapsody No. 1*
            Symphonie Concertante, Opus 88 (cello, orchestra)
Fauré, Gabriel, *La Viole du Bonheur, Opus 88* (incidental music)
Glazunov, Alexander, *Solemn Overture, Opus 73*
            Chant de Ménestral (cello, orchestra)
Grieg, Edvard, *Lyric Pieces, Book 10, Opus 71* (piano)
Hadley, Henry, *Symphony No. 2, "Four Seasons"*
Herbert, Victor, *Hero and Leander* (symphonic poem)
            Woodland Fancies (orchestra)
Ives, Charles, *From the Steeples and Mountains*
            The Children's Hour (song)
Koven, Reginald de, *Maid Marion* (operetta)
MacDowell, Edward, *Sonata No. 4, "Keltic"* (piano)
Mascagni, Pietro, *La Maschere* (opera)
Massenet, Jules, *Grisélidis* (opera)
Pierné, Gabriel, *Concertstücke for Harp and Orchestra*
Rachmaninoff, Serge, *Concerto No. 2, Opus 18, for Piano and Orchestra*
            Suite No. 2 for Two Pianos, Opus 17
Ravel, Maurice, *Jeux d'Eau* (piano)
Rimsky-Korsakov, Nicolai, *Servilia* (opera)
Saint-Saëns, Camille, *Les Barbares* (opera)
Schoenberg, Arnold, *Gurre-Lieder* (secular cantata)
Scriabin, Alexander, *2 Piano Preludes, Opus 27*
Sibelius, Jan, *Symphony No. 2 in D, Opus 43*
Stanford, Charles V., *Much Ado about Nothing* (opera)
Strauss, Richard, *Feuersnot, Opus 50* (opera)
Sullivan, Arthur, *The Emerald Isle* (opera completed by German)
Vaughan-Williams, Ralph, *Serenade for Small Orchestra*

1902

World Events:
In the U.S., the Chinese Exclusion Act limits the number of Chinese that may enter the country in any year; the Drago Doctrine promotes the protection of South American countries; the Carnegie Institution Foundation, the American Philosophical Association and Crater Lake National Park all are established. Internationally, Cuba becomes a republic when U.S. occupation ceases; the Boer War in South Africa ends with a British victory; England and Japan sign a treaty recognizing the independence of China and Korea; the International Women's Suffrage Alliance is formed; the Sinn Fein Party is founded in Ireland.

Cultural Highlights:
The Borghese villa and art collection is acquired by the Italian government. The Nobel Prize for Literature goes to the German scholar Theodor Mommsen. Births in the literature field include American novelist John Steinbeck and humorist poet Ogden Nash; deaths include American writers Edward Eggleston, Bret Harte and Frank Norris, German poets Hermann Allmers, Julius Grosse and Wilhelm Hertz, British poet Phillip J. Bailey and author Samuel Butler, Irish poet Aubrey T. de Vere and French novelist Émile Zola. The art world loses French sculptor Aimé Jules Dalou and artist James J. Tissot and American artist John Twachtman. Other highlights include:

Art: Thomas Eakins, *Self-Portrait*; Paul Gauguin, *The Call*; Robert Henri, *Fifty-Seventh Street*; Henri Matisse, *Notre Dame*; Claude Monet, *Waterloo Bridge*; Camille Pissarro, *Corner of the Meadow, Eragny*; Pierre Renoir, *Reclining Bather*; Auguste Rodin, *Romeo and Juliet*; Everett Shinn, *London Hippodrome*; John H. Twachtman, *Hemlock Pool*.

Literature: Arnold Bennett, *Anna of the Five Towns*; Arthur C. Doyle, *The Hound of the Baskervilles*; Rudyard Kipling, *Just-So Stories*; Maurice Maeterlinck, *Monna Vanna*; Alfred E. Mason, *The Four Feathers*; Beatrix Potter, *The Tale of Peter Rabbit*; Edith Wharton, *The Valley of Decision*; Owen Wister, *The Virginian*.

MUSICAL EVENTS

A. Births:

Jan 9	Rudolf Bing (Br-imp)	Jun 15	Max Rudolf (Ger-cd)
Jan 11	Maurice Duruflé (Fr-org)	Jun 23	Mimi Balkanska (Bul-sop)
Feb 11	Hans Redlich (Aus-mus)	Jun 26	Antonia Brico (Am-cd)
Feb 12	Anny Konetzni (Aus-sop)	Jun 26	Hugues Cuenod (Swi-ten)
Feb 16	Stefan Wolpe (Aus-cm)	Jun 28	Richard Rodgers (Am-cm)
Feb 17	Marian Anderson (Am-alto)	Aug	Gaby Casadesus (Fr-pn)
Mar 29	William Walton (Br-cm)	Aug 6	Margarete Kiose (Ger-alto)
Mar 31	Hans Albrecht (Ger-mus)	Aug 9	Zino Francescatti (Fr-vn)
Apr 8	Joseph Krips (Aus-cd)	Aug 9	Solomon (Br-pn)
May 5	Erick Schenk (Aus-mus)	Sep 28	Donald Jay Grout (Am-mus)
May 11	Bidú Sayao (Bra-sop)	Nov 1	Eugen Jochum (Ger-cd)
May 17	Fausto Cleva (Yug-cd)	Nov 7	Jesús M. Sanromá (P.R.-pn)
May 17	John Vincent (Am-cm-au)	Nov 22	Emanuel Feuermann (Aus-cel)
May 18	Meredith Willson (Am-cm)	Nov 22	Joaquin Rodrigo (Sp-cm)
May 20	Geneviève Thibault (Fr-mus)	Dec 19	Dusolina Gianini (Am-sop)
Jun 11	Vissarion Shebalin (Rus-cm)		

B. Deaths:

Jan 9	Gustav Rebling (Ger-org)	Jul 16	Heinrich Hoffmann (Ger-pn)
Feb 1	Solomon Jadassohn (Ger-the)	Aug 23	Teresa Stolz (Boh-sop)
Mar 21	Franz Nachbaur (Ger-ten)	Sep 7	Franz Wüllner (Ger-cm-cd)
Apr 18	Anna Schimon-Regan (Ger-sop)	Dec 3	Feodor Stravinsky (Rus-bs)

C. Débuts:

Met ---George Anthes (ten), Alexander Bandrowski-Sas (ten), Carlo Dani (ten), Signor Fanelli (bs), Emil Gerhäuser (ten), Alfred Hertz (cd), Estelle Liebling (sop), Helen Mapleson (mez), Emilio de Marchi (ten), Marie Maurer (mez), Luise Reuss-Belce (sop), Juliette Roslyn (mez), Andrés de Segurola (bs), Camille Seygard (sop)

U.S. --Maria Farnetti (tour), Antonio Paoli (N.Y.)

Other -Elsa Alsen (Heidelberg),Frederic Austin (London), Sergei Bortkiewicz (Munich), Fraser Gange (London), Eva Gauthier (Ottawa), Maria Gay (Brussels), Marie Hall (Prague), Melanie Kurt (Lübeck), Maria Labia (Milan), Paoli Martucci (Bologne), Richard Mayr (Bayreuth), Carmen Melis (Naples), Yolanda Merö-Irion (Dresden), Lucien Muratore (Paris), Antonia Nezhdanova (Moscow), Eva von der Osten (Dresden), Wilhelm Stenhammer (as pianist)

D. New Positions:

Conductors: Walter Damrosch (New York PO), Alfred Hertz (Met), Ernst Kunwald (Frankfurt SO)

Educational: Max Graf (musicology, Vienna Conservatory), Joseph Jongen (harmony, Liège Conservatory), Giuseppe Martucci (director, Naples Conservatory)

Others: Charles W. Cadman (music critic, *Pittsburgh Dispatch*), William Henderson (music critic, *New York Sun*), Oscar Sonneck (director, Library of Congress Music Division), Leopold Stokowski (organ, St. James), Karl Straube (organ, Thomaskirche, Leipzig)

E. Prizes and Honors:

Honors: Horatio Parker (honorary doctorate, Cambridge), Richard Strauss (honorary doctorate, Heidelberg), George F. Watts (Order of Merit)

F. Biographical Highlights:

Enrico Caruso makes his Covent Garden debut; Claude Debussy is prosecuted by his debtors; Manuel de Falla studies with Pedrell and decides to become a nationalist composer; Paul Hindemith's family moves to Frankfurt; Sigfrid Karg-Elert begins a short session of teaching in Magdeburg; Franz Lehár leaves the military and begins conducting at the Theater an der Wein; Pietro Mascagni spends time in the U.S. conducting his own operas; Sergei Rachmaninoff marries his cousin, Natalya Satina and honeymoons in Switzerland; Carl Reinecke retires from the active music field; Ottorino Respighi, while playing the in St. Petersburg Opera orchestra, begins studying composition with Rimsky-Korsakov; Igor Stravinsky, travelling in Germany, meets the sons of Rimsky-Korsakov who introduce him to their father; Alexandre Tansman enters the Conservatory at Lodz; Anton Webern graduates from Klagenfurt Gymnasium and visits Bayreuth.

G. Institutional Openings:

Performing Groups: Flonzaley String Quartet (N.Y.), Oxford Orchestral Society, Società Corale G.B. Martini (Bologna), Société des Festivals Lyriques (Paris), Stockholms Konsertförening, Sydsvenska Filharmoniska Forening (Malmö), Washington SO (D.C.)

Educational: Conservatoire Populaire Mimi Pinson (Paris), Florida State University School of Music, University of Minnesota Music Department

Other: Music and Drama Festival (Nottingham), National Theater of Helsinki, Tension-Resonator (patented by Mason & Hamlin), Theater am Habsburger (Cologne), Tulsa Commercial Club Band

H. Musical Literature:

Dickinson, Edward, *Music in the History of the Western Church*
Elson, Arthur, *Orchestral Instruments*
Friedlaender, Max, *Das Deutsche Lied in 18. Jahrhundert*
Fuller-Maitland, John, *English Music in the Nineteenth Century*

Goetschius, Percy, *Applied Counterpoint*
Grunsky, Karl, *Musikgeschichte des 19. Jahrhunderts*
Huneker, James, *Melomaniacs*
Mason, Daniel G., *From Grieg to Brahms*
Moos, Paul, *Moderne musikästhetik in Deutschland*
Riemann, Hugo, *Gross Kompositionslehre I*

I. Musical Compositions:
Bartók, Béla, *Scherzo for Orchestra*
Bloch, Ernst, *Symphony No. 1*
    Macbeth (opera)
Ciléa, Francesco, *Adriana Lecouvreur* (opera)
Coleridge-Taylor, Samuel, *Meg Blane* (opera)
Converse, Frederick, *La Belle Dame sans Merci* (baritone, orchestra)
Debussy, Claude, *Pelleas et Mélisande* (opera)
Delius, Frederick, *Appalachia* (chorus, orchestra)
Enescu, Georges, *Romanian Rhapsody No. 2*
Fauré, Gabriel, *Huit Pièces Brèves, Opus 84* (piano)
German, Edward, *Merrie England* (operetta)
Glazunov, Alexander, *Symphony No. 7, Opus 77*
    Ballade for Orchestra
Goldmark, Karl, *Götz von Berlichingen* (opera)
Grieg, Edvard, *Norwegian Peasant Dances, Opus 72* (piano)
Hadley, Henry, *In Bohemia, Opus 28* (symphonic poem)
Humperdinck, Engelbert, *Dornröschen* (opera)
Ives, Charles, *Symphony No. 2*
Lehár, Franz, *Wiener Frauen* (operetta)
MacDowell, Edward, *Fireside Tales, Opus 61* (piano)
    New England Idylls, Opus 62 (piano)
Magnard, Albéric, *Symphony No. 3, Opus 11*
Mahler, Gustave, *Kindertotenlieder* (soprano, orchestra)
    Five Rückert Songs
    Symphony No. 5
Massenet, Jules, *Le Jongleur de Notre Dame* (opera)
Nielsen, Carl, *Symphony No. 2, "The Four Temperaments"*
Novák, Vítezslav, *In der Tatra* (symphonic poem)
Rachmaninoff, Serge, *Twelve Songs, Opus 21*
    The Spring (cantata)
Respighi, Ottorino, *Concerto for Piano and Orchestra*
Reznicek, Emil von, *Til Eulenspiegel* (opera)
Rimsky-Korsakov, Nicolai, *Kaschei, the Immortal* (opera)
Saint-Saëns, Camille, *Concerto No. 2, Opus 119, for Cello and Orchestra*
Sibelius, Jan, *The Origin of Fire, Opus 72* (male voices, orchestra)
Suk, Josef, *Under the Apple Trees, Opus 20* (orchestra)
Vaughan-Williams, Ralph, *Fantasia for Piano and Orchestra*

1903

World Events:
In the U.S. the Wright Brothers make their famous flights at Kitty Hawk--the first flight covers 120 feet in 12 seconds; the first cross-country auto trip is made in 52 days; Canada and the U.S. settle their boundary dispute; the Hay-Bunau-Varilla treaty gives the Panama Canal Zone to the U.S. for the building of a canal across the isthmus. Internationally, Roosevelt aids the Panamanians in gaining independence from Colombia; the Russian Social Democratic Party splits into the Menshevik and Bolshevik factions.

Cultural Highlights:
John Singer Sargent opens a studio in Boston and Jacob Epstein goes to Paris for art study; the Nobel Prize in Literature goes to the Norwegian poet, dramatist and novelist Björnstrjerne Björnson. The literary field sees the deaths of British poet William Henley and novelist George Cissing and French dramatist Gabriel Legouvé and the births of American novelists Erskine Caldwell, James Cozzens and George Orwell. In the field of art the births include Russian artist Mark Rothko, British artist Graham Sutherland and art historian Kenneth Clark and American artist Adolf Gottlieb; deaths include French artists Paul Gauguin and Camille Pissaro and American artist James Whistler. Other highlights include:

Art: Barbara Hepworth, *Torso*; Hermann Knackfuss, *Emperor William II in Jerusalem*; Wilhelm Lehmbruck, *Standing Youth*; Henri Matisse, *Guitarist*; Claude Monet, *Houses of Parliament*; Pablo Picasso, *The Old Guitarist*; Georges Rouault, *The Bathers*; Augustus Saint-Gaudens, *General Sherman* (N.Y.); Abbott Thayer, *Stevenson Memorial Angel*.

Literature: Samuel Butler, *The Way of All Flesh*; Joseph Conrad, *Typhoon and Other Stories*; Thomas Hardy, *The Dynasts I*; Hugo von Hofmannsthal, *Electra*; Henry James, *The Ambassadors*; Tristan Klingsor, *Schéhérazade*; Jack London, *The Call of the Wild*; Frank Norris, *The Pit*; George Bernard Shaw, *Man and Superman*.

MUSICAL EVENTS

A. Births:

Jan 3	Boris Blacher (Ger-cm)	Jun 6	Aram Khatchaturian (Rus-cm)
Jan 5	Leighton Lucas (Br-cd)	Jun 20	Walter Graf (Aus-mus)
Jan 6	Maurice Abravanel (Gr-cd)	Jun 21	Louis Krasner (Rus-vn)
Jan 10	Jean Morel (Fr-cd)	Jul 4	Flor Peeters (Hol-org)
Jan 19	Ervin Nyiregyházi (Hun-pn)	Jul 25	André Fleury (Fr-org)
Feb 6	Claudio Arrau (Chil-pn)	Aug 17	Abram Chasins (Am-pn-cri)
Feb 22	Robert Weede (Am-bar)	Aug 23	William Primrose (Am-vla)
Mar 16	Nikolai Lopatnikoff (Rus-cm)	Oct 14	Jose Luccioni (Fr-ten)
Mar 28	Rudolf Serkin (Rus-pn)	Oct 19	Vittorio Giannini (Am-cm)
Apr 17	Gregor Piatigorsky (Rus-cel)	Nov 20	J.M. Coopersmith (Am-mus)
May 2	Oivin Fjeldsted (Nor-vn)	Dec 10	Winthrop Sargent (Am-cri)
May 2	Walter Goehr (Ger-cd)	Dec 12	Francisco C. Lange (Ger-mus)
Jun 4	Joel Berglund (Swe-bar)	Dec 13	Leo Schrade (Ger-mus)
Jun 4	Eugene Mravinsky (Rus-cd)		

B. Deaths:

Jan 28	Augusta Holmes (Fr-cm)	May 22	Theodor Reichmann (Ger-bar)
Jan 28	Jean Planquette (Fr-cm)	Jul 13	August Reissman (Ger-mus)
Feb 22	Hugo Wolf (Ger-cm)	Jul 28	Rosine Stoltz (Fr-mez)
Mar 5	Thomas Ryan (Am-cd)	Aug 29	Enrico Bevignani (It-cd)
Apr 10	Johann Bellermann (Ger-mus)	Nov 20	Hart P. Danks (Am-cm)
May 1	Luigi Arditi (It-cm-cd)	Dec 6	Frederick Gleason (Am-org)
May 15	Sibyl Anderson (Am-sop)	Dec 20	Kornél Abrányi (Hun-pn)

C. Débuts:

Met ---Julius Bayer (ten), Paula Braendle (mez), Alois Burgstaller (ten), Enrico Caruso (ten), Jessie Clevenger (sop), Minnie Egener (sop), Mildred Elliot (sop), Olive Fremstad (sop), Otto Goritz (bar), Willy Haupt (ten), Josephine Jacoby (mez), Louise Kirkby (alto), Ernst Kraus (ten), Katherine Moran (sop), Felix Mottl (cd), Johanna Poehlmann (mez), Archangelo Rossi (bs), Cleopatra Vicini (sop), Edyth Walker (mez), Marion Weed (sop)

U.S. --Dan Beddoe (N.Y.), Ada Crossley (tour), Rita Fornia (tour), Jacques Thibaud (N.Y.)

Other -Georg Baklanov (Kiev), Julia Claussen (Stockholm), Florence Easton (London), Elena Gerhardt (Leipzig), Allen Hinckley (Hamburg), Albert Huberty (Antwerp), Gertrude Kappel (Hanover), Barbara Kemp (Strasbourg), Francis MacMillan (Brussels), Alice Nielsen (Naples), Giannina Russ (Milan), Dmitri Smirnov (Moscow), Hans Tänzler (Danzig), Alfio Tedesco (Asti), Fritz Vogelstrom (Mannheim)

D. New Positions:

Conductors: Armas Järnefelt (Helsinki Opera), Felix Mottl (Munich Opera), Emil Oberhoffer (Minneapolis SO)

Educational: Samuel Coleridge-Taylor (composition, Trinity College), Josef B. Foerster (composition, Vienna Conservatory), Fritz Steinbach (director, Cologne Conservatory), Ermanno Wolf-Ferrari (director, Liceo Musicale, Venice)

Others: Heinrich Conried (manager, Met), Gabriel Fauré (music critic, *Le Figaro*), Philip Hale (music critic, *Boston Herald*)

E. Prizes and Honors:

Prizes: Albert Dupuis and Raoul Laparra (Prix de Rome), Felix Nowowiejski (Paderewski)

Honors: Camille Chevillard (Legion of Honor), August Mann (knighted), Hubert Parry (baronet)

F. Biographical Highlights:

Béla Bartók graduates from the Budapest Academy of Music; Charles W. Cadman moves with his family to Pennsylvania and begins work in a steel mill; Claude Debussy meets Emma Bardac, a banker's wife; Frederick Delius finally marries the artist Jelka Rosen; Amelita Galli-Curci takes first prize in piano at Milan Conservatory; Charles Griffes goes to Berlin and enrolls in the Stern Conservatory where he studies piano with Galston and composition with Humperdinck; John McCormack wins a songfest for tenors at the National Irish Festival in Dublin and joins the Cathedral Choir; Charles Santley makes a second concert tour of South Africa; Alexander Scriabin deserts his wife and children, leaves his work at the Conservatory and departs for Italy with Tatiana Schloezer; Václav Talich becomes concertmaster of the Odessa Orchestra in Russia; Donald Tovey acts as soloist in his own *Piano Concerto* in London; Anton Van Rooy is banned from Bayreuth for taking part in the New York performance of *Parsifal*; Edgard Varèse leaves Turin and moves to Paris.

G. Institutional Openings:

Performing Groups: Capet String Quartet II (Paris), La Chanterie de la Renaissance (Paris), London Choral Society, Minneapolis SO, New Haven Oratorio Society, Arthur Pryor Band (N.Y.), Russian SO of New York, Seattle SO, Société Symphonique de Québec

Educational: Cornell University Music Department, Hinshaw School of Music (Chicago), Liceo Musicale Giuseppe Tartini (Trieste), Mu Phi Epsilon Music Sorority (Cincinnati), Sigma Alpha Iota Music Sorority (Ann Arbor)

Other: Columbia Record Co. (N.Y.); Elkin and Co., Ltd., Music Publishers (London); Flenthrop Organ Co. (Holland), Municipal Theater (Bern), *Revue Musicale de Lyon*, (*Nouvelle Revue Musicale*), Société des Concerts Cortot (Paris), Société d'Études Musicales (Paris), Wetzler Symphony Concerts (N.Y.).

H. Musical Literature:

Burton, Frederick, *Songs of the Ojibway Indians*
Capellen, George, *Die musikalische Akustik als Grundlage der Harmonik und Melodik*
Elson, Arthur, *Women's Work in Music*
Farwell, Arthur, *A Letter to American Composers*
Hughes, Rupert, *The Musical Guide*
Knorr, Iwan, *Aufgaben für den Unterricht in der Harmonielehre*
Lussy, Mathis, *L'Anacrouse dans la musique moderne*
Reger, Max, *Beiträge zur Modulationslehre*
Rolland, Romaine, *The Life of Beethoven*

I. Musical Compositions:

Bartók, Béla, *Kossuth* (symphonic poem)
   Sonata for Violin and Piano
Bloch, Ernst, *Alpenkönig und Menschenfeind* (opera)
Chausson, Ernest, *Le Roi Arthur, Opus 23* (opera)
Converse, Frederick, *Euphrosyne Overture* (orchestra)
Debussy, Claude, *Estampes* (piano)
Dvořák, Antonin, *Armida, Opus 115* (opera)
Elgar, Edward, *The Apostles* (oratorio)
Enescu, Georges, *Orchestral Suite No. 1 in C, Opus 9*
Fauré, Gabriel, *3 Songs, Opus 85*
Foerster, Josef B., *Cyrano de Bergerac, Opus 55* (symphonic suite)
German, Edward, *The Princess of Kensington* (operetta)
Glazunov, Alexander, *From the Middle Ages, Opus 79* (orchestral suite)
Hadley, Henry, *Oriental Suite* (orchestra)
Herbert, Victor, *Babes in Toyland* (operetta)
   Columbus (symphonic poem)
d'Indy, Vincent, *Symphony No. 2 in B-flat*
   Choral Varié for Saxophone and Orchestra
Janácek, Leos, *Jenufa* (opera)
Koven, Reginald de, *Red Feather* (operetta)
Magnard, Albéric, *Hymn to Justice, Opus 14*
Massenet, Jules, *Concerto for Piano and Orchestra*
Napravnik, Eduard, *Francesca da Rimini* (opera)
Nielsen, Carl, *Helios Overture*
Paderewski, Ignace Jan, *Piano Sonata, Opus 14*
Rachmaninoff, Sergei, *Variations on a Theme of Chopin, Opus 22* (piano)
Ravel, Maurice, *String Quartet in F*
   Schéhérazade (song cycle)
Reznicek, Emil von, *A Comedy Overture*
Rimsky-Korsakov, Nicolai, *Pan Voyevoda* (opera)
Roussel, Albert, *Resurrection, Opus 4*
Satie, Erik, *Three Pieces in the Shape of a Pear* (piano)
Scriabin, Alexander, *Symphony No. 2, Opus 29*
Schoenberg, Arnold, *Pelleas und Mélisande, Opus 5* (symphonic poem)
Sibelius, Jan, *Concerto for Violin and Orchestra*
   Kuolema, Opus 44 (incidental music)
Strauss, Richard, *Sinfonia Domestica, Opus 53*
   Taillefer, Opus 52 (chorus, orchestra)
Suk, Josef, *Fantastic Scherzo, Opus 25* (orchestra)
Vierne, Louis, *Organ Symphony No. 2*
Wolf-Ferrari, Ermanno, *Le Donne Curiose* (opera)

1904

World Events:
In the U.S., Theodore Roosevelt is elected to his first full term as President; Roosevelt chooses William Howard Taft to be his Secretary of War; in St. Louis, the Louisiana Purchase Exposition opens; the New York subway begins limited operation; and the Cadillac Motor Car Co. is founded. Internationally, the Russo-Japanese War begins when the Japanese attack Port McArthur; in Europe, the Entente Cordiale is signed by France and England; in South America, the War of the Pacific ends with a treaty between Bolivia and Chile; W.C. Gorgas conquers Yellow Fever in Panama, thus opening the way for the completion of the Canal; Rolls Royce Co. founded in England.

Cultural Highlights:
French Poet Frédéric Mistral shares the Nobel Prize for Literature with the Spanish dramatist José Echegaray y Elizaguirre. *Caron*, a magazine of the Poetry Society, begins publication; the Kaiser Friedrich Museum (Bode Museum) opens in Berlin. Deaths in the field of art include American sculptors Erastus Palmer and John Rogers, French sculptor Frederic A. Bartholdi, American artist Martin J. Heade, German artist Franz von Lenbach and British artists Charles W. Furse, Valentine Prinsep and George Watts; the literary world loses Russian novelist Anton Chekhov and German poet Wilhelm Jordan. Births in the literary field include American author James T. Farrell, British poet Christopher Isherwood, Canadian novelist and poet Earle Birney and Chilean poet Pablo Neruda; the art world gains with the birth of Spanish artist Salvador Dali, French artist Henri Fantin-Latour and Dutch artist Willem de Kooning. Other highlights include:

Art: Mateo Alonso, *Christ of the Andes*; Albert Edelfelt, *Jan Sibelius* (sketch); Robert Henri, *Willie Gee*; Roland H. Perry, *Pennsylvania Capitol Dome*; Pablo Picasso, *The Two Sisters*; Pierre Renoir, *Still Life, Cup and Sugar Bowl*; Georges Rouault, *The Tragic Clown*; Henri Rousseau, *The Wedding*; Maurice Vlaminck, *Kitchen Interior*.

Literature: Gabriele d'Annunzio, *Alcyone*; James Barrie, *Peter Pan*; Max Beerbohm, *The Poet's Corner*; Anton Chekhov, *The Cherry Orchard*; Joseph Conrad, *Nostromo*; Joel C. Harris, *The Tar Baby*; William H. Hudson, *Green Mansions*; Jack London, *The Sea Wolf*; O'Henry, *Of Cabbages and Kings*; John Synge, *Riders to the Sea*.

MUSICAL EVENTS

A. Births:

Jan 2	James Melton (Am-ten)	Jul 24	Charles Fox (Am-mus)
Jan 3	Jan Peerce (Am-ten)	Sep 2	Set Svanholm (Swe-ten)
Jan 5	Erica Morini (Aus-vn)	Sep 21	Norbert Dufourcq (Fr-mus)
Jan 9	George Balanchine (Rus-bal)	Oct 1	Vladimir Horowitz (Rus-pn)
Feb 3	Luigi Dallapiccola (It-cm)	Oct 9	Carl Parrish (Am-mus)
Mar 8	Nikos Skalkottas (Ger-cm)	Nov 15	Mosco Carner (Aus-mus)
Mar 9	Gerald Abraham (Br-mus)	Nov 20	Alexander Danilova (Rus-bal)
Mar 19	Tadeusz Kassern (Pol-cm)	Nov 29	Hans Heinz (Aus-ten)
Apr 12	Lily Pons (Fr-sop)	Dec 14	Martin Bernstein (Aus-mus)
Apr 17	Joseph Ahrens (Ger-org)	Dec 20	Charles Haywood (Am-mus)
Jun 18	Manuel Rosenthal (Fr-cd)	Dec 25	Gladys Swarthout (Am-alto)
Jul 2	Carl Weinrich (Am-org)	Dec 26	Walter Gerstenberg (Ger-mus)
Jul 9	Robert Whitney (Br-cd)	Dec 30	Dmitri Kabalevsky (Rus-cm)
Jul 16	Goffredo Petrassi (It-cm)	Dec 31	Nathan Milstein (Am-vn)

B. Deaths:

Jan 3	Francesco Cortesi (It-cd-cm)	Feb 20	Gustav Heinze (Ger-cd-cm)
Jan 9	Antoinette Sterling (Am-alto)	Mar 11	Charles Grisart (Fr-cm)
Jan 10	Mitrophane Belaiev (Rus-pub)	May 1	Antonin Dvorák (Boh-cm)
Jan 15	Eduard Lassen (Den-cd-cm)	Jun 28	Daniel Emmett (Am-pop)

Feb 8   M. Schnoor von Carolsfeld   Aug 6   Edward Hanslick (Ger-cri)
         (Ger-sop)

C. Débuts:

Met ---Aïno Ackté (sop), Werner Alberti (bar), Bella Alten (sop), Susanne Baker (mez), Lucy Lee Call (sop), Maria DeMacchi (sop), Nahan Franko (cd), Eugenio Giraldoni (bar), Roberta Glanville (sop), Emil Greder (bs), Bessie Greenwood (sop), Emilie Herzog (sop), Gustav Hindrichs (cd), Heinrich Knote (ten), Lucille Lawrence (sop), Marguerite Lemon (sop), Otto Lörzsch (bs), Taurino Parvis (bar), Lloyd Rand (ten), Estelle Sherman (sop), Edith Vail (sop), India Waelchli (mez)

U.S. --Johannes Bischoff (N.Y.), Clara Clemens (Norfolk), Theodore Lierhammer (tour), Francis McLennan (tour), Agnes Nicholls (tour), Alois Pennarini (tour)

Other -Frances Alda (Paris), Lola Artôt de Padilla (Paris), Mme. Charles Cahier (Nice), Armand Crabbé (La Monnaie), Ruth Dezo (Berlin), Pauline Donalda (Nice), Misha Elman (Berlin), Carlo Galeffi (Rome), Putnam Griswold (Berlin), Eduard Habich (Koblenz), Clara Haskil (Bucharest), Pavel Ludikar (Prague), Riccardo Martin (Nantes), Jane Osborn-Hannah (Leipzig), Emil Schipper (Prague)

D. New Positions:

Conductors: Willy Hess (Boston SO), Emil Paur (Pittsburgh SO)

Educational: Emil Mlynarski (director, Warsaw Conservatory), Horatio Parker (dean, School of Music, Yale)

Others: John Ireland (organ, St. Luke's, Chelsea), Alexander Zemlinsky (director, Vienna Volksoper)

E. Prizes and Honors:

Honors: Fritz Kreisler (Beethoven Gold Medal), Martin Wegelius (Swedish Royal Academy)

F. Biographical Highlights:

Ernst Bloch returns to Geneva and enters the family clock business; Enrico Caruso makes his first recording with "Vesti la Giubba"; Claude Debussy leaves his wife and moves in with Emma Bardac; Emma Destinn and Pasquale Amato make their Covent Garden debuts; Florence Easton marries American tenor Francis MacLennan; Henry Hadley begins five years of conducting his own works around Germany; Paul Hindemith begins violin lessons with Rebner; Edward MacDowell quarrels with the president of Columbia University and resigns his post as professor of music--the first signs of his mental illness appear; John McCormack travels with the Dublin Cathedral Choir to the U.S.; Serge Prokofiev enters St. Petersburg Conservatory to study with Rimsky-Korsakov and Liadov; Curt Sachs receives his doctoral degree in the history of art; Jan Sibelius builds his country villa at Järvenpää into which he settles for the remainder of his life; Richard Strauss makes his first visit to the U.S. and conducts the premiere of his *Domestic Symphony* in New York; Anton Webern and Alban Berg become a part of Schoenberg's circle.

G. Institutional Openings:

Performing Groups: Arion Singing Society (Denver), Victor Herbert Orchestra (N.Y.), Irish Folk Song Society, London SO, Nashville SO (I), Pollard Opera Co. (New Zealand), Residentie-Orkest (The Hague)

Educational: Cadek School of Music (Chattanooga), Isadora Duncan School of Dancing (Berlin), Institute of Musical Art (N.Y.), McGill Conservatory of Music (Montreal), State Music Academy of Sofia

Other: Abbey Theater (Dublin), Aeolian Hall (London), American Academy of Arts and Letters, Bühnen der Stadt Bielefeld Opera House, French Society of Musicology (Paris), Heckelphone (by William Heckel), (New) Dallas Opera House, Orchestra Hall (Chicago)

H. Musical Literature:
Bustini, Alessandro, *La Sinfonia in Italia*
Dauriac, Lionel, *Essai sur l'Esprit Musical*
Gilman, Lawrence, *Phases of Modern Music*
Goetschius, Percy, *Lessons in Music Form*
Hervey, Arthur, *French Music in the Nineteenth Century*
Huneker, James, *Overtones*
Kienzl, Wilhelm, *Aus Kunst und Leben*
Mantuani, Josef, *Geschichte der Musik in Wien I*
Schmidt, Heinrich, *Die Orgel in unserer Zeit...*
Widor, Charles, *Technique de l'orchestre moderne*

I. Musical Compositions:
Alfvén, Hugo, *Swedish Rhapsody No. 1, "Midsummer Vigil"*
Arensky, Anton, *Nal and Damayanti (opera)*
Bartók, Béla, *Rhapsody for Piano, Opus 1*
    Scherzo for Piano and Orchestra, Opus 2
Busoni, Ferruccio, *Concerto for Piano, Male Chorus and Orchestra, Opus 39*
    Turandot Suite, Opus 41 (orchestra)
Chadwick, George, *Sinfonietta in D*
Cohan, George M., *Little Johny Jones* (musical)
Debussy, Claude, *Masques* (suite)
    Danses Sacrée et Profane (harp and strings)
    Fetes Galantes, Set II (songs)
Delius, Frederick, *Concerto for Piano and Orchestra*
Elgar, Edward, *Overture, In the South, Opus 50*
Giordano, Umberto, *Siberia* (opera)
Glazunov, Alexander, *Concerto, Opus 82, for Violin and Orchestra*
Harrington, Karl, *There's a Song in the Air* (Christmas song)
Herbert, Victor, *It Happened in Nordland* (operetta)
Ives, Charles, *Symphony No. 3, "Campmeeting"*
    Thanksgiving (from Holiday Symphony)
Leoncavallo, Ruggiero, *Roland* (opera)
Magnard, Albéric, *Chant Funebre, Opus 9* (orchestra)
    Guercoeur (opera)
    Overture, Opus 10
Mahler, Gustav, *Symphony No. 6*
Massenet, Jules, *La Cigale* (ballet)
Pierné, Gabriel, *The Children's Crusade* (oratorio)
Pizzetti, Ildebrando, *3 Symphonic Preludes on Sophocles*
Puccini, Giacomo, *Madame Butterfly* (opera)
Rachmaninoff, Serge, *Ten Preludes, Opus 23 for Piano*
Rimsky-Korsakov, Nicolai, *Invisible City of Kitezh* (opera)
Saint-Saëns, Camille, *Hélène* (opera)
Schmitt, Florent, *Psalm XLVII* (chorus and orchestra)
Scriabin, Alexander, *Piano Sonata No. 4, Opus 30*
    20 Preludes for Piano, Opus 33, 37, 39, 42
Stravinsky, Igor, *Piano Sonata*
Suk, Josef, *Prague, Opus 26* (orchestra)
Vaughan-Williams, Ralph, *In the Fen Country*
    Songs of Travel (song cycle)
    The House of Life (song cycle)
Webern, Anton, *Im Sommerwind* (symphonic poem)

1905

World Events:
In the U.S., the New York subway officially opens; the Rotary Clubs of America, the Industrial Workers of the World and the National Association of Audubon Societies are founded; New Orleans experiences an epidemic of Yellow Fever; Congress establishes Devil's Tower and Petrified Forest National Parks. Internationally, the Russo-Japanese War ends with the defeat of the Russian fleet; Bloody Sunday in St. Petersburg is followed by the October Manifesto; Albert Einstein makes public his special theory of relativity (E=mc).

Cultural Highlights:
"Les Fauves" exhibit in the Paris Salon d'Automne outrages the critics while in Dresden, the Bridge Group is formed; in London the Times Book Club comes into existence. The Nobel Prize for Literature is won by the Polish novelist Henryk Sienkiewicz; Robert Fry becomes director of the Metropolitan Museum of Art. The art world witnesses the deaths of German artists Adolphe Bouguereau and Adolf von Menzel and Belgian artist Constantin Meunier and the birth of American artists Arshile Gorky and Barnett Newman; the literary world loses French novelist Jules Verne, German poet Rudolf Baumbach, American novelist Lewis Wallace and poet John M. Hay but sees the births of Spanish novelist Jesús Bal y Gay, American dramatist Lillian Hellman, French author Jean Paul Sartre and Russian author Mikhail Sholokhov. Other highlights include:

Art: Muirhead Bone, *Demolition of Saint James' Hall*; Paul Cézanne, *Les Grandes Baigneuses*; André Derain, *River Seine at Chatou*; Childe Hassam, *Southwest Wind*; Aristide Maillol, *The Mediterranean* (bronze); Henri Matisse, *Luxe, Calme et Volupté*; Georges Rouault, *Head of Christ*; Henri Rousseau, *Jungle with Lion*.

Literature: David Belasco, *The Girl of the Golden West*; Arthur C. Doyle, *The Return of Sherlock Holmes*; Edward Forster, *Where Angels Fear to Tread*; Maxim Gorky, *Summer Folk*; Emmuska Orczy, *The Scarlet Pimpernel*; George Bernard Shaw, *Major Barbara*; H.G. Wells, *A Modern Utopia*; Edith Wharton, *The House of Mirth*.

MUSICAL EVENTS

A. Births:

Jan 2	Michael Tippett (Br-cm)	May 15	Hugo Rignold (Br-cd)
Jan 6	Mafalda Favero (It-sop)	Jun 6	Arthur Mendel (Am-mus)
Jan 27	John W. Schaum (Am-pn-ed)	Jul 19	Boyd Neel (Br-cd)
Feb 13	Leonard Ellinwood (Am-mus)	Aug 2	Karl A. Hartmann (Ger-cm)
Feb 14	Guillaume Landré (Hol-cm)	Aug 4	Boris Alexandrov (Rus-cd-cm)
Mar 18	John Kirkpatrick (Am-pn)	Aug 8	André Jolivet (Fr-cm)
Mar 24	Marc Blitzstein (Am-cm)	Aug 8	Nino Martini (It-ten)
Mar 26	André Cluytens (Fr-cd)	Aug 8	Carlton S. Smith (Am-mus)
Apr 3	Lili Kraus (Hun-pn)	Aug 23	Constant Lambert (Br-cd-cm)
Apr 12	Kurt H. Adler (Aus-cd)	Oct 15	Bruna Castagna (It-mez)
May 2	Alan Rawsthorne (Br-cm)	Oct 27	Genia Nemenoff (Rus-pn)
May 4	Mátyás Seiber (Hun-cm)	Nov 19	Tommy Dorsey (Am-pop)
May 5	Maria Caniglia (It-sop)	Dec 13	Luiz de Azevedo (Braz-mus)

B. Deaths:

Jan 4	Theodore Thomas (Ger-cd)	Jun 2	Franz Strauss (Ger-hn-cm)
Feb 2	Robert Eitner (Ger-mus)	Jun 30	Friedrich Ladegast (Ger-org.m)
Feb 13	Fanny Moran-Olden (Ger-sop)	Jul 27	John N. Pattison (Am-pn)
Feb 18	Arrey von Dommer (Ger-the)	Aug 31	Francesco Tomagno (It-ten)
Mar 3	Wilhelm Bäumker (Ger-mus)	Sep 22	Célestine Galli-Marie (Fr-mez)
May 9	Ernst Paur (Aus-pn-ed)	Nov 10	Jules Danbé (Fr-cd)

C. Débuts:

Met ---Lina Abarbanell (sop), Anna Arnaud (sop), Gustavo Berl-Resky (bar), Tony Franke (bar), Jeanne Jomelli (sop), Francisco Nuibo (ten), Giovanni Parolli (ten), Marie Rappold (sop), Cecile Talma (sop)

U.S. --Florence Easton (tour), Edward Lankow (N.Y.), Giorgio Polacco (San Francisco), Felix Weingartner (N.Y.)

Other -Thomas Beecham (London), Edmund Burke (Canada), Vladimir Cernikof (Mühlhausen), Marthe Chenal (Paris), Claire Croiza (Nancy), Freida Hempel (Berlin), Rued Langgard (as organist), Carmen Melis (Paris), Kathleen Parlow (London), Oscar Ralf (Stockholm), Gustav Schützendorf (Krefeld), Albert Spalding (Paris), Joseph Szigeti (Berlin), Giuseppe Taccani (Bologna), Hermann Wiedemann (Elberfeld)

D. New Positions:

Conductors: Frederick Stock (Chicago SO)

Educational: Ernst von Dohnányi (piano, Berlin Hochschule), Gabriel Fauré (director, Paris Conservatory), André Gédalge (counterpoint, Paris Conservatory), Alexander Glazunov (director, St. Petersburg Conservatory), Gustav Holst (music, St. Paul's Girls School), Mikhail Ippolitov-Ivanov (director, Moscow Conservatory), Willem Kes (director, Koblenz Conservatory), Daniel G. Mason (lecturer, Columbia)

Others: Ernest Newman (music critic, Manchester Guardian)

E. Prizes and Honors:

Prizes: Dominique Planchet (Chartier), Marcel Samuel Rousseau (Prix de Rome)

Honors: George Chadwick (honorary doctorate, Tufts), Edward Elgar (honorary doctorate, Yale), William Holman Hunt (Order of Merit)

F. Biographical Highlights:

Béla Bartók joins Zoltán Kodály in studying Eastern European folk music; Arnold Bax leaves the Royal Academy without finishing his courses; Claude Debussy's daughter, Chou-Chou, is born to Emma Bardac; Edward Elgar visits the U.S. and receives a doctorate from Yale; Alexandre Glazunov resigns his post over the firing of Rimsky-Korsakov from the St. Petersburg Conservatory but returns in December; Charles Griffes leaves the Berlin Conservatory to study composition privately with Humperdinck; Serge Koussevitsky marries tea fortune heiress Natalie Ushkov; Vítezslav Novák almost dies from a fall while climbing in the Tatras Mountains; Walter Piston's family moves to Boston; Artur Schnabel marries contralto Therese Behr; Ernestine Schumann-Heink marries her third husband, a Chicago lawyer, William Rapp, Jr.; Sergei Taneyev resigns in protest from the Moscow Conservatory; Joaquin Turina moves to Paris to study with Vincent d'Indy at the Schola Cantorum; Edgard Varèse enters the Paris Conservatory to study with Widor.

G. Institutional Openings:

Performing Groups: Georgian Philharmonic Society (Russia), Glasgow Grand Opera Co., Göteborg SO (Sweden), Komische Oper (Berlin), New SO of London, Nuremburg Music Theater and Opera Co., Ritter String Quartet (Würzburg), Salt Lake City SO, Société des Grands Concerts (Lyons)

Educational: Bergen Conservatory of Music, Institute of Musical Art (Juilliard), Schola de Montpelier, Scuola Nazionale di Musica (Rome)

Other: *L'Album Musical*, American Prix de Rome, Association of Young Polish Composers (Warsaw), *Mercure Musicale*, Minneapolis Auditorium; Rouart-Lerolle et Cie., Publishers (Paris); Society of British Composers (London), Young Polish Composers Publishing Co.

(Berlin)

H. Musical Literature:

Bennett, Joseph, *Forty Years of Music*
Curtis, Natalie, *Songs of Ancient America*
Elson, Arthur, *Modern Composers of Europe*
Foote, Arthur, *Modern Harmony*
Gevaert, François, *Traité d'Harmonie... I*
Grunsky, Karl, *Musikgeschichte des 17. und 18. Jahrhunderts*
Halm, August, *Harmonielehre*
Huneker, James, *Iconoclasts*
Kling, H., *Modern Orchestration*
Sankey, Ira, *My Life*

I. Musical Compositions:

Alfvén, Hugo, *Symphony No. 3, Opus 23*
Bartók, Béla, *Suite No. 1 for Orchestra, Opus 3*
Bloch, Ernst, *Hiver* (symphonic poem)
Casella, Alfredo, *Symphony No. 1*
Chadwick, Georges, *Cleopatra* (opera)
Converse, Frederick, *The Mystic Trumpeter* (tone poem)
Debussy, Claude, *La Mer*, (symphonic pictures)
       Images, Book I (piano)
       Rhapsody for Saxophone and Orchestra
Delius, Frederick, *A Mass of Life* (chorus, soloists, orchestra)
Elgar, Edward, *Introduction and Allegro for Strings, Opus 47*
       Pomp and Circumstance March No. 3
Falla, Manuel de, *La Vida Breve* (lyric drama)
Farwell, Arthur, *Symbolist Study No. 3* (orchestra)
Foerster, Josef B., *Symphony No. 4, Opus 54, "Easter"*
       Jessica, Opus 60 (opera)
Gilbert, Henry, *Comedy Overture on Negro Themes*
Herbert, Victor, *Madamoiselle Modiste* (operetta)
d'Indy, Vincent, *Jour d'été à la Montagne, Opus 61* (orchestra)
Ives, Charles, *Three Page Sonata for Piano*
Koussevitsky, Serge, *Concerto for Doublebass and Orchestra*
Lehár, Franz, *The Merry Widow* (operetta)
Loeffler, Charles, *La Mort de Tintagales* (dramatic poem)
Mahler, Gustav, *Symphony No. 7*
Massenet, Jules, *Chérubin* (lyric comedy)
Pfitzner, Hans, *Columbus, Opus 16* (a capella chorus)
Puccini, Giacomo, *Requiem* (soloists, chorus, orchestra)
Rachmaninoff, Sergei, *The Miserly Knight, Opus 24* (opera)
       Francesca da Rimini, Opus 25 (opera)
Ravel, Maurice, *Sonatine* (piano)
       Miroirs (piano)
       Introduction and Allegro (harp and orchestra)
Reger, Max, *Sinfonietta, Opus 90*
Respighi, Ottorino, *Re Enzo* (opera)
Reznicek, Emil von, *Symphonietta, "Ironic Symphony"*
Rimsky-Korsakov, Nicolai, *Dubinushka* (opera)
Satie, Erik, *Pousse l'Amour* (operetta)
Schoenberg, Arnold, *String Quartet No. 1, Opus 7*
Scriabin, Alexander, *Symphony No. 3, Opus 43, "Divine Poem"*
Sibelius, Jan, *Pelléas et Mélisande, Opus 46* (incidental music)
Stanford, Charles, *Symphony No. 6, Opus 94*
Strauss, Richard, *Salomé* (opera)

1906

World Events:
The San Francisco earthquake on April 18 takes 700 lives and causes $400,000,000 damage; Congress passes the Pure Food and Drug Act and the Meat Inspection Act and also approves sending troops into Cuba to quell riots; Victrolas first appear on the market. Internationally, Turkey gives up the Sinai Peninsula to Egypt; France and Spain take over control of Morocco; Britain launches its first large battleship, the *Dreadnaught*; Marie Curie becomes first woman professor at the Sorbonne; Frederick VIII becomes Danish monarch.

Cultural Highlights:
Italian poet Giosuè Carducci receives the Nobel Prize for Literature; in London the Central School of Speech Training and Dramatic Art opens its doors. The art world loses three French artists, Jules A. Breton, Eugène Carrière and Paul Cézanne and American artist Eastman Johnson; born are the American sculptor David Smith and the Russian-born artist, Peter Blume. The world of literature loses Norwegian dramatist Henrik Ibsen and novelist Alexander Kielland, Spanish novelist José de Pereda, American poet Paul D. Dunbar and Italian dramatist Giuseppe Giacosa; births include British poet John Betjeman and dramatist Samuel Beckett and Italian author Dino Buzzati. Other highlights include:

Art: Arthur Davies, *The Unicorns*; André Derain, *Turning Road, l'Estaque*; Childe Hassam, *Church at Old Lyme*; Aristide Maillol, *Chained Action*; Henri Matisse, *The Joy of Life*; Pierre Renoir, *Claude Renoir with His Toys*; Georges Rouault, *At the Mirror*; Maurice de Vlaminck, *The Banks of the Seine*.

Literature: Mary R. Andrews, *A Good Samaritan*; Leonid Andreyev, *The Life of Man*; James Breasted, *Ancient Records of Egypt*; Valeri Bryusov, *Stephanos*; Joseph Conrad, *Mirror of the Sea*; John Galsworthy, *The Man of Property*; Geronimo, *Autobiography*; O'Henry, *The Four Million*; Upton Sinclair, *The Jungle*; William Yeats, *Deirdre*.

MUSICAL EVENTS

A. Births:

Jan 3	Alessandro Ziliani (It-ten)	Jul 28	Gottlob Frick (Ger-bs)
Feb 10	Gianna Pederzini (It-mez)	Aug 11	Joseph Machlis (Am-mus)
Mar 27	Homer Ulrich (Am-mus)	Sep 1	Aksel Shiotz (Den-ten)
Mar 29	E. Power Biggs (Am-org)	Sep 4	Gilbert Chase (Am-mus)
Apr 9	Antal Dorati (Hun-cd)	Sep 19	Massimo Freccia (It-cd)
Apr 22	Eric Fenby (Br-cm-cd)	Sep 25	Dmitri Shostakovich (Rus-cm)
Apr 28	Paul Sacher (Swi-cd)	Oct 5	Alfred Frankenstein (Am-cri)
May 8	David Van Vactor (Am-cm)	Oct 10	Paul Creston (Am-mus)
May 17	Zinka Milanov (Yug-sop)	Oct 12	Herbert Alsen (Ger-bs)
May 28	Alexander Sved (Hun-bar)	Oct 31	Louise Talma (Am-cm)
Jun 8	Reginald Kell (Am-cri)	Dec 7	Elisabeth Höngen (Ger-alto)
Jun 15	Hans Schwieger (Ger-cd)	Dec 13	Hans Moldenhauer (Ger-mus)
Jun 24	Pierre Fournier (Fr-cel)	Dec 23	Ross Lee Finney (Am-cm)
Jul 19	Klaus Egge (Nor-cd-cm)	Dec 27	Oscar Levant (Am-pn)
Jul 26	Fritz Bose (Ger-mus)		

B. Deaths:

Jan 6	Marie G. Krauss (Aus-sop)	Jul 1	Manuel P. García (Sp-voc-ed)
Jan 21	Henry S. Edwards (Br-mus)	Jul 8	Ivan Melnikov (Rus-bar)
Feb 25	Anton Arensky (Rus-cm)	Jul 29	Alexandre Luigini (Fr-cm)
Mar 22	Martin Wegelius (Fin-cd)	Aug 26	Eugen Gura (Boh-bar)
Apr 25	John K. Paine (Am-cm-ed)	Sep 22	Julius Stockhausen (Ger-ten)
May 24	Anton Reicha (Cz-cm)	Oct 23	Vladimir Stasov (Rus-mus)
May 24	Heinrich Reichmann (Ger-mus)	Nov 27	Erich Valentin (Ger-mus)

C. Débuts:

Met ---Bessie Abott (sop), Celestina Boninsegna (sop), Samuel Bovy (cd), Carl Burrian (ten), Lina Cavalieri (sop), Victor Chalmin (bs), Geraldine Farrar (sop), Katherine Fleischer-Edel (sop), Otto Freitag (bs), Frederick Gunther (bs), Walter Koch (ten), Vittorio Navarini (bs), Helene Noldi (sop), Inge Oerner (sop), Lina Simeoli (sop), Riccardo Stracciari (bar)

U.S. --Amadeo Bassi (N.Y.), Alessandro Bonci (N.Y.), Florencio Constantino (New Orleans), Charles Dalmorès (N.Y.), Pauline Donalda (N.Y.), Josef Lhévinne (N.Y.), Francis MacMillan (N.Y.), Riccardo Martin (New Orleans), Maurice Renaud (N.Y.), Artur Rubinstein (N.Y.)

Other -Karl Armster (Essen), Margarethe Arndt-Ober (Frankfurt), Giuseppe Danise (Naples), Erna Denera (Kassel), Ilona Durigo (Vienna), Claire Dux (Cologne), Werner Engel (Berlin), Maude Fay (Munich), Helena Forti (Dessau), Amelita Galli-Curchi (Trani), Lillian Grenville (Nice), Nanny Larsén-Todsen (Stockholm), Mischa Levitzki (Antwerp), John McCormack (Savona), Geneviève Vix (Paris), Martha Winternitz-Dorda (Graz), Eric Wirl (Bayreuth)

D. New Positions:

Conductors: Volkmar Andreae (Zürich Tonhalle), Leo Blech (Berlin Opera), Karl Muck (Boston SO), Vassily Safonov (New York PO), Arturo Toscanini (La Scala)

Educational: Silas G. Pratt (Pratt Institute of Music and Art)

Others: Olin Downes (music critic, Boston *Post*), Samuel Langford (music critic, Manchester *Guardian*), Ernest Newman (music critic, Birmingham *Daily Post*)

E. Prizes and Honors:

Prizes: Jérôme Tharaud (Goncourt)

Honors: Edvard Grieg (honorary doctorate, Oxford), Edward C. Potter and Edmund Tarbell (National Academy), Jan Sibelius (Legion of Honor)

F. Biographical Highlights:

Frances Alda and Maria Gay make their Covent Garden debuts; John Alden Carpenter spends six months in Italy, studies composition with Elgar; Zoltán Kodály receives his Ph.D. degree with dissertation on Hungarian folk song; Nikolai Miaskovsky resigns from the Russian army and enters St. Petersburg Conservatory; Serge Rachmaninoff resigns from the Bolshoi and leaves for a tour of Italy before settling in Dresden; Igor Stravinsky marries his cousin, Katerina Nosenko; Karol Szymanowski moves to Berlin after having his first publication in Warsaw; Francisco Tárrega suffers from paralysis of the right side, causing his retirement from guitar playing in public; Deems Taylor receives his B.A. degree from New York University; Fartein Valen goes to the University of Oslo to study philology and music at the Conservatory.

G. Institutional Openings:

Performing Groups: Glasgow Orpheus Chorus, Manhattan Opera Co. and House I, Ravinia Park Concerts (Chicago), Toronto SO

Educational: Kansas City Conservatory of Music, Pratt Institute of Music and Art (Pittsburgh), Scuola Communale di Musica (Pisa)

Other: Deutsche Brahmsgesellschaft, Deutsch Musiksammlung; Sam Fox, Music Publisher (Cleveland); Grand Opera House (Tulsa); H. W. Gray Co., Inc., Music Publisher (N.Y.); Gulbranson Piano Co. (Chicago), Knud Larsen Musikforlag (Copenhagen), Los Angeles Philharmonic Auditorium, *Music Dealer* (*Music Industry*, N.Y.), Musikhistorisches Museum (Cologne), Presser Home for Retired Music Teachers (Philadelphia); W. A. Quinke & Co., Music Publishers (Los Angeles); Société des Concerts d'Autrefois (Paris), *Die Stimme: Centralblatt für Stimmung Tonbildung* (Berlin), Welsh Folk Song Society (Cardiff)

H. Musical Literature:

Capellen, George, *Ein neuer exotischer Musikstil*
Combarieu, Jules, *Éléments de grammaire musicale historique*
Dessoir, Max, *Aesthetik und allgemeine Kunstwissenschaft*
Hennig, Karl, *Einführung in das Wesen der Musik*
Mason, Daniel G., *The Romantic Composers*
Riemann, Hugo, *Hausmusik aus alter Zeit*
Rimsky-Korsakov, Nicolai, *My Musical Life*
Sankey, Ira, *Story of the Gospel Hymns*
Schenker, Heinrich, *Harmonielehre*
Vaughan-Williams, Ralph, *The English Hymnal*

I. Musical Compositions:

Alfvén, Hugo, *Symphony No. 3*
Bagley, E. E., *National Emblem March*
Bartók, Béla, *Orchestra Suite No. 2, Opus 4*
Cadman, Charles, *At Dawning* (song)
Chadwick, George, *Overture, Euterpe*
Converse, Frederick, *The Pipe of Desire* (opera)
Dinicu, Grigoras, *Hora Staccato* (violin)
Dohnányi, Ernst von, *Concerto for Cello and Orchestra*
Dukas, Paul, *Villanelle for Horn and Piano*
Elgar, Edward, *The Kingdom, Opus 51* (oratorio)
Enescu, George, *Symphony No. 1, Opus 13*
Fauré, Gabriel, *Piano Quintet No. 1, Opus 89*
Gilbert, Henry, *Dance in the Place Congo* (ballet)
Giordano, Umberto, *Fedora* (opera)
Glazunov, Alexander, *Symphony No. 8*
Hadley, Henry, *Symphony No. 3*
Herbert, Victor, *The Red Mill* (operetta)
Humperdinck, Engelbert, *The Tempest* (incidental music)
                          The Winter's Tale (incidental music)
d'Indy, Vincent, *Souvenirs, Opus 62* (tone poem)
Ives, Charles, *The Pond* (small orchestra)
Kodály, Zoltán, *Summer Evening* (symphonic poem)
Koven, Reginald de, *The Student King* (operetta)
Loeffler, Charles, *A Pagan Poem* (orchestra with piano)
Magnard, Albéric, *Hymn to Venus, Opus 17* (orchestra)
Malipiero, Gian F., *Sinfonia de Mare*
Massenet, Jules, *Ariane* (opera)
Nielsen, Carl, *Masquerade* (opera)
Rachmaninoff, Serge, *Fifteen Songs, Opus 26*
Ravel, Maurice, *Histoires Naturelles* (songs on Jules Renard)
Roussel, Albert, *Symphony No. 1, Opus 7, "Le Poeme de la Forêt"*
Saint-Saëns, Camille, *L'Ancêtre* (opera)
                       Psalm CL (double chorus and orchestra)
Schoenberg, Arnold, *Chamber Symphony No. 1, Opus 9*
Scriabin, Alexander, *4 Preludes for Piano, Opus 48*
                      3 Pieces for Piano, Opus 49
Sibelius, Jan, *Pohjola's Daughter, Opus 49* (symphonic poem)
              Belshazzar's Feast, Opus 51 (incidental music)
Suk, Josef, *Symphony No. 2, Opus 27, "Asrael"*
Vaughan-Williams, Ralph, *Norfolk Rhapsody No. 1*
Wolf-Ferrari, Ermanno, *I Quattro Rusteghi* (opera)

1907

World Events:
In the U.S., a financial panic; Oklahoma admitted as State number 46; President Roosevelt sends the "Great White Fleet" on a world cruise; United Press News Agency begins operation; Mother's Day first observed in Philadelphia. Internationally, Germany, Austria and Italy renew the Triple Alliance while England and France join with Russia in forming the Triple Entente; the *Lusitania* makes her maiden voyage; Austria introduces universal suffrage; Mohatmas Gandhi begins his civil disobedience crusade in Africa.

Cultural Highlights:
The National Museum of Wales opens in Cardiff; English novelist and story teller Rudyard Kipling receives the Nobel Prize for Literature and John Singer Sargent refuses a knighthood. Irish sculptor Augustus Saint-Gaudens dies but Russian artist Ilya Bolotowsky, Hungarian artist Zoltán Kemény and American sculptor George Rickey are born; births in the literary field include British poets W.H. Auden, Kurt Adler and Christopher Fry and novelist Daphne du Maurier and French poet René Char; deaths include Italian poet Giosuè Carducci, American author Thomas R. Aldrich, French novelist Joris Huysmans and British poet Francis Thompson. Other highlights include:

Art: George Bellows, *Stag at Sharkey's*; Claude Monet, *Water Lillies, Giverny*; Pablo Picasso, *Les Demoiselles d'Avignon*; Edward Poynter, *Lesbia and Sparrow*; Maurice Prendergast, *April Snow, Salem*; Frederic Remington, *Cavalry Charge on the Southern Plains*; Henri Rousseau, *The Snake Charmer*; John Sloan, *The Wake of the Ferry*.

Literature: Konstantin Balmont, *The Bird of Flame*; Hilary Belloc, *Cautionary Tales*; Theodore Dreiser, *Sister Carrie*; Henry James, *The American Scene*; Maurice Maeterlinck, *Ariane et Barbe-Bleue*; Rainer Rilke, *New Poems*; John Synge, *Playboy of the Western World*; Harold B. Wright, *The Shepherd of the Hills*.

MUSICAL EVENTS

A. Births:

Jan 4 Thyrasybulos Georgiades (Gr-mus)	May 8 Clifford Curzon (Br-pn)
Jan 7 Nicanor Zabaleta (Sp-hp)	Jun 18 Jeanette MacDonald (Am-sop)
Jan 17 Henk Badings (Hol-cm)	Jul 3 Gene Gutchë (Ger-cm)
Jan 18 János Ferencsik (Hun-cd)	Aug 20 Anatole Fistoulari (Gr-bs)
Feb 1 Camargo Guarnieri (Bra-cm)	Sep 23 Nicola Moscona (Gr-bs)
Feb 15 Jean Langlais (Fr-org)	Sep 23 Jarmila Novotná (Cz-sop)
Feb 16 Fernando Previtali (It-cd)	Oct 4 Alain Daniélou (Fr-mus)
Feb 17 Alec Wilder (Am-cm)	Oct 12 Wolfgang Fortner (Ger-cm)
May 4 Robert Donington (Br-mus)	Oct 27 Wilhelm Tappert (Ger-mus)
May 5 Yoritsune Matsudaira (Jap-cm)	Nov 9 Burrill Phillips (Am-cm)
May 15 Sigurd Rascher (Am-sax)	Nov 26 David Ewen (Am-mus)
	Dec 27 Willem van Otterloo (Hol-cd)

B. Deaths:

Mar 13 Fritz Scheel (Ger-cd)	Sep 4 Edvard Grieg (Nor-cm)
Apr 3 Marguerite Artôt (Fr-mez)	Sep 17 Ignaz Brüll (Aus-pn-cm)
Apr 15 Adolf Stern (Ger-mus)	Oct 5 James C. Culwick (Br-org)
Apr 26 Joseph Hellmesberger II (Aus-vn)	Nov 6 Johanne Cruvelli (Ger-sop)
Jun 2 Anastasius Dreszer (Pol-pn)	Nov 15 Antonia Mielke (Ger-sop)
Jun 4 Agathe Grondahl (Nor-pn-cm)	Nov 24 Theodor Bertram (Ger-bar)
Jun 4 Heinrich Köstlin (Ger-mus)	Nov 24 Max Hesse (Ger-pub)
	Nov 28 Enrico Delle Sedie (It-bar)

C. Débuts:

Met ---Frieda Altman (mez), Aristide Baracchi (bs), Alessandro Bonci (ten), Feodor Chaliapin (bs), Stephen Delwary (ten), Rodolfo Ferrari (cd), Rita Fornia (sop), Paul Lange (bar), Frieda Langendorff (sop), Riccardo Martin (ten), Primo Raimondi (ten), Giuseppe Tecchi (ten), Henriette Wakefield (mez), Herbert Waterous (bs), Paula Woening (mez)

U.S. --Ramon Blanchart (N.Y.), Richard Buhlig (Philadelphia), Armand Crabbé (N.Y.), Francesco Daddi (N.Y.), Adamo Didur (N.Y.), Mary Garden (N.Y.), Jeanne Gerville-Réache (N.Y.), Bernice de Pasquali (tour), Attilio Salvaneschi (tour), Mario Sammarco (N.Y.), Francesco Signorini (San Francisco), Giovanni Zenatello (N.Y.), Alice Zepilli (N.Y.)

Other -Karl Erb (Stuttgart), Paulo Gruppe (The Hague), Vittorio Gui (Rome), Beatrice Harrison (London), Myra Hess (London), Kathleen Howard (Metz), Serge Koussevitsky (Berlin, as conductor), Lydia Lipkovska (St. Petersburg), Frank Mullings (Coventry), Mignon Nevada (Rome), Alfred Peccaver (Prague), Maggie Teyte (Monte Carlo), Luisa Villani (Milan), Helene Wildbrunn (Dortmund), Efrem Zimbalist (Berlin)

D. New Positions:

Conductors: Armas Järnefelt (Stockholm Opera), Ernst Kunwald (Berlin PO), Gustav Mahler (Met), Karl Pohlig (Philadelphia Orchestra), Wilhelm Stenhammar (Göteborg SO)

Educational: Béla Bartók (piano, Budapest Academy), Charles Griffes (music director, Hackley School), Gustav Holst (music, Morley College), Hans Pfitzner (director, Strasbourg Conservatory), Ildebrando Pizzetti (composition, Parma Conservatory), Max Reger (composition, Leipzig Conservatory)

E. Prizes and Honors:

Prizes: Charles Radoux-Rogier (Prix de Rome)

Honors: Alexander Glazunov (honorary doctorate, Oxford), William Orchardson (knighted), Charles Santley (knighted)

F. Biographical Highlights:

Pasquale Amato and Maria Gay make their La Scala debuts; Frederick Converse withdraws from teaching to concentrate on composition; Frederick Delius meets Sir Thomas Beecham who becomes his champion; Emma Eames' divorce from painter Julian Story causes sensation; Manuel de Falla leaves Madrid to go to Paris; Charles Griffes returns to New York to teach at the Hackley School; Zoltán Kodály arrives in Paris, meets Debussy; John McCormack and Luisa Tetrazzini make their Covent Garden debuts; Gustav Mahler resigns as artistic director of the Vienna Opera, his daughter Maria dies and his own heart disease is first diagnosed; Leo Ornstein moves to the U.S.; Giacomo Puccini attends a Puccini festival at the Met; Wallingford Riegger graduates from the Institute of Musical Arts; Carl Ruggles moves to Winona, Minnesota; Leo Slezak begins voice study with Jean de Reszke; Wilhelm Stenhammar visits in Italy; Joseph Szigeti settles in London following his debut there; Edgard Varèse goes to Berlin to work with Busoni.

G. Institutional Openings:

Performing Groups: Blüthner Orchestra (Berlin), Choral Club of Hartford, Kiel Opera and Opera House, London String Quartet, St. Louis SO

Festivals: Concerts of British Chamber Music (London), Historic Concerts (Moscow)

Educational: Indiana College of Music and Fine Arts, Music Supervisor's National Conference (MENC today)

Other: Johann Sebastian Bach Home and Museum, Max Eschig Publishing Co. (Paris), Heckelphone-Clarinet (by Wilhelm Heckel), Hope-Jones Organ Co. (N.Y.), Malone Society (London), *Musica Sacro-Hispana* (Madrid), *Musical Observer* (N.Y.); Stainer and Bell, Music Publishers (London); Vinohrady Theater (Prague), *La Voz de la Musica*

H. Musical Literature:

Busoni, Ferruccio, *Toward a New Esthetic of Music*
Calvocoressi, Michel, *La Musique Russe*
Combarieu, Jules, *La Musique, ses lois, son évolution*
Curtis, Natalie, *The Indian's Book*
Kitson, Charles, *The Art of Counterpoint*
Lavignac, Albert, *Cours d'Harmonie...*
Louis, Rudolf, *Harmonielehre*
Mahillon, Victor, *Les Instruments à Vent*
Sonneck, Oscar, *Early Concert Life in America*
Terry, Richard, *Catholic Church Music*

I. Musical Compositions:

Alfvén, Hugo, *Swedish Rhapsody No. 2, "Uppsala"*
Bartók, Béla, *Two Portraits, Opus 5* (orchestra)
Chadwick, George, *Symphonic Sketches*
Converse, Frederick, *Job* (oratorio)
Debussy, Claude, *Images, Book II* (piano)
Delius, Frederick, *Songs of Sunset* (choral)
　　　　　　On Craig Dhu (chorus a capella)
　　　　　　Brigg Fair (violin and orchestra)
Dukas, Paul, *Ariane et Barbe-Bleu* (opera)
Elgar, Edward, *Pomp and Circumstance March No. 4*
　　　　　　The Wand of Youth Suites, Opus 1a and 1b
German, Edward, *Tom Jones* (operetta)
Giordano, Umberto, *Marcella* (opera)
Glazunov, Alexander, *Le Chant de Destin, Overture*
Glière, Reinhold, *Symphony No. 2, Opus 25*
Herbert, Victor, *The Tattooed Man* (operetta)
Humperdinck, Engelbert, *As You Like It* (incidental music)
Ives, Charles, *Calcium Light Night* (chamber orchestra)
　　　　　　Central Park in the Dark (orchestra)
Mahler, Gustav, *Symphony No. 8, "Symphony of a Thousand"*
Massenet, Jules, *Therese* (opera)
Paderewski, Ignace Jan, *Symphony, Opus 24*
Rachmaninoff, Serge, *Symphony No. 2, Opus 27*
　　　　　　The Isle of the Dead, Opus 29 (symphonic poem)
Ravel, Maurice, *L'Heure Espagnole* (one act opera)
　　　　　　Rhapsodie Espagnole (orchestra)
Rimsky-Korsakov, Nicolai, *Le Coq d'Or* (opera)
Schmitt, Florent, *La Tragedie de Salome* (orchestra)
Schoenberg, Arnold, *Friede auf Erden, Opus 13* (chorus)
Sibelius, Jan, *Two Songs, Opus 53*
　　　　　　Symphony No. 3, Opus 52
Stenhammar, Wilhelm, *Concerto No. 2 for Piano and Orchestra*
Stravinsky, Igor, *Symphony, Opus 1*
Suk, Josef, *A Summer Fairy Tale, Opus 29* (orchestra)
Szymanowski, Karol, *Symphony No. 1, Opus 15*
Vaughan-Williams, Ralph, *Toward the Unknown Region* (chorus, orchestra)
　　　　　　Norfolk Rhapsody No. 2 (orchestra)
　　　　　　Norfolk Rhapsody No. 3 (orchestra)

1908

World Events:
In the U.S., William Howard Taft becomes President No. 27; former President Grover Cleveland dies and future President Lyndon B. Johnson is born; New York's Singer Building becomes the first skyscraper; the Hudson River Tunnel opens; Henry Ford introduces the Model T; the *Christian Science Monitor* begins publication. Internationally, the Young Turks force restoration of the old constitution in the Ottoman Empire; Bulgaria declares its independence; Manuel II succeeds assassinated Carlos I in Portugal; the first Boy Scout Troop is introduced in England.

Cultural Highlights:
The "Ashcan" School of art makes its first exhibit and the Eight, a group of American painters, exhibits in New York; Allied Artists' Association is formed in London for exhibition of progressive painters; the *Friday Literary Review* begins publication. The German philosopher Rudolf Christian Eucken receives the Nobel Prize for Literature. The literary world loses the French poet François Coppée, Danish poet Holger Drachmann, American novelist Joel Chandler Harris and poet Ellen L. Moulton, Russian novelist Aleksei Potekhin, Canadian poet Louis Fréchette and French dramatist Victorien Sardou but gains by the birth of American novelist William Saroyan. The art world loses German artist Wilhelm Busch and Belgian sculptor Jef Lambeaux; Hungarian artist Victor Vasarely is born. Other highlights include:

Art: George Bellows, *Up the Hudson*; Umberto Boccioni, *Self-Portrait*; Constantin Brancusi, *The Kiss*; Georges Braque, *The Houses of l'Estaque*; Marsden Hartley, *Storm Clouds, Maine*; Henri Matisse, *The Girl with the Green Eyes*; Pierre Renoir, *Head of Coco* (bronze); John S. Sargent, *The Black Brook*; Maurice Vlaminck, *The Red Trees*.

Literature: Leonid Andreyev, *The Black Maskers*; Valeri Bryusov, *The Fiery Angel*; Edward Forster, *A Room with a View*; John W. Fox, *The Trail of the Lonesome Pine*; Anatole France, *Penguin Island*; Maurice Maeterlinck, *The Bluebird*; O'Henry, *The Voice of the City*; Ezra Pound, *A Lume Spento*; Henry Richardson, *Maurice Guest*.

MUSICAL EVENTS

A. Births:
Jan 12	Leopold Ludwig (Aus-cd)	Jun 20	LeRoy Anderson (Am-cm)
Feb 22	Irvin Kolodin (Am-cri)	Jun 23	Jussi Jalas (Fin-cd)
Mar 10	Owen Brannigan (Br-bs)	Jun 24	Hugo Distler (Ger-cm)
Mar 12	Eugene Conley (Am-ten)	Sep 26	Sylvia Marlowe (Am-hps)
Mar 14	Louise Cuyler (Am-mus)	Sep 30	David Oistrakh (Rus-vn)
Apr 5	Herbert von Karajan (Ger-cd)	Oct 2	Dénes Bartha (Hun-mus)
Apr 11	Karel Ancerl (Cz-cd)	Oct 21	Alexander Schneider (Rus-vn)
May 5	Kurt Böhme (Ger-bs)	Oct 26	Igor Gorin (Rus-bs)
May 15	Lars-Erik Larsson (Swe-cm)	Nov 28	Rose Bampton (Am-sop)
May 30	Beveridge Webster (Am-pn-cm)	Dec 3	Halsey Stevens (Am-cm)
May 31	Edith Coates (Br-mez)	Dec 10	Olivier Messiaen (Fr-cm)
Jun 7	Margherita Carosio (It-sop)	Dec 11	Elliott Carter (Am-cm)
Jun 7	Boris Goldovsky (Rus-pn)	Dec 13	Victor Babin (Rus-pn)
Jun 17	John Verrall (Am-cm)		

B. Deaths:
Jan 22	August E. Wilhelmj (Ger-vn)	Jun 21	Nicolai Rimsky-Korsakov (Rus-cm)
Jan 23	Edward MacDowell (Am-cm)	Jul 14	William Mason (Am-pn-ed)
Mar 12	Clara A. Novello (Br-sop)	Aug 13	Ira D. Sankey (Am-hymn)
Apr 4	Joseph Sucher (Hun-pn)	Sep 20	Pablo Sarasate (Sp-vn-cm)
May 12	Melesio Morales (Sp-cm)	Oct 21	Charles E. Norton (Am-au-ed)
Jun 13	"Blind Tom" Bethune (Am-pn)	Dec 24	François Gevaert (Fr-cm-mus)
Jun 18	Emil Vogel (Ger-mus)		

C. Débuts:

Met ---Frances Alda (sop), Pasquale Amato (bar), Angelo Bada (ten), Eduardo Cibelli (bar), Emmy Destinn (sop), Adamo Didur (bs), Fritz Feinhals (bar), Maria Gay (mez), Allen Hinckley (bs), Martha Leffler-Burckhard (sop), Gustav Mahler (cd), Eduardo Missiano (bar), Berta Morena (sop), Jean Noté (bar), Giulio Rossi (bs), Erik Schmedes (ten), Lenora Sparkes (sop), Arturo Toscanini (cd), Rosina Van Dyck (sop), Matja Van Niessen-Stone (mez), Herbert Witherspoon (bs)

U.S. --Hans Barth (N.Y.), Fannie Dillon (N.Y.), Hector Dufrane (N.Y.), Mischa Elman (N.Y.), Gustave Huberdeau (N.Y.), Maria Labia (N.Y.), Hans Letz (N.Y.), Gianna Ruff, Albert Spalding (N.Y.), Luisa Tetrazzini (N.Y.), Geneviève Vix (N.Y.), Ludwig Wüllner (N.Y.), Nicola Zerola (tour)

Other -Lucrezia Bori (Rome), Florica Cristoforeanu (Capodistria), Elvira de Hidalgo (Naples), Virgilio Lazzari (Vitale), Lucille Marcel (Vienna), Benno Moiseiwitsch (Reading), Marguerite Namara (Genoa), Leo Schützendorf (Düsseldorf), Andrés Segovia (Granada), Fritz Soot (Dresden), Giulia Tess (Venice), Carolina White (Naples)

D. New Positions:

Conductors: Max Fiedler (Boston SO), Carl Nielsen (Copenhagen Opera), Henryk Opiénski (Warsaw Opera), Max von Schillings (Stuttgart Opera), Arturo Toscanini (Met), Felix Weingartner (Vienna Opera)

Educational: Granville Bantock (professor, Birmingham University), Zoltán Kodály (composition, Budapest Academy), Walter Parratt (music chairman, Oxford), Ildebrando Pizzetti (harmony, Florence Conservatory)

Others: Charles W. Cadman (music critic, Pittsburgh *Dispatch*), Giulio Gatti-Casazza (director, Met), Hugo Riemann (director, Institute of Musical Science)

E. Prizes and Honors:

Prizes: André Gailhard (Prix de Rome)

Honors: George Clausen (Royal Academy), Julia Ward Howe (American Academy), Paolo Tosti (knighted)

F. Biographical Highlights:

Frances Alda makes her La Scala debut; Émile Cammaerts settles in London but keeps his Belgian citizenship; Claude Debussy finally marries Emma Bardac; Paul Hindemith is taken as a student by violinist Rebner; Charles Ives marries Harmony Twichell; Erich Kleiber goes to the University of Prague to study philosophy and music; Vanni Marcoux makes his Paris Opera debut; Alexander Scriabin meets Koussevitsky who becomes his ardent champion in conducting and in publishing; Jan Sibelius undergoes several throat operations; Richard Strauss builds his villa in Garmisch-Partenkirchen; Johan Svendsen forced to retire from active music life due to ill health; Maggie Teyte is personally selected by Debussy for the role of Melisande in his opera; Arturo Toscanini moves to New York to take over conducting at the Met; Ralph Vaughan-Williams studies composition and orchestration with Ravel; Anton Webern spends the summer conducting at Bad Ischl; Kurt Weill, at age 8, begins music study.

G. Institutional Openings:

Performing Groups: Boston Opera Co., Philharmonic Society of Buffalo, New Royal Opera Co. (Berlin), Sofia National Opera

Festivals: Belfast Music Festival

Educational: Musin Violin School (N.Y.), National Conservatory of Music (La Paz, Bolivia), Settlement Music School (Philadelphia)

Other: Allied Artist's Association (London), American Piano Co. (by consolidation), Association of Italian Musicologists, National Association of Organists, Philadelphia Opera House, Albert Schatz Collection of Original Opera Libretti (Library of Congress),

Opera House, Albert Schatz Collection of Original Opera Libretti (Library of Congress), Société Anonyme des Editions Maurice Senart (Paris), Teatro Colón (Buenos Aires), Théâtre du Jorat (Mézières)

H. Musical Literature:

Beck, Jean-Baptiste, *Die Melodien der Troubadours und Trouvéres*
Beyschlag, Adolf, *Die Ornamentik der Musik*
Expert, Henri, *Les Maîtres-Musiciens de la Renaissance Française (completed)*
Hamilton, Clarence, *Outlines of Music History*
Krehl, Stephan, *Kontrapunkt*
MacPherson, Stewart, *Evolution of Musical Design*
Mason, Daniel G., *Orchestral Instruments*
Riemann, Hugo, *Grundriss der Musikwissenschaft*
Rolland, Romain, *Musiciens d'Aujourd'hui*
   Musiciens d'Autrefois

I. Musical Compositions:

Balakirev, Mily, *Symphony No. 2*
Bartók, Béla, *String Quartet No. 1, Opus 7*
   Concerto No. 1 for Violin and Orchestra
Berg, Alban, *Sonata, Opus 1* (piano)
Cadman, Charles W., *From the Land of Sky-blue Waters* (song)
Debussy, Claude, *Iberia* (orchestra)
   Children's Corner (piano)
Delius, Frederick, *In a Summer Garden* (orchestral fantasy)
   Dance Rhapsody No. 1 (orchestra)
Dubois, Théodore, *Symphonie Française*
Elgar, Edward, *Symphony No. 1, Opus 55*
Fauré, Gabriel, *Serenade for Cello and Piano, Opus 98*
Foerster, Josef B., *From Shakespeare, Opus 76* (suite for orchestra)
Glière, Reinhold, *The Sirens, Opus 33* (symphonic poem)
Goldmark, Karl, *Ein Wintermärchen* (opera)
Herbert, Victor, *The Rose of Algeria* (operetta)
Humperdinck, Engelbert, *Lysistrata* (incidental music)
Ives, Charles, *The Unanswered Question* (trumpet, flute, strings)
   Sonata No. 1 for Violin and Piano
   The Anti-Abolitionist Riots (piano)
Liadov, Anatoli, *The Enchanted Lake* (symphonic poem)
MacDowell, Edward, *Lamia, Opus 29* (symphonic poem)
Mahler, Gustav, *Das Lied von der Erde* (soprano, tenor, orchestra)
Massenet, Jules, *Espade* (ballet)
Miaskovsky, Nicolai, *Symphony No. 1, Opus 3*
Nielsen, Carl, *Saga-Drom* (orchestra)
Prokofiev, Serge, *Suggestion Diabolique* (piano)
Ravel, Maurice, *Gaspard de la Nuit* (piano)
   Ma Mère l'Oye (piano, 4 hands)
Reger, Max, *Concerto, Opus 101, for Violin and Orchestra*
Satie, Erik, *Disagreeable Impressions* (piano)
Schoenberg, Arnold, *String Quartet No. 2, Opus 15*
Sibelius, Jan, *Swanwhite, Opus 52* (incidental music)
Straus, Oscar, *The Chocolate Soldier* (operetta)
Stravinsky, Igor, *Fireworks, Opus 4* (orchestra)
   Scherzo Fantastique, Opus 3 (orchestra)
Vaughan-Williams, Ralph, *3 Nocturnes* (baritone, chorus, orchestra)
Webern, Anton, *Passacaglia for Orchestra, Opus 1*
Widor, Charles, *Sinfonia Sacra for Organ and Orchestra*

1909

World Events:
In the U.S., Henry Ford introduces the assembly line into his plant; the Payne-Aldrich Tariff raises protective rates on imports; the National Conservation Association and the National Association for the Advancement of Colored People (NAACP) are both formed. Internationally, Robert Peary and his party become the first men to reach the North Pole; Louis Blériot becomes the first to fly the English Channel; the Union of South Africa is founded by British Parliament.

Cultural Highlights:
The Futurist movement in art is born in an article by the Italian poet Emilio Marinetti; the Knave of Diamonds group is formed in Russia and the Neue Künstlervereinigung (NKV) is founded in Munich. Selma Lagerlöf becomes the first woman to win the Nobel Prize for Literature. Deaths in the art world include British artist William Fritz and the artist of the American West, Frederic Remington. In the literary field, births include British novelist Eric Ambler and American author Eudora Welty; deaths include American authors Edward Everett Hale and Sarah Jewett, British poets George Meredith, Algernon Swinburne and dramatist John M. Synge, Scottish poet John Davidson, French poet Catulle Mendès and Italian novelist Alfredo Oriani. Other highlights include:

Art: Umberto Boccioni, *Riot in the Gallery*; Emile Bourdelle, *Hérkalès Archer* (bronze); Arthur B. Davies, *The Dream*; Wassily Kandinsky, *Blue Mountain*; Oskar Kokoschka, *Children Playing*; Henri Matisse, *Harmony in Red*; Emil Nolde, *Pentecost: Last Supper*; Pablo Picasso, *Harlequin*; Auguste Rodin, *Head of Mahler*.

Literature: Mary R. Andrews, *The Enchanted Forest*; Guillaume Apollinaire, *L'Enchanteur Pourrissent*; Sem Benelli, *L'Amore dei Tre Re*; John Galsworthy, *Strife*; Jack London, *Martin Eden*; Ferenc Molnár, *Liliom*; Ezra Pound, *Personae*; Rainer Maria Rilke, *Requiem*; Gertrude Stein, *Three Lives*; H.G. Wells, *Tono-Bungay*.

MUSICAL EVENTS

A. Births:

Jan 3	Victor Borge (Den-pn-hum)		Jul 27	Gianandrea Gavazzeni (It-cd)
Jan 11	Gunnar Berg (Den-cm)		Aug 16	Paul Callaway (Am-org)
Jan 15	Elie Siegmeister (Am-cm)		Aug 18	Arnold Franchetti (It-cm)
Jan 19	Hans Hotter (Ger-bar)		Aug 18	Howard Swanson (Am-cm)
Feb 5	Grazyna Bacewicz (Pol-cm-vn)		Aug 22	Vitya Vronsky (Rus-pn)
Feb 17	Marjorie Lawrence (Aust-sop)		Sep 22	Václav Dobiás (Cz-cm)
Mar 8	Anthony Donato (Am-cm)		Sep 27	Jean Berger (Ger-cm)
May 30	Benny Goodman (Am-pop)		Oct 8	Mack Harrell (Am-bar)
Jun 14	Burl Ives (Am-folk)		Nov 8	Alberto Erede (It-cd)
Jun 16	Willi Boskovsky (Am-cd)		Nov 28	Rose Bampton (Am-sop)
Jun 24	Milton Katims (Am-cd)		Dec 10	Otakar Kraus (Br-Cz-bar)
Jul 4	Alec Templeton (Br-pn-hum)		Dec 20	Vagn Holmboe (Den-cm)
				Agnes Demille (Am-bal)

B. Deaths:

Jan 13	Wilhelm Heckel (Ger-inst.m)		Jul 22	Oscar Byström (Swe-cm-pn)
Jan 14	Charles Meerens (Bel-acous)		Aug 6	Stepan Smolensky (Rus-mus)
Feb 8	Mieczyslav Karlovicz (Pol-cm)		Aug 17	Richard Hoffman (Br-pn)
Apr 3	Benjamin Lang (Am-pn-cd)		Oct 6	Dudley Buck (Am-cm)
Apr 27	Heinrich Conried (Aus-imp)		Nov 16	Francis Thomé (Fr-cm)
May 18	Isaac Albéniz (Sp-cm)		Dec 5	Ebenezer Prout (Br-the)
Jun 1	Giuseppe Martucci (It-cd-cm)		Dec 15	Francisco Tárrega (Sp-gui)

C. Debuts:

Met ---Ludwig Burgstaller (ten), Anna Case (sop), Edmond Clément (ten), Bernice DePasquali (sop), Marianne Flahaut (mez), Fernando Gianoli-Galletti (bs), Dinh Gilly (bar), Alma Gluck (sop), Rinaldo Grassi (ten), Carl Jörn (ten), Armando Lecomte (bar), Lydia Lipkovska (sop), Alice Nielsen (sop), Vittorio Podesti (cd), Marcelle Reiner (bs), Leo Slezak (ten), Egisto Tango (cd), Clarence Whitehill (bar), Florence Wickham (mez)

U.S. --Nazzareno de Angelis (N.Y.), Eugenia Bronskaja (Boston), Gervase Elwes (tour), Paulo Gruppe, Albert Huberty (New Orleans), Tilly Koenen (tour), Maria Kousnetzoff (N.Y.), Joseph Malkin (tour), John McCormack (N.Y.), Carmen Melis (N.Y.), Yolanda Mérö (N.Y.), Giovanni Polese (N.Y.), Sergei Rachmaninoff (tour), Marguerite Sylva (N.Y.)

Other -Jelly d'Aranyi (Vienna), Elvira Casazza (Varese), Marya Freund (Europe), Eva Gauthier (Parma), Marcel Grandjany (Paris), Morgan Kingston (London), Luigi Montesanto (Palermo), Wilhelm Rode (Erfurt), Minnie Saltzmann-Stevens (London), Richard Schubert (Strasbourg), Elisabeth Schumann (Hamburg), Fritz Windgassen (Hamburg), Benno Ziegler (Munich)

D. New Positions:

Conductors: Henry Hadley (Seattle SO), Gustav Mahler (New York PO), Tullio Serafin (La Scala), Leopold Stokowski (Cincinnati SO)

Educational: Henri Expert (librarian, Paris Conservatory), Nicolai Medtner (piano, Moscow Conservatory), Vítezslav Novák (composition, Prague Conservatory), Ignace Jan Paderewski (director, Warsaw Conservatory), Otakar Sevcík (violin, Vienna Academy)

Others: Carl Engel (editor, Boston Music Co.), Arthur Farwell (critic, *Musical America*)

E. Prizes and Honors:

Prizes: Paul Manship (American Prix de Rome)

Honors: Ivan A. Bunin (Russian Academy), Gabriel Fauré (French Institute), Daniel R. Knight (Legion of Honor), Arthur W. Pinero (knighted)

F. Biographical Highlights:

Charles W. Cadman spends his summer with the Omaha Indians; Claude Debussy begins to be bothered with cancer; Michel Fokine becomes chief choreographer for Diaghilev; Ossip Gabrilowitsch marries contralto Clara Clemens, daughter of Mark Twain; Charles Ives forms an insurance agency in New York with Julian Myrick; Gustav Mahler, gravely ill, quits the Met; Victor Maurel begins teaching voice in New York; Serge Prokofiev begins studying piano with Annette Espinova; Sergei Rachmaninoff makes his first concert tour of the U.S.; Fritz Reiner becomes coach at the Budapest Opera; Curt Sachs begins devoting full time to music; Carlos Salzedo moves to New York; Marcella Sembrich retires from the opera stage but continues her concert career; Arthur Shepherd leaves Salt Lake City for Boston; Ernst Toch wins the Mozart Prize and moves to Frankfurt; Fartein Valen enters Berlin Hochschule for further music study; Ermanno Wolf-Ferrari begins devoting full time to music.

G. Institutional Openings:

Performing Groups: Ballet Russe (Diaghilev), Beecham Orchestra (London), Berne Lehrergesangverein, English String Quartet, Koussevitsky Orchestra (Russia), Leeds String Quartet, MacDowell Chorus (Schola Cantorum), Memphis SO I (disbanded in 1920's), Mendelssohn Choir (Pittsburgh), Philadelphia Little Symphony, San Carlo Opera Co., Tollefsen Trio (N.Y.), Trondheim SO (Norway), Waldbauer-Kerpoly String Quartet (Budapest)

Festivals: Atlanta Music Festival, Chicago North Shore Festival

Educational: Delta Omicron International Music Fraternity (Cincinnati), Tulane University Music Dept. (New Orleans), Vander Cook College of Music (Chicago)

Other: Editions Russes de Musique, Frobenius Organ Co. (Copenhagen), Gamble Hinged Music Co. (Chicago), *Der Mercur, Musical Antiquary* (London), New Theater (N.Y.), Norsk Musikforlag, Société Musicale Independante (Paris), Symphony Club (Philadelphia), Tischer und Jagenberg Music Publishers (Cologne)

H. Musical Literature:
Burton, Frederick, *American Primitive Music*
Cooke, James, *Standard History of Music*
Elson, Louis, *Pocket Music Dictionary*
Farnsworth, Charles, *Education Through Music*
Goetschius, Percy, *Elementary Counterpoint*
Hilman, Lawrence, *Aspects of Modern Opera*
Hofmann, Joseph, *Piano Questions Answered*
Hofmann, Richard, *Katechismus der Musikinstrumente*
Kitson, Charles, *Studies in Fugue*
Landowska, Wanda, *Musique Ancienne*

I. Musical Compositions:
Albéniz, Isaac, *Iberia* (all four books finished)
Bax, Arnold, *In the Fairy Hills* (symphonic poem)
Berg, Alban, *Four Songs, Opus 2* (voice)
Bloch, Ernst, *MacBeth* (opera)
Cadman, Charles, *Four American Indian Songs*
Casella, Alfredo, *Symphony No. 2*
        Orchestral Suite in C
        Italie, Opus 11 (orchestra)
Coleridge-Taylor, Samuel, *Endymion's Dream* (opera)
Debussy, Claude, *Rondes de Printemps* (orchestra)
Elgar, Edward, *Elegy for Strings, Opus 58*
Foerster, Josef, *Enigma, Opus 99* (symphonic poem)
Foote, Arthur, *Piano Trio No. 2, Opus 65*
Holst, Gustav, *Suite No. 1 for Band*
Ives, Charles, *Sonata No. 1 for Piano*
        Washington's Birthday (from Holiday Symphony)
Lehár, Franz, *Count of Luxembourg* (operetta)
Liadov, Anatoli, *Kikimora* (symphonic poem)
Mahler, Gustav, *Symphony No. 9*
Massenet, *Jules Bacchus* (opera)
Prokofiev, Serge, *Piano Sonata No. 1 in F-sharp, Opus 1*
        Four Etudes, Opus 2 (piano)
Rachmaninoff, Serge, *Concerto No. 3, Opus 30, for Piano and Orchestra*
Schoenberg, Arnold, *Five Pieces for Orchestra, Opus 16*
        Erwartung, Opus 17 (monodrama)
        3 Pieces for Piano, Opus 11
Sibelius, Jan, *String Quartet, Opus 56, "Voces Intimae"*
        In Memoriam, Opus 59 (symphonic poem)
Strauss, Richard, *Elektra* (opera)
Szymanowski, Karol, *Lottery for Husbands* (operetta)
Vaughan-Williams, Ralph, *The Wasps* (incidental music)
        On Wenlock Edge (tenor, string quartet and piano)
        A Sea Symphony (soprano, baritone, chorus and orchestra)
Webern, Anton, *5 Songs from "Der Siebente Ring", Opus 3*
        5 Songs, Opus 4
        5 Movements for String Quartet, Opus 5
        6 Pieces for Orchestra, Opus 5
Wolf-Ferrari, Ermanno, *The Secret of Suzanne* (opera)

1910

World Events:

The U.S. census of 92,228,000 population in 46 states shows an increase of 21% in ten years; Halley's Comet makes its scheduled appearance; Glacier National Park is established by Congress; Kent State University is founded in Ohio; the Boy Scouts of America is incorporated; President William H. Taft begins the tradition of throwing out the first ball in opening ballgames. Internationally, George V takes the English throne on the death of Edward VII; Portugal and Mexico have revolutions that lead to establishment of republics; Japan annexes Korea in the Orient; Georges Claude introduces the Neon Light.

Cultural Highlights:

Several painters sign the Manifesto of the Futurist Painters as well as the Technical Manifesto; *Der Sturm* begins publication in Berlin. The Hall of Fame for Great Americans welcomes William Cullen Bryant, James Fenimore Cooper, Oliver Wendall Holmes, Edgar Allen Poe, and Harriet Beecher Stowe. The German novelist and poet, Paul von Heyse receives the Nobel Prize for Literature. Births include the American novelist Josephine Johnson and the French author Jean Genêt as well as American artist Franz Kline. Deaths in the literary world include Norwegian author Björnstjerne Björnson, German novelist Wilhelm Raabe, Russian novelist Leo Tolstoy and American authors Samuel Clemens (Mark Twain) and W.S. Porter (O'Henry); the art world mourns the deaths of American artists John La Farge and Winslow Homer and sculptors Larkin Meade and John Quincy Adams Ward, British artist William H. Hunt, Scottish artist William Orchardson and French artist Henri Rousseau. Other highlights include:

Art: Umberto Boccioni, *The City Rises*; Emile Bourdelle, *Rodin at Work*; Giorgio de Chirico, *Enigma of an Autumn Afternoon*; Frantisek Kupka, *Planes by Colors*; Fernand Léger, *Nues dans la Foret*; Wilhelm Lehmbruck, *Standing Woman*; Franz Marc, *Horse in Landscape*; Amedeo Modigliani, *The Cellist*.

Literature: Jane Addams, *Twenty Years at Hull House*; Leonid Andreyev, *Silence and Other Stories*; Theodor Däubler, *Das Nordlicht*; Sigmund Freud, *Five Lectures on Psychoanalysis*; Edward Robinson, *The Town Down the River*; John Synge, *Deirdre of the Sorrows*; H.G. Wells, *History of Mr. Polly*; William Yeats, *The Green Helmet*.

MUSICAL EVENTS

A. Births:

Jan 5	Erika Morini (Aus-vn)	Jun 21	Charles Jones (Can-cm)
Jan 10	Jean Martinon (Fr-cd)	Jun 22	Peter Pears (Br-ten)
Jan 11	Izler Solomon (Am-cd)	Aug 4	William Schuman (Am-cm)
Feb 3	Blas Galindo Dimas (Mex-cm)	Aug 5	Hans Nathan (Ger-mus)
Mar 9	Samuel Barber (Am-cm)	Aug 14	Pierre Schaeffer (Fr-acous)
Mar 13	Sammy Kaye (Am-pop)	Sep 3	Dorothy Maynor (Am-sop)
Mar 27	Manfred Bukofzer (Ger-mus)	Sep 14	Rolf Liebermann (Swi-cm)
Apr 9	Cloe Elmo (It-mez)	Sep 18	Leon Stein (Am-cm-ed)
May 23	Artie Shaw (Am-pop)	Dec 1	Alicia Markova (Br-bal)
Jun 10	Frederick Lechner (Ger-bar)	Dec 7	Richard F. Goldman (Am-cd)
Jun 14	Rudolf Kempe (Ger-cd)	Dec 15	Giulietta Simionato (It-alto)
Jun 17	H. Owen Reed (Am-cm)	Dec 20	Paul Bowles (Am-cm)
Jun 18	Jennie Tourel (Can-mez)		

B. Deaths:

Jan 13	Gustav Walter (Aus-ten)	Mar 31	Jean Moréas (Ger-cd)
Jan 19	Otakar Hostinsky (Cz-mus)	May 10	Benjamin Cutler (Am-the)
Mar 10	Carl Reinecke (Ger-pn-cm)	May 18	Pauline Viardot-García (Fr-mez)
Mar 17	Joaquin Valverde (Sp-cm)	May 29	Mily Balakirev (Rus-cm)
Mar 28	Edouard Colonne (Fr-cd)	Aug 31	Pierre Aubry (Fr-mus)

Sep 5   Franz Haberl (Ger-mus)

C. Debuts:

Met ---Mariska Aldrich (mez), Lamberto Belleri (ten), Max Bendix (cd), Francesco Cerri (bs), Gina Ciaparelli (sop), Maria Claessens (mez), Florencio Constantino (ten), Marie Delna (mez), Adolf Fuhrmann (bs), Elvira de Hidalgo (sop), William Hinshaw (bar), Herman Jadlowker (ten), John McCormack (ten), Jane Osborn-Hannah (sop), Maurice Renaud (bar), Léon Rothier (bs), Basil Ruysdael (bs), Dmitri Smirnov (ten), Lucy Weidt (sop)

U.S. --Adolphe Borchard, Luigi Cilla (Boston), David Devriès (N.Y.), Lillian Grenville (Chicago), Orville Harrold (N.Y.), Leo Sibiriakov (Boston), Marie Sundelius (Boston), Emilio Venturini (Chicago)

Other -Michael Bohnen (Düsseldorf), Eduardo Ferrari-Fontana (Turin), Fanny Heldy (Brussels), Maria Jeritza (Olmütz), Lotte Lehmann (Hamburg), Giovanni Martinelli (Milan), George Meader (Leipzig), Claudia Muzio (Arezzo), Giuseppe Nessi (Saluzzo); Rudolf Ritter (Vienna), Marcella Roeseler (Weisbaden), Vladimir Rosing (St. Petersburg), Theodor Scheidl (Vienna), Tito Schipa (Vercelli), Hertha Stolzenberg (Berlin), Conchita Supervia (Buenos Aires)

D. New Positions:

Conductors: Cleofonte Campanini (Manhattan Opera House), Otto Klemperer (Hamburg Opera), Gabriel Pierné (Concerts Colonne)

Educational: Paul Dukas (orchestration, Paris Conservatory)

Others: Andreas Dippel (manager, Chicago Opera), Harvey Gaul (organ, Calvary Church, Pittsburgh), Hans Pfitzner (director, Strasbourg Opera)

E. Prizes and Honors:

Prizes: Paul H. Allen (Paderewski), Ernst Toch (Mendelssohn)

Honors: Alexandre Guilmant (honorary doctorate, Manchester), Christian Sinding (Norwegian Government Grant), Charles Widor (French Academy)

F. Biographical Highlights:

Frances Alda marries Giulio Gatti-Casazza, manager of the New York Met; Arthur Farwell moves to New York and becomes supervisor of municipal music concerts; Amelita Galli marries her first husband, artist Luigi Curci; George Gershwin's family buys a new piano which the 12-year old George masters in a short time; Jacques Ibert enters Paris Conservatory; Zoltán Kodály marries composer and pianist Emma Sándor and receives his first public performance in Budapest; Bohuslav Martinu is expelled from the Prague Organ School for lack of interest in his studies; Serge Prokofiev's father dies, causing financial distress to the family; Alan Seeger graduates from Harvard; Sigmund Spaeth receives his Ph.D. from Princeton; Igor Stravinsky moves his family to Paris after receiving a commission from Diaghilev; Anton Webern conducts light music at Teplitz.

G. Institutional Openings:

Performing Groups: Barcelona SO, Barrère Ensemble of Wind Instruments (Little Symphony in 1914), Capet String Quartet III (Paris), Catterall String Quartet (London), Chicago-Philadelphia Opera Co., Denhof (Beecham) Opera Co. (London), Deutsche Oper (Berlin), Havana SO

Educational: Boston School of Music, Indiana University School of Music, Institute for Jewish Music (Jerusalem), Scuola Superiore de Musica Sacra (Rome), Shulamit Conservatory of Music (Tel Aviv), South African College of Music (Cape Town, later part of University of Cape Town)

Other: *Drei Masken Verlag* (Munich), *Muzika* (Moscow), *Orkestr* (Moscow); Rodeheaver-Ackley Co., Music Publishers (Chicago)

H. Musical Literature:
Elson, Louis, *Mistakes and Disputed Points in Music*
Findeisen, Nicolai, *Musical Antiquity*
Galpin, Francis, *Old English Instruments of Music*
Graf, Max, *Die innere werkstatt des Musikers*
Griesbacher, Peter, *Lehrbuch des Kontrapunkts*
Ivanov, Mikhail, *Historical Development of Music in Russia I*
Lehmann, Friedrich, *Harmonic Analysis*
Lomax, John, *Cowboy Songs and Frontier Ballads*
MacPherson, Stewart, *Music and Its Appreciation*
Schenker, Heinrich, *Kontrapunkt I*

I. Musical Compositions:
Bartók, Béla, *Roumanian Dances, Opus 8a* (piano)
                 Two Pictures, Opus 10 (orchestra)
Berg, Alban, *String Quartet, Opus 3*
Bond, Carrie Jacobs, *A Perfect Day* (song)
Cadman, Charles, *Vision of Sir Launfal* (cantata for male voices)
Debussy, Claude, *Preludes, Book I* (piano)
                 Rhapsody No. 1 for Clarinet
                 3 Ballades de François Villon
Dohnányi, Ernst von, *Suite in F-sharp for Orchestra*
Elgar, Edward, *Concerto, Opus 61 for Violin and Orchestra*
Fauré, Gabriel, *La Chanson d'Eve, Opus 95* (10 songs)
Foote, Arthur, *Suite in E, Opus 63* (strings)
Ganne, Louis, *Les Ailes* (opera)
Giordano, Umberto, *Mese Mariano* (opera)
Herbert, Victor, *Naughty Marietta* (operetta)
Holst, Gustav, *A Somerset Rhapsody, Opus 21* (orchestra)
Humperdinck, Engelbert, *Königskinder* (opera)
                 The Bluebeard (incidental music)
Ives, Charles, *Sonata Nos. 1 & 2 for Violin and Piano*
Mahler, Gustave, *Symphony No. 10* (first movement completed)
Massenet, Jules, *Don Quichotte* (opera)
Novák, Vítezslav, *Der Sturm* (chorus and orchestra)
Pierné, Gabriel, *On ne Badine pas Avec l'Amour* (opera)
Prokofiev, Serge, *Autumn Sketch* (orchestra)
Puccini, Giacomo, *Girl of the Golden West* (opera)
Rachmaninoff, Serge, *Liturgy of St. John Chrysostom, Opus 31* (chorus, orchestra)
                 Thirteen Preludes, Opus 32 for Piano
Rangström, Ture, *Dithyramb* (symphonic poem)
Reger, Max, *Concerto, Opus 114, for Piano and Orchestra*
                 Psalm 100, Opus 106
Respighi, Ottorino, *Semirama* (opera)
Saint-Saëns, Camille, *Ouverture de Fête, Opus 133*
Scriabin, Alexander, *Prometheus: Poem of Fire, Opus 60* (orchestra)
Strauss, Richard, *Der Rosenkavalier* (opera)
Stravinsky, Igor, *The Firebird* (ballet)
Szymanowski, Karol, *Symphony No. 2, Opus 19*
Varèse, Edgard, *Bourgogne* (symphonic poem)
Vaughan-Williams, Ralph, *Fantasia on a Theme by Thomas Tallis* (strings)
Webern, Anton, *Four Pieces for Violin and Piano, Opus 7*

1911

World Events:
C.P. Rogers makes the first transcontinental flight across the U.S. in 82 hours, 4 minutes; the U.S. Supreme Court breaks up Standard Oil Company and the American Tobacco Company; new inventions include the hydroplane, the self-starter for automobile engines, air conditioning and the Browning automatic pistol. Internationally, the Swedish explorer, Roald Amundsen becomes the first man to reach the South Pole; Chinese Revolution overthrows the Manchu government and Sun Yat-sen becomes president of the Republic; Parliament curtails the power of the House of Lords in England.

Cultural Highlights:
The Camden Town Group is formed in London while in Munich the Blaue Reiter Group and School of Abstract Art is established; the magazine *Poetry Review* begins publication. French poet Maurice Maeterlinck receives the Nobel Prize for Literature. Births this year include the American artist Edwin A. Abbey and sculptor Louise Bourgeois; in literature, American poets Elizabeth Bishop and Kenneth Patchen and novelist Tennessee Williams, Greek poet Odysseus Elytis, Polish poet Czeslav Milosz, British dramatist Terence Rattigan and French novelist Henri Troyat. Deaths include American sculptor Thomas Ball, German sculptor Reinhold Begas, Lithuanian artist Mikolajus Ciurlionis, French artist Alphonse Legros and Dutch artist Joseph Israëls. Other highlights include:

Art: Umberto Boccioni, *States of Mind*; Georges Braque, *Man with Guitar*; Marc Chagall, *I and the Village*; Lovis Corinth, *Golgotha*; Robert Delaunay, *The Eiffel Tower*; Marcel Duchamp-Villon, *Baudelaire*; Wilhelm Lehmbruck, *Kneeling Woman*, Henri Matisse, *Red Studio*; Maurice Utrillo, *Church at St. Hilaire*; Aston Webb, *Admiralty Arch* (London).

Literature: Guillaume Apollinaire, *Le Bestiare*; Katherine Bates, *America, the Beautiful and Other Poems*; Theodore Dreiser, *Jennie Gerhardt*; Edward Forster, *The Celestial Omnibus*; John Galsworthy, *The Patrician*; Hugo von Hofmannsthal, *Jedermann*; George Moore, *Hail and Farewell--Ave*; Ezra Pound, *Canzoni*; Edith Warton, *Ethan Frome*.

MUSICAL EVENTS

A. Births:

Jan 1	Roman Totenberg (Pol-vn)	Apr 21	Leonard Warren (Am-bar)
Jan 14	Helmuth Degen (Ger-cm)	Apr 28	Marie Tauberová (Cz-sop)
Jan 24	Muir Mathieson (Br-cd)	May 22	Janet Fraser (Scot-mez)
Jan 29	Bernard Herrmann (Am-cd-cm)	Jun 8	Bruno Bartolozzi (It-cm)
Jan 29	Bronislaw Gimpel (Pol-vn)	Jun 10	Dénes Agay (Hun-pn-ped)
Feb 2	Jussi Björling (Swe-ten)	Jun 10	Ralph Kirkpatrick (Am-hps)
Feb 3	Jehan Alain (Fr-org)	Jul 7	Gian Carlo Menotti (It-cm)
Mar 8	Alan Hovhaness (Arm-cd)	Jul 29	Ján Cikker (Cz-cm)
Mar 11	Howard Mitchell (Am-cd)	Aug 12	Edward Downes (Am-cri)
Mar 24	Enrique Jordá (Sp-cd)	Sep 19	Allan Pettersson (Swi-cm)
Mar 31	Elisabeth Grümmer (Ger-sop)	Nov 3	Vladimir Ussachevsky (Rus-cm)
Apr 13	Nino Sanzogno (It-cd)		

B. Deaths:

Mar 29	Alexandre Guilmant (Fr-cm)	Jul 4	Paul Runge (Ger-mus)
May 5	James Bland (Am-cm)	Jul 7	Samuel de Lange (Hol-org-cm)
May 18	Gustav Mahler (Aus-cm-cd)	Aug 14	Luigi Vannuccini (It-voc)
May 29	William S. Gilbert (Br-lib)	Oct 5	Charles T. Malherbe (Fr-mus)
Jun 14	Johan Svendsen (Nor-cm)	Oct 17	Alfred A. Giradet (Fr-bs)
Jul 2	Felix Mottl (Ger-cd)	Nov 8	Emma A. Osgood (Am-sop)

C. Debuts:

Met ---Amadeo Bassi (ten), Stefan Buckreus (bs), Giuseppe Cottino (bs), Elsa Foerster (sop), Cleo Gascoigne (sop), Giuseppina Giaconia (mez), Putnam Griswold (bs), Bernhard Heidenreich (bs), Heinrich Hensel (ten), Elvira Leveroni (mez), Gaston Martin (bar), Margarete Matzenauer (mez/sop), Lambert Murphy (ten), Giulio Romolo (bar), Giuseppe Sturani (cd), Luisa Tetrazzini (sop), Willy Tyroler (bs/cd), Hermann Weil (bar)

U.S. --Agustarello Affré (San Francisco), Georg Baklanov (Boston), Leonard Borwick(tour), Elvira Casazza (tour), Rafaelo Díaz (Boston), Jenny Dufau (Chicago), Frederick Frandkin, George Hamlin (Philadelphia), Mary Jordan (Boston), Leo Ornstein (N.Y.), Lila Robeson (Boston), Maggie Teyte (Chicago), Efrem Zimbalist (Boston)

Other -Maria Basilides (Budapest), Rosina Beckman (Australia), Luca Botta (Naples), Karin Branzell (Stockholm), Mildred Dibling (Paris), Jascha Heifetz (St. Petersburg), Hipolito Lazaro (Treviso), Miriam Licette (Rome), Ingeborg Liljeblad (Mannheim), Felice Lyne (London), Edith Mason (Barnes), Guiomar Novaës (Paris), Solomon (London), Mariano Stabile (Palermo), Emil Telmányi (Berlin), Cesar Vezzani (Paris)

D. New Positions:

Conductors: Wilhelm Furtwängler (Lübeck Opera), Juan Lamote de Grignon (Barcelona SO), Henry Hadley (San Francisco SO), Oskar Merikanto (Helsinki Opera), Pierre Monteux (Ballet Russe), Max Reger (Meiningen SO), Josef Stransky (New York PO)

Educational: Sylvain Dupuis (director, Liège Conservatory), Eugène Gigout (Paris Conservatory), Arnold Schoenberg (theory and compostion, Stern Conservatory, Berlin)

Others: Henry Burleigh (editor, *G. Ricordi*), Henry Colles (music critic, *London Times*)

E. Prizes and Honors:

Prizes: Paul Paray (Prix de Rome), Horatio Parker (Met Opera Prize)

Honors: Edward Elgar (Order of Merit), Franz Kniesel (honorary doctorate, Yale), Frederic Owen (knighted), Henry J. Wood (knighted)

F. Biographical Highlights:

Alban Berg, after a long 4-year wait due to her father's disapproval, finally marries his love, Helene Nahowski; Emma Eames marries her second husband, baritone Emilio de Gogorza, but soon fails in this marriage too; Artur Honegger goes to Paris and enters the Conservatory; Charles Ives decides to move out of New York and settles in Hartsdale, Connecticut; Alma Mahler, widow of the composer, begins an affair with Oscar Kokoschka; Minnie Saltzmann-Stevens makes her Bayreuth debut; Arnold Schoenberg moves his family to Berlin where he begins teaching at the Stern Conservatory and composition privately; William Grant Still leaves Arkansas to attend Wilberforce College in Ohio where he begins studying toward a science degree; Leopold Stokowski marries his first wife, pianist Olga Samaroff; Anton Webern joins Schoenberg in Berlin; Felix Weingartner resigns his opera post in Vienna but keeps the Philharmonic position; Ermanno Wolf-Ferrari visits the U.S.; Efrem Zimbalist emigrates to the U.S.

G. Institutional Openings:

Performing Groups: Austin SO, Bonn SO, Finnish Opera Co. (Helsinki), Goldman Band (N.Y.), Indianapolis Orchestral Association, Irish Orchestra of London, Kansas City SO, Portuguese SO, Ravinia Opera (Chicago), St. Olav Choir (Minnesota), San Francisco SO

Educational: Canadian Academy of Music, Cleveland Music School Settlement

Other: Birnbach Music Publishers (Berlin), Danish National Record Collection, English Folk Dance Society (London), London Opera House (Stoll Theater), *Musik-Pädagogische*, New Hungarian Music Society, *Pacific Coast Musician*, Rodewald Concerts Society (Liverpool), Society of Women Musicians (London)

H. Musical Literature:
Adler, Guido, *Der Stil in der Musik*
Dechevrens, Antoine, *Composition Musicale...*
Dickinson, Edward, *The Education of the Music Lover*
Duncan, William E., *The Story of the Carol*
Forsyth, Cecil, *Music and Nationalism*
Gastoué, Amédée, *L'Art Grégorien*
Hamilton, Clarence, *Sound and Its Relation to Music*
Leichtentritt, Hugo, *Musikalische Formenlehre*
Parry, Hubert, *Style in Musical Art*
Schoenberg, Arnold, *Harmonielehre*
Stanford, Charles, *Musical Composition*

I. Musical Compositions:
Bantock, Granville, *Dante and Beatrice* (symphonic poem)
Bartók, Béla, *Allegro Barbaro* (piano)
      Bluebeard's Castle (opera)
Berlin, Irving, *Alexander's Ragtime Band* (song)
Chadwick, George, *Symphonic Suite* (orchestra)
Cowell, Henry, *The Tides of Manaunaun* (piano)
Debussy, Claude, *The Martyrdom of St. Sebastian* (mystery play)
Delius, Frederick, *Summer Night on the River* (chamber orchestra)
Duparc, Henri, *Aux Étoiles* (symphonic poem)
Elgar, Edward, *Coronation March, Opus 65*
Fauré, Gabriel, *Nine Preludes, Opus 103, for Piano*
Foerster, Josef B., *Concerto No. 1 for Violin and Orchestra*
Gilbert, Henry, *Three American Dances* (orchestra)
Glazunov, Alexander, *Concerto No. 1, Opus 92, for Piano and Orchestra*
Glière, Reinhold, *Symphony No 3, Opus 42, "Ilya Mourometz"*
Granados, Enrique, *Goyescas* (piano)
Hadley, Henry, *Symphony No. 4, "North, East, South, West"*
Herbert, Victor, *Natouma* (opera)
Holst, Gustav, *Suite No. 2 for Band*
Ives, Charles, *Theater Orchestra Set*
      Robert Browning Overture
      Tone Roads No. 1 (chamber orchestra)
Magnard, Albéric, *Bérénice* (opera)
Mascagni, Pietro, *Isabeau* (opera)
Miaskovsky, Nicolai, *Symphony No. 2, Opus 11*
Nielsen, Carl, *Symphony No. 3, "Sinfonia Espansiva"*
      Concerto for Violin and Orchestra
Parker, Horatio, *Mona* (opera)
Pizzeti, Ildebrando, *Overture for a Tragic Farce*
Prokofiev, Serge, *Concerto No. 1, Opus 10, for Piano and Orchestra*
Rachmaninoff, Serge, *Etudes-Tableaux, Opus 33* (piano)
Rangström, Ture, *A Midsummer Piece* (symphonic poem)
Ravel, Maurice, *Valses Nobles et Sentimentales* (piano)
Saint-Saëns, Camille, *Déjanire* (opera)
Satie, Erik, *En Habit de Cheval* (piano)
Schoenberg, Arnold, *Six Little Pieces for Piano, Opus 19*
      Herzgewächse, Opus 20 (soprano, celesta, harmonium, harp)
Scriabin, Alexander, *Piano Sonata No. 5, Opus 53*
Sibelius, Jan, *Symphony No. 4, Opus 63*
Stravinsky, Igor, *Le Roi d'Étoiles* (cantata)
      Petrouchka (ballet)
Vaughan-Williams, Ralph, *Five Mystical Songs* (baritone, chorus)
Wolf-Ferrari, Ermanno, *The Jewels of the Madonna* (opera)

1912

World Events:
In the U.S., Woodrow Wilson becomes President no. 28 when Theodore Roosevelt, in disagreement with his former friend, President Taft, forms his own Bull Moose Party; New Mexico and Arizona become States Nos. 47 and 48 and Alaska is organized as a U.S. territory; Congress passes a bill mandating an 8-hour work day for all Federal employees; the Girl Scouts of America is founded. Internationally, the "unsinkable" Titanic, on its maiden voyage, hits an iceberg and sinks, taking with her more than 1500 people; British explorer Captain Scott and his party die on their way back from the South Pole; the First Balkan War begins and Albania declares its independence; the Sopwith Aviation Co. is founded in Great Britain.

Cultural Highlights:
In the U.S. the Authors League is founded and both Chicago and New York open Little Theaters; *Poetry: a Magazine of Verse* begins publication with Harriet Monroe as editor; art gallery, Der Sturm, opens in Berlin. The German philosopher, poet and dramatist, Gerhart Hauptmann, receives the Nobel Prize for Literature. Births this year includes American writers Arthur Berger and John Cheever and American artists William Baziotes and Morris Louis. Deaths in the world of art include British artist Lawrence Alma-Tadema, French artist Édouard Detaille, American sculptor Louis M. Potter and artist Robert MacCameron; in the literary field, British author Samuel Coleridge Taylor, German poet and historian Felix Dahn and novelist Karl May, Italian poet Giovanni Pascoli, Italian poet Mario Rapisardi and the Swedish author, August Strindberg. Other highlights include:

Art: Umberto Boccioni, *Amorpha, Fugue in Two Colors*; Emile Bourdelle, *Apollo and His Thought*; Wassily Kandinsky, *Montmartre: Le Passage Cottin*; Frantisek Kupka, *Development of Bottle in Space*; Louis Maurer, *September Morn*; Piet Mondrian, *Simultaneous Windows*; Pablo Picasso, *Nude Descending the Staircase*.

Literature: Eleanor Atkinson, *Greyfriars Bobby*; Rupert Brooke, *Poems*; Paul Ernst, *Ariadne auf Naxos*; Wassily Kandinsky, *Concerning the Spiritual in Art*; Amy Lowell, *A Dome of Many-Colored Glass*; George Moore, *Hail and Farewell-Salve*; Romain Rolland, *Jean Christophe*; George Bernard Shaw, *Pygmalion*; Rabindranath Tagore, *Gitanjali*.

MUSICAL EVENTS

A. Births:

Feb 4	Erich Leinsdorf (Aus-cd)	May 30	Alfred Deller (Br-c.ten)
Feb 8	Ilona Steingruber (Aus-sop)	Jun 3	Alois Pernerstorfer (Aus-bs)
Feb 11	Rudolf Firkusny (Cz-pn)	Jun 9	Ingolf Dahl (Ger-cm)
Feb 19	Stan Kenton (Am-pop)	Jun 17	Don Gillis (Am-cm)
Mar 4	Ferdinand Leitner (Am-cd)	Jul 27	Igor Markevitch (Rus-cd)
Mar 21	Gustav Neidlinger (Ger-bar)	Jul 28	Eleazar de Carvalho (Bra-cd)
Mar 22	Martha Mödl (Ger-sop)	Aug 18	Miliza Korjus (Pol-sop)
Mar 29	Fritz Ollendorf (Ger-bs)	Sep 5	John Cage (Am-cm)
Apr 22	Kathleen Ferrier (Br-alto)	Sep 19	Kurt Sanderling (Ger-cd)
May 3	Virgil Fox (Am-org)	Sep 21	György Sándor (Hun-pn)
May 12	Margaret Harshaw (Am-mez)	Oct 13	Hugo Weisgall (Cz-cm)
May 16	Felix Prohaska (Aus-cd)	Nov 26	Georg Solti (Hun-cd)
May 23	Jean Françaix (Fr-cm)	Dec 23	Josef Greindl (Ger-bs)
May 24	Joan Hammond (NZ-sop)	Dec 29	Peggy Glanville-Hicks (Aust-cm)

B. Deaths:

Jan 17	Antoine Dechevrens (Fr-mus)	Aug 13	Jules Massenet (Fr-cm)
Jan 18	Hermann Winkelmann (Ger-ten)	Oct 15	Charles R. Ruelle (Fr-mus)
Apr 1	William S. Mathews (Am-cri)	Nov 9	Gustav Jacobsthal (Ger-mus)
May 26	Jan Blockx (Hol-cm)		

C. Debuts:

Met ---Lucrezia Bori (sop), Sara Charles-Cahier (mez), Louise Cox (sop), Vera Curtis (sop), Maria Duchène (mez), Richard Hageman (cd), Carl Hager (bar), Charles Hargreaves (ten), Frieda Hempel (sop), Mary Jungmann (mez), Louis Kreidler (bar), Hans Morgenstern (cd), Ethel Parks (sop), Giorgio Polacco (cd), Giovanni Polese (bar), Lila Robeson (mez), Veni Warwick (sop)

U.S. --Wilhelm Backhaus (N.Y.), Marie-Louise Edvina (Boston), Mabel Garrison (N.Y.), Elena Gerhardt (tour), Aristodemo Giorgini (Chicago), Lucille Marcel (Boston), Vanni Marcoux (Boston), Edith Mason (Boston), Louis Persinger (tour), Titta Ruffo (Chicago), Evelyn Scotney (Boston), John Charles Thomas (N.Y.), Alfred Wallenstein (Los Angeles)

Other -Gilda Dalla Rizza (Bologna), Emanuel Feuermann (Vienna), Victor Fuchs (Breslau), Walter Gieseking (Hanover), Louis Gruenberg (Berlin), Edward Johnson (Padua), Germaine Lubin (Paris), Pierre Luboshutz (Moscow), Mischa Mischakoff (Berlin), Sigrid Onegin (Stuttgart), Aureliano Pertile (Vicenza), Vladimir Rosing (St. Petersburg), Ada Sari (Milan), Heinrich Schlusnus (Frankfurt), Lotte Schöne (Vienna), Friedrich Schorr (Graz), Vera Schwarz (Vienna)

D. New Positions:

Conductors: Erich Kleiber (Darmstadt Opera), Ernst Kunwald (Cincinnati SO), Karl Muck (Boston SO--return), Leopold Stokowski (Philadelphia Orchestra), Felix Weingartner (Hamburg Opera)

Others: Herbert Hughes (music critic, London *Daily Telegraph*)

E. Prizes and Honors:

Prizes: Felix Borowski (Rubinstein)

Honors: Gustave Charpentier (French Academy), Ignace Jan Paderewski (honorary doctorate, Lvov)

F. Biographical Highlights:

Henry Cowell presents the first known piano tone-clusters in a recital for the San Francisco Music Club; George Gershwin receives his first real music lessons, piano with Charles Hambitzer; Charles Ives buys a farm in Redding, Connecticut; Maria Jeritza makes her Vienna Opera debut; John McCormack begins to concentrate on recitals and begins to cut down his stage appearances; Charles Munch leaves Strasbourg and goes to Paris to study violin with Lucien Capet; Gregor Piatigorsky, age 9, is admitted to the Moscow Conservatory; Walter Piston enters the Massachusetts Normal Art School to study painting; organist Alexander Schreiner emigrates to the U.S.; Jan Sibelius is offered the chair of composition at the Vienna Academy but declines the offer; William Walton, age 10, enters the Oxford Choir School.

G. Institutional Openings:

Performing Groups: Max Jacobs String Quartet, Oratorio Society of Los Angeles, Pro-Arte String Quartet (Belgium), Sociedade de Concertos Sinfonicos de Rio de Janeiro, Württemburg State Opera and Theater

Educational: École Normale pour Pianistes (Paris), Phi Beta Music Fraternity (Evanston, IL)

Other: Berlin Opera House, Bosse Music Book Publishers (N.Y.), Confrère Liturgique (Paris), Enescu Prize in Composition (Bucharest), *Harvard Musical Review*

H. Musical Literature:

Boyd, Charles N., *Lectures on Church Music*
Chantavoine, Jean, *Musiciens et Poètes*
Gunn, Glenn, *History and Esthetics of Music*
Huberman, Bronislaw, *Aus der Werstatt des Virtuosen*
Hughes, Rupert, *The Music-Lover's Encyclopedia*

Schoenberg, Arnold, *Manual of Counterpoint*
Sharp, Cecil, *Folksongs of England*
Terry, Richard, *Westminster Hymnal*
Van den Borren, Charles, *Sources of Keyboard Music in England*

I. Musical Compositions:

Bartók, Béla, *Four Pieces for Orchestra, Opus 12*
Berg, Alban, *Five Orchestral Songs, Opus 4*
Bruch, Max, *Concerto for Two Pianos and Orchestra, Opus 88a*
Busoni, Ferruccio, *Sonatina No. 2 for Piano*
        Symphonic Nocturne, Opus 43
Casella, Alfredo, *Il Convento Veneziano* (ballet)
Chadwick, George, *Aphrodite* (symphonic fantasy)
Converse, Frederick, *Ormazd* (symphonic poem)
Debussy, Claude, *Jeux* (ballet)
        Syrinx (solo flute)
Delius, Frederick, *Song of the High Hills* (orchestra with wordless chorus)
        On Hearing the First Cuckoo in Spring (orchestra)
Dukas, Paul, *La Peri* (ballet)
Dupré, Marcel, *3 Preludes et Fugues, Opus 7* (organ)
Elgar, Edward, *Symphony No. 2, Opus 63*
        The Crown of India, Opus 66 (orchestral suite)
Farwell, Arthur, *3 Indian Songs, Opus 32*
Foote, Arthur, *4 Character Pieces after Omar Kháyyám, Opus 48*
Friml, Rudolf, *The Firefly* (operetta)
Glière, Reinhold, *Chrysis* (ballet)
Griffes, Charles, *Bacchanale, Opus 6* (orchestra)
Hadley, Henry, *The Atonement of Pan* (masque)
Herbert, Victor, *The Lady of the Slippers* (operetta)
Holst, Gustav, *Hymns from the Rig Veda* (voice, piano)
Ives, Charles, *The Gong on the Hook and Ladder* (orchestra)
        Putnam's Camp (from Three Places in New England)
        Decoration Day (from Holiday Symphony)
        Lincoln, the Great Commoner
Judge, Jack, *It's a Long, Long Way to Tipperary* (song)
Korngold, Erich, *Sinfonietta* (orchestra)
Leoncavallo, Ruggiero, *Zingari* (opera)
Massenet, Jules, *Roma* (opera)
Parry, Hubert, *Symphony No. 5*
Pierné, Gabriel, *Saint François d'Assise* (oratorio)
Pizzeti, Hildebrando, *Fedra* (**opera**)
Prokofiev, Serge, *Toccata, Opus 11* (piano)
        Sarcasms, Opus 17 (piano)
Rachmaninoff, Serge, *Fourteen Songs, Opus 34*
Rangström, Ture, *Ode to Autumn* (symphonic poem)
Ravel, Maurice, *Daphnis et Chloe* (ballet with chorus)
Satie, Erik, *Preludes flasque (Pour un chien)*
Schoenberg, Arnold, *Pierrot Lunaire, Opus 21* (soprano, chamber group)
Scriabin, Alexander, *Piano Sonatas No. 6 and 7*
Sibelius, Jan, *Scenes Historiques, Suite II, Opus 66*
Strauss, Richard, *Ariadne auf Naxos* (opera)
Turina, Joaquin, *La Processión del Rocío* (orchestra)
Vaughan-Williams, Ralph, *Fantasia on Christmas Carols*
Vierne, Louis, *Organ Symphony No. 3*
Webern, Anton, *Two Songs, Opus 8*

1913

World Events:

In the U.S., the ratification of the Sixteenth and Seventeenth Amendments provides for the establishment of a Federal income tax and for the direct election of Senators by the public; the Woolworth Building in New York becomes the world's tallest skyscraper; future President Richard Nixon is born; the Federal Reserve Act is passed and the Rockefeller Foundation is founded. Internationally, the Second Balkan War pits Bulgaria against Romania, Greece and Turkey-- the treaty of Bucharest takes territory away from Bulgaria; Turkey refuses to give up Crete; Albert Schweitzer opens a hospital in the French Congo; the Geiger Counter is introduced.

Cultural Highlights:

Beethoven's *Symphony No. 5* becomes the first classical recording to be made. The Cumberland Market Group is formed in London, the Omega Workshops are opened by Roger Fry while in New York the Armory Show introduces "modern" art to the masses; the Cleveland Museum of Art opens; Indian author Rabindranath Tagore receives the Nobel Prize for Literature. American poet Cincinnatus Miller and British poet Alfred Austin pass away. Births include American poet Karl Shapiro and author Irwin Shaw, Canadian author Robertson Davies and French novelist Albert Camus. Other highlights include:

Art: George Bellows, *The Cliffdwellers*; Umberto Boccioni, *Unique Forms of Continuity*; Marc Chagall, *The Musicians*; Giorgio de Chirico, *Soothsayer's Recompense*; Christian Eriksson, *The Little Mermaid*; Fernand Léger, *Contrast of Forms*; Wilhelm Lehmbruck, *Standing Youth*; Franz Marc, *Tower of Blue Horse*; Georges Rouault, *Three Judges*.

Literature: Willa Cather, *O Pioneers*; Joseph Conrad, *Chance*; John Fletcher, *Fire and Wine*; Robert Frost, *A Boy's Will*; Maxim Gorky, *My Childhood*; D.H. Lawrence, *Sons and Lovers*; Jack London, *John Barleycorn*; Thomas Mann, *Death in Venice*; John Masefield, *Dauber*; Stephen Phillips, *Lyrics and Dramas*; Eleanor Porter, *Pollyanna*.

MUSICAL EVENTS

A. Births:

Jan 2	Gardner Read (Am-cm-au)	Jun 24	Heinrich Hollreiser (Ger-cd)
Jan 24	Norman Dello Joio (Am-cm)	Jul 11	Risë Stevens (Am-mez)
Jan 25	Witold Lutoslawski (Pol-cm)	Jul 17	Everett Helm (Am-cm-mus)
Feb 17	René Leibowitz (Fr-cm)	Jul 22	Licia Albanese (It-sop)
Feb 19	Alvin Etler (Am-cm)	Aug 14	Ferruccio Tagliavini (It-ten)
Apr 14	Jean Fournet (Fr-cd)	Aug 28	Robert Irving (Br-cd)
Apr 18	Kent Kennan (Am-cm-au)	Sep 15	Henry Brant (Can-cm)
May 1	Walter Susskind (Can-cd)	Sep 28	Vivian Fine (Am-cm)
May 6	Gyula Dávid (Hun-cd)	Oct 10	Ljuba Welitsch (Bul-sop)
May 21	Gina Bachauer (Gr-pn)	Nov 19	Ataulfo Argenta (Sp-cd)
May 31	Constantin Silvestri (Rom-cd)	Nov 22	Benjamin Britten (Br-cm)
Jun 10	Thor Johnson (Am-cd)	Dec 10	Morton Gould (Am-cm-cd)
Jun 10	Tikhon Khrennikov (Rus-cm)	Dec 21	Andor Foldes (Hun-pn-cd)

B. Deaths:

Jan 6	Anton Schott (Ger-ten)	Aug 7	David Popper (Cz-cel-cm)
Feb 19	William Apthorp (Am-cri-mus)	Sep 5	Anton R. Grunicke (Ger-org)
Feb 26	Felix Draeske (Ger-cm)	Sep 13	Alfred R. Gaul (Br-org-cm)
Feb 28	Georges Houdard (Fr-mus)	Nov 17	Mathilde Marchesi (Ger-sop-cd)
Mar 12	Josef Bayer (Aus-cd-cm)	Nov 29	Ellsworth C. Phelps (Am-org)
May 28	Alexander Bandrowski-Sas (Pol-ten)		

C. Debuts:

Met ---Paul Althouse (ten), Margarethe Arndt-Ober (mez), Sophie Braun (mez), Carl Braun (bs), Italo Cristalli (ten), Lillian Eubank (mez), Adele Giordano (sop), Robert Leonhardt (bar), Leopoldo Mariani (ten), Giovanni Martinelli (ten), Anafesto Rossi (bar), Maurice Sapio (bs), Alfred Sappio (ten), Carl Schlegel (bs), Alice Sherman (sop), Jacques Urlus (ten)

U.S. --Fanny Anitua (tour), Luca Botta (California), Julia Claussen (Chicago), Julia Culp (N.Y.), Mildred Dilling (N.Y.), Cyrena van Gordon (Chicago), Beatrice Harrison (tour), Ethel Leginska (N.Y.), Arthur Loesser (N.Y.), Pavel Ludikar (Boston), José Mardones (Boston), Maria Moscisca (tour), Lucien Muratore (Chicago), Paul Reimers (N.Y.)

Other -Fernand Ansseau (Dijon), Conchita Badia (Barcelona), Fidela Campina (Madrid), Kirsten Flagstad (Oslo), Maria Ivogün (Munich), Oszkár Kálman (Budapest), Nina Koshetz (St. Petersburg), Rudolf Laubenthal (Berlin), Florence MacBeth (Braunschweig), Josef von Manowarda (Prague), Lauritz Melchior (Copenhagen), Isolde Menges (London), Rosa Raisa (Parma), Delia Reinhardt (Wroclaw), Manuel Salazar (Vicenza), Richard Tauber (Chemnitz)

D. New Positions:

Conductors: Hans Knappertsbusch (Eberfeld Opera), Bruno Walter (Munich Opera)

Educational: Ferrucio Busoni (director, Bologna Conservatory), Julián Carrillo (director, Mexico City Conservatory), Adolf Chybinski (musicology, Lvov University), Francesco Cilea (director, Palermo Conservatory), Arthur Foote (director, American Academy), Ottorino Respighi (composition, St. Cecilia's), Healy Willan (theory, Toronto Conservatory)

Others: Leo Blech (director, Berlin Opera), Cleofonte Camanini (manager, Chicago Opera)

E. Prizes and Honors:

Prizes: Lili Boulanger (Prix de Rome), Léon Jongen (Prix de Rome), Sergei Taneyev (Russian Musical Society)

Honors: James M. Barrie (baronet), Ferruccio Busoni (Legion of Honor), Johnston Forbes-Robertson (knighted)

F. Biographical Highlights:

Gian F. Malipiero, on a trip to Paris, meets with Casella and is influenced by his first hearing of Stravinsky's *Sacre*; Daniel Gregory Mason goes to Paris for further music studies with Vincent d'Indy; Lucian Muratore marries the soprano Lina Cavalieri; Ottorino Respighi decides to settle permanently in his favorite city, Rome; Igor Stravinsky meets with Arnold Schoenberg, is impressed by *Pierrot Lunaire*; Albert Schweitzer completes his medical studies and leaves for medical missionary work in Africa; Joaquin Turina completes his work at the Paris Schola Cantorum and, inspired by a meeting with Albéniz and Falla, returns to Madrid to write nationalistic music; Edgard Varèse, upon his return to Paris, begins working with Luigi Russolo in a search for new musical resources.

G. Institutional Openings:

Performing Groups: Century Opera Co. (N.Y.), Fort Worth SO, Houston SO, Kortschak (Berkshire) String Quartet, Lirico Arena Opera Co. (Verona), Lisbon PO, Scandinavian SO (N.Y.), Trio de Lutèce (N.Y.)

Educational: Institute of Musical Art (Rochester), Karl Wolfahrt Musikskola (Stockholm), London School of Dalcroze Eurythmics, Temple University School of Music (Philadelphia)

Other: Civic Music Association of Chicago, Decca Portable Gramophone Co., Duo-Art Reproducing Piano, Gesellschaft für Musik Freunde (Donaueschingen), Incorporated Association of Organists, Society of Friends of Music (N.Y.), Symphony Hall (Springfield, Massachusetts), Théâtre des Champs-Elysées (Paris)

H. Musical Literature:

Combarieu, Jules, *Histoire de la Musique I, II*
Deutsch, Otto, *Franz Schubert: Die Dokumente Seines Lebens und Schaffens*
Elsner, J., *The Musician's Guide*
Fellowes, Edmund, *English Madrigal School I*
Ferretti, Paolo, *Il Cursus Metrico e il ritmo delle melodie del Canto Gregoriano*
Ganz, Wilhelm, *Memories of a Musician*
Gasparini, Guido, *I caratteri peculiari del Melodramma italiano*
Goetschius/Tapper, *Essentials of Music History*
Halm, August, *Von Zwei Kulturen der Musik*
Lehmann, Lotte, *Mein Weg*

I. Musical Compositions:

Ball, Ernest R., *When Irish Eyes are Smiling* (song)
Berg, Alban, *Four Pieces for Clarinet and Piano, Opus 5*
Bloch, Ernst, *Three Jewish Poems* (orchestra)
Busoni, Ferruccio, *Indian Fantasy, Opus 44* (piano, orchestra)
Butterworth, George, *A Shropshire Lad* (song cycle)
Cadman, Charles, *Sayonara* (song cycle)
Carpenter, John Alden, *Gitanjali* (song cycle)
Charpentier, Gustav, *Impressions d'Italie* (suite)
Debussy, Claude, *Preludes, Book II* (piano)
        Three Poems of Mallarmé (voice)
Dohnányi, Ernst von, *Variations on a Nursery Song* (piano, orchestra)
Elgar, Edward, *Falstaff, A Symphonic Study, Opus 68* (orchestra)
Enescu, Georges, *Symphony No. 2*
Fauré, Gabriel, *Penelope* (opera)
Gilbert, Henry, *Negro Rhapsody* (orchestra)
Hauer, Josef, *Symphony No. 1, "Nomos"*
Herbert, Victor, *Sweethearts* (operetta)
Holst, Gustav, *St. Paul's Suite* (strings)
Ireland, John, *The Forgotten Rite* (symphonic prelude)
Ives, Charles, *Chromatimelodtune* (chamber orchestra)
        String Quartet No. 2
Magnard, Albéric, *Symphony No. 4*
Milhaud, Darius, *Agamemnon* (Part I of Aeschylus' *Orestes*)
Prokofiev, Serge, *Concerto No. 2, Opus 16, for Piano and Orchestra*
        Piano Sonata No. 2, Opus 14
Rachmaninoff, Serge, *The Bells* (soloists, chorus, orchestra- after Poe)
        Piano Sonata No. 2, Opus 36 (revised, 1931)
Ravel, Maurice, *Trois Poèmes de Mallarmé* (voice, piano, string quartet, woodwinds)
Reger, Max, *Four Tonepaintings after Böcklin, Opus 124* (orchestra)
Satie, Erik, *Descriptions Automatiques* (piano)
        Embryons Desséchés (piano)
Schmidt, Franz, *Symphony No. 2*
Schoenberg, Arnold, *Die Glückliche Hande, Opus 18* (chamber opera)
Scriabin, Alexander, *Piano Sonatas No. 8, 9 and 10*
Sibelius, Jan, *The Bard, Opus 64* (tone poem)
        Luonnotar, Opus 70 (tone poem)
Stenhammer, Wilhelm, *Serenade for Orchestra, Opus 31*
Strauss, Richard, *Festival Prelude* (organ and orchestra)
Stravinsky, Igor, *Le Sacre du Printemps, Opus 61* (ballet)
Vaughan-Williams, Ralph, *A London Symphony*
Webern, Anton, *Six Bagatelles for String Quartet, Opus 9*
        Five Pieces for Orchestra, Opus 10

1914

World Events:

In the U.S., transcontinental telephone service from New York to San Francisco is introduced; Henry Ford introduces both the 8-hour day and the profit-sharing plan in his factory; in the U.S. Congress, the Clayton Antitrust Act is passed, the Federal Trade Commission is formed and the Army Air Service is established. Internationally, World War I begins after the assassination of Archduke Ferdinand and his wife at Sarajevo-- trench warfare begins on the Western Front; Great Britain takes over Nigeria and Egypt as protectorates; the British Parliament gives home rule to Ireland; Panama Canal is finished.

Cultural Highlights:

The Nobel Prize for Literature was not awarded this year but Selma Lagerlöf was inducted into the Swedish Academy; Carl Sandburg was given an award by *Poetry* magazine and Alexander Woollcott becomes drama critic for the *New York Times*. Births this year include American novelists Ralph Ellison and Bernard Malamud and poet John Berryman as well as British poet Dylan Thomas. Deaths include German author Paul von Heyse, French poet Frédéric Mistral, British poet and critic, Theodore Watts-Dunton and American sculptor Vinnie Hoxie. Other highlights include:

Art: Ernst Barlach, *The Avenger*; Emile Bourdelle, *The Dying Centaur*; Georges Braque, *Music*; Giorgio de Chirico, *Gare Montparnasse*; Marcel Duchamp-Villon, *Horse*; Oskar Kokoschka, *Die Windsbraut*; Franz Marc, *Deer in Forest II*; Pierre Renoir, *The Judgement of Paris*; Anne Whitney, *Titanic Memorial*.

Literature: Edgar Rice Burroughs, *Tarzan of the Apes*; Theodore Dreiser, *The Titan*; Robert Frost, *North of Boston*; James Joyce, *Dubliners*; Alfred Joyce Kilmer, *Trees and Other Poems*; Vachel Lindsay, *The Congo and Other Poems*; Gertrude Stein, *Tender Buttons*; Booth Tarkington, *Penrod*; Max Weber, *Cubist Poems*.

MUSICAL EVENTS

A. Births:

Jan 16	Roger Wagner (Am-cd)	Jul 2	Frederick Fennell (Am-cd)
Jan 18	Catherine Crozier (Am-org)	Jul 22	Cecil Effinger (Am-cd-ed)
Jan 23	Pina Carmirelli (It-vn)	Aug 9	Ferenc Fricsay (Hun-cd)
Jan 25	William Strickland (Am-cd)	Aug 10	Witold Malcuzynski (Pol-pn)
Feb 26	Witold Rowicki (Pol-cd)	Aug 25	Alexei Haieff (Rus-cm)
Mar 20	Sviatoslav Richter (Rus-pn)	Aug 28	Richard Tucker (Am-ten)
Apr 17	Janine Micheau (Fr-sop)	Sep 5	Gail Kubik (Am-cm-vn)
May 5	Kyrill Kondrashin (Rus-cd)	Sep 16	Herta Glaz (Aus-alto)
May 9	Carlo Maria Giulini (It-cd)	Sep 24	Andrzej Panufnik (Pol-cm)
May 10	Richard Lewis (Br-ten)	Nov 15	Jorg Bolet (Cub-pn)
Jun 14	Geoffrey Sharp (Br-cri)	Dec 3	Irving Fine (Am-cm)
Jun 26	Wolfgang Windgassen (Ger-ten)	Dec 14	Rosalyn Tureck (Am-pn-hps)
Jun 29	Rafael Kubelik (Cz-cd)		

B. Deaths:

Jan 3	Raoul Pugno (Fr-pn)	Aug 12	Pol-Henri Plançon (Gr-bs)
Jan 11	Georgina Weldon (Br-sop)	Aug 28	Anatoli Liadov (Rus-cm)
Jan 19	Rudolf Genée (Ger-cri-mus)	Sep 3	Albéric Magnard (Fr-cm)
Feb 6	Karl R. Hennig (Ger-the-cm)	Sep 10	Wilhelm Ganz (Ger-pn)
May 10	Lillian Nordica (Am-sop)	Sep 13	Robert Hope-Jones (Br-org.m)
May 10	Ernst von Schuch (Aus-cd)	Nov 9	Jean Baptiste Faure (Fr-bar)
Jun 28	Surindro Tagore (Ind-mus)	Dec 14	Giovanni Sgambati (It-pn-cm)
Aug 11	Emil Fischer (Ger-bs)	Dec 18	Gustav Mollenhauer (Ger-ww.m)

C. Debuts:

Met ---Rudolf Berger (ten), Carl von Bitterl (bs), Max Bloch (ten), Luca Botta (ten), Luigi Conti (bs), Désiré Defrère (bar), Raymonde Delaunois (mez), Eduardo Ferrari-Fontana (ten), Mabel Garrison (sop), Margarete Märkl (mez), Freida Martin (sop), Elisabeth Schumann (sop), Johannes Sembach (ten), Riccardo Tegani (bar)

U.S. --Clarence Adler (N.Y.), Guido Ciccolini (Boston), Ferruccio Corradetti (tour), Carl Flesch (tour), Kathleen Howard (N.Y.), Florence MacBeth (Chicago), Ottokar Marák (Chicago), Rosa Raisa (Chicago), Minnie Saltzmann-Stevens (Chicago), Martha Winternitz-Dorda (Chicago)

Other -Claudio Arrau (Berlin), Beniamino Bibli (Rovigo), Mercedes Capsir (Barcelona), Apollo Granforte (Argentina), Käthe Herwig (Berlin), Joseph Hislop (Stockholm), Parry Jones (England), Maria Kurenko (Kharkov), Forrest Lamont (Rome), Virgilio Lazzari (Rome), Karl Norbert (Prague), Karl Oestvig (Stuttgart), Ezio Pinza (Soncino)

D. New Positions:

Conductors: Fritz Reiner (Dresden State Opera), Hermann Scherchen (Riga SO), Fritz Stiedry (Berlin Opera)

Educational: Reinhold Glière (director, Kiev Conservatory), Julius Röntgen (director, Amsterdam Conservatory), Franz Schmidt (piano, Vienna Academy), Donald Tovey (Reid Chair, Edinburgh)

Others: Harvey Gaul (music critic, Pittsburgh *Post-Gazette*), Manfred Gurlitt (director, Bremen Opera), Oscar Sonneck (editor, *The Musical Quarterly*)

E. Prizes and Honors:

Prizes: Marcel Dupré (Prix de Rome), Beniamino Gigli (Parma)

Honors: Henri Bergson (French Academy), Enrique Granados (Legion of Honor), George Henschel (knighted), Jan Sibelius (honorary doctorate, Yale), Richard Strauss (honorary doctorate, Oxford)

F. Biographical Highlights:

Adrian Boult receives his doctorate; Henry Cowell begins formal music education with Seeger; Walter Damrosch receives doctorate from Columbia; Claude Debussy on last trip abroad to London; Manuel de Falla along with Joaquin Turina returns to Spain; Olive Fremstad gives her farewell Met performance; Alma Gluck marries her second husband, Efrem Zimbalist; Percy Grainger leaves Australia for the U.S.; Edward Johnson debuts at La Scala; Hans Kindler leaves Holland for the U.S.; Fritz Kreisler joins the Austrian army; Lotte Lehmann makes her Vienna Opera debut; Charles Munch is drafted into the German army; Carl Orff graduates from the Munich Academy; Serge Prokofiev, after graduation, travels to London; Igor Stravinsky moves his family to Switzerland; Karol Szymanowski visits North Africa; Paul Wittgenstein loses his right arm in the war.

G. Institutional Openings:

Performing Groups: Amici della Musica (Ancona), Baltimore SO, Cape Town SO, Chamber Music Society of New York, Detroit SO, Newark SO, Société des Concerts Populaires (Paris)

Educational: Concord Summer School of Music, Detroit Institute of Musical Arts, Beit Leviyim Music School (Tel Aviv), *Music Educator's Journal*

Other: American Society of Composers, Authors and Publishers (ASCAP); *L'Arte Pianistica* (Naples); Valentin de Carvalho, Music Publisher (Lisbon); Lewisohn Stadium (N.Y.), Performing Right Society of Great Britain, Society of St. Gregory of America

H. Musical Literature:

Carrillo, Julián, *Tratado Sintético de Harmonia*
Duncan, William, *Encyclopedia of Musical Terms*
Forsyth, Cecil, *Orchestration*

Gehrkens, Karl, *Music Notation and Terminology*
Hadden, James, *Modern Musicians*
Hull, Arthur, *Modern Harmony*
Idelsohn, Abraham, *Thesaurus of Hebrew-Oriental Melodies*
Kitson, Charles, *Evolution of Harmony*
Molnár, Antal, *The Spirit of the History of Music*
Preobrazhensky, Anton, *Sacred Music in Russia*
Prunières, Henry, *Le Ballet de Cour en France...*
Tapper, Thomas, *The Education of the Music Teacher*

I. Musical Compositions:
Alford, Kenneth, *Colonel Bogey March* (band)
Bloch, Ernest, *Psalm XXII*
Cadman, Charles, *Thunderbird Suite* (orchestra)
          From Wigwam and Tepee (song cycle)
Carpenter, John Alden, *Adventures in a Perambulator* (orchestral suite)
Delius, Frederick, *North Country Sketches* (orchestra)
Foote, Arthur, *Night Piece* (flute)
Griffes, Charles T., *Fantasy Pieces, Opus 6, for Piano*
Hadley, Henry, *Lucifer* (tone poem)
Handy, William, *St. Louis Blues* (song)
Hauer, Josef, *Symphony No. 3*
Herbert, Victor, *Madeleine* (opera)
Holst, Gustav, *The Planets* (orchestra)
Humperdinck, Engelbert, *Die Marketenderin* (opera)
Ives, Charles, *General Booth Enters into Heaven* (song)
          Sonata No. 3 for Violin and Piano
Janácek, Leos, *The Excursions of Mr. Broucek* (opera)
MacKenzie, Alexander, *The Cricket on the Hearth* (opera)
Mason, Daniel G., *Symphony No. 1, Opus 11*
Massenet, Jules, *Cleopatra* (opera)
Miaskovsky, Nicolai, *Symphony No. 3, Opus 15*
Pizzetti, Ildebrando, *Fire Symphony* (orchestra)
Prokofiev, Serge, *Concerto No. 1, Opus 19, for Violin and Orchestra*
          Scythian Suite, Opus 20 (orchestra)
Rangström, Ture, *The Sea Sings* (symphonic poem)
Ravel, Maurice, *Deux Mélodies Hébraïques*
Romberg, Sigmund, *The Midnight Girl* (operetta)
Satie, Erik, *Cinq Grimaces pour le Longe d'une Nuit d'Été*
          Sports et Divertissements
Schmidt, Franz, *Notre Dame* (opera)
Scriabin, Alexander, *5 Preludes, Opus 74, for Piano*
          2 Poems for Piano, Opus 71
Sibelius, Jan, *The Oceanides, Opus 73* (tone poem)
Strauss, Richard, *Joseph Legende* (ballet)
Stravinsky, Igor, *Le Rossignol* (opera)
          3 Pieces for String Quartet
Taylor, Deems, *The Chambered Nautilus* (cantata)
          The Highwayman (cantata)
Turina, Joaquin, *Margot* (opera)
Vierne, Louis, *Organ Symphony No. 4*
Webern, Anton, *Three Little Pieces for Cello and Piano*
Weingartner, Felix, *Cain and Abel* (opera)

1915

World Events:
The U.S. warns Germany about her unrestricted submarine warfare against U.S. and other neutral shipping; the U.S. Coast Guard service is formed; Congress sends troops to help quell an uprising in Haiti; Rocky Mountain and Dinosaur National Parks are established by Congressional action; the first Kiwanis Club is founded in Detroit. Internationally, World War I rages on -- the *Lusitania* is sunk off the coast of Ireland and poison gas is used for the first time at the battle of Ypres; the Dardanelles campaign against Turkey fails; Hugo Junkers develops the first fighter airplane; Rasputin gains control over the Royal family of Russia; China receives the Twenty-one demands from Japan.

Cultural Highlights:
The West Virginia Folklore Society is founded while in Zurich, the Dadaist movement is founded by Hans Arp and others; Rabindranath Tagore is knighted and French biographer, dramatist and novelist Romain Rolland receives the Nobel Prize for Literature. D.W. Griffith's *The Birth of a Nation* takes the U.S. by storm. The Art world witnesses the deaths of American sculptor Anne Whitney and artist John W. Alexander and French sculptor Henri Gaudier-Brzeska; births include the American sculptor Karl Bitter and artists Jack Levine and Robert Motherwell. Deaths in the literary field include British poets Rupert Brooke and Stephen Phillips, Italian authors Luigi Capuana and Enrico Castelnuovo and French author Remy de Gourmont; births include Canadian author Saul Bellow and Americans Nathaniel Benchley and Arthur Miller. Other highlights include:

Art: Carlo Carrà, *Lot's Daughter*; Giorgio de Chirico, *The Seer*; Raoul Dufy, *Hommage à Mozart*; Lyonel Feininger, *Self-Portrait*; Marsden Hartley, *Painting No. 5*; Henri Matisse, *Goldfish*; Maurice Prendergast, *Promenade*; Pierre Renoir, *Nude Resting*; Joseph Stella, *Battle of Light: Coney Island*; Max Weber, *Rush Hour, New York*.

Literature: Eleanor Atkinson, *Johnny Appleseed*; Rupert Brooke, *1914*; Joseph Conrad, *Victory*; Theodore Dreiser, *The Genius*; Edgar Masters, *Spoon River Anthology*; W. Somerset Maugham, *Of Human Bondage*; John McCrae, *In Flander's Field*; Ezra Pound, *Cathy*; Rafael Sabatini, *The Sea Hawk*; Edith Sitwell, *The Mother and Other Poems*.

MUSICAL EVENTS

A. Births:

Jan 10	Dean Dixon (Am-cd)	Jun 2	Robert Palmer (Am-cm)
Jan 15	Alan Lomax (Am-folk)	Jun 6	Vincent Persichetti (Am-cm)
Jan 18	Hans Tischler (Aus-mus)	Jul 9	David Diamond (Am-cm)
Feb 3	Richard Bales (Am-cm)	Aug 26	Gré Brouwenstijn (Hol-sop)
Mar 4	Carlos Surinach (Sp-cm)	Aug 26	Humphrey Searle (Br-cm)
Mar 10	Charles Groves (Br-cd)	Sep 3	Knut Nystedt (Nor-cm)
Mar 14	Alexander Brott (Can-cd-cm)	Oct 24	Tito Gobbi (It-bar)
Mar 19	Nancy Evans (Br-sop)	Nov 8	Lamberto Gardelli (It-cd)
Mar 20	Gabor Carelli (It-ten)	Nov 27	Victor Alessandro (Am-cd)
Apr 23	Italo Tajo (It-bs)	Nov 29	Harold C. Schonberg (Am-cri)
May 6	George Perle (Am-cm)	Dec 9	Elisabeth Schwarzkopf (Ger-sop)
May 29	Karl Münchinger (Ger-cd)	Dec 13	Paul Hume (Am-cri)

B. Deaths:

Jan 2	Karl Goldmark (Hun-cm)	May 1	John S.B. Hodges (Br-org-rel)
Jan 15	Guillaume Couture (Can-cm)	Jun 6	William Cummings (Br-org)
Feb 12	Fanny Crosby (Am-hymn)	Jun 19	Sergei Taneyev (Rus-cm-pn)
Feb 16	Emil Waldteufel (Ger-cm)	Jun 25	Rafael Joseffy (Hun-pn)
Apr 14	Carl F. Glasenapp (Ger-mus)	Sep 29	Luther O. Emerson (Am-cd-cm)
Apr 27	Alexander Scriabin (Rus-cm)	Oct 7	Samuel P. Warren (Am-org)

Nov 14   Theodor Leschetizky
         (Aus-ped)

Nov 14   Booker T. Washington (Am-ed)
Dec 24   William H. Doane (Am-hymn)

C. Debuts:

Met ---Gaetano Bavagnoli (cd), Artur Bodanzky (Cd), Ina Bourskaya (mez), Giacomo Damacco (ten), Marie-Louise Edvina (sop), Charles Garden (ten), Julia Heinrich (sop), Melanie Kurt (sop), Giuseppe de Luca (bar), Nazzarena Malaspina (sop), Pompilio Malatesta (bs), Edith Mason (sop), Flora Perini (mez), Henri Scott (bs), Luisa Villani (sop), Helen Warrum (sop), Erma Zarska (sop)

U.S. --Richard Benelli (N.Y.), Octave Dua (Chicago), Povla Frijsh (N.Y.), Eva Gauthier (tour), Percy Grainger (N.Y.), William Kroll (N.Y.), Tamaki Miura (Boston), Guiomar Novaës (N.Y.), Conchita Supervia (Chicago), Alice Verlet (Chicago)

Other -Robert Burg (Prague), Antonio Cortis (Valencia), Irene Eden (Zurich), Hermann Gallos (Vienna), Charles Hackett (Pavia), Percy Heming (London), Frida Leider (Halle), Kathleen Long (London), Erwin Nyiregyházi (Berlin), Maria Olczewska (Krefeld), Elizabeth Rethberg (Dresden), Max Rosen (Dresden), Heinrich Schlusnus (Hamburg), Rudolf Serkin (Vienna), Hina Spani (Milan), Igor Stravinsky (as conductor)

D. New Positions:

Conductors: Ernest Ansermet (Geneva SO), Wilhelm Furtwängler (Mannheim Opera), Alfred Hertz (San Francisco SO)

Educational: Henri Verbrugghen (director, New South Wales Conservatory, Australia)

Others: Lawrence Gilman (music & literature critic, *North American Review*), André Marchal (organ, St. Germain-des-Pres), Leonide Massine (choreographer, Diaghilev's Ballet Russe)

E. Prizes and Honors:

Prizes: Ilona Kabos (Liszt)

Honors: Franz Kniesel (honorary doctorate, Princeton), Francis Parkman (Hall of Fame)

F. Biographical Highlights:

Ernst von Dohnányi leaves Berlin and returns to Hungary seeking to reform its music education program; Sigfrid Karg-Elert enlists in the German Army; Alma Mahler marries the German architect and designer Walter Gropius; Wilfrid Pelletier sent to Paris after winning the Prix d'Europe for music study with Widor and Philipp; Camille Saint-Saëns visits the U.S. and represents the French government at the Panama-Pacific Exposition; Arnold Schoenberg, rejected for army duty, takes his family to Vienna; Leopold Stokowski becomes a naturalized American citizen; George Szell joins the staff of the Berlin Opera as an assistant conductor; Arturo Toscanini resigns his Met position and returns to Italy; Edgard Varèse arrives in the U.S. and meets the American author Louise Norton; Anton Webern begins a short army career in the Austrian army.

G. Institutional Openings:

Performing Groups: American SO, Denver Grand Opera Co., Little Symphony of New York, Palestrina Choir (Philadelphia)

Educational: American Association of University Professors, Denishawn School of Dancing and Related Arts (N.Y.), Hans Hoffman School of Fine Arts (Munich), Institute Jaques-Dalcroze (Geneva), Louisiana State University Music Department, Louisville Conservatory of Music (Kentucky), Osaka Music School (Japan), Salonica State Conservatory of Music, San Francisco Conservatory of Music

Other: Atlanta Music Club, *The Catholic Choirmaster*, Arthur Judson Concert Management (N.Y.), *Musical Contemporary*, *Musical Quarterly*, Nordiska Musikförlaget (Stockholm)

H. Musical Literature:

Dickinson, Edward, *Music and Higher Education*
Dolmetsch, Arnold, *Interpretation of the Music of the 17th and 18th Centuries*
Fischer, Wilhelm, *Zur Entwicklungsgeschichte des Wiener klassischen Stils*
Goetschius, Percy, *Larger Forms of ... Composition*
Goldschmidt, Hugo, *Der Musikästhetik des 18. Jahrhunderts*
Huneker, James, *Ivory Apes and Peacocks*
Jean-Aubrey, Georges, *Musique francais d'aujourd'hui*
Mason, Daniel G., *The Art of Music*
Sonneck, Oscar, *Early Opera in America*
Work, John W., Sr., *Folk Song of the American Negro*

I. Musical Compositions:

Bartók, Béla, *Piano Sonatina*
Berg, Alban, *Three Pieces for Orchestra, Opus 6* (revised 1929)
Bloch, Ernst, *Schelomo* (cello, orchestra)
Busoni, Ferruccio, *Rondo Arlecchinesco, Opus 46* (orchestra)
                    Indian Diary, Opus 47 (orchestra)
Cadman, Charles W., *Garden of Mystery* (opera)
Chadwick, George, *The Padrone* (opera)
                    Tam O'Shanter (symphonic ballad)
Debussy, Claude, *Etudes, Book I and II* (piano)
                    Sonata No. 1 for Cello and Piano
Elgar, Edward, *Polonia, Opus 76* (symphonic prelude)
Enescu, Georges, *Orchestral Suite No. 2*
Falla, Manuel de, *El Amor Brujo* (ballet)
                    Nights in the Gardens of Spain (piano and orchestra)
Giordano, Umberto, *Madame Sans-Gene* (opera)
Glazunov, Alexander, *Karelische Legende* (symphonic poem)
Glière, Reinhold, *Trizna, Opus 66* (symphonic poem)
Hadley, Henry, *Azora* (opera)
Herbert, Victor, *Princess Pat* (operetta)
Holst, Gustav, *Japanese Suite* (orchestra)
Hubay, Jenö, *Anna Karenina* (opera)
                    Symphony No. 2, Opus 93
d'Indy, Vincent, *Legend of St. Christopher, Opus 67* (opera)
Ives, Charles, *Violin Sonata No. 4, "Children's Day at the Camp Meeting"*
                    Orchestral Set No. 2
                    Concord Sonata (piano, completed)
Leoncavallo, Ruggiero, *La Candida* (opera)
Novák, Vítezslav, *Der Burgkobold* (opera)
Pijper, Willem, *Rhapsody for Piano and Orchestra*
Prokofiev, Serge, *Chout, Opus 21* (ballet)
Rachmaninoff, Serge, *Vesper Mass, Opus 37* (boy's chorus, men's chorus, orchestra)
Rangström, Ture, *Symphony No. 1, "In Memoriam August Strindberg"*
Reger, Max, *Mozart Variations* (orchestra)
Respighi, Ottorino, *Sinfonia Drammatica* (orchestra)
Sibelius, Jan, *Symphony No. 5, Opus 82*
Stenhammer, Wilhelm, *Symphony in g*
Strauss, Richard, *Eine Alpensinfonie, Opus 64* (orchestra)
Villa-Lobos, Heitor, *Concerto No. 1 for Cello and Orchestra*

1916

World Events:

In the U.S., Woodrow Wilson is re-elected President; General Pershing wages an unsuccessful campaign against Pancho Villa in Mexico; General Motors is incorporated in Delaware; the Federal Farm Loan Act is passed to help the nation's farmers; Flag Day is proclaimed; Lassen Volcanic National Park is established by Congress. Internationally, the British Fleet suffers severe damage in the Battle of Jutland while the battles of Verdun and the Somme take place on the battlefields of France; David Lloyd George becomes British Prime Minister; the Easter uprising takes place in Dublin against British rule; Rasputin is assassinated in Moscow.

Cultural Highlights:

Dadaism begins in Zurich with a show meant to scandalize. Three art magazines begin publication, *Dada*, *Ars Nova* (Italy) and the *Theatre Arts Magazine* of England. Swedish author and poet Verner von Heidenstam receives the Nobel Prize for Literature and Henri Barbusse wins the Goncourt Prize with his war story, *Le Feu*. The Society of Independent Artists is formed in the U.S. Births in the year include American author Irving Wallace, British sculptor Kenneth Armitage, German sculptor Peter Fingesten and American artist Richard Pousette-Dart. Deaths in the art field include German sculptor Karl Begas, Jr. and artist Franz Marc, Italian artist Umberto Boccioni, American artists William M. Chase and Thomas Eakins and French artist Odilon Redon; the literary field loses American novelists Henry James and Jack London and poets James Whitcomb Riley and Alan Seger, Polish novelist Henryk Sienkiewicz and Belgian poet Émile Verhaeren. Other highlights include:

Art: Jean (Hans) Arp, *Squares Arranged by Laws of Chance*; Giorgio de Chirico, *The Jewish Angel*; Robert Delauney, *The Flamenco Singer*; Frantisek Kupka, *Irregular Forms*; Wilhelm Lehmbruck, *The Fallen*; Henri Matisse, *The Three Sisters* and *Bathers by a River*; Pierre Renoir, *Venus* (bronze); Joseph Wright, *Imperial Hotel, Tokyo*.

Literature: Harold Brighouse, *Hobson's Choice*; Robert Frost, *Mountain Interval*; Vicente Ibañez, *The Four Horsemen of the Apocalypse*; James Joyce, *Portrait of the Artist as a Young Man*; Ring Lardner, *You Know Me, Al*; Amy Lowell, *Men, Women and Giants*; Carl Sandburg, *Chicago Poems*; Booth Tarkington, *Penrod and Sam*.

MUSICAL EVENTS

A. Births:

Jan 22	Henri Dutilleux (Fr-cm)	Jul 5	Gabriella Gatti (It-sop)
Feb 12	Abraham Veinus (Am-mus)	Jul 6	Walther Siegmund-Schultze (Ger-mus)
Apr 6	Martha Lipton (Am-alto)	Jul 17	Eleanor Steber (Am-sop)
Apr 11	Alberto Ginastera (Arg-cd)	Jul 23	Ben Weber (Am-cm)
Apr 22	Yehudi Menuhin (Am-vn-cd)	Aug 2	Hans Hopf (Ger-ten)
Apr 30	Alda Noni (It-sop)	Aug 16	Maura Lympany (Br-pn)
Apr 30	Robert Shaw (Am-cd)	Sep 10	Barbara Troxell (Am-sop)
May 10	Milton Babbit (Am-cm)	Sep 26	Robert Kelly (Am-cm)
May 12	Ellis B. Kohs (Am-cm)	Oct 10	Scott Huston (Am-cm)
May 22	Gordon Binkerd (Am-cm)	Oct 19	Emil Gilels (Rus-pn)
Jun 26	Giuseppe Taddei (It-bar)	Dec 22	Fernando Corena (Swi-bs)
Jul 3	Robert Stevenson (Am-mus)		

B. Deaths:

Jan 22	Iwan Knorr (Ger-cm-cu)	May 28	Albert Lavignac (Fr-mus)
Feb 19	Ernst Mach (Ger-acous)	Jul 7	Jules Combarieu (Fr-mus)
Feb 20	Giovanni Sbriglia (It-ten)	Jul 27	Karl Klindworth (Ger-pn-cd)
Mar 24	Enrique Granados (Sp-cm)	Aug 5	Georges Butterworth (Br-cm)
May 11	Max Reger (Ger-cm)	Aug 13	Fritz Steinbach (Ger-cd)
May 23	Clara L. Kellogg (Am-sop)	Sep 25	Emil Krause (Ger-cri)

Oct 30 Silas G. Pratt (Am-pn)	Dec 20 Hans Richter (Ger-cd)
Nov 23 Eduard Napravnik (Cz-cd-cm)	Dec 25 William W. Gilchrist (Am-cm-cd)
Dec 2 Francesco Tosti (It-cm)	

C. Debuts:

Met ---Maria Barrientos (sop), Sophie Barton (mez), Fernando Carpi (ten), Paul Eisler (cd), Maud Fay (sop), Anna Fitziu (sop), Kathleen Howard (mez), Mario Laurenti (bar), Claudia Muzio (sop), Gennaro Papi (cd), Lavinia Puglioli (sop), Marie Sundelius (sop), Marie Tiffany (sop), Phyllis White (sop)

U.S. --Ernest Ansermet (N.Y.), Mario Camlee (Los Angeles), Giulio Crimi (Chicago), Amelita Galli-Curci (Chicago), Virgilio Lazzari (Boston), Mischa Levitzki (N.Y.), Isolde Menges (N.Y.), Giacomo Rimini (Chicago)

Other -Norman Allin (London), Toti Dal Monte (Milan), Zbigniew Drzewiecki (Warsaw), Karl Elmendorff (Düsseldorff), Ilona Kabos (Budapest), Alexander Kipnis (Hamburg), Elfriede Marherr (Berlin), José Riavez (Zagreb), Christy Solari (Mantua), Ebe Ticozzi (Genoa), Eva Turner (London), Renato Zanelli (Santiago)

D. New Positions:

Conductors: Gustav Strube (Baltimore SO and director, Peabody Institute)

Educational: Felix Borowski (president, Chicago Musical College), Francesco Cilea (director, Naples Conservatory), Ernst von Dohnányi (piano, Budapest Academy), Carl Nielsen (theory & composition, Copenhagen Conservatory)

Others: Ernest Grosjean (organ, Versailles)

E. Prizes and Honors:

Honors: Thomas Beecham (knighted), Henry James (Order of Merit)

F. Biographical Highlights:

Ernst Bloch makes his first visit to the United States as accompanist to singer Maud Allen; Enrique Granados, following the torpedoing of their oceanliner, loses his life attempting to rescue his wife; Charles Hackett makes his debut at La Scala; Lotte Lehmann moves to Vienna; Darius Milhaud is invited by Claudel to go to Rio de Janeiro as his secretary; Pierre Monteux leaves the French army and tours the United States as conductor with the Ballet Russe; Ervin Nyiregyházi studies music in Berlin with Dohnányi; Edmund Rubbra begins the study of music with Cyril Scott; Marcella Sembrich retires from active music life; William Grant Still begins arranging and playing for W.C. Handy in Memphis; Fartein Valen returns to Norway and settles in Valevåg.

G. Institutional Openings:

Performing Groups: City of Birmingham SO (England), Dessoff Madrigal Singers (N.Y.), People's Chorus of New York

Educational: Lambda Phi Delta Music Sorority (Evanston), Limburg Organ School, Longy School of Music (Boston), David Mannes School of Music (N.Y.), National Central Library (England), New South Wales Conservatorium of Music and State Orchestra (Australia), Philippines Conservatory of Music

Other: Finnish Musicological Society; Hill, Norman and Beard, Organ Builders (London); Presser Foundation (Philadelphia)

H. Musical Literature:

Burleigh, Henry, *Jubilee Songs of the U.S.A.*
Forsyth/Stanford, *A History of Music*
Goldman, Edwin, *Band Guide and Aid to Teachers*
Halm, August, *Von Grenzen und Ländern der Musik*
Hull, Arthur, *Modern Musical Styles*

Kitson, Charles, *Applied Strict Counterpoint*
Langenus, Gustave, *Complete Clarinet Method*
Lomax, John W. Jr., *Plantation Songs of the Negro*
Mason, Daniel, *Great Modern Composers*
Miller, Dayton, *Science of Musical Sounds*

I. Musical Compositions:

Bantock, Granville, *The Hebridean Symphony*
Bartók, Béla, *Suite, Opus 14, for Piano*
    The Wooden Prince (ballet)
    10 Songs, Opus 15 and 16
Bax, Arnold, *The Garden of Fand* (symphonic poem)
Bloch, Ernst, *Israel Symphony* (with soloists and chorus)
    String Quartet No. 1
Busoni, Ferruccio, *Arlecchino* (opera)
Casella, Alfredo, *Elegia Eroica* (orchestra)
Debussy, Claude, *Sonata for Flute, Viola and Harp*
Delius, Frederick, *Dance Rhapsody No. 2* (orchestra)
    Requiem (chorus, orchestra)
    Concerto for Violin and Orchestra
    Concerto for Violin, Cello and Orchestra
Dohnányi, Ernst von, *Etudes de Concert, Opus 28* (piano)
Friml, Rudolf, *Rose Marie* (operetta)
Grainger, Percy, *In a Nutshell* (piano and orchestra)
Granados, Enrique, *Goyescas* (opera)
Griffes, Charles, *Four Roman Sketches, Opus 7* (piano)
    The Kairn of Koridwen (dance-drama)
    3 Songs, Opus 10
Hadley, Henry, *The Ocean* (tone poem)
    Bianca (one-act opera)
Hanson, Howard, *Symphonic Prelude* (orchestra)
Holst, Gustav, *Savitri* (one-act opera)
Ives, Charles, *Symphony No. 4*
Janácek, Leos, *The Diary of One Who Vanished* (opera)
Korngold, Erich, *Violanta* (opera)
    Der Ring des Polykrates (opera)
Leoncavallo, Ruggiero, *Goffredo Mameli* (opera)
Milhaud, Darius, *Les Choéphores* (part II of Aeschylus' Orestes)(incidental music)
Nielsen, Carl, *Symphony No. 4, "Inextinguishable"*
Prokofiev, Serge, *The Gambler, Opus 24* (opera)
Schoenberg, Arnold, *Four Orchestral Songs, Opus 22*
Sibelius, Jan, *Jedermann, Opus 83* (incidental music)
Stanford, Charles, *The Critic* (opera)
Stravinsky, Igor, *Berceuses du Chat*
Szymanowski, Karol, *Symphony No. 3, Opus 27, "Song of the Night"*
    Concerto No. 1, Opus 35, for Violin and Orchestra
Turina, Joaquin, *Navidad* (opera)
Villa-Lobos, Heitor, *Symphony No. 1, "The Unforeseen"*
Webern, Anton, *Five Songs, Opus 13*

1917

World Events:

In the U.S., Congress declares war on Germany on April 4 and proceeds to pass the Selective Service Act, the Espionage Act and the Trading with the Enemy Act; a Literacy Test for Aliens is passed over the president's veto; Puerto Rico becomes a U.S. territory; the International Association of Lion's Clubs is founded. Internationally, Germany begins unrestricted U-boat warfare on any and all shipping; in Russia, the Bolshevik Revolution forces Nicholas II to abdicate while Vladimir Lenin and Leon Trotsky seize power; the Bolsheviks then sue for peace with Germany; Finland declares its independence of Russia; Trans-Siberian Railway is finished; the Balfour Declaration gives British support to a Jewish Palestine.

Cultural Highlights:

The Dutch magazine *De Stijl* begins publication as does the Dadaist journal *291*; the November Group of Finnish artists is formed; Marc Chagall becomes Commissioner of Fine Arts in Vitebsk; the Danish authors Karl Gjellerup and Henrik Pontoppidan share the Nobel Prize for Literature; The Museum of New Mexico opens its doors in Santa Fe. Births include British novelist Anthony Burgess, Italian novelist Carlo Cassola and the American poets Gwendolyn Brooks and Robert Lowell and authors Jessica Mitford, Peter Taylor and Carson McCullars, German author Heinrich Böll and American artist Andrew Wyeth. Deaths in the art world include French artist Edgar G. Degas and sculptor Auguste Rodin, American sculptors Moses J. Ezekiel and Bela Pratt and artist Albert P. Ryder; the literary world loses British poet Edward Thomas, American poet John Piatt and Irish novelist Jane Barlow. Other highlights include:

Art: Emile Barnard, *Abraham Lincoln;* Pierre Bonnard, *Nude at the Fireplace;* Charles Burchfield, *Church Bells, Winter Night*; Marc Chagall, *The Grey House*; Giorgio de Chirico, *Grand Metaphysical Interior*; Amedeo Modigliani, *Girl with Braids*; Emil Nolde, *The Family*; Georges Rouault, *The Three Clowns*; Joseph Stella, *The Brooklyn Bridge*.

Literature: T.S. Elliot, *Prufrock*; Hamlin Garland, *Son of the Middle Border*; Carl G. Jung, *Psychology of the Unconscious*; Alfred Joyce Kilmer, *Main Street and Other Poems*; Vachel Lindsay, *The Chinese Nightingale*; Archibald MacLeish, *The Tower of Ivory*; Edward Robinson, *Merlin*; Upton Sinclair, *King Coal*; Booth Tarkington, *Seventeen*.

MUSICAL EVENTS

A. Births:

Jan 4 William Latham (Am-cm)	May 4 Edward T. Cone (Am-the-cri)
Jan 5 Wieland Wagner (Ger-imp)	May 14 Lou Harrison (Am-cm)
Jan 7 Ulysses Kay (Am-cm)	May 23 Sidney Foster (Am-pn-ed)
Jan 12 Walter Hendl (Am-cd)	May 25 Heinz Rehfuss (Ger-bar)
Feb 5 Otto Edelmann (Aus-bar)	Jun 4 Robert Merrill (Am-bar)
Feb 13 Thomas Scherman (Am-cd)	Jul 6 Dorothy Kirsten (Am-sop)
Feb 21 Francis Madeira (Am-cd)	Aug 16 Roque Cordero (Pan-cm)
Feb 22 Louis Auriacombe (Fr-cd)	Sep 13 Robert Ward (Am-cm)
Mar 7 Robert Erickson (Am-cm)	Sep 15 Hilde Gueden (Aus-sop)
Mar 16 Walter Goldschmidt (Aus-cd)	Sep 20 Goeran Gentele (Swe-imp)
Mar 19 Dinu Lipatti (Rom-pn)	Oct 4 Lawrence Davidson (Am-bs)
Apr 5 Richard Yardumian (Am-cm)	Oct 21 "Dizzy" Gilespie (Am-pop)

B. Deaths:

Jan 12 Maria Teresa Carreño (Ven-pn)	Feb 13 Harry E. Woolridge (Br-mus)
Jan 13 Albert Niemann (Ger-ten)	Apr 4 Scott Joplin (Am-pop-cm)
Feb 10 Emile-Louis Pessard (Fr-cm)	Apr 14 Richard Wallaschek (Aus-the)
Feb 11 Bernhard Listemann	Apr 17 Barton M'Guckin (Ir-ten)
(Ger-vn-cd)	May 25 Edouard de Reszke (Pol-bs)

Jul 16   Phillip Scharwenka (Pol-cm)   Dec 7   Alois Minkus (Aus-cm)
Sep 8   Charles E. Lefebvre (Fr-cm)   Dec 16   Henry Barnabee (Am-voc-imp)

C. Debuts:

Met ---Louis d'Angelo (bar), Thomas Chalmers (bar), Julia Claussen (mez), Florence Easton (sop), Helene Kanders (sop), Morgan Kingston (ten), Sante Mandelli (ten), José Mardones (bs), Giuseppina Mazza (mez), Ruth Miller (sop), Pierre Monteux (cd), Roberto Moranzoni (cd), May Peterson (sop), Maria Savage (sop/mez), Albert Scholl (bar)

U.S. --Joseph Bonnet (N.Y.), Roland Hayes (Boston), Jascha Heifetz (N.Y.), Carel van Hulst (Chicago), Forrest Lamont (Chicago), Edgard Varèse (as conductor)

Other -Karl Böhm (Graz), Dino Borgioli (Milan), Thomas Burke (Milan), Maria Carina (Turin), Maria Hussa (Vienna), Alfred Jerger (as baritone), Fritzi Jokl (Frankfurt), Dora Labette (London), Imre Palló (Budapest), Gabrielle Ritter-Ciampi (Paris), Bianca Scacciati (Milan), Grete Stückgold (Nuremburg), Tossy Spivakovsky (Berlin), Vilem Zitek (Prague)

D. New Positions:

Conductors: Otto Klemperer (Cologne Opera), Serge Koussevitsky (Petrograd State SO), Pierre Monteux (Met)

Educational: Bernhard Paumgartner (director, Salzburg Mozarteum), Ildebrando Pizzetti (director, Florence Conservatory), Roger Sessions (theory, Smith College), Joseph Szigeti (violin, Geneva Conservatory)

Others: Walter Alcock (organ, Salisbury Cathedral)

E. Prizes and Honors:

Honors: Harry T. Burleigh (Spingarn Medal), Edgar S. Kelley (honorary doctorate, Cincinnati), Ignace Jan Paderewski (honorary doctorate, Yale)

F. Biographical Highlights:

Charles W. Cadman takes up residence in Los Angeles; Johanna Gadski gives her farewell Met performance; Paul Hindemith when called to the military works with the regimental band and forms a soldier's string quartet to entertain the troops; Serge Koussevitsky is given the post of conductor of the State SO in Petrograd (new name for St. Petersburg); Fernando de Lucia retires from the opera stage; Gian F. Malipiero flees the war, settles in Rome; John McCormick becomes a naturalized American citizen; Wallingford Riegger gives up his position with the Bluethner Orchestra in Berlin and returns to the U.S.; Carl Ruggles settles in New York and begins working for the promotion of modern music; Roger Sessions receives his bachelor degree from Yale; Oliver Strunk begins studying at Cornell University; Karol Szymanowski's manor house is destroyed by the Russian revolutionists, all his possessions including two grand pianos are dumped in the lake.

G. Institutional Openings:

Performing Groups: Budapest String Quartet, George Enescu SO (Bucharest), Guy Lombardo Band (Toronto), Philadelphia Chamber Music Association

Festivals: Salzburg Music Festival

Educational: Manhattan School of Music

Other: Chilean Bach Society, Finnish Composer's Union (Helsinki); Harold Flammer, Inc., Music Publishers (N.Y.); Music Society of University College (Dublin), Musical Alliance of America, Società Italiana de Musique Moderna (by A. Cassella), Société Française de Musicologie (Paris), Society of Norwegian Composers, *Tesoro Musical*

H. Musical Literature:

Dickinson, Charles, *Excursions in Musical History*
Duncan, William E., *Ultra-Modernism in Music*

Einstein, Alfred, *A Short History of Music*
Huneker, James, *The Philharmonic Society of New York and its 75th Anniversary*
Kurth, Ernst, *Grundlagen des Linearen Kontrapunkt*
McGill, Josephine, *Folk Songs of the Kentucky Mountains*
Metcalf, Frank, *American Psalmody*
Sharp/Campbell, *English Folksongs from the Southern Appalachians*
Turina, Joaquin, *Enciclopedia abreviada de música*
Watt, Henry, *The Psychology of Sound*

I. Musical Compositions:
Bartók, Béla, *String Quartet No. 2, Opus 17*
Bax, Arnold, *Tintagel* (tone poem)
Berlin, Irving, *Yip, Yip, Yaphank* (musical)
Busoni, Ferruccio, *Turandot* (opera)
        Suite, Die Brautwahl, Opus 45 (orchestra)
Cadman, Charles, *Oriental Rhapsody* (orchestra)
Carpenter, John Alden, *Concertino* (piano and orchestra)
        Symphony
Cohan, George M., *Over There* (song)
Converse, Frederick, *Ave Atque Vale* (tone poem)
Debussy, Claude, *Violin Sonata No. 3* (with piano)
Delius, Frederick, *Eventyr* (orchestra)
Hadley, Henry, *Ode to Music* (soloists, chorus and orchestra)
Hanson, Howard, *Symphonic Legend* (orchestra)
Holst, Gustav, *Hymn of Jesus* (two choruses and orchestra)
Koven, Reginald de, *Canterbury Pilgrims* (opera)
Malipiero, Gian, *Ditirambo Tragico* (orchestra)
Mascagni, Pietro, *Lodoletta* (opera)
Pfitzner, Hans, *Palestrina* (opera)
Pijper, Willem, *Symphony No. 1, "Pan"*
Pizzetti, Ildebrando, *La Sacra Rappresentazione d'Abraham ed Isaac* (incidental music)
Poulenc, Francis, *Rapsodie Negre* (piano, string quartet, flute, clarinet, voices)
Prokofiev, Serge, *Visions Fugitive, Opus 22* (piano)
        Symphony No. 1, Opus 25, "Classical"
        Piano Sonatas No. 3 and 4, Opus Nos. 28 and 29
Rachmaninoff, Serge, *Etudes-Tableaux, Opus 39* (piano)
Ravel, Maurice, *Le Tombeau de Couperin* (orchestrated 1919)
Respighi, Ottorino, *The Fountains of Rome* (orchestra)
Reznicek, Emil von, *Eros and Psyche* (opera)
Romberg, Sigmund, *Maytime* (operetta)
Satie, Erik, *Parade* (ballet)
Sibelius, Jan, *12 Songs, Opus 88 and 90*
Sinding, Christian, *Concerto No. 3, Opus 119, for Violin and Orchestra*
Stravinsky, Igor, *Renard* (a "barnyard opera")
        Les Noces (ballet)
Suk, Josef, *Ripening* (orchestra)
Villa-Lobos, Heitor, *Uirapuru* (ballet)
        Symphony No. 2, "Ascension"
        Amazonas (ballet)
Webern, Anton, *Five Songs, Opus 12*

1918

World Events:

World War I ends and U.S. President Wilson presents his Fourteen Points, his own plan for a lasting peace; the passing of the Sedition Act in Congress causes the jailing of many Socialists; first Air Mail service begins; the Browning automatic rifle is invented; the U.S. Supreme Court upholds the Selective Service Act. Internationally, Kaiser Wilhelm flees Germany while the new government signs the Armistice agreement; Poland, Austria, Hungary and Czechoslovakia are declared to be independent states; civil war between the Whites and the Reds (Bolsheviks) in Russia leads to the murder of the royal family.

Cultural Highlights:

Pulitzer Prizes: Drama, Jesse L. Williams (*Why Marry?*); Fiction, Ernest Poole (*His Family*); Poetry, Sara Teasdale (*Love Songs*). Henry Hall Caine and John Lavery are knighted but John Galsworthy refuses his knighthood. The Albertina collection of old masterpieces is taken over by the Austrian State; the Novembergruppe of German artists is formed in Berlin. Russian author Alexander Solzhenitsyn is born this year as is Canadian poet Louis Dudek. Deaths in the literary world includes French poets Guillaume Apollinaire, Henri Chantavoine and Edmond Rostand, Canadian poets William W. Campbell and John McCrae, Italian novelist Salvatore Farina, American poet Alfred Joyce Kilmer and historian Henry Adams and German dramatist Frank Wedekind; the art world mourns the passing of French sculptor Raymond Duchamp-Villon, Swiss artist Ferdinand Hodler, Austrian artist Gustav Klimt and American artist Joseph Pickett and Henry G. Dearth. Other highlights include:

Art: Pierre Bonnard, *Le Jardin Sauvage*; Robert Delauney, *Igor Stravinsky*; Paul Klee, *Gartenplan*; Oskar Kokoschka, *Saxonian Landscape*; Ferdinand Léger, *Le Moteur*; Max Liebemann, *Richard Strauss*; George Luks, *Armistice Night*; Henri Matisse, *Odalisques*; Amedeo Modigliani, *The Peasant Boy*; Maurice Prendergast, *Autumn Festival*.

Literature: Benjamin Brawley, *The Negro in Literature and Art*; Rupert Brookes, *Collected Poems*; Émile Cammaerts, *Messines and Other Poems*; Willa Cather, *My Antonia*; James Joyce, *Exiles*; Windham Lewis, *Tarr*; Carl Sandburg, *The Corn Huskers*; Oswald Spangler, *The Decline of the West*; Booth Tarkington, *The Magnificent Ambersons*.

MUSICAL EVENTS

A. Births:

Jan 6 José A. Alegría (Por-mus)	Jun 4 Jan van Dijk (Hol-cm-pn)
Jan 18 Amalie Materna (Aus-sop)	Jul 5 George Rochberg (Am-cm)
Jan 21 Antonio Janigro (It-cel-cd)	Jul 6 Eugene List (Am-pn)
Jan 24 Gottfried von Einem (Aus-cm)	Jul 26 Leonard Rose (Am-cel)
Mar 3 Frank Wigglesworth (Am-cm)	Aug 25 Leonard Bernstein (Am-cm-cd)
Mar 15 Zara Dolukhanova (Rus-sop)	Sep 11 Gertrude Ribla (Am-sop)
Mar 20 Bernd Zimmermann (Ger-cm)	Sep 19 Blanche Thebom (Am-alto)
Mar 28 Anselmo Colzani (It-bar)	Sep 22 Henryk Szeryng (Pol-vn)
Apr 3 Sixten Ehrling (Swe-cd)	Nov 14 Jean Madeira (Am-alto)
Apr 25 Astrid Varnay (Swe-sop)	Nov 18 Stig Westerburg (Swe-cd-pn)
May 17 Birgit Nilsson (Swe-sop)	Dec 8 Gérard Souzay (Fr-bar)

B. Deaths:

Feb 7 Alexander Taneyev (Rus-cm)	Apr 22 Antonio Pini-Corsi (It-bar)
Feb 23 Sophie Menter (Ger-pn)	Jun 1 Jaroslav Novotny (Cz-cm)
Feb 27 Vassily Safonov (Rus-cd)	Jun 10 Arrigo Boito (It-cm-lib)
Mar 15 Lili Boulanger (Fr-cm)	Jun 27 Gustav Kobbé (Am-cri)
Mar 25 Claude Debussy (Fr-cm)	Aug 19 Henry G. Hanchett (Am-org)
Mar 26 César Cui (Rus-cm)	Oct 7 Hubert Parry (Br-cm)

Oct 18 Charles Converse (Am-cm)   Nov 4   Michael Brenet (Fr-mus)
Oct 24 Alexander Lecocq (Fr-cm)   Dec 13 Nicolai Figner (Rus-ten)

C. Debuts:

Met ---Cecilia Arden (mez), Kitty Beale (sop), Marguerite Belleri (mez), Constanze Bitterl (sop), Robert Couzinou (bar), Giulio Crimi (ten), Rafaelo Diaz (ten), Mary Ellis (sop), Alice Gentle (mez), Hipolito Lazaro (ten), Mary Mellish (sop), Luigi Montesanto (bar), Giordano Paltrinieri (ten), Rosa Ponselle (sop), Margaret Romaine (sop), Louise Tozier (sop)

U.S. --Alfred Cortot (N.Y.), Alessandro Dolci (Chicago), Yvonne Gall (Chicago), Queena Mario (N.Y.), Greta Masson, John O'Sullivan (Chicago), Max Rosen (N.Y.), Toscha Seidel (N.Y.)

Other -Adrian Boult (London), Vina Bovy (Ghent), Samuel Dushkin, Zino Francescatti (Marseilles), Benvenuto Franci (Rome), Göta Ljungberg (Stockholm), Lauritz Melchior (as tenor), Irene Minghini-Cattaneo (Savona), Rosa Pauly (Vienna), Nino Piccaluga (Novara), Meta Seinemeyer (Berlin), Margaret Sheridan (Rome), Oda Slobodskaya (Leningrad), Violetta de Strozzi (Zagreb), Erich Zimmermann (Dresden)

D. New Positions:

Conductors: Ernest Ansermet (Orchestre de la Suisse Romande), Fritz Busch (Stuttgart Opera), Ossip Gabrilowitsch (Detroit SO), Hans Knappertsbusch (Leipzig Opera), Henri Rabaud (Boston SO), Nicolai Sokoloff (Cleveland SO), Eugène Ysaye (Cincinnati SO)

Educational: Hugh Allen (director, Royal Conservatory), Willem Pijper (theory, Amsterdam Conservatory), Nicolas Tcherepnin (director, Tbilisi Conservatory)

Others: Sydney Nicholson (organ, Westminster Abbey)

E. Prizes and Honors:

Honors: Max Bruch (honorary doctorate, Berlin), John Alden Carpenter (National Institute of Arts and Letters), William Hadow (knighted), Nellie Melba (Dame), Henri Rabaud (French Institute)

F. Biographical Highlights:

Leopold Auer moves to the U.S. where he settles permanently; George Bundy buys the American distributorship for Selmer instruments; Aaron Copland graduates from Boys High School; Henry Cowell enlists in the army, spends time as arranger for the U.S. Army Band; Josef Foerster returns to the new Czech Republic to teach in the Conservatory; Percy Grainger becomes a naturalized American citizen; Alois Hába begins the study of composition with Schreker; Gustav Holst visits the Middle East as music advisor to the Y.M.C.A.; Charles Ives suffers a massive heart attack and is forced to cut back on business and music activities; Charles Koechlin makes a lecture tour of the U.S.; Margarete Matzenauer becomes a naturalized U.S. citizen; Darius Milhaud returns to Paris; Karl Muck is placed in a Georgia internment camp for the duration of the war; Sergei Rachmaninoff moves his family to the U.S.; Václav Talich becomes second conductor of the Czech PO; Alexander Tcherepnin's family flees St. Petersburg, settles in Tiflis; Jennie Tourel flees with her family and settles in Danzig; Anton Webern returns to Vienna; Kurt Weill goes to Berlin for music study.

G. Institutional Openings:

Performing Groups: Beethoven Association of New York, Berlin Society for New Music, Cleveland SO, Herbert Ware (Cardiff) SO, Léner String Quartet (Budapest), Orchestre de la Suisse Romande (Switzerland), Rotterdam SO, Washington Community Opera (Wash. National Opera Association)

Festivals: Coolidge Chamber Music Festival (Massachusetts)

Educational: Institute of Music (Jerusalem), Neuchatel Conservatory of Music, Pi Kappa Lambda Honor Society (Evanston Illinois)

Other: *American Organist*; Belwin, Inc., Music Publishers (N.Y.); *La Critica Musicale*, Lewisohn Stadium Concerts (N.Y.), Neue Musikgesellschaft (Berlin), Society of Private Music Performance (Vienna), Society of Swedish Composers, *Der Spiegel, Zeitschrift für Musikwissenschaft*

H. Musical Literature:

Downes, Olin, *The Lure of Music*
Elson, Louis, *Women in Music*
Farmer, Henry, *Heresy in Art*
Fisher, William, *Notes on Music in Old Boston*
Gennrich, Friedrich, *Musikwissenschaft und Romanische Philologie*
Hanchett, Henry G., *Introduction to the Theory of Music*
Henschel, George, *Musings and Memories of a Musician*
Howard, Kathleen, *Confessions of an Opera Singer*
Huré, Jean, *La Technique de l'Orgue*
Mason, Daniel, *Contemporary Composers*

I. Musical Compositions:

Bartók, Béla, *Three Studies, Opus 18* (piano)
Berlin, Irving, *God Bless America* (song)
Boito, Arrigo, *Nerone* (opera, unfinished)
Cadman, Charles, *Shanewis* (opera)
Casella, Alfredo, *Pagine di Guerra* (orchestra)
            Pupazzetti (orchestra)
Cowell, Henry, *Symphony No. 1*
Delius, Frederick, *A Song before Sunrise* (orchestra)
Elgar, Edward, *String Quartet, Opus 83*
            Piano Quintet, Opus 83
Fauré, Gabriel, *Le Jardin Clos, Opus 106* (eight songs)
            Cello Sonata No. 1. Opus 109
Foerster, Josef, *The Conquerors* (opera)
Griffes, Charles, *Poem for Flute and Orchestra*
            Three Poems by MacLeod, Opus 11 (voice, orchestra)
            Piano Sonata
Hadley, Henry, *Cleopatra's Night* (opera)
Hill, Edward, *A Child's Garden of Verse* (symphonic suite)
Janácek, Leos, *Taras Bulba* (symphonic poem)
Lehár, Franz, *Wo die Lerche Singt* (operetta)
Malipiero, Gian, *Grottesco for Orchestra*
Martin, Frank, *Les Dithyrambes* (chorus, orchestra)
Martinu, Bohuslav, *Magic Night* (voice, orchestra)
Medtner, Nicolai, *Concerto No. 1, Opus 33, for Piano and Orchestra*
Miaskovsky, Nicolai, *Symphony No. 4, Opus 17*
            Symphony No. 5, Opus 18
Milhaud, Darius, *L'Homme et son Désir* (ballet)
Nielsen, Carl, *Pan and Syrinx* (orchestra)
Poulenc, Francis, *Mouvements Perpétuels* (piano)
Prokofiev, Serge, *They are Seven* (tenor, chorus, orchestra)
Puccini, Giacomo, *Gianni Schicchi* (opera)
            Il Tabarro (opera)
Respighi, Ottorino, *La Boutique Fantasque* (ballet after Rossini)
Roussel, Albert, *Padmavati, Opus 18* (opera-ballet)
Satie, Erik, *Socrates* (opera)
Strauss, Richard, *Le Bourgeois Gentilhomme* (incidental music)
Stravinsky, Igor, *L'Histoire du Soldat* (narrator, dancers, chamber group)
            Ragtime for Eleven Instruments
Szymanowski, Karol, *12 Etudes, Opus 33, for Piano*
Taylor, Deems, *Through the Looking Glass* (chamber orchestra)

1919

World Events:
U.S. President Wilson, on a tour promoting the League of Nations, suffers a stroke--Congress rejects the League; the American Legion is formed at the same time as the American Communist Party; the Prohibition Amendment is ratified and Grand Canyon National Park is established; former President Theodore Roosevelt passes away early in January. Internationally, the Treaty of Versailles officially ends World War I and Geneva becomes the site of the League of Nations; Switzerland is recognized by all powers as a permanent neutral country and Danzig becomes a free city; the first non-stop flight across the Atlantic takes 16 hours and 27 minutes.

Cultural Highlights:
Pulitzer Prizes: Fiction, Booth Tarkington (*The Magnificent Ambersons*); Poetry, Carl Sandburg (*The Corn Huskers*), and Margaret Widemer (*Old Road to Paradise*). Carl Spitteler receives the Nobel Prize for Literature and Frank Brangwyn is inducted into the Royal Academy; Rabindranath Tagore gives up his knighthood in protest over the massacre of Indians. The Bauhaus school is founded in Weimar by Walter Gropius while the British Drama League is formed in England; the Louis Comfort Tiffany Foundation for art students is established in New York. Literary births include Doris Lessing, Iris Murdoch and Jerome Salinger; deaths include Russian author Leonid Andreyev and British novelist Amelia Barr. Deaths in the art field include Americans Ralph Blakelock, Kenyon Cox and Frank Duveneck, German sculptor Wilhelm Lehmbruck, British artist Edward J. Poynter and French artist Pierre Renoir. Other highlights include:

Art: Constantin Brancusi, *Bird in Space*; Vasili Kandinsky, *Dreamy Improvisations*; Paul Klee, *Dream Birds*; Fernand Léger, *The City*; Frederick MacMonnies, *Civic Virtue*; Henri Matisse, *The Artist and His Model*; Amedeo Modigliani, *Self-Portrait*; Georgia O'Keefe, *Over Blue*; Pablo Picasso, *Sketch to Stravinsky's Ragtime*; Grant Wood, *Psyche* (bronze).

Literature: Sherwood Anderson, *Winesburg, Ohio*; Leonid Andreyev, *S.O.S.*; Joseph Conrad, *The Arrow of Gold*; Theodore Dreiser, *Twelve Men*; T.S. Elliot, *Poems*; Thomas Hardy, *Collected Poems*; Hermann Hesse, *Demian*; Vicente Ibañez, *Blood and Sand*; W. Somerset Maugham, *The Moon and the Sixpence*; Albert Terhune, *Lad, a Dog*.

MUSICAL EVENTS

A. Births:

Jan 24	Leon Kirchner (Am-cm)	Jul 28	Milan Horvat (Yug-cd)
Jan 30	Robert Suter (Swi-cm)	Jul 31	Norman Del Mar (Br-cd-cm)
Feb 2	Lisa Della Casa (Swi-sop)	Aug 7	Kim Borg (Fin-bs)
Feb 2	Waldemar Kementt (Aus-ten)	Aug 11	Ginette Neveu (Fr-vn)
Feb 6	Arthur Gold (Am-pn)	Aug 24	Niels Bentzon (Den-cm)
Mar 28	Jacob Avshalomov (Chi-cm)	Sep 11	Lex van Delden (Hol-cm)
Apr 9	Noah Greenberg (Am-cd-mus)	Sep 14	Deryck Cooke (Br-mus)
May 10	Peter Maag (Swi-cd)	Sep 24	Vaclav Nelhybel (Cz-cm)
May 14	Jindrich Rohan (Cz-cd)	Oct 4	Geneviève Joy (Fr-pn)
May 18	Margot Fonteyn (Br-bal)	Oct 9	Irmgard Seefried (Ger-sop)
May 19	Boris Christoff (Bul-bs)	Nov 17	Hershey Kay (Am-cm)
May 30	George London (Can-bar)	Nov 27	Roman Haubenstock-Ramati (Pol-cm)
Jun 5	Akeo Watanabe (Jp-cm)	Dec 21	Ernst Wiemann (Ger-bs)
Jul 6	Ernst Haeflinger (Swi-ten)		

B. Deaths:

Feb 2	Xavier Leroux (Fr-cm)	Aug 1	Oscar Hammerstein (Am-imp)
Feb 14	M.H. van't Kruis (Hol-org)	Aug 9	Ruggiero Leoncavallo (It-cm)
Apr 19	Barbara Marchisio (It-alto)	Aug 11	Andrew Carnegie (Am-ind-pat)
May 8	Philipp Wolfrum (Ger-mus)	Sep 20	Pavel Khokhlov (Rus-mus)
Jul 10	Hugo Riemann (Ger-mus)	Sep 27	Adelina Patti (Sp-sop)

Nov 15 Henry L. Higginson
       (Am-bk-pat)
Dec 18 Horatio Parker (Am-cm)

Dec 19 Cleofonte Campanini (It-cd)
Dec 21 Louis Diemer (Fr-pn-cm)
Dec 31 Marie Van Zandt (Am-sop)

C. Debuts:

Met ---Gladys Axman (sop), Giuseppe Bamboschek (cd), Louise Bêrat (mez), Gabriella Besanzoni (mez), Octave Dua (ten), Margaret Farnham (sop), Jeanne Gordon (mez), Charles Hackett (ten), Orville Harrold (ten), Frances Ingram (mez), Edna Kellogg (sop), Katherine Kennedy (sop), Eugenie Manetti (sop), Helena Marsh (mez), Giovanni Martino (bs), Millo Picco (bar), Evelyn Scotney (sop), Albert Wolff (cd), Renato Zanelli (bar)

U.S. --Howard Barlow (New Hampshire), Cornelis Bronsgeest (tour), Borghild Bryhn-Langaard (Chicago), John Corigliano (N.Y.), Anis Fuleihan (N.Y.), Edward Johnson (Chicago), Benno Moiseiwitsch (N.Y.), José Mojica (Chicago), Manuel Salazar (tour), Tito Schipa (Chicago)

Other -Ivar Andrésen (Stockholm), Mimi Balkanska (Sofia), Ewa Bandrowska-Turka (Krakow), Valeria Barsova (Moscow), Alexander Brailowsky (Paris), Madeleine Grey (Paris), Adolph Hallis (London), Henry Holst (Copenhagen), Felicie Hüni-Mihacek (Vienna), Erika Morini (Leipzig), Maria Müller (Linz), Ella Némethy (Budapest), Augusta Oltrabella (Mondovi), Charles Panzéra (Paris), Tancredi Pasero (Vincenza), Alexander Pirogov (Moscow), Heinrich Rehkemper (Coburg), Hans Reinmar (Olomouc)

D. New Positions:

Conductors: Hans Knappertsbusch (Dessau Opera), Max von Schillings (Berlin Opera), Richard Strauss (Vienna Opera), Felix Weingartner (Vienna Volksoper)

Educational: Charles van den Borren (librarian, Brussels Conservatory), Frederick Converse (theory, New England Conservatory), Josef Foerster (composition, Prague Conservatory), Sigfrid Karg-Elert (theory, Leipzig Conservatory), Otakar Sevcík (violin, Prague Master School)

Others: James Huneker (music critic, New York *World*), Ignace Jan Paderewski (Prime Minister of Poland)

E. Prizes and Honors:

Prizes: Jacques Ibert (Prix de Rome)

Honors: Gerald Berners (baronet), Charles M. Loeffler & Alberto Williams (Legion of Honor), Ralph Vaughan-Williams (honorary doctorate, Oxford)

F. Biographical Highlights:

Ernst von Dohnányi removed as head of Budapest Conservatory after six months by the pro-fascist regime; Alexander Kipnis joins the Berlin State Opera; Wanda Landowska makes Paris her home and opens a school for interpretation of early music; Olivier Messiaen, age 12, enters Paris Conservatory; Joan Miró leaves Spain for Paris; Karl Muck is deported from the U.S. and returns to a sanatorium in Austria; Carl Orff leaves the army and returns to Munich; Walter Piston enrolls as special student at Harvard; Katherine Anne Porter leaves Colorado for New York; Abraham Rattner given a traveling scholarship by the Pennsylvania Academy; Dmitri Shostakovich enters the Leningrad Conservatory; Karol Szymanowski's family moves to Poland; Virgil Thomson enters Harvard; Thornton Wilder graduates from Yale.

G. Institutional Openings:

Performing Groups: Belgrade National Opera, Bratislava National Opera, Busch String Quartet, Glasgow SO, Golschman Concerts (Paris), Los Angeles PO, New SO (N.Y.), Oslo PO, Philharmonic Choir of London

Educational: Eastman School of Music (Rochester), École Normale de Musique (Paris), Hellenic Conservatory of Music (Greece), Idelsohn Music School (Jerusalem), Institute for the History of Music (Brno), Kappa Psi Fraternity (Oklahoma), Latvian Conservatory of Music (Riga), New Orleans Conservatory of Music, University of Iowa School of Music, University of North Carolina Music Department

Other: Canto, Hanssler Music Publishers (Stuttgart), Harcourt, Brace and Co., Publishers, *Mercury*, National Association of Harpists, National Association of Music Merchants, National Association of Negro Musicians (Chicago), Orchestra Hall (Detroit), Società Polifonica Romana, Society for the Publication of American Music (N.Y.), Vincent Bach Corporation (N.Y.)

H. Musical Literature:

Cowell, Henry, *New Musical Resources* (published 1930)
Foote, Arthur, *Modulation & Related Harmonic Questions*
Gehrkens, Karl, *Introduction to School Music Teaching*
          Essentials in Conducting
Jachimecki, Zdzislaw, *Outlines, Polish History of Music*
Kretzschmar, August, *Geschichte der Oper*
Niemann, Walter, *Meister des Klaviers*
Seashore, Carl, *Psychology of Musical Talent*
Watt, Henry, *The Foundations of Music*

I. Musical Compositions:

Alfvén, Hugo, *Symphony No. 4, Opus 39*
Bartók, Béla, *The Miraculous Mandarin, Opus 19* (ballet)
Carpenter, John Alden, *Birthday of the Infanta* (ballet)
Delius, Frederick, *A Poem of Life and Love* (orchestra)
Elgar, Edward, *Cello Concerto, Opus 85*
Enescu, Georges, *Symphony No. 3*
Falla, Manuel de, *The Three Cornered Hat* (ballet)
Fauré, Gabriel, *Fantasie, Opus 111* (piano and orchestra)
          Masque et Bergamasque, Opus 112 (orchestra)
Hadley, Henry, *Othello* (symphonic poem)
Hanson, Howard, *Symphonic Rhapsody* (orchestra)
Humperdinck, Engelbert, *Gaudeamus* (opera)
Mason, Daniel, *String Quartet on Negro Themes* (revised 1930)
          Prelude and Fugue for Piano and Orchestra
Milhaud, Darius, *Le Boeuf sur le Toit* (ballet)
Nielsen, Carl, *Alladin* (incidental music)
Poulenc, Francis, *Le Bestiaire* (songs after Apollinaire)
          Cocardes (song cycle)
Prokofiev, Serge, *The Love of Three Oranges, Opus 33* (opera)
Rangström, Ture, *Symphony No. 2, "My Country"*
          The Crown Bride (opera)
Reznicek, Emil von, *Symphony No. 2*
Saint-Saëns, Camille, *Morceau de Concert, Opus 154* (harp, orchestra)
Satie, Erik, *Quatre petites pieces Montées* (piano)
Stanford, Charles, *Concerto No. 3, Opus 171, for Piano and Orchestra*
Strauss, Richard, *17 Songs, Opus 67, 68 and 69*
          Die Frau ohne Schatten (opera)
Stravinsky, Igor, *Pulcinella* (ballet)
          Piano Rag Music
          Le Rossignol (fairy-tale opera)
Villa-Lobos, Heitor, *Symphony No. 3, "The War"*
          Symphony No. 4, "The Victory"

1920

World Events:

The U.S. census shows a population of 106,022,000 in 48 states, a 15% increase in ten years; Warren G. Harding becomes President No. 29; Prohibition goes into effect while the Nineteenth Amendment gives suffrage to women; Congress rejects the League of Nations; transcontinental airmail goes into service. Internationally, the League of Nations convenes in January; Palestine, Syria and Lebanon become British mandates; Thomas Masaryk becomes president of Czechoslovakia who along with Yugoslavia and Romania forms the Little Entente; DeHaviland Aircraft Co. founded in England.

Cultural Highlights:

The Pulitzer Prize for Drama goes to Eugene O'Neill for his work, *Beyond the Horizon*; no prizes are given for poetry or fiction. Norwegian author Knut Hamsun receives the Nobel Prize for Literature. Augustus Saint-Gaudens and Mark Twain are inducted into the Hall of Fame for Great Americans. The Société Anonyme, Inc. is formed for the promotion of American art; the Group of Seven (Toronto) holds its first exhibit. Deaths in the literary field include American novelist William D. Howells, German poet Richard Dehmel and Spanish novelist Benito Pérez Galdós; in the art field, American sculptor Thomas Clarke and artists Samuel Colman and Henry Mosler as well as German sculptor Max Klinger and Italian artist Amadeo Modigliani. Births include Romanian poet Paul Celan and American artist George Tooker. Other highlights include:

Art: Charles Burchfield, *February Thaw*; Jacob Epstein, *Christ* (bronze); Max Ernst, *Here Everything is Floating*; Rockwell Kent, *Wilderness*; Paul Klee, *They're Biting*; Paul Manship, *Diana*; Piet Mondrian, *Composition in Red, Yellow and Blue*; Otto Mueller, *Three Girls in the Woods*; Stanley Spencer, *Christ on the Cross*.

Literature: Sherwood Anderson, *Poor White*; Jaroslav Hasek, *Good Soldier Schweik*; Sinclair Lewis, *Main Street*; Eugene O'Neill, *Beyond the Horizon*; Edward Robinson, *Lancelot*; Carl Sandburg, *Smoke and Steel*; George Bernard Shaw, *Heartbreak House*; H.G. Wells, *The Outline of History*; Edith Wharton, *The Age of Innocence*.

MUSICAL EVENTS

A. Births:

Jan 5	Arturo Michelangeli (It-pn)	Apr 29	Harold Shapero (Am-cm)
Jan 18	William W. Austin (Am-mus)	May 20	Hephzibah Menuhin (Am-vn)
Jan 19	Luciano Chailly (It-cm)	Jun 4	Fedora Barbieri (It-mez)
Jan 22	William Warfield (Am-bar)	Jul 16	Ivo Jirásek (Cz-cm)
Feb 15	Eileen Farrell (Am-sop)	Jul 19	Robert Mann (Am-vn)
Feb 21	Daniza Ilitsch (Yug-sop)	Jul 21	Isaac Stern (Am-vn)
Feb 23	Hall Overton (Am-cm)	Jul 24	Ruggiero Ricci (Am-vn)
Feb 29	Ivan Petrov (Rus-bs)	Aug 9	Reinhard Pauly (Am-mus)
Mar 2	Ingmar Bengtsson (Swe-mus)	Sep 5	Peter Fricker (Br-cm)
Apr 12	Robert Fizdale (Am-pn)	Oct 8	Dorothy Dow (Am-sop)
Apr 21	Bruno Maderna (It-cm)	Dec 6	Dave Brubeck (Am-pop)
Apr 25	Ella Fitzgerald (Am-pop)	Dec 18	Rita Streich (Ger-sop)
Apr 27	Guido Cantelli (It-cd)	Dec 23	Paul Franke (Am-ten)
Apr 28	Nan Merriman (Am-mez)		

B. Deaths:

Jan 8	Maud Powell (Am-vn)	Jul 22	Robert Lienau (Ger-pub)
Jan 16	Reginald de Koven (Am-cm)	Aug 4	Vladimir Rebikov (Rus-cm)
Feb 2	Riccardo Gandolfi (It-cm)	Aug 20	Etelka Gerster (Hun-bar)
Feb 12	Emile Sauret (Fr-vn-cm)	Sep 15	Andrew Black (Scot-bar)
Feb 14	Louis C. Elson (Am-mus)	Sep 18	Luigi Torchi (It-mus)
Apr 4	Karl Bohm (Ger-pn)	Oct 2	Max Bruch (Ger-vn-cm)
Apr 8	Charles Griffes (Am-cm)	Oct 9	Selma Kronold (Pol-sop)

Nov 4 Paul Knüpfer (Ger-bs)   Dec 26 Hugo Goldschmidt (Ger-mus)
Nov 4 Paul H. LeBrun (Bel-cd-cm)   Dec 28 Theodor Helm (Aus-mus)
Dec 6 Karel Kovarovics (Cz-cd-cm)

C. Debuts:

Met ---Mario Chamlee (ten), Ellen Dalossy (mez), Giuseppe Danise (bar), Beniamino Gigli (ten), William Gustafsen (bs), Henry Hadley (cd), Sue Harvard (sop), Carolina Lazzari (mez), Adam Lellman (ten), Alice Miriam (sop), Nina Morgana (sop), Frances Peralta (sop), Anne Roselle (sop), Marion Telva (mez)

U.S. --Albert Coates (N.Y.), Joseph Fuchs (N.Y.), Joseph Hislop (tour), Kathryn Meisle (Minneapolis), Erwin Nyiregyházi (N.Y.)

Other -Rosette Anday (Budapest), Giannina Arangi-Lombardi (Rome), Ella Fleisch (Vienna), Louis Kentner (Budapest), Giacomo Lauri-Volpi (Rome), Tiana Lemnitz (Heilbronn), René Maison (Geneva), Nathan Milstein (Odessa), Mieczyslaw Munz (Berlin), Hans Nissen (Berlin), Iva Pacetti (Prato), Rosetta Pampanini (Rome), Alessio de Paolis (Bologna), Paul Paray (Paris), Ludwig Weber (Vienna), Carlo Zecchi (Berlin)

D. New Positions:

Conductors: Hamilton Harty (Hallé Orchestra), Václav Talich (Czech PO)

Educational: Ernst Bloch (director, Cleveland Institute), Julián Carrillo (director, Mexico National Conservatory), Reinhold Glière (composition, Moscow Conservatory), Joseph Jongen (counterpoint, Brussels Conservatory), Marguerite Long (piano, Paris Conservatory), Hans Pfitzner (composition, Prussian Academy of Arts), Henry Rabaud (director, Paris Conservatory)

Others: Ernest Newman (music critic, London *Sunday Times*)

E. Prizes and Honors:

Prizes: Marc Jean Delmas (Prix de Rome)

Honors: Hugh Percy Allen (knighted), Clara Butt (Dame), Gabriel Fauré and Maurice Ravel (Legion of Honor), Joseph Jongen (Belgian Royal Academy)

F. Biographical Highlights:

Henri Collet coins the name "Les Six" for six French composers; Aaron Copland travels to Paris to study with Nadia Boulanger; Walter Damrosch takes the New York PO on its first European tour; Edward Elgar loses his wife, Alice; Gabriel Fauré retires from the Paris Conservatory; Josef Gingold emigrates to the U.S.; Henry Hadley becomes associate conductor of the New York PO; Lilli Lehmann retires; Josef Lhévinne settles in the U.S.; Erwin Nyiregyházi sails for the U.S.; Serge Prokofiev leaves Russia for Paris; Arthur Shepherd becomes assistant conductor of the Cleveland SO; Igor Stravinsky moves his family back to Paris; Karol Szymanowski makes his first trip to the U.S.; Randall Thompson graduates from Harvard; Astrid Varnay emigrates with her family to the U.S.; Bernard Wagenaar moves to the U.S.; William Walton leaves Oxford without a degree; Hugo Weisgall's family emigrates to the U.S.; Kurt Weill studies with Busoni.

G. Institutional Openings:

Performing Groups: Cincinnati Summer Opera Association, Hartford Oratorio Society, Koussevitsky Concerts (Paris), Lithuanian Opera Theater, Moscow State PO, Musica Sacra Society (Buffalo), Nashville SO (II), Paul Whiteman Orchestra (N.Y.), People's SO (Boston), Prague String Quartet, Society for Modern Music (Prague), Zagreb PO

Educational: Cleveland Institute of Music, Deutsche Akademie für Musik (Prague), Julius Hartt School of Music (Hartford, CT), Juilliard Musical Foundation (N.Y.), Pergolesi Musical Institute (Ancona), Tartu Music Academy (Estonia)

Other: American Orchestral Society, *Music and Letters*, *Musical Digest*, *Il Pianoforte*, *La Revue Musicale*, *The Sackbut*, Società Amici della Musica (Pisa), Society of Romanian

Composers, Young Composer's Society (Denmark)

H. Musical Literature:

Davidson, Archibald, *Protestant Church Music in America*
Dickinson, Clarence, *Troubadour Songs*
Forsyth, Cecil, *Choral Orchestration*
Gedalge, André, *L'Ensignement de la Musique par l'Éducation Méthodique de l'Orielle*
Hauer, Josef, *Über die Klangfarbe*
MacPherson, Stewart, *Melody and Harmony*
Mason, Daniel, *Music as a Humanity*
Moser, Hans, *Geschichte der Deutschen Musik I*
Rosenfeld, Paul, *Musical Portraits*
Schenker, Heinrich, *Kontrapunkt*

I. Musical Compositions:

Bantock, Granville, *The Great God Pan* (soloists, chorus, orchestra)
Bliss, Arthur, *Two Studies for Orchestra*
Busoni, Ferruccio, *Divertimento for Flute and Orchestra*
            Waltzes, Opus 20, for Orchestra
Chávez, Carlos, *Symphony No. 1*
Converse, Frederick, *Symphony No. 1*
Copland, Aaron, *Scherzo: The Cat and the Mouse* (piano)
Griffes, Charles, *Pleasure Dome of Kubla Khan* (symphonic poem)
Hadley, Henry, *The Ocean* (symphonic poem)
            Piano Quintet, Opus 50
Hanson, Howard, *Exultation* (symphonic poem with piano)
            Before the Dawn (symphonic poem)
Hindemith, Paul, *Eight Songs for Soprano, Opus 18*
Honegger, Artur, *Pastorale d'Été* (orchestra)
            Horace Victorieux (orchestra)
Ibert, Jacques, *The Ballad of Reading Gaol* (orchestra)
Janácek, Leos, *The Ballad of Blanik* (orchestra)
Korngold, Erich, *Die Töte Stadt* (opera)
Koven, Reginald de, *Rip Van Winkle* (opera)
Milhaud, Darius, *5 Etudes for Piano and Orchestra*
Poulenc, Francis, *Piano Suite in C*
Prokofiev, Serge, *Overture on Hebrew Themes* (clarinet, string quartet, piano)
Ravel, Maurice, *La Valse* (orchestra)
Reznicek, Emil von, *Ritter Blaubart* (opera)
Roussel, Albert, *Pour une Fête de Printemps, Opus 22* (symphonic poem)
Satie, Erik, *La Belle Excentrique* (piano, four hands, or orchestra)
Schmitt, Florent, *Antoine et Cléopâtre* (incidental music)
Sibelius, Jan, *3 Pieces for Orchestra, Opus 96*
Sinding, Christian, *Symphony No. 3, Opus 121*
Stravinsky, Igor, *Symphonies of Wind Instruments*
Szymanowski, Karol, *Mandragora, Opus 43* (ballet)
Turina, Joaquín, *Danzas Fantasticas* (orchestra)
            Sinfonia Sevillana
Vaughan-Williams, Ralph, *The Lark Ascending* (violin, orchestra)
Villa-Lobos, Heitor, *Choros No. 1* (Brazilian guitar)
            Symphony No. 5, "The Peace"
Weingartner, Felix, *Die Dorfschule* (opera)
            Meister Andrea (opera)

1921

World Events:

In the U.S., former President William Howard Taft is sworn in as Chief Justice of the Supreme Court; the Limitation of Armaments Conference meets in Washington; the Tomb of the Unknown Soldier is created in Arlington National Cemetery in Washington, D.C.; KOKA in Pittsburgh begins regular radio programming; the Quota Act limits the number of immigrants allowed into the U.S.; *Reader's Digest* magazine begins publication. Internationally, the Irish Free State is created out of southern Ireland; the Paris Conference sets up German reparation payments; Benito Mussolini's Fascist Party makes a considerable gain in seats in the Italian parliament; Hermann Rorschach introduces his famous inkblot tests.

Cultural Highlights:

Pulitzer Prizes: Fiction, Edith Wharton (*The Age of Innocence*); Drama, Zona Gale (*Miss Lulu Betts*). The Nobel Prize for Literature goes to French novelist and critic Anatole France; John Lavery is inducted into the Royal Academy in England; Diego Rivera, after 12 years in Europe, returns to Mexico; Maurice Maeterlinck embarks on a lecture tour of the U.S. Births in the art world include Dutch artist and sculptor Karel Appel and French artist Georges Matthieu; deaths include German artist Adolf von Hildebrand, American artists John F. Murphy and Abbott Thayer, Spanish artist Francisco Pradilla and British artist Marcus Stone. The world of literature loses Russian poets Alexander A. Blok and Nikolai Gumilyov, Bulgarian poet Ivan Vazov and German poet and critic Max Kalbeck. Other highlights include:

Art: Joseph Albers, *Figure*; Paul Bartlett, *Benjamin Franklin*; Max Beckmann, *The Dream*; Louis Corinth, *Apocalypse*; Raoul Davis, *Lucky Strike*; Otto Dix, *The Artist's Parents*; George Grosz, *Gray Day*; Vasili Kandinsky, *Comedy*; Fernand Léger, *Three Women*; Henri Matisse, *Still Life with Lemon*; Pablo Picasso, *Three Musicians*.

Literature: Sherwood Anderson, *Triumph of the Egg*; John Dos Passos, *Three Soldiers*; Edna Ferber, *The Girls*; F. Scott Fitzgerald, *Flappers and Philosophers*; Federico García-Lorca, *Libro de Poemas*; Nikolai Gumilyov, *Pillar of Fire*; Luigi Pirandello, *Six Characters in Search of an Author*; Eugene O'Neill, *Emperor Jones*; Rafael Sabatini, *Scaramouche*.

MUSICAL EVENTS

A. Births:

Jan 21	Hilde Rössl-Majdan (Aus-alto)		Aug 7	Karel Husa (Cz-cm)
Jan 31	Mario Lanza (Am-ten)		Aug 8	Roger Nixon (Am-cm)
Feb 5	John Pritchard (Br-cd)		Aug 10	Agnes Giebel (Ger-sop)
Feb 11	Israel Baker (Am-vn)		Sep 3	Thurston Dart (Br-mus)
Mar 2	Robert Simpson (Br-cm)		Sep 25	Edith Farnadi (Aus-pn)
Mar 4	Halim El-Dabh (Egy-cm)		Oct 1	Margaret Hillis (Am-cd)
Mar 6	Julius Rudel (Am-cd)		Oct 21	Malcolm Arnold (Br-cm)
Mar 21	Arthur Grumiaux (Bel-vn)		Oct 23	Denise Duval (Fr-sop)
Apr 1	William Bergsma (Am-cm)		Oct 24	Sena Jurinac (Yug-sop)
Apr 6	Andrew Imbrie (Am-cm)		Nov 8	Jerome Hines (Am-bs)
May 17	Dennis Brain (Br-hn)		Nov 9	Pierette Alarie (Can-sop)
May 26	Inge Borkh (Ger-sop)		Nov 19	Géza Anda (Hun-pn)
Jul 15	Jack Beeson (Am-cm)		Nov 24	Claude Palisca (Am-mus)
Jul 24	Giuseppe di Stefano (It-ten)		Dec 18	Cesare Valletti (It-ten)
Jul 30	Grant Johanneson (Am-pn)		Dec 22	Robert Kurka (Am-cm)

B. Deaths:

Jan 12	Gervase Elwes (Br-ten)		Mar 24	Joseph M. Sévérac (Fr-cm)
Feb 2	Luigi Mancinelli (It-cd)		Apr 5	Alphons Diepenbrock (Hol-cm)
Feb 9	James H. Huneker (Am-cri)		May 10	Shukichi Mitsukuri (Jap-cm)

Jun 22	Lucille Marcel (Am-sop)	Sep 27	Engelbert Humperdinck (Ger-cm)
Jul 1	Teresa Brambilla-Ponchielli	Oct 23	Natalie Curtis (Am-folk)
	(It-sop)	Dec 16	Camille Saint-Saëns (Fr-cm)
Aug 2	Enrico Caruso (It-ten)	Dec 25	Hans Huber (Swi-cm)

C. Debuts:

Met ---Grace Anthony (sop), Yvonne d'Arle (sop), Grace Bradley (mez), Chief Caupolkan (bar), Cora Chase (sop), Marie Escobar (sop), Amelita Galli-Curci (sop), Maria Jeritza (sop), Suzanne Keener (sop), George Meader (ten), Aureliano Pertile (ten), Viola Philo (sop), Paolo Quintina (bs), Vezio Righi (bar), Manuel Salazar (ten), Myrtle Schaaf (mez), Giuseppe Sterzini (bar), Gaetano Tomasini (ten)

U.S. --Marcel Dupré (N.Y.), Claire Dux (Chicago), Nina Koshetz (N.Y.), Selma Kurtz (N.Y.), Erica Morini (N.Y.), José Palet (tour), Graziella Pareto (Chicago), Artur Schnabel (N.Y.), Joseph Schwarz (N.Y.), Rosina Storchio (Chicago)

Other -Isobel Baillie (Manchester), Rudolf Bockelmann (Leipzig), George Cehanovsky (Leningrad), Oivin Fjeldstad (Oslo, as violinist), Szymon Goldberg (Warsaw), Josef Krips (Vienna), Efrem Kurtz (Berlin), Elisabeth Ohms (Mainz), Kálmán Pataky (Budapest), André Pernet (Nice), Mark Reyzen (Kharkov), Helge Roswaenge (Neustrelitz), Anna Rózsa (Cluj), Maria Zamboni (Piacenza)

D. New Positions:

Conductors: Alfred Alessandrescu (Romanian Opera), Karl Böhm (Munich Opera), Rudolf Ganz (St. Louis SO), Arturo Toscanini (La Scala)

Educational: Arthur Benjamin (professor, Royal College), Nadia Boulanger (Fontainebleau American Academy), Marcel Grandjany (harp, American School, Fontainbleau), Gian F. Malipiero (composition, Moscow Conservatory)

Others: Paul Pisk (music editor, *Wiener Arbeiter-Zeitung*), Deems Taylor (music critic, New York *World*)

E. Prizes and Honors:

Prizes: Howard Hanson and Leo Sowerby (Prix de Rome), William J. McCoy (Bispham)

Honors: Ivor Atkins (knighted), John Alden Carpenter (Legion of Honor)

F. Biographical Highlights:

Robert Casadesus marries pianist Gaby L'Hôte; Feodor Chaliapin leaves Russia for the West; William Dawson graduates from Tuskegee Institute; Ernst von Dohnányi makes his first tour of the U.S.; Edward Elgar sells his home and moves into a London apartment; Amelita Galli-Curci receives American citizenship; Hans Kindler becomes an American citizen; Harl McDonald receives his bachelor degree from USC; Eugene Ormandy arrives in the U.S.; Gregor Piatigorsky sneaks out of Russia; Quincy Porter returns to the U.S.; Francis Poulenc begins music study with Koechlin; Jan Sibelius makes his last appearance outside Finland; Karol Szymanowski visits the U.S. twice as concert emissary from Poland; Alexander Tcherepnin's family leaves Russia for good, settles in Paris; Virgil Thomson studies with Nadia Boulanger in Paris.

G. Institutional Openings:

Performing Groups: Artistic (Ondrícek) String Quartet (Vienna), City of Birmingham Choir, Buffalo SO, Denver String Quartet, Detroit Symphony Choir, Lisbon Philharmonic, London Chamber Orchestra, Milwaukee Civic Orchestra, South Australia Orchestra, Westminster Choir (N.Y.), Yale Glee Club

Festivals: Donaueschingen Contemporary Music Festival

Educational: American Academy in Rome, American Conservatory at Fontainebleau, Bulgarian State Music Academy, Diller-Quaile School of Music, Ulms Conservatory of Music

Other: American Music Guild (N.Y.), Danish Musicological Society; E.C. Schirmer Co. (Boston); *Eolian Review*, International Composers Guild (N.Y.), Jerusalem Musical Society; Jonathan Cape, Publisher (London); *The Organ*, Sarajevo National Theater, Slingerland Banjo and Drum Co. (Chicago), Town Hall (N.Y.)

H. Musical Literature:

Asafiev, Boris, *Russian Poets in Russian Music*
Auer, Leopold, *Violin Playing as I Teach It*
Boult, Adrian, *Handbook on Technique of Conducting*
Engel, Carl, *Alla Breve: Bach to Debussy*
Fellowes, Edmund, *English Madrigal Composers*
Gastoué, Amédée, *L'Orgue en France de l'antiquité au début de la période Classique*
Gérold, Théodore, *La Musicologie médiévale*
        L'Art du chant en France au XVIIIe siècle
Pratt, Waldo, *Music of the Pilgrims*
Salzedo, Carlos, *Modern Study of the Harp*

I. Musical Compositions:

Bartók, Béla, *Violin Sonata No. 1*
Bax, Arnold, *Symphony No. 1*
Berg, Alban, *Wozzeck* (opera)
Cadman, Charles, *Rubayyát of Omar Khayyám* (piano)
Chávez, Carlos, *El Fuego Nuevo* (ballet)
Converse, Frederick, *Symphony No. 2*
Delius, Frederick, *Concerto for Cello and Orchestra*
Fauré, Gabriel, *Piano Quintet No. 2, Opus 115*
Gilbert, Henry, *Indian Sketches* (orchestra)
Giordano, Umberto, *Giove a Pompei* (opera)
Glière, Reinhold, *The Cossacks of Zaporozh* (symphonic poem)
Hanson, Howard, *Concerto for Organ, Harp and Orchestra*
Hindemith, Paul, *Morder, Hoffnung der Frauen* (opera)
        Sancta Susanna (opera)
Holst, Gustav, *The Perfect Fool* (ballet)
Honegger, Artur, *King David* (dramatic oratorio)
        Skating Rink (ballet)
d'Indy, Vincent, *Le Poème des Rivages, Opus 77* (orchestra)
Ireland, John, *The Land of Lost Content* (song cycle)
        Mai-Dun (symphonic rhapsody)
Janácek, Leos, *Kata Kabanova* (opera)
Krenek, Ernst, *Symphony No. 1, Opus 7*
Martinu, Bohuslav, *Istar* (ballet)
Mascagni, Pietro, *Il Piccolo Marat* (opera)
Milhaud, Darius, *Saudados do Brazil* (piano)
Pfitzner, Hans, *Von Deutscher Seele* (soloists, chorus, organ, orchestra)
Pijper, Willem, *Symphony No. 2*
Prokofiev, Serge, *Piano Concerto No. 3, Opus 26*
Rangström, Ture, *The Middle Ages* (opera)
Romberg, Sigmund, *Blossom Time*
Roussel, Albert, *Symphony No. 2, Opus 23*
Ruggles, Carl, *Angels* (brass, strings - revised 1939)
Stravinsky, Igor, *Suite No. 2 for Small Orchestra*
Vaughan-Williams, Ralph, *A Pastoral Symphony*
Villa-Lobos, Heitor, *Malazarte* (opera)
Webern, Anton, *Six Songs, Opus 14*

1922

World Events:
In the U.S. the Teapot Dome Scandal erupts over leasing of oil deposits without competitive bidding; the Washington Conference of the Far East and on Disarmament convenes; first commercial radio station, WEAF, begins broadcasting; H.T. Calmus develops Technicolor for films; the Lincoln Memorial in Washington, D.C. is dedicated; American inventor Alexander Graham Bell passes away in August. Internationally, in Italy, Mussolini's Brown Shirts march on Rome where he is given dictatorial powers; fourteen Russian States form the Union of Soviet Socialist Republics (USSR); the British Broadcasting Co. (BBC) is formed; Kemal Ataturk becomes president of the Turkish Republic.

Cultural Highlights: /
Pulitzers: Drama, Eugene O'Neill (*Anna Christie*); Fiction, Booth Tarkington (*Alice Adams*); Poetry, Edwin A. Robinson (*Collected Poems*). The Nobel Prize for Literature goes to the Spanish dramatist Jacinto Benavente y Martínez; James Barrie is given the Order of Merit; Howard Carter, working for Lord Carnavon, discovers the lost tomb of the Egyptian pharaoh Tutankhamen; the Novecento Italiano, urging return to classical Italian traditions, is founded. Deaths in the literary field include French poet Félix Bataille, British poet Wilfred Blunt and novelist W.H. Hudson, French novelist Marcel Proust and Italian novelist Giovanni Verga; births include British authors Kingsley Amis and John Braine, French novelist Alain R. Grillet and American novelist William Gaddis. Births in the art world include American sculptor Leonard Baskin and artists Leon Golub and Richard Diebenkorn and Russian artist Jules Olitski; American sculptor Alexander Doyle dies. Other highlights include:

Art: George Bellows, *The White Horse*; André Derain, *Boy with a Hat*; Daniel French, *Abraham Lincoln Memorial*; Paul Klee, *The Twittering Machine*; Ferdinand Léger, *Women in an Interior*; Homer Dodge Martin, *Lower Manhattan*; Henri Matisse, *The Music Lesson*; Joan Miró, *The Farm*; Joseph Stella, *New York Interpreted*.

Literature: Bertolt Brecht, *Drums in the Night*; e.e. cummings, *The Enormous Room*; T.S. Elliot, *The Waste Land*; F. Scott Fitzgerald, *Tales of the Jazz Age*; John Galsworthy, *The Forsythe Saga*; Hermann Hesse, *Gedichte*; A.E. Housman, *Last Poems*; James Joyce, *Ulysses*; D.H. Lawrence, *Aaron's Rod*; Sinclair Lewis, *Babbitt*.

MUSICAL EVENTS

A. Births:

Jan 7 Jean Pierre Rampal (Fr-fl)	Jul 3 David Ward (Am-bs)
Feb 1 Renata Tebaldi (It-sop)	Jul 24 Leo Kraft (Am-cm)
Feb 16 Geraint Evans (Br-bar)	Aug 15 Lukas Foss (Ger-cm-cd)
Feb 23 Ilse Hollweg (Ger-sop)	Aug 20 Regina Resnik (Am-sop)
Mar 3 Kazimierz Serocki (Pol-pn-cm)	Sep 20 William Kapell (Am-pn)
Mar 12 Ralph Shapey (Am-cm)	Sep 24 Ettore Bastianini (It-bar)
Mar 21 Roger Gardes (Fr-ten)	Sep 24 Cornell MacNeil (Am-bar)
Mar 30 Peter J. Horn (Ger-cm)	Oct 28 Gershon Kingley (Ger-cm)
Apr 4 Frederick Koch (Am-cm)	Nov 22 Fikret Amirov (Azer-cm)
May 24 Sadao Bekku (Jp-cm)	Dec 3 Phyllis Curtin (Am-sop)
May 29 Iannis Xenakis (Ger-cm)	Dec 10 Allen D. Sapp (Am-cm)
Jun 4 Irwin Bazelon (Am-cm)	Dec 18 Cesare Valletti (It-ten)
Jun 6 Iain Hamilton (Scot-cm)	

B. Deaths:

Jan 23 Arthur Nikisch (Hun-cd)	Mar 27 Nikolai Sokolov (Rus-cm)
Jan 26 Luigi Denza (It-cm)	Apr 6 Arabella Goddard (Br-pn)
Jan 31 Heinrich Reinhardt (Ger-cm)	Apr 21 Alessandro Moreschi (It-cas)

Jun 6   Lillian Russell (Am-act-sop)
Aug 19   Felipe Pedrell (Sp-mus)
Aug 22   Sofia Scalchi (It-mez)
Oct 27   Rita Fornia (Am-sop)

C. Debuts:

Met ---Paul Bender (bar), Edmund Burke (bar), Louis Hasselmans (cd), Edward Johnson (ten), Rafaele Lipparini (ten), Queena Mario (sop), Augusto Monti (ten), Sigrid Onegin (mez), Augusto Ordognez (bar), Angeles Ottein (sop), Italo Picchi (bar), Elisabeth Rethberg (sop), Laura Robertson (sop), Louis Rozsa (bar), Titta Ruffo (bar), Charlotte Ryan (sop), Gustav Schützendorf (bar), Curt Taucher (ten), Muriel Tindal (sop)

U.S. --Richard Crooks (N.Y.), Cesare Formichi (Chicago), Myra Hess (tour), Maria Ivogün (tour), Ulysses Lappas (Chicago), Ottilie Metzger-Lattermann (tour), Angelo Minghetti (Chicago), Mieczyslaw Munz (N.Y.), Vladimir Rosing (Rochester), Felix Salmond (N.Y.), Emil Schipper (tour)

Other -Florence Austral (London), Salvatore Baccaloni (Rome), Roger Bourdin (Paris), Gustav Cloez (Paris), Rudolf Firkusny (Prague), Annie Fischer (Budapest), Vladimir Horowitz (Kharkov), Herbert Janssen (Berlin), Emanuel List (Vienna), Giovanni Manurita (Rome), Carlo Morelli (Florence), Jaro Prohaska (Lübeck), Carlo Tagliabue (Lodi), Alexander Tcherepnin (London), Viorica Ursuleac (Agram), Gertrud Wettergren (Stockholm)

D. New Positions:

Conductors: Fritz Busch (Dresden Opera), Wilhelm Furtwängler (Berlin PO & Leipzig Gewandhaus), Hans Knappertsbusch (Munich Opera), Clemens Krauss (Vienna Opera), Karl Muck (Hamburg PO), Fritz Reiner (Cincinnati SO)

Educational: Florent Schmitt (director, Lyons Conservatory), Josef Suk (composition, Prague Conservatory)

Others: Carl Engel (director, Music Division, Library of Congress), Joseph Messner (organ, Salzburg Cathedral)

E. Prizes and Honors:

Prizes: Wallingford Riegger (Paderewski), Leopold Stokowski (Bok), Leo Weiner (Coolidge)

Honors: Alexander MacKenzie, Landon Ronald and Richard Terry (knighted), George Huë (French Academy), Ignace Jan Paderewski (Legion of Honor), Ethel Smyth (Dame)

F. Biographical Highlights:

Béla Bartók begins his virtuoso career with a European tour; Ferruccio Busoni gives his last public performance; George Cehanovsky flees Russia and emigrates to the U.S.; Luigi Dallapiccola moves to Florence and enters the Cherubini Conservatory; Pauline Donalda retires from the stage; Geraldine Farrar gives her farewell Met performance; Howard Hanson. the first American to win the Prix de Rome, begins a three-year stay in Rome; Abraham Idelssohn moves to the U.S. from Jerusalem; Eugen Jochum leaves the Augsburg Conservatory for the Munich Academy; Aram Khatchaturian is admitted to the Gnessin Music Academy; André Kostelanetz leaves Russia and settles in the U.S.; Darius Milhaud makes a concert tour of the U.S. and lectures at several universities; Iva Pacetti makes her La Scala debut; Ignace Jan Paderewski, out of politics, resumes his concert career; Aureliano Pertile makes his La Scala debut; Tibor Serly returns to Hungary to study with Kodály; Randall Thompson receives his M.A. from Harvard; Eugène Ysaÿe quits his post as conductor of the Cincinnati SO and returns to Belgium.

G. Institutional Openings:

Performing Groups: British National Opera Company (Bradford), Jerusalem String Quartet, Kolisch String Quartet (Vienna), Lenox String Quartet, New Jersey SO, Rochester SO, St. Nikolaichor (Kiel), San Francisco Opera Company

Educational: American Academy of Teachers of Singing, Helsinki Folk Conservatory

Other: Club of Moravian Composers (Brno), Danish Hymn Society, Hollywood Bowl

Concerts, Hymn Society of America (Ohio), International Society for Contemporary Music, Ondes Martenot (patent obtained), Quarter-tone Clarinet

H. Musical Literature:

Coeuroy, André, *La Musique française moderne*
Gastoué, Amédée, *Les Primitifs de la musique française*
Hába, Alois, *Harmonic Foundation of the Quarter-tone System*
Ives, Charles, *114 Songs*
Jaques-Dalcroze, Emile, *Rhythm, Music and Education*
Jeppesen, Knud, *The Style of Palestrina and the Dissonance*
Krehl, Stephan, *Theorie der Tonkunst und Kompositionslehre*
Lahee, Henry, *Annals of Music in America*
Morris, R.O., *Contrapuntal Technique in the XVIth Century*
Schoenberg, Arnold, *Composing with Twelve Tones*
Wedge, George, *Advanced Ear Training*

I. Musical Compositions:

Bantock, Granville, *Song of Songs* (soloists, chorus, orchestra)
Bliss, Arthur, *Color Symphony*
Busoni, Ferruccio, *Sarabande and Cortège, Opus 51, from "Doktor Faust"* (orchestra)
Cadman, Charles, *Willow Wind* (song cycle)
Carpenter, John Alden, *Krazy Kat* (ballet)
Chadwick, George, *Anniversary Overture*
Dohnányi, Ernst von, *The Tower of the Voyvod* (opera)
Fauré, Gabriel, *Cello Sonata No. 2, Opus 117*
Glazunov, Alexander, *Piano Concerto No. 2*
Grainger, Percy, *Shepherd's Hey* (orchestra)
Hanson, Howard, *Symphony No. 1, "Nordic"*
Hindemith, Paul, *Kleine Kammermusik I, Opus 24, No. 1*
                Der Dämon, Opus 28 (ballet)
                Die Junge Magd, Opus 23, No. 2 (chamber group)
Ibert, Jacques, *Escales* (orchestra)
Krenek, Ernst, *Symphonies No. 2 and 3*
Malipiero, Gian, *Cimarosiana* (orchestra)
Martinu, Bohuslav, *Vanishing Midnight* (symphonic poem)
Milhaud, Darius, *Les Eumenides* (part III of Aeschylus' *Orestes*)
Nielsen, Carl, *Symphony No. 5*
Pfitzner, Hans, *Concerto in B-flat for Piano and Orchestra*
Pijper, Willem, *Antigone* (incidental music)
Pizzetti, Ildebrando, *Debora e Jaele* (opera)
                Requiem Mass for A Capella Chorus
Ravel, Maurice, *Orchestration of Pictures at an Exhibition* (Mussorgsky)
Respighi, Ottorino, *Concerto Gregoriano* (violin, orchestra)
Roussel, Albert, *Symphony No. 3, Opus 42*
Salzedo, Carlos, *Sonata for Harp and Orchestra*
Shostakovich, Dmitri, *Fantastic Dances, Opus 5* (piano)
Sibelius, Jan, *Suite Caracteristique, Opus 100* (orchestra)
Stravinsky, Igor, *Mavra* (opera)
                Le Baiser de la Fee (ballet)
Szymanowski, Karol, *Hagith* (opera)
Varèse, Edgard, *Offrandes*
Vaughan-Williams, Ralph, *Mass in g*
                Communion Service in g
                The Shepherds on the Delectable Mountains (cantata)
Walton, William, *String Quartet*

1923

World Events:

In the U.S. Calvin Coolidge becomes President No. 30 on the death of Warren G. Harding; U.S. troops are recalled from Germany; an antitoxin for scarlet fever is discovered; inventions include the electric razor, the bulldozer and cellophane; New York boasts the first neon sign; Carlsbad Caverns National Park is established. Internationally, Adolf Hitler is imprisoned following the failure of his "Beer Hall Putsch" in Munich; the Treaty of Lausanne limits Turkey to Asia and internationalizes the Dardanelles; France and Belgium invade the Ruhr to seek war reparations; Japanese earthquake kills over 100,000 people.

Cultural Highlights:

Pulitzers: Drama, Owen Davis (*Icebound*); Fiction, Willa Cather (*One of Ours*); Poetry, Edna St. Vincent-Millay (*The Ballad of the Harp Weaver and Other Poems*). The Nobel Prize for Literature goes to the British poet, William B. Yeats. The Freer Gallery of Art opens in the Smithsonian and *Time* magazine begins publication. Births in the literary field include Irish author Brendan Behan and American poet Anthony Hecht; deaths include Dutch novelist Louis Couperous and British novelist Katherine Mansfield. Births in the realm of art include American artists Sam Francis, Roy Lichtenstein and Larry Rivers; deaths include American artists Henry Krehbiel and Elihu Vedder and sculptor Edward C. Potter. Also passing away is the well-known actress Sarah Bernhardt. Other highlights include:

Art: Max Beckmann, *Charnel House*; Marc Chagall, *Love Idyll*; Nikolaus Geiger, *Hans Pfitzner;* Vasili Kandinsky, *Composition with Chessboard*; Käthe Kollwitz, *War*; László Moholy-Nagy, *Space Segments*; Pablo Picasso, *Woman in White*; Stanley Spencer, *The Resurrection*; Maurice de Vlaminck, *Village in Northern France.*

Literature: Sherwood Anderson, *Horses and Men*; Ivan Bunin, *The Village*; Joseph Conrad, *The Rover*; e.e. cummings, *Tulips and Chimneys*; Robert Frost, *New Hampshire*; Hermann Hesse, *Siddhartha*; Aldous Huxley, *Antic Hay*; Ferenc Molnár, *The Red Mill*; George Bernard Shaw, *St. Joan*; Wallace Stevens, *Harmonium.*

MUSICAL EVENTS

A. Births:

Jan 8	Giorgio Tozzi (Am-bs)	Jul 11	Ludmilla Dvoráková (Cz-sop)
Jan 22	Leslie Bassett (Am-cm)	Aug 4	Arthur Butterworth (Br-cm)
Feb 6	Maurice LeRoux (Fr-cm-cd)	Aug 26	Wolfgang Sawallisch (Ger-cd)
Feb 10	Cesare Siepi (It-bs)	Aug 29	Lester Trimble (Am-cm)
Feb 12	Mel Powell (Am-cm)	Sep 1	Frank Erickson (Am-cm)
Apr 6	Mimi Benzell (Am-sop)	Sep 6	William Kraft (Am-cm)
Apr 8	Franco Corelli (It-ten)	Oct 3	Stanislaw Skrowaczewski (Pol-cd)
May 17	Peter Mennin (Am-cm)	Oct 20	Robert Kraft (Am-cm)
May 23	Alicia de Larrocha (Sp-pn)	Oct 23	Ned Rorem (Am-cm)
May 28	György Ligeti (Hun-cm)	Nov 1	Victoria de los Angeles (Sp-sop)
Jun 5	Daniel Pinkham (Am-org)	Nov 5	Biserka Czejic (Yug-sop)
Jun 5	Henryk Czyz (Pol-cd)	Nov 6	Renato Capecchi (It-bar)
Jun 29	Chou Wen Chung (Chi-cm)	Dec 3	Maria Callas (It-sop)
Jul 3	Jean E. Ivey (Am-cm)	Dec 25	Louis Lane (Am-cd)

B. Deaths:

Jan 5	Emmanuel Wirth (Boh-vn)	May 30	Camille Chevillard (Fr-cd-cm)
Feb 19	Joseph Peinbaur Sr. (Aus-cm)	Jun 26	Karl Scheidemantel (Ger-bar)
Apr 11	Edoardo Caudello (Rom-vn-cm)	Jul 13	Asgar Hamerik (Den-cd-cm)
May 23	Heinrich Schmidt (Ger-mus)	Jul 14	Louis Ganne (Fr-cm)
May 26	Lionel A. Dauriac (Fr-mus)	Aug 31	Ernest Van Dyck (Bel-ten)

Sep 16   Emilie Hertzog (Ger-sop)   Oct 22   Victor Maurel (Fr-bar)
Oct 14   George E. Whiting (Am-org)   Dec 2   Tomas Bretón (Sp-cm-cd)

C. Debuts:

Met ---Merle Alcock (mez), Michael Bohnen (bs), Flora Cingolani (sop), Raimondo Ditello (ten), Miguel Fleta (ten), Arnold Gabor (bar), Virginia Grassi (sop), Nannette Guilford (sop), Louise Hunter (sop), Barbara Kemp (sop), Rudolf Laubenthal (ten), Giacomo Lauri-Volpi (ten), Delia Reinhardt (sop), Marcella Röseler (sop), Thalia Sabanieeva (sop), Anna Staber (sop), Lawrence Tibbett (bar), Armand Tokatyan (ten), Phradie Wells (sop), James Wolfe (bs)

U.S. --Elsa Alsen (tour), Fernand Ansseau (Chicago), Claudio Arrau (N.Y.), Georges Enescu (N.Y.), Dusolina Giannini (N.Y.), Alexander Kipnis (Baltimore), Wanda Landowska (Philadelphia), Alfred Piccaver (Chicago), Carmela Ponselle (N.Y.), Adolf Schoepflin (tour), Meta Seinemeyer (tour), Bruno Walter (N.Y.)

Other -Raya Garbousova (Moscow), Gerhard Hüsch (Osnabrück), Paul Kletzki (Berlin), Mary Lewis (Vienna), Mariya Maxakova (Moscow), Angus Morrison (London), Maria Nemeth (Budapest), Jean Pournet (London), Max Rudolph (Freiburg), Karl Schmitt-Walter (Nuremburg), Mihály Székely (Budapest), Roman Totenberg (Warsaw), Adolf Vogel (Klagenfurt), Rudolf Watzke (Karlsruhe), Walter Widdop (London)

D. New Positions:

Conductors: Eugene Goosens (Rochester PO), Erich Kleiber (Berlin Opera), Paul Paray (Lamoureux Concerts), Henri Verbrugghen (Minneapolis SO)

Educational: Jan Kunc (director, Brno Conservatory), Selim Palmgren (composition, Eastman), Flor Peeters (professor, Mechelen Institute), Nicholas Slonimsky (professor, Eastman)

Others: Eric Blom (music critic, Manchester *Guardian*), Lawrence Gilman (music critic, New York *Herald-Tribune*)

E. Prizes and Honors:

Prizes: Herbert Elwell & Jeanne Leleu (Prix de Rome)

Honors: Cecil Sharp (honorary doctorate, Cambridge)

F. Biographical Highlights:

Béla Bartók divorces his first wife and marries pianist Ditta Pásztory; Arthur Bliss begins a two-year stay teaching music in California; Georges Enescu visits U.S. for the first time playing and conducting his own works; Michel Fokine makes his home in New York; Alois Hába leaves his study with Schenker and returns to Prague; Gustav Holst falls, suffers serious head injury but makes his first tour of the U.S. as conductor and lecturer; Nanny Larsen-Todsen makes her La Scala debut; Bohuslav Martinu, again failing to graduate from Prague Conservatory, leaves Czechoslovakia for Paris where he studies privately with Roussel; Carlos Salzedo becomes a naturalized American citizen; Dmitri Shostakovich completes the piano course at the Leningrad Conservatory; Nicolas Slominsky emigrates to the U.S.; William Grant Still given a scholarship by Chadwick to study with Varèse; Margaret Sutherland leaves Australia to study in London and Vienna; Virgil Thomson graduates from Harvard; Michael Tippett enters the Royal College of Music; Heitor Villa-Lobos begins studying music in Paris on state and private grants.

G. Institutional Openings:

Performing Groups: Belgrade PO, Czech Nonet, Hungarian State SO, Israel Opera Co., Moravian String Quartet (Brno), Moscow Conservatory (Beethoven) String Quartet, New SO of Toronto, Portland (Maine) SO, Sarajevo Philharmonic Society, Vlach String Quartet (Prague), Winnipeg SO

Festivals: Würzburg Mozart Festival

Educational: École l'Arcuiel (Paris), International Academy of Fine Arts, Orchesterschule der Sachsischen Staatskapelle (Dresden)

Other: Association of Contemporary Music (Moscow), Bärenreiter-Verlag (Augsburg), *The Gramophone, Moderne Music, L'Orgue et les Organistes*, Swedish Performing Rights Society, *Symphonia* (Netherlands)

H. Musical Literature:
Calvocoressi, Michel, *Musical Criticism*
Carse, Adam, *Harmony Exercises*
Caruso/Tetrazzini, *How to Sing*
Coeuroy, André, *Musique et littérature comparées*
Damrosch, Walter, *My Musical Life*
Dickinson, George, *Foretokens of the Tonal Principle*
Dykema, Peter, *School Music Handbook*
Emmanuel, Maurice, *La Polyphonie sacrée*
Hughes, Dom Anselm, *Latin Hymnody*
Myers, Rollo, *Modern Music: Its Aims and Tendencies*

I. Musical Compositions:
Bartók, Béla, *Dance Suite* (orchestra)
Bath, Hubert, *Bubbles* (opera)
Bloch, Ernst, *Baal Shem* (violin, piano)
Falla, Manuel de, *Master Peter's Puppet Show* (chamber opera)
Farwell, Arthur, *Navajo War Dance* (chamber orchestra)
Fauré, Gabriel, *String Quartet, Opus 121*
Gruenberg, Louis, *Daniel Jazz* (chamber group)
Hanson, Howard, *Lux Aeterna* (symphonic poem)
Hindemith, Paul, *Das Marienleben* (voice, piano)
Honegger, Artur, *Pacific 231* (Symphonic Movement No. 1)
    Chant de Joie (orchestra)
    Prelude to the Tempest
Kodály, Zoltán, *Psalmus Hungaricus, Opus 13* (chorus, orchestra)
Krenek, Ernst, *Concerto No. l, Opus 18, for Piano and Orchestra*
Malipiero, Gian F., *Pause del Silenzio* (orchestra)
Miaskovsky, Nicolai, *Symphonies Nos. 6 and 7, Opus 23, 24*
Milhaud, Darius, *La Creation du Monde* (ballet)
Pierné, Gabriel, *Cydalise et le Chèvre-Pied* (ballet)
Poulenc, Francis, *Les Biches* (ballet)
Prokofiev, Serge, *The Flaming Angel* (opera)
    Piano Sonata No.5, Opus 38
Rangström, Ture, *Sotto Voce* (symphonic poem)
Respighi, Ottorino, *La Primavera* (soloists, chorus, orchestra)
Reznicek, Emil von, *Holofernes* (opera)
Riegger, Wallingford, *La Belle Dame Sans Merci* (women's voices, orchestra)
Schoenberg, Arnold, *Five Piano Pieces, Opus 23*
    Serenade, Opus 24
    Suite for Piano, Opus 25
Sessions, Roger, *The Black Maskers* (orchestra)
Sibelius, Jan, *Symphony No. 6, Opus 104*
Stravinsky, Igor, *Octet for Winds*
Turina, Joaquin, *Jardin de Oriente* (opera)
Varèse, Edgard, *Hyperprisms* (orchestra)
Vaughan-Williams, Ralph, *Old King Cole* (ballet)
    English Folk Song Suite (band)
Walton, William,   *Façade*
Webern, Anton, *Five Sacred Songs, Opus 15*

1924

World Events:
In the U.S., Calvin Coolidge is elected President for his first full term; former president Woodrow Wilson dies; American Indians are given full citizenship by Congress; the first coast-to-coast radio hook-up is made; the Dawes Plan is introduced to help Germany with war reparations; the Holland Tunnel is finished in New York; J. Edgar Hoover becomes head of the F.B.I. Internationally, in Russia, Lenin dies and Joseph Stalin begins a bloody bath against all opponents including Trotsky; Benito Mussolini consolidates his hold on the Italian government in the elections; Greece once again becomes a republic; the Olympic games are held in Paris and Chamonix, France.

Cultural Highlights:
Pulitzers: Drama, Hatcher Hughes (*Hell-Bent for Heaven*); Fiction, Margaret Wilson (*The Able McLaughlins*); Poetry, Robert Frost (*New Hampshire*); Polish novelist Wladyslaw Stanislaw Reymont receives the Nobel Prize for Literature; the First Surrealist Manifesto is introduced in France; Alexei Jawlensky forms the Blue Four with Feininger, Kandinsky and Klee; the *Saturday Review of Literature* begins publication. Deaths in the world of literature include Russian poet Valery Bryusov, Polish-born novelist Joseph Conrad, Belgian poet Iwan Gilkin, French novelist Anatole France, Austrian novelist Franz Kafka, British novelist Marie Corelli and Swiss poet Carl Spitteler; births include the American writers James Baldwin and Truman Capote. The art world loses American artists Daniel Knight, Maurice Prendergast and sculptor Victor Brenner; born is American sculptor George Segal and British sculptor Anthony Caro. Other highlights include:

Art: George Bellows, *The Dempsey-Firpo Fight*; Constantin Brancusi, *The Beginning of the World*; Georges Braque, *Sugar Bowl*; Marc Chagall, *Daughter Ida*; Charles Despiau, *Faunesse* (bronze); Oskar Kokoschka, *Venice*; Gaston Lachaise, *Dolphin Fountain*; Joan Miró, *Catalan Landscape*; Anne Whitney, *War Memorial* (Texas).

Literature: Maxwell Anderson, *What Price Glory?*; Edna Ferber, *So Big*; Edward H. Forster, *A Passage to India*; Ernest Hemingway, *In Our Time*; Thomas Mann, *The Magic Mountain*; John Masefield, *Sard Harker*; Herman Melville, *Billy Budd*; Sean O'Casey, *Juno and the Paycock*; Eugene O'Neill, *Desire Under the Elms*.

MUSICAL EVENTS

A. Births:

Jan 8	Benjamin Lees (Chi-cm)	May 17	Gabriel Bacquier (Fr-bar)
Jan 8	Charles Starer (Aus-cm)	May 18	Samson François (Fr-pn)
Jan 26	Warren Benson (Am-cd)	Jun 17	Edward Downes (Br-cd)
Jan 29	Luigi Nono (It-cm)	Jul 5	Oscar Czerwenka (Aus-bs)
Feb 23	Lejaren Hiller (Am-cm)	Jul 5	Janos Starker (Hun-cel)
Feb 26	Silvio Varviso (Swi-cd)	Jul 9	Leonard Pennario (Am-pn)
Apr 3	Joseph Kerman (Am-mus)	Aug 8	Thomas Beversdorf (Am-cm)
Apr 14	Neville Marriner (Br-cd)	Aug 14	Georges Prêtre (Fr-cd)
Apr 16	Henry Mancini (Am-pop)	Sep 30	Giuseppe Campora (It-ten)
Apr 19	Hertha Töpper (Aus-alto)	Oct 17	Rolando Panerai (It-bar)
Apr 21	Franz Mazura (Aus-bar)	Nov 14	Leonid Kogan (Rus-vn)
Apr 23	Arthur Frankenpohl (Am-cm)	Dec 24	Zara Nelsova (Can-cel)
May 2	John R. White (Am-mus)		Berthe Monmart (Fr-sop)

B. Deaths:

Jan 24	Klaus G. Roy (Aus-mus-cm)	May 26	Victor Herbert (Am-cm-cd)
Mar 27	Walter Parratt (Br-org)	Jun 11	Théodore Dubois (Fr-org)
Mar 29	Charles V. Stanford (Ir-cm)	Jun 23	Eugenio Giraldoni (It-bar)
May 10	August Kretschmar (Ger-mus)	Jun 23	Cecil Sharp (Br-folk)
May 12	Henri C. Maréchal (Fr-cm)	Jul 27	Ferruccio Busoni (It-cm)

Aug 13 Julián Aguirre (Arg-cm)
Nov 4   Gabriel Fauré (Fr-cm)
Nov 16 Alexander Archangelski
        (Rus-cm)

Nov 29 Giacomo Puccini (It-cm)
Dec 8   Xavier Scharwenka (Ger-cm)
Dec 9   Bernard Zweers (Hol-cm)

C. Debuts:

Met ---Max Altglass (ten), Vincente Ballester (bar), Mary Bonetti (mez), Karin Branzell (mez), Ralph Errolle (ten), G. Marinelli (ten), Toti dal Monte (sop), Martin Oehman (ten), Joan Ruth (sop), Friedrich Schorr (bar), Tullio Serafin (cd), Paolina Tomasini (sop)

U.S. --Jules Bledsoe (N.Y.), Alexander Brailowsky (N.Y.), George Cehanovsky (San Carlo), Antonio Cortis (Chicago), Fraser Gange (N.Y.), Vladimir Golschmann (N.Y.), Marcel Grandjany (N.Y.), Charles Kullman (N.Y.), Georg Liebling (N.Y.), Eugene Ormandy (N.Y.), Gladys Swarthout (Chicago), John Charles Thomas (N.Y.)

Other -Edith Coates (London), Giuseppina Cobelli (Piacenza), Ivan Galamian (Paris), Frederik Jagel (Livorno), Adele Kern (Munich), Jan Kiepura (Lvov), Marta Krásová (Bratislava), Galliano Masini (Livorno), Heddle Nash (Milan), Maria Nezadál (Olomouc), Dennis Noble (London), Gianna Pederzini (Messina), Gertrude Rünger (Erfurt), Margarete Teschemacher (Cologne), Georges Thill (Paris), Kerstin Thorborg (Stockholm), Renato Zanelli (as tenor)

D. New Positions:

Conductors: Adrian Boult (Birmingham SO), Serge Koussevitsky (Boston SO), Clemens Krauss (Frankfurt Opera), Efrem Kurtz (Stuttgart SO), Pierre Monteux (Amsterdam Concertgebuouw), Tullio Serafin (Met), George Szell (Berlin Opera)

Educational: Howard Hanson (director, Eastman), Abraham Idelsohn (Jewish music, Hebrew Union College), Wilhelm Kempff (director, Württemberg Hochschule für Musik), Ildebrando Pizzetti (director, Milan Conservatory), Ottorino Respighi (director, Conservatory St. Cecilia)

Others: Olin Downes (music critic, New York *Times*)

E. Prizes and Honors:

Prizes: Arthur Benjamin (Carnegie)

Honors: Charles Wakefield Cadman (honorary doctorate, Wolcott Conservatory, Denver), Edward Elgar (Master of the King's Music)

F. Biographical Highlights:

Samuel Barber begins music study at Curtis Institute; Ernst Bloch and Toscha Seidel become naturalized American citizens; Benjamin Britten, age 13, is taken on as a composition student by Frank Bridge; Aaron Copland leaves Paris after three years of music study to return to the U.S.; Antal Dorati graduates from the Liszt Academy of Music and makes his conducting debut in Budapest; Paul Hindemith marries Gertrude, daughter of the Jewish conductor Ludwig Rottenberg; Lotte Lehman and Frida Leider make their Covent Garden debuts; Pierre Monteux gives up his post with the Boston SO and decides to return to Europe; Gregor Piatigorsky becomes cellist in the Berlin PO under Furtwängler; Walter Piston graduates *summa cum laude* from Harvard; Arnold Schoenberg marries his second wife, Gertrud Kolisch; Eva Turner makes her La Scala debut.

G. Institutional Openings:

Performing Groups: Adesi Chorus (N.Y.), Boston Sinfonietta, Bulgarian National PO, Copenhagen Boy's Choir, Hart House String Quartet (Toronto), Kutcher String Quartet (London), Los Angeles Grand Opera Association, Munich PO, Philadelphia Civic Opera Company

Educational: Buenos Aires Conservatory of Music, Curtis Institute of Music (Philadelphia),

Institut Grégorien (Paris)

Other: Associated Glee Clubs of America, Guggenheim Foundation, Kleines Festspielhaus (Salzburg), Lillenas Music Publishing Co., *Muzika* (Poland), *Note d'Archivio*, Polish Society of Music Writers and Critics, *Schweizerisches Jahrbuch für Musikwissenschaft*; Simon and Schuster, Publishers (N.Y.); Swedish Composer's Society

H. Musical Literature:

Dumesnil, René, *Le Monde des Musiciens*
Dyson, George, *The New Music*
Expert, Henri, *Monuments de la musique française au temps de la Renaissance I*
Gray, Cecil, *A Survey of Contemporary Music*
Hill, Edward, *Modern French Music*
Idelson, Abraham, *A History of Jewish Music*
Kitson, Charles, *The Art of Counterpoint*
Schenker, Heinrich, *Der Tonwille*
Spaeth, Sigmund, *The Common Sense of Music*
Wedge, George, *Keyboard Harmony*

I. Musical Compositions:

Bantock, Granville, *The Seal Woman* (opera)
Bax, Arnold, *Symphony No. 2*
Bloch, Ernst, *From Jewish Life* (cello, piano)
Busoni, Ferruccio, *Doktor Faust* (unfinished opera)
Cadman, Charles, *A Witch of Salem* (opera)
Converse, Frederick, *Song of the Sea* (orchestra)
Copland, Aaron, *Symphony for Organ and Orchestra*
Dohnányi, Ernst von, *Ruralia Hungarica* (piano, also orchestra)
Gershwin, George, *Rhapsody in Blue* (piano, orchestra)
Glière, Reinhold, *Two Poems for Soprano and Orchestra, Opus 60*
Ives, Charles, *Three Quarter-Tone Pieces* (quarter-tone piano)
Janácek, Leos, *Cunning Little Vixen* (opera)
Milhaud, Darius, *Les Malheurs d'Orphée* (opera)
    Salade (ballet)
Pfitzner, Hans, *Concerto for Violin and Orchestra*
Prokofiev, Serge, *Symphony No. 2, Opus 40*
Puccini, Giacomo, *Turandot* (unfinished opera)
Ravel, Maurice, *Tzigane* (violin, piano)
Respighi, Ottorino, *Pines of Rome* (symphonic poem)
Ruggles, Carl, *Men and Mountains* (orchestra)
Satie, Erik, *Relâche* (ballet)
    Mercure (ballet)
Schoenberg, Arnold, *Wind Quintet, Opus 26*
Sibelius, Jan, *Symphony No. 7, Opus 105*
Strauss, Richard, *Schlagobers* (ballet)
Stravinsky, Igor, *Concerto for Piano and Winds*
Szymanowski, Karol, *King Roger* (opera)
Varèse, Edgard, *Octandre* (chamber group)
Vaughan-Williams, Ralph, *Hugh, the Drover* (opera)
Webern, Anton, *Five Canons, Opus 16* (voice, clarinet, bass clarinet)
    Three Sacred Folksongs, Opus 17 (voice, clarinet, bass clarinet, violin)

1925

World Events:
In the U.S., attention is focused on Dayton, Tennessee, where the Scopes Evolution Trial is taking place; Billy Mitchell is court-martialled for criticizing neglect of air power; Chrysler Corporation is formed; the first motion telecast is made in Washington D.C.; the new Madison Square Garden opens in New York; latest fads are the Charleston and Crossword puzzles. Internationally, Paul von Hindenburg becomes President of the new German Republic; the Locarno Pacts on arms limitations and arbitration are drawn up; Cyprus becomes a British Crown Colony and Albania becomes a Republic; the Pahlavi dynasty founded in Iran.

Cultural Highlights:
Pulitzers: Drama, Sydney Howard (*They Knew What They Wanted*); Fiction, Edna Ferber (*So Big*); Poetry, Edwin A. Robinson (*The Man Who Died Twice*). British author and critic George Bernard Shaw receives the Nobel Prize for Literature; Francis Dicksee is knighted for his contribution to the art world; the *New Yorker* magazine begins publication. American novelist Flannery O'Connor and author Gore Vidal are born this year; dead are American novelist James Allen and poet Amy Lowell, French poet Pierre Louijs and Polish novelist Wladyslaw Reymont. The art world sees the deaths of American artists George W. Bellows, George W. Cable, Willard Metcalf and John Sargent, British sculptor Hamo Thornycroft, Russian artist Lovis Corinth and Scotch artist William Brymner and the birth of American artist Robert Rauschenberg. Other highlights include:

Art: Joseph Albers, *Fugue*; Ernst Barlach, *Death* (bronze); Charles Despiau, *Eve* (bronze); Arthur Dove, *The Critic*; Paul Klee, *A Tiny Tale of a Tiny Dwarf*; Frantisek Kupka, *Around a Point*; Henri Matisse, *Decorative Figure*; Joan Miró, *Harlequin's Carnival*; Pablo Picasso, *Three Dancers*; Georges Rouault, *The Apprentice*.

Literature: John Dos Passos, *Manhattan Transfer*; Theodore Dreiser, *An American Tragedy*; T.S. Elliot, *The Hollow Men*; F. Scott Fitzgerald, *The Great Gatsby*; DuBose Heyward, *Porgy*; Adolf Hitler, *Mein Kampf*; Sinclair Lewis, *Arrowsmith*; Liam O'Flaherty, *The Informer*; Mikhail Sholokhov, *The Don Stories*; William Yeats, *A Vision*.

MUSICAL EVENTS

A. Births:

Jan 15	Ruth Slenczynska (Am-pn)	Aug 15	Aldo Ciccolini (It-pn)
Mar 12	Helga Pilarczyk (Ger-sop)	Sep 11	Harry Somers (Can-cm)
Mar 26	Pierre Boulez (Fr-cm-cd)	Oct 11	Russell Oberlin (Am-c.ten)
May 14	Patrice Munsel (Am-sop)	Oct 24	Luciano Berio (It-cm)
May 22	James King (Am-ten)	Oct 29	Donald Waxman (Am-cm)
May 28	Dietrich Fischer-Dieskau	Nov 13	Paul W. Whear (Am-cm)
	(Ger-bar)	Nov 15	Jurriaan Andriessen (Hol-cm)
Jun 21	Larisa Audeyeva (Rus-sop)	Nov 17	Charles J. Hall (Am-cm-ed)
Jun 28	Giselher Klebe (Ger-cm)	Nov 17	Charles Mackerras (Am-cd)
Jun 28	Marilyn Mason (Am-org)	Nov 18	William Mayer (Am-cm)
Jul 4	Cathy Berberian (Am-sop)	Nov 22	Gunther Schuller (Am-cm)
Jul 11	Nicolai Gedda (Swe-ten)	Nov 23	Nicole Henriot (Fr-pn)
Jul 12	Yasushi Akutagawa (Jap-cm)	Nov 26	Eugene Istomin (Am-pn)
Jul 24	Adele Adison (Am-sop)	Dec 2	Irina Arkhipova (Rus-mez)
Jul 28	André Boucourechliev		
	(Bul-au-cm)		

B. Deaths:

Jan 6	Ferdinand Löwe (Aus-cd)	Mar 4	Moritz Moskowski (Pol-cm)
Feb 17	Alwina Valleria (Am-sop)	Apr 3	Jean de Reszke (Pol-ten)
Feb 23	Fernando de Lucia (It-ten)	Apr 25	George Stephanescu (Rom-cm-cd)

Jun 11	Louis Fleury (Fr-fl)	Oct 27	Theodore Presser (Am-ed)
Jul 1	Erik Satie (Fr-cm)	Oct 27	Wilhelm Gericke (Aus-ed)
Sep 12	Leonard Bertwick (Br-pn)	Dec 9	Eugène Gigout (Fr-org)

C. Debuts:

Met ---Mario Basiola (bar), Victorio Fullin (ten), Nanny Larsen-Todsen (sop), Agnes Moore (sop), Maria Müller (sop), Carmela Ponselle (alto), Frederick Vajda (bs)

U.S. --Marian Anderson (N.Y.), Florence Austral (tour), Richard Bonelli (Chicago), Wilhelm Furtwängler (N.Y.), Carroll Hollister (N.Y.), Irene Scharrer (tour), Oscar Shumsky (Philadelphia), Joseph Szigeti (Philadelphia), Helen Traubel (St. Louis), Isabelle Vengerova (Detroit)

Other -Joseph Bentonelli (Nice), Erna Berger (Dresden), Bruna Castagna (Mantua), Antal Dorati (Budapest), Pierre Fournier (Paris), Roy Henderson (London), Walter Herbert (Bern), Anny Konetzni (Vienna), Jarmila Novotná (Prague), Robert Riefling (Oslo), Bidú Sayao (Rio de Janeiro), Erna Schlüter (Mannheim), Paul Schöffler (Dresden), Bernard Shore (London), Ebe Stignani (San Carlo), Fritz Wolff (Bayreuth), Nicanor Zabaleta (Paris)

D. New Positions:

Conductors: Zdenek Chalabala (Brno Opera), Willem van Hoogstraten (Portland SO)

Educational: Ernst Bloch (director, San Francisco Conservatory), Joseph Jongen (director, Brussels Conservatory), Willem Pijper (composition, Amsterdam Conservatory), François Rasse (director, Liège Conservatory), Leo Sowerby (composition, American Conservatory, Chicago)

Others: Samuel Chotzinoff (music critic, New York *World*), Jean Huré, (organ, St. Augustine, Paris)

E. Prizes and Honors:

Prizes: Adeline Masino, Bernard Ocko and Catherine Wade Smith (Naumberg)

Honors: Emma Albani (Dame), Henry Hadley (honorary doctorate, Tufts), Hamilton Hardy (knighted), Gabriel Pierné (French Academy)

F. Biographical Highlights:

Frances Alda divorces Giulio Gatti-Casazza; William Dawson goes to Chicago for further music study at the American Conservatory; Maxim Gorky moves to New York; Jascha Heifetz becomes a U.S. citizen; Dmitri Kabalevsky transfers to the Moscow Conservatory; Igor Markevich goes to Paris for further music studies; Nathan Milstein leaves Russia on a concert tour and decides to stay in the West; Herman Schlicker moves to the U.S.; Friedrich Schorr makes his Covent Garden debut; Dmitri Shostakovich completes the Conservatory composition course; Igor Stravinsky makes his first U.S. tour as composer and performer; Margaret Sutherland leaves London to return to Australia; Gladys Swarthout marries Harry Kern (divorced 1931); Joseph Szigeti leaves Switzerland for the U.S.; Virgil Thomson moves to Paris for a fifteen-year stay; Donald Tovey appears in the U.S. as a pianist.

G. Institutional Openings:

Performing Groups: Barbirolli Chamber Orchestra (Chelsea), Boston Civic SO, Civic Music Association (Des Moines, IA), Florentine Wind Sextet, Hall Johnson Choir (California), Harp Ensemble of London, Hirsch String Quartet (Hallé), Philadelphia Chamber String Sinfonietta, Stratton String Quartet (London)

Educational: Denver College of Music, Günther Schule (Munich), Leopold Mozart Conservatorium (Augsburg), Massine Ballet School (London), Mu Beta Psi Music Fraternity, School for Catholic Church Music

Other: American Composer's Project, Canadian Performing Rights Society, Elizabeth Sprague Coolidge Foundation and Coolidge Auditorium (Library of Congress), Fair Park

Music Hall (Dallas), Franz Liszt Memorial Hall (Budapest), Kawai Piano Co. (Japan), Protective Collective of Composers (Russia), *La Revue Musicale Belge*, Symphony Hall (Newark, NJ)

H. Musical Literature:
Dickinson, Edward, *The Spirit of music*
Fellowes, Edmund, *The English Madrigal*
Hába, Alois, *Von der Psychologie der musikalischen Gestaltung*
Johnson, James, *American Negro Spirituals*
Lászlo, Alexander, *Die Farblichtmusik*
Mason, Daniel G., *Artistic Ideals*
Molnár, Antal, *New Music*
Newman, Ernest, *A Music Critic's Holiday*

I. Musical Compositions:
Bloch, Ernst, *Concerto Grosso No. 1* (piano, strings)
Cadman, Charles, *The Willow Tree* (opera)
Chávez, Carlos, *Energia for Nine Instruments*
Copland, Aaron, *Music for the Theater* (orchestra)
       Dance Symphony
       Grogh (ballet)
Cowell, Henry, *The Banshee* (piano)
Gade, Jacob, *Jalousie Tango*
Gershwin, George, *Piano Concerto in F*
Hadley, Henry, *A Night in Old Paris*
Hanson, Howard, *Lament for Beowolf* (chorus, orchestra)
Hindemith, Paul, *Concerto for Orchestra*
Holst, Gustav, *At the Boar's Head* (one-act opera)
Honegger, Artur, *Concertino for Piano and Orchestra*
       Judith (opera)
Janácek, Leos, *Concertino for Piano and Chamber Orchestra*
       The Makropoulos Affair (opera)
Kodály, Zoltán, *Ballet Music for Orchestra*
Krenek, Ernst, *Symphony No. 4, Opus 34*
Loeffler, Charles, *Memories of My Childhood* (orchestra)
Nielsen, Carl, *Symphony No. 6, "Sinfonia Semplice"*
Pizzetti, Ildebrando, *Lo Straniero* (opera)
Prokofiev, Serge, *Le Pas d'Acier, Opus 41* (ballet)
Ravel, Maurice, *L'Enfant et les Sortilèges* (opera-ballet)
       Chansons Madécasses (voice, flute, cello, piano)
Rogers, Bernard, *Symphony Adonais*
Schmitt, Florent, *Salammbo, Six Symphonic Episodes, Opus 76*
Schoenberg, Arnold, *Four Pieces for Orchestra*
       Suite, Opus 29 (chamber orchestra)
Shostakovich, Dmitri, *Symphony No. 1, Opus 7*
Sibelius, Jan, *Tapiola, Opus 112* (tone poem)
Strauss, Richard, *Intermezzo* (opera)
Toch, Ernst, *Wegwende* (opera)
Vaughan-Williams, Ralph, *Flos Campi* (viola, chorus, chamber orchestra)
       Sancta Civitas (oratorio)
       Concerto Accademico (violin, orchestra)
Walton, William, *Overture, Portsmouth Point*
Webern, Anton, *Three Songs, Opus 18*

1926

World Events:
In the U.S., the first practical solid-fuel rocket is launched by R.H. Godard; the National Broadcasting Co. (NBC) is organized as the first radio network; the Army Air Corps is created by Congressional action; Admiral Richard Byrd flies over the North Pole; Congress establishes the Great Smoky Mountains, Mammoth Cave and Shenandoah National Parks. Internationally, the British Parliament outlaws general strikes after being paralyzed for several days; Chiang Kai-Shek overthrows the Manchu dynasty in China; Portugal becomes a military dictatorship; Gertrude Ederle becomes the first woman to swim the English Channel from France to England; future Queen Elizabeth II of England is born.

Cultural Highlights:
Pulitzers: Drama, George Kelly (*Craig's Wife*); Fiction, Sinclair Lewis (*Arrowsmith*-- prize refused by author); Poetry, Amy Lowell (*What's O'Clock*). Italian novelist Grazia Deledda receives the Nobel Prize for Literature; the Civic Repertory Theater is formed in New York. In the literary field, births include American poets A.R. Ammons and Allen Ginsburg and author James P. Donleavy; deaths include British novelists H. Rider Haggard and Israel Zangwill, French author Jean Richepin, German poet Rainer M. Rilke and American author Henry T. Finck. The art world loses American artist Mary Cassatt, French artist Claude Monet and British artist Thomas Moran. Other highlights include:

Art: Marc Chagall, *Lover's Bouquet*; Raymond Duchamp-Villon, *The Great Horse*; Jacob Epstein, *The Visitation* (bronze); Lyonel Feininger, *Victory of the Sloop Maria*; Vasili Kandinsky, *Several Circles*; John Marin, *Stonington Harbor, Maine, IV*; Henri Matisse, *Odalisque with Tambourine*; Georgia O'Keefe, *Black Iris*. William Zorach, *Child with Cat*.

Literature: Edna Ferber, *Show Boat*; Ernest Hemingway, *The Sun also Rises*; Will James, *Smoky*; Thomas Lawrence, *Seven Pillars of Wisdom*; Anita Loos, *Gentlemen Prefer Blondes*; Sean O'Casey, *The Plough and the Stars*; Carl Sandburg, *Abraham Lincoln, the Prairie Years*; Edna St. Vincent-Millay, *The King's Henchmen*.

MUSICAL EVENTS

A. Births:

Jan 12	Morton Feldman (Am-cm)	Jul 3	Meyer Kupferman (Am-cm)
Feb 11	Alexander Gibson (Scot-cd)	Jul 5	Kenneth Gaburo (Am-cm)
Feb 17	Lee Hoiby (Am-cm)	Aug 1	Theo Adam (Ger-bar)
Feb 18	Rita Gorr (Bel-mez)	Aug 10	Marie Claire Alain (Fr-org)
Feb 28	Seymour Shifrin (Am-cm)	Aug 15	Julius Katchen (Am-pn)
Mar 6	H.C. Robbins Landon (Am-mus)	Aug 29	Raymond Lewenthal (Am-pn)
Mar 11	Ilhan Mimaroglu (Tur-cm)	Sep 1	Franco Gulli (It-vn)
Apr 11	Gervase de Peyer (Br-cl)	Oct 1	Gerhard Stolze (Ger-ten)
May 17	Marc Honegger (Fr-mus)	Oct 25	Galina Vishnevskaya (Rus-sop)
May 19	Paul Cooper (Am-cm)	Oct 29	Jon Vickers (Can-ten)
May 30	Edouard van Remoortel (Bel-cd)	Nov 7	Joan Sutherland (Aust-sop)
		Nov 16	Ton de Leeuw (Hol-cm)
Jun 6	Klaus Tennstedt (Ger-cd)	Dec 15	Denis Arnold (Br-mus)
Jun 6	Denis Vaughn (Aust-cd)	Dec 16	James McCracken (Am-ten)
Jun 12	Carlisle Floyd (Am-cd)	Dec 18	Rita Streich (Ger-sop)
Jun 15	Jan Carlstedt (Swe-cm)	Dec 26	Earle Brown (Am-cm)
Jul 1	Hans Werner Henze (Ger-cm)		

B. Deaths:

Jan 8	Emile Paladilhe (Fr-cm)	Mar 15	Aglaja Orgeni (Hun-sop)
Feb 5	André Gédalge (Fr-cm)	Mar 30	Eugenia Mantelli (It-alto)
Feb 27	Helena Teodorini (Rom-sop)	May 23	Hans Koessler (Ger-cm)

Jun 1	Vassili Metallov (Rus-mus)	Sep 9	Anton Andersen (Nor-cel-cm)
Jun 21	Marie-Hippolyte Rôse (Fr-sop)	Sep 11	Ernest Eulenberg (Ger-pub)
Jul 12	Charles Wood (Ir-cm)	Oct 15	Matilde Bauermeister (Ger-sop)

C. Debuts:

Met ---Martha Attwood (sop), Vincenzo Bellezza (cd), George Cehanovsky (bar), Edytha Fleischer (sop), Dorothea Flexer (mez), Maria Ivogün (sop), Elizabeth Kandt (sop), Louise Lerch (sop), Mary Lewis (sop), Pavel Ludikar (bs), Joseph MacPherson (bs), Lauritz Melchior (ten), Ezio Pinza (bs), Marion Talley (sop), Alfio Tedesco (ten), Elda Vettori (sop)

U.S. --Lillian Fuchs (N.Y.), Walter Gieseking (N.Y.), Aroldo Lindi (Chicago), Alexander McCurdy (N.Y.), Yehudi Menuhin (San Francisco, age 9), Aaltje Noordewier-Reddingius (tour), Eide Norena (Chicago), Solomon (tour), Alexander Tcherepnin (tour)

Other -John Brownlee (London), Noël Eadie (London), Irene Eisinger (Basel), Desző Ernster (Düsseldorf), Mafalda Favero (Cremona), Eugen Jochum (Munich), Maryla Jonas (Warsaw), Sergei Lemeshev (Sverdlovsk), Max Lorenz (Dresden), Ginette Neveu (Paris), Julius Patzak (Reichenberg), Lea Piltti (Helsinki), Afro Poll (Pisa), Joachim Sattler (Wuppertal), Eugenia Verbitskaya (Kiev), Franz Völker (Frankfurt)

D. New Positions:

Conductors: Alfred Alessandrescu (Bucharest PO), Eugen Jochum (Kiel Opera), Josef Krips (Karlsruhe), Karl Krueger (Seattle SO), Nikolai Malko (Leningrad SO)

Educational: Hendrik Andriessen (composition, Amsterdam Conservatory), Josef Hofmann (director, Curtis Institute), Ernest MacMillan (director, Toronto Conservatory)

E. Prizes and Honors:

Prizes: Phyllis Draeuter (Naumberg), Margaret Hamilton (Naumberg), Albert Huybrechts (Coolidge), Sonia Skalka (Naumberg)

Honors: Henry Coward (knighted), Serge Koussevitsky (honorary doctorate, Brown), Charles M. Loeffler (honorary doctorate, Yale), Henry J. Wood (honorary doctorate, Oxford)

F. Biographical Highlights:

Béla Bartók's *Miraculous Mandarin* causes a scandal as members of the audience walk out; Gerald Finzi is found to be suffering from tuberculosis; Josef Hofmann becomes a naturalized American citizen; Dmitri Kabalevsky begins studying composition with Miaskovsky at the Moscow Conservatory; Gian F. Malipiero begins his edition of the complete works of Monteverdi; Ester Mazzoleni retires from the stage; Colin McPhee leaves his studies in Paris and returns to New York; Ervin Nyiregyházi marries his first wife (first of nine); Tancredi Pasero makes his La Scala debut; Walter Piston returns from France to accept a position at Harvard; Ottorino Respighi resigns his conservatory post to devote full time to composition; Artur Rodzinski comes to the U.S. to be assistant to Stokowski in Philadelphia; Leopold Stokowski marries heiress to the Johnson and Johnson drug forture, Evangeline Johnson; Igor Stravinsky rejoins the Russian Orthodox Church; Alexander Tcherepnin concertizes in the U.S.; Virgil Thomson meets Gertrude Stein; Helen Traubel passes up the opportunity to sing at the Met; Hugo Weisgall becomes a naturalized American citizen.

G. Institutional Openings:

Performing Groups: Bach Cantata Club (London), Basle Chamber Orchestra, Bratislava Radio Orchestra, Brussels String Quartet, Chamber Music Society of Bordeaux, Elman String Quartet (N.Y.), Lithuanian Radio SO (Vilnius), London Junior Orchestra, Madrigalist Romani, New SO (Japan SO in 1942, NHK SO in 1951; Tokyo), Philadelphia Grand Opera Co., Pittsburgh SO

Educational: Jacksonville (Florida) College of Music, Macedonian Conservatory of Music, National Conservatory of Music (Athens), Westminster Choir School (N.Y.)

Other: Edwin F. Kalmus, Music Publisher; Elkan Publishing Co. (Philadelphia), Hamburg Opera House, Konserthus (Stockholm Concert Hall), Naumberg Music Foundation (N.Y.), *New Music*, Oxford University Opera Club, Shea's Buffalo Theater

H. Musical Literature:
Almeida, Renato, *Historia da musica Brasileira*
Davison, Archibald, *Music Education in America*
Finck, Henry, *My Adventures in the Golden Age...*
Haas, Robert, *Die Wiener Oper*
Hadow, William, *Church Music*
Hamilton, Clarence, *Epochs in Musical Progress*
Hauer, Josef, *Zwölftontechnik...*
Howes, Frank, *The Borderland of Music and Psychology*
Molnár, Antal, *The New Hungarian Music*
Spaeth, Sigmund, *Words and Music*

I. Musical Compositions:
Antheil, George, *Ballet Méchanique*
    Symphony No. 1
Bartók, Béla, *Piano Concerto No. 1*
Berg, Alban, *Lyric Suite* (string quartet)
Bliss, Arthur, *Introduction and Allegro* (orchestra)
Bloch, Ernst, *America: An Epic Rhapsody* (orchestra)
Carpenter, John Alden, *Skyscrapers* (ballet)
Casella, Alfredo, *Scarlattiana* (piano, orchestra)
Chávez, Carlos, *Los Cuatro Soles* (ballet)
Copland, Aaron, *Piano Concerto*
Hanson, Howard, *Pan and the Priest* (symphonic poem)
Hindemith, Paul, *Cardillac* (opera)
Ibert, Jacques, *Jeux* (orchestra)
d'Indy, Vincent, *Diptyque Méditerranean* (orchestra)
Janácek, Leos, *Sinfonietta* (orchestra)
    Glagolitic Mass (soloists, chorus, organ, orchestra)
Kodály, Zoltán, *Háry János* (opera)
Krenek, Ernst, *Johnny Spielt Auf, Opus 45* (opera)
Mason, Daniel G., *Chanticleer Overture, Opus 27*
Milhaud, Darius, *Carnaval d'Aix* (piano, orchestra)
    Les Malheurs d'Orphée (opera)
Moore, Douglas, *Pageant of P.T. Barnum* (orchestra)
Nielsen, Carl, *Flute Concerto*
Pijper, Willem, *Symphony No. 3*
Rachmaninoff, Serge, *Piano Concerto No. 4, Opus 40*
Respighi, Ottorino, *Trittico Botticelliano* (small orchestra)
Riegger, Wallingford, *Rhapsody for Orchestra, Opus 5*
Roussel, Albert, *Suite in F for Orchestra, Opus 33*
Ruggles, Carl, *Portals for String Orchestra*
Sibelius, Jan, *The Tempest, Opus 109* (incidental music)
Varèse, Edgard, *Intégrales* (chamber orchestra, percussion)
Webern, Anton, *Two Songs for Chorus, Opus 19*
    Piano Variations, Opus 27
Weill, Kurt, *Der Protagonist* (opera)

1927

World Events:

Charles Lindberg flies the Atlantic solo in 33½ hours; the first sound movie, "The Jazz Singer", is released; work begins on the presidential faces on Mount Rushmore in South Dakota; Ford discontinues the popular Model T; Babe Ruth sets the home run record of 60 in one season. Internationally, Stalin expels Trotsky and his followers from the Russian Communist Party and assumes total control; Allied military control ends in Germany; the British Broadcasting Co. (BBC) is chartered; the Tokyo subway opens; Pavlov publishes his famous dog-conditioning experiments.

Cultural Highlights:

Pulitzers: Drama, Paul Green (*In Abraham's Bosom*); Fiction, Louis Bromfield (*Early Autumn*); Poetry, Leonora Speyer (*Fiddler's Farewell*). French philosopher Henri Bergson receives the Nobel Prize for Literature. The art world loses Spanish artist Juan Gris but gains by the birth of American sculptors John Chamberlain and Edward Kienholz and artist Alex Katz. The literary world loses American author John L. Long and Polish poet Gustav Danilowski but witnesses the birth of American poet John Ashbury and author Peter Matthiessen and German author Günther Grass. Other highlights include:

Art: Ernst Barlach, *Hovering Angel*; Constantin Brancusi, *Bird in Space*; Georges Braque, *The Black Rose*; Stuart Davis, *Egg Beater No. 1*; Jacob Epstein, *Madonna and Child* (bronze); Max Ernst, *The Great Forest*; Paul Klee, *Seaside Town, South of France*; Gaston Lachaise, *Standing Woman* (bronze); Henri Matisse, *Decorative Figure, Ornamental Back*.

Literature: Maxwell Anderson, *Saturday's Children*; Willa Cather, *Death Comes for the Archbishop*; Ernest Hemingway, *Men without Women*; Hermann Hesse, *Steppenwolf*; Sinclair Lewis, *Elmer Gantry*; Donald Marquis, *Archy and Mehibatel*; Eugene O'Neill, *Lazarus Laughed*; Edward A. Robinson, *Tristram*; Thornton Wilder, *The Bridge of San Luis Rey*.

MUSICAL EVENTS

A. Births:

Jan 12 Salvatore Martirano (Am-cm)	May 5 Charles Rosen (Am-pn-mus)
Jan 17 Donald Erb (Am-cm)	May 7 Elisabeth Söderström (Swe-sop)
Feb 1 Flaviano Labo (It-ten)	Jul 7 Jean Casadesus (Fr-pn)
Feb 3 Claire Watson (Am-sop)	Jul 8 Kurt Masur (Ger-cd)
Feb 10 Leontyne Price (Am-sop)	Jul 16 Serge Baudo (Fr-cd)
Feb 10 Brian Priestman (Br-cd)	Jul 20 Michael A. Gielen (Aus-cd)
Feb 23 Régine Crespin (Fr-sop)	Jul 24 Wilfred Josephs (Br-cm)
Feb 26 Donald Gramm (Am-bs)	Aug 11 Raymond Leppard (Br-cd)
Mar 1 Lucine Amara (Am-sop)	Sep 25 Colin Davis (Br-cd)
Mar 6 Norman Treigle (Am-bs)	Oct 6 Paul Badura-Skoda (Aus-pn)
Mar 27 Mstislav Rostropovich	Nov 8 Ingrid Bjoner (Nor-sop)
(Rus-cel-cd)	Nov 24 Emma Lou Diemer (Am-cm)
Apr 10 Luigi Alva (Peru-ten)	Nov 24 Alfredo Krauss (Sp-ten)
Apr 16 Marie Collier (Aust-sop)	Dec 7 Helen Watts (Br-alto)
Apr 23 Russell Smith (Am-cm)	Dec 24 Teresa Stich-Randall (Am-sop)
Apr 25 Siegfried Palm (Ger-cel)	Dec 25 Bethany Beardslee (Am-sop)
May 1 Gary Bertini (Is-cd)	

B. Deaths:

Jan 25 Hugo Riemann (Ger-mus)	May 31 Giuseppe Campanari (It-bar)
Feb 19 Robert Fuchs (Aus-cm)	Aug 10 Adolph M. Foerster (Am-cm)
Mar 28 Karl Prohaska (Aus-cm-ed)	Aug 13 Hermann Abert (Ger-mus)
Apr 16 Rosa Sucher (Ger-sop)	Sep 14 Isadora Duncan (Am-bal)
May 3 Ernest R. Ball (Am-cm)	Oct 20 Mikhail M. Ivanov (Rus-mus)

Nov 20 Wilhelm Stenhammer (Swe-cm)   Dec 12 Heinrich Reitach (Aus-mus)
Nov 29 Henry W. Savage (Am-imp)

C. Debuts:

Met ---Leonora Corona (sop), Philine Falco (sop), Frederick Jagel (ten), Walter Kirchoff (ten), Dorothee Manski (sop), Everett Marshall (bs), Richard Mayr (bs), Mildred Parisette (sop), Elena Rakowska (sop), Grete Stückgold (sop)

U.S. --Jelly d'Aranyi (N.Y.), Robert Goldsand (N.Y.), Hans Kindler (Philadelphia; as conductor), Benno Rabinof (N.Y.), Victor de Sabata (N.Y.), Jesús María Sanromá (Boston), Heinrich Schlusnus (Chicago), Robert Weede (N.Y.)

Other -William Busch (London), André Cluytens (Antwerp), Gina Cigna (Milan), Richard Crooks (Hamburg), Maria Res Fischer (as alto), Ferdinand Frantz (Kassel), Margarete Klose (Ulm), Franz Konwitschny (Leipzig), Cléontine de Meo (Paris), Zinka Milanov (Ljubljana), Gerhard Pechner (Berlin), Margherita Perras (Berlin), Sydney Rayner (Rome), Franca Somigli (Rovigo), René Verdière (Paris)

D. New Positions:

Conductors: Howard Barlow (CBS SO), Karl Böhm (Darmstadt), Otto Klemperer & Alexander von Zemlinsky (Kroll Opera)

Educational: Paul Dukas (composition, Paris Conservatory), Arthur Farwell (theory & composition, Michigan State University), Paul Hindemith (composition, Berlin Hochschule), Gustave Reese (professor, New York University), Franz Schmidt (director, Vienna Musikhochschule), Karol Szymanowski (director, Warsaw Conservatory)

Others: Walter Damrosch (NBC Music Advisor), Deems Taylor (editor, *Musical America*)

E. Prizes and Honors:

Prizes: Claudio Arrau (Geneva), Julia Kahn (Naumberg), Dorothy Kendrick (Naumberg), Lev Oborin (Chopin), Daniel Saidenberg (Naumberg), William Sauber (Naumberg), Sadie Schwartz (Naumberg), Sadah Stuchari (Naumberg)

Honors: André Messager (Commander, Legion of Honor), Deems Taylor (honorary doctorate, New York University)

F. Biographical Highlights:

Jehan Alain enters Paris Conservatory; Béla Bartók takes a concert tour of the U.S.; Paul Creston begins playing organ in movie theaters; William Dawson receives a master's degree with honors; Hugo Distler begins study at the Leipzig Conservatory; John Ireland's near disastrous marriage is annulled; André Jolivet begins teaching in Paris; Eugene Ormandy takes on U.S. citizenship; Serge Prokofiev, after nine years in the West, returns to Russia; Lotte Schöne makes her Covent Garden debut; Elie Siegmeister receives his B.A. degree from Colombia; Oliver Strunk spends a study year in Berlin; Set Svandholm studies at the Swedish Royal Conservatory; Fartein Valen becomes director of the Norwegian music Collection of Oslo University; Bernard Wagenaar becomes a U.S. citizen; Kurt Weill begins his collaboration with Brecht; Hugo Weisgall begins music study at Peabody.

G. Institutional Openings:

Performing Groups: Aeolian String Quartet (England), Birmingham Philharmonic String Orchestra, Brussels Philharmonic Society, CBS SO (N.Y.), Chamber Orchestra of Boston, Downtown Glee Club (N.Y.), Finnish Royal Orchestra (Helsinki), Havana String Quartet, Pennsylvania Grand Opera Co. (Philadelphia)

Educational: Beethoven Archives Research Institute (Bonn), Biscay Conservatory of Music (Spain), International Society for Musicology (Basel), Michigan State University Dept. of Music, School of English Church Music (Royal School in 1945; London)

Other: Associated Music Publishers (N.Y.), Heinz Hall for the Performing Arts (Pittsburgh), International Frédéric Chopin Piano Competition (Warsaw), Meisterarchiv of the

Austrian National Library, Shrine Auditorium (Los Angeles), Sixth-Tone Harmonium (by A. Förster), Society for Contemporary Music (Philadelphia)

H. Musical Literature:

Bekker, Paul, *The Story of Music*
Calvocoressi, Michel, *Principles and Methods of Musical Criticism*
Dickinson, George, *Growth and Use of Harmony*
Hába, Alois, *Neue Harmonielehre...*
Hipsher, E., *American Opera and Its Composers*
Kwalwasser, Jacob, *Tests and Measurements in Music*
Rosenfeld, Paul, *Modern Tendencies in Music*
Wellesz, Egon, *Byzantinische Musik*

I. Musical Compositions:

Bartók, Béla, *String Quartet No. 3*
Chávez, Carlos, *HP (Horsepower)* (ballet)
Converse, Frederick, *Flivver Ten Million* (orchestra)
Farwell, Arthur, *The Gods of the Mountain* (orchestral suite)
Gershwin, George, *Three Preludes for Piano*
    Funny Face (musical)
    Strike Up the Band (musical)
Glière, Reinhold, *Red Poppy Ballet*
Hindemith, Paul, *Hin und Zurück* (one-act opera)
    Concert Music for Winds
Honegger, Artur, *Antigone* (lyric tragedy)
Ibert, Jacques, *Angélique* (opera)
Kern, Jerome, *Showboat* (musical)
Kodály, Zoltán, *Theatre Overture*
Medtner, Nicolai, *Concerto No. 2 for Piano and Orchestra*
Miaskovsky, Nicolai, *Symphonies Nos. 9, Opus 28, and 10, Opus 30*
Milhaud, Darius, *Le Pauve Matelot* (one-act opera)
Mossolov, Alexander, *The Iron Foundry* (orchestra)
Pijper, Willem, *Concerto for Piano and Orchestra*
Piston, Walter, *Symphonic Piece* (orchestra)
Respighi, Ottorino, *Church Windows* (orchestra)
    Brazilian Impressions (orchestra)
Riegger, Wallingford, *Study in Sonority, Opus 7* (orchestra)
Romberg, Sigmund, *The New Moon* (musical)
Roussel, Albert, *Concerto, Opus 36, for Piano and Orchestra*
Schoenberg, Arnold, *String Quartet No. 3*
Sessions, Roger, *Symphony No. 1*
Shostakovich, Dmitri, *Symphony No. 2, Opus 13, "To October"*
Strauss, Richard, *Die Ägyptische Helena* (opera)
Stravinsky, Igor, *Oedipus Rex* (opera-oratorio)
    Apollon Musagètes (ballet)
Szymanowski, Karol, *String Quartet No. 2, Opus 56*
Taylor, Deems, *The King's Henchmen* (opera)
Thomson, Virgil, *Capital, Capitals* (four men's voices, piano)
Varèse, Edgard, *Arcana* (orchestra)
Webern, Anton, *Trio, Opus 20* (violin, viola, cello)
Weill, Kurt, *Rise and Fall of the City of Mahoganny*
Weinberger, Jaromir, *Schwanda, The Bagpiper* (opera)

1928

World Events:

In the U.S., Herbert Hoover is elected as President No. 31; Admiral Byrd begins exploration of the Antarctic; Amelia Earhart becomes the first woman to fly the Atlantic; Mount Palomar Observatory installs the first 200-inch telescope; Mickey Mouse first appears as "Steamboat Willie." Internationally, the Kellogg-Briand Pact, outlawing war, is signed by 65 nations; Stalin's first "Five-Year Plan" is introduced to Russian farms and industries; the Olympic Games are held in Amsterdam; first flight is made by the autogiro; newly re-elected President Obrégon of Mexico is assassinated.

Cultural Highlights:

Pulitzers: Drama, Eugene O'Neill (*Strange Interlude*); Fiction, Thornton Wilder (*Bridge of San Luis Rey*); Poetry, Edwin A. Robinson (*Tristram*). Norwegian novelist Sigrid Undset is the recipient of the Nobel Prize for Literature; William Llewellyn becomes president of the Royal Academy of Art. Births in the literary field include American authors Edward Albee and Alvin Toffl; deaths include American novelist George McCutcheon, Swiss novelist Heinrich Federer, Russian novelist Nikolai Findeisen, British authors Thomas Hardy and Arthur E. Hull, Spanish novelist Vincente Ibañez and German novelist Hermann Sudermann. The art world loses French sculptor Paul Bartholomé, American artist Arthur B. Davies and British sculptor George Frampton; births include sculptor Georg Baselitz and American artists Helen Frankenthaler, Al Held and Robert Indiana. Other highlights include:

Art: Georges Braque, *Still Life with Jug*; Carlo Carrá, *Morning by the Sea*;   John S. Curry, *Baptism in Kansas*; Stuart Davis, *Eggbeater No. 4*; Charles Demuth, *I Saw the Figure 5 in Gold*; Alberto Giacometti, *Observing Head*; Henri Matisse, *Seated Odalisque*; Louis Maurer, *Still Life With Fish*; Georgia O'Keeffe, *Nightwave*.

Literature: Stephen V. Benét, *John Brown's Body*; Bertolt Brecht, *The Three-Penny Opera*; John Galsworthy, *A Modern Comedy*; Aldous Huxley, *Point Counter Point*; D.H. Law-rence, *Lady Chatterley's Lover*; W. Somerset Maugham, *Ashenden*; Eugene O'Neill, *Strange Interlude*; Upton Sinclair, *Boston*; Lytton Strachey, *Elizabeth and Essex*.

MUSICAL EVENTS

A. Births:

Jan 8 Evelyn Lear (Am-sop)	May 30 Gustav Leonhardt (Hol-hps-cd)
Jan 10 Wallace Berry (Am-cm-au)	May 31 Jacob Lateiner (Am-pn)
Jan 16 Pilar Lorengar (Sp-sop)	Jun 16 Sergiu Comissiona (Rom-cd)
Jan 17 Jean Barraqué (Fr-cm)	Jun 26 Jacob Druckman (Am-cm)
Jan 20 Antonio de Almeida (Fr-cd)	Jul 11 Robert Washburn (Am-cm)
Feb 9 Franz Crass (Ger-bs)	Jul 23 Leon Fleisher (Am-pn)
Feb 10 Donald Johanos (Am-cd)	Jul 26 Tadeusz Baird (Pol-cm)
Feb 29 McHenry Boatwright (Am-bar)	Aug 4 Jess Thomas (Am-ten)
Mar 4 Samuel Adler (Ger-cm)	Aug 14 Anshel Brusilow (Am-vn-cd)
Mar 15 Nicholas Flagello (It-cm)	Aug 22 Karlheinz Stockhausen (Ger-cm)
Mar 16 Christa Ludwig(Ger-sop)	Aug 29 Thomas J. Stewart (Am-bar)
Mar 24 Byron Janis (Am-pn)	Sep 6 Evgeny Svetlanov (Rus-cd)
Apr 2 Yolanda Marcoulescou	Sep 23 Robert Helps (Am-cm)
(Rom-sop)	Oct 12 Jerzy Semkov (Pol-cd)
Apr 12 Jean François Paillard	Oct 14 Gary Graffman (Am-pn)
(Fr-cd)	Nov 14 Leonie Rysanek (Aus-sop)
May 2 Horst Stein (Ger-cd)	Nov 27 Walter Klein (Aus-pn)
May 27 Thea Musgrave (Br-cm)	Dec 2 Jörg Demus (Aus-pn)

B. Deaths:

Jan 9 Jean E. Lemaire (Fr-cm)	Feb 27 Emma Steiner (Am-cd)
Feb 18 Celeste Heckscher (Am-cm)	Apr 11 Arthur Seidl (Ger-mus)

Apr 15	Vittorio Arimondi (It-bs)	Aug 12	Leos Janácek (Cz-cm)
May 19	Henry F. Gilbert (Am-cm)	Oct 30	Oscar G. Sonneck (Am-mus)
Jun 17	Karl Pohlig (Ger-cd)	Nov 7	Mattia Battistini (It-bar)
Jul 22	W.C. Brownell (Am-cri)	Dec 25	Théodor von Frimmel (Aus-mus)
Aug 6	William H. Flood (Ir-mus)		

C. Debuts:

Met ---Pearl Besuner (sop), Jane Carrol (mez), Grace Divine (mez), Aida Doninelli (sop), Gina Gola (sop), Clara Jacobo (sop), Gertrude Kappel (sop), Grace Moore (sop), Fred Patton (bs), Wilfrid Pelletier (cd), Aaron Weisberg (ten), Marek Windheim (ten)

U.S. --Thomas Beecham (N.Y.), Vladimir Horowitz (N.Y.), José Iturbi (Philadelphia), Helen Jepson (Philadelphia), Victor Labunski (N.Y.), Frida Leider (Chicago), René Maison (Chicago), Hephziba Menuhin (San Francisco), Bernardino Molinari (N.Y.), Ruggiero Ricci (San Francisco), Andrés Segovia (N.Y.), Mariano Stabile (Chicago), Thelma Votipka (Philadelphia)

Other -Anna Báthy (Budapest), Hugues Cuenod (Paris), Margaret Field-Hyde (Cambridge), Marta Fuchs (Aachen), Karl Hartmann (Elberfeld), Herbert von Karajan (Vienna), Moura Lympany (London), David Oistrakh (Leningrad), Lily Pons (Mühlhausen), Hans Richter-Haaser (Dresden), Wilhelm Schirp (Cologne), Joseph Schmidt (Berlin), Ina Souez (Ivrea), Ludwig Suthaus (Aachen), Alexander Sved (Budapest), Enid Szantho (Vienna)

D. New Positions:

Conductors: Carlos Chávez (Mexican SO), Vladimir Golschmann (Scottish SO), Paul Paray (Monte Carlo SO), Fernando Previtali (Maggio Musicale, Florence), Arturo Toscanini (New York PO)

Educational: Carlos Chávez (director, Mexican National Conservatory), Herbert Elwell (composition, Cleveland Institute), Edward Burlingame Hill (professor, Harvard), Efrem Zimbalist (violin, Curtis Institute)

Others: Arthur Shepherd (music critic, Cleveland *Press*)

E. Prizes and Honors:

Prizes: Helen Berlin, Louis Kaufman, Adele Marcus, George Rasely, August Werner and Olga Zundel (Naumberg)

Honors: Edward German (knighted), Willem Mengelberg (honorary doctorate, Columbia), Maurice Ravel (honorary doctorate, Oxford), Václav Talich (Swedish Royal Academy)

F. Biographical Highlights:

Samuel Barber travels to Italy on a Bearns Prize; Jussi Björling enters Stockholm Conservatory; Alexander Glazunov travels in Western Europe; Charles Koechlin makes a second lecture visit to the U.S.; Ervin Nyiregyházi, returning to Los Angeles, begins to work for Hollywood; Goffredo Petrassi enters the Conservatorio di S. Cecilia in Rome; Gregor Piatigorsky leaves the Berlin PO to enter a solo career; Quincy Porter returns to Paris for a three-year stay; Maurice Ravel makes a tour of the U.S.; Joseph Schillinger emigrates to the U.S. and settles in New York; Isaac Stern enters the San Francisco Conservatory; Oliver Strunk begins work at the Library of Congress; Henryk Szeryng sent to Berlin for violin study; Michael Tippett leaves the Royal College and moves to Exted, Surrey; Edgard Varèse goes to Paris for a five-year stay.

G. Institutional Openings:

Performing Groups: Barkel String Quartet (Stockholm), Dessoff A Capella Singers (N.Y.), Detroit Civic Opera Co., Gastspieloper (Berlin), Griller String Quartet (London), Hewitt String Quartet (Paris), Mexican SO (Mexico City), New Jersey SO, Orchestrale Florentina, Prague Wind Quintet, Red Army Song and Dance Ensemble (Moscow), Soviet PO (Moscow), Suzuki String Quartet (Nagoya, Japan)

Festivals: Asheville Mountain Dance & Folk Festival (North Carolina)

Educational: Arthur Jordan Conservatory of Music (Indianapolis), Cincinnati Institute of Fine Arts, National Music Camp (Interlochen, Michigan), Bedrich Smetana Museum (Prague).

Other: Accademia dei Dilettanti di Musica (Philadelphia), Archive of American Folk Song (Library of Congress); J. Obermayer, Harp Maker (Munich); Masonic Auditorium (Detroit); Mills Music, Inc. (N.Y.); Music Appreciation Hour (radio, with Walter Damrosch), *Die Musikpädagogische Bibliothek,* Peer-Southern Music Publishing Co., Quarter-Tone Piano (by Hans Barth), *La Rassegna Musicale,* Stanislavsky Opera Theater (Moscow), Teatro Comunale di Firenze

H. Musical Literature:

Blom, Eric, *The Limitations of Music*
Dumesnil, René, *Musiciens romantiques*
Findeisen, Nicolai, *History of Russian Music*
Geiringer, Karl, *Vorgeschichte und Geschichte der europäischen Läute*
Haas, Robert, *Die Musik des Barocks*
Hadow, Willliam, *Collected Essays*
Mason, Daniel, *The Dilemma of American Music*
Metcalf, Frank, *Stories of Hymn Tunes*
Widor, Charles, *L'Orgue moderne*

I. Musical Compositions:

Badings, Henk, *Concerto No. 1 for Violin and Orchestra*
Bantock, Granville, *Pilgrim's Progress* (chorus, orchestra)
Bartók, Béla, *String Quartet No. 4*
Bax, Arnold, *Symphony No. 3*
Cadman, Charles W., *Father of Waters* (cantata)
Carpenter, John Alden, *String Quartet*
Converse, Frederick, *Elegiac Poem* (orchestra)
Gershwin, George, *An American in Paris* (orchestra)
Holst, Gustav, *Egdon Heath* (orchestra)
Honegger, Artur, *Rugby, Symphonic Movement No. 2*
Janácek, Leos, *From the House of the Dead* (opera)
Milhaud, Darius, *Christopher Columbus* (opera)
Moore, Douglas, *Moby Dick* (symphonic poem)
Nielsen, Carl, *Concerto for Clarinet and Orchestra*
Pijper, Willem, *Six Symphonic Epigrams* (orchestra)
Pizzetti, Ildebrando, *"Summer" Concerto* (orchestra)
Poulenc, Francis, *Concerto Champêtre* (harpsichord and piano, orchestra)
Prokofiev, Serge, *Symphony No. 3, Opus 44*
Ravel, Maurice, *Bolero*
Rogers, Bernard, *Symphony No. 2*
Schmidt, Franz, *Symphony No. 3*
Schoenberg, Arnold, *Variations for Orchestra, Opus 31*
Shostakovich, Dmitri, *The Nose, Opus 15* (opera)
Stravinsky, Igor, *The Fairy's Kiss* (ballet)
　　　　　Cappriccio for Piano and Orchestra
Thomson, Virgil, *Symphony on a Hymn Tune*
Toch, Ernst, *Egon and Emilie, Opus 46* (opera)
Vaughan-Williams, Ralph, *Sir John in Love* (opera)
　　　　　Te Deum in G
Webern, Anton, *Symphony, Opus 21*
Weill, Kurt, *The Three Penny Opera*

1929

World Events:
Black Friday on Wall Street in the U.S.--stock market collapse brings on a world-wide depression; in Chicago, the St. Valentine's Day massacre occurs; U.S. warships are sent to Shanghai to protect U.S. citizens; Admiral Byrd flies over the South Pole; radio program "Amos and Andy" begins broadcasting. Internationally, the Lateran Treaties return the Papal Territory to the Pope; Leon Trotsky, now exiled from Moscow, flees for his life; the Graf Zeppelin takes a round-the-world flight; A. Fleming discovers penicillin; the French withdraw their troops from the Rheinland.

Cultural Highlights:
Pulitzers: Drama, Elmer L. Rice (*Street Scene*); Fiction, Julia Peterkin (*Scarlet Sister Mary*); Poetry, Stephen Vincent Benét (*John Brown's Body*). The Nobel Prize for Literature goes to Thomas Mann; and John Galsworthy receives the Order of Merit. In New York, the Museum of Modern Art (MOMA) and the Baltimore Museum of Art open their doors. American author Chaim Potok and poet Adrienne Rich are born as is British dramatist John Osborne; Norwegian dramatist Gunnar Heiberg and German author Arno Holz pass away. The art field mourns the deaths of French sculptor Léonard Beguine and artist Émile-Antoine Bourdelle and American artist Robert Henri. Other highlights include:

Art: Georges Braque, *The Round Table*; John S. Curry, *Tornado over Kansas*; Salvador Dali, *Ilumined Pleasures*; Jacob Epstein, *Night and Day*; Paul Klee, *Fools in a Trance*; Le Corbusier, *The City of Tomorrow*; Fernand Léger, *Les Deux Danseuses*; Pablo Picasso, *Woman in an Armchair*; Grant Wood, *Woman with Plants*.

Literature: Jean Cocteau, *Les Enfants Terribles*; Lloyd Douglas, *The Magnificent Obsession*; William Faulkner, *The Sound and the Fury*; Ernest Hemingway, *A Farewell to Arms*; Erich Remarque, *All Quiet on the Western Front*; Elmer L. Rice, *Street Scene*; Thomas Wolfe, *Look Homeward, Angel*; William Yeats, *The Winding Stair*.

MUSICAL EVENTS

A. Births:

Jan 15	Eva Badura-Skoda (Aus-mus)	Jun 13	Alan Civil (Br-hn)
Jan 15	Teizo Matsumura (Jp-cm))	Jul 9	Eberhard Wächter (Aus-bar)
Jan 16	Marilyn Horne (Am-mez)	Jul 11	Hermann Prey (Ger-bar)
Feb 2	Waldemar Kmentt (Aus-ten)	Jul 15	Charles Anthony (Am-ten)
feb 14	Wyn Morris (Br-cd)	Jul 23	Henri Pousseur (Bel-cm)
Feb 20	Toshiro Mayuzumi (Jp-cm)	Jul 26	Alexis Weissenberg (Bul-pn)
Mar 3	Robert Nagy (Am-ten)	Aug 8	Josef Suk (Cz-vn-cm)
Mar 4	Bernard Haitink (Hol-cd)	Aug 11	Wilfred Boettcher (Ger-cd)
Mar 18	John Macurdy (Am-bs)	Aug 28	István Kertész (Hun-cd)
Mar 19	Robert Muczynski (Am-cm)	Sep 8	Christoph von Dohnányi (Ger-cd)
Apr 6	André Previn (Am-cd)	Sep 13	Nicolai Ghiaurov (Bul-bs)
Apr 8	Walter Berry (Aus-bar)	Oct 24	George Crumb (Am-cm)
Apr 14	Paavo Berglund (Fin-cd)	Nov 3	Arkady Aronov (Rus-pn)
Apr 29	Peter Sculthorpe (Aust-cm)	Nov 9	Piero Cappuccilli (It-bar)
May 18	Roger Matton (Can-cm)	Nov 20	Kenneth Schermerhorn (Am-cd)
May 25	Beverly Sills (Am-sop)	Dec 3	Paul Turok (Am-cm)
Jun 1	Yehudi Wyner (Am-cm)	Dec 16	Donald Grobe (Am-ten)
Jun 6	Boguslaw Schäffer (Pol-the)		

B. Deaths:

Jan 11	Elfrida Andrée (Swe-org-cm)	Feb 17	Anton Preobrazhensky (Rus-mus)
Feb 6	Minnie Hauk (Am-sop)	Feb 24	André Messager (Fr-cm-cd)
Feb 6	Siegfried Ochs (Ger-cd)	Apr 16	Otto Goritz (Ger-bar)

May 27	Lilli Lehmann (Ger-sop)	Jul 15	Hugo von Hofmannsthal (Aus-lib)
May 21	Elise Hensler (Am-sop)	Aug 19	Sergei Diaghilev (Rus-imp)
May 27	Giuseppe Anselmi (It-ten)	Sep 26	Karl Weinmann (Ger-mus)
Jul 4	Jean Gerárdy (Bel-cel)	Oct 17	Willibald Nagel (Ger-mus)
Jul 13	Eusebius Mandyczewski	Nov 9	Theodor Pfeiffer (Ger-pn-mus)
	(Aus-mus)	Dec 31	Alexander Lambert (Pol-pn)

C. Debuts:

Met ---Dreda Aves (sop), Santa Biondo (sop), Carlo Coscia (bs), Alfredo Gandolfi (bar), Eleanor LaMance (mez), Augusta Oltrabella (sop), Tancredi Pasero (bs), Wilfrid Pelletier (cd), Edward Ransome (ten), Karl Riedel (cd), Joseph Rosenstock (cd), Gladys Swarthout (mez)

U.S. --Rose Bampton (N.Y.), Giovanni Inghilleri (Chicago), José Iturbi (tour), Nathan Milstein (Philadelphia), Gregor Piatigorsky (Oberlin, OH), Margherita Salvi (Chicago), Emil Schipper (Chicago), Eva Turner (Chicago)

Other -Mathieu Ahlersmeyer (Mönchengladbach), Webster Aitken (Vienna), Joel Berglund (Stockholm), Kurt Böhme (Bautzen), Arthur Carron (London), Andor Foldes (Vienna), Emil Gilels (Odessa), Joan Hammond (Sydney), Caterina Jarboro (Milan), Edward Kilenyi, Hilde Konetzni (Chemnitz), Dorothea Lawrence (Quebec), Nicola Moscona (Athens), Alfred Poell (Düsseldorf), Arno Schellenberg (Düsseldorf), Paul-Henri Vergnes (Paris), Alessandro Ziliani (Milan)

D. New Positions:

Conductors: Henry Hadley (Manhattan SO), Jascha Horenstein (Düsseldorf Opera), Otakar Jeremiás (Prague Radio SO), Herbert von Karajan (Ulm Opera), Clemens Krauss (Vienna Opera & PO), Pierre Monteux (Paris SO), Artur Rodzinski (Los Angeles PO)

Educational: Rudolf Ganz (Chicago Musical College)

Others: Carl Engel (President, G. Schirmer), Florent Schmitt (music critic, *Le Temps*), Hans Stuckenschmidt (music critic, *Berliner Zeitung am Mittag*)

E. Prizes and Honors:

Prizes: Elsa Barraine, Werner Janssen & Norman Lockwood (Prix de Rome)

Honors: Laura Knight (Dame), Arthur Somervell (knighted)

F. Biographical Highlights:

Henry Cowell becomes first American composer to be invited to Soviet Russia; Mafalda Favera makes her La Scala debut; Roy Harris returns to the U.S. after three years in Europe; José Iturbi makes his first tour of the U.S.; Aram Khachaturian goes to the Moscow Conservatory; Lars-Erik Larsson is given a state composer's grant; Witold Lutoslawski enters Warsaw University to study mathematics; Alma Mahler marries Franz Werfel; Nicolai Malko leaves the U.S. to return to Russia; Serge Prokofiev injures his hand in an auto accident; Sylvestre Revueltas becomes assistant conductor to the Mexican SO; Grete Stückgold divorces her first husband and marries baritone Gustav Schützendorf; Ernst Toch moves to Berlin; Arturo Toscanini resigns his La Scala post in protest of the fascist regime of Mussolini; Kurt Weill gives up all side jobs to devote full time to composition; Eugène Ysaÿe loses a foot to diabetes.

G. Institutional Openings:

Performing Groups: Esplanade Concerts (Boston), Loewenguth String Quartet; Manhattan SO, Orpheus Male Choir (Phoenix), Symphony Orchestra of Paris, Tucson SO

Festivals: Delius Music Festival (London)

Educational: National Guild of Piano Teachers (Austin, TX), *The School Musician*

Other: American Bandmasters Association (ABA), American Society of Ancient Instruments (Philadelphia), Association for Contemporary Music (Munich), Broude Brothers Music

Publishers (N.Y.), Chicago Opera House, *Das Chorwerk*, Cincinnati Chamber Music Society, *The Consort*, Cos-Cob (Arrow) Press (N.Y.), Dolmetsch Foundation (England), Edwin A. Fleischer Collection of Scores (Philadelphia), Friends and Enemies of Modern Music (Hartford, CT), Hammond Instrument Co. (Chicago), International Bruckner Society (Vienna), *Journal of the Acoustical Society of America*

H. Musical Literature:
Andersen, Arthur, *Practical Orchestration*
Carse, Adam, *Orchestral Conducting*
Cobbett, Walter, *Cyclopaedia of Chamber Music*
Dykema, Peter, *Music Tests*
Forsyth, Cecil, *Orchestration*
Gastoué, Amédéo, *La Vie musicale de l'église*
Macpherson, Stewart, *A Simple Introduction to the Principles of Tonality*
Molnár, Antal, *Introduction to Contemporary Music*
Rosenfeld, Paul, *An Hour with American Music*
Scherchen, Hermann, *Lehrbuch des Dirigierens*

I. Musical Compositions:
Berg, Alban, *Le Vin* (soprano, orchestra)
Bloch, Ernst, *Helvetia, Land of Mountains and Its People* (symphonic fresco)
Copland, Aaron, *Symphonic Ode for Orchestra*
Delius, Frederick, *A Song of Summer* (orchestra)
Dupré, Marcel, *Organ Symphony No. 1*
Foerster, Josef, *Symphony No. 5, Opus 141*
Giordano, Umberto, *Il Re* (opera)
Gershwin, George, *Show Girl* (musical)
Harris, Roy, *American Portraits* (orchestra)
Hindemith, Paul, *Neues von Tagen* (opera)
Honegger, Artur, *Concerto for Cello and Orchestra*
Ibert, Jacques, *Persée et Andromède* (opera)
Kabalevsky, Dmitri, *Concerto No. 1 for Piano and Orchestra*
Lambert, Constant, *The Rio Grande* (chorus, piano, orchestra)
Mason, Daniel, *Symphony No. 2, Opus 30*
McPhee, Colin, *Sea Shanty Suite* (orchestra)
Milhaud, Darius, *Concerto for Violin and Orchestra*
Piston, Walter, *Suite No. 1 for Orchestra*
Poulenc, Francis, *Aubade* (piano, eighteen instruments)
Prokofiev, Serge, *Divertimento for Orchestra, Opus 43*
                  The Prodigal Son, Opus 46 (ballet)
Rangström, Ture, *Symphony No. 3, "Song Under the Stars"*
Respighi, Ottorino, *Roman Festivals* (orchestra)
Roussel, Albert, *Petite Suite, Opus 39* (orchestra)
Schoenberg, Arnold, *Von Heute auf Morgen, Opus 32* (opera)
Strauss, Richard, *Gesange des Orients, Opus 77* (song cycle)
Stravinsky, Igor, *Four Etudes for Orchestra*
Thompson, Randall, *Symphony No. 1*
Turina, Joaquin, *Evocaciones, Opus 46* (piano)
Vaughan-Williams, Ralph, *Benedicite* (soprano, chorus, orchestra)
Villa-Lobos, Heitor, *Côros No. 9* (orchestra)
                  Twelve Studies for Guitar
Walton, William, *Concerto for Viola and Orchestra*

1930

World Events:

The U.S. census shows a population of 122,775,000, a 16% increase; former President William H. Taft dies; the Hawley-Smoot Tariff raises import taxes to a new high; the Bureau of Narcotics is formed by the Treasury Dept.; the Veteran's Administration is formed; founding of the W.W. Kellogg Foundation, the American Interplanetary Society and the University of Kansas City. Internationally, the Nazi Party gains a majority in the German Reichstag; the London Naval Treaty seeks limited naval forces for the U.S., Great Britain and Japan; the last allied troops leave the Rhineland; Haile Selassie becomes emperor of Ethiopia; discovery of the Planet Pluto.

Cultural Highlights:

Pulitzers: Drama, Marc Connelly (*The Green Pastures*); Fiction, Oliver La Farge (*Laughing Boy*); Poetry, Conrad Aitken (*Selected Poems*). Sinclair Lewis becomes the first American to win a Nobel Prize for Literature; John Mansfield is appointed British Poet Laureate; James Whistler and Walt Whitman are inducted into the Hall of Fame for Great Americans. Deaths in the field of art include American artist Charles Hawthorne and German artist Karl Oesterley; births include American artist Jasper Johns and Polish artist Richard Anuszkiewicz. Births in the literary field include British dramatist Harold Pinter and poet Ted Hughes, Irish author Edna O'Brien and French author Françoise Mallet-Joris; deaths include British poet Robert Bridges and authors Arthur Conan Doyle and D.H. Lawrence, French poet Adolphe Retté and Russian poet Vladimir Mayakovsky. Other highlights include:

Art: Charles Burchfield, *The Rainy Night*; Charles Demuth, *Buildings, Lancaster*; Raoul Dufy, *Chateau and Horses*; Jacob Epstein, *Genesis* (marble); Marsden Hartley, *Beaver Lake, Lost River*; Edward Hopper, *Early Sunday Morning*; Reginald Marsh, *The Bowery*; Louis Maurer, *Still Life with Doily*; Grant Wood, *American Gothic*.

Literature: Maxwell Anderson, *Elizabeth, the Queen*; W.H. Auden, *Poems*; Ivan Bunin, *The Well of Days*; Noel Coward, *Private Lives*; Hart Crane, *The Bridge*; John Dos Passos, *The 42nd Parallel*; T.S. Eliot, *Ash Wednesday*; Edna Ferber, *Cimarron*; W. Somerset Maugham, *The Summing Up*; Robert Sherwood, *Waterloo Bridge*.

MUSICAL EVENTS

A. Births:

Jan 4	Gábor Gabos (Hun-pn)	Jul 10	Josephine Veasey (Br-mez)
Feb 7	David Bar-Illan (Is-pn)	Jul 25	Maureen Forrester (Can-alto)
Feb 11	Hilde Somer (Aus-pn)	Aug 11	Heinz Zimmerman (Ger-cm)
Feb 22	Marni Nixon (Am-sop)	Sep 13	Larry Austin (Am-cm)
Feb 26	Lazar Berman (Rus-pn)	Sep 27	Igor Kipnis (Ger-hps)
Mar 5	Lorin Maazel (Am-cd)	Sep 29	Richard Bonynge (Aust-cd)
Mar 9	Thomas Schippers (Am-cd)	Sep 30	Fritz Wunderlich (Ger-ten)
Mar 18	Maurice Peress (Am-cd)	Oct 3	David Epstein (Am-cm-cri)
Mar 25	David Burge (Am-pn-cm)	Oct 8	Toru Takemitsu (Jp-cm)
Mar 28	Robert Ashley (Am-cm)	Oct 18	Barry McDaniel (Am-bar)
Apr 8	John Reardon (Am-bar)	Oct 28	Gilbert Trythall (Am-cm)
May 4	Gennady Rozhdestvensky	Oct 30	Stanley Sadie (Br-mus)
	(Rus-cd)	Nov 2	Harold Farberman (Am-cm)
May 4	Roberta Peters (Am-sop)	Nov 9	Ivan Moravec (Cz-pn)
May 8	Heather Harper (Br-sop)	Nov 17	David Amram (Am-cm)
Jun 25	Carol Bogard (Am-sop)	Dec 7	Richard Felciano (Am-cm)
Jul 3	Carlos Kleiber (Ger-cd)	Dec 10	Rey Longyear (Am-mus)

B. Deaths:

Jan 18	André Mocquereau (Fr-mus)	Jan 28	Emmy Destinn (Cz-sop)
Jan 27	Jean Huré (Fr-org-cm)	Feb 13	Conrad Ansorge (Ger-pn)

Feb 21	George W. Stebbins (Am-org)	Sep 28	Daniel Guggenheim (Am-ind-pat)
Apr 3	Emma Albani (Can-sop)	Oct 1	Riccardo Drigo (It-cm)
Jun 7	Nahan Franko (Am-vn-cd)	Oct 3	Friedrich Ludwig (Ger-mus)
Jun 22	Mary Davies (Br-sop)	Oct 4	Camille Bellaique (Fr-mus)
Jul 15	Leopold Auer (Hun-vn-ed)	Dec	Marie Fillunger (Aus-sop)
Aug 4	Siegfried Wagner (Ger-cm-cd)	Dec 7	Robert Blass (Am-bs)
Sep 26	Willem De Haan (Hol-cd-cm)	Dec 17	Peter Warlock (Br-cm)

C. Debuts:

Met ---Ivar Andrésen (bs), Beatrice Belkin (sop), Hans Clemens (ten), Olga Didur (mez), Claudio Frigerio (bs), Elisabeth Ohms (sop), Faina Petrova (mez), Myrna Sharlow (sop), Siegfried Tappolet (bs), Antonin Trantoul (ten)

U.S. --Margarete Baumer (tour), Rudolf Bockelmann (Chicago), Arthur Fiedler (Boston), Sascha Gorodnitzki (tour), Eduard Habich (Chicago), Karl Hartmann (tour), Ralph Kirkpatrick (Cambridge, MA), Erich Kleiber (N.Y.), Lotte Lehmann (Chicago), Eugene List (Los Angeles), Giovanni Manurita (Chicago), Hans Nissen (Chicago), Nino Piccaluga (tour), Carlo Scattola (tour), Jan Smeterlin (tour)

Other -Jussi Björling (Stockholm), Maria Caniglia (Turin), Alberto Erede (Rome), Hans Hotter (Troppau), Raoul Jobin (Paris), Giuseppe Lugo (Paris), Georgii Nelepp (Leningrad), Afro Poli (Pisa), Torsten Ralf (Stettin), György Sándor (Budapest), Martial Singher (Amsterdam), Set Svanholm (as baritone), Sándor Svéd (Budapest), Pia Tassinari (Milan), Frank Valentino (Italy)

D. New Positions:

Conductors: Adrian Boult (BBC SO), Arthur Fiedler (Boston Pops), Erich Kleiber (New York PO), Franz Konwitschny (Stuttgart Opera), Fritz Mahler (Copenhagen Radio SO)

Educational: Luigi Dallapiccola (piano, Florence Conservatory), William Dawson (director, Tuskegee School of Music), Gerald Finzi (composition, Royal Academy), Joaquin Turina (composition, Madrid Conservatory)

Others: André Fleury (organ, St. Augustin, Paris), Olivier Messiaen (organ, Trinity Church, Paris), Henry Pleasants (music critic, Philadelphia *Evening Bulletin*)

E. Prizes and Honors:

Prizes: Louise Bernhardt (Naumberg), Ruth Culbertson (Naumberg), Annie Fischer (Liszt), Helen McGraw (Naumberg), Mila Wellerson (Naumberg)

Honors: Granville Bantock (knighted)

F. Biographical Highlights:

Ernst Bloch goes to Europe for a nine-year stay; Benjamin Britten enters the Royal College of Music; John Cage leaves college to spend a year travelling in Europe; Luigi Dallapiccola visits in Germany & Austria; Hans Hoffman travels to the U.S., begins teaching in California; André Jolivet begins music study with Varèse; Dmitri Kabalevsky graduates from Moscow Conservatory; René Leibowitz begins studies with Schoenberg in Berlin; William Schuman, upon hearing the New York PO for the first time, enters Malkin Conservatory; Michael Tippet begins a year of composition study with R.O. Morris; Arturo Toscanini becomes the first non-German to conduct at Bayreuth; Heitor Villa-Lobos returns to Brazil.

G. Institutional Openings:

Performing Groups: BBC SO (London), Indianapolis SO, Intimate Opera Co. (London), Shinko Sakkyokuka (Japan), Venezuela SO

Festivals: Venice Festival of Contemporary Music

Educational: Lima Academy of Music (Peru)

Other: Association of Polish Composers (Warsaw), Boosey and Hawkes, Ltd (by Merger), Cambridge Theater (London), Dallas Civic Music Association, Hermann Moeck Publishing Co. (Celle), Horace Bushnell Memorial Opera House (Hartford), John Challis Harpsichord Co. (Michigan), *Musical Review for the Blind*, National Orchestral Association (N.Y.), Netherlands Society for Contemporary Music, Neue Schütz Gesellschaft (Augsburg), New York Philharmonic Broadcasts, Suvini Zerboni (Italian Music Publishers)

H. Musical Literature:

Asafiev, Boris, *Musical Form as Process I*
Dumesnil, René, *Musique contemporaine en France*
Fisher, William, *Ye Olde New England Psalm Tunes*
Grabner, Hermann, *Der lineare Satz*
Jeppesen, Knud, *Kontrapunkt*
Molnár, Antal, *Physics and Music*
Orff, Carl, *Orff-Schulwerk I*
Rolland, Romain, *Goethe et Beethoven*

I. Musical Compositions:

Antheil, George, *Transatlantic* (opera)
Bartók, Béla, *Cantata Profana* (tenor, baritone, double chorus, orchestra)
Bax, Arnold, *Symphony No. 4*
Copland, Aaron, *Piano Variations*
Delius, Frederick, *Songs of Farewell* (soprano, orchestra)
Elgar, Edward, *Pomp and Circumstance March No. 5*
Grainger, Percy, *Handel in the Strand* (two pianos)
Hanson, Howard, *Symphony No. 2, Opus 30, "Romantic"*
Hindemith, Paul, *Concert Music for Viola and Orchestra*
   Concert Music for Strings and Brass, Opus 50
Holst, Gustav, *Choral Fantasia, Opus 51* (soprano, chorus, organ, orchestra)
   Hammersmith, Prelude and Scherzo (orchestra)
Honegger, Artur, *Symphony No. 1*
Ibert, Jacques, *Divertissement* (chamber orchestra)
   Le Roi d'Yvetot (opera)
Kodály, Zoltán, *Marosszék Dances* (orchestra)
Martinu, Bohuslav, *Concerto No. 1 for Cello and Chamber Orchestra*
Messiaen, Olivier, *Les Offrandes Oubliées* (orchestra)
Milhaud, Darius, *Maximilian* (opera)
   Concerto for Percussion and Small Orchestra
Moore, Douglas, *A Symphony of Autumn*
Pijper, Willem, *The Tempest* (incidental music)
Prokofiev, Serge, *Symphony No. 4, Opus 47*
Respighi, Ottorino, *Metamorphosen* (orchestra)
   Lauda per la Nativita del Signore (soloists, chorus, orchestra)
Revueltas, Silvestre, *Cuauhnahuac* (orchestra)
Roussel, Albert, *Symphony No. 4, Opus 53*
   Bacchus et Ariane, Opus 43 (ballet)
Schmitt, Florent, *Symphonic Concertante for Piano and Orchestra, Opus 82*
Schoenberg, Arnold, *Begleitungmusik, Opus 34* (orchestra)
Shostakovich, Dmitri, *Symphony No. 3, Opus 20, "May Day"*
   Golden Age Ballet, Opus 22
Stravinsky, Igor, *Symphony of Psalms* (chorus, orchestra)
Taylor, Deems, *Peter Ibbetson* (opera)
Toch, Ernst, *Der Fächer, Opus 51* (opera)
Vaughan-Williams, Ralph, *Job, a Masque for Dancing*
Villa-Lobos, Heitor, *Bachianas Brasileiras No. 1 for Eight Celli*
   Bachianas Brasileiras No. 2 for Orchestra
Webern, Anton, *Quartet, Opus 22* (violin, clarinet, saxophone, piano)

1931

World Events:
In the U.S. Congress officially adopts the *Star Spangled Banner* as the National Anthem; inventor Thomas Edison dies; the President proposes a one-year moratorium on all war debts; the Empire State and Chrysler buildings are finished in New York City; the first cyclotron is invented by E. Lawrence. Internationally, the Statute of Westminster sets up the British Commonwealth of Nations; Japan invades Manchuria and renames it Manchukuo; the second Spanish Republic is formed as Alphonso XIII abdicates; Haile Selasie gives constitutional government to Ethiopia; A. Picard reaches a 10-mile altitude in his sealed cockpit balloon.

Cultural Highlights:
Pulitzers: Drama, Susan Glaspell (*Alison's House*); Fiction, Margaret A. Barnes (*Years of Grace*); Poetry, Robert Frost (*Collected Poems*). The Nobel Prize for Literature goes to Erik A. Karlfeldt; British artist William Robertson is knighted; artist Philip W. Steer is given the Order of Merit; Sybil Thorndike is made a Dame of the British Empire. The Courtauld Institute of Art opens in London and the Whitney Museum of American Art opens in New York; Abstraction-Création, a group of abstract painters and sculptors, is formed in Paris. The literary world loses British novelists E. Arnold Bennet and Thomas Caine, Irish poet Alfred Graves, Swedish authors Tor Hedberg and Hjalmar Bergman and poet Erik Karlfeldt and American poet Vachel Lindsay; British novelist John Le Carré is born. The art world sees the birth of German artist Frank Auerbach, American sculptor Robert Morris and British artist Malcolm Morley but mourns the passing of Italian artist Giovanni Boldini and Americans Daniel French and Robert Spencer. Other highlights include:

Art: Salvador Dali, *The Persistence of Memory*; Julio Gonzalez, *Harlequin Pierrot*; Ernest Graham, *Blue Abstraction*; John Kane, *The Monongahela Valley*; Henri Matisse, *Girl in a Yellow Dress*; Joan Miró, *Man, Woman and Child*; Georgia O'Keefe, *Cow's Skull: Red, White and Blue*; José Orozco, *Zapalistas*; Grant Wood, *Midnight Ride of Paul Revere*.

Literature: Vicki Baum, *Grand Hotel*; Pearl Buck, *The Good Earth*; Willi Cather, *Shadows on the Rock*; Daphne du Maurier, *The Loving Spirit*; William Faulkner, *Sanctuary*; Ogden Nash, *Hard Lines*; Eugene O'Neill, *Mourning Becomes Electra*; Erich Remarque, *The Road Back*; Edmund Wilson, *Axel's Castle*; Virginia Woolf, *The Waves*.

MUSICAL EVENTS

A. Births:

Jan 4 Gordon Peters (Am-perc-ed)	May 6 Donald Martino (Am-cm)
Jan 5 Alfred Brendel (Aus-pn)	May 7 Helge Brilioth (Swe-ten)
Jan 20 Birgit Finnila (Swe-alto)	May 28 Peter Westergaard (Am-cm)
Jan 29 Ezio Flagello (Am-bs)	May 31 Shirley Verrett (Am-mez)
Feb 20 Margareta Hallim (Swe-sop)	Jun 16 Lucia Dlugoszewski (Am-cm)
Mar 5 Barry Tuckwell (Aust-hn)	Jun 20 Arne Nordheim (Nor-cm)
Mar 7 Mady Mesplé (Fr-sop)	Jun 30 James Loughran (Scot-cd)
Mar 13 Rosalind Elias (Am-mez)	Aug 21 Gregg Smith (Am-cd)
Mar 16 Theo Altmeyer (Ger-ten)	Aug 28 John Shirley-Quirk (Br-bs)
Mar 27 Yoriaki Matsudaira (Jp-cm)	Oct 1 Sylvano Bussotti (It-cm)
May 29 Gloria Davy (Am-sop)	Oct 16 Valery A. Klimov (Rus-vn)
Apr 4 Arthur Weisberg (Am-bn-cd)	Nov 4 Jindrich Jindrak (Cz-bar)
Apr 6 Joan Carlyle (Br-sop)	Nov 21 Malcolm Williamson (Aust-cm)
Apr 7 Donald Harris (Am-cm)	Nov 30 Günther Herbig (Cz-cd)
Apr 13 Anita Cerquetti (It-sop)	Dec 24 Mauricio Kagel (Arg-cm)
Apr 27 Igor Oistrakh (Rus-vn)	Jeanette Pilou (It-sop)

B. Deaths:

Feb 12 Karl L. Schaefer (Ger-acous)	Feb 22 Mario Ancona (It-bar-cm)

Feb 23	Nellie Melba (Aust-sop)	Jul 10	Amédée Reuchsel (Fr-org)
Mar 10	William Gustafsen (Am-bs)	Sep 2	Franz Schalk (Aus-cd)
Mar 21	Erik Schmedes (Den-ten)	Oct 2	Carl Nielsen (Den-cm)
Apr 4	George Chadwick (Am-cm)	Oct 17	Peter Wagner (Ger-mus)
May 12	Eugène Ysaÿe (Bel-vn)	Dec 2	Vincent d'Indy (Fr-cm)
Jul 2	André Tessier (Fr-mus)	Dec 27	Peter C. Lutkin (Am-org)

C. Debuts:

Met ---Marie von Essen (mez), Carlton Gauld (bs), Max Lorenz (ten), Lily Pons (sop), Maria Ranzow (mez), Georges Thill (ten)

U.S. --Salvatore Baccaloni (Chicago), Augusto Beuf (Chicago), Marion Claire (Chicago), Noël Eadie (Chicago), Hamilton Harty (tour), Hedwig Jungkurth (tour), Jan Kiepura (Chicago), John Kirkpatrick (N.Y.), Nino Martini (Philadelphia), Rosetta Pampanini (Chicago), Isaac Stern (San Francisco, age 11), Risë Stevens (N.Y.), George Szell (St. Louis), Jennie Tourel (Chicago)

Other -Peter Anders (Berlin), Maria Cebotari (Dresden), Frederick Dalberg (Leipzig), Herta Glaz (Breslau), Joan Hammond (Sydney), Harriet Henders (Graz), Charles Kullman (Berlin), Ray Lev (London), Nino Martini (Milan), Tatiana Menotti (Vienna), André Navarra (Paris), Gustav Neidlinger (Mainz), Maria Reining (Vienna), Tibór Varga (Budapest), Ramón Vinay (Mexico City)

D. New Positions:

Conductors: Vladimir Golschmann (St. Louis SO), Eugene Goosens (Cincinnati SO), Odd Grünner-Hegge (Oslo PO), Hans Kindler (National SO), Kyrill Kondrashin (Moscow Children's Theater), Ernest MacMillan (Toronto SO), Eugene Ormandy (Minneapolis SO)

Educational: Carl Nielsen (director, Copenhagen Conservatory), Flor Peeters (organ, Ghent conservatory)

Others: Eric Blom (music critic, Birmingham *Post*), Hugo Distler (organ, Jacobkirche, Lübeck), Deems Taylor (music critic, New York *American*)

E. Prizes and Honors:

Prizes: Kurtis Brownell, Edwina Eustis, Lillian Rehberg Goodman, and Marguerite Hawkins (Naumburg)

Honors: Béla Bartók (Legion of Honor), Bernard T. Heinze (Royal Academy), John B. McEwen & Hugh Roberton (knighted)

F. Biographical Highlights:

Milton Babbitt studies math, but soon switches to music; Eduard von Beinum becomes Mengelberg's assistant at the Amsterdam Concertgebouw; Peggy Glanville-Hicks wins a scholarship to the Royal College in London; Sigfrid Karg-Elert begins a year-long organ tour of the U.S.; Bohuslav Martinu marries Charlotte Quennegen; Eugene Mravinsky graduates from Leningrad Conservatory; Luisa Tetrazzini makes her final New York appearance; Vladimir Ussachevsky settles in California and enters Pasadena Junior College; Dag Wirén finishes his studies at the Stockholm Conservatory and goes to Paris to study composition with Sabaneyev.

G. Institutional Openings:

Performing Groups: Albuquerque Civic SO, Brussels SO, Cologne Bach Choir, English National Opera (from Sadler's Wells), Gertler (Brussels) String Quartet, Menges String Quartet (London), Montevideo SO, National SO (Washington, D.C.), Rio de Janeiro PO, Vancouver SO

Educational: Buenos Aires Institute of Musicology, Loyola University College of Music, Music Library Association (Canton, MA), Salzedo Harp Colony (Camden, ME)

Other: *Der Blockflötenspiegel*, Bruckner Society of America, *Forum*, Galaxy Music

Corporation (N.Y.), G.B. Dealy Award Competition (Dallas), MacNaughton Concerts London), Metropolitan Opera Broadcasts, Quarter-Tone Trumpet, Severance Hall (Cleveland)

H. Musical Literature:

Blume, Friedrich, *Die evangelische Kirchenmusik*
Dykema, Peter, *Music for School Administrators*
Engel, Carl, *Discords Mingled*
Gastoué, Amédée, *La Liturgie et la musique*
Hadow, William, *English Music*
Howard, John Tasker, *Our American Music*
Jacob, Gordon, *Orchestral Technique*
Kurth, Ernst, *Musikpsychologie*
Schering, Arnold, *Geschichte der Musik in Beispielen*
Tovey, Donald, *Companion to Bach's Art of the Fugue*

I. Musical Compositions:

Barber, Samuel, *Dover Beach* (voice, string quartet)
Bartók, Béla, *Concerto No. 2 for Piano and Orchestra*
Bax, Arnold, *Symphony No. 5*
Benjamin, Arthur, *The Devil Take Her* (opera)
Carpenter, John Alden, *Patterns for Piano and Orchestra*
Casella, Alfredo, *La Donna Serpente* (opera)
Cowell, Henry, *Synchrony* (orchestra)
Dawson, William, *Negro Folk Symphony*
Foerster, Josef, *Concerto for Cello and Orchestra*
Gershwin, George, *Rhapsody No. 2 for Piano and Orchestra*
Gruenberg, Louis, *Jack and the Beanstalk* (opera)
Hába, Alois, *The Mother* (quarter-tone opera)
Hadley, Henry, *Aurora Borealis Overture*
Harris, Roy, *Toccata for Orchestra*
Hindemith, Paul, *Concert Music for Harp, Piano and Brass, Opus 49*
Honegger, Artur, *Les Cris du Monde* (oratorio)
Martinu, Bohuslav, *Concerto for String Quartet and Orchestra*
Moore, Douglas, *Overture on an American Tune*
Pfitzner, Hans, *Das Herz* (opera)
Pizzetti, Ildebrando, *Introduction to Agamemnon* (incidental music)
Prokofiev, Serge, *Concerto No. 4, Opus 53, for Piano, Left Hand*
Rangström, Ture, *Symphony No. 3, "Song under the Stars"*
Ravel, Maurice, *Concerto for Piano and Orchestra*
                Concerto for Piano, Left Hand
Shostakovich, Dmitri, *The Bolt, Opus 27* (ballet)
Sousa, John P., *The Kansas Wildcat March*
Still, William Grant, *Afro-American Symphony*
Stravinsky, Igor, *Concerto for Violin and Orchestra*
Suk, Josef, *Mass in B-flat*
Thomson, Randall, *Symphony No. 2*
Thompson, Virgil, *Symphony No. 2*
Turina, Joaquin, *Rapsodia Sinfónica* (piano, strings)
Varèse, Edgard, *Ionisation* (percussion ensemble)
                Hyperprism (percussion, winds)
Vaughan-Williams, Ralph, *Concerto for Piano and Orchestra*
Vierne, Louis, *Organ Symphony No. 6*
Walton, William, *Belshazzar's Feast* (oratorio)
Wellesz, Egon, *Die Bacchantinnen* (opera)
Wolf-Ferrari, Ermanno, *La Vedova Scaltra* (opera)

1932

World Events:
In the U.S., Franklin D. Roosevelt becomes President number 32; Charles Lindberg's son is kidnapped and slain by kidnappers; the "Veteran's Army," camping out in Washington, is dispersed by troops; the Reconstruction Finance Corporation is established; first Winter Olympics take place in Lake Placid, New York. Internationally, the death of a Japanese Buddhist priest in Shanghai becomes the excuse for the invasion of China by Japanese troops; Antonio Salazar becomes dictator of Portugal for 36 years; British scientist James Chadwick discovers the neutron; Geneva Conference seeks further military reduction.

Cultural Highlights:
Pulitzers: Drama, shared by Ira Gershwin, George S. Kaufman and Morrie Ryskind (*Of Thee I Sing*); Fiction, Pearl S. Buck (*The Good Earth*); Poetry, George Dillon (*The Flowering Stone*). John Galsworthy receives the Nobel Prize for Literature and Maurice Maeterlinck and Edward Bairstow are knighted. The Unit One group of British artists opens its exhibit in London; Samuel Courtauld donates his art collection to the University of London. Deaths in the literary field include American authors Charles Chesnutt and Hart Crane and French author René Bazin; births include American authors Stephen Birmingham and John Updike and British author Antonio Fraser. Births in the art world include American artist Ron B. Kitaj, Columbian artist Fernando Botero and British artist Peter Blake. Other highlights include:

Art: Thomas Hart Benton, *Arts of the West*; Peter Blume, *Light of the World*; Barbara Hepworth, *Reclining Figure*; John Kane, *From My Studio Window*; Pablo Picasso, *Girl before a Mirror*; Georges Rouault, *Christ Mocked by Soldiers*; Ben Shahn, *The Passion of Sacco and Vanzetti*; Grant Wood, *Daughters of the American Revolution*.

Literature: Erskine Caldwell, *Tobacco Road*; T.S. Elliot, *Selected Essays*; William Faulkner, *Light in August*; Edna Ferber, *Dinner at Eight*; J. Hall and C. Nordhoff, *Mutiny on the Bounty*; Ernest Hemingway, *Death in the Afternoon*; Aldous Huxley, *Brave New World*; Eugene O'Neill, *Ah! Wilderness*; John Steinbeck, *The Pastures of Heaven*.

MUSICAL EVENTS

A. Births:

Jan 27 Lothar Klein (Ger-cm)	Jun 30 Martin Mailman (Am-cm)
Feb 4 Ivan Davis (Am-pn)	Jul 13 Per Norgård (Den-cm)
Feb 8 John Williams (Am-cd-cm)	Jul 17 Niccolò Castigliono (It-pn)
Feb 27 Roger Boutry (Fr-pn-cm)	Aug 2 Marvin D. Levy (Am-cm)
Mar 10 Carlos Paita (Arg-cd)	Aug 4 Gabriella Tucci (It-sop)
Mar 21 Joseph Silverstein (Am-vn-cd)	Aug 10 Alexander Goehr (Ger-cm)
Apr 5 Mary Costa (Am-sop)	Aug 28 Cristina Deutekom (Hol-sop)
Apr 21 Henri Lazarof (Bul-cm)	Sep 6 Gilles Tremblay (Can-cm)
Apr 22 Michael Colgrass (Am-cm)	Sep 17 Daniel Majeske (Am-vn)
May 8 Carlo Cossutta (It-ten)	Sep 25 Glenn Gould (Can-pn)
May 13 Yuri Ahronovich (Rus-cd)	Oct 16 Henry Lewis (Am-cd)
May 29 Karl Ridderbusch (Ger-bs)	Oct 17 Gundaris Poné (Rus-cm-cd)
May 30 Pauline Oliveros (Am-cm)	Nov 26 Alan Stout (Am-cm)
Jun 17 Mignon Dunn (Am-mez)	Dec 16 Rodion Shchedrin (Rus-cm)
Jun 21 Judith Raskin (Am-sop)	Dec 25 Bonaldo Giaiotti (It-bs)

B. Deaths:

Feb 22 Johanna Gadski (Ger-sop)	Jun 7 Emil Paur (Cz-cd)
Mar 3 Eugène d'Albert (Scot-pn-cm)	Jun 8 Clementine Schuch-Proska (Hun-sop)
Mar 6 John P. Sousa (Am-cd-cm)	Jun 9 Nathalie Janotha (Pol-pn)
Mar 18 Richard Specht (Aus-cri)	Jul 24 Marie Delna (Fr-alto)
May 3 John Orth (Am-org-cm)	Aug 16 Pietro Floridia (It-pn)

Sep 1 Irene Abendroth (Aus-sop)   Nov 29 Agide Jacchia (It-cd)
Oct 19 Arthur Friedheim (Ger-pn-cm)   Dec 12 Alma Haas (Ger-pn)
Nov 28 Anton von Rooy (Hol-bar)   Dec 19 Clarence Whitehill (Am-bs)

C. Debuts:

Met ---Arthur Anderson (bs), Rose Bampton (alto/sop), Richard Bonelli (bar), Armando Borgioli (bar), Pietro Comara (cd), Doris Doe (mez), Helen Gleason (sop), Margaret Halstead (sop), Ludwig Hoffmann (bs), Göta Ljunberg (sop), Gustaaf de Loor (ten), Francesco Merli (ten), Tito Schipa (ten)

U.S. --E. Power Biggs (N.Y.), Sigfrid Karg-Elert (tour), Carlo Morelli (Chicago), Egon Petri (N.Y.), Izler Solomon (Lansing, MI)

Other -Kurt Baum (Zurich), Bertrand Etcheverry (Paris), Sylvia Fisher (Melbourne), Margherita Grandi (Milan), Marjorie Lawrence (Monte Carlo), José Luccioni (Rouen), Charles Munch (Paris), Zara Nelsova (London), Mercedes Olivera (Montevideo), William Pleeth (Leipzig), Frantisek Rauch (Prague), Aulikki Rautawaara (Helsinki), Martha Rohs (Aachen), Marko Rothmüller (Hamburg), Carla Spletter (Berlin), Erich Witte (Bremerhaven)

D. New Positions:

Conductors: Eugene Mravinsky (Leningrad Opera and Ballet)

Educational: Roy Harris (composition, Juilliard), Dmitri Kabalevsky (composition, Moscow Conservatory), Gian F. Malipiero (composition, Venice Conservatory), Quincy Porter (professor, Vassar College)

Others: André Cluytens (music director, Toulouse Opera), Herbert Elwell (music critic, Cleveland *Plain Dealer*), Armas Järnefelt (director, Helsinki Opera), Leonide Massine (producer, Ballet Russe de Monte Carlo), Jan A. Maklakiewicz (organ, Holy Cross, Warsaw)

E. Prizes and Honors:

Prizes: Dalies Frantz, Huddie Johnson, Inez Lauritano, Foster Miller and Milo Miloradovich (Naumberg), Vittorio Giannini (Prix de Rome), Bohuslav Martinu (Coolidge), Roman Totenburg (Mendelssohn), Alexandre Uninski (Chopin)

Honors: Georges Enescu (Romanian Academy), Ottorino Respighi (Italian Royal Academy)

F. Biographical Highlights:

Elliott Carter receives his M.A. from Harvard, goes to Paris for further study; Aaron Copland visits Mexico; Alexander Glazunov, in poor health, settles in Paris; Gustav Holst, while a visiting professor at Harvard, suffers ulcer attacks; Tikhon Khrennikov transfers to the Moscow Conservatory; Witold Lutoslawski enters the Warsaw Conservatory; Galliano Masini makes his La Scala debut; Alfred Maurer commits suicide; Andrzej Panufnik studies at the Warsaw Conservatory; Carl Parish studies at the American Conservatory in Fontainebleau; Gladys Swarthout marries her second husband, Frank Chapman, Jr.; Karol Szymanowski is forced to resign as director of the Warsaw Conservatory; Alexandre Tansman begins a long tour of the Far East; Fartein Valen spends a year in Majorca; Ralph Vaughan-Williams visits the U.S. and lectures at Bryn Mawr; Heitor Villa-Lobos begins planning music programs for the public schools in Rio de Janeiro.

G. Institutional Openings:

Performing Groups: Alex Cohen String Quartet, The Andrews Sisters Trio, Ballet Russe de Monte Carlo, Baltimore Opera Co., Boyd Neel Orchestra (London), Buffalo PO, Curtis String Quartet (Philadelphia), London PO, MacNaughton String Quartet (London), Maganini Chamber Symphony (N.Y.), Milwaukee Opera Co., North Carolina SO, Providence SO

Festivals: Central City Opera Festival (Colorado), Strasbourg International Music Festival

Educational: École Monteux (Paris), University of Louisville School of Music

Other: Aeolian American Corporation (N.Y., by merger), Australian Broadcasting Commission, Chamber Music Society of America, *Chord and Discord*, Commission des Orgues des Monuments Historiques, Congrès International de Organologie (Strasbourg); L'Oiseau-Lyre, Music Publishers (Paris); Radio City Music Hall (N.Y.), Schlicker Organ Co. (Buffalo), War Memorial Opera House (San Francisco), *Eine Weiner Musikzeitschrift*

H. Musical Literature:
Apel, Willi, *Der Fuge*
Chaliapin, Feodor, *Man and Mask*
Gérold, Théodore, *La Musique au moyen âge*
Idelsohn, Abraham, *Jewish Liturgy and Its Development*
Kwalwasser, Jacob, *Problems in Public School Music*
Pratt, Carroll, *The Meaning of Music*
Sharp/Karpeles, *English Folksongs from the Southern Appalachians*
Shaw, George Bernard, *Music in London, 1890-2904*
Strunk, Oliver, *State and Resources of Musicology in the United States*

I. Musical Compositions:
Bacon, Ernst, *Symphony No. 1*
Badings, Henk, *Symphony No. 2*
Barber, Samuel, *Overture to "A School for Scandal", Opus 5*
Britten, Benjamin, *Sinfonietta* (orchestra)
Chávez, Carlos, *Antigone* (incidental music)
Converse, Frederick, *Prophecy* (soprano, orchestra)
Delius, Frederick, *Prelude to Irmelin* (opera of 1892)
Farwell, Arthur, *Prelude to a Spiritual Drama* (orchestra)
Fortner, Wolfgang, *Concerto for Organ and Strings*
Guarnieri, Camargo, *Pedro Malazarte* (opera)
Hadley, Henry, *Belshazzar* (cantata)
Hindemith, Paul, *Morgen Musik*
            Philharmonic Concerto (orchestra)
Ibert, Jacques, *Paris, Suite Symphonique*
Kabalevsky, Dmitri, *Symphony No. 1, "Proletarians, Unite"*
Martinu, Bohuslav, *Sinfonia for Two Orchestras*
McDonald, Harl, *Symphony No. 1, "The Santa Fe Trail"*
Miaskovsky, Nicolai, *Symphonies Nos. 11, Opus 34, and 12, Opus 35*
Orff, Carl, *Ein Sommernachtstraum* (incidental music)
Poulenc, Francis, *Concerto for Two Pianos and Orchestra*
Prokofiev, Serge, *Concerto No. 5, Opus 55, for Piano and Orchestra*
Rachmaninoff, Serge, *Variations on a Theme of Corelli, Opus 42* (piano)
Ravel, Maurice, *Three Songs of Don Quichotte à Dulcinée*
Respighi, Ottorino, *Maria Egiziaca* (opera)
Riegger, Wallingford, *Dichotomy, Opus 12* (orchestra)
Ruggles, Carl, *Sun Treader* (orchestra)
Schoenberg, Arnold, *Moses and Aaron, Acts 1 and 2* (opera)
Shostakovich, Dmitri, *Lady MacBeth of Minsk, Opus 29* (opera)
Strauss, Richard, *Arabella* (opera)
Toch, Ernst, *Symphony No. 2, Opus 11* (with piano)
Vaughan-Williams, Ralph, *Magnificat* (contralto, women's chorus, orchestra)
Weinberger, Jaromir, *The Outcasts of Poker Flat* (opera)

1933

World Events:
In the U.S., the 20th Amendment, providing for an earlier swearing in of the elected president and the 21st Amendment, repealing prohibition, are ratified; President Roosevelt begins his "Fireside Chats" to the public; a national Bank Holiday is declared; the National Recovery Administration is formed; the Tennessee Valley Authority is established; the Civilian Conservation Corps is formed; future president Calvin Coolidge is born. Internationally, President Hindenburg is forced to appoint Adolf Hitler as Chancellor of Germany; Hitler pulls Germany out of the League of Nations and begins rearmament; Stalin begins new purges in the Russian Communist Party; the London Economic Conference seeks cures for the worldwide depression.

Cultural Highlights:
Pulitzers: Drama, Maxwell Anderson (*Both Your Houses*); Fiction, T.S. Stribling (*The Store*); Poetry, Archibald MacLeish (*Conquistador*). The Nobel Prize for Literature goes to Russian novelist and poet Ivan Bunin who becomes the first Russian to do so. The Federal Arts Project is instigated in Washington and the Canadian Group of Artists has their first exhibit. Births in the literary world include American author John Gardner and Polish writer Jerzy Kosinski; deaths include British novelists John Galsworthy and Anthony Hope, German poets Paul Ernst and Stefan George, Norwegian poet Olaf Bull, Irish novelist George Moore and Americans Ring Lardner and Sara Teasdale. Deaths in the art world include Americans James Kelly and George Luks; born is American artist Dan Flavin. Other highlights include:

Art: Gifford Beal, *Equestrian*; Max Beckmann, *Departure*; Charles Burchfield, *Ice Glare*; Jacob Epstein, *Ecco Homo*; Alberto Giacometti, *Place at 4 A.M.*; Paul Manship, *Prometheus* (Rockefeller Center); Henri Matisse, *The Dance*; Joan Miró, *Composition;* Horace Pippin, *The Buffalo Hunt*; Maurice de Vlaminck, *Les Gerber*.

Literature: Hervey Allen, *Anthony Adverse*; W.S. Auden, *Dance of Death*; Erskine Caldwell, *God's Little Acre*; T.S. Eliot, *The Use of Poetry and the Use of Criticism*; James Hilton, *Lost Horizon*; Thomas Mann, *Joseph and His Brothers*; Mikhail Sholokhov, *Seeds of Tomorrow*; Horace Walpole, *Vanessa*; H.G. Wells, *The Shape of Things to Come*.

MUSICAL EVENTS

A. Births:

Jan 10	Akira Miyoshi (Jp-cm)	Jul 18	R. Murray Schafer (Can-cm)
Feb 3	Yoshimi Takeda (Jp-cd)	Jul 18	Yevgeny Yevtushenko (Rus-cd)
Feb 4	Tochi Ichiyanagi (Jp-cm)	Aug 15	Rita Hunter (Br-sop)
Feb 7	Stuart Burrows (Br-ten)	Aug 18	Bela Rudenko (Rus-sop)
Mar 23	Norman Bailey (Br-bar)	Aug 21	Janet Baker (Br-mez)
Apr 12	Monserrat Caballé (Sp-sop)	Sep 8	Eric Salzman (Am-cm-cri)
Apr 14	Morton Subotnick (Am-cm)	Sep 15	Rafael Frühbeck de Burgos (Sp-cd)
Apr 21	Easley Blackwood (Am-cm)	Sep 22	Leonardo Balada (Sp-cm)
May 21	Maurice André (Fr-tpt)	Oct 2	Guy Chauvet (Fr-ten)
May 22	John Browning (Am-pn)	Oct 2	Michel Plasson (Fr-cd)
May 29	Helmuth Rilling (Ger-cd-org)	Oct 18	Jacques Charpentier (Fr-cm)
Jun 8	Raymond Michalski (Am-bs)	Oct 28	Ronald Lo Presti (Am-cm)
Jun 17	Christian Ferras (Fr-vn)	Nov 7	Danica Mastilovic (Yug-sop)
Jun 26	Claudio Abbado (It-cd)	Nov 12	Jean Papineau-Couture (Can-cm)
Jun 29	John Obetz (Am-org)	Nov 19	Siegfried Behrend (Ger-gui)
Jul 10	Jan De Gaetani (Am-mez)	Nov 23	Krzystof Penderecki (Pol-cm)
Jul 15	Julian Bream (Am-gui)	Dec 6	Henryk Górecki (Pol-cm)

B. Deaths:

Jan 6	Vladimir de Pachmann (Rus-pn)	Feb 8	Oskar Fleisher (Ger-mus)

Feb 12	Henri Duparc (Fr-cm)	Jul 23	Max von Schillings (Ger-cd)
Feb 17	Henri Viotta (Hol-cd-mus)	Aug 18	Katherina Fleischer-Edel (Ger-sop)
Mar 18	Josef Mantuani (Aus-mus)	Sep 29	Jean François Delmas (Fr-bs)
Apr 9	Sigfrid Karg-Elert (Ger-cm)	Oct 16	Maurice Renaud (Fr-bar)
May 22	Emil Oberhoffer (Ger-cd)	Nov 21	Lionel de la Laurencie (Fr-mus)
Jul 6	Robert Kajanus (Fin-cd-cm)	Dec 22	Frances Peralta (Br-sop)

C. Debuts:

Met ---Lillian Clark (sop), Richard Crooks (ten), Virgilio Lazzari (bs), Frida Leider (sop), Emanuel List (bs), Nino Martini (ten), Eide Norena (sop), Maria Olszewska (alto), Irra Petina (mez)

U.S. --Isobel Baillie (Cornell University), Norman Cordon (Chicago), Julius Huen (N.Y.), Caterina Jarboro (Philadelphia), Ray Lev (N.Y.)

Other -Nancy Evans (Liverpool), Lászlo Halász (Vienna), Elisabeth Höngen (Wuppertal), Miliza Korjus (Berlin), Heinz Kraayvanger (Lübeck), Paul Kuen (Konstanz), Erich Kunz (Troppau), Erich Leinsdorf (Vienna), Igor Markevich (Amsterdam), Ruth Michaelis (Halberstadt), Janine Micheau (Paris), Magda Olivero (Turin), Kurt Preger (Prague), Hilde Reggiani (Modena), Phyllis Sellick (Harrogate), Henryk Szeryng (Warsaw), Jennie Tourel (Paris)

D. New Positions:

Conductors: John Barbirolli (Scottish SO), Robert Heger (Berlin Opera), Heinrich Hollreiser (Weisbaden SO), Otto Klemperer (Los Angeles PO), Josef Krips (Vienna Opera), Karl Krueger (Kansas City PO), Paul Paray (Concerts Colonne), Artur Rodzinski (Cleveland Orchestra), Georg Solti (Budapest Opera), Hans Weisbach (Leipzig Radio SO)

Educational: Jan van Gilse (director, Utrecht Conservatory)

Others: Deems Taylor (director, ASCAP)

E. Prizes and Honors:

Prizes: Catherine Carver (Naumberg), Annie Fischer (Liszt-Bartók), Andor Foldes (Liszt), Harry Katzman (Naumberg)

Honors: Walter Alcock (knighted), Gina Bachauer (Vienna Medal of Honor), John Alden Carpenter (honorary doctorate, Wisconsin University)

F. Biographical Highlights:

George Balanchine, invited by Lincoln Kirstein, arrives in the U.S. to open a school of ballet; Béla Bartók refuses to perform in Nazi Germany; John Cage studies with Weiss in New York; Henri Dutilleux enters Paris Conservatory; Edward Elgar submits to a tumor operation; Lukas Foss moves with his family to Paris when the Nazis take over in Germany; George Grosz settles in the U.S.; Otto Klemperer leaves Germany for the U.S. as does Hugo Leichtentritt; Witold Lutoslawski begins composition study with Maliszewski at the Warsaw Conservatory; Artur Rodzinski becomes an American citizen; Curt Sachs, deprived of all music positions in Germany, goes to Paris; Antonio Scotti gives his farewell performance at the Met; Fritz Stiedry, forced out of Germany by the Nazis, goes to Russia; Ernst Toch moves to England; Bruno Walter leaves Germany for Austria; Kurt Weill, together with Maurice Abravanel, flees to Paris; Alexander von Zemlinsky flees Germany to Vienna.

G. Institutional Openings:

Performing Groups: Birmingham (Alabama) SO, Blech String Quartet (London), Chicago Grand Opera Co. II, Dayton PO, Erevan Theater of Opera and Ballet; Kansas City PO, Little Rock SO, Pro Musica Antiqua (Belgium), St. Paul Opera Association (Minnesota), Schola Cantorum Basiliensis, Sons of the Pioneers (Pioneer Trio; Los Angeles),

Festivals: Florence Music Festival (Italy)

Educational: Accademia Musical Napoletana, Banff Centre and School of Fine Arts

(Alberta, Canada), Cali Conservatory and School of the Fine Arts (Colombia), Falsenreitschule (Salzburg), Lithuanian Conservatory of Music, Palestine Conservatory of Music and Dramatic Art

Other: Federal Arts Project, International Liszt Piano Competition (Liszt-Bartók in 1956), National Association for American Composers and Conductors (N.Y.), Palacio Nacional de Bella Artes (Mexico City), Wagner Museum (Tribschen)

H. Musical Literature:
Abraham, Gerald, *This Modern Stuff*
Bauer, Marion, *Twentieth Century Music*
Cowell, Henry, *American Composers on American Music*
Forsyth, Cecil, *Clashpans*
Foss, Hubert, *Music in My Time*
Goetschius, Percy, *The Structure of Music*
Jackson, George, *White Spirituals in the Southern Uplands*
Moser, Hans, *Musiklexikon*
Spaeth, Sigmund, *The Art of Enjoying Music*
Terry, Charles S., *The Revised English Hymnal*

I. Musical Compositions:
Antheil, George, *Archipelago* (orchestra)
Bliss, Arthur, *Concerto for Two Pianos and Orchestra*
Cadman, Charles, *Dark Dancers of the Mardi Gras*
Carpenter, John Alden, *Sea Drift* (symphonic poem)
Casella, Alfredo, *Concerto for Violin, Cello and Piano*
Chávez, Carlos, *Sinfonia di Antigone* (Symphony No. 1)
Coates, Eric, *London Suite* (orchestra)
Copland, Aaron, *A Short Symphony*
Dohnányi, Ernst von, *Symphonic Minutes, Opus 36* (orchestra)
Fernandez, Oscar, *Malazarte* (opera)
Gruenberg, Louis, *Emperor Jones* (opera)
Harris, Roy, *Symphony: 1933*
Honegger, Artur, *Symphonic Movement No.3* (orchestra)
Jongen, Joseph, *Symphonie Concertante* (organ and orchestra)
Kabalevsky, Dmitri, *Symphony No. 2*
Kern, Jerome, *Roberta* (musical)
Khrennikov, Tikhon, *Concerto for Piano and Orchestra*
Kodály, Zoltán, *Dances of Galanta* (orchestra)
Messiaen, Olivier, *L'Ascension* (orchestra)
Miaskovsky, Nicolai, *Symphonies Nos. 13, Opus 36; and 14, Opus 37*
Phillips, Burrill, *Princess and Puppet* (ballet)
Pijper, Willem, *Halewijn* (symphonic drama)
Piston, Walter, *Concerto for Orchestra*
Poulenc, Francis, *Intermezzo* (incidental music)
Read, Gardner, *The Painted Desert, Opus 22* (tone poem)
Riegger, Wallingford, *Evocation* (orchestra)
Rogers, Bernard, *Three Japanese Dances for Orchestra*
Roussel, Albert, *Le Testament de la Tante Caroline* (opera)
Schmidt, Franz, *Symphony No. 4*
Shostakovich, Dmitri, *Twenty-four Preludes for Piano, Opus 34*
            Concerto No. 1, Opus 35, for Piano and Strings (with trumpet)
Suk, Josef, *Epilogue* (orchestra)
Szymanowski, Karol, *Concerto No. 2, Opus 61, for Violin and Orchestra*

1934

World Events:
In the U.S., President Roosevelt unveils his "Good Neighbor Policy" towards Latin America; the Federal Housing Administration is formed to insure loans by private institutions; the Federal Communications Commission (FCC) is created; the Export-Import Bank begins operation; Everglades National Park is created. Internationally Adolf Hitler seizes complete authority and declares himself "Führer" of a New Germany; Austrian Chancellor Dollfuss is assassinated by the Nazis in a take-over attempt; the S.S. Queen Mary is launched in Great Britain; the Dionne Quintuplets in Canada become the first known to have survived; Leopold III becomes King of Belgium.

Cultural Highlights:
Pulitzers: Drama, Sidney Kingsley (*Men in White*); Fiction, Caroline Miller (*Lamb in His Bosom*); Poetry, Robert Hillyer (*Collected Verse*). The Nobel Prize for Literature goes to Italian dramatist and novelist, Luigi Pirandello. British artist and critic Roger E. Fry dies as do the German poet Theodor Däubler and author Theodore Baker, British dramatist Arthur W. Pinero and Russian novelist Andrei Byely; American author Willie Morris is born. Other highlights include:

Art: Charles Burchfield, *November Evening*; Alexander Calder, *A Universe*; Salvador Dali, *The Metamorphosis of Narcissus*; George Grosz, *The Couple*; Edward Hopper, *House on the Pamet River*; José Orozco, *American Civilization*; Ben Shahn, *The W.C.T.U. Parade*; Robert Spencer, *The Angel*; Maurice de Vlaminck, *Letter to Bertha*.

Literature: James Cain, *The Postman Always Rings Twice*; René Char, *Le Marteau sans Maître*; T.S. Eliot, *Elizabethan Essays*; F. Scott Fitzgerald, *Tender is the Night*; James Hilton, *Goodbye Mr. Chips*; James O'Hara, *Appointment in Samarra*; Robert Sherwood, *The Petrified Forest*; Irving Stone, *Lust for Life*; Pamela Travers, *Mary Poppins*.

MUSICAL EVENTS

A. Births:

Jan 16	Richard Wernick (Am-cm)		Jul 5	Tom Krause (Fin-bar)
Feb 11	Jerome Lowenthal (Am-pn)		Jul 12	Van Cliburn (Am-pn)
Feb 18	Aldo Ceccato (It-cd)		Jul 15	Harrison Birtwistle (Br-cm)
Feb 24	Renata Scotto (It-sop)		Jul 18	Roger Reynolds (Am-cm)
Feb 28	Sylvia Geszty (Hun-sop)		Jul 30	André Prévost (Can-cm)
Mar 2	Bernard Rands (Br-cm)		Aug 4	Gabriel Tacchino (Fr-pn)
Mar 4	Mario Davidovsky (Arg-cm)		Sep 9	Peter Maxwell Davies (Br-cm)
Mar 8	Christian Wolff (Am-cm)		Sep 21	Gloria Saarinen (N.Z.-pn)
Apr 11	Henry Holt (Am-cd)		Oct 3	Benjamin Boretz (Am-the-cm)
Apr 18	George Shirley (Am-ten)		Oct 22	Donald McIntyre (N.Z.-bs)
May 6	Jane Berbié (Fr-mez)		Nov 14	Reinhard Gerlach (Ger-mus)
May 23	Robert Moog (Am-inv)		Nov 24	Alfred Schnittke (Rus-cm)
Jun 6	Phillippe Entremont (Fr-pn)		Dec 15	Raina Kabaivanska (Bul-sop)
Jun 11	Augustin Anievas (Am-pn)		Dec 17	Mariella Adam (It-sop)
Jun 19	Donald Bell (Can-bar)		Dec 23	Claudio Scimone (It-cd-mus)
Jun 27	Anna Moffo (Am-sop)			

B. Deaths:

Jan 18	Ottokar Sevcik (Boh-pn)		Jun 15	Louis Bruneau (Fr-cm)
Feb 21	William Kes (Hol-vn-cd)		Jul 8	Alfred V. Heuss (Swi-mus)
Feb 23	Edward Elgar (Br-cm)		Sep 1	Fanny Davies (Br-pn)
Mar 21	Franz Schreker (Aus-cm)		Sep 10	George Henschel (Br-bar-cd)
Mar 30	Henry T. Parker (Am-cri)		Sep 24	Edwin H. Lemare (Br-org)
May 2	Max Friedlaender (Ger-mus)		Sep 28	Oscar von Riesemann (Ger-mus)
May 25	Gustav Holst (Br-cm)		Oct 3	Henri Marteau (Fr-vn)
Jun 10	Frederick Delius (Br-cm)		Nov 12	Henri Verbrugghen (Bel-cd)

Nov 30 Philip Hale (Am-cri)   Dec 30 Peter Cornelius (Den-ten)

C. Debuts:

Met ---Dino Borgioli (ten), Carlo Del Corso (ten), Cyrena van Gordon (alto), Anny Konetzni (sop), Lotte Lehmann (sop), Ettore Panizza (cd), John Charles Thomas (bar)

U.S. --Joseph Bertonnelli, Robert Duncan (N.Y.), Emmanuel Feuermann (Chicago), Eva Hadrabová (tour), Margaret Harshaw (Atlantic City), Maria Hussa (Chicago), Werner Janssen (N.Y.), Theodate Johnson (N.Y.), Franca Somigli, Violetta de Strozzi (N.Y.), Ninon Vallin (tour), Beveridge Webster (N.Y.)

Other -Licia Albanese (Milan), Maud Cunitz (Gotha-Sonderhausen), Cloe Elmo (Cagliari), Gottlob Frick (Coberg), Gabriella Gatti (Rome), Antonio Janigro (Paris), Rafael Kubelik (Prague), Rudolf Neuhaus (Neustrelitz), Sviatoslav Richter (Odessa), Stella Roman (Italy), Hilde Scheppan (Darmstadt), Hjordis Schymberg (Stockholm), Shulamith Shafir (London), Maria Tauberová (Prague)

D. New Positions:

Conductors: Eugen Jochum (Hamburg Opera), Herbert von Karajan (Aachen Opera), Jonel Perlea (Bucharest Opera), Tullio Serafin (Teatro Reale, Rome)

Educational: Flor Alpaerts (director, Antwerp Conservatory), David Oistrakh (violin, Moscow Conservatory)

Others: Joseph Ahrens (organ, St. Hedwig, Berlin), Karl Böhm (director, Dresden Opera), Samuel Chotzinoff (music critic, San Francisco *Chronicle*), Oliver Strunk (director, Music Division, Library of Congress)

E. Prizes and Honors:

Prizes: Eugene Bozza & José Muñoz Molleda (Priz de Rome), Joseph Knitzer & Ruby Mercer (Naumberg)

Honors: Arnold Bax (honorary doctorate, Oxford), Henry W. Davies (Master of the King's Music), Paul Dukas (French Academy), Eugene Goosens (Legion of Honor)

F. Biographical Highlights:

Béla Bartók is relieved of all teaching duties at Budapest Academy of Music; Benjamin Britten, in Vienna, considers studying with Berg; John Cage studies with Schoenberg; Kirsten Flagstad debuts at Bayreuth; Paul Hindemith's music is boycotted by the Nazis; Charles Ives undergoes successful cataract surgery; Herbert von Karajan joins Nazi Party to keep conducting job in Aachen; Aram Khachaturian graduates from Moscow Conservatory; Alexander Kipnis becomes an American citizen; Erich Kleiber resigns from the Berlin Opera; Erich Korngold settles in Hollywood; Colin McPhee begins a two-year stay in Bali; Eugene Ormandy makes his first recording with the Minneapolis SO on RCA; Andrzej Panufnik enters Warsaw Conservatory; Willi Reich receives a doctorate from Vienna University; Arnold Schoenberg arrives in the U.S.; Igor Stravinsky becomes a French citizen; Walter Susskind graduates from the German Academy in Prague; Karol Szymanowski gives up composition; Alexander Tcherepnin begins concert tours in the Far East; Luisa Tetrazzini retires from the stage; Ernst Toch, invited to the U.S., teaches in New York.

G. Institutional Openings:

Performing Groups: Bach Choir (Philadelphia), BBC Northern SO, Benny Goodman Band, Hartford SO, The Ink Spots, New York Cantata Singers, Orchestra National de la Radiodiffusion Française, Toronto SO, Tudor Singers of Toronto, Walden String Quartet (Illinois)

Festivals: Berkshire Music Festival, Glyndebourne Opera Festival and House

Educational: Academia de Musica Euterpe (Costa Rica), Frederick Chopin Institute (Warsaw), Hans Hoffman School of the Fine Arts (N.Y.), Phaleron Conservatory of Music (Athens), School of American Ballet, University of Arizona School of Music

Other: American Musicological Society (Philadelphia), Anthologie Sonore (Paris), *Chor*, Decca Record Co., Göteborg Concert Hall (Sweden), Hammond Organ Co. (Chicago), *Revista Brasileira de Musica*, Wadsworth Atheneum (Hartford, CT)

H. Musical Literature:

Apel, Willi, *Musik aus früher Zeit I, II*
Dumesnil, René, *Histoire illustrée de la musique*
Ferretti, Paolo, *Estètica gregoriana I*
Grabner, Hermann, *Anleitung zur Fugencomposition*
Ippolitov-Ivanov, Mikhail, *50 Years of Russian Music*
Jonas, Oswald, *Das Wesen des musikalischen Kunstwerk*
Koechlin, Charles, *Théorie de la musique*
Niles, John Jacob, *Songs of the Hill People*
Scholes, Percy, *The Puritans and Music in England and New England*
Thomas, O., *Practical Music Criticism*

I. Musical Compositions:

Badings, Henk, *Symphony No. 3*
Bartók, Béla, *String Quartet No. 5*
Bax, Arnold, *Symphony No. 6*
Bloch, Ernst, *Sacred Service* (chorus, soloist, orchestra)
Britten, Benjamin, *Simple Symphony* (strings)
Copland, Aaron, *Statements for Orchestra*
Creston, Paul, *Out of the Cradle Endlessly Rocking* (chamber orchestra)
Dawson, William, *Negro Folk Symphony*
Enescu, Georges, *Symphony No. 4* (unfinished)
Farwell, Arthur, *Rudolph Gott Symphony*
Gershwin, George, *Cuban Overture*
Glazunov, Alexander, *Concerto for Saxophone and Orchestra*
Hanson, Howard, *Merry Mount* (opera)
Hindemith, Paul, *Mathis der Maler* (opera)
Honegger, Artur, *Sémirámis* (ballet)
Ibert, Jacques, *Diane de Poitiers* (opera)
Kabalevsky, Dmitri, *Symphony No. 3, "Requiem for Lenin"*
Khachaturian, Aram, *Symphony No. 1*
Malipiero, Gian F., *Concerto No. 1 for Piano and Orchestra*
McDonald, Harl, *Symphony No. 2, "Rhumba"*
Miaskovsky, Nicolai, *Symphony No. 15, Opus 38*
Phillips, Burrill, *Selections from McGuffey's Reader* (orchestra)
Piston, Walter, *Prelude and Fugue for Orchestra*
Pizzetti, Ildebrando, *Concerto for Cello and Orchestra*
Porter, Quincy, *Symphony No. 1*
Prokofiev, Serge, *Lt. Kijé Suite, Opus 60*
       Concerto, Opus 58, for Cello and Orchestra
Rachmaninoff, Serge, *Rhapsody on a Theme of Paganini* (piano and orchestra)
Rogers, Bernard, *Once Upon a Time* (small orchestra)
Roussel, Albert, *Sinfonietta for String Orchestra, Opus 52*
Rubbra, Edmund, *Sinfonia Concertante for Piano and Orchestra*
Shostakovich, Dmitri, *The Limpid Stream, Opus 30* (ballet)
Stravinsky, Igor, *Divertimento* (orchestra)
Thomson, Virgil, *Four Saints in Three Acts* (opera)
Varèse, Edgard, *Ecuatorial* (therominovox, baritone, brass, percussion, organ)
Vaughan-Williams, Ralph, *Symphony No. 4*
       Suite for Viola and Orchestra
Webern, Anton, *Three Songs, Opus 23*
       Concerto for Nine Instruments, Opus 24

1935

World Events:
In the U.S., the Works Progress Administration (WPA) makes jobs available on public projects; the Social Security Act is passed; the National Labor Relations Board is set up; George Gallup founds the American Institute of Public Opinion; the Committee for Industrial Organization (CIO) is formed; Alcoholics Anonymous is organized. Internationally, Adolf Hitler deprives all German Jews of citizenship and begins universal military training; Benito Mussolini orders the invasion of Ethiopia; the India Act provides for a separate legislature in Delhi; Burma becomes a separate state; the Moscow Subway opens.

Cultural Highlights:
Pulitzers: Drama, Zoe Akins (*The Old Maid*); Fiction, Josephine W. Johnson (*Now in November*); Poetry, Audrey Wurdemann (*Bright Ambush*). The Federal Writer's Project becomes a part of the government WPA program. John Masefield is given the Order of Merit. Births in the field of art include Bulgarian artist Christo, American sculptor Carl Andre and artist Jim Dine; deaths include American artists Charles Demuth and Childe Hassam, French artist Paul Signac and sculptor Gaston Lachaise, German artist Max Liebermann and Russian artist Kasimir Malevich. Deaths in the literary world include American poet Edwin A. Robinson, novelist Anne Sedgwick and French novelist and critic Charles Bourget. Other highlights include:

Art: Salvador Dali, *Giraffe on Fire*; Arthur Dove, *The Goat*; Julio González, *Angel*; William Gropper, *The Senate*; Edward Hopper, *Shakespeare at Dusk*; Vasili Kandinsky, *Movement I*; Henri Matisse, *The Pink Nude*; Pablo Picasso, *Minotauromachy*; Grant Wood, *Death on the Ridge Road*.

Literature: Maxwell Anderson, *Winterset*; Enid Bagnold, *National Velvet*; T.S. Eliot, *Murder in the Cathedral*; James Farrell, *Studs Lonigan*; C.S. Forester, *The African Queen*; Robert Graves, *I, Claudius*; Sinclair Lewis, *It Can't Happen Here*; John Steinbeck, *Tortilla Flat*; Thomas Wolfe, *Of Time and the River*.

MUSICAL EVENTS

A. Births:

Jan 10 Sherrill Milnes (Am-bar)	Jun 21 Diego Masson (Fr-cd)
Jan 12 Margherita Rinaldi (It-sop)	Jun 24 Jerry Riley (Am-cm)
Jan 14 James Fleetwood (Am-ten)	Jul 2 Gilbert Halisch (Am-pn)
Jan 15 Malcolm Frager (Am-pn)	Jul 17 Peter Schickele (Am-hum-cm)
Jan 23 Teresa Zylis-Gara (Pol-sop)	Jul 19 Gerd Albrecht (Ger-cd)
Feb 4 Martti Talvela (Fin-bs)	Jul 27 Richard Noitach (Am-cd)
Feb 27 Mirella Freni (It-sop)	Jul 29 Peter Schreier (Ger-ten)
Mar 16 Teresa Berganza (It-mez)	Aug 2 Mary Thomas (Br-sop)
Mar 30 Gordon Mumma (Am-cm)	Aug 29 Victor Braun (Can-bar)
Mar 30 John Eaton (Am-cm)	Sep 1 Seiji Ozawa (Can-cd)
Apr 9 Aulis Sallinen (Fin-cm)	Oct 2 Peter Frankl (Hun-pn)
Apr 10 Jorge Mester (Am-cd)	Oct 5 Arlene Saunders (Am-sop)
Apr 22 Fiorenza Cossotto (It-alto)	Oct 13 Luciano Pavarotti (It-ten)
May 28 Richard Van Allen (Br-bs)	Nov 23 William Lewis (Am-ten)
Jun 5 Peter Schat (Hol-cm)	Dec 26 Viorica Cortez (Rom-sop)
Jun 20 Norman Paige (Am-ten)	Dalia Atlas (Is-cd)

B. Deaths:

Jan 11 Marcella Sembrich (Pol-sop)	Apr 5 Emil Elynarski (Pol-cd-vn)
Jan 15 Lucien Fugère (Fr-bar)	Apr 20 Rudolf Schwartz (Ger-mus)
Jan 22 Heinrich Schenker (Ger-the)	Apr 28 Alexander McKenzie (Br-cm)
Jan 28 Mikhail Ippolitov-Ivanov (Rus-cm)	May 10 Herbert Witherspoon (Am-bs)
	May 17 Paul Dukas (Fr-cm)

May 19	Charles M. Loeffler (Am-cm)	Nov 14	Paul Bergmans (Bel-mus)
May 29	Josef Suk (Boh-vn-cm)	Nov 28	Erich von Hornbostel (Aus-mus)
Sep 23	Vincenzo Bellini (It-cm)	Dec 1	Richard Mayr (Aus-bs)
Oct 4	Marie Gutheil-Schoder	Dec 4	Johan Halvorsen (Nor-cm)
	(Ger-mez)	Dec 9	Nina (Hagerup) Grieg (Nor-sop)
Oct 6	Frederick H. Cowen	Dec 24	Alban Berg (Aus-cm)
	(Br-pn-cm)		

C. Debuts:

Met ---Chase Baromeo (bs), Hilde Burke (sop), Susanne Fisher (sop), Kirsten Flagstad (sop), Mario Gili (bs), Eduard Habich (bar), Julius Huehn (bar), Helen Jepson (sop), Charles Kullman (ten), Marjorie Lawrence (sop), Myrtle Leonard (mez), Kathryn Meisle (mez), Carlo Morelli (bar), Helen Olheim (mez), Hubert Raidich (bs), Charlotte Symons (sop), Thelma Votipka (sop), Gertrud Wettergren (alto)

U.S. --Webster Aitken (N.Y.), Winifred Cecil (N.Y.), Raya Garbousova (N.Y.), Beata Malkin, Bidú Sayao (N.Y.), Joseph Schuster (N.Y.), Isaac Stern (San Francisco), Roman Totenberg (N.Y.), Rosalyn Tureck (N.Y.)

Other -Gina Bachauer (Athens), Jorge Bolet (Amsterdam), Giorgio Ciampi (Milan), Tito Gobbi (Gubbio), Joseph Greindl (Munich), Rudolf Kempe (Leipzig), Otakar Kraus (Brno), Alicia de Larrocha (Madrid), Giulio Neri (Rome), Edith Picht-Axenfeld (Berlin), Ester Réthy (Budapest), Antonio Salvarezza (Italy), Giulietta Simionato (Florence), Italo Tajo (Turin), Horst Taubmann (Chemnitz)

D. New Positions:

Conductors: Wilhelm Furtwängler (Berlin PO), Ernest Schelling (Baltimore SO), Hans Schmidt-Isserstedt (Hamburg Opera), Václav Talich (Prague Opera)

Educational: Nadia Boulanger (École Normale, Paris), Paul Hindemith (advisor, Turkish School Music), Daniel Lesur (counterpoint, Schola Cantorum, Paris), Roger Sessions (professor, Princeton)

Others: Rudolf Bing (manager, Glyndebourne Opera), Edward Johnson (manager, Met), Clemens Krauss (director, Berlin Opera), Howard Taubman (music editor, New York *Times*)

E. Prizes and Honors:

Prizes: Benjamin de Loache (Naumberg), Yoritsune Matsudaira (Weingartner), Marshall Moss (Naumberg), Ginette Neveu (Wieniawski), Harvey Shapiro, Aniceta Shea, Judith Sidorsky, and Florence Vickland (Naumberg

Honors: Béla Bartók (Hungarian Academy), Ernest C. MacMillan & Donald Tovey (knighted), Fartein Valen (Norwegian Government Grant)

F. Biographical Highlights:

Milton Babbitt receives his B.A. degree from New York University; Samuel Barber goes to Europe again on a Prix de Rome; Benjamin Britten meets W.H. Auden while working on film music; Elliott Carter returns to the U.S.; Leon Fleisher, age 6, first appears in public recital; Amelita Galli-Curchi has operation to remove a throat tumor; Paul Hindemith given a "leave of absence" from his Hochschule position; Maria Jeritza marries her second husband, Winfield Sheehan; Erich Kleiber moves his family to Buenos Aires; Raphael Kubelik visits the U.S. as an accompanist to his father; Franz Lehár founds his own publishing firm; Gian Carlo Menotti goes to the U.S.; William Schuman receives his B.S. degree from Columbia; Rudolf Serkin marries Irene Busch; Igor Stravinsky makes a second tour of the U.S.; Ernst Toch moves to the U.S.; Vladimir Ussachevsky graduates from Pomona College; Kurt Weill goes to New York to oversee the performance of his stage works.

G. Institutional Openings:

Performing Groups: BBC Scottish SO, Belgian Radio Orchestra, Benny Goodman Trio,

Bergen Kammermusik-forening, Bombay SO, Chattanooga SO, Cleveland Women's Orchestra, English Consort of Viols (London), Hungarian String Quartet (Budapest), Knoxville SO, New York Women's SO, Paris SO, Soirées de Bruxelles, Stalingrad PO

Educational: Academy of Vocal Arts (Philadelphia)

Other: *The American Music Lover,* Archive of Oriental Music (Jerusalem), Composer's Forum (N.Y.), Composer's Press (N.Y.), Federal Music Project (WPA), Lüdenscheider Musikvereiningung, Metropolitan Opera Guild, National Association of Performing Artists, National Federation of Music Societies (England), Société des Concerts Symphoniques de Montreal, Southern Music Co. (San Antonio)

H. Musical Literature:

Abraham, Gerald, *Studies in Russian Music*
Ameln, Konrad, *Handbuch der deutschen Evangelischen Kirchenmusik*
Ferguson, Donald, *A History of Musical Thought*
Miller, Dayton, *Anecdotal History of the Science of Sound*
Morris, R., *The Structure of Music*
Prunières, Henry, *Nouvelle histoire de la musique I*
Stravinsky, Igor, *Chroniques de ma vie*
Tovey, Donald, *Essays in Musical Analysis I*

I. Musical Compositions:

Badings, Henk, *Violin Concerto No. 2*
Berg, Alban, *Violin Concerto*
    Lulu (unfinished opera)
Casella, Alfredo, *Cello Concerto*
Chávez, Carlos, *Obertura Republicana* (orchestra)
Converse, Frederick, *American Sketches* (symphonic suite)
Cowell, Henry, *Sinister Resonance* (piano)
Gershwin, George, *Porgy and Bess* (folk opera)
Harris, Roy, *Overture, When Johnny Comes Marching Home*
Hindemith, Paul, *Der Schwanendreher* (violin, orchestra)
    Concerto for Orchestra, Opus 38
Honegger, Artur, *Joan of Arc at the Stake* (stage oratorio)
Ibert, Jacques, *Concertino de Camera for Saxophone and Orchestra*
Malotte, Albert Hay, *The Lord's Prayer* (song)
Martinu, Bohuslav, *Overture to a Comedy*
    Piano Concerto No. 2
Mascagni, Pietro, *Nerone* (opera)
McDonald, Harl, *Symphony No. 3, "Tragic Cycle"*
Messiaen, Olivier, *La Nativité du Seigneur* (organ)
Moore, Douglas, *White Wings* (chamber orchestra)
Poulenc, Francis, *Suite Française* (orchestra)
Prokofiev, Serge, *Romeo and Juliet, Opus 64* (ballet)
    Concerto No. 2 for Violin and Orchestra, Opus 63
Respighi, Ottorino, *Lucrezia* (opera)
Schmidt, Franz, *Piano Concerto No. 2 for the Left Hand*
Sessions, Roger, *Violin Concerto*
Strauss, Richard, *Die Schweigsame Frau* (opera)
Stravinsky, Igor, *Concerto for Two Pianos and Orchestra*
Walton, William, *Symphony No. 1*
Webern, Anton, *Three Songs, Opus 25*
    Das Augenlicht, Opus 26 (chorus, orchestra)

1936

World Events:

In the U.S., Franklin D. Roosevelt is re-elected President; the Ford Foundation is founded to support education, culture and welfare; Boulder (Hoover) Dam is completed; mandatory 40-hour week is enforced for all companies with government contracts; the Merchant Marine Act is passed. Internationally, the Spanish Civil War begins and Francisco Franco takes command of the Falangists; Hitler reoccupies the Rhineland while Europe watches; King George V of England dies--George VI becomes King when Edward VIII abdicates to marry American divorcee, Wally Simpson; the Rome-Berlin Axis Agreement is signed; King Farouk comes to the throne in Egypt.

Cultural Highlights:

Pulitzers: Drama, Robert Sherwood (*Idiot's Delight*); Fiction, Harold L. Davis (*Honey in the Horn*); Poetry, Robert P. Coffin (*Strange Holiness*). Eugene O'Neill is the recipient of the Nobel Prize for Literature. the Society of American Abstract Art is founded and the magazines, *Life* and *New Directions in Literature*, begin publication. In the field of art, births include German artist Horst Antes, American artist Frank Stella, German artist Hans Haacke and Greek sculptor Lucas Samaras; deaths include American artist John Hamilton, French artist Auguste Delacroix and Canadian artist Homer Watson. In the literary field, deaths include Italian novelist Grazia Deledda and poet Luigi Pirandello, Spanish poet Frederico García Lorca, Russian author Maxim Gorky, British poet A.E. Housman and author Rudyard Kipling, French poets Gustave Kahn and Henri de Regnier; American Larry MacMurtry is born. Other highlights include:

Art: Pierre Bonnard, *The Garden*; Salvador Dali, *Autumn Cannibalism*; William Gropper, *For the Record*; Thomas Jones, *The American Farm*; Piet Mondrian, *Composition in White, Black and Red*; Henry Moore, *Two Forms*; Maurice de Vlaminck, *The Pot of Coffee*; Grant Wood, *Spring Turning*; Frank Lloyd Wright, *Falling Water House*.

Literature: Daphne du Maurier, *Jamaica Inn*; T.S. Eliot, *Essays Ancient and Modern*; William Faulkner, *Absalom, Absalom!*; Robert Frost, *A Further Range*; Aldous Huxley, *Eyeless in Gaza*; George Kaufman and Moss Hart, *You Can't Take It with You*; Margaret Mitchell, *Gone with the Wind*; Carl Sandburg, *The People, Yes*.

MUSICAL EVENTS

A. Births:

Jan 1	Eve Queler (Am-cd)	Jun 15	Edward Tarr (Am-tp-mus)
Jan 13	Renato Bruson (It-bar)	Jun 24	Rod McWherter (Am-ten)
Jan 14	Thomas Bricetti (Am-cd-cm)	Jul 9	David Zinman (Am-ten)
Jan 19	Elliot Schwartz (Am-cm)	Jul 21	Ursula Schröder-Feinen (Ger-sop)
Jan 28	Robert Suderberg (Am-cm)	Aug 17	Nicola Ghiuselev (Bul-bs)
Feb 2	Martina Arroyo (Am-sop)	Aug 29	Gilbert Amy (Fr-cm-cd)
Feb 16	Eliahu Inbal (Is-cd)	Aug 30	Peter van der Bilt (Hol-bar)
Mar 3	G. van der Horst (Hol-org)	Sep 13	Werner Hollweg (Ger-ten)
Mar 4	Aribert Reimann (Ger-cm)	Sep 16	Piero Gamba (It-cd)
Mar 29	Richard Russell Bennett (Am-cm)	Oct 1	Edward Villella (Am-bal)
		Oct 3	Steve Reich (Am-cm)
Apr 8	Lawrence Smith (Am-cd)	Oct 7	Charles Dutoit (Swe-cd)
Apr 15	Héctor Quintanar (Mex-cm-cd)	Nov 6	David Ward-Steinman (Am-cm)
Apr 19	Bernhard Klee (Ger-cd)	Nov 7	Gwyneth Jones (Br-sop)
Apr 22	Pierre Hétu (Can-cd)	Nov 10	Peter Marx (-cd)
Apr 29	Zubin Mehta (Ind-cd)	Nov 21	James de Preist (Am-cd)
May 2	Michael Rabin (Am-vn)	Dec 5	Jeanette Scovotti (Am-sop)
May 5	Anna Alberghetti (It-sop)	Dec 31	Noel Tyl (Am-bar)
May 7	Cornelius Cardew (Br-cm)		Zdenek Macal (Cz-cd)

B. Deaths:

Jan 23 Clara Butt (Br-alto)

Feb 26 Antonio Scotti (It-bar)

Mar 6 Rubin Goldmark (Am-cm)

Mar 6 Josef Stransky (Boh-cm)

Mar 21 Alexander Glazunov (Rus-cm)

Mar 30 J.A. Fuller-Maitland (Br-mus)

Apr 18 Ottorino Respighi (It-cm)

May 24 Claudia Muzio (It-sop)

Jul 20 Arthur Whiting (Am-pn-cm)

Aug 4 Henry Schoenefeld (Am-cm-pn)

Sep 14 Ossip Gabrilowitsch (Rus-pn)

Oct 12 Félia Litvinne (Rus-sop)

Nov 11 Edward German (Br-cm)

Nov 17 Ernestine Schumann-Heink (Ger-alto)

Dec 25 Carl Stumpf (Ger-acous)

Dec 28 Ernest Grosjean (Fr-org-cm)

C. Debuts:

Met ---Josephine Antoine (sop), Joseph Bentonelli (ten), Alois Blum (bar), Natalie Bodanskaya (sop), Vina Bovy (sop), Lucille Browning (mez), Arthur Carron (ten), Bruna Castagna (mez), Maurice Abravanel (cd), Muriel Dickson (sop), Wilfred Engelman (bar), Norman Fisher (bs), Dusolina Giannini (sop), John Gurney (bs), Emily Hardy (sop), Irene Jessner (sop), Anna Kaskas (mez), René Maison (ten), Nicholas Massue (ten), Lodovico Oliviero (ten), Jarna Paull (mez), Jeanne Pengelly (sop), George Rasely (ten), Sydney Rayner (ten), Joseph Royer (bar), Maxine Stellman (sop), Rosa Tentoni (sop), Kerstin Thorborg (mez)

U.S. --Gitta Alpar (N.Y.), John Barbirolli (N.Y.), Charles Bruck, Ania Dorfmann (N.Y.), Deszö Ernster (tour), Hertha Glaz (tour), Gary Graffman (Philadelphia), Rudolf Serkin (N.Y.), Jenny Tourel (Chicago)

Other -Anton Dermota (Vienna), Karl Doench (Goerlitz), Boris Gmirya (Kharkov), Hans Hopf (Munich), Max Lichtegg (Bern), Elena Nikolaidi (Vienna), Alois Pernerstorfer (Graz), Ruth Railton (Liverpool), Georg Solti (Budapest), Walter Susskind (Prague), Giuseppe Taddei (Rome), Günther Treptow (Berlin), Hermann Uhde (Bremen), Giuseppe Valdengo (Parma), Ljuba Welitsch (Sofia)

D. New Positions:

Conductors: Franco Autori (Buffalo SO), Issay Dobrowen (Budapest Opera), José Iturbi (Rochester SO), Rafael Kubelik (Czech PO), Pierre Monteux (San Francisco SO), Eugene Ormandy (co-director, Philadelphia Orchestra), Bruno Walter (Vienna Opera), Arthur Zack (New Orleans PO)

Educational: Ildebrando Pizzetti (composition, Accademia de S. Cecilia, Rome), Arnold Schoenberg (theory, UCLA)

Others: Deems Taylor (music consultant, CBS), Oscar Thompson (editor, *Musical America*)

E. Prizes and Honors:

Prizes: Jehan Alain (Prix des Amis de l'Orgue), Frederick Buldrini (Naumberg), Kent Kennan (Prix de Rome), Charles Koechlin (Cressent)

F. Biographical Highlights:

Lucretia Bori and Florence Easton give their farewell Met performances; Henry Cowell, taken into court on a morals charge is sent to San Quentin; Lyonel Feininger returns to the U.S.; Roy Harris marries Beula Duffey (Johana); Elvira de Hidalgo retires from the stage; Felix Labunski leaves Poland for the U.S.; Igor Markevitch marries Nijinsky's sister, Kira; Pierre Monteux decides to return to the U.S.; Andrzej Panufnik graduates with distinction from Warsaw Conservatory; Paul Pisk emigrates to the U.S.; Rosa Ponselle marries Charles A. Jackson; Paul Robeson makes a concert tour of Russia; Joseph Schillinger becomes an American citizen; Georg Solti begins working with Toscanini; William Steinberg emigrates to Israel; Kerstin Thorborg makes her Covent Garden debut; Ernst Toch settles in California, begins teaching at USC; Vladimir Ussachevsky receives his M.A. from Eastman.

G. Institutional Openings:

Performing Groups: Adelaide Singers (Australia), BBC Welsh SO, Budapest Radio

Orchestra, Israel (Palestine) SO, National SO of Colombia; Negro Chorus of Los Angeles; New Orleans PO, USSR State SO, Woody Herman Band

Festivals: Les Festivals de Montreal, Ravinia Festival (Chicago)

Educational: Brazilian Conservatory of Music (Rio de Janeiro), Brevard Music Center (North Carolina), Music Department of Manchester University

Other: American Guild of Musical Artists, Ford Foundation, Metropolitan Opera Auditions, Neil A. Kjos Music Co.; New Friends of Music, Inc. (N.Y.); N.P. Mander, Ltd., Organ Builders (London); Society for Research in Asiatic Music (Tokyo), Society of the Classic Guitar (N.Y.), Teatro Comunale dell'Opera (Genoa), Whittall Foundation (Library of Congress)

H. Musical Literature:
Abraham/Calvocoressi, *Masters of Russian Music*
Einstein, Alfred, *A Short History of Music*
Gérold, Théodore, *Histoire de la musique des origines à la fin du XIVe siècle*
Kolodin, Irving, *The Metropolitan Opera, 1883-1936*
Molnár, Antal, *Music Today*
Niles, John Jacob, *More Songs of the Hill People*
Rosenfeld, Paul, *Discoveries of a Music Critic*
Schaeffner, André, *Origines des instruments de musique*

I. Musical Compositions:
Barber, Samuel, *Symphony No. 2, Opus 9*
Bartók, Béla, *Music for Strings, Percussion and Celesta*
Blitzstein, Marc, *The Cradle Will Rock* (opera)
Bloch, Ernst, *The Voice in the Wilderness* (orchestra)
Chávez, Carlos, *Sinfonia India*
Converse, Frederick, *Symphony No. 3*
Copland, Aaron, *El Salón México* (orchestra)
Diamond, David, *Concerto No. 1 for Violin and Orchestra*
Harris, Roy, *Symphony No. 2*
Hovhaness, Alan, *Prelude and Quadruple Fugue* (orchestrated 1955)
Kabalevsky, Dmitri, *Concerto No. 2 for Piano and Orchestra*
Khachaturian, Aram, *Concerto for Piano and Orchestra*
Kodály, Zoltán, *Te Deum* (soloists, chorus, orchestra)
Martinon, Jean, *Symphony No. 1*
Mason, Daniel G., *Symphony No. 3, "A Lincoln Symphony"*
Messiaen, Olivier, *Poémes pour mi* (soprano, orchestra)
Milhaud, Darius, *Suite Provençale* (orchestra)
Orff, Carl, *Carmina Burana* (secular cantata)
Prokofiev, Serge, *Peter and the Wolf, Opus 67* (narrator and orchestra)
Rachmaninoff, Serge, *Symphony No. 3*
Rangström, Ture, *Symphony No. 4, "Invocations"*
Read, Gardner, *Symphony No. 1, Opus 30*
Rogers, Bernard, *Symphony No. 3*
Rubbra, Edmund, *Symphony No. 1*
Schoenberg, Arnold, *Concerto, Opus 36, for Violin and Orchestra*
    String Quartet No. 4, Opus 37
Schuman, William, *Symphony No. 1* (eighteen instruments)
Shostakovich, Dmitri, *Symphony No. 4, Opus 43*
Skalkottas, Nikos, *36 Greek Dances for Orchestra* (completed)
Stravinsky, Igor, *The Card Game* (ballet)
Thompson, Randall, *The Peaceable Kingdom* (cantata)
Varèse, Edgard, *Density 21.5* (solo flute)
Vaughan-Williams, Ralph, *Dona Nobis Pacem* (soprano, baritone, chorus, orchestra)
    Riders to the Sea (opera)
Webern, Anton, *Variations for Piano, Opus 27*

1937

World Events:
> In the U.S. the Neutrality Act forbids dealing in munitions and permits sale of food supplies for cash only; San Francisco's Golden Gate Bridge officially opens; Amelia Earhart Putnam disappears on a flight across the Pacific; DuPont Laboratories synthesizes nylon; Polaroid Corporation is founded by Edwin H. Land. Internationally the Japanese take Peking and Shanghai, sinks the U.S. gunboat, *Panay*, and attacks both U.S. and British ships; Mussolini takes Italy out of the League of Nations; Neville Chamberlain becomes Prime Minister of Great Britain; the dirigible *Hindenburg* blows up while mooring at Lakehurst, New Jersey.

Cultural Highlights:
> Pulitzers: Drama, Moss Hart and George S. Kaufman (*You Can't Take It with You*); Fiction, Margaret Mitchell (*Gone With the Wind*); Poetry, Robert Frost (*A Further Range*). Roger Martin du Gard receives the Nobel Prize for Literature. László Moholy-Nagy opens the New Bauhaus in Chicago; the Euston Road "School of Drawing and Painting" seeks a return to naturalism. Deaths in the literary world include American authors Paul Bekker, Donald R. Marquis and Edith Wharton, British novelist James Barrie and dramatist John Drinkwater; American author Joseph Wambaugh is born. Deaths in the art world include American artists Bruce Crane and Henry O. Tanner and sculptor Frederick Macmonnies and British sculptor Allen Jones; British artist David Hockney is born. Other highlights include:

> Art: Max Beckmann, *Triptych, Temptation*; Peter Blume, *The Eternal City*; Georges Braque, *Woman with a Mandolin*; Salvador Dali, *Inventions of the Monsters*; Edward Hopper, *Cape Cod Evening*; Jack Levine, *Feast of Pure Reason*; Henri Matisse, *Lady in Blue*; Pablo Picasso, *Guernica*; Georges Rouault, *The Old King*.

> Literature: Louis Bromfield, *The Rains Came*; Archibald Cronin, *The Citadel*; Ernest Hemingway, *To Have and Have Not*; John P. Marquand, *The Late George Apley*; Erich Remarque, *Three Comrades*; John Steinbeck, *The Red Pony* and *Of Mice and Men*; J.R.R. Tolkien, *The Hobbit*; Lawrence Watkin, *On Borrowed Time*.

MUSICAL EVENTS

A. Births:

Jan 4	Grace Bumbry (Am-sop)	Jul 7	Elena Obraztsova (Rus-sop)
Jan 8	Robert L. Moran (Am-cm)	Aug 4	David Bedford (Br-cm)
Jan 27	John Ogdon (Br-pn)	Aug 13	Felicia Weathers (Am-sop)
Jan 29	Horst Adams (Ger-mus)	aug 25	Nancy Tatum (Am-sop)
Jan 31	Philip Glass (Am-cm)	Sep 1	Paul M. Palombo (Am-cm)
Feb 6	Wieslaw Ochman (Pol-ten)	Sep 22	Francesco Petracchi (It-bs)
feb 9	Hildegard Behrens (Ger-sop)	Oct 18	Catarina Ligendza (Swe-sop)
Mar 16	David Del Tredici (Am-cm)	Oct 29	Michael Ponti (Am-pn)
Mar 24	Benjamin Luxon (Br-bar)	Nov 2	Gerard Béhaque (Fr-mus)
May 1	Bo Nilsson (Swe-cm)	Nov 7	Patricia Brooks (Am-sop)
May 13	Judith Somogi (Am-cd)	Nov 20	René Kollo (Ger-ten)
May 26	Yehuda Yannay (Rom-cm)	Nov 20	Ruth Laredo (Am-pn)
May 28	Wilfried Koch (Ger-cd)	Nov 22	Theophil Antonicek (Aus-mus)
Jun 3	M. Valerie Masterson (Br-sop)	Dec 26	Jiri Kout (Cz-cd)
Jun 7	Neeme Järvi (Est-cd)	Dec 26	Teresa Kubiak (Pol-sop)
Jun 20	Stafford Dean (Br-bs)		Loris Tjeknavorian (Iran-cd)
Jul 6	Vladimir Ashkenazy (Rus-pn-cd)		

B. Deaths:

Jan 10	Clarence Eddy (Am-org)	Mar 12	Jenö Hubay (Hun-vn-cm)
Jan 22	Walter W. Cobbett (Br-cd)	Mar 12	Charles Widor (Fr-org-cm)

Mar 29	Karol Szymanowski (Pol-cm)	Jun 5	William Henderson (Am-cri)
Apr 8	Arthur Foote (Am-cm)	Jul 11	George Gershwin (Am-pop)
Apr 9	William H. Hadow (Br-cm)	Jul 17	Gabriel Pierné (Fr-cm)
Apr 18	R.R. Terry (Br-mus)	Jul 24	Julie Rivé-King (Am-pn)
Apr 27	Gustave Schützendorf	Jul 25	Georges Servières (Fr-mus)
	(Ger-bar)	Aug 23	Albert Roussel (Fr-cm)
May 6	Sam Franko (Am-cd-vn)	Sep 6	Henry Hadley (Am-cm)
Jun 2	louis Vierne (Fr-cm-org)	Dec 28	Maurice Ravel (Fr-cm)

C. Debuts:

Met ---Stella Andreva (sop), John Brownlee (bar), Gina Cigna (sop), Donald Dickson (bar), Marita Farell (sop), Daniel Harris (bar), Karl Hartmann (ten), Mária Mátyás (mez), Ruby Mercer (sop), Zinka Milanov (sop), Nicola Moscona (bs), Bidú Sayao (sop), Carlo Tagliabue (bar), Thomas L. Thomas (bar), Jennie Tourel (sop), Helen Traubel (sop), Adolf Vogel (bs), Robert Weede (bar)

U.S. --Jussi Björling (Chicago), Jorge Bolet (Philadelphia), Antál Dorati (tour), Ivan Galamian (Philadelphia), Paul Hindemith (D.C.), Byron Janis (N.Y.), Julius Katchen (N.Y.), Marta Krásová (tour), José Luccioni (Chicago), Luboshutz & Nemenoff (N.Y.), Galliano Masini (Chicago), Dmitri Mitropoulos (Providence, RI), Rosa Pauly (N.Y.), Erna Sack (tour)

Other -Marie-Claire Alain (Ste. Germaine-en-Laye), Scipio Colombo (Italy), Fernando Corena (Italy), Otto Edelman (Gera), Maria Gyurkovics (Budapest), Ida Haendel (London), Richard Holm (Kiel), Franz Klarwein (Berlin), Georgina von Milinkovic (Zurich), Alda Noni (Ljubljana), Fritz Ollendorff (Basel), Mariana Radev (Trieste), Marianne Schech (Coblenz), Richard Schock (Braunschweig), Frans Vroons (Paris)

D. New Positions:

Conductors: John Barbirolli (New York PO), Hans Knappertsbusch (Vienna Opera and PO), Clemens Krauss (Munich Opera), Lars-Erik Larsson (Swedish Radio SO), Dmitri Mitropoulos (Minneapolis SO), Willem van Otterloo (Utrecht SO), Fabien Sevitzky (Indianapolis SO), Arturo Toscanini (NBC SO), Robert Whitney (Louisville Orchestra)

Educational: Hendrik Andriessen (director, Utrecht Conservatory), Felix Borowski (musicology, Northwestern University), Karl Höller (composition, Frankfurt Conservatory), Jacques Ibert (director, French Academy, Rome), Magda Tagliaferro (piano, Paris Conservatory)

E. Prizes and Honors:

Prizes: Maurice Bialkin (Naumberg),Jorge Bolet (Naumberg & Hofmann), Charles Koechlin (Halphan), Ida Krehm (Naumberg), David Oistrakh (Brussels), Pauline Pierce (Naumberg)

Honors: Arnold Bax, Adrian Boult & Percy Buck (knighted), Frederick Converse (American Academy), Wilfrid Pelletier (Legion of Honor)

F. Biographical Highlights:

Rose Bampton and Edith Coates make their Covent Garden debuts; Béla Bartók forbids the performance of any of his works in any Axis country; John Cage moves to Seattle and begins work with the Bird dance class; Hugo Distler moves to Stuttgart; Georges Enescu makes his second visit to the U.S.; Lukas Foss moves to the U.S. with his family; Charles Koechlin makes his last lecture visit of the U.S.; Raphael Kubelik, substituting for an ailing Talich, takes the Czech PO on its English tour; Afro Poll makes his La Scala debut; William Primrose becomes first violist of the NBC SO under Toscanini; Sviatoslav Richter enters the Moscow Conservatory; Curt Sachs emigrates to the U.S.; Paul Schöffler makes his Vienna Opera debut; William Schuman receives his M.A. degree from Columbia; Risë Stevens sings her first Carmen in Prague.

G. Institutional Openings:

Performing Groups: Dayton Ballet Company, Daytona Philharmonic Youth Orchestra,

Lisbon PO, Louisville SO, NBC SO, Schneiderhan String Quartet (Vienna), Swedish Radio SO, Tokyo SO

Festivals: Saratoga Springs Festival (N.Y.)

Educational: Belgrade Academy of Music, National Bandmasters Fraternity (Arlington, TX), Phi Beta Mu

Other: American Composer's Alliance (N.Y.), Concours Musical Reine Elisabeth (Belgium), *Der Dreiklang* (Vienna), Electric Piano, Japanese Society for Contemporary Music, Teatro delle Novita (Bergamo)

H. Musical Literature:

Alda, Frances, *Men, Women and Tenors*
Bairstow, Edward, *Counterpoint and Harmony*
Chávez, Carlos, *Toward a New Music*
Galpin, Francis, *Music of the Sumerians, Babylonians and Assyrians*
Hindemith, Paul, *Craft of Musical Composition I*
Krenek, Ernst, *Über neue Musik*
Sachs, Curt, *World History of Dance*
Slominsky, Nicholas, *Music Since 1900*

I. Musical Compositions:

Andriessen, Hendrik, *Symphony No. 2*
Antheil, George, *Symphony No. 2, "American"*
Bacon, Ernst, *Symphony No. 2*
Badings, Henk, *Symphonic Variations* (orchestra)
Barber, Samuel, *Essay No. 1 for Orchestra, Opus 12*
Bartók, Béla, *Sonata for Two Pianos and Percussion* (also in Concerto form)
Bergsma, William, *Paul Bunyan Suite* (orchestra)
Bloch, Ernst, *Evocations* (symphonic suite)
Britten, Benjamin, *Variations on a Theme of Frank Bridge* (strings)
Cadman, Charles, *American Folksong Suite* (orchestra)
Carpenter, John Alden, *Concerto for Violin and Orchestra*
Casella, Alfredo, *Concerto for Orchestra*
Copland, Aaron, *The Second Hurricane* (opera)
Damrosch, Walter, *The Man Without a County* (opera)
Egge, Klaus, *Concerto No. 1, Opus 9, for Piano and Orchestra*
Gillis, Don, *The Panhandle Suite* (orchestra)
Gruenberg, Louis, *Green Mansions* (radio opera)
Hindemith, Paul, *Nobilissima Visione* (ballet)
Kabalevsky, Dmitri, *Master of Clamency* (opera)
McDonald, Harl, *Symphony No. 4*
Menotti, Gian Carlo, *Amelia Goes to the Ball* (opera)
Milhaud, Darius, *Scaramouche Suite* (two pianos)
Moore, Douglas, *The Headless Horsemen* (opera)
Piston, Walter, *Symphony No. 1*
Poulenc, Francis, *Tel Jour Telle Nuit* (song cycle after Eluard)
Rubbra, Edmund, *Symphony No. 2, Opus 45*
Schuman, William, *Symphony No. 2*
Shostakovich Dmitri, *Symphony No. 5, Opus 47*
Strauss, Richard, *Daphne* (opera)
Thomson, Virgil, *The River* (film music)
          Filling Station (ballet)
Varèse, Edgard, *Etude pour Espace* (chorus, two pianos, percussion)
Vaughan-Williams, Ralph, *Festival Te Deum* (chorus, orchestra)

1938

World Events:

The United States severs relations with Germany by recalling its ambassador--Germany retaliates in kind; Congress creates the Federal National Mortgage Association (FNMA) and establishes the House Committee on Un-American Activities; Orson Wells creates a national panic with his broadcast of H.G. Wells' *War of the Worlds*. Internationally, in the Anschluss, German troops occupy Austria; Neville Chamberlain negotiates the Munich Pact giving the Czech Sudetenland to Hitler; Stalin's third five-year plan increases armament and defense in Russia; Eire becomes a sovereign nation in the British Commonwealth; *Queen Elizabeth* launched; Mexico nationalizes all oil companies.

Cultural Highlights:

Pulitzers: Drama, Thornton Wilder (*Our Town*); Fiction, John P. Marquand (*The Late George Apley*); Poetry, Marya Zaturenska (*Cold Morning Sky*). Pearl S. Buck receives the Nobel Prize for Literature; French writer André Maurois in knighted and Edwin L. Lutyens becomes President of the Royal Academy of Art. In Mexico the Federation de l'Art Révolutionaire Indépendant is formed. Deaths in the art world include American artists Thomas Dewing, Edmund Tarbell and sculptors George Bernard and Sergeant Kendall, German sculptor Ernst Barlach and artist Ernst Kirchner. Deaths in the literary field include American novelist Thomas Wolfe and author James W. Johnson, Italian poet Gabriele d'Annunzio, Russian novelist Alexander Kuprin and Czech novelist Karel Capek. Other highlights include:

Art: Jean Arp, *Growth*; Salvador Dali, *Apparition of Face and Fruit-Dish*; Jo Davidson, *Will Rogers Monument*; Charles Despiau, *Assis* (terra-cotta); Raoul Dufy, *Regatta*; Marsden Hartley, *Fisherman's Last Supper*; Paul Klee, *A Park Near Lucerne*; Jacques Lipchitz, *Prometheus with a Vulture*; Henry Moore, *Recumbent Figures*.

Literature: Maxwell Anderson, *Knickerbocker Holiday*; Taylor Caldwell, *Dynasty of Death*; Daphne du Maurier, *Rebecca*; Margaret Rawlings, *The Yearling*; Jean Paul Sartre, *Nausea*; Robert Sherwood, *Abe Lincoln in Illinois*; John Steinbeck, *The Long Valley*; Thornton Wilder, *Our Town*; Richard Wright, *Uncle Tom's Children*.

MUSICAL EVENTS

A. Births:

Jan 8	Yevgeni Nesterenko (Rus-bs)		Jun 13	Gwynne Howell (Br-bs)
Feb 6	Ellsworth Milburn (Am-cm)		Jun 15	Jean-Claude Eloy (Fr-cm)
Feb 8	Elly Ameling (Hol-sop)		Jul 21	Anton Kuerti (Aus-pn)
Feb 11	Edith Mathis (Swi-sop)		Aug 4	Simon Preston (Br-org)
Feb 13	Johanna Meier (Am-sop)		Aug 8	Jacques Hétu (Can-cm)
Feb 16	John Corigliano (Am-cm)		Aug 9	Micheline Saint-Marcoux (Can-cm)
Mar 2	Simon Estes (Am-bar)		Aug 12	Huguette Tourangeau (Can-alto)
Mar 17	Rudolf Nureyev (Rus-bal)		Aug 13	Oscar Ghiglia (It-gui)
Apr 11	Kurt Moll (Ger-bs)		Sep 6	Joan Tower (Am-cm)
Apr 29	Kenneth Riegel (Am-ten)		Sep 20	Jane Manning (Br-sop)
May 10	Maxim Shostakovich		Sep 21	Yuji Takahashi (Jp-pn-cm)
	(Rus-pn-cd)		Nov 16	Akira Endo (Jp-cd)
May 13	Ludovic Spiess (Rom-ten)		Nov 17	Alvaro Cassuto (Por-cd)
May 21	Michael Halász (Hun-cd)		Dec 3	José Serebrier (Urg-cd)
May 26	William Bolcom (Am-cm)		Dec 4	Yvonne Minton (Aust-sop)
May 26	Teresa Stratas (Can-sop)		Dec 9	Tatiana Troyanos (Am-sop)
May 27	Elizabeth Harwood (Br-sop)		Dec 20	John Harbison (Am-cm)
Jun 9	Charles Wuorinen (Am-cm)			

B. Deaths:

Jan 21	Marie Wurm (Br-pn-cd)		Apr 12	Feodor Chaliapin (Rus-bs)
Mar 19	Ludwig Wüllner (Ger-voc)		May 30	Miguel Fleta (Sp-ten)

Jun 2   Hans Wolzogen (Ger-mus)
Aug 14   Abraham Idelsohn (Lat-mus)
Aug 14   Landon Ronald (Br-cd)
Oct 27   Alma Gluck (Hun-sop)
Oct 27   Eva Tetrazzini (It-sop)

Nov 11   Franco Leoni (It-cm)
Nov 21   Leopold Godowsky (Pol-pn)
Dec 8   Georg Baklanov (Rus-bar)
Dec 14   Maurice Emmanuel (Fr-cm-mus)
Dec 26   Irene von Chavanne (Aus-alto)

C. Debuts:

Met ---Jussi Björling (ten), Maria Caniglia (sop), Glenn Darwin (bar), Mafalda Favero (sop), Jan Kiepura (ten), Bruno Landi (ten), Erich Leinsdorf (cd), Galliano Masini (ten), Marisa Morel (sop), Hans Nissen (bar), Alessio de Paolis (ten), Rosa Pauly (sop), Risë Stevens (mez), Enid Szantho (mez), Erich Witte (ten)

U.S. --Simon Barere (N.Y.), Joel Berglund (Chicago), Dean Dixon (N.Y.), Rudolf Firkusny (N.Y.), Massimo Freccia (N.Y.), Carroll Glenn (N.Y.), Szymon Goldberg (N.Y.), Mack Harrell (N.Y.), Hilde Konetzni (tour), Lorin Maazel (Los Angeles), James Melton (Cincinnati), Janine Micheau (San Francisco), Jan Peerce (Philadelphia), Hilde Reggiani (Chicago), Maria Reining (Chicago), Ebe Stignani (San Francisco), Jenö Takács (tour), Alessandro Ziliani (San Francisco)

Other -Martha Angelici (Paris), Hans Braun (Königsberg), Michel Dens (Lille), Irene Joachim (Paris), Germaine Lubin (Berlin), Enzo Mascherini (Florence), Elena Nicolai (Milan), Heinz Rehfuss (Biel-Solothurn), Otto von Rohe (Duisburg), Elisabeth Schwarz-kopf (Berlin), Josef Simándy (Szeged), Ferruccio Tagliavini (Florence), Ramón Vinay (Mexico City), Ernst Wiemann (Kiel)

D. New Positions:

Conductors: Kurt Adler (Chicago Opera), Herbert von Karajan (Berlin Opera), Erich Leinsdorf (Met), Lovro von Matacic (Belgrade PO), Eugene Mravinsky (Leningrad SO), Charles Munch (Paris Conservatory Concerts), Fritz Reiner (Pittsburgh SO), Nino Sanzogno (Liceo Musicale, Venice)

Educational: Catharine Crozier (organ, Eastman), Giorgio Ghedini (composition, Parma Conservatory), Grant Johannesen (artist-in-residence, Wisconsin University), Quincy Porter (dean, N.E. Conservatory), Carl Ruggles (composition, University of Miami)

Others: Abraham Veinus (music research, RCA)

E. Prizes and Honors:

Prizes: Henri Dutilleux (Prix de Rome), Emil Gilels (Brussels), Carroll Glenn (Naumberg)

Honors: Henri Busser (French Academy), Arnold Dolmetsch (Legion of Honor), Newman Flower (knighted), Artur Honegger (French Institute)

F. Biographical Highlights:

Malcolm Arnold given scholarship to Royal College; Milton Babbitt begins teaching at Princeton; Gottfried von Einem becomes a coach at the Berlin Opera; Alberto Ginastera graduates from the Brazilian National Conservatory; Paul Hindemith leaves Germany for Switzerland; Ernst Krenek emigrates to the U.S.; Lotte Lehmann flees Nazi Austria and settles in California; Thomas Mann moves to the U.S.; John McCormack retires from active concert life; Hans Moldenhauer emigrates to the U.S.; Magda Olivero makes her La Scala debut; Egon Petri moves to the U.S.; Lily Pons marries André Kostelanetz; André Previn leaves Germany with his family, goes to the U.S.; Serge Prokofiev makes his last tour outside of Russia; Rudolf Réti settles in the U.S.; William Steinberg invited to the U.S. by Toscanini; Igor Stravinsky loses his oldest daughter; Edgard Varèse unsuccessfully tries to interest Hollywood in his musical ideas; Stefan Wolpe arrives in the U.S.; Alexander von Zemlinsky flees Nazi Austria.

G. Institutional Openings:

Performing Groups: Berne Chamber Orchestra, Bulgarian (Aramov) String Quartet (Sofia), Collegium Musicum Antwerpiense, Glenn Miller Orchestra, New York Chamber Orchestra, PBS Choral Society (Palestine)

Festivals: Ibero-American Music Festival (Bogotá), Kleine Musikfeste (Lüdenscheid), Lucerne Festival

Other: American Accordionists' Association, Arrow Music Press (N.Y.), Boston Society of Ancient Instruments, Drinker Library of Choral Music (Philadelphia), Griffith Music Foundation (Newark NJ), Henry Hadley Foundation for the Advancement of American Music (N.Y.), Instituto Interamericano de Musicología (Montevideo), National Association of Choir Directors, *Revue Internationale de Musique*, Society for the Preservation and Encouragement of Barber Shop Quartet Singing in America, Tanglewood Music Shed, Teatro Nuovo (Milan), World Center for Jewish Music

H. Musical Literature:

Abraham, Gerald, *A Hundred Years of Music*
Casella, Alfredo, *Il Pianoforte*
Farrar, Geraldine, *Such Sweet Compulsion*
Harding, Rosamond, *Origins of Musical Time and Expression*
Leichtentritt, Hugo, *Music, History and Ideas*
Moser, Hans, *Kleine Deutsche Musikgeschichte*
Scholes, Percy, *Oxford Companion to Music*
Stuckenschmidt, Hans, *The History of Dissonance*

I. Musical Compositions:

Barber, Samuel, *Adagio for Strings, Opus 11*
Bartók, Béla, *Concerto No. 2 for Violin and Orchestra*
Bloch, Ernst, *Concerto for Violin and Orchestra*
Britten, Benjamin, *Concerto No. 1 for Piano and Orchestra*
Chávez, Carlos, *Concerto for Four Horns and Orchestra*
Copland, Aaron, *Outdoor Overture* (orchestra)
    Billy the Kid (ballet)
Glière, Reinhold, *Concerto for Harp and Orchestra*
Hanson, Howard, *Symphony No. 3*
Hindemith, Paul, *Symphonic Dances for Orchestra*
Kabalevsky, Dmitri, *Colas Breugnon* (opera)
Kennan, Kent, *Night Soliloquy* (flute and orchestra)
Lutoslawski, Witold, *Symphonic Variations* (orchestra)
Malipiero, Gian, *Antonio e Cleopatra* (opera)
Martinu, Bohuslav, *Double Concerto* (two string orchestras, piano, timpani)
Milhaud, Darius, *Médée* (opera)
Orff, Carl, *Der Mond* (opera)
Pijper, Willem, *Concerto for Violin and Orchestra*
Piston, Walter, *The Incredible Flutist* (ballet)
Poulenc, Francis, *Concerto for Organ, Strings and Timpani*
Prokofiev, Serge, *Alexander Nevsky, Opus 78* (cantata based on film music)
Revueltas, Silvestre, *Sensemaya* (orchestra)
Schmidt, Franz, *The Book with the Seven Seals* (oratorio)
Schoenberg, Arnold, *Kol Nidre, Opus 39* (speaker, chorus, orchestra)
Skalkottas, Nikos, *Concerto No. 2 for Piano and Orchestra*
Strauss, Richard, *Der Friedenstag* (opera)
Stravinsky, Igor, *Dumbarton Oaks Concerto* (sixteen wind instruments)
Vaughan-Williams, Ralph, *Serenade to Music* (soloists, chorus and small orchestra)
    Partitia for Double String Orchestra
Villa-Lobos, Heitor, *Bachianas Brasilieras No. 3 for Piano and Orchestra*
    Bachianas Brasilieras No. 5 for Voice and Orchestra
Webern, Anton, *String Quartet, Opus 28*

1939

World Events:
In the U.S., the atom is split for the first time at Columbia University; the Neutrality Act of 1939 permits the sale of arms to France and Great Britain; Igor Sikorsky introduces the helicopter; Fairs are held on both coasts, the New York World's Fair is held on the east coast and the San Francisco International Exposition is held on the west coast. Internationally, the Nazis occupy the remainder of Czechoslovakia and invade Poland to start World War II; the Russo-Finnish War begins and Russia invades Poland from the east; the Spanish Civil War comes to an end; the first jet plane is tested in Germany; George VI becomes the first British monarch to visit the U.S.

Cultural Highlights:
Pulitzers: Drama, Robert E. Sherwood (*Abe Lincoln in Illinois*); Fiction, Marjorie Rawlings (*The Yearling*); Poetry, John G. Fletcher (*Selected Poems*). The Nobel Prize for Literature goes to the Finnish writer Frans Emil Sillanpää; British essayist Max Beerbohm is knighted. Pocket Books are introduced by Robert de Graff. Deaths include British poet William B. Yeats, German author Ludwig Fulda, Norwegian poet Olav Dunn, Spanish poet Antonio Ruiz, novelist of the American West, Zane Grey, and American artist Ernest Lawson; births include Irish poet Seamus Heaney and British dramatists Shelagh Delaney and Alan Ayckbourn and American artist Larry Bell. Other highlights include:

Art: Thomas Hart Benton, *Threshing Wheat*; Alexander Calder, *Lobster Trap and Fish Tail*; André Derain, *Young Girl Peeling Fruit*; Jacob Epstein, *Adam Jacob and the Angel*; Paul Klee, *Conquest of the Mountains*; Jean Paul Laurent, *The Hunt and the Forester*; Antoine Pevsner, *Projection in Space*; Ben Shahn, *The Vacant Lot*.

Literature: Maxwell Anderson, *Key Largo*; Lillian Hellman, *The Little Foxes*; James Joyce, *Finnegan's Wake*; George Kaufman and Moss Hart, *The Man Who Came to Dinner*; Richard Llewellyn, *How Green Was My Valley*; Katherine Porter, *Pale Horse, Pale Rider*; Carl Sandburg, *Abraham Lincoln--The War Years*; John Steinbeck, *The Grapes of Wrath*.

MUSICAL EVENTS

A. Births:

Jan 29 Lorna Haywood (Br-sop)	Jun 6 Louis Andriessen (Hol-cm)
Feb 3 Helga Dernesch (Aus-sop)	Jun 6 Giacomo Aragall (Sp-ten)
Feb 8 Gundula Janowitz (Ger-sop)	Jun 9 Ileana Cotrubas (Rom-sop)
Feb 10 Barbara Kolb (Am-cm)	Jul 3 Brigitte Fassbaender (Ger-sop)
Feb 11 Catherine Gayer (Am-sop)	Jul 31 Steuart Bedford (Br-cd)
Feb 18 Marek Janowski (Pol-cd)	Aug 6 Rodney Friend (Br-vn)
Feb 19 Vladimir Atlantov (Rus-ten)	Aug 26 Nicholas Braithwaite (Br-cd)
Mar 3 Edith Peinemann (Ger-vn)	Aug 28 Robert Aitken (Can-cd)
Mar 7 Donald McInnes (Am-vn)	Sep 5 Kenneth Klein (Am-cd)
Mar 8 Robert Tear (Br-ten)	Sep 10 Judith Nelson (Am-sop)
Mar 12 Veriano Luchetti (It-ten)	Sep 13 Arleen Augér (Am-sop)
Mar 20 Ralph Votapek (Am-pn)	Sep 17 David Griffith (Am-ten)
Mar 25 Lawrence Bernstein (Am-mus)	Sep 28 Harry Theyard (Am-ten)
Mar 26 Peter Schneider (Aus-cel)	Oct 19 Benita Valente (Am-sop)
Apr 21 John McCabe (Br-pn-cm)	Nov 5 Marcia Baldwin (Am-sop)
Apr 30 Ellen T. Zwillich (Am-cm)	Nov 12 Lucia Popp (Aus-sop)
May 9 Bruce Mather (Can-cm)	Nov 30 Walter Weller (Aus-cd)
May 11 Harvey Sollberger (Am-fl-cm)	Dec 6 Ilana Vered (Is-pn)
May 14 Joan Grillo (Am-sop)	Dec 8 James Galway (Ir-fl)
May 21 Heinz Holliger (Swi-cm-ob)	

B. Deaths:

Jan 12	Hariclea Darclée (Rom-sop)	Aug 25	Geneviève Vix (Fr-sop)
Jan 12	Eugenio Pirani (It-pn-cm)	Sep 8	Lawrence Gilman (Am-cri)
Jan 28	William S. Haynes (Am-fl.m)	Oct 29	Giulio Crimi (It-ten)
Feb 11	Franz Schmidt (Aus-cm)	Nov 3	Charles Tournemire (Fr-org)
Feb 17	Willy Hess (Ger-vn-cd)	Nov 23	Arthur Bodanski (Aus-cd)
May 8	Robert Lachmann (Ger-mus)	Dec 6	Charles Dalmorès (Fr-ten)
Jun 3	Enrique Arbós (Sp-cm-cd)	Dec 8	Ernest H. Schelling (Am-cm)
Jul 29	Waldo S. Pratt (Am-ped)		

C. Debuts:

Met ---Lina Aimaro (sop), Herbert Alsen (bs), Douglas Beattie (bs), John Carter (ten), Annamary Dickey (sop), Harriet Handers (sop), Mack Harrell (bar), Edith Herlick (sop), Herbert Janssen (bar), Eyvind Laholm (ten) Emil Lange (ten), Walter Olitzki (bar), Hilde Reggiani (sop), Leonard Warren (bar)

U.S. --Kurt Baum (Chicago), Margit Boker (Chicago), Clifford Curzon (tour), William Masselos (N.Y.), Dorothy Maynor (N.Y.), Jarmila Novotná (San Francisco), Sigurd Rascher (Boston), György Sándor (N.Y.), Leo Smit (N.Y.), Patricia Travers (Detroit)

Other -Beno Blachut (Olomouc), Zara Dolukhanova (Erevan), Hilde Gueden (Vienna), Benno Kusche (Heidelberg), Denis Matthews (London), Helmut Melchert (Wuppertal), Mario del Monaco (Pesaro), Clara Petrella (Milan), Aksel Schiotz (Copenhagen), Irmgard Seefried (Aachen), Paolo Silveri (Rome), Polyna Stoska (Berlin), Wolfgang Windgassen (Pforzheim)

D. New Positions:

Conductors: Howard Barlow (Baltimore SO), Rafael Kubelik (Brno SO), Malcolm Sargent (Hallé Orchestra)

Educational: Samuel Barber (composition, Curtis Institute), Léon Jongen (director, Brussels Conservatory), Ernst Krenek (composition, Vassar), Gian F. Malipiero (director, Venice Conservatory), Rudolf Serkin (piano, Curtis Institute), Randall Thompson (director, Curtis Institute), Ermanno Wolf-Ferrari (composition, Salzburg Mozarteum)

Others: Paul Callaway (organ, Washington Cathedral), Harold Schonberg (music critic, *American Music Lover*)

E. Prizes and Honors:

Prizes: Gertrude Gibson (Naumberg), Arthur Grumiaux (Vieuxtemps), William Horne (Naumberg), Arturo Michelangeli (Geneva), Mara Sebriansky & Zadel Skolovsky (Naumberg), Maria Stader (Geneva)

Honors: Charles van den Borren (Belgian Royal Academy), Robert Mayer (knighted), Richard Wright (Guggenheim)

F. Biographical Highlights:

Benjamin Britten and Peter Pears follow Auden to the U.S.; Mario Castelnuovo-Tedesco leaves Italy for the U.S.; Andor Foldes settles in the U.S.; Otto Klemperer undergoes serious brain surgery; Fritz Kreisler returns permanently to the U.S.; Leonard Rose becomes principal cellist with the Cleveland SO; György Sándor, Artur Schnabel and Rudolf Serkin all take up residency in the U.S.; Georg Solti leaves Hungary for Switzerland; Risë Stevens marries Walter Surovy who becomes her manager; Igor Stravinsky, losing both his wife and mother, spends time in a sanitarium; Henryk Szeryng goes to London to join the Army of Free Poland; Yves Tanguy moves to the U.S.; Bruno Walter decides to stay in the U.S.; Paul Wittgenstein settles in New York; Alexander von Zemlinsky arrives in the U.S.

G. Institutional Openings:

Performing Groups: All-American Youth Orchestra (Philadelphia), American Ballet Theater, Athens National Opera, Brooklyn Chamber Music Society, Chigi Quintet (Siena, Italy),

Dublin Orchestral Players, Harry James Band, Israel String Quartet, King Cole Trio (Hollywood), Koeckert String Quartet (Prague), Orchestre de Chambre Hewitt (Paris), Pittsburgh Opera Co., Prague German PO, Primrose String Quartet (N.Y.), San Antonio SO, Schola Cantorum (Mexico), Tucson Boys Choir

Educational: Brunswick Staatsmusikschule, Tau Beta Sigma Music Sorority (Texas Tech)

Other: Allen Organ Co. (Allentown, PA), American Recorder Society (N.Y.), Amigos de Musica (Mexico); Broadcast Music, Inc. (BMI, N.Y.); Electric Metronome, Geneva International Competition for Musical Performers, Getzen Co. (Elkhorn, WI), *Horizon*, Liverpool Philharmonic Hall, Novachord (by Lawrence Hammond)

H. Musical Literature:

Allen, Warren, *Philosophies of Music History*
Carse, Adam, *Musical Wind Instruments*
Copland, Aaron, *What to Listen for in Music*
Hindemith, Paul, *Craft of Musical Composition II*
Jeppesen, Knud, *Counterpoint*
Thompson, Oscar, *International Cyclopedia of Music and Musicians*
Thomson, Virgil, *The State of Music*
H. Weinstock/W. Brockway, *Men of Music*

I. Musical Compositions:

Barber, Samuel, *Concerto for Violin and Orchestra, Opus 14*
Bartók, Béla, *String Quartet No. 6*
         Mikrokosmos, Vol. VI (piano)
         Divertimento for Strings
Bax, Arnold, *Symphony No. 7*
Britten, Benjamin, *Les Illuminations* (voice, strings)
Cadman, Charles, *Symphony*
Carter, Elliott, *Pocahontas* (ballet)
Chávez, Carlos, *Four Nocturnes* (voice and orchestra)
Copland Aaron, *The Quiet City* (film music)
Cowell, Henry, *Symphony No. 2, "Anthropos"*
Fortner, Wolfgang, *Capriccio and Finale* (orchestra)
Gretchaninov, Alexander, *Symphony No. 5, Opus 153*
Harris, Roy, *Symphony No. 3*
Hindemith, Paul, *Concerto for Violin and Orchestra*
Holmboe, Vagn, *Symphony No. 2*
Kabalevsky, Dmitri, *Symphony No. 4*
Kodály, Zoltán, *Peacock Variations* (orchestra)
         Concerto for Orchestra
McDonald, Harl, *Legend of the Arkansas Traveller* (orchestra)
Menotti, Gian Carlo, *The Old Maid and the Thief* (opera)
Moore, Douglas, *The Devil and Daniel Webster* (opera)
Piston, Walter, *Concerto for Violin and Orchestra*
Poulenc, Francis, *Four Motets for a Time of Penitence* (chorus)
Prokofiev, Serge, *Simeon Kotka* (opera)
Schoenberg, Arnold, *Chamber Symphony No. 2, Opus 38*
Schuman, William, *American Festival Overture* (orchestra)
Shostakovich, Dmitri, *Symphony No. 6, Opus 54*
Skalkottas, Nikos, *Orchestral Suite No. 1*
Tippett, Michael, *Concerto for Double String Orchestra*
Vaughan-Williams, Ralph, *Five Variants of "Dives and Lazarus"*
Walton, William, *Concerto for Violin and Orchestra*
Webern, Anton, *Cantata No. 1, Opus 29* (soprano, chorus, orchestra)

1940

World Events:

The U.S. census shows a population of 132,165,000, a 7.3% increase in ten years. Franklin D. Roosevelt is elected for a third term as President; the Selective Training and Service Act is passed by Congress who also passes the Smith Alien Act limiting the American Communists; the President begins a defense build-up; the Fair Labor Standards Act goes into effect. Internationally, World War II continues with the fall of Norway, France and the Netherlands; the Battle of Britain begins following the evacuation of Dunkirk; Neville Chamberlain resigns as Prime Minister of England and Winston Churchill succeeds him; the Russo-Finish War ends and the Battle of Africa begins; Leon Trotsky is assassinated in Mexico.

Cultural Highlights:

Pulitzers: Drama, William Saroyan (*The Time of Your Life*); Fiction, John Steinbeck (*The Grapes of Wrath*); Poetry, Mark Van Doren (*Collected Poems*). Francis Taylor becomes director of the Metropolitan Museum of Art. *Angry Penguins*, an Australian journal for avant-garde art and literature appears. Births in the literary field include Russian poet Joseph Brodsky, British author Bruce Chatwin and American author Peter Benchley; deaths include American novelists F. Scott Fitzgerald, Hamlin Garland, Edwin Markham and poet DuBose Heyward, Swedish novelist and poet Selma Lagerlöf, poet Verner von Heidenstam and Russian novelist Mikhail Bulgakov. Births in the art field include American artists Chuck Close and Nancy Graves and Venezuelan sculptor Alberto Collie; deaths include French artist Édouard Vuillard and Swiss artist Paul Klee. Other highlights include:

Art: Max Beckmann, *Circus Caravan*; Thomas Crawford, *Whitestone Bridge*; Ludwig von Hofmann, *Spring*; Edward Hopper, *Gas*; Vasili Kandinsky, *Sky Blue*; Oskar Kokoschka, *Polperro, Cornwall*; Carl Milles, *The Meeting of the Waters*; John Piper, *St. Mary le Port, Bristol*; Max Weber, *The Hasidic Dance*; William Zorach, *The Head of Christ*.

Literature: Lloyd Douglas, *Invitation to Live*; Graham Greene, *The Power and the Glory*; Ernest Hemingway, *For Whom the Bell Tolls*; Carson McCullers, *The Heart is a Lonely Hunter*; Mikhail Sholokhov, *The Quiet Don*; James Thurber, *Fables for Our Time*; Thomas Wolfe, *You Can't Go Home Again*; William Yeats, *Last Poems and Plays*.

MUSICAL EVENTS

A. Births:

Jan 3	Motohiko Adachi (Jp-cm)
Jan 6	Shirley Love (Am-mez)
Jan 14	Siegmund Nimsgern (Ger-bar)
Jan 29	Justino Díaz (P.R.-bs)
Feb 20	Christoph Eschenbach (Ger-pn)
Mar 2	Robert Lloyd (Br-bs)
Mar 17	Elizabeth Steiner (Ger-sop)
Mar 28	André de Groote (Bel-pn)
Apr 3	Anja Silja (Ger-sop)
Apr 17	Siegfried Jerusalem (Ger-ten)
Apr 27	Tom McDonnell (Aus-bar)
May 24	Christoff Wolff (Ger-mus)
May 30	Olivia Stapp (Am-sop)
Jun 4	Katherine Pring (Br-sop)
Jun 6	Phillip Rhodes (Am-cm)
Jul 5	Donald Shanks (Aust-bs)
Jul 10	Helen Donath (Am-sop)
Jul 22	Michael Heise (Ger-cd)
Aug 18	Michelangelo Veltri (Arg-cd)
Aug 25	José Van Dam (Bel-bar)
Sep 2	Rudolph Angermüller (Ger-mus)
Sep 22	Edward Boguslawski (Pol-cm)
Sep 27	Josephine Barstow (Br-sop)
Oct 4	Alain Lombard (Fr-cd)
Oct 17	Stephen Bishop-Kovacevich (Br-pn)
Oct 20	Joanna Simon (Am-mez)

B. Deaths:

Jan 19	Albert Reisse (Ger-ten)
Feb 2	Arnold Volpe (Rus-cd)
Feb 23	Gerald Warfield (Am-cm)
Feb 29	Arnold Dolmetsch (Br-mus)
Mar 3	Karl Muck (Ger-cd)
Apr 4	Luisa Tetrazzini (It-sop)
Jun 8	Frederick Converse (Am-cm)
Jun 20	Jehan Alain (Fr-org)
Jun 20	Emma Nevada (Am-sop)
Jul 4	Bertram Shapleigh (Am-cm)

Jul 10	Donald Tovey (Br-mus)	Oct 5	Silvestre Revueltas (Mex-cm)
Jul 28	Lucy Weidt (Ger-sop)	Nov 26	Ivar Andrésen (Nor-bs)
Aug 8	Alessandro Bonci (It-ten)	Dec 5	Jan Kubelik (Cz-vn)
Sep 2	Guilio Gatti-Casazza (It-imp)	Dec 11	Theodor Gerlach (Ger-cd)
Sep 24	Frank T. Arnold (Br-mus)	Dec 15	Blanche Marchesi (Fr-sop)

C. Debuts:

Met ---Licia Albanese (sop), Salvatore Baccaloni (bs), Emery Darcy (ten), Jean Dickinson (sop), John Dudley (ten), Norina Greco (sop), Raoul Jobin (ten), Arthur Kent (bar), Alexander Kipnis (bs), Anthony Marlowe (ten), Jarmila Novotná (sop), Josef Santoro (ten), Eleanor Steber (sop), Alexander Sved (bar), Frank Valentino (bar)

U.S. --Eugene Conley (N.Y.), Andor Foldes (N.Y.), Herta Glaz (Chicago), Jascha Horenstein (N.Y.), Edward Kilenyi (N.Y.), Dorothy Kirsten (Chicago), Nan Merriman (tour), Gerhard Pechner (San Francisco), Abbey Simon (N.Y.)

Other -Pierrette Alarie (Montreal), Fedora Barbieri (Florence), Lazar Berman (Moscow), Gré Brouwenstijn (Amsterdam), Sixten Ehrling (Stockholm), Gianandrea Gavazzeni (Italy), Arthur Grumiaux (Brussels), Elisabeth Grümmer (Aachen), Geraint Jones (London), Emmy Lowe (Hanover), Witold Malcuzynski (Paris), Nicola Monti (Cagliari), Petre Munteanu (Bucharest), Rosl Schwaiger (Salzburg), Walburga Wegner (Düsseldorf), Zvi Zeitlin (Palestine)

D. New Positions:

Conductors: Sixten Ehrling (Stockholm Opera), Georg Jochum (Linz SO), Thor Johnson (Grand Rapids SO), Enrique Jordá (Madrid SO), Ole Windingstad (New Orleans PO)

Educational: Aaron Copland (Berkshire), Hugo Distler (organ, composition, Berlin Hochschule), Douglas Moore (director, Columbia Music Department), Lodovico Rocca (director, Turin Conservatory), Michael Tippet (music director, Morley College)

Others: Gustave Reese (publication director, Schirmer), Virgil Thomson (music critic, New York *Herald Tribune*)

E. Prizes and Honors:

Prizes: Harry Cykman (Naumberg), Sidney Foster (Leventritt), Theodore Lettvin and Thomas Richner (Naumberg)

Honors: Stephen Foster (Hall of Fame)

F. Biographical Highlights:

Béla Bartók arrives in the U.S.; Leonard Bernstein studies with Koussevitsky at Tanglewood; Henry Cowell is paroled from San Quentin; Walt Disney produces *Fantasia* with Stokowski and the Philadelphia Orchestra; Kathleen Ferrier gives up a telephone operator job on winning a local singing competition; Paul Hindemith arrives in the U.S.; Nikolai Malko settles in Chicago; Bohuslav Martinu flees Nazi-held Paris; Olivier Messiaen taken prisoner and sent to a POW camp; Darius Milhaud, forced from France, is offered a teaching position at Mills College; Egon Petri flees Poland, goes to the U.S.; Igor Stravinsky marries Vera de Bosset, settles in Hollywood; Joseph Szigeti settles in the U.S.; Michael Tippet refuses to be drafted on conscientious grounds; Ernst Toch becomes an American citizen; Arturo Toscanini takes the NBC SO on South American tour.

G. Institutional Openings:

Performing Groups: Alexandra Choir of London, Arkansas State SO, Baltimore Civic Opera Co., Berne Chamber Choir, Bolivian National Orchestra (La Paz), Brazilian SO (Rio de Janeiro), Choral Guild of Atlanta, Houston Youth SO, Janssen SO (Hollywood), Lithuanian State PO (Vilnius), Opera Guild of Canada (Montreal), Tokyo PO, Vegh String Quartet (Budapest)

Educational: Centro de Studi Rossiniani (Pesaro), Escuela Moderna de Musica (Santiago

Chile)

Other: Alice M. Ditson Fund (Columbia University), Berkshire Music Center (Lenox MA), Council for the Encouragement of Music and the Arts (CEMA, London), Edgar M. Leventritt Foundation International Competition, Kleinhaus Music Hall (Buffalo NY), *Music Review*, Society of Musical Artists (Iceland), Solovox (by L. Hammond), Van Vulpen Brothers, Organ Builders (Utrecht)

H. Musical Literature:

Carse, Adam, *The Orchestra of the 18th Century*
Garbuzov, Nicolai, *Musical Acoustics*
Krenek, Ernst, *Studies in Counterpoint Based on the Twelve-Tone Technique*
Levant, Oscar, *A Smattering of Ignorance*
Molnár, Antal, *Popular Musical Aesthetics*
Reese, Gustave, *Music in the Middle Ages*
Sachs, Curt, *History of Musical Instruments*
Schoenberg, Arnold, *Theory of Composition*

I. Musical Compositions:

Britten, Benjamin, *Sinfonia da Requiem* (orchestra)
Carpenter, John Alden, *Symphony No. 2*
Casella, Alfredo, *Symphony No. 3, Opus 63*
Castelnuovo-Tedesco, Mario, *Midsummer Night's Dream Overture*
Chávez, Carlos, *Concerto for Piano and Orchestra*
Copland, Aaron, *Our Town* (film music)
Cowell, Henry, *Ancient Desert Drone* (orchestra)
Diamond, David, *Concert Piece for Orchestra*
Dello Joio, Norman, *Prairie* (ballet)
Gillis, Don, *Symphonies Nos. 1 and 2*
Ginastera, Alberto, *Panambi* (ballet)
Goosens, Eugene, *Symphony No. 1*
Gould, Morton, *Spirituals for Orchestra*
            American Symphonette No. 4, "Latin-American"
Harris, Roy, *Symphony No. 4, "Folksong"*
Hindemith, Paul, *Concerto for Cello and Orchestra*
            The Four Temperaments (piano and orchestra)
Kabalevsky, Dmitri, *The Comedians, Opus 26* (ballet)
Kay, Ulysses, *Concerto for Oboe and Orchestra*
Khachaturian, Aram, *Concerto for Violin and Orchestra*
Koechlin, Charles, *Les Bandar-Log, Opus 176* (symphonic poem)
Martinu, Bohuslav, *Sinfonietta Giocoso for Piano and Orchestra*
Miaskovsky, Nicolai, *Symphonies Nos. 20 and 21*
Milhaud, Darius, *Symphony No. 1* (large orchestra)
Pfitzner, Hans, *Symphony No. 2, Opus 46*
Poulenc, Francis, *Banalités* (song)
Prokofiev, Serge, *Betrothal in a Convent* (opera)
Rachmaninoff, Serge, *Symphonic Dances* (orchestra)
Rodgers, Richard, *Pal Joey* (musical)
Rubbra, Edmund, *Symphony No. 3*
Strauss, Richard, *Die Liebe de Danae* (opera)
Stravinsky, Igor, *Tango* (arrangement for orchestra)
            Symphony in C
Walton, William, *Scapino, a Comedy Overture*
Webern, Anton, *Variations for Orchestra, Opus 30*

1941

World Events:
In the U.S., President Roosevelt proclaims the Four Freedoms (of worship, of speech, from want, from fear); Pearl Harbor is attacked by the Japanese on December 7; Congress declares war on Japan; Germany and Italy declare war on the U.S.; first commercial television broadcast made in New York. Internationally, Japan carries the war to the South Pacific; Douglas MacArthur is made Supreme Allied Commander in the Pacific; Hitler invades Russia in June; Roosevelt and Churchill meet and sign the Atlantic Charter; Hitler begins the extermination of the Jews in Germany and the occupied countries.

Cultural Highlights:
Pulitzers: Drama, Robert E. Sherwood (*There Shall Be No Night*); Poetry, Leonard Bacon (*Sunderland Capture*). British artist Frank Brangwyn is given a knighthood. *Poets of the Year* begins publication and the National Gallery of Art opens in the Smithsonian. Births in the literary field include American authors Paul Theroux and Anne Tyler; deaths include Indian poet Rabindranath Tagore, Irish author James Joyce, British novelist Virginia Woolf, Swedish author Hjalmar Soderberg, French poet Tristan Derème, novelist Hugh Walpole and American author Sherwood Anderson. Deaths in the art field include French artist Robert Delaunay and American sculptor Roland H. Perry. Other highlights include:

Art: Max Beckmann, *Perseus*; Constantin Brancusi, *Cock Greeting the Sun*; Charles Davis, *New York Under Gaslight*; Lyonel Feininger, *The City at Night*; Naum Gabo, *Spiral Theme, Construction in Plastic*; Louis Guglielmi, *Terror in Brooklyn*; Malvina Hoffmann, *Paderewski*; Edward Hopper, *Nighthawks*; Joseph Nash, *Bombers Over Britain*.

Literature: James Agee, *Let Us Praise Famous Men*; Noel Coward, *Blithe Spirit*; Archibald Cronin, *The Keys of the Kingdom*; Edna Ferber, *Saratoga Trunk*; Lillian Hellman, *Watch on the Rhine*; James Hilton, *Random Harvest*; Mary O'Hara, *My Friend Flicka*; William L. Shirer, *Berlin Diary*; James Thurber, *The Male Animal*.

MUSICAL EVENTS

A. Births:

Jan 2 Kazuyoshi Akiyama (Jp-cd)	Aug 6 Doris Hayes (Am-pn)
Jan 3 David Atherton (Br-cd)	Aug 28 Paul Plishka (Am-bs)
Jan 12 Anne Howells (Br-mez)	Aug 31 Walter Verdehr (Yug-pn)
Jan 21 Placido Domingo (Sp-ten)	Sep 1 Julia Varady (Rom-sop)
Feb 6 Stephen Albert (Am-cm)	Sep 10 Christopher Hogwood (Br-mus)
Mar 4 Yuri Simonov (Rus-cd)	Sep 22 William Powers (Am-bs)
Apr 3 Jorma Hynninen (Fin-bar)	Sep 22 Anna Tomowa-Sintow (Bul-sop)
Apr 13 Margaret Price (Br-sop)	Sep 24 Pablo Elvira (P.R.-bar)
Apr 24 John Williams (Aust-gui)	Sep 26 Salvatore Accardo (It-vn)
Apr 27 Judith Blegen (Am-sop)	Oct 3 Ruggero Raimondi (It-bs)
May 12 Anthony Newman (Am-hps)	Oct 23 Lawrence Foster (Am-cd)
May 17 David Cope (Am-cm-the)	Oct 27 Edda Moser (Ger-sop)
May 24 Bob Dylan (Am-pop)	Nov 6 James Bowman (Br-c.ten)
Jun 1 Edo de Waart (Hol-cd)	Nov 16 Paul Katz (Am-cel)
Jun 5 Martha Argerich (Arg-pn)	Nov 20 Gary Karr (Am-cb)
Jun 7 Jaime Laredo (Bol-vn)	Dec 6 John Nelson (Am-cd)
Jun 8 Paula Robison (Am-fl)	Dec 7 Edward Auer (Am-pn)
Jun 16 Dino Ciani (It-pn)	Dec 8 Ingrid Dingfelder (Ger-fl)
Jul 28 Riccardo Muti (It-cd)	Dec 14 Karan Armstrong (Am-sop)

B. Deaths:

Jan 2 Mischa Levitzki (Rus-pn)	Feb 15 Guido Adler (Aus-mus)
Jan 10 Frank Bridge (Br-cm)	Feb 19 Hamilton Harty (Br-cd)

Mar 11	Melanie Kurt (Aus-sop)	Jun 29	Ignace Jan Paderewski (Pol-pn)
Mar 12	Charles Skilton (Am-cm)	Jul 10	Jelly Roll Morton (Am-pop)
Mar 24	Angelo Bada (It-ten)	Aug 16	John Coates (Br-ten)
Mar 27	Stewart MacPherson (Br-the)	Sep 6	Ernst Kraus (Ger-ten)
Apr 16	Pearl G. Curran (Am-cm)	Oct 3	Wilhelm Kienzl (Aus-cm)
May 18	Milka Ternina (Yug-sop)	Dec 3	Christian Sinding (Nor-cm)
Jun 17	John Wagenaar (Hol-cm)	Dec 7	Cecil Forsyth (Br-mus)

C. Débuts:

Met ---Kurt Baum (ten), Paul Breisach (cd), Nadine Conner (sop), Maria Van Delden (sop), Lansing Hatfield (bs), Mary Van Kirk (mez), Edwin McArthur (cd), Italo Montemezzi (cd), Mona Paulee (mez), Gerhard Pechner (bs), Jan Peerce (ten), Stella Roman (sop), Frank St. Leger (cd), May Savage (mez), Josephine Tuminia (sop), Astrid Varnay (sop), Bruno Walter (cd), Elsa Zebranska (sop)

U.S. --Catherine Crozier (Washington, D.C.), Ella Flesch (N.Y.), Jerome Hines (San Francisco), William Kapell (N.Y.), George London (Los Angeles), Robert Mann (N.Y.), James Pease (Philadelphia), Luigi Silva (Rochester), Tossy Spivakovsky (tour), Polyna Stoska (tour), Blanche Thebom (N.Y.), Theodor Uppman (Philadelphia)

Other -Inge Borkh (Lucerne), Lisa della Casa (Biel), Rudolf Christ (Innsbruck), Mercel Cordes (Eger), Suzanne Danco (Genia), Horst Günther (Leipzig), Jacques Jansen (Paris), Piet Kee (Zaandam), Leonid Kogan (Moscow), Lisa Otto (Beuthen), Clara Petrella (Alessandria), Cesare Siepi (Schio), Leopold Simoneau (Montreal), Eugenia Zareska (Milan)

D. New Positions:

Conductors: Rafael Kubelik (Czech PO), Karl Munchinger (Hanover SO), Kurt Sanderling (Leningrad PO)

Educational: Richard Bonelli (Curtis Institute), Giorgio Ghedini (composition, Milan Conservatory), Alberto Ginastera (composition, Buenos Aires Conservatory), Olivier Messiaen (harmony, Paris Conservatory), Boris Schwarz (professor, Queen's College), Reginald Stewart (director, Peabody Institute), Randall Thompson (music chairman, University of Virginia), Efrem Zimbalist (director, Curtis Institute)

Others: Frederick L. Allen (editor, Harper's Magazine)

E. Prizes and Honors:

Prizes: Paul Creston (New York Critic's Circle), William Kapell (Naumberg), Robert Mann (Naumberg), André Pernet (Geneva), Harold Shapero (Prix de Rome), Lura Stover (Naumberg), Alexandre Tansman (Coolidge), Erno Valasek (Leventritt)

Honors: Arnold Bax (Master of the King's Music), George Dyson (knighted), Myra Hess (Dame)

F. Biographical Highlights:

Ernest Bloch returns to the U.S. and settles in California; Pierre Boulez begins studying higher math at Lyons; Aaron Copland visits Latin-America as an envoy for the Department of Inter-American Affairs; Gottfried von Einem studies with Boris Blacher while helping many people escape from the Nazis; Karel Husa enters Prague Conservatory when all other schools are closed by the Nazis; Serge Koussevitsky becomes an American citizen; Felix Labunski becomes an American citizen; Bohuslav Martinu escapes the Nazis and arrives in New York; Birgit Nilsson studies voice at the Royal Academy in Stockholm; Magda Olivera retires from the stage after her marriage; Jean Papineau-Couture receives his B.Mus. from New England Conservatory; Serge Prokofiev suffers the first of a series of heart attacks; Arnold Schoenberg becomes an American citizen.

G. Institutional Openings:

Performing Groups: Bergen Trade Union Orchestra (Norway), Choral Society of Lisbon

(Portugal), Collegiate Chorale of New York, Dublin Grand Opera Society, Festival Negro Chorus of Los Angeles, Greater Miami Opera Association, London Baroque Ensemble, Longine Symphonette (N.Y.), New London Orchestra, Philharmonia String Quartet (London), Symphony Orchestra of Chile (Santiago)

Educational: College Band Director's National Association (Chicago)

Other: International Music Co. (New York Publishers), New York Music Critics' Circle Award, Pan-American Union, Music Division

H. Musical Literature:

Aldrich, Richard, *Concert Life in New York, 1902-23*
Copland, Aaron, *Our New Music*
Fellowes, Edmund, *English Cathedral Music...*
Haydon, Glen, *Introduction to Musicology*
Howard, John T., *Our Contemporary Composers*
Lang, Paul, *Music in Western Civilization*
Piston, Walter, *Harmony*
Tovey, Donald, *A Musician Talks*

I. Musical Compositions:

Bergsma, William, *Gold and the Señor Commandante* (ballet)
Blomdahl, Karl-Birger, *Concerto for Viola and Orchestra*
Britten, Benjamin, *String Quartet No. 1*
Carpenter, John Alden, *Symphony No. 3*
Creston, Paul, *Symphony No. 1*
      Concerto for Saxophone and Orchestra
Dallapiccola, Luigi, *Canti di Prigoniera* (opera)
Dello Joio, Norman, *Concerto for Two Pianos and Orchestra*
      Sinfonietta (orchestra)
Diamond, David, *Symphony No. 1*
Enescu, Georges, *Symphony No. 5* (unfinished)
Fortner, Wolfgang, *Ernste Musik* (orchestra)
Gillis, Don, *Symphony No. 3, "Symphony of Free Men"*
Ginastera, Alberto, *Estancia* (ballet)
      Concierto Argentino (orchestra)
Guarnieri, Camargo, *Brazilian Dance* (orchestra)
Hindemith, Paul, *Symphony in E-flat*
Honegger, Artur, *Symphony No. 2 for Strings*
Leibowitz, René, *Symphony No. 4*
Mennin, Peter, *Symphony No. 1*
Messiaen, Olivier, *Quartet for the End of Time*
Miaskovsky, Nicolai, *Symphonies No. 22 and 23*
Milhaud, Darius, *Concerto for Clarinet and Orchestra*
      Chansons de Ronsard (voice and orchestra)
Piston, Walter, *Sinfonietta* (orchestra)
Poulenc, Francis, *Les Animaux Modeles* (ballet)
Prokofiev, Serge, *The Duenna* (opera)
      Symphonic Suite, 1941, Opus 90
Riegger, Wallingford, *Canon and Fugue for Strings*
Schoenberg, Arnold, *Variations on a Recitative, Opus 40* (organ)
Schuman, William, *Symphony No. 3*
Strauss, Richard, *Capriccio* (opera)
Thomson, Virgil, *Oedipus Tyrannus* (incidental music)
Tippett, Michael, *A Child of Our Time* (oratorio)
Weill, Kurt, *Lady in the Dark* (musical)

1942

World Events:

In the U.S., Enrico Fermi produces the first nuclear chain reaction at the University of Chicago; General Dwight D. Eisenhower is made Commander of the U.S. forces in Europe; the Merchant Marine Academy is founded at Kings Point, New York; women's auxiliary corps are formed in all the services; the Congress of Racial Equality (CORE) is founded. Internationally, the Battle of Stalingrad begins; Allied troops invade North Africa; the Battles of the Coral Sea (in May) and Midway (in June) blunt the Japanese naval advance; U.S. troops invade Guadalcanal; Tokyo bombed in August; 26 nations sign the United Nations agreement; German massacre of all the males in Lidice, Poland.

Cultural Highlights:

Pulitzers: Fiction, Ellen Glasgow (*In This Our Life*); Poetry, William Rose Benét (*The Dust Which Is God*). Births in the literary field include American authors J. Michael Crichton, John Irving and Erica Jong; deaths include Austrian novelist Stefan Zweig, French author Léon Daudet and Czech poet Josef S. Machar. Deaths in the world of art include American sculptors Frederic Ruckstull and Gertrude Whitney and artist Grant Wood and Spanish sculptor Julio Gonzáles; American artist Jonathan Borofsky is born. Other highlights include:

Art: Max Beckmann, *The Actors*; Pierre Bonnard, *L'Oiseau Bleu*; George Braque, *Patience*; Alexander Calder, *Red Petals*; Max Ernst, *Europe after the Rain*; Marsden Hartley, *Mt. Katahdin, Autumn, I*; Horace Pippin, *The Hanging of John Brown*; Jackson Pollack, *Male and Female*; Graham Sutherland, *Red Landscapes*; Jack B. Yeats, *Two Travellers*;

Literature: Sally Benson, *Meet Me in St. Louis*; James Cozzens, *The Just and the Unjust*; Lloyd C. Douglas, *The Robe*; Robert Frost, *A Witness Tree*; Daphne du Maurier, *Frenchman's Creek*; C.S. Lewis, *Screwtape Letters*; Elliot Paul, *The Last Time I Saw Paris*; James Steinbeck, *The Moon Is Down*; Thornton Wilder, *The Skin of Our Teeth*.

MUSICAL EVENTS

A. Births:

Jan 5	Maurizio Pollini (It-pn)	Jul 29	Bernd Weikl (Aus-bar)
Jan 26	Robert Preston (Am-pn)	Aug 1	Claes Ahnsjö (Swe-ten)
Mar 28	Samuel Ramey (Am-bs)	Aug 4	Reinhard Strohm (Ger-mus)
Apr 10	June Card (Am-sop)	Aug 13	Sheila Armstrong (Br-sop)
Apr 18	Richard Angas (Br-bar)	Sep 15	Eduardo Mata (Mex-cd)
Apr 25	Martin Dalby (Scot-cm)	Oct 31	Daniel Roth (Fr-org)
Apr 29	Susan Starr (Am-pn)	Nov 12	David Holloway (Am-bar)
May 4	Enrique Batiz (Mex-cd)	Nov 16	Daniel Barenboim (Arg-pn-cd)
May 6	Richard Stilwell (Am-ten)	Nov 18	Jeffrey Siegel (Am-pn)
Jun 5	Charles Dodge (Am-cm)	Nov 23	Jenny Abel (Ger-vn)
Jun 18	Hans T. Vonk (Hol-cd)	Nov 27	Michael Devlin (Am-bar)
Jun 23	Thom Ritter George (Am-cm)	Dec 8	Sylvia Sebastiani (It-sop)
Jul 5	Matthias Bamert (Swi-cd-cm)	Dec 19	Tirimo Martino (Br-pn)
Jul 12	Richard Stolzman (Am-clar)	Dec 26	Adriana Maliponte (It-sop)

B. Deaths:

Jan 1	Charles Hackett (Am-ten)	Jun 18	Arthur Pryor (Am-bs)
Jan 6	Emma Calvé (Fr-sop)	Aug 4	Alberto Franchetti (It-cm)
Jan 21	Henryk Opiénski (Pol-mus)	Aug 13	Pasquale Amato (It-bar)
Feb 20	Guido Gasperini (It-mus)	Aug 22	Michel Fokine (Rus-bal)
Mar 16	A. von Zemlinsky (Aus-cm)	Oct 20	Frederick Stock (Ger-cd)
Apr 11	Henry Prunières (Fr-mus)	Nov 1	Hugo Distler (Ger-org)
Apr 17	Alfred Hertz (Ger-cd)	Nov 5	George M. Cohan (Am-pop)
May 7	Felix Weingartner (Aus-cd)	Dec 3	W. Peterson-Berger (Swi-cm)
May 25	Emanuel Feuermann (Aus-cel)	Dec 12	Hugo Holle (Ger-mus)

C. Debuts:

Met ---Lorenzo Alvary (bar), Thomas Beecham (cd), Walter Cassel (bar), Fausto Cleva (cd), Lily Djanel (sop), Doris Doree (sop), John Garris (ten), Hertha Glaz (alto), Frances Greer (sop), Margaret Harshaw (mez), Osie Hawkins (bar), Maria Markan (sop), James Melton (ten), Lillian Raymond (sop), George Szell (cd), Marie Wilkins (sop)

U.S. --Lawrence Davidson (Chicago), Ellabelle Davis (N.Y.), Kathleen Ferrier (Newcastle), Marjorie Lawrence (return debut), Witold Malcuzynski (N.Y.), Zara Nelsova (N.Y.), Regina Resnik (N.Y.)

Other -Ana Maria de Botazzi (Buenos Aires), Aldo Ciccolini (Naples), Ernst Haefliger (Vienna), Manfred Jungwirth (Bucharest), Sena Jurinac (Zagreb), Suzanne Juyol (Paris), Libero de Luca (Biel-Solothurn), Martha Mödl (Remscheid), Peter Pears (London), Giacinto Prandelli (Bergamo), Mstislav Rostropovich (Leningrad), Ilona Steingruber (Tilsit), Josef Traxel (Mainz)

D. New Positions:

Conductors: Tibor Freso (Bratislava Opera), Tauno Hannikainen (Duluth SO), Armas Järnefelt (Helsinki SO), Ernst Märzendorfer (Graz SO), Fernando Previtali (La Scala), Malcolm Sargent (Liverpool PO), Reginald Stewart (Baltimore SO)

Educational: Mieczyslaw Horszowski (piano, Curtis Institute), Wilfrid Pelletier (director, Montreal Conservatory), Quincy Porter (director, New England Conservatory), Vissarion Shebalin (director, Moscow Conservatory)

Others: Karl Elmendorff (director, Dresden Opera), Max de Schauensee (music critic, Philadelphia Evening Bulletin), Deems Taylor (President, ASCAP)

E. Prizes and Honors:

Prizes: Norman Dello Joio (Town Hall), Annette Elkanova (Naumberg), Roy Harris (Coolidge), Jane Rogers (Naumberg), David Sarser (Naumberg), Georg Solti (Geneva)

Honors: John Alden Carpenter (American Academy), William Walton (honorary doctorate, Oxford)

F. Biographical Highlights:

Malcolm Arnold becomes first trumpet with the London PO; Pierre Boulez, against his father's wishes, moves to Paris and begins music study at the Paris Conservatory; Benjamin Britten leaves the U.S. to return to England; John Cage moves to New York; Boris Christoff is given a scholarship by the King of Bulgaria to study voice in Italy; Henry Cowell is given a full pardon by the Governor of California; Emil Gilels becomes an official member of the Communist Party in Russia; Peggy Glanville-Hicks settles in the U.S. for the war years; Margaret Harshaw wins in the Met auditions; Lili Kraus and her family are arrested and confined in a Japanese POW camp; Lorin Maazel, at the age of 12, conducts a full program with the New York PO; Nathan Milstein, Pierre Monteux and Gregor Piatigorsky all become naturalized American citizens; Elisabeth Rethberg makes her final Met appearance.

G. Institutional Openings:

Performing Groups: Cardiff Municipal Choir, Cathedral Choral Society (Washington, D.C.), Chilean National Ballet, Dallas Chamber Music Society, Hartt Opera Theater (Hartford), London Wind Players, Parrenin String Quartet (Paris), U.S.S.R. State Choir (Moscow), Youth Symphony of Seattle

Educational: Conservatoire de Musique et de l'Art Dramatique (Montreal), National Catholic Music Educators' Association (Washington, D.C.), National Conservatory of Music (Rio de Janeiro), Spokane Conservatory of Music

Other: American Symphony Orchestra League (Washington, D.C.), Koussevitsky Music Foundation (N.Y.), Opera Guild of Montreal, *Revista Musical Mexicana*, Rocky Ridge Music Center (Colorado)

H. Musical Literature:

Apel, Willi, *The Notation of Polyphonic Music, 900-1600*
Blom, Eric, *Music in England*
Carner, Mosco, *Study in Twentieth Century Harmony*
Dorian, Frederick, *History of Music in Performance*
Ewen, David, *Music Comes to America*
Gleason, Harold, *Examples of Music before 1400*
Howard, John T., *This Modern Music*
Lomax, Alan, *American Folk Song and Folk Lore*
Moore, Douglas, *From Madrigal to Modern Music*
Parrish, Lillian, *Slave Songs of the Georgia Slave Islands*
Reese, Gustave, *Music in the Middle Ages*

I. Musical Compositions:

Addinsell, Richard, *Warsaw Concerto*
Antheil, George, *Symphony No. 3*
Barber, Samuel, *Essay No. 2 for Orchestra*
Berlin, Irving, *This is the Army* (musical)
Bernstein, Leonard, *Jeremiah Symphony* (with mezzo-soprano)
Bloch, Ernest, *Symphonic Suite* (orchestra)
Britten, Benjamin, *A Ceremony of Carols*
Cadman, Charles W., *Aurora Borealis* (piano and orchestra)
Carter, Elliott, *Symphony No. 1*
Casella, Alfredo, *Paganiniana* (orchestra)
Chávez, Carlos, *Toccata for Percussion*
Copland, Aaron, *Rodeo* (ballet)
    Danzon Cubano (two pianos)
    A Lincoln Portrait (speaker and orchestra)
Cowell, Henry, *Symphony No. 3, "Gallic"*
Creston, Paul, *Dance Variations* (soprano and orchestra)
Damrosch, Walter, *The Opera Clerk* (opera)
Dello Joio, Norman, *Prairie* (ballet)
    The Duke of Sacramento (ballet)
Egge, Klaus, *Symphony No. 1, Opus 17*
Ginastera, Alberto, *Sinfonica Porteña*
Glière, Reinhold, *Concerto for Soprano and Orchestra*
Gould, Morton, *Symphony No. 1*
Guarnieri, Camargo, *Concerto No. 1 for Violin and Orchestra*
Khachaturian, Aram, *Gayne* (ballet)
Khrennikov, Tikhon, *Symphony No. 2*
Martinu, Bohuslav, *Symphony No. 1*
Milhaud, Darius, *Concerto for Two Pianos and Orchestras*
Orff, Carl, *Die Kluge* (opera)
    Catulli Carmina (secular cantata)
Prokofiev, Serge, *War and Peace* (opera)
Riegger, Wallingford, *Passacaglia and Fugue, Opus 36*
Rubbra, Edmund, *Symphony No. 4*
Schoenberg, Arnold, *Concerto for Piano and Orchestra, Opus 42*
Schuman, William, *Concerto for Piano and Orchestra*
    Symphony No. 4
Shostakovich, Dmitri, *Symphony No. 7, Opus 60, "Leningrad"*
Strauss, Richard, *Concerto No. 2 for Horn and Orchestra*
Stravinsky, Igor, *Danses Concertantes* (orchestra)
    Circus Polka (orchestra)
Villa-Lobos, Heitor, *Bachianas Brasileiras No. 7* (orchestra)

1943

World Events:
President Roosevelt meets with Prime Minister Churchill in Casablanca and later the two meet with Stalin at Teheran; the "pay-as-you-go" Income Tax Bill is passed by Congress; the Pentagon building is finished in Washington; the "Big Inch" pipeline begins operation between Texas and Pennsylvania; the Jefferson Memorial is dedicated in Washington; educator and inventor George Washington Carver is born. Internationally, General Eisenhower is named as Supreme Allied Commander in Europe; the Allies invade Sicily and southern Italy--Italy withdraws from the conflict; the Germans surrender at Stalingrad and in North Africa; island-hopping campaign begins in the South Pacific.

Cultural Highlights:
Pulitzers: Drama, Thornton Wilder (*The Skin of Our Teeth*); Fiction, Upton Sinclair (*Dragon's Teeth*); Poetry, Robert Frost (*A Witness Tree*). Osbert Sitwell is given a baronet. Deaths in the art field include American artist Marsden Hartley and French artist Maurice Denis; Russian artist Vitaly Komar is born. Deaths in the literary field include American poet Stephen Vincent Benét, Russian poet Konstantin Balmont, Danish novelist Henrik Pontoppidan, Austrian dramatist Karl Schönherr, British poet Lawrence Binyon and Italian poet and writer, Guido Mazzoni. Other highlights include:

Art: Max Beckmann, *Carnaval*; Constantin Brancusi, *The Flying Turtle*; Marsden Hartley, *The Dead Plover*; Willem de Kooning, *The Queen of Hearts*; Jacques Lipschitz, *Prometheus*; Reginald Marsh, *Coney Island I*; Henri Matisse, *Tabac Royal*; Piet Mondrian, *Broadway Boogie-Woogie*; Jackson Pollack, *The She-Wolf*.

Literature: Louis Bromfield, *Mrs. Parkington*; T.S. Eliot, *Four Quartets*; Hermann Hesse, *Das Glasperlenspiel*; Mary O'Hara, *Thunderhead, Son of Flicka*; Ayn Rand, *The Fountainhead*; William Saroyan, *The Human Comedy*; Jean Paul Sartre, *The Flies*; Betty Smith, *A Tree Grows in Brooklyn*; P. Tregaskis, *Guadalcanal Diary*.

MUSICAL EVENTS

A. Births:

Jan 7	Richard Armstrong (Br-cd)	Jun 23	James Levine (Am-cd)
Jan 16	Brian Ferneyhough (Br-cm)	Jun 28	Cherry Rhodes (Am-mus)
Feb 5	John Owings (Am-pn)	Jul 27	Patricia Jones (Am-mus)
Feb 5	Ivan Tcherepnin (Am-cm)	Aug 13	Estela Olevsky (Arg-pn)
Feb 9	Ryland Davies (Br-ten)	Sep 2	Gayle Smith (Am-cel)
Feb 20	Nancy Mandel (Am-vn)	Sep 21	James Tocco (Am-pn)
Mar 22	Joseph Schwantner (Am-cm)	Sep 23	Janet E. Jacques (Br-sop)
Apr 4	Sergiu Luca (Rom-vn)	Oct 6	Udo Zimmermann (Ger-cm)
Apr 14	Nikolai Petrov (Rus-pn)	Oct 14	Anthony Iannaccone (Am-cm)
Apr 20	John E. Gardiner (Br-cd)	Oct 22	Paul Zukofsky (Am-vn)
Apr 27	James Atherton (Am-ten)	Nov 7	Trudeliese Schmidt (Ger-alto)
May 7	Stephen Kates (Am-cel)	Nov 20	Meredith Monk (Peru-cm)
May 28	Elena Souliotis (Gr-sop)	Dec 19	Yehuda Hanani (Is-cel)
Jun 1	Richard Goode (Am-pn)	Dec 24	Leon Gregorian (Iran-cd)
Jun 14	Edith Guillaume (Den-sop)		Michael Murray (Am-org)

B. Deaths:

Jan 14	Adolf Sandberger (Ger-mus)	Jun 1	Amédée Gastoué (Fr-mus)
Jan 18	Maria Mikhailova (Rus-sop)	Jun 6	Sigrid Onegin (Ger-alto)
Mar 23	Joseph Schillinger (Rus-the)	Jul 13	Kurt Huber (Swi-mus)
Mar 28	Serge Rachmaninoff (Rus-pn)	Jul 29	Maria Gay (Sp-alto)
Apr 15	Raffaele Casimiri (It-mus)	Aug 2	Karl Grunsky (Ger-cri)
Apr 19	Gustav Doret (Swe-cm-cd)	Aug 21	William L. Phelps (Am-cri)
May 29	Hermann Wetzler (Am-org-cd)	Sep 30	Naoum Aronson (Rus-cel)

Oct 29 Percy Goetschius (Br-the)
Nov 11 André Pirro (Fr-mus)
Nov 12 Paul Stefan (Aus-mus)

Nov 16 Winthrop Sterling (Am-org)
Nov 22 Pietro A. Yon (It-org)
Dec 25 Raymond Woodman (Am-org)

C. Debuts:

Met ---Thelma Altman (mez), John Baker (bar), Christina Carroll (sop), Donald Dame (ten), Elwood Gary (ten), Jacques Gérard (ten), Frederick Lechner (bs), Patrice Munsel (sop), Martial Singher (bar)

U.S. --Leonard Bernstein (N.Y.), John Browning (Denver, age 10), Leon Fleisher (San Francisco), Eugene Istomin (Philadelphia), Byron Janis (N.Y.), Jean Madeira (N.Y.), Henryk Szeryng (N.Y.)

Other -Owen Brannigan (London), Jörg Demus (Vienna), Carla Henius (Kassel), Colin Horsley (Manchester), Luigi Infantino (Parma), Magda Laszló (Budapest), Wilma Lipp (Vienna), Johanna Martzy (Budapest), Ivan Petrov (Moscow), Anneliese Rothenberger (Koblenz), Rita Streich (Aussig), Ramón Vinay (as tenor)

D. New Positions:

Conductors: Kurt H. Adler (chorus, San Francisco Opera), John Barbirolli (Hallé SO), Karl Böhm (Vienna Opera), Désiré Defauw (Chicago SO), André Jolivet (Comédie Française), Kyrill Kondrashin (Bolshoi Ballet), Karl Krueger (Detroit SO), Efrem Kurtz (Kansas City PO), Erich Leinsdorf (Cleveland Orchestra), Artur Rodzinski (New York PO), Hans Schmidt-Isserstedt (Berlin Opera), Alfred Wallenstein (Los Angeles PO)

Education: Marcel Grandjany (harp, Montreal Conservatory)

E. Prizes and Honors:

Prizes: David Diamond (Paderewski), Samson François (Long-Thibaud), Ruth Geiger (Naumberg), Eugene Istomin (Leventritt), Constance Keene (Naumberg), Jean Louel (Prix de Rome), Dolores Miller (Naumberg), Gardner Read (Paderewski), William Schuman (Pulitzer--Cantata, *A Free Song*), Béla Siki (Liszt)

Honors: Stanley Marchant (knighted)

F. Biographical Highlights:

Samuel Barber enters the U.S. Air Force; Béla Bartók makes his last public appearance as a pianist; Boris Christoff returns to Bulgaria from Italy, then goes to Salzburg for further study; Ross Lee Finney enters the Office of Strategic Services for the U.S. Government; Herbert von Karajan leaves Berlin after Furtwängler is reinstated at the Opera; Fritz Kreisler, André Previn and Boris Schwarz become naturalized American citizens; Charles Mackerras, upon graduating, becomes first oboist with the Sydney SO; Leonard Rose joins the cello section of the New York PO; Mstislav Rostropovich enters Moscow Conservatory; Friedrich Schorr gives his farewell Met performance; Michael Tippett serves time in prison for his views as a conscientious objector.

G. Institutional Openings:

Performing Groups: Liverpool SO, New Orleans Opera Association, New York City Opera, Valencia Municipal Orchestra (Spain)

Educational: Instituto Español de Musicología

Other: Committee for the Promotion of New Music (London), Concours International Marguerite Long-Jacques Thibaud (Paris), New York City Center of Music and Drama, Société de Musique de Chambre de la Société des Concerts du Conservatoire de Paris

H. Musical Literature:

Ansermet, Ernest, *La Geste du Chef d'Orchestre*
Beecham, Thomas, *A Mingled Chime*
Ewen, David, *Dictators of the Baton*
Geiringer, Karl, *Musical Instruments, Their History*

Hindemith, Paul, *A Concentrated Course in Traditional Harmony*
Moore, Gerald, *The Unashamed Accompanist*
Sachs, Curt, *Rise of Music in the Ancient World*
Stringham, Edwin, *Listening to Music Creatively*

I. Musical Compositions:
Antheil, George, *Symphony No. 4*
Bacon, Ernst, *Ford's Theater* (symphonic suite)
      From These States (symphonic suite)
Bartók, Béla, *Concerto for Orchestra*
Bergsma, William, *Music on a Quiet Theme* (orchestra)
Bernstein, Leonard, *Five Kid Songs*
Blomdahl, Karl-Birger, *Symphony No. 1*
Britten, Benjamin, *Serenade for Tenor, Horn and Strings*
Carpenter, John Alden, *The Anxious Bugler* (orchestra)
Casella, Alfredo, *Concerto for Strings, Piano and Percussion*
Castelnuovo-Tedesco, Mario, *The Princess and the Pea* (opera)
      An American Rhapsody (orchestra)
Cowell, Henry, *American Pipers* (orchestra)
Creston, Paul, *Frontiers* (orchestra)
Dello Joio, Norman, *The Mystic Trumpeter* (Chorus and horn)
      Magnificat (orchestra)
Finney, Ross Lee, *Symphony No. 1*
Gillis, Don, *Symphony No. 4*
Hanson, Howard, *Symphony No. 4, "Sinfonia da Requiem"*
Harris, Roy, *Symphony No. 5*
Hindemith, Paul, *Ludus Tonalis* (piano)
      Cupid and Psyche Overture
Honegger, Artur, *Jour de Fête Suisse* (orchestra)
Kabalevsky, Dmitri, *24 Preludes for Piano*
Khachaturian, Aram, *Symphony No. 2*
Martinu, Bohuslav, *Memorial to Lidice* (orchestra)
      Symphony No. 2
Messiaen, Olivier, *Visions de l'Amen* (piano)
Miaskovsky, Nicolai, *Symphony No. 24, Opus 63*
Milhaud, Darius, *Bolivar* (opera)
Piston, Walter, *Symphony No. 2*
      Prelude and Allegro for Organ and Strings
Poulenc, Francis, *Métamorphoses* (song cycle)
Read, Gardner, *Symphony No. 2*
Rodgers, Richard, *Oklahoma* (musical)
Schoenberg, Arnold, *Theme and Variations, Opus 43a* (band)
Schuman, William, *William Billings Overture*
      Symphony No. 5 (strings)
Shostakovich, Dmitri, *Symphony No. 8, Opus 65*
Skalkottas, Nikos, *Orchestral Suite No. 2*
Thompson, Randall, *The Testament of Freedom* (men's voices)
Vaughan-Williams, Ralph, *Symphony No. 5*
Webern, Anton, *Cantata No. 2, Opus 31*

1944

World Events:
In the U.S., Franklin D. Roosevelt is elected to an unprecedented fourth term as President; the Dumbarton Oaks and Bretton Woods Conferences are held by the world leaders; Eisenhower, Marshall, MacArthur and Arnold are given the new rank of General of the Armies; the GI Bill of Rights is passed by Congress; the American Veterans of World Wars (AMVET) is founded. Internationally, D-Day takes place on June 6 when the Allies invade France; the Battle of the Bulge is the last push by German troops; Germany uses rockets, the V-1 and V-2 against England; an attempt by German generals to assassinate Hitler fails; the Allies return to the Philippines; the Japanese fleet is destroyed in the Battle of Leyte Gulf.

Cultural Highlights:
Pulitzers: Fiction, Martin Flavin (*Journey in the Dark*); Poetry, Stephen Vincent Benét (*Western Star*). Danish poet and novelist Johannes Vilhelm Jensen receives the Nobel Prize for Literature; Alfred J. Munnings becomes president of the Royal Academy of Art; Sir William Burrell presents his art collection to the city of Glasgow. In the literary field American author Carl Bernstein is born; deaths include American authors George Ade, John Peale Bishop, Irvin Cobb and Harold Wright and French novelist Jean Giraudoux. The art field witnesses the death of American sculptor Cyrus E. Dallin, French sculptor Aristide Maillol, American artist Edgar Cameron, British artist George Clausen, Russian artist Vasili Kandinsky, Dutch artist Piet Mondrian and Norwegian artist Edvard Munch. Other highlights include:

Art: Melvin M. Albright, *The Picture of Dorian Gray*; Georges Braque, *Pumpkin Slice*; Alexandre Colin, *Liberation*; Arshile Gorky, *The Liver is the Cock's Comb*; Henri Matisse, *The White Dress*; Henri Moore, *Madonna (Northampton)*; Georges Rouault, *Homo Homini Lupus*; Ben Shahn, *The Red Stairway*; Andrew Wyeth, *Rum Runner*.

Literature: Ivo Andric, *The Bridge on the Drina*; Saul Bellow, *The Dangling Man*; Albert Camus, *Caligula*; John R. Hersey, *A Bell for Adano*; W. Somerset Maugham, *The Razor's Edge*; Katherine Ann Porter, *The Leaning Tower*; Anya Seton, *Dragonwyck*; Franz Werfel, *Jacobowsky and the Colonel*; Kathleen Windsor, *Forever Amber*.

MUSICAL EVENTS

A. Births:

Jan 28	John Tavener (Br-cm)	Jul 12	Judith de Paul (Am-sop)
Jan 30	Lynn Harrell (Am-cel)	Jul 19	Lorin Hollander (Am-pn)
Feb 1	Aage Haugland (Den-bs)	Jul 30	Teresa M. Cahil (Br-sop)
Feb 2	Ursula Oppens (Am-pn)	Aug 12	Peter Hofmann (Ger-ten)
Feb 4	Andrew F. Davis (Br-cd)	Sep 1	Leonard Slatkin (Am-cd)
Mar 2	Leif Segerstam (Fin-cd)	Sep 10	Thomas Allen (Br-bar)
Mar 3	Florence Quivar (Am-mez)	Sep 16	Caspar Richter (Ger-cd)
Mar 6	Kiri Te Kanawa (N.Z.-sop)	Oct 17	Anne-Marie Antoine (Bel-sop)
Mar 17	John R. Lill (Br-pn)	Oct 18	Nelson Freire (Bra-pn)
Mar 19	Myung-Wha Chung (Kor-cel)	Oct 20	William Albright (Am-pn-cm)
Apr 6	Felicity Palmer (Br-sop)	Oct 23	Barbara Dix (Br-alto)
Apr 16	Dennis R. Davies (Am-cd)	Nov 11	Jennifer Bate (Br-sop)
Apr 21	Julian Smith (Br-cd)	Nov 19	Agnes Baltsa (Gr-mez)
Apr 24	Norma Burrowes (Br-sop)	Nov 26	Susanne Marsee (Am-mez)
Apr 25	John Sebastian (Am-harm)	Dec 21	Michael T. Thomas (Am-cd)
Apr 26	Richard Bradshaw (Br-cd)		Ellen Shade (Am-sop)
Jun 17	Anthony Paratore (Am-pn)		Vladimir Spivakov (Rus-vn)
Jun 20	Jenny Hill (Br-sop)		

B. Deaths:

Jan 19	Charles Douglas (Am-org)	Aug 8	Aïno Ackté (Fin-sop)
Feb 1	Michel Calvocoressi (Fr-mus)	Aug 10	Henry J. Wood (Br-cd)
Apr 18	Cécile Chaminade (Pol-cm)	Sep 3	Franz Drdla (Cz-vn-cm)
May 6	Carl Engel (Fr-mus)	Nov 12	Edgar Kelley (Am-cm)
May 8	Ethel Smyth (Br-cm)	Nov 14	Karl Flesch (Hun-vn-ped)
May 13	Charles H. Kitson (Br-the)	Dec 2	Josef Lhévinne (Rus-pn)
May 16	Leone Sinigaglia (It-cm)	Dec 12	Ferencz Hegedus (Hun-vn)
Jun 5	Riccardo Zandonai (It-cm)	Dec 15	Glenn Miller (Am-pop)
Jun 14	Georges Barrère (Fr-fl)	Dec 27	Mrs. H.H.A. Beach (Am-cm)
Aug 2	Joseph Bonnet (Fr-org)	Dec 30	Romain Rolland (Fr-mus)

C. Debuts:

Met ---Morton Bowe (ten), Audrey Bowman (sop), Emil Cooper (cd), Ella Flesch (sop), William Harshaw (bar), Christine Johnson (sop), Florence Kirk (sop), Martha Lipton (alto), Richard Manning (ten), Jeanne Palmer (sop), Regina Resnik (mez), Anton Schubel (bs), Blanche Thebom (mez), Hugh Thompson (bar), Philip Whitfield (bs)

U.S. --Donald Gramm (Chicago), Grant Johannesen (N.Y.), Miliza Korjus (N.Y.), Robert Merrill (Trenton, N.J.), Leonard Rose (N.Y.), Richard Tucker (N.Y.)

Other -Victoria de los Angeles (Barcelona), Elisabetta Barbato (Rome), Mimi Benzell (Mexico City), Carlo Maria Giulini (Rome), Friedrich Gulda (Vienna), Bengt Johnsson (Copenhagen); Martin Lawrence (Hull), Miriam Pirazzini (Rome), Constance Shacklock (London), Renata Tebaldi (Rovigo), Silvio Varviso (St. Gall), Galina Vishnevskaya (Leningrad)

D. New Positions:

Conductors: Massimo Freccia (New Orleans PO); Charles Groves (BBC Northern SO); Erich Kleiber (Havana PO); Paul Paray (Cologne SO); George Szell (Met)

Educational: Roger Sessions (composition, U. of California, Berkeley)

Others: William Schuman (publication director, Schirmer)

E. Prizes and Honors:

Prizes: Carol Brice (Naumberg), Jean Carlton (Naumberg), Harry Datyner (Geneva), Raymond Gallois-Montbrun (Prix de Rome), Howard Hanson (Pulitzer--*Symphony No. 4*), Walter Piston (New York Music Critics' Circle), Jeanne Therrien (Naumberg and Leventritt)

F. Biographical Highlights:

Marie Claire Alain enters the Conservatory of Paris; John Alexander joins the U.S. Air Force; Leonard Bernstein makes a last minute substitution for an ailing Bruno Walter for a phenomenal debut with the New York PO; Boris Christoff is arrested and put into a Nazi prison camp; Ernst von Dohnányi leaves Hungary for Vienna but ends up in the U.S.; Vladimir Horowitz, Nikolai Lopatnikoff, Vittorio Rieti and Artur Schnabel all become naturalized American citizens; Eugene Ormandy leaves RCA and begins a 25-year association with Columbia Records; Andrzej Panufnik's early works are all destroyed in the Warsaw uprising; Alexander Schneider quits the Budapest String Quartet; Peter Schreier, age 9, debuts in Dresden as a genie in the Magic Flute; Eduard Tubin flees Communist Estonia and settles permanently in Sweden; Heitor Villa-Lobos makes his first visit to the U.S.

G. Institutional Openings:

Performing Groups: Atlanta Youth Symphony (Atlanta SO in 1947); Chelsea SO (England); City of Birmingham SO (England); Société de Musique de Chambre de Versailles; Wichita SO (Kansas)

Educational: National Association of Teachers of Singing (NATS; Cincinnati)

Other: Agrupación Nueva Música (Buenos Aires), Arts Council of Australia (Sydney); Composer's Guild of Great Britain (London); Hinrichson's Musical Year Book; National Society of Arts and Letters (Washington, D.C.)

H. Musical Literature:

Apel, Willi, *The Harvard Dictionary of Music*
Blume, Friedrich, *Wesen und Werden deutscher Musik*
Carner, Mosco, *On Men and Music*
Downes, Edward O., *Adventures in Symphonic Music*
Dumesnil, René, *La Musique romantique français*
Jacob, Gordon, *How to Read a Score*
Messiaen, Olivier, *Technique of My Musical Language*
Morris, R.O., *Introduction to Counterpoint*
Veinus, Abraham, *Pocket Book of Great Operas*

I. Musical Compositions:

Arnold, Malcolm, *Concerto for Horn and Orchestra*
Barber, Samuel, *Symphony No. 2, Opus 19*
    Capricorn Concerto
Bernstein, Leonard, *Fancy Free* (ballet)
    On the Town (ballet)
Blomdahl, Karl-Birger, *Concerto Grosso* (orchestra)
Cadman, Charles W., *A Mad Empress Remembers* (cello and orchestra)
Chávez, Carlos, *Daughter of Colquide* (ballet)
Copland, Aaron, *Appalachian Spring* (ballet)
Egge, Klaus, *Concerto No. 2 for Piano and Orchestra*
Einem, Gottfried von, *Concerto for Orchestra, Opus 4*
Foss, Lukas, *Concerto No. 1 for Piano and Orchestra*
Gillis, Don, *The Alamo* (orchestra)
Ginastera, Alberto, *Twelve American Preludes for Piano*
Harris, Roy, *Symphony No. 6, "Gettysburg Address"*
Hindemith, Paul, *Symphonic Metamorphoses on Themes of Carl Maria von Weber*
Ibert, Jacques, *Capriccio for Small Orchestra*
Kay, Ulysses, *Of New Horizons Overture*
Khachaturian, Aram, *Masquerade Suite*
Martinu, Bohuslav, *Symphony No. 3*
McDonald, Harl, *Symphonic Suite, "My Country at War"*
Mennin, Peter, *Symphony No. 2*
    Concerto for Orchestra
Messiaen, Olivier, *Vingt Regards sur l'Enfant Jésus* (piano)
    Trois Petites Liturgies de la Présence Divine (voices, orchestra)
Milhaud, Darius, *Suite Française*
Prokofiev, Serge, *Cinderella* (ballet)
    Symphony No. 5, Opus 100
Rangström, Ture, *Festival Prelude*
Riegger, Wallingford, *Symphony No. 1*
Schuller, Gunther, *Concerto for Horn and Orchestra*
Schuman, William, *Circus Overture*
Stravinsky, Igor, *Norwegian Moods* (orchestra)
    Scenes de Ballet (orchestra)
Thomson, Virgil, *Orchestra Suite No. 2, "Portraits"*
Tippett, Michael, *The Weeping Babe* (soprano and chorus a capella)
Villa-Lobos, Heitor, *Symphony No. 6*
    Bachianas Brasileiras No. 8 (orchestra)

1945

World Events:
In the U.S., President Roosevelt dies and Harry S. Truman becomes President No. 33; the first trial explosion of an atom bomb takes place at Alamogordo, New Mexico; the United Nations opens in San Francisco; a B-25 Bomber hits the Empire State Building in New York; the Cooperative for American Relief in Europe (CARE) is founded. Internationally, World War II ends with the unconditional surrender of Germany and of Japan following the dropping of atomic bombs on Hiroshima and Nagasaki; the Big Three leaders meet at Yalta and Potsdam; Clement Atlee becomes British Prime Minister; the Act of Chapultepec, a Latin American defense league, is signed.

Cultural Highlights:
Pulitzers: Drama, Mary Chase (*Harvey*); Fiction, John Hersey (*A Bell for Adano*); Poetry, Karl Shapiro (*V-Letter and Other Poems*). Chilean poet and educator Gabriela Mistral becomes the first Latin-American woman to receive a Nobel Prize for Literature; Edward Hopper is inducted into the National Institute and Sidney Lanier is entered into the Hall of Fame for Great Americans. Births in the art field include the American artists John Alexander and Susan Rothenberg and Russian artist Alexander Melamid; deaths include American sculptor Alexander Calder. Deaths in the literary field include American novelists Theodore Dreiser and Ellen Glasgow, British poet and critic Arthur Symons, Russian author Alexei Tolstoy, French poet Paul Valery and Austrian author Franz Werfel. Other highlights include:

Art: Max Beckmann, *Blindman's Bluff*; Otto Dix, *Saul and David*; Max Ernst, *The Temptation of St. Anthony*; Francis Gruber, *Job*; Jacques Lipschitz. *Mother and Child*; John Marin, *Junk Mountains*; Ben Shahn, *Liberation; Reconstruction*; Yves Tanguy, *Rapidity of Sleep*; Max Weber, *The Brass Band*; William Zorach, *Victory*.

Literature: *New Testament--Revised Standard Version*; Mary Chase, *Harvey*; Robert Frost, *A Masque of Reason*; Jean Giraudoux, *The Madwoman of Chaillot*; Sinclair Lewis, *Cass Timberlane*; George Orwell, *Animal Farm*; John Steinbeck, *Cannery Row*; Evelyn Waugh, *Brideshead Revisited*; Tennessee Williams, *The Glass Menagerie*.

MUSICAL EVENTS

A. Births:

Jan 1	Noel A. Davies (Br-cd)	Jul 7	Matti Salminen (Fin-bs)
Jan 19	Charles Amirkhanian (Am-cm)	Jul 9	Manfred Jung (Ger-ten)
Jan 26	Jacqueline du Pré (Br-cel)	Aug 16	Evelyn Mandac (Phil-sop)
Feb 5	Phyllis Bryn-Julson (Am-sop)	Aug 18	Lars Anders Roos (Swe-pn)
Feb 11	Lenus J. Carlson (Am-bar)	Aug 31	Itzhak Perlman (Is-vn)
Feb 21	D'Anna Fortunato (Am-sop)	Sep 12	John Mauceri (Am-cd)
Mar 9	Carol Ann Wilcox (Am-sop)	Sep 15	Jessye Norman (Am-sop)
Mar 16	Douglas Ahlstedt (Am-ten)	Sep 27	Misha Dichter (Am-pn)
Mar 20	Christine Edinger (Ger-vn)	Oct 20	Thomas Pasatieri (Am-cm)
Apr 9	Neil Jenkins (Br-ten)	Oct 28	Alan W. Titus (Am-bar)
Apr 10	Robert Wittinger (Ger-cm)	Nov 25	Håkan Hagegård (Swe-bar)
Apr 27	Carolyne James (Am-sop)	Nov 27	Martin Katz (Am-pn)
May 6	Victoria Bond (Am-cd-cm)	Nov 30	Radu Lupu (Rom-pn)
Jun 1	Frederica von Stade (Am-mez)	Dec 13	Anne Shasby (Br-pn)
Jun 25	Jane Marsh (Am-sop)		Jean-Jacques Kantorow (Fr-vn)

B. Deaths:

Jan 12	Theodor Kroyer (Ger-mus)	Jun 26	Nicolas Tcherepnin (Rus-cm)
Jan 30	Herbert Clarke (Am-tpt)	Aug 2	Pietro Mascagni (It-cm)
Mar 5	Luise Reuss-Belce (Aus-sop)	Aug 2	Emil Reznicek (Aus-cm)
Apr 12	Peter Raabe (Ger-mus)	Sep 15	Anton Webern (Aus-cm)
Apr 24	Hubert Bath (Br-cm)	Sep 16	John McCormack (It-ten)

Sep 26   Béla Bartók (Hun-cm)
Oct 6   George C. Stebbins (Am-hymn)
Nov 11   Jerome Kern (Am-pop)

Dec 1   Harvey Gaul (Am-m.ed)
Dec 8   Alexander Siloti (Rus-pn)
Dec 30   Francis Galpin (Br-mus)

C. Debuts:

Met ---Pierrette Alarie (sop), Mimi Benzell (sop), Fritz Busch (cd), Wellington Ezekiel (bs), Frederick Gynrod (bar), Thomas Hayward (ten), Dorothy Kirsten (sop), Robert Merrill (bar), Torsten Ralf (ten), Kenneth Schon (bar), Richard Tucker (ten)

U.S. --Jacob Lateiner (Philadelphia), Jerome Lowenthal (Philadelphia), Florence Quartararo (Hollywood), Malcolm Sargent (N.Y.), Russell Sherman (N.Y.), Betty K. Stasson (Chicago), Ramón Vinay (N.Y.), Camilla Williams (Philadelphia)

Other -Ettore Bastianini (Ravenna), Piero Gamba (Rome), Severino Gazzelloni (Rome), Maurice Gendron (London), Walter Goldschmidt (Graz), Walter Kreppel (Nuremburg), Josef Metternich (Berlin), Anna Pollack (London), Dorothea Siebert (Marburg), Béla Siki (Budapest), Eugenia Smolenskaya (Stalingrad), Gérard Souzay (London), Hertha Töpper (Graz), Ivo Zidek (Ostrava)

D. New Positions:

Conductors: Ataulfo Argenta (Madrid National Orchestra), Edward van Beinum (Amsterdam Concertgebouw), Antal Dorati (Dallas SO), Jussi Jalas (Helsinki Opera), Ferdinand Leitner (Hamburg Opera), Witold Rowicki (Polish Radio SO), Hans Schmidt-Isserstedt (North German SO), William Steinberg (Buffalo SO)

Educational: William Schuman (President, Juilliard)

Others: Klaus Egge (President. Society of Norwegian Composers), Jean Langlais (organ, Ste. Clothilde, Paris), André Marchal (organ, St. Eustache, Paris), Gustave Reese (publication director, Carl Fischer)

E. Prizes and Honors:

Prizes: Jane Boedeker (Naumberg), Aaron Copland (Pulitzer--*Appalachian Spring*), Howard Hanson (Ditson), Paula Lenchner (Naumberg), Louise Meiszner (Leventritt), Alexander Schneider (Coolidge)

Honors: John Alden Carpenter (American Academy), Léon Jongen (Belgian Royal Academy), Serge Koussevitsky (honorary doctorate, Boston U.), Charles Munch (Legion of Honor)

F. Biographical Highlights:

Licia Albanese, Ernst Krenek, Lotte Lehmann, Carl Milles and Igor Stravinsky all become naturalized American citizens; Boris Christoff, freed from the Nazi POW camp, goes to Rome for further voice study; Alberto Ginastera, dismissed from his Argentine music post by Juan Perón, goes to the U.S.; Bruno Maderna returns to Venice and the Conservatory; Giovanni Martinelli retires from the stage; Peter Mennin receives his M.Mus. degree; John Ogdon begins music study at the Royal Manchester College; Serge Prokofiev suffers a concussion from a fall following a heart attack; George Rochberg, discharged from the Army, enrolls at Curtis Institute; Gunther Schuller becomes principle horn in the Met orchestra; Stanislaw Skrowaczewski completes his graduate studies in music; Leopold Stokowski marries heiress Gloria Vanderbilt; Iannis Xenakis loses the sight in one eye from a war injury.

G. Institutional Openings:

Performing Groups: French Wind Quintet (Paris), Hungarian Radio and Television SO (Budapest), Katowice Radio SO, Mississippi Opera Association (Jackson), North German SO (Hamburg), Philharmonia Orchestra of London, Pittsburgh Youth Symphony, Rheinische PO (Koblenz), Rhode Island PO (Providence), San Antonio Opera Co., Smetana String Quartet (Prague), Stuttgart Chamber Orchestra

Festivals: Cheltenham Music Festival (England)

Educational: American Institute of Musicology (Cambridge, Massachusetts), Berklee School of Music (Boston), Halle Hochschule für Theater und Musik, Israel Academy of Music, Krakow College of Music, Ohio State University School of Music, Rouen Municipal Conservatory of Music, Tel Aviv Music Teacher's Training School

Other: La Fédération Internationale des Jeunesses Musicales, Gaudeamus Foundation (Netherlands), Internationales Musiker-Brief-Archiv (Berlin), Leipzig State Theater and Opera Co., *Music Survey*, Musica Viva (Australia)

H. Musical Literature:
Antheil, George, *Bad Boy of Music*
Davison, Archibald, *Choral Conducting*
Eschmann, Karl, *Changing Forms in Modern Music*
Graf, Max, *Legend of a Musical City*
Niles, John J., *Anglo-American Ballad Book*
Slonimsky, Nicolas, *Music of Latin-America*
Thomson, Virgil, *The Musical Scene*
Wood, Henry, *About Conducting*

I. Musical Compositions:
Antheil, George, *Symphony No. 5*
Barber, Samuel, *Concerto for Cello and Orchestra, Opus 22*
Bartók, Béla, *Concerto No. 3 for Piano and Orchestra*
        Concerto for Viola and Orchestra
Britten, Benjamin, *Peter Grimes* (opera)
        Festival Te Deum
Cadman, Charles W., *Overture, Huckleberry Finn Goes Fishing*
Carpenter, John Alden, *The Seven Ages* (symphonic suite)
Carter, Elliott, *Holiday Overture*
Creston, Paul, *Symphony No. 2, Opus 35*
Dello Joio, Norman, *Concert Music* (orchestra)
Diamond, David, *Symphonies No. 3 and 4*
Foss, Lukas, *Symphony in G*
        The Gift of the Magi (ballet)
Gillis, Don, *Symphony No. 5*
Kay, Ulysses, *Suite for Orchestra*
Kodály, Zoltán, *Missa Brevis*
Malipiero, Gian F., *Symphony No. 3*
Martinu, Bohuslav, *Symphony No. 4*
        Concerto No. 2 for Cello and Orchestra
Menotti, Gian C., *Concerto for Piano and Orchestra*
Orff, Carl, *Die Bernauderin* (opera)
Riegger, Wallingford, *Symphony No. 2, Opus 41*
Rodgers, Richard, *Carousel* (musical)
Schuller, Gunther, *Concerto for Cello and Orchestra*
Schuman, William, *Undertow* (ballet)
Shostakovich, Dmitri, *Symphony No. 9, Opus 70*
Siegmeister, Elie, *Western Suite* (orchestra)
Stevens, Halsey, *Symphony No. 1*
Strauss, Richard, *Metamorphosen for 23 strings*
Stravinsky, Igor, *Ebony Concerto* (clarinet and swing band)
        Symphony in Three Movements
Tippett, Michael, *Symphony No. 1*
Villa-Lobos, Heitor, *Symphony No. 7*
        Bachianas Brasileiras No. 5 for Soprano and 8 Celli

1946

World Events:

In the U.S., Winston Churchill delivers his "Iron Curtain" speech in Fulton, Missouri and coins the "cold war" that begins between Russia and the West; independence is given to the Philippines; the Atomic Energy Commission is established by Congress and most price and wage controls are lifted. Internationally, Trygve Lie is elected as first Secretary-General of the United Nations in its London meeting; the Italians force the abdication of Umberto II and establish a republic; General Charles DeGaulle resigns as French President; the War Criminal Trials are held in Nuremburg; Juan Perón is elected as President of Argentina.

Cultural Highlights:

Pulitzers: Drama, Russel Crouse and Howard Lindsay (*State of the Union*). German author Hermann Hesse receives the Nobel Prize for Literature; Ezra Pound, indicted for treason, enters a mental asylum; Les Automatistes exhibition takes place in Montreal, the first abstract showing in Canada. Deaths in the literary field include American authors Thomas Dixon, Damon Runyon, Gertrude Stein and Booth Tarkington, British author H.G. Wells and German author Gerhart Hauptmann; deaths in the art world include American artists John S. Curry and Arthur Dove, Italian artist Joseph Stella, French sculptor Charles Despiau, Hungarian sculptor László Moholy-Nagy and Polish sculptor Elie Nadelman. Other highlights include:

Art: Charles Burchfield, *The Sphinx and the Milky Way*; Willem de Kooning, *Light in August*; Otto Dix, *Crucifixion*; Arshile Gorky, *Charred Beloved I*; Georg Grosz, *The Pit*; Jacques Lipschitz, *Benediction*; Henry Moore, *Reclining Figure*; Jackson Pollack, *The Blue Unconscious*; Andrew Wyeth, *Winter*.

Literature: Theodore Dreiser, *The Bulwark*; Lillian Hellman, *Another Part of the Forest*; Robinson Jeffers, *Medea*; Nikos Kazantzakis, *Zorba, the Greek*; Robert Lowell, *Lord Weary's Castle*; John Marquand, *B.F.'s Daughter*; Eugene O'Neill, *The Iceman Cometh*; Robert Penn Warren, *All the King's Men*; Frank Yerby, *The Foxes of Harrow*.

MUSICAL EVENTS

A. Births:

Jan 15	Joseph Kalichstein (Is-pn)
Jan 16	Katia Ricciarelli (It-sop)
Feb 1	Carol Neblett (Am-sop)
Feb 3	Adolovni Acosta (Phil-pn)
Feb 18	Helen M. Attfield (Br-alto)
Feb 24	Jiri Belohlávek (Cz-cd)
Feb 26	Anthony Peebles (Br-pn)
Mar 4	Ralph Kirshbaum (Am-cel)
Mar 4	Peter Vronsky (Cz-vn-cd)
Mar 7	Okko Kamu (Fin-cd)
Apr 13	Kari Tikka (Fin-cd-cm)
May 7	Barbara Daniels (Am-sop)
May 10	Kun-Woo Paik (Kor-pn)
Jun 15	François Huybrechts (Bel-cd)
Jun 20	André Watts (Am-pn)
Aug 18	Barry Busse (Am-ten)
Aug 31	Pamela Hebert (Am-sop)
Sep 9	Miriam Fried (Rom-vn)
Sep 22	John Tomlinson (Br-bs)
Oct 1	Sandra Walker (Am-mez)
Oct 19	Ray Morrison (Am-bs)
Oct 27	Peter Martins (Den-bal)
Nov 2	Giuseppe Sinopoli (It-cd)
Nov 29	Carole Ann Farley (Am-sop)
Dec 4	James Boswell (Am-vn)
Dec 5	José Carreras (Sp-ten)
Dec 16	Trevor Pinnock (Br-hps)
Dec 21	Christopher Keene (Am-cd)
Dec 23	Edita Gruberová (Cz-sop)
Dec 30	David Arnold (Am-ten)
	Stanislav Macura (Cz-cd)

B. Deaths:

Jan 7	Adam Didur (Pol-bs)
Jan 10	Cornelia Van Zanten (Hol-sop)
Jan 25	Edward Dickinson (Am-org)
Feb 20	Hugh Percy Allen (Br-mus)
Apr 5	Vincent Youmans (Am-pop)
May 20	Emil Frey (Swi-pn)
Jun 1	Leo Slezak (Aus-ten)
Jun 3	Margaret Glyn (Br-mus)
Jul 19	Dominique Planchet (Fr-cm)
Jul 21	Paul Rosenfeld (Am-cri)

Aug 2 Ernst Kurth (Aus-mus)
Aug 8 Maria Barrientos (Sp-sop)
Sep 3 Moritz Rosenthal (Pol-pn)
Sep 20 Mária Basilides (Hun-alto)
Oct 16 Granville Bantock (Br-cm)

Nov 14 Manuel de Falla (Sp-cm)
Dec 26 Hans Volkman (Ger-mus)
Dec 28 Carrie Jacobs Bond (Am-cm)
Dec 30 Charles Cadman (Am-cm)

C. Debuts:

Met ---Joel Berglund (bar), Mario Berini (ten), Leslie Chabay (ten), Dezsö Ernster (bs), Louis Fourestier (cd), Stella Gentile (sop), Mary Henderson (sop), Jerome Hines (bs), Irene Jordan (mez), Philip Kinsman (bs), Felix Knight (ten), René Mazella (sop), Florence Quartararo (sop), Max Rudolf (cd), Fritz Stiedry (cd), Set Svanholm (ten), Francisco Tortolero (ten), Claramae Turner (mez), Giacomo Vaghi (bs), Ramón Vinay (ten/bar), Gladys Zeiher (mez)

U.S. --Lucine Amara (San Francisco), Gold & Fizdale (N.Y.), Bernard Greenhouse (N.Y.), Maryla Jonas (N.Y.), Meyer Kupferman (N.Y.), Charles Munch (Boston), Patricia Neway (Chautauqua), James Pease (N.Y.), Italo Tajo (Chicago), Giuseppe Valdengo (tour)

Other -Martha Argerich (Buenos Aires), David Bar-Illan (Israel), Boris Christoff (Rome), Sergiu Comissiona (Bucharest), Anita Corridori (Como), Kathleen Ferrier (Glyndebourne), Glenn Gould (Toronto), Christa Ludwig (Frankfurt), Ivan Moravec (Prague), Birgit Nilsson (Stockholm), Juan Oncino (Barcelona), Georges Prêtre (Marseilles), Nicola Rossi-Lemeni (Venice), Giuseppe di Stefano (Milan)

D. New Positions:

Conductors: Oivin Fjeldstad (Norwegian Radio SO), Lamberto Gardelli (Stockholm Opera), Carlo Maria Giulini (Italian Radio SO), Werner Janssen (Utah SO), Felix Prohaska (Vienna Opera), Constantin Silvestri (Bucharest PO), Walter Susskind (Scottish National Orchestra), George Szell (Cleveland Orchestra)

Educational: Elliott Carter (composition, Peabody), Mario Castelnuovo-Tedesco (composition, Los Angeles Conservatory), Knud Jeppeson (musicology, Arhus University), Jean Papineau-Couture (professor, Quebec Conservatory), Randall Thompson (professor, Princeton)

E. Prizes and Honors:

Prizes: Anahid Ajemian (Naumberg), Aaron Copland (New York Critics' Circle), Friedrich Gulda (Geneva), Leonid Hambro (Naumberg), Jerome Hines (Caruso), David Nadien (Leventritt), Jeanne Rosenblum (Naumberg), Heidi Schneider (Long-Thibaud), Harold Shapero (Gershwin)

F. Biographical Highlights:

Eduard van Beinum, substituting for an ailing Albert Coates, makes his London debut; Georges Enescu moves to New York and begins teaching; Alexander Gretchaninov, Paul Hindemith, Christopher Isherwood, Herbert Janssen, Nikolai Malko, Dmitri Mitropoulos, Artur Rubinstein, Jennie Tourel and Paul Wittgenstein all become naturalized American citizens; Elisabeth Grümmer joins the Berlin Opera company; Zoltán Kodály returns to concert life with a concert tour of Europe; Franz Lehár moves to Switzerland, loses his wife; Bohuslav Martinu invited to Prague Conservatory but Communists veto the move; Mstislav Rostropovich graduates from Moscow Conservatory; Aksel Schiotz undergoes operation to remove tumor from his voice box; H.H. Stuckenschmidt, released from a POW camp, returns to Germany; Renata Tebaldi makes her La Scala debut;

G. Institutional Openings:

Performing Groups: Anchorage SO (Alaska), Bamburg SO, Fine Arts String Quartet (Chicago), Fort Worth Opera Co., Jeunesses Musicales (Brussels), Juilliard String Quartet (N.Y.), Mobile Opera Guild, Moscow Philharmonic Quartet, Nashville SO (III), New England Opera Co., Paganini String Quartet, Portland (Oregon) Symphonic Choir, Roger Wagner Chorale (Los Angeles), Rome Opera Co., Royal PO (London), Sofia State PO, Southwest German Radio SO, Sydney SO (Australia), Taneyev String Quartet

(Leningrad), Texas Boys Choir (Fort Worth), Welsh National Opera Co. (Cardiff)

Festivals: Caramoor Festival (Katonah, N.Y.), Darmstadt Contemporary Music Festival and Center, Prague Spring Festival

Educational: American String Teachers Association (ASTA, Athens GA), Cambridge Summer School of Music

Other: British Arts Council, Galpin Society (London), Hal Leonard Music Inc. (Winona, MN), *The Instrumentalist*, London Bach Society, *Nuestra Música* (Mexico), *Revue Belge da Musicologie*, Supraphon Records (Czechoslovakia)

H. Musical Literature:
Apel, Willi, *Historical Anthology of Music I*
Blom, Eric, *Everyman's Dictionary of Music*
Deutsch, Otto, *Schubert: A Documentary Biography*
Dumesnil, René, *Music in France between the Wars*
Hindemith, Paul, *Elementary Training for Musicians*
Sachs, Curt, *The Commonwealth of Art*
Schillinger, Joseph, *The Schillinger Method of Musical Composition*
Stravinsky, Igor, *Poetics of Music*
Turina, Joaquin, *Tratado de composición*

I. Musical Compositions:
Andriessen, Hendrik, *Symphony No. 3*
Arnold, Malcolm, *Symphony for Strings*
Barber, Samuel, *Medea* (ballet)
Berlin, Irving, *Annie, Get Your Gun* (musical)
Bernstein, Leonard, *Facsimile* (ballet)
Blitzstein, Marc, *Symphony: the Airbourne* (with narrator, soloists, male chorus)
Boulez, Pierre, *Piano Sonata No. 1*
Britten, Benjamin, *The Rape of Lucrecia* (opera)
          Young Person's Guide to the Orchestra
Copland, Aaron, *Symphony No. 3*
Cowell, Henry, *Symphony No. 4, "Short Symphony"*
Dohnányi, Ernst von, *Concerto No. 2 for Piano and Orchestra*
Guarnieri, Camargo, *Symphony No. 2*
          Concerto No. 2 for Piano and Orchestra
Harris, Roy, *Concerto for Accordian and Orchestra*
          Concerto for Two Pianos and Orchestra
Hindemith, Paul, *When Lilacs Last in the Dooryard Bloomed* (chorus, orchestra)
Honegger, Artur, *Symphony No. 3, "Liturgique"*
Khachaturian, Aram, *Concerto for Cello and Orchestra*
Krenek, Ernst, *Concerto No. 3 for Piano and Orchestra*
Martinu, Bohuslav, *Symphony No. 5*
Mennin, Peter, *Symphony No. 3*
Menotti, Gian Carlo, *The Medium* (opera)
Miaskovsky, Nicolai, *Symphony No. 25*
Milhaud, Darius, *Concerto No. 3 for Piano and Orchestra*
          Concerto No. 2 for Cello and Orchestra
Piston, Walter, *Orchestral Suite No. 2*
Prokofiev, Serge, *Symphony No. 6, Opus 111*
Schoenberg, Arnold, *Prelude for Orchestra, Opus 44*
Sessions, Roger, *Symphony No. 2*
Strauss, Richard, *Concerto for Oboe and Orchestra*
Stravinsky, Igor, *Concerto for String Orchestra*

1947

World Events:
In the U.S., the President proclaims the Truman Doctrine against Communist agression in the Americas; the Taft-Hartley Law limits Union power in strikes; the Marshall Plan is introduced to help developing countries; the C.I.A. is formed to work directly for the Administration; the U.S. Air Force becomes a separate service; Jackie Robinson becomes the first black to play major league baseball. Internationally, Russia forms the Cominform in occupied countries to offset the U.S. Marshall Plan; India and Pakistan become separate independent states; the Dead Sea Scrolls are discovered in Palestine; Thor Heyerdahl sails his raft, Kon-Tiki, from South America to Polynesia.

Cultural Highlights:
Pulitzers: Fiction, Robert Penn Warren (*All the King's Men*); Poetry, Robert Lowell (*Lord Weary's Castle*). André Gide receives the Nobel Prize for Literature. The Institute of Contemporary Arts is founded in London. Births include three Americans, author Ann Beattie, novelist Stephen King and dramatist David Mamet. Deaths include American novelist Willa Cather, French dramatist Tristan Bernard, French artist Pierre Bonnard, British sculptor Henry Kitson and German sculptor George Kolbe. Other highlights include:

Art: William Baziotes, *The Dwarf*; Alberto Giacometti, *The Pointing Man*; Edward Hopper, *Cornbelt City*; Henry Moore, *Three Standing Figures*; Jackson Pollack, *Cathedral*; Theodore Roszak, *The Spectre of Kitty Hawk*; William Zorach, *The Future Generation*.

Literature: W.H. Auden, *The Age of Anxiety*; Saul Bellow, *The Victim*; Anne Frank, *The Diary of Anne Frank*; Thomas Mann, *Dr. Faustus*; Arthur Miller, *All My Sons*; John Steinbeck, *The Wayward Bus*; Tennessee Williams, *A Streetcar Named Desire*.

MUSICAL EVENTS

A. Births:

Jan 4	Irene Gubrud (Am-sop)	Jul 7	Paul Polivnick (Am-cd)
Jan 10	James Morris (Am-bar)	Jul 24	Peter Serkin (Am-pn)
Jan 10	Mischa Maisky (Rus-cel)	Aug 2	Ruth Bakke (Nor-cm-org)
Feb 15	John Adams (Am-cm)	Aug 19	Gerard Schwartz (Am-cd)
Feb 27	Gidon Kremer (Lat-vn)	Aug 28	Gustav Kuhn (Aus-cd)
Mar 15	Jonathan Abramowitz (Am-cel)	Aug	Dmitri Alexeyev (Rus-pn)
Mar 15	Jean Kars (Aus-pn)	Sep 1	Young Uck Kim (Kor-vn)
Mar 25	Gabriela Benachková (Cz-sop)	Sep 13	John Mills (Br-gui)
Mar 30	James Kreger (Am-cel)	Nov 2	David Ahern (Aust-cm-cd)
Apr 19	Murray Perahia (Am-pn)	Nov 5	Christopher Kite (Br-hps)
Apr 30	Elizabeth Hynes (Am-sop)	Nov 12	Sheri Greenawald (Am-sop)
May 8	Felicity Lott (Br-sop)	Dec 10	Christian Badea (Rom-cd)
Jun 5	Laurie Anderson (Am-cm)	Dec 14	Christopher Parkening (Am-gui)
Jun 5	Michele Campanella (It-pn)		Paul Griffiths (Br-cri)
Jun 8	Joan La Barbara (Am-cm)		Thomas Igloi (Hun-cel)

B. Deaths:

Jan 2	Ellen Gulbranson (Swe-sop)	May 6	Louise Homer (Am-alto)
Jan 26	Grace Moore (Am-sop)	May 11	Ture Rangström (Swe-cm)
Jan 27	Anna von Mildenburg (Aus-sop)	May 22	Charles Farnsworth (Am-m.ed)
Jan 29	Marthe Chenal (Fr-sop)	May 25	Johannes Wolf (Ger-mus)
Feb 14	Celestina Boninsegna (It-sop)	Jun 11	Frieda Langendorff (Ger-alto)
Mar 5	Alfredo Casella (It-cm)	Jun 15	Bronislaw Huberman (Pol-vn)
Mar 11	Victor Hely-Hutchinson (Br-cm)	Aug 29	Lillian Blauvelt (Am-sop)
		Nov 27	William Hinshaw (Am-bar)
Mar 19	Willem Pijper (Hol-cm)	Dec 26	Marguerite Carré (Fr-sop)

C. Debuts:

Met ---Giuseppe Antonicelli (cd), Lawrence Davidson (bs), Elen Dosia (sop), Cloe Elmo (mez), Clifford Harvuot (bar), Daniza Ilitsch (sop), Paula Lenchner (sop), Melchiorre Luise (bs), Inge Manski (sop), Wolfgang Martin (cd), Claudia Pinza (sop), Evelyn Sachs (mez), Erna Schlüter (sop), Hjördis Schymberg (sop), Polyna Stoska (sop), Mihály Székely (bs), Ferruccio Tagliavini (ten), Pia Tassinari (sop), Giuseppe Valdengo (bar)

U.S. --Pablo Civil (tour), Eileen Farrell (Florida), Ellen Faull (N.Y.), Samson François (N.Y.), Claude Frank (N.Y.), Orazio Frugoni (N.Y.), Gary Graffman (Philadelphia), William Horne (N.Y.), Helen Kwalwasser (N.Y.), Ginette Neveu (Boston), Michael Rabin, Nell Rankin (N.Y.), Norman Scott, Berl Senofsky, Beverly Sills (Philadelphia), Norman Treigle (New Orleans), Alexis Weissenberg (N.Y.)

Other -Kim Borg (Helsinki), Julian Bream (Cheltenham), Maria Callas (Verona), Anselmo Colzani (Bologna), Oskar Czerwenka (Graz), Denise Duval (Paris), Mindru Katz (Bucharest), Richard Lewis (Glyndebourne), Rolando Panerai (Naples), Gianni Raimondi (Bologna), Elisabeth Söderstrom (Drottningholm), Erna Spoorenberg (Hilversum), Joan Sutherland (Sydney), Richard Tucker (Verona), Cesare Valletti (Bari)

D. New Positions:

Conductors: Eugene Goosens (Sydney SO), Thor Johnson (Cincinnati SO), Otto Klemperer (Budapest Opera), Erich Leinsdorf (Rochester SO), Fritz Mahler (Erie SO), Artur Rodzinski (Chicago SO), Georg Solti (Munich Opera), Bruno Walter (New York PO)

Educational: Blas Galindo (director, Mexico Conservatory), Jean Coulthard (theory & composition, University of British Columbia), Lars-Erik Larsson (composition, Stockholm Conservatory), Bruno Maderna (composition, Venice Conservatory), Leonard Rose (cello, Juilliard), Edmund Rubbra (lecturer, Oxford)

Others: Vina Bovy (director, Royal Opera, Ghent), Thurston Dart (editor, *Galpin Society Journal*)

E. Prizes and Honors:

Prizes: Victoria de los Angeles (Geneva), Abba Bogin and Jane Carlson (Naumberg), Alexei Haieff & Andrew Imbrie (Prix de Rome), Charles Ives (Pulitzer in music, *Symphony No. 3*), Vladimir Orloff (Bucharest), Andrzej Panufnik & Stanislaw Skrowaczewski (Szymanowski), Berl Senofsky (Naumberg), Alexis Weissenberg (Leventritt)

Honors: Paul Badura-Skoda (Austrian State), Percy Hull & Malcolm Sargent (knighted), Serge Koussevitzky (honorary doctorate, Harvard), Aksel Schiotz (knighted, Denmark)

F. Biographical Highlights:

Aaron Copland visits Latin-America again as a representative of the U.S. State Department; Alberto Ginastera returns to Buenos Aires; Margaret Hillis graduates from Indiana University; Arthur Honegger suffers a serious heart attack; Karel Husa receives his D.M.A. from Prague Academy; Adele Kern retires from the stage; Paul Kletzki takes up Swiss citizenship; Serge Koussevitsky marries his first wife's niece, Olga Naumov; Charles Mackerras receives a scholarship to study with Talich in Prague; Lauritz Melchior becomes an American citizen; Peter Mennin receives his Ph.D. degree from Eastman; Henri Pousseur studies music at the Liège Conservatory; George Rochberg receives his B.Mus. degree; Richard Strauss given "official clearance" at the British Festival arranged by Beecham; Iannis Xenakis is condemned to death and flees to Paris.

G. Institutional Openings:

Performing Groups: Amadeus String Quartet (London), English Opera Group (London), Hollywood String Quartet, Israel National Opera, Janácek String Quartet (Brno), Little Orchestra Society (N.Y.), Memphis SO II, National Arts Foundation, National Youth Orchestra of Great Britain (London), New Music Quartet (N.Y.), New York Woodwind Quintet, Osaka PO (Japan), Queensland SO (Brisbane), Tulsa SO, Winnipeg SO

Festivals: Edinburgh Music Festival, Holland Festival (Amsterdam), Ojai Festival (Ojai CA)

Educational: Institut für Neue Musik und Musikerziehung (Darmstadt), Janácek Academy of the Arts (Brno), Jerusalem Academy and Conservatory of Music II, Music Academy of the West (Los Angeles), Prague Academy of the Arts, Stanford U. Music Department.

Other: *Galpin Society Journal*, G. Henle Verlag (Munich), International Folk Music Council (London), *Der Kirchenchor*, London Records, Midwest National Band and Orchestra Clinic (Chicago), *Musica, Musik und Altar, Polyphonie*, Societas Universalis Sanctae Caeciliae (Rome)

H. Musical Literature:
Apel, Willi, *Masters of the Keyboard*
Bukofzer, Manfred, *Music of the Baroque Era*
Einstein, Alfred, *Music in the Romantic Era*
Grout, Donald, *A Short History of the Opera*
Leibowitz, René, *Schoenberg and His School*
McHose, Allen, *Contrapuntal Harmonic Technique*
Piston, Walter, *Counterpoint*
Slonimsky, Nicolas, *Thesaurus of Scales and Melodic Patterns*

I. Musical Compositions:
Badings, Henk, *Symphony No. 4*
Barber, Samuel, *Knoxville: Summer of 1915* (soprano, orchestra)
Blomdahl, Karl-Birger, *Symphony No. 2*
Britten, Benjamin, *Albert Herring* (opera)
Carter, Elliott, *The Minotaur* (ballet)
Copland, Aaron, *In the Beginning* (mezzo-soprano and chorus a cappella)
Duruflé, Maurice, *Requiem, Opus 9* (chorus and orchestra)
Egge, Klaus, *Symphony No. 2, Opus 22*
Egk, Werner, *Abraxas* (ballet)
Einem, Gottfried von, *Dantons Tod, Opus 6* (opera)
Foss, Lukas, *Song of Songs* (cantata)
Gillis, Don, *Symphony No. 5½, "Symphony for Fun"*
            Symphony No. 6
Gould, Morton, *Symphony No. 3*
Henze, Hans Werner, *Symphony No. 1*
            Concerto for Violin and Orchestra
Hindemith, Paul, *Concerto for Piano and Orchestra*
            Symphonia Serena
Honegger, Artur, *Symphony No. 4, "Deliciae Basiliensis"*
Khatchaturian, Aram, *Symphony No. 3*
Lutoslawski, Witold, *Symphony No. 1*
Malipiero, Gian F., *Symphony No. 5*
Menotti, Gian Carlo, *The Telephone* (opera)
Moore, Douglas, *Farm Journal* (chamber orchestra)
            Symphony in A
Piston, Walter, *Symphony No. 3*
Poulenc, Francis, *Sinfonietta* (orchestra)
Riegger, Wallingford, *Symphony No. 3, Opus 42*
Rubbra, Edmund, *Festival Overture, Opus 62*
Schoenberg, Arnold, *A Survivor from Warsaw* (narrator, chorus, orchestra)
Schuman, William, *Night Journey* (ballet)
            Concerto for Violin and Orchestra
Sessions, Roger, *The Trial of Lucullus* (opera)
Siegmeister, Elie, *Symphony No. 1*
Stravinsky, Igor, *Orpheus* (ballet)
Thomson, Virgil, *The Mother of Us All* (opera)
Vaughan-Williams, Ralph, *Symphony No. 6*

1948

World Events:

In the U.S., Harry S. Truman scores a surprising defeat over Thomas Dewey and is re-elected to a full term as President; the Organization of American States (OAS) is organized; Mt. Palomar Observatory installs a new two-hundred inch lens; Bell Laboratories unveil the first electric transistor. Internationally, Israel is proclaimed a Jewish state and David Ben-Gurion becomes its first Prime Minister; the Communists take over Czechoslovakia and Hungary; the Berlin Air Lift begins when the Russians blockade Berlin access routes on the ground; Yugoslavia is expelled from Russia's good graces; Mahatma Gandhi is assassinated in India.

Cultural Highlights:

Pulitzers: Drama, Tennessee Williams (*A Streetcar Named Desire*); Fiction, James A. Michener (*Tales of the South Pacific*); Poetry, W.H. Auden (*The Age of Anxiety*). American author T.S. Eliot receives the Nobel Prize for Literature and Ngaio Marsh is knighted. Arshile Gorky commits suicide after cancer operation and auto wreck; the Cobra Group of expressionists hold their first exhibit in Copenhagen. American artist Eric Fischl is born; French novelist Georges Bernanos, German artist Kurt Schwitters and Armenian artist Arshile Gorky die. Other highlights include:

Art: Peter Blume, *The Rock*; Alberto Giacometti, *The City Square*; George Grosz, *Waving the Flag*; Edward Hopper, *Seven O'Clock*; Fernand Léger, *Homage to David*; Jacques Lipschitz, *The Sacrifice*; Marino Marini, *Horse and Rider*; Henri Matisse, *Large Interior in Red*; Jackson Pollack, *No. I*; Andrew Wyeth, *Christiana's World*.

Literature: Truman Capote, *Other Voices, Other Rooms*; Christopher Fry, *The Lady's Not for Burning*; Norman Mailer, *The Naked and the Dead*; James Michener, *Tales of the South Pacific*; Alan Paton, *Cry, the Beloved Country*; Irving Shaw, *The Young Lions*; Evelyn Waugh, *The Loved One*; Tennessee Williams, *Summer and Smoke*.

MUSICAL EVENTS

A. Births:

Jan 27	Mikhail Baryshnikov (Rus-bal)	Jul 4	Clamma Dale (Am-sop)
Feb 6	Monica Gaylord (Am-pn)	Jul 6	Elizabeth Altman (Br-pn)
Feb 14	Thomas Pinschof (Aus-fl)	Jul 16	Pinchas Zukerman (Is-vn)
Mar 4	Sigmund Cowan (Am-bar)	Jul 28	Michael Ponder (Br-vla)
Mar 19	Joseph Paratore (Am-pn)	Aug 13	Kathleen Battle (Am-sop)
Mar 26	Kyung-Wha Chung (Kor-vn)	Aug 17	John Cheek (Am-bar)
Apr 3	Garrick Olsson (Am-pn)	Aug 19	Elisabeth Mead (Aust-pn)
Apr 6	Joan Atherton (Br-cm)	Aug 28	Horacio Gutiérrez (Cuba-pn)
Apr 11	Erich Louis Graf (Am-fl)	Aug 28	Lucia Valentini (It-mez)
Apr 18	Catherine Malfitano (Am-sop)	Sep 8	Peter Strummer (Can-bar)
May 2	Jeannine Altmeyer (Am-sop)	Nov 1	James Fields (Am-pn)
May 10	Ani Kavafian (Turk-vn)	Nov 20	Daniel Heifetz (Am-vn)
May 29	Linda Gray (Scot-sop)	Nov 20	Barbara Hendricks (Am-sop)
Jun 5	Sergio Abreu (Bra-gui)	Dec 20	Mitsuko Uchida (Jp-pn)
Jun 9	Nathaniel Rosen (Am-cel)		Arpad Joó (Hun-cd)
Jun 18	Eva Marton (Hun-sop)		Paul Schenly (Ger-pn)
Jul 3	Peter Ruzicka (Ger-cm-cd)		

B. Deaths:

Jan 1	William Landré (Hol-cm)	Apr 24	Manuel Ponce (Mex-cd)
Jan 8	Richard Tauber (Aus-ten)	May 17	Olga Samaroff (Am-pn)
Jan 21	Ermanno Wolf-Ferrari (It-cm)	Jun 7	Georges Huë (Fr-cm)
Jan 26	John A. Lomax (Am-folk)	Jul 27	Susan Glaspell (Am-nov)
Feb 11	Serges Eisenstein (Rus-film)	Aug 27	Oscar Ferdandez (Bra-cm)
Apr 13	Max Seiffert (Ger-mus)	Aug 27	Oley Speaks (Am-bar-cm)

Sep 2   Giuseppina Cabilli (It-sop)
Sep 4   Alice Barbi (It-mez)
Oct 10 Siegmund von Hausegger
        (Aus-cd)
Oct 24 Franz Lehár (Aus-cm)

Nov 12 Umberto Giordano (It-cm)
Nov 13 Josephine Jacoby (Am-alto)
Dec 17 Edgar Istel (Ger-mus)
Dec 30 Rosina Buckman (N.Z.-sop)

C. Debuts:

Met ---Marilyn Cotlow (sop), Paul Franke (ten), Carmen Gracia (sop), Frank Guarrera (bar), Jean Madeira (c.alto), Giuseppe di Stefano (ten), Brian Sullivan (ten), Italo Tajo (bs), Luben Vichey (bs)

U.S. --Adele Addison (Boston), Frances Bible (N.Y.), Giorgio Ciompi, Paul Doktor (N.Y.), Tito Gobbi (San Francisco), Nicole Henriot (N.Y.), Anton Kuerti (Cleveland), Raymond Lewenthal, Marko Rothmüller (N.Y.), Robert Rounseville (N.Y.), Aksel Schiotz (N.Y.), Thomas Schippers (N.Y.), Giorgio Tozzi (N.Y.). Lawrence Winters (N.Y.), Frances Yeend (N.Y.)

Other -Paul Badura-Skoda (Austria), Alfred Brendel (Graz), Henryk Czyz (Warsaw), Geraint Evans (London), Dietrich Fischer-Dieskau (Berlin), Claude Holffer (Paris), Peter Katin (London), István Kertész (Hungary), Aase Loveberg (Oslo), Charles Mackerras (London), Yolanda Marcoulescou (Bucharest), Elsie Morison (London), Václav Neumann (Prague), Igor Oistrakh (Moscow), Norma Proctor (Southwart)

D. New Positions:

Conductors: Maurice Abravanel (Utah SO), Ferenc Fricsay (Berlin Opera), Herbert von Karajan (Vienna PO), Efrem Kurtz (Houston SO), Charles Munch (Boston SO), Fritz Reiner (Met), Hans Rosbaud (SW German Radio SO), Hans Schwieger (Kansas City PO)

Educational: Joseph Fuchs (violin, Juilliard), Bohuslav Martinu (composition, Princeton), Flor Peeters (organ, Antwerp Conservatory), Paul Pisk (music chairman, Redlands).

Others: Tikhon Khrennikov (chairman, Union of Soviet Composers), Harold C. Schonberg (music critic, *Musical Courier*)

E. Prizes and Honors:

Prizes: Aldo Ciccolini (St. Cecilia, Rome), Norman Dello Joio (New York Critics' Circle), Dean Dixon (Ditson), Jean Graham and Alexis Weissenberg (Leventritt), Sidney Harth and Paul Olefsky (Naumberg), Erich Kahn (Coolidge), Theodore Lettvin (Naumberg), Walter Piston (Pulitzer, music, *Symphony No. 3*), Peter Wollfisch (Liszt-Bartók)

Honors: Steuart Wilson (knighted)

F. Biographical Highlights:

Milton Babbitt rejoins the staff at Princeton; Leonard Bernstein Joins the staff at Tanglewood; Christoph von Dohnányi enters the Munich Musikhochschule; Andor Foldes and Peggy Glanville-Hicks become American citizens; Joonas Kokkonen graduates with his Masters degree from Helsinki University; Raphael Kubelik leaves Czechoslovakia after the Communist takeover; Ruth Laredo, age 10, plays a Beethoven concerto with the Detroit SO; Charles Mackerras marries Helena Wilkins, "honeymoons" in Czechoslovakia studying with Talich; Pierre Schaeffer formulates his theory of *musique concrète*; Rodion Shchedrin enrolls in Moscow Choral School; Dmitri Shostakovich, along with Khachaturian and Prokofiev, is called upon to suffer another official Soviet rebuke; Janos Starker settles in the U.S.; Igor Stravinsky meets Robert Craft who becomes his aide and biographer; Giuseppe Taddei makes his La Scala debut; Astrid Varnay makes her Covent Garden debut; William Walton marries Susana Gil and settles on the Italian isle of Ischia.

G. Institutional Openings:

Performing Groups: C.B.C. Opera Co. (Toronto), Chamber Society of Baltimore; Deller Consort (London), Goldsbrough Orchestra (English Chamber Orchestra in '60; London), Grass Roots Opera Co. (North Carolina), Lithuanian Opera & Ballet Theater (Vilnius),

London Consort of Winds, Los Angeles New Orchestra, Orchestra of the Scuola Veneziana, Radio Eireann (RTE) SO, Robert Shaw Chorale (N.Y.), Tulsa Opera Co., Vienna Octet, The Weavers Folk Group (N.Y.)

Festivals: Aldeburgh Festival, Ansbach Bach Festival, Bath Festival (London), Besançon International Music Festival

Other: Boelke-Bomart, Music Publishers (N.Y.); C.F. Peters Corporation, *Journal of the American Musicological Society*, K.G. Geimeinhardt Co. (Elkhart, IN), Long Play Record (by Columbia Records), Louisville Orchestra Commissioning Project, Music Association of Ireland (Dublin), *Die Musikforschung, Die Neue Schau, Revue Musicale de la Suisse Romande, Symphony Magazine*, Teatro Margherita (Genoa), *Zeitschrift für Spielmusik*

H. Musical Literature:
Ansermet, Ernest, *Débat sur l'art contemporaine*
Carse, Adam, *The Orchestra from Beethoven*
Furtwängler, Wilhelm, *Gespräche über Musik*
Ives, Burl, *Wayfaring Stranger*
Molnár, Antal, *The Spirit of New Music*
Niles, John Jacob, *Anglo-American Carol Study Book*
Sachs, Curt, *Our Musical Heritage*
Ulrich, Homer, *Chamber Music*

I. Musical Compositions:
Blacher, Boris, *Concerto No. 1 for Piano and Orchestra, Opus 28*
Blitzstein, Marc, *The Little Foxes* (opera)
Bloch, Ernest, *Concerto Symphonique* (piano and orchestra)
Boulez, Pierre, *Les Soleil des Eaux* (soprano and orchestra)
Britten, Benjamin, *The Beggar's Opera* (on John Gay's original)
Carpenter, John Alden, *Carmel Concerto* (orchestra)
Copland, Aaron, *Concerto for Clarinet and Orchestra*
Cowell, Henry, *Symphony No. 5*
Dallapiccola, Luigi, *Il Prigioniero* (opera)
Diamond, David, *Concerto No. 2 for Violin and Orchestra*
Einem, Gottfried von, *Orchestra Music, Opus 9*
Finney, Ross Lee, *Concerto for Piano and Orchestra*
Gould, Morton, *Fall River Legend* (ballet)
Hanson, Howard, *Concerto for Piano and Orchestra*
Henze, Hans Werner, *Symphony No. 2*
                   Whispers from Heavenly Death
Kabalevsky, Dmitri, *Concerto for Violin and Orchestra*
Maderna, Bruno, *Concerto for Piano and Orchestra*
Mennin, Peter, *Symphony No. 4, "The Cycle"* (with chorus)
Messiaen, Olivier, *Turangalila Symphony*
                   Concerto No. 2 for Violin and Orchestra
Milhaud, Darius, *Kentuckiana* (orchestra
Moore, Douglas, *The Emperor's New Clothes* (opera)
Prokofiev, Serge, *A Tale of a Real Man* (opera)
Schuman, William, *Symphony No. 6*
Stravinsky, Igor, *Mass* (male and boys' choirs and ten instruments)
Thomson, Virgil, *Louisiana Story* (film music)
Tippett, Michael, *Suite in D for Orchestra*
Vaughan-Williams, Ralph, *Scott of the Antarctic* (film music)
Weill, Kurt, *Down in the Valley* (opera)

1949

World Events:

In the U.S., Congress ratifies the North Atlantic Treaty Organization (NATO); New York becomes the permanent home of the United Nations; President Truman outlines his Point Four Proposal for aiding underdeveloped nations; a WAC corporal rocket becomes the first to reach outer space; the "bikini" bathing suit is introduced. Internationally, the Berlin Air-lift ends after 328 days and Germany is divided into Communist East Germany and free West Germany; Russia explodes its first atomic bomb; Hungary nationalizes all major industries; the Greek Civil War ends; the Communists take over in China and the Nationalists are driven off the mainland to Formosa (Taiwan).

Cultural Highlights:

Pulitzers: Drama, Arthur Miller (*Death of a Salesman*); Fiction, James G. Cozzens (*Guard of Honor*); Peter Viereck (*Terror and Decorum*). The Nobel Prize for Literature goes to American novelist William Faulkner; the abstract art gallery, Salon de Mai, opens in Paris. Deaths in the literary field include American author Margaret Mitchell, Belgian poet Maurice Maeterlinck and Norwegian novelist Sigrid Undset; born is American novelist Mary Gordon. Deaths in the art field include American sculptor Robert Aitken and artist Walt Kuhn, British artist William Nicholson, Mexican artist José Orozco and Belgian artist James Ensor. Other highlights include:

Art: Max Beckmann, *The Tempest*; Marc Chagall, *Red Sun*; Jacob Epstein, *Lazarus*; Henry Moore, *The Family Group*; Robert Motherwell, *Five in the Afternoon*; Louise Nevelson, *Archaic Figure with Star*; Richard Pousette-Dart, *Number 11: A Presence*; Kenneth Price, *Bird by the Sea*; Yves Tanguy, *Fear*; Maurice Vlaminck, *Les Blés*.

Literature: Nelson Algren, *The Man with the Golden Arm*; Maxwell Anderson, *Lost in the Stars*; Gwendolyn Brooks, *Annie Allen*; John Marquand, *The Point of No Return*; Arthur Miller, *The Death of a Salesman*; John O'Hara, *A Rage to Live*; George Orwell, *1984*; Eleanor Roosevelt, *This I Remember*; Albert Schweitzer, *Hospital in the Jungle*.

MUSICAL EVENTS

A. Births:

Jan 4	Margaret Marshall (Scot-sop)	Aug 28	Imogen Cooper (Br-pn)
Feb 15	Christopher Rouse (Am-cm)	Sep 9	Adam Fischer (Hun-cd)
Feb 26	Emma Kirkby (Br-sop)	Sep 19	Eduardo Abreu (Bra-gui)
May 11	Ruth Welting (Am-sop)	Oct 4	John Aler (Am-ten)
May 14	Alan Marks (Am-pn)	Oct 13	Leona Mitchell (Am-sop)
May 16	Lawrence Ferrara (Am-pn)	Oct 21	Shumalit Ran (Is-cm)
May 21	Rosalind Plowright (Br-sop)	Nov 7	Robin McCabe (Am-pn)
Jun 2	Neil Shicoff (Am-ten)	Nov 15	Angela East (Br-cel)
Jun 8	Emmanuel Ax (Pol-pn)	Dec 2	Sharon Robinson (Am-cel)
Jun 23	Peter Barcza (Swe-bar)	Dec 14	Gita Karasik (Am-pn)
Jun 29	Pierre Amoyal (Fr-vn)	Dec 15	Graham Titus (Br-bar)
Jun 29	Carol Wincenc (Am-fl)	Dec 27	Isola Jones (Am-mez)
Jul 23	Carlos Bonell (Br-gui)		Gregory Allen (Am-pn)
Aug 24	Stephen Paulus (Am-cm)		Christian Blackshaw (Br-pn)

B. Deaths:

Jan 14	Joaquin Turina (Sp-cm)	May 10	Emilio de Gogorza (Am-bar)
Jan 22	Helen Hood (Am-cm)	May 22	Hans Pfitzner (Ger-cm)
Jan 27	Boris Asafiev (Rus-cm-mus)	Jun 9	Maria Cebotari (Rom-sop)
Feb 11	Giovanni Zenatello (It-ten)	Jun 18	Maurice D'Oisley (Br-ten)
Mar 11	Juan Lamote de Grignon	Jul 6	Herman Weil (Ger-bar)
	(Sp-cm)	Jul 18	Vítezslav Novák (Cz-cm)
Mar 28	Grigoras Dinicu (Rom-cm)	Aug 11	Karl Weigl (Aus-cm)

Aug 30   Hans Kindler (Hol-cd)
Sep 8   Richard Strauss (Ger-cm)
Sep 11   Henri Rabaud (Fr-cd-cm)

Sep 12   Harry T. Burleigh (Am-cm)
Sep 20   Nikos Skalkottas (Gr-cm)
Oct 28   Ginette Neveu (Fr-vn)

C. Debuts:

Met ---Elisabetta Barbato (sop), Erna Berger (sop), Anne Bollinger (sop), Helena Braun (sop), Ferdinand Frantz (bar), Denis Harbour (bs), Lois Hunt (sop), Jacques Jansen (ten), Peter Klein (ten), Enzo Mascherini (bs), Frank Murray (ten), Jonel Perlea (cd), Fritz Reiner (cd), Gertrude Ribla (sop), Ljuba Welitsch (sop)

U.S. --Bethany Beardslee (N.Y.), Guido Cantelli (N.Y.), Joan Hammond (N.Y.), Sidney Harth (N.Y.), Luigi Infantino (N.Y.), Lili Kraus (N.Y.), Yvonne Loriod (N.Y.), Daniel Majeske (Detroit), Frederick Marvin (N.Y.), Elena Nikolaidi (tour), Elizabeth Rich (N.Y.), Samuel Sanders

Other -Theo Adam (Dresden), Renato Capecchi (Reggio), Mary Curtis-Verna (Milan), Ludmila Dvořáková (Ostrava), Pierre Fleta (Barcelona), Rita Gorr (Antwerp), Ernst Haefliger (Salzburg), Pilar Lorengar (Madrid), Peter Maag (Biel), Leonie Rysanek (Innsbruck), José Serebrier (Montevideo), Amy Shuard (Johannesburg), Gerhard Stolze (Dresden), Robert Veyron-Lacroix (Paris), Nicola Zaccaria (Athens)

D. New Positions:

Conductors: André Cluytens (Paris Conservatory SO), Antal Dorati (Minneapolis SO), Walter Hendl (Dallas SO), Eugen Jochum (Munich Radio SO), Rudolf Kempe (Dresden Opera), Franz Konwitschny (Leipzig Gewandhaus), Howard Mitchell (National SO), Willem van Otterloo (The Hague SO)

Educational: Hendrik Andriessen (director, Hague Conservatory), John Kirkpatrick (music chair, Cornell), George Rochberg (professor, Curtis Institute)

Others: Joel Berglund (director, Stockholm Opera), William Glack (editor, *The Score*)

E. Prizes and Honors:

Prizes: Milton Babbitt (New York Critics' Circle), Alfred Brendel (Busoni), Bella Davidovich (Chopin), Peter Frisker (Koussevitsky), Gary Graffman (Leventritt), Grant Johannesen (Ostend), Lorne Munroe (Naumberg), Virgil Thomson (Pulitzer, music, *Louisiana Story*)

Honors: John Barbirolli & Bernard Heinze (knighted), Sviatoslav Richter (Stalin)

F. Biographical Highlights:

Ernst von Dohnányi settles in Florida and becomes composer-in-residence and pianist at Florida State University; Max Ernst returns to France; György Ligeti graduates from the Budapest Academy of Music; George London makes his Vienna Opera debut; Bruno Maderna studies with Hermann Scherchen; Leontyne Price wins a scholarship to Juilliard School of Music; Serge Prokofiev suffers a stroke; George Rochberg receives his M.A. degree from University of Pennsylvania; Ned Rorem studies music composition with Honegger; Joseph Rosenstock becomes an American citizen; Georg Solti makes his concert debut in London; William Grant Still becomes first black to have an opera performed by a major opera company; Zoltán Székely decides to settle in the U.S.

G. Institutional Openings:

Performing Groups: Bavarian Radio SO (Munich), Berliner Ensemble (Brecht), Boccherini Quintet (Rome), Bulgarian Radio and Television SO (Sofia), Cleveland Chamber Music Society, Haydn Orchestra of London, Hungarian State PO (Bucharest), La Salle String Quartet (Juilliard), Mannes Trio (N.Y.), NBC Television Opera Co., Phoenix Boys Choir, Rackham Symphony Choir (Detroit), Slovak Philharmonic Society (Bratislava), SO of Rio de Janeiro, Victorian Melbourne SO (Australia)

Educational: *Schweitzerische Musikpädagogische Blätter*, Tokyo University of Arts

Other: Busoni International Piano Competition (Italy), Centre de Documentation de Musique Internationale (Paris), Centro dell'Oratorio Musicale (Rome), Chopin Piano Competition (Warsaw), Greater Louisville Foundation for the Arts, Group 49 (Poland), *The Hymn*, International Music Council (UNESCO; Paris), Israeli Music Publications (Tel Aviv), *The Music Index*, Naumberg Recording Award, New Composer's Association (Tokyo), *Schwann Record Catalog*, *The Score*, Vanguard Recording Society (N.Y.)

H. Musical Literature:

Blume, Friedrich, *Musik in Geschichte und Gegenwart I*
Dumesnil, René, *L'Envers de la Musique*
Einstein, Alfred, *The Italian Madrigal*
Lawrence, Marjorie, *Interrupted Melody*
Leibowitz, René, *Introduction to 12-tone Music*
Partch, Harry, *Genesis of a New Music*
Tovey, Donald, *The Mainstream of Music*
Ulrich, Homer, *The Education of a Concertgoer*

I. Musical Compositions:

Antheil, George, *Symphony No. 6*
Arnold, Malcolm, *Concerto for Clarinet and Orchestra*
Badings, Henk, *Symphony No. 5*
Baird, Tadeusz, *Concerto for Piano and Orchestra*
Bernstein, Leonard, *The Age of Anxiety* (piano and orchestra)
Blitzstein, Marc, *Regina* (opera)
Brian, Havergal, *Symphony No. 8*
Britten, Benjamin, *Spring Symphony* (soloists, chorus, orchestra)
Creston, Paul, *Concerto for Piano and Orchestra*
Dello Joio, Norman, *New York Profiles* (orchestra)
Egk, Werner, *French Suite* (orchestra)
Finzi, Gerald, *Concerto for Clarinet and Orchestra*
Glière, Reinhold, *The Bronze Horseman* (ballet)
Hamilton, Lou, *Symphony in G*
Hanson, Howard, *Cherubic Hymn* (chorus and orchestra)
Henze, Hans Werner, *Symphony No. 3*
Jolivet, André, *Concerto No. 1 for Flute and Orchestra*
Kabalevsky, Dmitri, *Concerto for Cello and Orchestra*
Martin, Frank, *Golgotha* (oratorio)
Martinu, Bohuslav, *Concerto for Orchestra*
Milhaud, Darius, *String Quartet No. 15* (forms Octet with *Quartet No. 14*)
Orff, Carl, *Antigonae* (opera)
Phillips, Burrill, *Don't We All* (opera)
Rodgers, Richard, *South Pacific* (musical)
Schoenberg, Arnold, *Fantasia, Opus 47* (violin and piano)
                       Dreimal Tausend Jahre, Opus 50a (chorus a capella)
Shostakovich, Dmitri, *Song of the Forests, Opus 81* (cantata)
Sieber, Mátyás, *Ulysses* (cantata)
Surinach, Carlos, *Symphony No. 2*
Thompson, Randall, *Symphony No. 3*
Thomson, Virgil, *Concerto for Cello and Orchestra*
Vaughan-Williams, Ralph, *Fantasia on "Old 104" Psalm Tune* (piano and orchestra)
Weill, Kurt, *Lost in the Stars* (musical)

1950

World Events:
The U.S. Census shows a population of 151,326,000, a 14% increase; Senator Joseph McCarthy begins his communist witch-hunt in Washington; the Alger Hiss spy case takes place; the McCarran Internal Security Act toughens controls on communists; President Truman approves the building of the Hydrogen Bomb; the National Science Foundation is created. Internationally, the Korean War begins as North Korea invades South Korea; U.S. troops are sent in and drive the communists back to the Yalu River; the Chinese enter the conflict and drive the Allies back to the dividing line; Sukarno becomes President of Indonesia; riots begins in South Africa over apartheid.

Cultural Highlights:
Pulitzers: Drama, Richard Rodgers, Oscar Hammerstein II and Joshua Logan (*South Pacific*); Fiction, A.B. Guthrie, Jr. (*The Way West*); Poetry, Gwendolyn Brooks (*Annie Allen*) becomes the first black woman to win a Pulitzer Prize. The Nobel Prize for Literature goes to Bertrand Russell. Deaths in the art field include American sculptor Allan Clark, Canadian sculptor Alexander Proctor and German artist Max Beckmann. Deaths in the literary field include American poets John C. Fletcher, Edgar L. Masters and Edna St. Vincent Millay and author Carl Van Doren and George Orwell, Italian novelist Rafael Sabatini, Irish novelist James Stephens and British dramatist and critic, George Bernard Shaw; American author Frances Lebowitz is born. Other highlights include:

Art: Milton Avery, *Maternity*; Marc Chagall, *King David*; Stuart Davis, *Little Giant Still Life*; Alberto Giacometti, *Chariot*; Ludwig von Hofmann, *Elegy*; Marino Marini, *Igor Stravinsky*; Henry Moore, *Double Standing Figure*; Pablo Picasso, *The She-Goat*; Jackson Pollack, *Lavender Mist*; Samuel Scott, *Haitian Market*; Yves Tanguy, *Chess Set*.

Literature: e.e. cummings, *XAIPE*; Christopher Fry, *Venus Observed*; Thor Heyerdahl, *Kon Tiki*; William Inge, *Come Back, Little Sheba*; Eugene Ionesco, *The Bald Soprano*; Ezra Pound, *Seventy Cantos*; Harold Robinson, *The Cardinal*; Robert Warren, *World Enough and Time*; Richard Wilbur, *Ceremony and Other Poems*.

MUSICAL EVENTS

A. Births:

Feb 19 Leslie Richards (Am-mez)	Aug 12 Lia Frey-Rabine (Am-sop)
Mar 5 Eugene Fodor (Br-pn)	Aug 17 Anton Del Forno (Am-gui)
Mar 9 Howard Shelley (Br-pn)	Sep 16 Kay George Roberts (Am-cd)
Mar 18 James Conlon (Am-cd)	Sep 19 Jeffrey Gall (Am-c.ten)
Mar 21 James W. Dietsch (Am-bar)	Oct 4 Francisco Araiza (Mex-ten)
Mar 27 Maria Ewing (Am-sop)	Oct 13 Katherine Ciesinski (Am-mez)
Apr 17 Cristina Ortiz (Bra-pn)	Oct 27 Susanna Ross (Br-sop)
Apr 27 Calvin Simmons (Am-cd)	Nov 25 Yvonne Kenny (Aust-sop)
May 9 Michel Béroff (Fr-pn)	Dec 7 Kathleen Kuhlmann (Am-mez)
Jun 8 Elmar Oliveira (Am-vn)	Dec 24 Libby Larsen (Am-cm)
Jun 28 Philip F. Fowke (Br-pn)	Dec 26 Krzystof Baculewski (Pol-cm)
Aug 8 Anna Sandor (Hun-cel)	Katia Labèque (Fr-pn)
Aug 11 Terrence Farrell (Am-gui)	

B. Deaths:

Feb 9 Edyth Walker (Am-mez)	Oct 18 Giuseppe Borgatti (It-ten)
Apr 3 Kurt Weill (Ger-cm)	Nov 20 Francesco Cilea (It-cm)
Apr 8 Vaclav Nijinsky (Rus-bal)	Dec 1 Ernest J. Moeran (Br-cm)
Jul 1 Émile Jaques-Dalcroze (Fr-cm)	Dec 2 Dinu Lipatti (Rom-pn)
Aug 9 Nicolai Miaskovsky (Rus-cm)	Dec 22 Walter Damrosch (Ger-cd)
Aug 26 Giuseppe de Luca (It-bar)	Dec 23 Vincenzo Tommasini (It-cm)
Oct 14 Richard Kountz (Am-cm)	Dec 31 Charles Koechlin (Fr-cm)

C. Debuts:

Met ---Lucine Amara (sop), Fedora Barbieri (mez), Eugene Conley (ten), Alberto Erede (cd), Hans Hotter (bar), Mario del Monaco (ten), Sven Nilsson (bs), Eugene Ormandy (cd), Roberta Peters (sop), Delia Rigal (sop), Margaret Roggero (mez), Paul Schöffler (bar), Cesare Siepi (bs), Paolo Silveri (bar), Barbara Troxell (sop), Genevieve Warner (sop)

U.S. --Victoria de los Angeles (N.Y.), Gina Bachauer (N.Y.), Aldo Ciccolini (N.Y.), Suzanne Danco, Marjorie Gordon (N.Y.), Friedrich Gulda (N.Y.), Vera Little (N.Y.), David Lloyd (N.Y.), Cornell MacNeil (Philadelphia), Carla Martinis (N.Y.), Gérard Souzay (N.Y.), Renata Tebaldi (San Francisco), William Warfield (N.Y.)

Other -Joaquín Achucarro (Masavou), Marie Claire Alain (Paris), Walter Berry (Vienna), Giuseppe Campora (Milan), Régine Crespin (Mühlhausen), Peter Frankl (Budapest), Leyla Gencer (Ankara), Giangiacomo Gulfi (Spoleto), Joonas Kokkonen (Helsinki), Gustav Leonhardt (Vienna), Arthur Lima (Rio de Janeiro), Nell Rankin (Zurich), Hilde Rössl-Majdan (Vienna), André Turp (Montreal), Alexander Young (Edinburgh)

D. New Positions:

Conductors: Karel Ancerl (Czech PO), Adrian Boult (London PO), Colin Davis (Chelsea Opera Group), Carlo Maria Giulini (Milan Radio SO), Josef Krips (London SO), Rafael Kubelik (Chicago SO), Dmitri Mitropoulos (New York PO), Malcolm Sargent (BBC SO)

Educational: György Ligeti (harmony & counterpoint, Budapest Academy), Carl Orff (composition, Berlin Hochschule), Gunther Schuller (professor, Manhattan School of Music)

Others: Rudolf Bing (general manager, Met), David Willcocks (organ, Worcester Cathedral)

E. Prizes and Honors:

Prizes: Margaret Barthel, Angelene Collins, Esther Glazer Betty Jean Hagen (Naumberg), Karel Husa (Boulanger), Leon Kirchner (New York Critics' Circle), Gian Carlo Menotti (Pulitzer, Music), George Rochberg (Prix de Rome), Jacques Villon (Carnegie).

Honors: Arthur Bliss (knighted)

F. Biographical Highlights:

Luciano Berio marries soprano Cathy Berberian; Lukas Foss studies in Rome on a fellowship; Carlos Kleiber begins music lessons in Buenos Aires; Ernst Krenek marries composer Gladys Nordenstrom; Bruno Maderna makes his conducting debut in Munich; Lauritz Melchior, at odds with Rudolph Bing, leaves the Met never to return; Thea Musgrave goes to Paris to study with Boulanger; Andrzej Panufnik studies Soviet teaching methods in Russia; Ezio Pinza moves to Broadway to star in *South Pacific*; Italo Tajo makes his Covent Garden debut; Alexander Tcherepnin and his family settle in Chicago; Arturo Toscanini takes the NBC SO on a nationwide tour; Barry Tuckwell and Malcolm Williamson leave Australia for England; Benita Valente begins voice study with Lotte Lehmann; Iannis Xenakis begins studying composition with Messiaen.

G. Institutional Openings:

Performing Groups: Baltimore Chamber Music Society, Belfast SO, Berlin Motet Choir, Canadian Opera Co. (Toronto), Chelsea Opera Group, Golden Age Singers (London), Hilltop Opera Co. (Baltimore), Hungarian State Folk Ensemble (Budapest), I Solisti di Zagreb, Melos Ensemble (London), Norwegian Opera Co. (Oslo), Portland (Oregon) Opera Association, Utah Chorale (Salt Lake City), West Australian SO (Perth)

Festivals: Aspen Music Festival (Colorado), Bordeaux May Festival, Marlboro Music Festival (Vermont), Prades Music Festival (France)

Educational: Catholic University Music Department (D.C.), Deutsche Hochschule für Musik (East Berlin), Idyllwild School of Music (California), Institute for Folk Music (Weimar), International Association of Music Libraries (Lünebeck)

Other: Ars Viva, Music Publishers; *The Church Musician*, Essen Opera House, Groupe de Recherche de Musique Concrète (Paris), Hammond Chord Organ (by Lawrence Hammond), Inspiration Point Fine Arts Colony (Eureka Springs, AR), The Norfolk and Norwich Music Club, Sheffield Bach Society, Weintraub Music Co. (N.Y.)

H. Musical Literature:
Barzun, Jacques, *Berlioz and the Romantic Century*
Bukofzer, Manfred, *Studies in Medieval and Renaissance Music*
Chantavoine, Jean, *The Symphonic Poem*
Demuth, Norman, *The Symphony: History and Development*
Malko, Nikolai, *The Conductor and His Baton*
Schoenberg, Arnold, *Style and Idea*
Sessions, Roger, *The Musical Experience of Composer, Performer, and Listener*
Strunk, Oliver, *Source Readings in Music History*

I. Musical Compositions:
Anderson, Leroy, *Syncopated Clock* (orchestra)
Avshalomov, Aaron, *Symphony No. 3*
Blomdahl, Karl-Birger, *Symphony No. 3, "Facetter"*
Boulez, Pierre, *Le Visage Nuptial* (two solo voices, chorus, orchestra)
Chávez, Carlos, *Concerto for Violin and Orchestra*
Copland, Aaron, *Twelve Poems by Emily Dickinson* (songs)
                Old American Songs, Set I (voice, orchestra)
Creston, Paul, *Symphony No. 3, Opus 48*
Diamond, David, *Concerto for Piano and Orchestra*
Fortner, Wolfgang, *The White Rose* (ballet)
Foss, Lukas, *The Celebrated Jumping Frog of Calaveras County* (opera)
Hamilton, Iain, *Concerto for Clarinet and Orchestra*
Harris, Roy, *Concerto for Violin and Orchestra*
Henze, Hans Werner, *Concerto for Piano and Orchestra*
Hindemith, Paul, *Concerto for Horn and Orchestra*
Honegger, Artur, *Symphony no. 5, "Di Tre Re"*
Jolivet, André, *L'Inconnue* (ballet)
Kabalevsky, Dmitri, *The Family of Taras* (opera)
Korngold, Erich, *Symphony, Opus 40*
Krenek, Ernst, *Concerto No. 4 for Piano and Orchestra*
Leibowitz, René, *La Rumeur de L'Espace*
Mennin, Peter, *Symphony No. 5*
Menotti, Gian Carlo, *The Consul* (opera)
Milhaud, Darius, *Concerto No. 4 for Piano and Orchestra*
Orff, Carl, *The Triumph of Aphrodite* (secular cantata)
Piston, Walter, *Symphony No. 4*
Poulenc, Francis, *Concerto for Piano and Orchestra*
Prokofiev, Serge, *The Stone Flower* (ballet)
Rawsthorne, Alan, *Symphony*
Rorem, Ned, *Symphony No. 1*
Schoenberg, Arnold, *Psalm CXXX, Opus 50b* (chorus a capella)
Schuman, William, *Judith* (ballet)
Siegmeister, Elie, *Symphony No. 2*
Stravinsky, Igor, *The Rake's Progress* (opera)
Toch, Ernst, *Symphony No. 1*
Vaughan-Williams, Ralph, *Concerto Grosso for Strings*
Villa-Lobos, Heitor, *Symphony No. 8*
                Erosion of the Amazon (orchestra)

1951

World Events:
In the U.S., the 22nd Amendment, limiting the President to only two terms, is ratified; the U.S. signs the ANZUS Pact with Australia and New Zealand; President Truman removes General MacArthur from his Far East command; Julius and Ethel Rosenberg are sentenced to death for spying; the Heart-Lung machine is perfected. Internationally, formal peace treaties are signed with Germany and Japan; the Korean Armistice fails but peace talks begin at Panmunjom; Winston Churchill again becomes Prime Minister of Great Britain and halts the nationalization of British industry; Iran nationalizes all its oil fields.

Cultural Highlights:
Pulitzers: Fiction, Conrad Richter (*The Town*); Poetry, Carl Sandburg (*Complete Poems*). The Nobel Prize for Literature goes to Pär F. Lagerkvist; the Matisse Museum opens in Nice, France. Deaths include the American novelists Lloyd C. Douglas, James N. Hall and Sinclair Lewis, British author Cecil Gray, German novelist Bernhard Kellermann, French novelist André Gide and German author and critic, Wilhelm Altmann. American artist Julian Schnabel is born. Other highlights include:

Art: Gifford Beal, *Mending the Nets*; Peter Blume, *Man of Sorrows*; Salvador Dali, *Christ on the Cross*; Stuart Davis, *The Mellow Pad*; Naum Gabo, *Translucent Variations on a Spheric Theme*; Barnett Newman, *Cathedra*; Pablo Picasso, *Baboon and Young*; Ben Shahn, *Silent Music*; Matthew Smith, *Hudson River Landscape*.

Literature: Rachel Carson, *The Sea Around Us*; William Faulkner, *Requiem for a Nun*; James Jones, *From Here to Eternity*; Robert Lowell, *Mills of the Kavanaughs*; Norman Mailer, *Barbary Shore*; Catherine Marshall, *A Man Called Peter*; Jerome Salinger, *The Catcher in the Rye*; Hermann Wouk, *The Caine Mutiny*.

MUSICAL EVENTS

A. Births:

Jan 7	Jonathan Del Mar (Br-cd)	Oct 1	Timothy C. Michaels (Am-ten)
Jan 19	Benjamin Bakkegard·(Am-hn)	Oct 23	Marianne Häggander (Swe-sop)
Jan 20	Ivan Fischer (Hun-cd)	Oct 25	Ransom Wilson (Am-fl)
Mar 28	Karen Kain (Can-bal)	Nov 2	Jeremy Menuhin (Am-pn-cd)
Apr 6	Pascal Rogé (Fr-pn)	Nov 18	Heinrich Schiff (Am-cel)
Apr 14	Julian Lloyd Webber (Br-cel)	Nov 22	Kent Nagano (Am-cd)
May 7	Janina Fialkowska (Can-pn)	Dec 6	Daniel Adni (Is-pn)
Jun 17	Sergio Cardenas (Mex-cd)	Dec 16	Carroll B. Freeman (Am-ten)
Jul 12	Sylvia Sass (Hun-sop)		Peter Altrichter (Cz-cm)
Aug 16	Douglas Riva (Am-pn)		Steve Ingham (Br-cm)
Sep 8	Dezso Ránki (Hun-pn)		Cyprien Katsaris (Fr-pn)
Sep 25	Peter Dvorsky (Cz-ten)		Lubov Timofeeva (Rus-pn)

B. Deaths:

Feb 26	George Oldroyd (Br-org)	Aug 21	Constant Lambert (Br-cm-cd)
Mar 21	Willem Mengelberg (Hol-cd)	Sep 14	Fritz Busch (Ger-cd)
Apr 21	Olive Fremstad (Swe-sop)	Nov 9	Sigmund Romberg (Hun-pop)
Apr 26	John A. Carpenter (Am-cm)	Nov 13	Hugo Leichtentritt (Ger-mus)
May 29	Josef B. Foerster (Boh-cm)	Nov 13	Nicholas Medtner (Rus-cm)
Jun 4	Serge Koussevitsky (Rus-cd)	Nov 25	Paul Hirsch (Ger-mus)
Jul 13	Arnold Schoenberg (Aus-cm)	Dec 13	Selim Palmgren (Fin-cm)
Jul 26	Giuseppe Agostini (It-ten)	Dec 21	Edmund Fellowes (Br-mus)
Aug 15	Artur Schnabel (Aus-pn)	Dec 22	Powell Weaver (Am-cm)

C. Debuts:
Met ---Kurt Adler (cd), Victoria de los Angeles (sop), Algerd Brazis (bar), Renato

Capecchi (bar), Gabor Carelli (ten), Frank d'Elia (ten), Hilde Gueden (sop), Tibor Kozma (cd), Fritz Krenn (bs), George London (bar), Mildred Miller (mez), Elena Nikolaidi (alto), Alois Pernerstorfer (bs), Marguerite Piazza (sop), Giacinto Prandelli (ten), Nell Rankin (mez), Norman Scott (bar), Carlo Tomanelli (bs), Günther Treptow (ten)

U.S. --Stephen Bishop-Kovacevich (San Francisco), Donald Gramm (N.Y.), Grace Hoffman, Leonard Hungerford (N.Y.), Michael Isador, Paul Jacobs (N.Y.), Magda Olivero (San Antonio), Charles Rosen (N.Y.), Nicola Rossi-Lemeni (tour), Susan Starr, Frans Vroons (San Francisco), Zvi Zeitlin (N.Y.)

Other -Carlo Bergonzi (as baritone), Anita Cerquetti (Spoleto), Franco Corelli (Spoleto), Nicolai Gedda (Stockholm), Thomas Hemsley (London), Waldemar Kmentt (Vienna), Sándor Konya (Bielefeld), Gladys Kuchta (Florence), Malcolm Lipkin (Holland), Bertha Monmart (Paris), Helga Pilarczyk (Brunswick), Nello Santi (Padua), Graziella Sciutti (Aix-en-Provence), Josef Suk (Prague), Gabriella Tucci (Lucca), Claire Watson (Graz)

D. New Positions:

Conductors: Charles Groves (Bournemouth SO), Guy Fraser Harrison (Oklahoma City SO), Jan Krenz (Polish Radio SO), Leopold Ludwig (Hamburg Opera), Wilfrid Pelletier (Quebec SO), Edouard van Remoortel (Belgian National SO), Horst Stein (Hamburg Opera)

Educational: Giorgio Ghedini (director, Milan Conservatory), Aarre Merikanto (composition, Sibelius Academy, Helsinki), Leonard Rose (cello, Curtis Institute), Vissarion Shebalin (composition, Moscow Conservatory)

Others: George Rochberg (publication director, Theodore Presser)

E. Prizes and Honors:

Prizes: Janine Dacosta (Long-Thibaud), Christoph von Dohnányi (Strauss), Philippe Entremont (Thibaud), Joyce Flissler (Naumberg), Iain Hamilton (Koussevitsky), Laurel Hurley (Naumberg), June Kovach (Naumberg), László Lajtha (Kossuth), Frank Wigglesworth (Prix de Rome)

Honors: Ernest Bullock & William Walton (knighted), Henry Cowell (National Institute)

F. Biographical Highlights:

Luciano Berio makes his first U.S. visit; Pierre Boulez turns to magnetic tape composition; Luigi Dallapiccola makes his first U.S. visit; Gerald Finzi first learns of his leukemia; Otakar Kraus makes his Covent Garden debut; Lotte Lehmann gives her farewell concert; George London debuts at La Scala as well as the Met; Lorin Maazel goes to Italy on a Fulbright Scholarship; Toshiro Mayuzumi goes to Paris and enrolls in the Conservatory; Krzystof Penderecki enters Krakow University to study classical antiquity; Leonard Rose begins touring as a soloist; Rodion Shchedrin enters Moscow Conservatory; Karlheinz Stockhausen is inspired to explore new paths by attending the Darmstadt Festival; Joan Sutherland goes to England to study at the Royal College; Evgeny Svetlanov graduates from Gnessin Institute; Joseph Szigeti becomes a U.S. citizen; Michael Tippett resigns from Morley College to work for the BBC; Barry Tuckwell leaves Australia for England; Astrid Varnay appears at Bayreuth; Ralph Vaughan-Williams loses his wife of 54 years.

G. Institutional Openings:

Performing Groups: Bulgarian State Folksong and Dance Ensemble (Sofia), Dvořák String Quartet (Prague), Haifa SO, Philip Jones Brass Ensemble (London), Moravian PO, Orquesta Radio Naciónal (Argentina), Vlach String Quartet (Prague), Worcester Concert Club

Festivals: Bilbao Festival (Spain), Birmingham Festival of the Arts (Alabama), Wexford Festival (Ireland), Wiener Festwochen

Educational: Teresa Carreño Conservatory of Music (Caracas), Marlboro Music School (Massachusetts)

Other: American Opera Society (N.Y.), Arts Council of Ireland (Dublin), Brattleboro Music Center, British Institute of Recorded Sound (London), Canadian League of Composers (Toronto), Centre Belge de Documentation Musicale, Concert Artists Guild (N.Y.), Electronic Music Studio of the West German Radio (Cologne), Hungarian Recording Co. (Budapest), *Journal Musical Française*, Mermaid Theater (London), Royal Festival Hall (London)

H. Musical Literature:

Deutsch, Otto, *Schubert: Thematic Catalogue*
Honegger, Artur, *Je suis Compositeur*
Hanson, Howard, *Music in Contemporary American Civilization*
Leichtentritt, Hugo, *Musical Form*
Réti, Rudolf, *The Thematic Process in Music*
Rogers, Bernard, *The Art of Orchestration*
Thomson, Virgil, *Music, Right and Left*
Vincent, John, *The Diatonic Modes in Modern Music*

I. Musical Compositions:

Avshalomov, Aaron, *Symphony No. 4*
Bloch, Ernest, *Suite Hébraique* (viola, orchestra)
Boulez, Pierre, *Polyphonie for Eighteen Instruments*
Brian, Havergal, *Symphony No. 9*
Britten, Benjamin, *Billy Budd* (opera)
Cage, John, *Music of Changes* (piano)
　　　　　Concerto for Prepared Piano
Carter, Elliott, *String Quartet No. 1*
Chávez, Carlos, *Symphony No. 3*
Cowell, Henry, *Symphony No. 6*
Creston, Paul, *Concerto for Two Pianos and Orchestra*
Dello Joio, Norman, *The Triumph of St. Joan Symphony*
Diamond, David, *Symphony No. 5*
Dutilleux, Henri, *Symphony No. 1*
Floyd, Carlisle, *Fugitives* (opera)
Fortner, Wolfgang, *Concerto for Cello and Orchestra*
Hamilton, Iain, *Symphony No. 2*
Harris, Roy, *Symphony No. 7*
Henze, Hans Werner, *Rosa Silber* (ballet)
Hindemith, Paul, *Symphony: Harmonie der Welt*
　　　　　Symphony in B-flat for Band
Ibert, Jacques, *Barbe-bleue* (opera)
Jolivet, André, *Concerto for Piano and Orchestra*
Jongen, Joseph, *Three Symphonic Movements*
Kay, Ulysses, *Sinfonia in E*
Krenek, Ernst, *Concerto for Two Pianos and Orchestra*
Menotti, Gian Carlo, *Amahl and the Night Visitors* (opera)
Messiaen, Olivier, *Le Livre d'Orgue* (piano)
Moore, Douglas, *Giants in the Earth* (opera)
Pizzetti, Ildebrando, *Ifigenia* (opera)
Poulenc, Francis, *Stabat Mater* (chorus a capella)
Rodgers, Richard, *The King and I* (musical)
Rogers, Bernard, *Leaves from the Tale of Pinocchio* (narrator, chamber orchestra)
Schoenberg, Arnold, *De Profundis, Opus 50b* (choir)
Shostakovich, Dmitri, *Twenty-four Preludes and Fugues, Opus 87* (piano)
Stockhausen, Karlheinz, *Kreuzspiel* (orchestra)
Vaughan-Williams, Ralph, *The Pilgrim's Progress* (opera)
Villa-Lobos, Heitor, *Symphony No. 9*

1952

World Events:

In the U.S., General Dwight D. Eisenhower declares for the Republican Party and is elected President No. 34; the first Hydrogen Bomb is exploded at Eniwetok Atoll in the South Pacific; the McCarran-Walter Act reforms the immigration laws; the G.I. Bill of Rights for Korean Veterans is signed; Puerto Rico becomes a U.S. Commonwealth. Internationally, King George of England dies and Elizabeth II becomes Queen; King Farouk is overthrown in Egypt and a republic is proclaimed; Juan Batista seizes power in Cuba; Jetliner service begins in Europe; the European Defense Community is formed; Mau-mau terrorism begins in Kenya; Armistice is declared in Korea.

Cultural Highlights:

Pulitzers: Drama, Joseph Kramm (*The Shrike*); Fiction, Hermann Wouk (*The Caine Mutiny*); Poetry, Marianne Moore (*Collected Poems*). François Mauriac receives the Nobel Prize for Literature; Albert Schweitzer receives the Nobel Peace Prize. The Stratford Shakespeare Festival begins in Ontario and the Cinerama Process is introduced into the movie world. The art world loses American sculptor Jo Davidson and artist Howard C. Christy; the literary world loses British novelist Norman Douglas, French novelist Jean Tharaud and poet Paul Éluard, Norwegian author Knut Hamsun, Hungarian author Ferenc Molnár and Spanish philosopher George Santayana. Other highlights include:

Art: William Baziotes, *Primeval Landscape*; Marc Chagall, *Green Night*; Roberto Crippa, *Aurora Borealis*; Willem de Kooning, *Woman I*; Jacob Epstein, *Madonna and Child*; Helen Frankenthaler, *Mountains and Seas*; Barbara Hepworth, *Evocation*; Jackson Pollack, *No. 12*: Theodore Roszak, *Whaler of Nantucket*; Georges Rouault, *End of Autumn*.

Literature: *Bible: Revised Standard Version*; Jean Anouilh, *Waltz of the Toreadors*; Samuel Beckett, *Waiting for Godot*; Pierre Boulle, *The Bridge on the River Kwai*; Ralph Ellison, *The Invisible Man*; Edna Ferber, *Giant*; Ernest Hemingway, *The Old Man and the Sea*; Eugene O'Neill, *A Moon for the Misbegotten*; John Steinbeck, *East of Eden*.

MUSICAL EVENTS

A. Births:

Jan 8 Vladimir Feltsman (Rus-pn)	Aug 16 Gianna Rolandi (Am-sop)
Jan 18 Paul Arden-Griffith (Br-ten)	Aug 30 Simon Bainbridge (Br-cm)
Jan 27 Sylvia Ho (Chi-pn)	Oct 23 Jay M. Gottlieb (Am-pn)
Feb 16 Judith G. Kellock (Am-sop)	Oct 29 Ida Kavafian (Turk-vn)
Feb 23 William Black (Am-pn)	Nov 5 Steven D. Black (Br-pn)
Mar 17 Beverly Morgan (Am-sop)	Nov 6 Antoni R. Bonetti (Br-cd)
May 8 Wyn Davies (Br-cd)	Nov 22 Toby Appel (Am-vn)
May 30 Zoltán Kocsis (Hun-pn)	Nov 30 Semyon Bychkov (Rus-cd)
May 30 Alexander Toradze (Rus-pn)	Dec 2 James Lancelot (Br-org)
Jun 7 Václav Hudecek (Cz-vn)	Dec 26 André-Michel Schub (Am-pn)
Jun 12 Oliver Knussen (Br-cm)	Dec 29 Gelsey Kirkland (Am-bal)
Jul 5 Kristine Ciesinki (Am-sop)	Ian Hobson (Br-pn)
Jul 19 Dominic Muldowney (Br-cm-cd)	Marielle Labèque (Fr-pn)
Jul 21 Janis Gail Eckhart (Am-mez)	Silvia Marcovici (Rom-vn)
Jul 27 Carol Vaness (Am-sop)	Santiago Rodriguez (Cuba-pn)
Aug 10 Ashley Putnam (Am-sop)	

B. Deaths:

Jan 11 Aureliano Pertile (It-ten)	Apr 13 Margarete Siems (Ger-sop)
Jan 20 Arthur Farwell (Am-cm-pub)	Apr 20 Frederic Austin (Br-bar-cm)
Feb 13 Alfred Einstein (Ger-mus)	Apr 23 Elisabeth Schumann (Ger-sop)
Feb 15 Max Altglass (Pol-ten)	May 21 Frances Alda (N.Z.-sop)
Apr 2 Antonio Cortis (Sp-ten)	Jun 9 Adolf Busch (Ger-vn)

Jun 13	Emma Eames (Am-sop)	Aug 18	Henry Expert (Fr-mus)
Jun 17	Alberto Williams (Arg-cm)	Oct 7	Berta Morena (Ger-sop)
Jun 19	Heinrich Schlusnus (Ger-bar)	Oct 24	Frederick Jacobi (Am-cm)
Jul 8	Medea Figner (Rus-sop)	Oct 31	Adolf Chybínski (Pol-mus)
Jul 16	Jean Chantavoine (Fr-mus)	Dec 14	Fartein Valen (Nor-cm)
Aug 11	Riccardo Martin (Am-ten)	Dec 25	Bernardino Molinari (It-cd)

C. Debuts:

Met ---Ernesto Barbini (cd), Sigurd Björling (bar), Arthur Budney (bar), Laura Castellano (sop), Renato Cellini (cd), Josef Greindl (bs), Richard Holm (ten), Elisabeth Höngen (mez), Hans Hopf (ten), Erich Kunz (bar), Brenda Lewis (sop), Graciela Rivera (sop), John Tyers (bar), Walburga Wegner (sop), Hilde Zadek (sop)

U.S. --John Alexander (Cincinnati), Augustin Anievas (N.Y.), Van Cliburn, Donald Grobe (Chicago), Jean Langlais (tour), John Macurdy (New Orleans), James McCracken (Central City, Colorado), Gerald Tarack (N.Y.)

Other -Serge Baudo (Paris), Ingrid Bjoner (Oslo), Charles Craig (London), Gábor Gabos (Budapest), Nicolai Gedda (Stockholm), Alexander Gibson (London), Michael Gielen (Vienna), Peter Glossop (London), Marga Höffgen (Berlin), Grace Hoffman (Zurich), Carlos Kleiber (La Plata), Raymond Leppard (London), Pilar Lorengar (Madrid), Kerstin Meyer (Stockholm), Hermann Prey (Wiesbaden), Teresa Stich-Randall (Vienna), Klaus Tennstedt (Halle), Fritz Uhl (Graz)

D. New Positions:

Conductors: Victor Alessandro (San Antonio SO), Edward T. Downes (Covent Garden), Massimo Freccia (Baltimore SO), Alexander Hilsberg (New Orleans PO), Heinrich Hollreiser (Vienna Opera), Rudolf Kempe (Munich Opera), Peter Maag (Düsseldorf Opera), Paul Paray (Detroit SO), Georg Solti (Frankfurt Opera), William Steinberg (Pittsburgh SO)

Educational: Hendrik Andriessen (music history, Nijmegen University), Peter R. Fricker (director, Morley College), Edward Steuermann (piano, Juilliard)

E. Prizes and Honors:

Prizes: Ernest Bloch (New York Critics' Circle), Leon Fleisher (Brussels), Gail Kubik (Pulitzer, music, *Symphony Concertante*), Lois Marshall, Yoko Matsuo and Diana Steiner (Naumberg), Igor Oistrakh (Wienawski), Sergio Perticaroli (Busoni)

Honors: Franz André (Schoenberg Medal), Edmond Appia & Eugene Ormandy (Legion of Honor), Edward Steuermann (Schoenberg Medal)

F. Biographical Highlights:

Carlos Kleiber abandons chemistry to work in a Munich Theater; Sergiu Luca moves with his parents to Israel; Arne Nordheim leaves the Oslo Music Conservatory; Per Norgård begins music study at the Copenhagen Conservatory of Music; Leontyne Price marries baritone William Warfield; Karlheinz Stockhausen moves to Paris to study music composition with Olivier Messiaen; Joan Sutherland signs a contract with the management of Covent Garden; Galina Vishnevskaya begins her association with the Bolshoi Opera Co.; John Williams wins a guitar audition and begins study with Andrés Segovia.

G. Institutional Openings:

Performing Groups: Canadian Broadcasting Co. SO (Toronto), Eden-Tamir Piano Duo, Edmonton SO, Helsinki Chamber Orchestra, Kammermusik der Staats-Kapelle Dresden, Kentucky Opera Association (Louisville), Modern Jazz Quartet, New York Pro musica, Quito Philharmonic Society (Ecuador), RTF Chamber Orchestra, Tokyo Opera (Niki Kai)

Festivals: Hallé Handel Festival, Pittsburgh International Festival

Educational: Archiv Für Musikwissenschaft (revival), Free Academy of Music (Sao Paulo, Brazil), Fromm Music Foundation (Harvard), Piccola Accademi a Musicale (Florence)

Other: *African Music, Ars Organi,* Association des Amis d'Henry Expert et de la musique Française Ancienne (Paris), Alfredo Casella International Competition, Gilbert & Sullivan Society (Houston), Japanese Musicological Society (Tokyo), Modern Music Masters Society (Park Ridge, IL), *Music and Musician,* Queen Elizabeth Music Competition (Brussels), *Repertoire International des Sources Musicales,* Southeastern Composer's League (South Carolina)

H. Musical Literature:

Cooper, Martin, *British Musicians of Today*
Davison, Archibald, *Church Music, Illusion and Reality*
Hindemith, Paul, *A Composer's World*
Jelinek, Hanns, *Anleitung zur Zwölftonkomposition*
Kennan, Kent, *The Technique of Orchestration*
Leibowitz, René, *The Evolution of Music*
Rufer, Josef, *Die Komposition mit zwölf Tönen*
Ulrich, Homer, *Symphonic Music*

I. Musical Compositions:

Barber, Samuel, *Souvenirs, Opus 28* (ballet)
Bernstein, Leonard, *Trouble in Tahiti* (opera)
Blacher, Boris, *Piano Concerto No. 2, "Variable Meters"*
Boulez, Pierre, *Structures I* (two pianos)
　　　　Piano Sonata No. 2
Cage, John, *4'33"* (any instrument, tacet)
　　　　Music for Piano, 1952
Chávez, Carlos, *Symphony No. 4, "Romantic"*
Copland, Aaron, *Old American Songs, Set II* (voice, orchestra)
Cowell, Henry, *Symphony No. 7*
Creston, Paul, *Symphony No. 4*
Dohnányi, Ernst von, *Concerto for Harp and Orchestra*
Floyd, Carlisle, *Out of the Cradle Endlessly Rocking* (soprano and orchestra)
Fortner, Wolfgang, *Die Witwe von Ephesus* (opera)
Gould, Morton, *Concerto for Tap Dancer and Orchestra*
Hamilton, Iain, *Concerto for Violin and Orchestra*
Henze, Hans Werner, *Boulevard Solitude* (opera)
Holmboe, Vagn, *Symphony No. 8, "Sinfonia Boreale"*
Kabalevsky, Dmitri, *Concerto No. 3 for Piano and Orchestra*
Kirchner, Leon, *Sinfonia for Orchestra*
Maderna, Bruno, *Musica per Due Dimensioni* (orchestra)
Mennin, Peter, *Concertato, Moby Dick* (orchestra)
Prokofiev, Serge, *Symphony No. 7*
Rodgers, Richard, *Victory at Sea* (television film music)
Stockhausen, Karlheinz, *Spiel* (opera)
Stravinsky, Igor, *Cantata* (soloists, women's chorus, chamber orchestra)
　　　　Septet (clarinet, bassoon, horn, violin, viola, cello, piano)
Tippett, Michael, *The Midsummer Marriage* (opera)
Toch, Ernst, *Symphony No. 2*
Vaughan-Williams, Ralph, *Sinfonia Antarctica* (No. 7, with soprano and women's chorus)
Villa-Lobos, Heitor, *Symphony No. 10*
　　　　Concerto No. 4 for Piano and Orchestra

1953

World Events:

In the U.S., the experimental Bell X-1A reaches a speed in excess of 1,600 miles per hour; the Communist Party is forced to register as an agent of the U.S.S.R.; the Refugee Relief Act allows refugees from Communist countries to enter the U.S.; the Department of Health, Education and Welfare (HEW) is formed. Internationally, Joseph Stalin dies and Georgi Malenkov becomes Russian Premier with Nikita Khrushchev as first secretary; Russian tanks crush an East Berlin uprising; Dag Hammarskjold is elected as United Nations Secretary-General; the official Korean Armistice is signed; the coronation of Queen Elizabeth is held in England.

Cultural Highlights:

Pulitzers: Drama, William Inge (*Picnic*); Fiction, Ernest Hemingway (*The Old Man and the Sea*); Poetry, Archibald MacLeish (*Collected Poems*). The Nobel Prize for Literature goes to Winston Churchill; Foundation Maeght, the Modern Art Museum is opened in Nice; the Painters Eleven group is founded in Toronto. Deaths in the art world include American artists John Marin and Everett Shinn and sculptor James E. Fraser and French artist Raoul Dufy; in the literary world, deaths include Americans Eugene O'Neill, Marjorie Rawlings and Ben A. Williams, French novelist Jérôme Tharaud and poet-historian Hilaire Belloc, Belgian poet Émile Cammaerts, Russian poet and novelist Ivan A. Bunin and British poet Dylan Thomas. Other highlights include:

Art: Albers, *Homage to the Square; Ascending*; Georges Braque, *Apples*; Marc Chagall, *The Eiffel Tower*; Stuart Davis, *Semé*: Jean Dubuffet, *The Busy Life*; Helen Frankenthaler, *Open Wall*; Naum Gabo, *Construction in Space*; Jackson Pollack, *Portrait and a Dream*.

Literature: James Baldwin, *Go Tell It on the Mountain*; Saul Bellow, *Adventures of Augie March*; Charles B. Catton, *A Stillness at Appomattox*; Jacques Cousteau, *Silent World*; Arthur Miller, *The Crucible*; Leon Uris, *Battle Cry*; Tennessee Williams, *Camino Real*.

MUSICAL EVENTS

A. Births:

Jan 20	Timothy Lowe (Br-pn)	Aug 18	Kenneth Kiesler (Am-cd)
Jan 22	Myung-Whun Chung (Kor-pn-cd)	Aug 22	David Burgess (Am-gui)
Jan 25	Roger Guy Steptoe (Br-cm)	Sep 1	Richard Buckley (Am-cd)
Feb 20	Riccardo Chailly (It-cd)	Oct 23	Marak Choloniewski (Pol-cm)
Feb 27	David E. Francis (Br-hps)	Nov 24	Tod Machover (Am-cel-cm)
Apr 6	Pascal Devoyon (Fr-pn)	Dec 4	Barbara Gorzynska (Pol-vn)
Apr 16	Eva Lundgren (Swe-sop)	Dec 21	Andras Schiff (Hun-pn)
May 8	Jennifer Rhys-Davies (Br-sop)		Jacques Gauthier (Fr-pn)
May 14	Lynne Lewandowski (Am-hp.m)		Steven de Groote (S.Af.-pn)
Jun 18	Peter Donohoe (Br-pn-cd)		Robert Saxton (Br-cm)
Aug 5	Alison Pearce (Br-sop)		Ilona Tokody (Hun-sop)
Aug 16	Stephen Robinson (Am-gui)		Hugh Wolff (Am-cd)

B. Deaths:

Jan 1	Ludomir Rozycki (Pol-cm)	Jul 12	Joseph Jongen (Bel-cm)
Jan 15	Heinrich Knote (Ger-ten)	Aug 14	Friedrich Schorr (Hun-bar)
Jan 22	Andrés de Segurola (Sp-bs)	Sep 1	Jacques Thibaud (Fr-vn)
Feb 5	Suzanne Adams (Am-sop)	Sep 15	Frank Ward (Am-cm)
Mar 4	Serge Prokofiev (Rus-cm)	Oct 3	Arnold Bax (Br-cm)
Mar 17	Conrado del Campo (Sp-cm)	Oct 8	Kathleen Ferrier (Br-alto)
May 4	T. Tertius Noble (Br-org-cm)	Oct 27	Zdzislaw Jachimecki (Pol-mus)
May 19	Frank Mullings (Br-ten)	Oct 29	William Kapell (Am-pn)
May 19	Albert Spaulding (Am-vn)	Nov 4	Elizabeth S. Coolidge (Am-pat)
Jun 17	Walter Niemann (Ger-mus)	Nov 18	Ruth Crawford Seeger (Am-folk)

Nov 26 Ivor Atkins (Br-org-cd)   Dec 9   Issay Dobrowen (Rus-cd)
Dec 4   Daniel G. Mason (Am-cm-ed)   Dec 11 Albert Coates (Br-cd-cm)

C. Debuts:

Met ---Ettore Bastianini (bar), Lisa Della Casa (sop), Jean Fenn (sop), Joseph Folmer (ten), Giulio Gari (ten), Vilma Georgiou (sop), Heidi Krall (sop), Maria Leoni (sop), Rudolf Mayreder (bs), James McCracken (ten), Andrew McKinley (ten), Josef Metternich (bs), Herva Nelli (sop), Nicola Rossi-Lemeni (bs), Irmgard Seefried (sop), Dorothy Shaw (mez), Theodor Uppman (bar), Cesare Valletti (ten), Sandra Warfield (mez)

U.S. --Paul Badura-Skoda (N.Y.), Inge Borkh (San Francisco), Jean Cox (Boston), Philippe Entremont (N.Y.), Ferenc Fricsay (Boston), Margarete Klose (San Francisco), James Levine (age 10, as pianist), Richard Lewis (San Francisco), John McCollum, Karl Münchinger (San Francisco), Elisabeth Schwarzkopf (San Francisco), Georg Solti (San Francisco), Ludwig Suthaus (San Francisco), Daniel Wayenberg (N.Y.)

Other -Bruno Bartoletti (Firenze), Irene Dalis (Oldenburg), Jörg Demus (Vienna), Maureen Forrester (Montreal), Friedrich Lenz (Düsseldorf), Barry McDaniel (Stuttgart), Mady Mesplé (Liège), Gustav Neidlinger (Milan), Jane Rhodes (Nancy), Marisa Robles (Madrid), Mario Sereni (Maggio), Renata Scotto (Milan), Gabriel Tacchino (Paris), Giorgio Tadeo (Palermo), Valerie Tryon (London), Eberhard Wächter (Vienna)

D. New Positions:

Conductors: Kurt Adler (San Francisco Opera), Dean Dixon (Göteborg SO), Sixten Ehrling (Stockholm Opera), Carlo Maria Giulini (La Scala), Franz Konwitschny (Dresden Opera), Fritz Mahler (Hartford SO), Fritz Reiner (Chicago SO), Wolfgang Sawallisch (Aachen SO)

Educational: Boris Blacher (director, Berlin Hochschule), Roque Cordero (director, Panama Music Institute), Lukas Foss (composition, UCLA), Roger Sessions (Conant Professor, Princeton)

Others: János Ferencsik (music director, Budapest Opera)

E. Prizes and Honors:

Prizes: Jacob Avshalomov (New York Critics' Circle), Elliott Carter (Prix de Rome), Lee Cass (Naumberg), Ella Goldstein (Busoni), Jacques Klein (Geneva), Georgia Laster (Naumberg), Gilda Muhlbauer (Naumberg)

Honors: Karl-Birger Blomdahl (Swedish Royal Academy), Arthur Bliss (Master of the Queen's Music), Frank Dobson (Royal Academy)

F. Biographical Highlights:

Mattiwilda Dobbs becomes the first black to sing at La Scala; Nicolai Gedda and Giorgio Tozzi make their La Scala debuts; Margaret Harshaw makes her Covent Garden debut; Hans Werner Henze moves to the Isle of Ischia; Paul Hindemith settles in Switzerland; William Kapell dies in an airplane crash; István Kertész graduates from Liszt Academy; James Levine, age 10, conducts the Cincinnati SO; Charles Mackerras begins free-lance conducting; Bohuslav Martinu begins a two-year stay in Nice; Andrzej Panufnik travels to China as a delegate for Polish Cultural program; Kryzstoff Penderecki adds composition to his other studies; Henri Pousseur graduates from Brussels Conservatory; Steve Reich enters Cornell University; Vissarion Shebalin suffers a stroke; Rita Streich makes her London debut; Helen Traubel quarrels with Rudolf Bing over her Broadway roles and quits the Met; Norman Treigle joins the N.Y. City Opera; Ralph Vaughan-Williams marries Ursula Wood.

G. Institutional Openings:

Performing Groups: Academic Choral Society (Helsinki), Allegri String Quartet, Concentus Musicus of Vienna, Elizabethan Singers (London), Ensemble Baroque de Paris, Lyric Art Quartet-Quintet (Houston), Miami Beach SO, National Chamber Orchestra (Toulouse), National Radio Orchestra of Madrid, Jean-François Paillard Chamber Orchestra (Paris),

RTE Singers (Dublin), Santa Fe (Rio Grande) SO, Schola Cantorum of Copenhagen

Festivals: Bergen International Music Festival

Educational: American School Band Directors' Association (Iowa), Electronic Music Center at Columbia-Princeton, International Society for Music Education (Brussels), National Catholic Bandmasters' Association (Notre Dame, IN), Yugoslav Academy of Arts and Sciences, Music Section (Zagreb)

Other: International Library for African Music (Transvaal), Louisville Records (by special grant), Romanian Opera House (Bucharest), Theater der Stadt Bonn

H. Musical Literature:

Dickinson, George, *The Study of Music as Liberal Art*
Farmer, Henry, *Oriental Studies, Mainly Musical*
Goldovsky, Boris, *Accents on Opera*
Graf, Max, *Geschichte und Geist der modernen Musik*
Moser, Hans, *Musikästhetik*
Peeters, Flor, *Ars Organi I*
Read, Gardner, *Thesaurus of Orchestral Devices*
Sachs, Curt, *Rhythm and Tempo, A Study in Music History*
Slonimsky, Nicolas, *Lexicon of Musical Invective*

I. Musical Compositions:

Adler, Samuel, *Symphony No. 1*
Alfvén, Hugo, *Symphony No. 5, Opus 54*
Arnold, Malcolm, *Symphony No. 2*
Badings, Henk, *Symphony No. 6, "Symphony of Psalms"*
Bernstein, Leonard, *Wonderful Town* (musical)
Bloch, Ernest, *Concerto Grosso* (string quartet and string orchestra)
                    Sinfonia Brève
Britten, Benjamin, *Gloriana* (opera)
Cage, John, *Music for Piano, 1953*
Chávez, Carlos, *Symphony for Strings* (No. 5)
Copland, Aaron, *The Tender Land* (opera)
Cowell, Henry, *Symphonies Nos. 8, 9, 10, and 11*
Egk, Werner, *The Chinese Nightingale* (ballet)
Foss, Lukas, *A Parable of Death* (cantata)
Gerhard, Roberto, *Symphony No. 1*
Ginastera, Alberto, *Concert Variations* (orchestra)
Hamilton, Iain, *Symphonic Variations*
Harris, Roy, *Concerto for Piano and Orchestra*
Honegger, Artur, *Christmas Cantata*
Husa, Karel, *Symphony No. 3*
Kay, Ulysses, *Concerto for Orchestra*
Khachaturian, Aram, *Spartacus Ballet*
Kirchner, Leon, *Concerto for Piano and Orchestra*
Lees, Benjamin, *Symphony No. 1*
Leibowitz, René, *Ricardo Gonfolano* (opera)
Martinu, Bohuslav, *Symphony No. 6, "Fantaisies Symphoniques"*
Mennin, Peter, *Symphony No. 6*
Messiaen, Olivier, *Réveil des oiseaux* (piano, orchestra)
Riegger, Wallingford, *Concerto for Piano and Woodwind Quintet*
Schuman, William, *Mighty Casey* (baseball opera)
Shostakovich, Dmitri, *Symphony No. 10*
Stockhausen, Karlheinz, *Punkte* (ten instruments)
Villa-Lobos, Heitor, *Concerto No. 2 for Cello and Orchestra*
Walton, William, *Orb and Scepter* (coronation march)

1954

World Events:

In the U.S., the first atomic powered submarine, the Nautilus, is launched; the Communist Control Act ends the legal status of the American Communist Party; the Supreme Court outlaws racial segregation in public schools; the Air Force Academy opens in Colorado Springs; the U.S. signs a mutual defense treaty with Japan. Internationally, the Communist forces under Ho Chi Minh defeat the French who withdraw from Vietnam which now is divided into North and South; the Southeast Asia Treaty Organization (SEATO) is created; the Big Four ministers meet in Berlin but Russia blocks all moves to unify Germany; Nassar seizes control of Egypt.

Cultural Highlights:

Pulitzers: Drama, John Patrick (*Teahouse of the August Moon*); Poetry, Theodore Roethke (*The Waking*); Autobiography, Charles Lindbergh (*The Spirit of St. Louis*). The Nobel Prize for Literature goes to American author Ernest Hemingway; Edith Sitwell is made a Dame of the British Empire; A.E. Richardson becomes President of the Royal Academy of Art; the J. Paul Getty Museum opens in Malibu, California; the Gutai Group of abstract artists is founded in Osaka, Japan. Deaths include French artists André Derain and Henri Matisse, American artist Reginald Marsh, American novelist Joseph Hergesheimer and poet Leonard Bacon, Swedish poet-novelist Frans Bengtsson and British novelist James Hilton. Other highlights include:

Art: Marc Chagall, *The Red Roofs*; Salvador Dali, *The Crucifixion*; Stuart Davis, *Colonial Cubism*; Jasper Johns, *Construction with a Piano*; Fernand Léger, *Acrobat on a Horse*; Pablo Picasso, *Sylvette*; Mark Rothko, *Light, Earth and Blue*; Ben Shahn, *The Blind Botanist*; Weldon, *Marine Corps Monument: Raising of the Flag on Iwo Jima*.

Literature: William Golding, *The Lord of the Flies*; Evan Hunter, *The Blackboard Jungle*; Robinson Jeffers, *The Cretan Woman*; James Michener, *Sayonara*; Max Shulman, *The Tender Trap*; John Steinbeck, *Sweet Thursday*; J.R.R. Tolkein, *The Lord of the Rings*; Thornton Wilder, *The Matchmaker*; Tennessee Williams, *Cat on a Hot Tin Roof.*

MUSICAL EVENTS

A. Births:

Jan 5 Thomas G. Dickinson (Am-pn)	May 9 Lawrence Dutton (Am-vla)
Feb 4 Patricia Schuman (Am-sop)	May 28 Yuri Egorov (Rus-pn)
Feb 27 Jo Ann Falletta (Am-cd)	Jul 18 Tobias Picker (Am-cm)
Mar 8 Evelyn de la Rosa (Am-sop)	Aug 10 Eliot Fisk (Am-gui)
Mar 15 Susan Finger (Am-mus-pn)	Sep 18 Lawrence Amundrud (Can-pn)
Mar 15 Michael Lipman (Am-cel)	Oct 2 Shizuka Ishikawa (Jp-vn)
Mar 17 Mischa Lefkowitz (Rus-vn)	Nov 6 Cheryl Ann Parrish (Am-sop)
Apr 19 Richard Heller (Aus-cm)	Tedd Joselson (Bel-pn)
Apr 22 Joel E. Fried (Am-cd)	Francesco Nicolosi (It-pn)
Apr 28 Dong-Suk Kang (Kor-vn)	Peter Zazofsky (Am-vn)

B. Deaths:

Jan 11 Oscar Straus (Ger-cm)	May 16 Clemens Krauss (Ger-cd)
Jan 25 Yvonne de Tréville (Am-sop)	May 19 Charles Ives (Am-cm)
Jan 27 Paul Marie Masson (Fr-mus)	Jul 16 Lucien Muratore (Fr-ten)
Jan 28 Allen C. Hinckley (Am-bs)	Jul 20 Jean Roger-Ducasse (Fr-cm)
Jan 31 Edward Maryon (Br-cm)	Sep 19 Tibor Harsányi (Hun-cm)
Feb 6 Paul Althouse (Am-ten)	Oct 27 Franco Alfano (It-cm)
Mar 1 Mable Wood Hill (Am-cm)	Nov 3 Jean Périer (Fr-ten-act)
Mar 24 Harry L Freeman (Am-cm)	Nov 30 Wilhelm Furtwängler (Ger-cd)
Apr 8 Fritzi Scheff (Aus-sop)	Dec 31 Peter van Anrooy (Hol-cd-cm)

C. Debuts:

Met ---Charles Anthony (ten), Kurt Böhme (bs), Fernando Corena (bs), Jon Crain (ten), Otto Edelmann (bar), Rosalind Elias (mez), Christel Goltz (sop), Elizabeth Holiday (mez), Calvin Marsh (bar), Dmitri Mitropoulos (cd), Marquita Moll (sop), Gino Penno (ten), Cyril Ritchard (bar), Louis Sgarro (bs), Shakeh Vartenissian (sop), Benjamin Wilkes (ten), Dolores Wilson (sop)

U.S. --David Bar-Illan (tour), Maria Callas (Chicago), Richard Cassilly (N.Y.), Mary Curtis-Verna (San Francisco), Gloria Davy (N.Y.), Natalie Hinderas (N.Y.), Marilyn Horne (Los Angeles), Josef Krips (Buffalo), John Reardon (N.Y.), Giulietta Simionato (Chicago), Leopold Simoneau (tour), Thomas Stewart (N.Y.), Eduard van Beinem (Philadelphia), Regina Sarfaty

Other -Luigi Alva (Milan), Maurice André (Paris), Irina Arkhipova (Sverdlovsk), Heather Begg (New Zealand), Monserrat Caballé (Barcelona), Marie Collier (Melbourne), Franz Crass (Krefeld), Roger Gardes (Paris), Lina Lalandi (London), Flaviano Labo (Piacenza), Ilse Ludwig (Dresden), Forbes Robinson (London), Allan Schiller (Leeds), Alain Vanzo (Paris), Jon Vickers (Toronto), Fritz Wunderlich (Freiburg)

D. New Positions:

Conductors: Karl Böhm (Vienna Opera), Luis Herrera de la Fuente (Mexican SO), Antonio Janigro (Zagreb Radio SO), Enrique Jordá (San Francisco SO), Herbert von Karajan (Berlin PO), Milton Katims (Seattle SO), Carlos Kleiber (Potsdam SO), Josef Krips (Buffalo PO), Charles Mackerras (BBC SO), Stanislaw Skrowaczewski (Krakow SO)

Educational: Marcel Dupré (director, Paris Conservatory), Karel Husa (composition, Cornell)

Others: Paul H. Lang (music critic, New York *Herald Tribune*)

E. Prizes and Honors:

Prizes: Roger Boutry (Prix de Rome), John Browning (Steinway), William Doppmann (Naumberg), Jules Eskin (Naumberg), Martha Flowers (Naumberg), Ingrid Haebler (Munich), Paul Hindemith (Sibelius), Aldo Mancinelli (Busoni), Quincy Porter (Pulitzer, music; *Concerto Concertante*), Jean Wentworth (Naumberg)

Honors: Norman Demuth (Legion of Honor)

F. Biographical Highlights:

Grace Bumbry is a winner on Arthur Godfrey's Talent Scouts program; William Dawson retires as director of the Tuskegee Choir; George Enescu suffers a stroke which makes him an invalid till his death; Karel Husa leaves Paris for the U.S.; Eduardo Mata begins study at the National Conservatory of Mexico; Zubin Mehta enters the Vienna Academy of Music; Andrzej Panufnik moves to England; Krzystoff Penderecki enters the State Academy of Music in Krakow; José Serebrier, at age 15, wins a composition contest sponsored by the Uruguayan National Orchestra; Joan Sutherland marries Richard Bonynge; Gladys Swarthout retires to Florence, Italy; Henryk Szeryng is encouraged by Rubinstein to resume his concert career; Arturo Toscanini gives his farewell concert and retires to Italy; Gilles Tremblay leaves Canada for further study in Paris with Messiaen; Ralph Vaughan-Williams makes a second lecture-tour of the U.S.; Charles Wuorinen wins New York Philharmonic's Young Composers Award.

G. Institutional Openings:

Performing Groups: Les Ballets de L'Étoile (by M. Béjart), Boston Camerata, Carmirelle String Quartet, Chicago Lyric Opera, Domaine Musical Concerts (Paris), Festival Singers of Canada, Gaudeamus String Quartet (Bilthoven, Netherlands), National SO of the South African Broadcasting Corporation (Johannesburg), New Zealand Opera Co., Ostrava (Janácek) PO, Pittsburgh Youth SO

Festivals: Cork International Choral Festival (Ireland), Newport (Kool) Jazz Festival (Newport, Rhode Island), Nutida Musik (Swedish Contemporary Music Festival), St.

Pancras (Camden) Festival (London)

Educational: Göteborg School of Music, Louisville Academy of Music

Other: Ahrend & Burnzema, Organ Builders (Leer), *Black Mountain Review*, Central Opera Service (N.Y.), Compagnia dei Giovanni (Italy); Composer's Recordings, Inc. (N.Y.); Deutscher Verlag für Musik (Leipzig), International Rostrum for Composers (UNESCO), R.A. Moog Co. (Trumansburg, N.Y.), Musicwriter

H. Musical Literature:

Bernstein, Leonard, *The Joy of Music*
Dart, Thurston, *The Interpretation of Music*
Deutsch, Otto, *Handel: Documentary History*
Ferguson, Donald, *Masterworks of the Orchestral Repertoire*
Georgiades, Thrasybulos, *Musik und Sprache*
Munch, Charles, *Je suis chef d'orchestre*
Reed, H. Owen, *Basic Music*
Reese, Gustave, *Music in the Renaissance*
Searle, Humphrey, *Twentieth Century Counterpoint*

I. Musical Compositions:

Andriessen, Hendrik, *Symphony No. 4*
Arnold, Malcolm, *Concerto for Harmonica and Orchestra*
Barber, Samuel, *Prayers of Kierkegård* (soprano, chorus, orchestra)
Beeson, Jack, *Hello, Out There* (opera)
Bloch, Ernest, *Symphony for Trombone and Orchestra*
Blomdahl, Karl-Birger, *Sisyphos* (ballet)
Brian, Havergal, *Symphonies 10 and 11*
Britten, Benjamin, *The Turn of the Screw* (opera)
Creston, Paul, *Dance Overture*
Crumb, George, *Eleven Echoes of Autumn* (violin, alto flute, clarinet, piano)
Dallapiccola, Luigi, *Variations for Orchestra*
Diamond, David, *Symphony No. 6*
Dohnányi, Ernst von, *American Rhapsody* (orchestra)
Farberman, Harold, *Evolution* (percussion)
Floyd, Carlisle, *Susannah* (opera)
Hanson, Howard, *Chorale and Alleluia* (band)
Hovhaness, Alan, *Concerto for Orchestra I*
Imbrie, Andrew, *Concerto for Violin and Orchestra*
Kay, Ulysses, *Serenade for Orchestra*
Leibowitz, René, *Concerto for Piano and Orchestra*
Luening/Ussachevsky, *Poem in Cycles and Bells*
Lutoslawski, Witold, *Concerto for Orchestra*
Mayuzumi, Toshiro, *Bacchanale* (orchestra)
Menotti, Gian Carlo, *The Saint of Bleeker Street* (opera)
Milhaud, Darius, *David* (opera)
Rosenberg, Hilding, *Louisville Concerto*
Sessions, Roger, *Idyll of Theocritus* (soprano, orchestra)
Stockhausen, Karlheinz, *Kontrapunkt* (ten instruments and orchestral version)
Stravinsky, Igor, *In Memoriam: Dylan Thomas* (tenor, string and trombone quartets)
Thomson, Virgil, *Concerto for Flute, Strings and Percussion*
Varèse, Edgard, *Deserts* (orchestra, tape)
Vaughan-Williams, Ralph, *Hodie* (Christmas cantata)
          Concerto for Tuba and Orchestra
Villa-Lobos, Heitor, *Concerto No. 5 for Piano and Orchestra*
Walton, William, *Troilus and Cressida* (opera)
Xenakis, Iannis, *Metastasis* (orchestra)

1955

World Events:
In the U.S. the labor unions A.F. of L. and C.I.O. merge with George Meany becoming the first president; the U.S. and Canada approve the Distant Early Warning Line (DEW); the Supreme Court orders public school desegregation; blacks boycott Alabama buses; U.S. advisors enter South Vietnam; approved oral contraceptive ("the pill") is introduced. Internationally, Winston Churchill resigns as British Prime Minister and is replaced by Anthony Eden; Malenkov resigns as Soviet Premier and Nikolai Bulganin becomes his replacement; the first International Conference on the Peaceful Uses of Atomic Energy meets in Geneva; the Central Treaty Organization (CENTO) is formed; the Warsaw Pact is ratified.

Cultural Highlights:
Pulitzers: Drama, Tennessee Williams (*Cat on a Hot Tin Roof*); Fiction, William Faulkner (*A Fable*); Poetry, Wallace Stevens (*Collected Poems*). Icelandic novelist Haldór K. Laxness receives the Nobel Prize for Literature. American novelist Jay McInerney is born; deaths in the literary field include American author Bernard de Voto, dramatist Robert Sherwood and poet Wallace Stevens, German novelists Heinrich Hauser and Thomas Mann, French poet Paul Claudel and Spanish philosopher José Ortega. Deaths in the art field include French artists Émile Bernard, Fernand Léger, Yves Tanguy and Maurice Utrillo, German artist Willi Baumeister and Swedish sculptor Carl Milles. Other highlights include:

Art: Salvador Dali, *The Lord's Supper*; Willem de Kooning, *Police Gazette*; Richard Diebenkorn, *Berkeley No. 3*; Max Ernst, *Bottled Moon*; Leon Golub, *Damaged Man*; Hans Hofmann, *Exuberance*; Oskar Kokoschka, *Thermopylae Triptych*; Lee Krasner, *Blue Level*; Pablo Picasso, *Women of Algiers*.

Literature: Enid Bagnold, *The Chalk Garden*; James Donlevy, *The Ginger Man*; Jean Genêt, *The Balcony*; William Inge, *The Bus Stop*; Mackinlay Kantor, *Andersonville*; Norman Mailer, *Deer Park*; Arthur Miller, *A View from the Bridge*; Vladimir Nabokov, *Lolita*; Flannery O'Connor, *A Good Man Is Hard to Find*; Herman Wouk, *Marjorie Morningstar*.

MUSICAL EVENTS

A. Births:

Jan 19	Simon Rattle (Br-cd)	Jul 30	Roberto De Clara (Can-cd)
Feb 7	John E. Holmquist (Am-gui)	Oct 1	Benjamin Verdery (Am-gui)
Mar 9	Fernando Bujones (Am-bal)	Oct 7	Yo Yo Ma (Chi-cel)
Mar 30	Margaret Fingerhut (Br-pn)	Dec 25	Robert David Taub (Am-pn)
Apr 23	Henk van der Meulen (Hol-cm)		Michel Dalberto (Fr-pn)
Jul 10	Milan Langer (Cz-pn)		Randall Hodgkinson (Am-pn)
Jul 27	Ronald Braunstein (Am-cd)		

B. Deaths:

Jan 22	Lydia Lipkovska (Rus-sop)	Jun 18	Willy Burkhard (Swi-cm)
Feb 11	Juan B. Fuentes (Mex-cm-the)	Aug 13	Florence Easton (Br-sop)
Mar 30	Harl McDonald (Am-cm)	Aug 22	Olin Downes (Am-art)
May 4	Georges Enescu (Rom-cm-cd)	Oct 7	Frieda Hempel (Ger-sop)
May 31	Raoul Gunsbourg (Rom-imp)	Nov 25	Jacques Handschin (Swi-mus)
Jun 1	Melius Christiansen (Nor-cd)	Nov 26	Fausto Torrefranca (It-mus)
Jun 15	Franz Ludwig (Boh-mus)	Dec 7	Manfred Bukofzer (Ger-mus)

C. Debuts:
Met ---Bernd Aldenhoff (ten), Marian Anderson, (alto), Giuseppe Campora (ten), Albert de Costa (ten), Matthew Farruggio (ten), Ralph Herbert (bar), Laurel Hurley (sop), Rudolph Kempe (cd), Paul Marko (bs), Robert McFerrin (bar), Mario Ortica (ten), Gianni Poggi (ten), Martin Rich (cd), Thomas Schippers (cd), Renata Tebaldi (sop), Giorgio Tozzi

(bs), Hermann Uhde (bar)

U.S. --Géza Anda (Philadelphia), Carlo Bergonzi (Chicago), Jörg Demus (N.Y.), Sergio Fiorentino (N.Y.), Dietrich Fischer-Dieskau (Cincinnati), Ezio Flagello (N.Y.), Emil Gilels (tour), Carlo Maria Giulini (Chicago), Glenn Gould (Washington, D.C.), Lorin Hollander (N.Y.), Alicia de Larrocha (Los Angeles), Evelyn Lear (N.Y.), Pilar Lorengar (N.Y.), Igor Markevich (Boston SO), David Oistrakh (N.Y.), Teresa Stich-Randall (Chicago), André Watts (age 9, Philadelphia)

Other -Teresa Berganza (Madrid), Mimi Coertse (Naples), Mirella Freni (Modena), Nicolai Ghiaurov (Sofia), André de Groote (Johannesburg), Nan Merriman (Milan), Jorge Mester (Mexico City), Anna Moffo (Spoleto), Tony Poncet (Liège), Anja Silja (Brunswick), Josephine Veasey (London), Helen Watts (London), Ingvar Wixell (Gävle), Erwin Wohlfahrt (Aachen), Giuseppe Zampieri (Berlin)

D. New Positions:

Conductors: Charles Bruck (Strasbourg Radio SO), Sergiu Comissiona (Romanian Opera), Lamberto Gardelli (Danish Radio SO), Margaret Hillis (N.Y. City Opera), István Kertész (Budapest Opera), Otto Klemperer (Philharmonia Orchestra, London), Peter Maag (Bonn Opera), Kurt Masur (Dresden PO), Hans Schmidt-Isserstedt (Stockholm PO), Horst Stein (Berlin Opera), Leopold Stokowski (Houston SO)

Educational: Vagn Holmboe (composition, Copenhagen Conservatory), Menahem Pressler (piano, Indiana University)

Others: Jacques Ibert (director, Paris Opera)

E. Prizes and Honors:

Prizes: Maurice André (Geneva), John Browning and Betty Jean Hagen (Leventritt), Nancy Cirillo (Naumberg), Sergiu Comissiona (Besançon), Pierre Dubois (Prix de Rome), Nicolai Ghiaurov (Paris), Adam Harasiewicz (Chopin), Ronald Leonard (Naumberg), Mary MacKenzie (Naumberg), Gian Carlo Menotti (Pulitzer, music, *The Saint of Bleeker Street*)

Honors: Eugene Goosens (knighted), George London (Kammersänger, Vienna), Walter Piston (American Academy)

F. Biographical Highlights:

Marian Anderson becomes first black vocalist to sing at the Met; Vladimir Ashkenazy takes second prize in the Chopin Competition; Benjamin Britten takes Peter Pears on a recital tour of the Far East; Pierre Boulez becomes a part of the Darmstadt group; David Del Tredici enters the University of California; Grace Hoffman makes her La Scala debut; Neeme Järvi enters Leningrad Conservatory; Herbert von Karajan voted conductor-for-life by the Berlin PO; Bohuslav Martinu moves to the U.S. but has trouble adjusting to the American way of life; John La Montaine travels to Paris to study with Nadia Boulanger; Zara Nelsova takes American citizenship; Arne Nordheim studies in Paris; Tancredi Pasero retires from the stage; William Primrose becomes a naturalized American citizen; Regina Resnik begins concentrating on the soprano repertoire; Mstislav Rostropovich marries Galina Vishnevskaya; Beverly Sills joins the New York City Opera; Elisabeth Söderstrom debuts at Salzburg; Evgeny Svetlanov becomes assistant conductor of the Bolshoi Theater; Joan Tower returns to the U.S. to study at Bennington College; Barry Tuckwell becomes principle horn of the London SO; Shirley Verrett wins on Arthur Godfrey's Talent Scouts program.

G. Institutional Openings:

Performing Groups: Anchorage Civic Opera (Alaska), Antwerp PO, Beaux Arts Trio (Indiana University), Borodin String Quartet (Moscow), Brooklyn PO, Cleveland Orchestra Chorus, Festival Piano Quartet (Aspen), Handel Opera Society of London, Hebrew University SO, Houston Ballet, Houston Grand Opera Co., Kontarsky Brothers Piano Duo; National Opera Co. (Raleigh, NC), Netherlands Chamber Orchestra, Santiago Municipal PO (Chile), State PO of Romania (Bucharest)

Festivals: Athens Festival of the Arts, Empire State Musical Festival, Lausanne International Festival, Heinrich Schütz Tage (Dresden)

Educational: Joseph Haydn Institut (Cologne), Institute of Puerto Rican Culture

Other: Alexander Broude, Inc. (N.Y.); Johann Joseph Fux Society (Graz), *Gazzetta Musicale de Napoli*, International Gustav Mahler Society (Vienna), League of Filipino Composers, Milan Studio di Fonologia Musicale, Musician's Memorial Chapel (London), National Philharmonic Hall (Warsaw), Neue Mozart Ausgabe (Bärenreiter), NHK Electronic Music Studio (Tokyo), Society for Ethnomusicology (Philadelphia)

H. Musical Literature:
Chase, Gilbert, *America's Music*
Forte, Allen, *Contemporary Tone Structures*
Kwalwasser, Jacob, *Exploring the Musical Mind*
Machlis, Joseph, *The Enjoyment of Music*
MacMillan, Ernest, *Music in Canada*
Mann, Alfred, *The Theory of Fugue*
Piston, Walter, *Orchestration*
Rufer, Joseph, *Musiker über Musik*
Stevens, Denis, *Tudor Church Music*

I. Musical Compositions:
Adler, Richard, *Damn Yankees* (musical)
Badings, Henk, *Louisville Symphony* (Symphony No. 7)
Bergsma, William, *The Wife of Martin Guerre* (opera)
Binkerd, Gordon, *Symphony No. 1*
Blacher, Boris, *Concerto for Viola and Orchestra*
Bloch, Ernest, *Symphony in E-flat*
Boulez, Pierre, *Le Marteau sans Maître* (contralto, chamber group)
Carter, Elliott, *Variations for Orchestra*
Copland, Aaron, *Canticle of Freedom* (ballet)
Dahl, Ingolf, *Tower of Santa Barbara* (ballet)
Dallapiccola, Luigi, *Canti di Liberazione* (mixed chorus, orchestra)
Egk, Werner, *Irisch Legende* (opera)
Hanson, Howard, *Symphony No. 5, "Sinfonia Sacra"*
Henze, Hans Werner, *Symphony No. 4*
Hovhaness, Alan, *Mysterious Mountain* (symphony)
Jolivet, André, *Transoceanic Suite*
Kabalevsky, Dmitri, *Nikita Vershinin* (opera)
Kay, Ulysses, *The Boor* (opera)
Leibowitz, René, *Trauersymphonie* (orchestra)
Read, Gardner, *Symphony No. 4*
Reed, H. Owen, *Peter Homan's Dream*
Riegger, Wallingford, *Dance Rhythms, Opus 58* (orchestra)
          Overture, Opus 60
Rochberg, George, *Symphony No. 1*
Rorem, Ned, *Symphony No. 2*
Schuman, William, *Credendum* (orchestra)
Shchedrin, Rodion, *The Humpback Horse* (ballet)
Shostakovich, Dmitri, *Concerto No. 1 for Violin and Orchestra*
Thompson, Randall, *A Trip to Nahant* (orchestra)
Tippett, Michael, *Concerto for Piano and Orchestra*
Toch, Ernst, *Symphony No. 3*
Vaughan-Williams, Ralph, *Symphony No. 8*
Villa-Lobos, Heitor, *Symphony No. 11*
          Concerto for Harmonica and Orchestra

1956

World Events:
In the U.S. President Dwight Eisenhower beats Adlai Stevenson for a second term as President; the Federal Aid Highway Act authorizes beginning work on the Interstate Highway system; the Agricultural (Soil Bank) Act pays farmers to remove croplands from production; Albert B. Sabin perfects his oral vaccine for polio. Internationally, the Hungarian Freedom Uprising is crushed by the entrance of Russian tanks and troops; Egypt nationalizes the Suez Canal--fighting with England and France is ended by the intervention of the U.N.; Fidel Castro begins an anti-Batista campaign in Cuba; first transatlantic telephone cable begins use; "De-Stalinization" begins in Russia.

Cultural Highlights:
Pulitzers: Drama, Frances Goodrich and Albert Hackett (*The Diary of Anne Frank*); Fiction, MacKinlay Kantor (*Andersonville*); Poetry, Elizabeth Bishop (*Poems, North and South*). The Spanish poet Juan Ramón Jiménez receives the Nobel Prize for Literature; W.H. Auden begins teaching poetry at Oxford. Deaths in the literary field include French novelist Julien Benda, British poet Alan A. Milne, German dramatist Berthold Brecht and American novelist Louis Bromfield; in the art field, American sculptor Chester Beach and artists Gifford R. Beal, Lyonel Feininger and Jackson Pollack, British artists Max Beerbohm and Frank Brangwyn, Egyptian-born Louis Guglielmi and German artist Emil Nolde. Other highlights include:

Art: Leonard Baskin, *Man with a Dead Bird*; Mary Brooks, *Karrig*; Chryssa, *Bronze Tablet No. 2*; Willem de Kooning, *Easter Monday*; Barbara Hepworth, *Orpheus*; Richard Lippold, *Variations within a Sphere 10;* Theodore Roszak, *Sea Sentinal*; William Scott, *Red Nude*; George Tooker, *The Government Bureau*; Joern Utzon, *Sydney Opera House*.

Literature: Nelson Algren, *A Walk on the Wild Side*; Winston Churchill, *History of the English Speaking People*; Patrick Dennis, *Auntie Mame*; John F. Kennedy, *Profiles in Courage*; Ira Levin, *No Time for Sergeants*; Ann Lindbergh, *The Unicorn and Other Poems*; Grace Metalious, *Peyton Place*; Eugene O'Neill, *Long Day's Journey into Night*.

MUSICAL EVENTS

A. Births:

Jan 4	Richard L. Harris (Br-hps)	Sep 6	Makiko Kawahito (Jap-vla)
Mar 3	Stuart Hutchinson (Br-cd-pn)	Sep 12	Valerie Ashworth (Br-pn)
Mar 21	Ann MacKay (Br-sop)	Sep 12	Jeffrey Kahane (Am-pn)
Apr 16	Michael Lewin (Am-pn)	Oct 12	Penelope Walker (Br-sing)
Jun 23	Sylvia McNair (Am-sop)	Nov 6	Andrea Matthews (Am-sop)
Aug 5	Adrian Goss (Br-ten)	Dec 5	Krystian Zimerman (Pol-pn)
Aug 7	Sharon Isbin (Am-gui)	Dec 28	Nigel P. Kennedy (Am-vn)
Aug 16	Angela-Maria Blasi (Am-sop)		Andrei Gavrilov (Rus-pn)

B. Deaths:

Jan 3	Alexander Gretchaninov (Rus-cm)	Sep 9	Rupert Hughes (Am-mus)
Jan 27	Erich Kleiber (Ger-cd)	Sep 27	Gerald Finzi (Br-cm)
Feb 16	Théodore Gérold (Fr-mus)	Oct 26	Walter Gieseking (Fr-pn)
Feb 18	Gustave Charpentier (Fr-cm)	Nov 2	Jacob Weinberg (Rus-pn-cm)
Feb 21	Edwin F. Goldman (Am-band)	Nov 4	Art Tatum (Am-pop)
Mar 1	Henriette Renié (Fr-hp)	Nov 11	Marie Hall (Br-vn)
Mar 11	Sergi Vassilenko (Rus-cm)	Nov 24	Guido Cantelli (It-cd)
Mar 28	Cecil Smith (Am-cri)	Nov 26	Tommy Dorsey (Am-pop)
Jun 25	Reinhold Glière (Rus-cm)	Dec 7	Henry Fillmore (Am-band)
Sep 6	Felix Borowski (Br-cm-cri)	Dec 8	Hans Barth (Ger-pn-cm)
		Dec 11	Stefi Geyer (Hun-vn)

C. Debuts:

Met ---Belén Amparán (alto), Henry Arthur (ten), Daniele Barioni (ten), Carlo Bergonzi (ten), Rose Byrum (sop), Maria Callas (sop), Madelaine Chambers (sop), Emilia Cundari (sop), Mattiwilda Dobbs (sop), John Frydel (bs), Tito Gobbi (bar), Florence Holland (sop), Gladys Lansing (mez), Jean Morel (cd), Hal Roberts (ten), Enzo Sordello (bar), Antonietta Stella (sop), Helen Vanni (mez)

U.S. --McHenry Boatwright (Boston), Karl Böhm (Chicago), John Browning (N.Y.), Boris Christoff (San Francisco), André Cluytens (D.C.), Mignon Dunn (N.Y.), Maureen Forrester (N.Y.), George L. Katz (N.Y.), Louis Kentner (N.Y.), Birgit Nilsson (Hollywood), Louis Quilico (N.Y.), Mstislav Rostropovich (N.Y.), Leonie Rysanek (Los Angeles), Paul Zukofsky (N.Y.)

Other -Gerd Albrecht (Hamburg), Janet Baker (Glyndebourne), Annelies Burmeister (Weimar), José Carreras (Barcelona), György Cziffra (Vienna), Norma Fisher (London), Jana Frenklova (Prague), Ingeborg Hallstein (Passau), Hiroyuki Iwaki (Tokyo), Hans Kaart (Karlsruhe), Alfredo Kraus (Cairo), Mario Lippert (Hagen), Edith Mathis (Lucerne), Paolo Montarsolo (Bologna), William Murray (Spoleto), Edith Peineman (Munich)

D. New Positions:

Conductors: Eduard van Beimun (Los Angeles PO), Carlos Kleiber (Düsseldorf Opera), Kyrill Kondrashin (Moscow SO), Nikolai Malko (Sydney SO), Igor Markevitch (Montreal SO), Felix Prohaska (Frankfurt Opera), Stanislaw Skrowaczewski (Warsaw PO), Izler Solomon (Indianapolis SO), Walter Susskind (Toronto SO)

Educational: John Brownlee (president, Manhattan School), Hans Heinz (voice, Juilliard), Charles Kullman (voice, Indiana University), Robert Whitney (Dean of Music, Louisville University)

Others: Set Svanholm (director, Stockholm Opera)

E. Prizes and Honors:

Prizes: Salvatore Accardo (Geneva), Vladimir Ashkenazy (Brussels), Janet Baker (Ferrier), Wayne Connor (Naumberg), Jörg Demus (Busoni), George Katz (Naumberg), Alfredo Kraus (Geneva), Donald McCall (Naumberg), Gerard Poulet (Paganini), Ernst Toch (Pulitzer, music, *Symphony No. 3*)

Honors: Margot Fonteyn (Dame), Jacques Ibert (French Institute), Ernst Toch (National Institute)

F. Biographical Highlights:

Elly Ameling wins a local Holland singing competition; Leonardo Balada goes to the U.S. and enters New York School of Music; John Browning places second in the Queen Elizabeth Competition in Brussels; Ivan Davis wins second prize in the Busoni Competition; William Dawson is sent by the U.S. State Department to train choral groups in Spain; Mirella Freni begins a two-year leave from her career on the birth of her daughter; Hans Werner Henze moves to Naples; Eliahu Inbal graduates from the Jerusalem Academy of Music; Ani and Ida Kavafian move with their family to the U.S.; György Ligeti leaves Hungary and settles in Vienna; Neville Marriner joins the London SO as a violinist; Bohuslav Martinu accepts the professorship of the American Academy in Rome; Per Norgård studies with Nadia Boulanger in Paris; José Serebrier moves to the U.S. and enters Curtis Institute; Solomon suffers a stroke and retires from concertizing; Isaac Stern becomes the first major performer to visit Russia during the Cold War.

G. Institutional Openings:

Performing Groups: Australian Opera Co. (Sydney), Brno State PO (by merger), Dave Brubeck Quartet, Central Philharmonic Society (Peking), Clarion Concerts (New York), Deutsche Oper am Rhein (Düsseldorf), Diamov String Quartet (Sofia), Japan State PO (Tokyo), Kammermusikkreis Ferdinand Conrad, Koblenz Madrigal Choir, Lucerne Festival Strings, Rhode Island Civic Chorale, Rome Piano Quartet, Washington D.C. Opera

Society, West Bay Opera (San Francisco)

Festivals: Alaska Festival of Music (Anchorage), Warsaw Autumn Festival of Contemporary Music

Educational: Brisbane Conservatory of Music, Hanoi Conservatory of Music (Vietnam)

Other: Ford Auditorium (Detroit), Gulbenkian Foundation, Memphis Opera Theater, Moravian Music Foundation (Winston-Salem, NC), Music Promotion Foundation of the Philippines, Organ Historical Society (Richmond, VA), *Quadrivium*, Robert Schumann International Piano Competition (E. Germany), Tivoli Gardens Concert Hall (Copenhagen)

H. Musical Literature:

Adorno, Theodor, *Dissonanzen: Musik in der verwalteten Welt*
Barzun, Jacques, *Music in American Life*
Coeuroy, André, *Dictionaire critique de la musique ancienne et moderne*
Hume, Paul, *Catholic Church Music*
Karpeles, Maud, *Folk Songs of Europe*
Kerman, Joseph, *Opera as Drama*
Nettl, Bruno, *Music in Primitive Cultures*
Newman, Ernest, *From the World of Music*
Sessions, Roger, *Reflections on the Music life in the United States*

I. Musical Compositions:

Badings, Henk, *Symphony No. 8, "Hannover"*
Barber, Samuel, *Vanessa* (opera)
          Medea's Meditation and Dance of Vengeance (orchestra)
Berio, Luciano, *Nones* (orchestra)
Bernstein, Leonard, *Candide* (opera)
Britten, Benjamin, *Prince of the Pagodas* (ballet)
Cowell, Henry, *Symphony No. 12*
Creston, Paul, *Lydian Ode* (orchestra)
Dello Joio, Norman, *Meditations on Ecclesiastes* (string orchestra)
Einem, Gottfried von, *Concerto for Piano and Orchestra, Opus 20*
Glanville-Hicks, Peggy, *Tapestry* (orchestra)
Henze, Hans Werner, *König Hirsch* (opera)
Kabalevsky, Dmitri, *Symphony No. 5*
Kay, Ulysses, *String Quartet No. 2*
Lees, Benjamin, *Concerto No. 1 for Piano and Orchestra*
Loewe, Frederick, *My Fair Lady* (musical)
Martin, Frank, *The Tempest* (opera)
Martinu, Bohuslav, *Concerto No. 4 for Piano and Orchestra*
Mennin, Peter, *Concerto for Cello and Orchestra*
Menotti, Gian Carlo, *The Unicorn, the Gorgon and the Manicore* (ballet)
Moore, Douglas, *The Ballad of Baby Doe* (opera)
Piston, Walter, *Symphony No. 5*
Reed, H. Owen, *La Fiesta Mexicana* (band)
Schuman, William, *New England Triptych* (orchestra)
Sessions, Roger, *Piano Concerto*
Stockhausen, Karlheinz, *Zeitmesse* (oboe, flute, english horn, clarinet, bassoon)
          Gesang der Jünglinge (boy soprano, electronics)
Stravinsky, Igor, *Canticum Sacrum* (tenor, baritone, chorus, orchestra)
          Chorale Variations on "Von Himmel Hoch"
Vaughan-Williams, Ralph, *Fen and Flood* (cantata)
Villa-Lobos, Heitor, *Symphony No. 12*
          Emperor Jones (ballet)
Walton, William, *Concerto for Cello and Orchestra*
Xenakis, Iannis, *Pithroprakta* (fifty instruments)

1957

World Events:

In the U.S., the President unfolds his Eisenhower Doctrine for aid to Middle Eastern countries in their fight against Communism; the Civil Rights Commission is formed; the phrase, "under God," is added to the U.S. Pledge of Allegiance; the Southern Christian Leadership Conference is founded; the bridge over the Straits of Mackinac is opened in Michigan. Internationally, the European Economic Community (the European Common Market) is formed; the Russians launch the first space craft to orbit the earth, Sputnik I and II; the International Atomic Energy Agency is founded; the International Geophysical Year begins; air service begins between London and Moscow; the Federation of Malaysia becomes an independent state.

Cultural Highlights:

Pulitzers: Autobiography, John F. Kennedy (*Profiles in Courage*); Drama, Eugene O'Neill (*Long Day's Journey into Night*); Poetry, Richard Wilbur (*Things of This World*). The Nobel Prize for Literature goes to French novelist Albert Camus; e.e. cummings receives the Bollingen Prize; Charles P. Snow is knighted. Deaths include British author Percy W. Lewis and novelist Joyce Cary, American author Anne Parrish and poet Badger Clark, Danish novelist Johannes Anker Larsen, Romanian sculptor Constantin Brancusi and Mexican artist Diego Rivera. Other highlights include:

Art: Henri-Georges Adam, *Beacon of the Dead (Auschwitz)*; Marc Chagall, *Self Portrait*; Sam Francis, *Middle Blue*; Norbert Kricke, *Water Forest (Gelsenkirchen)*; Le Corbusier, *Tokyo Art Museum*; Pablo Picasso, *Las Meninas*; Richard Pousette-Dart, *Spanish Presence*; Mark Rothko, *Light Red over Black*; Andrew Wyeth, *Brown Swiss*.

Literature: James Agee, *A Death in the Family*; John Cheever, *The Wapshot Chronicle*; James G. Cozzens, *By Love Possessed*; Kettl Frings, *Look Homeward, Angel*; William Inge, *Dark at the Top of the Stairs*; Jack Kerouac, *On the Road*; John Osborne, *The Entertainer*; Boris Pasternak, *Doctor Zhivago*; Max Shulman, *Rally 'Round the Flag, Boys*.

MUSICAL EVENTS

A. Births:

Jan 28	John Gough (Br-pn)	Sep 17	Michael Morgan (Am-cd)
Feb 14	Sandro de Palma (It-pn)	Oct 25	Colin Carr (Br-cel)
Jun 1	J. Patrick Raftery (Am-bar)	Oct 30	Shlomo Mintz (Rus-vn)
Jun 4	Mark Beudert (Am-ten)	Dec 2	Elena Filipova (Rom-sop)
Jul 6	Craig S. Goodman (Am-fl)		Mikhail Pletnev (Rus-pn)

B. Deaths:

Jan 16	Arturo Toscanini (It-cd)	Jun 6	Ella Fleisch (Hun-sop)
Feb 7	Rudolf Réti (Serb-mus-the)	Jun 12	Jimmy Dorsey (Am-pop)
Feb 16	Josef Hofmann (Pol-pn)	Sep 1	Dennis Brain (Br-hn)
Mar 8	Othmar Schoeck (Swi-cm-cd)	Sep 20	Jan Sibelius (Fin-cm)
Apr 30	Ludwig Schiedermair (Ger-mus)	Nov 4	Maria J. Canteloube (Fr-pn)
May 2	Tadeusz Kassern (Pol-cm)	Nob 29	Erich Korngold (Boh-cm)
May 6	Rudolf Gerber (Ger-mus)	Nov 30	Beniamino Gigli (It-ten)
May 9	Ezio Pinza (It-bar)	Dec 12	Robert Kurka (Am-cm)
May 26	Ernst Flade (Ger-mus)	Dec 21	Eric Coates (Br-cd-cm)

C. Debuts:

Met ---Mildred Allen (sop), Cesare Bardelli (bar), Karl Böhm (cd), Mary Curtis-Verna (sop), Irene Dalis (mez), Ezio Flagello (bs), Nicolai Gedda (ten), Norman Kelly (ten), Charles Kuestner (ten), Flaviano Labo (ten), Gloria Lind (sop), Jean Melatti (sop), Martha Mödl (sop), Robert Nagy (ten), Carlotta Ordassy (sop), Marianne Schech (sop), Mario Sereni (bar), Wolfgang Windgassen (ten)

U.S. --Daniel Bahrenboim (N.Y.), Lili Chookasian (Chicago), Loren Driscoll (N.Y.), Erich Kunzel (Santa Fe), Aase Loveberg (Philadelphia), Jean Martinon (Boston), Johanna Martzy (tour), Anna Moffo (Chicago), Paolo Montarsolo, Ticho Parly (New Orleans), Leontyne Price (San Francisco), Rafael Puyana (N.Y.), Gianni Raimondi (tour), Judith Raskin (Ann Arbor), Rita Streich (San Francisco), Jess Thomas (San Francisco)

Other -Virginia Babikian (Spoleto), Cathy Berberian (Naples), Malcolm Binns (London), Piero Cappuccilli (Milan), Kyung-Wha Chung (Seoul), Fiorenza Cossotto (Milan), Justino Díaz (Puerto Rico), Placido Domingo (as baritone), Heather Harper (Glyndebourne), Mindru Katz (Paris), Tom Krause (Helsinki), Radu Lupu (Romania), Alberto Remedios (London), Teresa Zylis-Gara (Krakow)

D. New Positions:

Conductors: Antonia de Almeida (Lisbon Radio SO), Colin Davis (BBC Scottish SO), Alexander Gibson (Sadler's Wells), Bernard Haitink (Netherlands Radio SO), Margaret Hillis (Chicago Symphony Chorus), Igor Markevitch (Lamoureux Concerts), Andrzej Panufnik (Birmingham SO), Julius Rudel (N.Y.,City Opera)

Educational: George Perle (theory, University of California), Bernd Zimmermann (Cologne Musikhochschule)

Others: Christoph von Dohnányi (music director, Lübeck Opera), Hans Stuckenschmidt (music critic, *Frankfurter Allgemeine Zeitung*)

E. Prizes and Honors:

Prizes: Jenö Adám and Gyula David (Kossuth), Martha Argerich (Busoni), Norman Dello Joio (Pulitzer, music, *Meditations on Ecclesiastes*), Peter Frankl (Long-Thibaud), Mirella Freni (Viotti), Michael Grebanier (Naumberg), Anton Kuerti (Leventritt), Jerome Lowenthal (Busoni and Darmstadt), Angelica Lozada (Naumberg), Dominique Merlet (Geneva), Wyn Morris (Koussevitsky), Leslie Parnas (Casals), Regina Sarfaty (Naumberg)

Honors: Jenö Adám (Kossuth), Paul Ben-Haim (Israel State), Maggie Teyte (Legion of Honor)

F. Biographical Highlights:

Dominick Argento earns his Ph.D. from Eastman; Fiorenza Cossotto makes her La Scala debut; Peter Maxwell Davies receives government scholarship for study in Italy; Colin Davis becomes assistant conductor of the BBC Scottish SO; Ivan Davis wins second prize in the Busoni Competition but ties with Jerome Lowenthal; Malcolm Frager graduates from Columbia with a degree in Russian; Mauricio Kagel leaves Argentina and settles in Cologne; István Kertész moves to Germany; Alfredo Kraus makes his London debut; Raphael Kubelik conducts the Vienna PO, the first engagement in a German-speaking country since WW II; James McCracken leaves the Met and moves to Europe; Jonel Perlea suffers a heart attack; Steve Reich graduates from Cornell with honors; Regina Resnik makes a successful Covent Garden debut; Elliott Schwartz receives a B.A. from Columbia; Renata Scotto makes her English debut; Robert Starer becomes a U.S. citizen; Robert Suderburg graduates *summa cum laude* from the University of Minnesota; Martti Talvela, in teacher training, begins voice lessons at Lahti Academy; Edgard Varèse goes to Paris to work in the Philips laboratories on a piece for the Brussels World Fair.

G. Institutional Openings:

Performing Groups: Amsterdam Chamber Orchestra, Bartók String Quartet (Budapest), The Beatles (Liverpool), Dallas Civic Opera Co., Grupo Nueva Musica (Madrid), Hungarian Chamber Orchestra (Budapest), Improvisation Chamber Ensemble (by Lukas Foss), Intimate Opera Group (Adelaide, Australia), The Kingston Trio, Omaha Opera Co., Opera da Camera di Milano, Philharmonia Hungarica, Santa Fe Opera Co

Festivals: Casals Festival (Puerto Rico)

Educational: College Music Society (Harvard), Institute of Medieval Music (N.Y.), Instituto di Storia della Musica dell'Università (Palermo), Orense Conservatory of Music

Other: Cologne Opera House, Institute for Twentieth Century Music (Tokyo), International Society of Organ Builders (Amsterdam), *Journal of Music Theory*, Mannheim National Theater, Merola Opera Program, Music Critics Association (Rockville, MD), Summy-Birchard Co. (by merger), World Music Bank

H. Musical Literature:

Apel, Willi, *Gregorian Chant*
Chasins, Abram, *Speaking of Pianists*
Dallin, Leon, *Techniques, 20th Century Composition*
Howard/Bellows, *Short History of Music in America*
Hume, Paul, *Our Music, Our Schools and Our Culture*
McCutchan, Robert, *Hymn Tune Names: Sources and Significance*
Parrish, Carl, *Notation of Medieval Music*
Reese, Gustave, *Fourscore Classics of Music Literature*
Stuckenschmidt, H.H., *Glanz und Elend der Musikkritik*
Wittgenstein, Paul, *School for the Left Hand*

I. Musical Compositions:

Adler, Samuel, *Symphony No. 2*
Argento, Dominick, *The Boor* (opera)
Arnold, Malcolm, *Symphony No. 3*
Bernstein, Leonard, *West Side Story* (musical)
Binkerd, Gordon, *Symphony No. 2*
Blacher, Boris, *Music for Cleveland* (orchestra)
Boulez, Pierre, *Piano Sonata No. 3*
Brian, Havergal, *Symphony No. 12*
Britten, Benjamin, *Noye's Fludde* (one-act opera)
Dello Joio, Norman, *Air Power* (suite)
Dorati, Antal, *Symphony*
Egge, Klaus, *Symphony No. 3, Opus 28*
Egk, Werner, *Der Revisor* (opera)
Einem, Gottfried von, *Medusa* (ballet)
Fortner, Wolfgang, *Die Bluthochzeit* (opera)
Ginastera, Alberto, *Concerto for Harp and Orchestra*
Gould, Morton, *Jekyll and Hyde Variations* (orchestra)
Hanson, Howard, *Song of Democracy* (soli, chorus, orchestra)
Hindemith, Paul, *Die Harmonie der Welt* (opera)
Ibert, Jacques, *Tropisms for Imaginary Loves* (ballet)
Mayuzumi, Toshiro, *Campanologie* (orchestra)
Milhaud, Darius, *Aspen Serenade* (nine instruments)
Poulenc, Francis, *Dialogues of the Carmelites* (opera)
            Elegy for Horn and Orchestra
Riegger, Wallingford, *Symphony No. 2, Opus 63*
            Festival Overture, Opus 68
Rorem, Ned, *Symphony No. 3*
Sessions, Roger, *Symphony No. 3*
Shostakovich, Dmitri, *Concerto No. 2 for Piano and Orchestra*
            Symphony No. 11, "1905"
Stockhausen, Karlheinz, *Gruppen for Three Orchestras*
Stravinsky, Igor, *Agon* (ballet)
Toch, Ernst, *Symphony No. 4*
Vaughan-Williams, Ralph, *Symphony No. 9*
Walton, William, *Partita for Orchestra*
Willson, Meredith, *The Music Man* (musical)
Yardumian, Richard, *Passacaglia, Recitatives and Fugue* (piano concerto)

1958

World Events:

In the U.S., Alaska becomes State No. 49; the National Aeronautics and Space Administration (NASA) is formed and *Pioneer I* and *Explorer I* are launched; the Defense Reorganization Act improves defense against unexpected attack; the submarine *Nautilus* crosses the North Pole under the ice; trans-atlantic jet service begins. Internationally, Charles DeGaulle is elected President under the new French Constitution; the United Arab Republic is formed by merger of Egypt and Syria; Russia agrees to back the building of the Aswan Dam on the Nile; the Western powers reject Khrushchev's demand to end the co-occupation of Berlin.

Cultural Highlights:

Pulitzers: Drama, Ketti Frings (*Look Homeward, Angel*); Fiction, James Agee (*A Death in the Family*); Poetry, Robert Penn Warren (*Promises: Poems, 1954-1956*). Russian author Boris Pasternak is the recipient of the Nobel Prize for Literature. Stereo Recordings make their appearance. Deaths in the art field include French artists Georges Rouault and Maurice de Vlaminck, Italian sculptor Giacomo Balla and British sculptor John Gregory; in the literary field, deaths include American novelist Mary Roberts Rinehart and poet Grace W. Conkling, British poet Alfred Noyes and dramatist Harold Brighouse and German novelist Lion Feuchtwanger. Other highlights include:

Art: Mary Brooks, *Acanda*; Jacob Epstein, *St. Michael and the Devil*; Ivor Hitchens, *Woodland, Vertical and Horizontal*; Johann Hofmann, *Golden Blaze*; R.B. Kitaj, *Erasmus*; Ellsworth Kelly, *Ralph Vaughan-Williams*; Henry Moore, *Reclining Figure* (UNESCO); Louise Nevelson, *Sky Cathedral*; Abraham Rattner, *Song of Esther*.

Literature: Edward Albee, *The Zoo Story*; Louis Auchincloss, *Venus in Sparta*; Truman Capote, *Breakfast at Tiffany's*; e.e. cummings, *95 Poems*; Samuel R. Delaney, *A Taste of Honey*; T.S. Eliot, *The Elder Statesman*; Jack Kerouac, *The Subterraneans*; Archibald MacLeish, *J.B.*; Leon Uris, *Exodus*; E.B. White, *The Once and Future King*.

MUSICAL EVENTS

A. Births:

Apr 10 Yefim Bronfman (Rus-pn)	Sep 7 Christopher Black (Br-pn)
Apr 14 Aprile Millo (Am-sop)	Sep 13 Carl A. Jackson (Br-org)
Apr 14 Tamara Smirnova (Rus-vn)	Oct 5 Galina Stamenova (Bul-vn)
Jun 30 Esa-Pekka Salonen (Fin-cd)	Oct 20 Ivo Pogorelich (Yug-pn)
Jul 7 Michala Petri (Den-rec)	Nov 18 Bernard d'Ascoli (Fr-pn)
Aug 30 Claire Fox Hillard (Am-cd)	Dang Thai Son (Kor-pn)

B. Deaths:

Jan 12 Arthur Shepherd (Am-cm)	Jul 31 Percy A. Scholes (Br-cri)
Jan 21 Ataulfo Argenta (Sp-cd)	Aug 17 Florent Schmitt (Fr-cm)
Feb 20 Isidor Philipp (Fr-pn-ed)	Aug 24 Leo Blech (Ger-cd-cm)
Feb 24 Thomas Topper (Am-m.ed)	Aug 25 Hans Clemens (Ger-ten)
Mar 13 Maria Müller (Aus-sop)	Aug 26 Ralph Vaughan-Williams (Br-cm)
Mar 25 Emerson Whithorne (Am-cm)	Sep 11 Robert Lach (Aus-mus-cm)
Mar 28 W.C. Handy (Am-pop)	Sep 27 Adolfo Salazar (Sp-mus)
Apr 1 Bretislav Bakala (Cz-cd)	Nov 2 Adam Carse (Br-cm-au)
Jun 23 Max Graf (Aus-cri)	Nov 27 Artur Rodzinsky (Pol-cd)
Jun 23 Armas Järnefelt (Fin-cm)	Dec 11 Paul Bazelaire (Fr-cel)
Jul 19 Erwin Stein (Aus-cd-au)	Dec 26 Eva Gauthier (Can-sop)

C. Debuts:

Met ---Max Alperstein (ten), Arthur Backgren (bs), Inge Borkh (sop), Luigi de Cesare (ten), Gloria Davy (sop), Mignon Dunn (mez), Eugenio Fernandi (ten), Walter Hemmerly (bs), Grace Hoffman (mez), Kunie Imai (sop), Arnold Knight (ten), William Lewis (ten),

Lou Marcella (ten), Giulio Mollica (ten), Barry Morell (ten), William Olvis (ten), Marcella Pobbè (sop), Thomas Powell (bs), William Starling (bs), Sam Sternberg (bs), John Trehy (bs), Dimiter Uzunov (ten), William Wildermann (bs), Primo Zambruno (ten), Mario Zanasi (bar)

U.S. --Martina Arroyo (N.Y.), Vladimir Ashkenazy (tour), Teresa Berganza (Dallas), Mary Costa (Los Angeles), James Fleetwood, Jan de Gaetani (N.Y.), Joan Grillo, Bernard Haitink (Los Angeles), Janice Harsanyi (Philadelphia), Eugene Haynes, Jr. (N.Y.), Gita Karasik (San Francisco), Leonid Kogan (Boston), Kyrill Kondrashin, Raymond Michalski (Philadelphia), Arlene Sanders, Jeffery Siegel (Chicago), Stanislaw Skrowaczewski (Cleveland)

Other -Donald Bell (London), Jane Berbie (Milan), Gene Boucher (Milan), Carlo Cossutta (Buenos Aires), Bonaldo Giaiotti (Milan), Choo Hoey (Brussels), Jindrich Jindrak (Prague), Vera Little-Augustithis (Berlin), Adriana Maliponte (Milan), Norman Paige (Linz), Ian Partridge (Bexhill), Jeannette Pilou (Milan), Margherita Rinaldi (Spoleto), Ann Schein (London), Thomas Stewart (Berlin), Teresa Stratas (Toronto), John Williams (London)

D. New Positions:

Conductors: Leonard Bernstein (New York PO), Sergiu Comissiona (Haifa SO), Robert Irving (N.Y. City Ballet), Thor Johnson (Northwestern University), Edouard van Remoortel (St. Louis SO), Max Rudolf (Cincinnati SO), Nello Santi (Zurich Opera), Klaus Tennstedt (Dresden Opera)

Educational: Kees van Baaren (director, Hague Conservatory), Raymond Leppard (lecturer, Cambridge), Peter Mennin (director, Peabody), Krzystof Penderecki (composition, Polish Academy), Janos Starker (cello, Indiana University)

Others: Kirsten Flagstad (director, Norwegian State Opera), Eric Salzman (music critic, New York *Times*)

E. Prizes and Honors:

Prizes: Claudio Abbado (Koussevitsky), Salvatore Accardo (Paganini), Elly Ameling (Geneva), Samuel Barber (Pulitzer, music, *Vanessa*), Ana Maria de Botazzi (Liszt), Van Cliburn (Tchaikovsky), Ivan Davis (Casella), Peter Frankl (Liszt), Mirella Freni (Vercelli), Valery Klimov (Tchaikovsky), Elaine Lee, Joseph Schwartz and Shirley Verrett (Naumberg), Arnold Steingardt (Leventritt)

Honors: Leonard Bernstein (Ditson Award), Klaus Egge (Order of King Olav), Maggie Teyte (Dame of the British Empire)

F. Biographical Highlights:

Vladimir Ashkenazy makes his first American tour; Ernest Bloch undergoes cancer surgery; Gene Boucher wins opera audition in Cincinnati; Grace Bumbry shares her Met audition prize with Martina Arroyo; Régine Crespin debuts at Bayreuth; Alberto Ginastera becomes dean of arts at Argentine Catholic University; Jerome Hines makes his La Scala debut; Kyrill Kondrashin becomes the first Soviet conductor to visit the U.S.; Bohuslav Martinu discovers he has cancer; Ermanno Mauro leaves Italy for Canada; Zubin Mehta enters the Royal Liverpool PO and wins a major conducting prize; Krzystoff Penderecki graduates *cum laude* from Polish State Academy of Music; Ezra Pound, released from the hospital, returns to Italy; Ned Rorem returns to the U.S.; Bidú Sayao retires from the stage; Janos Starker resumes his concert career; Karlheinz Stockhausen begins a concert-lecture tour of the U.S.; Alexander Tcherepnin and his family become U.S. citizens; Rosalyn Tureck becomes the first woman to conduct the New York PO; Edo de Waart is given a scholarship to study at Amsterdam Conservatory; Claire Watson makes her Covent Garden debut; Helen Watts makes her London operatic debut.

G. Institutional Openings:

Performing Groups: Austral String Quartet (Sydney), Bach & Madrigal Society (Phoenix),

Boston Grand Opera Co., Denver Lyric Theater, Kansas City Lyric Theater (Opera in 1977), Lenox Quartet (Berkshire), Milwaukee SO, Musique de Notre Temps (Montreal), Northern Sinfonia (Newcastle-upon-Tyne), Puerto Rico SO, Sicilian SO (Palermo), Weller String Quartet (Vienna)

Festivals: George Enescu Festival (Romania), Festival of Two Worlds (Spoleto), Fort Wayne Fine Arts Festival, Musique d'Aujourd'hui (Paris), Osaka International Festival, Vancouver International Festival (British Columbia)

Educational: National School Orchestra Association

Other: *American Choral Review*, Clarion Music Society (N.Y.), Cooperative Studio for Electronic Music (Ann Arbor), Piano Technicians' Guild and *Journal* (Seattle), Rodgers Organ Co., Society for the Preservation of the American Musical Heritage, *Stereo Review*, Studio de Musique Electronique (Brussels), Tchaikovsky Competitions (Moscow)

H. Musical Literature:

Blom, Eric, *Classics, Major and Minor*
Chominski, Józef, *History of Harmony and Counterpoint*
Ives, Burl, *Burl Ives Book of Irish Songs*
Krenek, Ernst, *Tonal Counterpoint*
Mann, Alfred, *The Study of the Fugue*
Parrish, Carl, *A Treasury of Early Music*
Réti, Rudolf, *Tonality, Atonality and Pantonality*
Wellesz, Egon, *Origin of Schoenberg's Twelve-Tone System*

I. Musical Compositions:

Berio, Luciano, *Thema, Omaggio a Joyce* (electronic)
Boulez, Pierre, *Doubles* (orchestra)
Britten, Benjamin, *Nocturne* (tenor, string orchestra)
Cage, John, *Fontana Mix* (musique concrète)
Cowell, Henry, *Symphony No. 13, "Madras"*
Creston, Paul, *Concerto for Accordion and Orchestra*
Floyd, Carlisle, *Wuthering Heights* (opera)
Hanson, Howard, *Mosaics* (orchestra)
Ibert, Jacques, *Bacchanale* (orchestra)
Imbrie, Andrew, *Concerto for Violin and Orchestra*
Lees, Benjamin, *Symphony No. 2*
            Concerto for Violin and Orchestra
Lutoslawski, Witold, *Funeral Music* (string ensemble)
Martirano, Salvatore, *O,O,O,O, That Shakespeherian Rag* (chorus, ensemble)
Mayuzumi, Toshiro, *Nirvana Symphony* (with male chorus)
Mennin, Peter, *Concerto for Piano and Orchestra*
Menotti, Gian Carlo, *Maria Golovia* (opera)
Messiaen, Olivier, *Catalogue d'Oiseaux* (piano)
Milhaud, Darius, *Symphony No. 8*
Moore, Douglas, *Gallantry* (soap opera)
Norgård, Per, *Constellations* (strings)
Penderecki, Krzystof, *Emanationen* (two string orchestras)
Piston, Walter, *Concerto for Viola and Orchestra*
Poulenc, Francis, *La Voix Humaine* (one-act opera)
Read, Gardner, *Symphony No. 4*
Rorem, Ned, *Symphony No. 3*
Stravinsky, Igor, *Threni* (soloists, chorus, orchestra)
Surinach, Carlos, *Concerto for Orchestra*
Tcherepnin, Alexander, *Symphony No. 4*
Tippett, Michael, *Symphony No. 2*
Varèse, Edgard, *Poème Electronique* (electronic)
Vaughan-Williams, Ralph, *Four Last Songs*
Xenakis, Iannis, *Achorripsis* (twenty-one instruments)

1959

World Events:

In the U.S., Hawaii is admitted as State No. 50; Nikita Khruschev and Fidel Castro take good-will tours of the U.S.; the St. Lawrence Seaway officially opens for traffic; NASA begins its astronaut program; the first nuclear-powered cargo ship, the *Savannah*, is launched; *Vanguard II* becomes the first weather station in space. Internationally, the Chinese crush a Tibetan freedom uprising; border warfare flares up between China and India; Cyprus is given independence and Archbishop Makarios is elected as President; Russia hits the moon and takes photographs from close up; the Antarctica Treaty insuring neutrality of the continent is signed by twelve nations.

Cultural Highlights:

Pulitzers: Drama, Archibald MacLeish (*J.B.*); Fiction, Robert L. Taylor (*The Travels of Jaimie McPheeters*); Poetry, Stanley Kunitz (*Selected Poems, 1928-1958*). Italian poet Salvatore Quasimodo receives the Nobel Prize for Literature. The Whitney Gallery of Western Art opens in Cody, Wyoming and El Museo de Arte de Lima opens in Peru; the Guggenheim Museum opens in New York. American-born sculptor Jacob Epstein, architect Frank Lloyd Wright and German artist George Grosz die. Other highlights include:

Art: Herbert Bayer, *White Moon and Structure*; André Beaudin, *La Lune de Mai*; Fernando Botero, *Mona Lisa, Age 12*; Marc Chagall, *La Champ de Mars*; Zoltán Kemény, *Fluctuations*; Joan Miró, *Murals for UNESCO (Paris)*; Ben Nicholson, *February 1959*; Victor Vasarely, *Supernovae*; Andrew Wyeth, *Groundhog Day*.

Literature: Jean Anouilh, *Becket*; Saul Bellow, *Henderson, the Rain King*; Allen Drury, *Advise and Consent*; William Faulkner, *The Mansion*; Günther Grass, *The Tin Drum*; Lillian Hellman, *The Little Foxes*; Denise Levertov, *With Eyes at the Back of Our Head*; James Michener, *Hawaii*; Philip Roth, *Goodbye, Columbus*.

MUSICAL EVENTS

A. Births:

Feb 25	Pamela Nash (Br-hps)	Dec 25	Jon Kimura Parker (Can-pn)
May 5	Bohumil Kulínsky (Cz-cd)		David Buechner (Am-pn)
May 18	Sally Ann Bottomley (Br-pn)		Michael Gurt (Am-pn)
Jun 15	Robert Cohen (Br-cel)		Louis Lortie (Can-pn)
Jul 25	Helen Willis (Br-mez)		André Nikolsky (Rus-pn)
Nov 27	Viktoria Mullova (Rus-vn)		Jonathan Plowright (Br-pn)

B. Deaths:

Jan 9	Edwin A. Fleisher (Am-pat)	Jul 7	Ernest Newman (Br-cri)
Feb 5	Curt Sachs (Ger-mus)	Jul 10	Eugen Schmitz (Ger-mus)
Feb 12	George Antheil (Am-cm)	Jul 16	Ernest Bloch (Ger-cm)
Feb 16	F. Charles Adler (Br-cd)	Aug 16	Wanda Landowska (Pol-hps)
Mar 20	Ernst Knoch (Ger-cd)	Aug 17	Pedro H. Allenda (Chil-cm-mus)
Apr 11	Eric W. Blom (Br-cri)	Aug 28	Bohuslav Martinu (Cz-cm)
Apr 13	Eduard van Beinum (Hol-cd)	Sep 22	Josef M. Hauer (Ger-the-cm)
Apr 17	Barbara Kemp (Ger-sop)	Oct 7	Mario Lanza (Am-ten)
Apr 22	Theodor Scheidl (Ger-bar)	Nov 11	Heitor Villa-Lobos (Bra-cm)
Apr 25	David Mannes (Am-cm-cd)	Nov 26	Albert W. Ketelby (Br-cm)
Jul 3	Maryla Jonas (Pol-cm)	Dec 1	Max Unger (Ger-mus)

C. Debuts:

Met ---Martina Arroyo (sop), Kim Borg (bar), Charleen Clark (sop), Oscar Czerwenka (bs), Karl Doench (bar), Mary Fercana (sop), Edward Ghazal (bs), Alexandra Jones (mez), Kurt Kessler (ten), Karl Liebl (ten), Christa Ludwig (sop), Cornell MacNeil (bar), Frank Mandile (ten), Anna Moffo (sop), Birgit Nilsson (sop), Leonie Rysanek (sop), Dina de Salvo (mez), George Schich (Cd), Giulietta Simionato (mez), Elisabeth Söderström (sop), Ignace Strasfogel (cd), Teresa Stratas (sop), Nino Verchi (cd), Joan Wall (mez)

U.S. --Ivan Davis (N.Y.), Geraint Evans (San Francisco), Sylvia Fisher (Chicago), Reri Grist (Santa Fe), Sena Jurinac (San Francisco), Robert Kearns (N.Y.), Igor Kipnis (Radio Broadcast), Ralph Kirschbaum (Dallas), Spiro Malas (Baltimore), Jeanette Scovotti (N.Y.), Peter Serkin (age 11), George Shirley (N.Y.), Gabriela Tucci (San Francisco), Silvio Varviso (San Francisco), Jon Vickers (Dallas), Ralph Votapek (N.Y.), Giuseppe Zampieri (San Francisco)

Other -Norman Bailey (Vienna), Guy Chauvet (Paris), Colin Davis (Canada), Nelson Freire (Vienna), Horacio Gutiérrez (Havana), Paul Jorgensen (Copenhagen), Zoltán Kelemen (Augsburg), Evelyn Lear (Berlin), Danica Mastilovic (Frankfurt), Donald McIntyre (Cardiff), György Melis (Budapest), Norman Paige (Lina), Bruno Prevedi (Milan), Janos Solyom (Sweden), Margaret Tynes (Montreal)

D. New Positions:

Conductors: Peter Adler (Baltimore SO), André Cluytens (Vienna Opera), Colin Davis (Sadler's Wells), Massimo Freccia (Rome Radio SO), Rafael Frühbeck de Burgos (Bilbao SO), Alexander Gibson (Scottish National Orchestra), Wolfgang Sawallisch (Cologne SO), Jerzy Semkov (Warsaw Opera)

Educational: Dominick Argenta (composition, University of Minnesota), Joonas Kokkonen (composition, Sibelius Academy), Alicia de Larrocha (director, Marshall Academy, Barcelona), Russell Sherman (piano, Pomona College)

Others: Rolf Liebermann (director, Hamburg Opera), Jack A. Westrup (editor, *Music and Letters*)

E. Prizes and Honors:

Prizes: Howard Aibel (Naumberg), Stuart Canin (Paganini), Ivan Davis (Busoni), Malcolm Frager (Leventritt), Grant Johannesen (Cohen), Jaime Laredo (Brussels), John La Montaine (Pulitzer, music, *Piano Concerto*), Sophia Steffan (Naumberg), Ralph Votapek (Naumberg)

Honors: Leonard Bernstein (Gold Baton), Aram Khachaturian (Lenin), Martial Singher (Legion of Honor), Henri Troyat (French Academy)

F. Biographical Highlights:

Emanuel Ax's family moves from Warsaw to Winnipeg, Canada; Stephen Bishop-Kovacevich moves to London to study with Myra Hess; Eduardo Chillida moves back to his home town of San Sebastián; Régine Crespin, Cornell MacNeil and Gabriela Tucci make their La Scala debuts; Placido Domingo auditions as a baritone for the Mexican National Opera but is accepted as a tenor; Grace Hoffman and Alfredo Kraus make their Covent Garden debuts; Karel Husa and Carlos Surinach become American citizens; Mindru Katz settles in Israel; Leo Nucci goes to Bologna to study voice but works as an auto mechanic; Cécile Ousset ties for second place in the Busoni Competition; Thomas Schippers takes the N.Y. PO on a concert tour of Russia; Gunther Schuller quits teaching to devote full time to composition; Teresa Stratas graduates from the University of Toronto; Matti Talvela, age 24, hears his first opera; David Del Tredici enters Princeton University; Benita Valente marries bassoonist Anthony Checchia.

G. Institutional Openings:

Performing Groups: Academy of St. Martin-in-the-Fields (London), Agrupación Coral Nuestra Señora de la Almudena (Madrid), Chicago Little Symphony, I Solisti Veneti (Padua), Montevideo Municipal SO, Nederlands Danstheater (The Hague), Northern Greece SO (Salonica), Philadelphia String Quartet, St. Paul Chamber Orchestra (Minn.), Vancouver Opera Co. (British Columbia), Wiener Solisten

Educational: Centre Français d'Humanisme Musical (Aix-en-Provence), Houston Ballet Academy, Institute of Verdi Studies (Parma)

Other: American Choral Director's Association (Lawton, OK), Bannister Harpsichord Co.,

Beethoven Halle (Bonn), Canadian Music Centre (Toronto), Falkoner Center Theater (Copenhagen); Grant, Degens and Bradbeer, Organ Builders (London); Houston Friends of Music, International Congress of Strings (Oklahoma), International Harp Contest (Israel), Internationale Arbeitsgemeinschaft für Hymnologie, Kassel State Theater, Studio de Musique Contemporaine (Geneva)

H. Musical Literature:

Adorno, Theodor, *Klangfiguren*
Bernstein, Leonard, *The Infinite Variety of Music*
Cooke, Deryck, *The Language of Music*
Craft, Robert, *Conversations with Igor Stravinsky*
Hiller/Isaacson, *Experimental Music*
Kennan, Kent, *Counterpoint*
Krenek, Ernst, *Modal Counterpoint*
Newman, William, *The Sonata in the Baroque Era*
Siegmeister, Elie, *Invitation to Music*
Wagner, Joseph, *Orchestration: A Practical Handbook*

I. Musical Compositions:

Adler, Samuel, *The Outcasts of Poker Flat* (opera)
Beeson, Jack, *Symphony in A*
Binkerd, Gordon, *Symphony No. 3*
Blomdahl, Karl-Birger, *Aniara* (opera)
Brian, Havergal, *Symphony No. 13*
Carter, Elliott, *String Quartet No. 2*
Crumb, George, *Variazoni* (orchestra)
Diamond, David, *Symphony No. 7*
Dutilleux, Henri, *Symphony No. 2, "Le Double"*
Fine, Vivian, *Valedictions*
Finney, Ross Lee, *Symphony No. 2*
Flanagan, William, *The Lady of Tearful Regret* (cantata after Edward Albee)
Gerhard, Roberto, *Symphony No. 2*
Hamilton, Iain, *Sinfonia for Two Orchestras*
Hanson, Howard, *Summer Seascapes for Orchestra*
Harris, Roy, *Give Me the Splendid, Silent Sun* (cantata)
Hindemith, Paul, *Pittsburgh Symphony*
Hovhaness, Alan, *Magnificat*
            Symphony No. 4 (band)
Imbrie, Andrew, *Legend for Orchestra* (symphonic poem)
Kay, Hersey, *Good Soldier Schweik* (opera)
Khrennikov, Tikhon, *Concerto for Violin and Orchestra*
Martin, Frank, *Mystère de la Nativité* (oratorio)
Orff, Carl, *Oedipus der Tyrann* (opera)
Penderecki, Krzystoff, *Psalms of David* (chorus, two pianos, harp, percussion)
Piston, Walter, *Concerto No. 2 for Violin and Orchestra*
            Concerto for Two Pianos and Orchestra
Poulenc, Francis, *Gloria* (soprano, chorus, orchestra)
Rodgers, Richard, *The Sound of Music* (musical)
Rorem, Ned, *Symphonies No. 2 and 3*
Schuller, Gunther, *Seven Studies on Themes of Paul Klee* (orchestra)
Sessions, Roger, *Divertimento for Orchestra*
Shostakovich, Dmitri, *Concerto No. 1 for Cello and Orchestra*
Stockhausen, Karlheinz, *Zyklus* (percussion)
Stravinsky, Igor, *Movements for Piano and Orchestra*
            Double Canon for String Quartet
Van Vactor, David, *Symphony No. 2*
Xenakis, Iannis, *Dual* (game for two orchestras)
            Terrêtektorh (orchestra)

1960

World Events:
The U.S. Census shows a population of 179,323,000, an 18% increase in ten years; John F. Kennedy, the first Catholic to be so elected, becomes President No. 35; the U.S. spy plane, the U-2, is shot down by the Russians over their territory; the Civil Rights Act is passed by Congress; the Peace Corp is founded; the nuclear sub, *Triton*, travels around the world underwater. Internationally, the Belgian Congo receives independence, but Civil War breaks out between rival factions, requiring U.N. troops to restore order; France explodes its first atomic bomb; the European Free Trade Association is formed; work begins on Egypt's Aswan Dam; Brasilia becomes the new capital of Brazil; the Olympic Games are held in Rome.

Cultural Highlights:
Pulitzers: Drama, George Abbott, Jerome Weidman, Sheldon Harnick and Jerry Bock (*Fiorello*); Fiction, Allen Drury (*Advise and Consent*); Poetry, William Snodgrass (*Heart's Needle*). The Nobel Prize for Literature goes to Saint-John Perse; Gwendolyn Brooks becomes the first black woman to be taken into the National Institute; the Fernand Léger Museum opens in Biot, France, and the Groupe de Recherche d'Art Visuel (GRAV) is formed in Paris. Deaths include French novelist Albert Camus and poet Paul Fort, Italian poet Massimo Bontempelli, Russian novelist Boris Pasternak, American novelists John P. Marquand and Richard Wright, British dramatist Eden Phillpotts and Canadian poet Jean Charbonneau. Other highlights include:

Art: Karel Appel, *Woman with Ostrich*; John Bratby, *Gloria with Sunflower*; Charles Burchfield, *The Four Seasons*; Alexander Calder, *Guillotine for Eight*; Philip Evergood, *Virginia in the Grotto*; Lucio Fontana, *Spatial Fantasy R. 230*; Leon Golub, *The Burnt Man*; R.B. Kitaj, *Pariah*; Morris Louis, *Alpha Pi*; Louise Nevelson, *Royal Tide IV*.

Literature: J. Adamson, *Born Free*; W.H. Auden, *Homage to Clio*; Gwendolyn Brooks, *The Bean Eaters*; James L. Herlihy, *All Fall Down*; Ezra Pound, *Thrones*; Irwin Shaw, *Two Weeks in Another Town*; John Updike, *Rabbit, Run*; Gore Vidal, *The Best Man*; Irving Wallace, *The Chapman Report*; Tennessee Williams, *Period of Adjustment*.

MUSICAL EVENTS

A. Births:

Jan 29	Cho-Laing Lio (Tai-vn)	George Benjamin (Br-pn-cm)
Apr 23	Barry Douglas (Ir-pn)	Boyan Vodenicharov (Bul-pn)
Jul 22	Sergei Edelmann (Rus-pn)	Avedis Kouyoumdjian (Leb-pn)
Aug 6	Wolfgang Manz (Ger-pn)	Kazune Shimizu (Jap-pn)
Dec 29	Grant Llewellyn (Br-cd)	István Székely (Hun-pn)

B. Deaths:

Jan 20	Ernst F. Schmid (Ger-mus)		Jul 25	Désiré Defauw (Bel-cd)
Jan 24	Edwin Fischer (Swi-pn-cm)		Sep 9	Jussi Björling (Swe-ten)
Jan 29	Mack Harrell (Am-bar)		Sep 12	Dino Borgioli (It-ten)
Feb 9	Ernst von Dohnányi (Hun-cm)		Sep 14	Otto Ursprung (Ger-mus)
Mar 2	Emile Vuillermoz (Fr-cri)		Sep 25	Mátyás Seiber (Hun-cm)
Mar 7	Leonard Warren (Am-bar)		Oct 4	Robert Haas (Aus-mus)
Mar 30	Joseph Haas (Ger-cm-ped)		Nov 2	Dmitri Mitropoulos (Gr-cd)
Apr 9	Arthur Benjamin (Aust-cm)		Nov 27	Ernest M. Skinner (Am-org.m)
May 8	Hugo Alfvén (Swe-cm)		Dec 4	Walter Goehr (Ger-cd)
May 14	Lucrezia Bori (Sp-sop)		Dec 7	Clara Haskil (Rom-pn)
Jul 9	Edward B. Hill (Am-cm)		Dec 7	Lila Robeson (Am-alto)
Jul 15	Lawrence Tibbett (Am-bar)		Dec 13	John Charles Thomas (Am-bar)

C. Debuts:
Met ---Anthony Balestrieri (ten), Nicola Barbusci (bs), Piero Cappuccilli (bar), Anselmo

Colzani (bar), Charles Cooke (ten), Eileen Farrell (sop), Dino Formichini (ten), Bonaldo Giaiotti (bs), Ethel Greene (mez), Kerstin Meyer (mez), Pamela Munson (mez), Paul de Paola (bs), Meridith Parsons (sop), Hermann Prey (bar), Jane Rhodes (sop), Anneliese Rothenberger (sop), Georg Solti (cd), Walter Taussig (cd), Lorenzo Testi (bar), Gabriela Tucci (sop), Jon Vickers (ten)

U.S. --Antonio de Almeida (N.Y.), Cathy Berberian (Berkshire), Patricia Brooks (N.Y.), Eugene Fodor (Denver), Lawrence Foster (Los Angeles), Lynn Harrell (N.Y.), Joao Carlos Martins (N.Y.), Sviatoslav Richter (tour), Renata Scotto (Chicago), Amy Shuard (N.Y.), Joan Sutherland (Dallas), Benita Valente (N.Y.)

Other -Claudio Abbado (Milan), Janet Baker (Edinburgh), Peter van der Bilt (Amsterdam), Grace Bumbry (Paris), Myung-Whun Chung (Seoul, as pianist), Placido Domingo (as tenor), Elizabeth Harwood (Glyndebourne), Rita Hunter (London), Gundula Janowitz (Vienna), Robert Kerns (Spoleto), Anna Reynolds (Parma), Peter Schneider (Salzburg), Olivia Stapp (Spoleto), Erika Szikaly (Budapest)

D. New Positions:

Conductors: Michael Gielen (Stockholm Opera), Paul Kletzki (Dallas SO), Kyrill Kondrashin (Moscow PO), Jean Martinon (Düsseldorf Opera), Zubin Mehta (Montreal So), Kurt Sanderling (East Berlin SO), Stanislaw Skrowaczewski (Minnesota SO), David Willcocks (London Bach Choir)

Educational: Elliott Carter (composition, Yale), Josef Gingold (violin, Indiana University), George Rochberg (music chairman, University of Pennsylvania)

Others: Harold Schonberg (music editor, New York *Times*)

E. Prizes and Honors:

Prizes: Elliott Carter (Pulitzer--*String Quartet III*), Malcolm Frager (Belgium), Elizabeth Harwood (Ferrier), Leon Kirchner (New York Music Critics' Circle), Jerome Lowenthal (Queen Elizabeth), Adriana Maliponte (Geneva), Maurizio Pollini (Chopin), Joseph Silverstein (Naumberg, recording)

Honors: Leonard Bernstein (Musician of the Year, *Musical America* and Einstein Award), Edward MacDowell (Hall of Fame for Great Americans)

F. Biographical Highlights:

Gwendolyn Brooks becomes the first black woman in the National Institute; Deryck Cooke begins reconstruction of Mahler's *Symphony No. 10*; Mario Davidovsky moves to the U.S.; Gloria Davy makes her Covent Garden debut; Roberto Gerhard takes British citizenship; Marilyn Horne marries conductor Henry Lewis and becomes part of the Sutherland Opera Group; Byron Janis tours the U.S.; Jaime and Ruth Laredo are married; Lorin Maazel becomes the first American to conduct at Bayreuth; Eduardo Mata begins study with Chávez; Santiago Rodriguez is taken from Cuba to the U.S. for further music study; Peter Sculthorpe returns to Australia; Anja Silja debuts at Bayreuth and begins an affair with Wieland Wagner; Isaac Stern leads a campaign to save Carnegie Hall from destruction; Joan Sutherland takes up residency in Switzerland; Zoltán Székely becomes a U.S. citizen; Joseph Szigeti retires from the concert stage; Martti Talvela wins a local singing competition and leaves Finland; Benita Valente graduates from Curtis Institute and wins a Met Opera Audition.

G. Institutional Openings:

Performing Groups: American Brass Quintet, American Wind SO (Pittsburgh), Camerata Singers (N.Y.), Contemporary Chamber Ensemble of New York, Dayton Opera Association, English Chamber Orchestra (London), Israel Chamber Orchestra, National SO of Havana, National Youth Orchestra of Canada (Toronto), Netherlands Wind Ensemble (Amsterdam), Nuova Consonanza (Rome), Oxford Schola Cantorum, Pittsburgh Oratorio Society, Slovak Chamber Orchestra (Bratislava), Stuttgart Schola Cantorum, Tucson Youth SO

Festivals: Adelaide Festival of Arts (Australia)

Educational: Gaylord Music Library (Washington University), Puerto Rico Conservatory of Music

Other: Associated Councils of the Arts, Contemporary Music Society (ONCE), Donaueshingen Concert Hall, Hawaii Opera Theater (Honolulu), *Hungarian Music*, Metropolitan Opera Studio (N.Y.), *L'Organo: Revista di Cultura Organaria e Organistica*, Percussive Arts Society, Salzburg Grosses Festspielhaus, Society for Asian Music (N.Y.)

H. Musical Literature:
Craft, Robert, *Memories and Commentaries*
Grout, Donald, *A History of Western Music*
Hanson, Howard, *Harmonic Materials of Modern Music*
Kauder, Hugo, *Counterpoint*
Kodály, Zoltán, *Folk Music of Hungary*
Lang, Paul Henry, *Problems of Modern Music*
Nettl, Bruno, *An Introduction to Folk Music in the United States*
Rubbra, Edmund, *Counterpoint*
Shaw, George Bernard, *How to Become a Music Critic*

I. Musical Compositions:
Adler, Samuel, *Symphony No. 3, "Diptych"*
Arnold, Malcolm, *Symphony No. 4*
Badings, Henk, *Symphony No. 9* (strings)
Barber, Samuel, *Toccata Festiva, Opus 36*
Bazelon, Irwin, *Symphony No. 1*
Berio, Luciano, *Circles* (voice, harp, percussion)
Boulez, Pierre, *Pli Selon Pli*
Brian, Havergal, *Symphony No. 14*
Britten, Benjamin, *Midsummer Night's Dream* (opera)
Casals, Pablo, *El Pessebre* (oratorio)
Cowell, Henry, *Symphony No. 12*
Davies, Peter M., *O Magnum Mysterium*
Diamond, David, *Symphony No. 8*
Foss, Lukas, *Time Cycle* (soprano and orchestra)
　　　　　Concerto for Improvising Instruments and Orchestra
Ginastera, Alberto, *Cantata para América Magica*
Henze, Hans Werner, *Prinz von Homburg* (opera)
Hovhaness, Alan, *Symphonies No. 6, 7 and 8*
Mayuzumi, Toshiro, *Mandala Symphony*
Messiaen, Olivier, *Chronochromie* (orchestra)
Miyoshi, Akira, *Three Symphonic Movements* (orchestra)
Nono, Luigi, *Intolleranza* (opera)
Nystedt, Knut, *The Seven Seals* (orchestra)
Penderecki, Krzysztof, *Anaklasis* (40 strings, percussion)
　　　　　Threnody for the Victims of Hiroshima (52 strings)
Piston, Walter, *Symphony No. 7*
Reed, H. Owen, *Earth Trapped* (opera)
Schuman, William, *Symphony No. 7*
Shostakovich, Dmitri, *String Quartets No. 7 and 8*
Stockhausen, Karlheinz, *Carré* (4 orchestras, 4 choruses, 4 conductors)
　　　　　Kontakte (electronics, piano, percussion)
Stravinsky, Igor, *Monumentum pro Gesualdo*
Walton, William, *Symphony No. 2*

1961

World Events:
The United States breaks relations with Cuba and fails in the attempted invasion of Cuba at the Bay of Pigs; the first sub-orbital space flights are made by Alan Shepard and Gus Grissom; the Twenty-Third Amendment gives District of Columbia residents the right to vote; Yankee slugger Roger Maris breaks Babe Ruth's home-run record of 60 in one season. Internationally, Yuri Gagarin, a Russian Cosmonaut, becomes the first man into space in *Vostok I*; the Communists begin building the Berlin Wall to stop the flow of refugees from East Germany; United Nations Secretary-General Dag Hammarskjold is killed in a plane crash in Africa; the Union of South Africa elects to leave the British Commonwealth to become a republic; the Communists begin revolts in Angola.

Cultural Highlights:
Pulitzers: Drama, Tad Mosel (*All the Way Home*); Fiction, Harper Lee (*To Kill A Mockingbird*); Poetry, Phyllis McGinley (*Times Three: Selected Verse*). The Nobel Prize for Literature goes to Ivó Andric; the Los Angeles County Art Museum opens its doors. Deaths in the literary field include American humorist James Thurber and novelists Ernest Hemingway and Julia Peterkin, French poet Blaise Cendars and author Louis F. Céline, Canadian novelist Mazo de la Roche; in the art field, Russian artist Max Weber and sculptor Antoine Pevsner, American "primitive" artist Grandma Moses, French sculptor Paul Landowski and British artist Vanessa Bell. Other highlights include:

Art: Joseph Albers, *Silent Hall*; Marc Chagall, *The 12 Tribes of Israel* (stained glass); Adolph Gottlieb, *Black Black*; Robert Indiana, *American Dream I*; Jasper Johns, *Mop*; Yves Klein, *Monochrome Blue*; Morris Louis, *Moving In*; Henry Moore, *Reclining Mother and Child*; Richard Pousette-Dart, *Earth Mystery*; Andrew Wyeth, *Distant Thunder*.

Literature: *New Testament: New English Version*; Edward Albee, *The American Dream*; Joseph Heller, *Catch-22*; Harold Robbins, *The Carpetbaggers*; Pierre Sallinger, *Franny and Zooey*; Muriel Spark, *The Prime of Miss Jean Brodie*; John Steinbeck, *The Winter of Our Discontent*; Irving Stone, *The Agony and the Ecstasy*; Tennessee Williams, *Night of the Iguana*; Yevgeny Yevtushenko, *Babi Yar*.

MUSICAL EVENTS

A. Births:

Jan 10	Nadja Salerno-Sonnenberg (It-vn)	Sep 7 Jean-Yves Thibaudet (Fr-pn)
May 11	Cecile Licad (Phil-pn)	Oct 18 Heidrun Holtman (Ger-pn)
May 14	Dylana Jenson (Am-vn)	Oct 18 Wynton Marsalis (Am-tpt)
		Nov 22 Stephen Hough (Br-pn)

B. Deaths:

Jan 11	Elena Gerhardt (Ger-mez)	Mar 16 Václav Talich (Cz-cd)
Jan 19	William T. Upton (Am-mus)	Apr 2 Wallingford Riegger (Am-cm)
Jan 20	Hans Albrecht (Ger-mus)	Apr 21 James Melton (Am-ten)
Jan 21	John Becker (Am-cm)	Apr 23 Hans Weisbach (Ger-cd)
Feb 3	Archibald Davison (Am-m.ed)	Jun 23 Nikolai Malko (Rus-cd)
Feb 12	Edmond Appia (Swi-cd)	Aug 10 Alexander Hilsberg (Pol-cd)
Feb 20	Percy Grainger (Aus-pn)	Aug 17 Carlos Salzedo (Fr-hp)
Mar 3	Paul Wittgenstein (Ger-pn)	Nov 14 Fritz Stein (Ger-mus)
Mar 8	Thomas Beecham (Br-cd)	Edith de Lys (Am-sop)

C. Debuts:
Met ---John Alexander (ten), Gianna d'Angelo (sop), Ingrid Bjoner (sop), Lynn Blair (sop), Franco Corelli (ten), Phyllis Curtin (sop), Biserka Cvejic (sop), William Dembaugh (ten), Gottlob Frick (bs), Sándor Konya (ten), Gladys Kriese (mez), Gladys Kuchta (sop), Mary Ellen Pracht (sop), Leontyne Price (sop), George Shirley (ten), Teresa

Stich-Randall (sop), Leopold Stokowski (cd), Joan Sutherland (sop), Silvio Varviso (cd), Andrea Velis (ten), Galina Vishnevskaya (sop), Eberhard Wächter (bar), Ernst Wiemann (bs), Frances Yeend (sop), Giuseppe Zampieri (ten)

U.S. --Dominic Cossa (N.Y.), Dennis R. Davies (N.Y.), Justino Díaz (Boston), Sixten Ehrling (Detroit), Henry Holt (Los Angeles), James King (San Francisco), Alfredo Kraus (tour), James Levine (as conductor), Seiji Ozawa (N.Y.), Thomas Paul (N.Y.), Paul Plishka (New Jersey), Paula Robison (N.Y.), Graziella Sciutti (San Francisco), Joseph Silverstein (as conductor), Richard Woitach

Other -Elly Ameling (Amsterdam), Klara Barlow (Bern), Renato Bruson (Spoleto), Helga Dernesch (Bern), Brigitte Fassbaender (Munich), Nicola Ghiuselev (Sofia), Raina Kabaivanska (Milan), James Loughran (London), Kari Nurmela (Helsinki), Rita Orlandi-Malaspina (Milan), Luciano Pavarotti (Reggio), Jacqueline du Pré (London), Karl Ridderbusch (Münster), Peter Schreier (Dresden), John Shirley-Quirk (Glyndebourne), Martti Talvela (Stockholm), José Van Dam (Paris)

D. New Positions:
Conductors: Dean Dixon (Hesse Radio SO), Jean Fournet (Dutch Radio PO), Bernard Haitink and Eugen Jochum (Amsterdam Concertgebouw), Rafael Kubelik (Bavarian Radio SO), Lovro von Matacic (Frankfurt Opera), Pierre Monteux (London SO), Constantin Silvestri (Bournemouth SO), Georg Solti (Covent Garden), Walter Weller (Vienna PO)

Educational: Henri Dutilleux (composition, École Normal, Paris), Roy Harris (composer-in-residence, UCLA), Sergei Lemeshev (voice, Moscow Conservatory), George Perle (composition, Queen's College), Edmund Rubbra (composition, Guildhall School), Gilles Tremblay (composition, Montreal Conservatory), John Williams (guitar, Royal College)

E. Prizes and Honors:
Prizes: Maurice Abravanel (Ditson), Agustin Anievas (Mitropoulos), Ivan Davis (Liszt), Gábor Gabos (Liszt-Bartók), Alicia de Larrocha (Paderewski), Yvonne Minton (Ferrier), John Ogdon (Liszt), Walter Piston (Pulitzer--*Symphony No. 7*), Jerome Rose (Busoni)

Honors: Gerald Abraham (honorary doctorate, Durham), Leonard Bernstein (National Institute), Aaron Copland (MacDowell Medal), Leontyne Price (Musician of the Year, *Musical America*), Jack Allen Westrup (knighted)

F. Biographical Highlights:
Emanuel Ax's family leaves Canada for New York; Stephen Bishop-Kovacevich makes his London debut; Grace Bumbry becomes the first black artist to sing at Bayreuth; Kyung-Wha Chung follows her sister, Myung-Wha, to New York where they both enter Juilliard; Mirella Freni and Teresa Stratas make their Covent Garden debuts; Edita Gruberová enters Bratislava Conservatory; Horacio Gutiérrez leaves Castro's Cuba for the U.S.; Hans Werner Henze leaves Naples for the Roman countryside; Mauricio Kagel makes an extensive lecture tour of the U.S.; Ton de Leeuw makes his first trip to Italy; James Levine enters Juilliard; Rudolph Nureyev defects to the West; Andrzej Panufnik becomes a British citizen; Gianna Pederzini gives her farewell performance in Rome; Vladimir Spivakov enters Moscow Conservatory; Risë Stevens sings her last Carmen at the Met; Joan Sutherland makes her La Scala debut; Shirley Verrett graduates from Juilliard but refuses a Met contract; Edo de Waart becomes oboist with the Amsterdam PO; Charles Wuorinen receives his B.A. degree from Columbia; Pinchas Zukerman is brought to the U.S. by Isaac Stern for further violin study.

G. Institutional Openings:
Performing Groups: Accademia Monteverdiana (N.Y.), Aeolian Chamber Players (N.Y.), The Beach Boys (California), Hungarian Wind Quintet (Budapest), Japanese PO of Los Angeles, Musica Aeterna Orchestra and Chorus; Philadelphia Chamber Orchestra, Piccola Opera Co. (Detroit), Rose-Stern-Istomin Trio; Vancouver Opera Association; Giuseppe Verdi Choir (Pisa)

Festivals: Farnham Festival (England), Zagreb Festival of Contemporary Music

Educational: California Institute of the Arts, Duke University Music Department, Mu Beta Psi Fraternity (North Carolina)

Other: British Liszt Piano Competition (London), Connoisseur Society (Record Co.), International Beethoven Piano Competition (Austria), International Music Center (Vienna), *RMA Research Chronicle*, San Francisco Tape Music Center, Studio Musicologia (Hungary), Ten Centuries Concerts (Toronto), Young Concert Artists (N.Y.)

H. Musical Literature:
Ansermet, Ernest, *Fundamentals of Music in the Human Consciousness*
Cage, John, *Silence*
Chávez, Carlos, *Musical Thought*
Chybinski, Adolf, *On Polish Folk Music*
Ehmann, Wilhelm, *Alte Musik in der neuen Welt*
Forte, Allen, *The Compositional Matrix*
Kohs, Ellis B., *Music Theory, A Syllabus*
Machlis, Joseph, *Introduction to Contemporary Music*
Persichetti, Vincent, *Twentieth Century Harmony*
Read, Gardner, *Style and Orchestration*

I. Musical Compositions:
Arnold, Malcolm, *Symphony No. 5*
Badings, Henk, *Symphony No. 10*
Brian, Havergal, *Symphonies No. 17, 18 and 19*
Brown, Earle, *Available Forms*
Carter, Elliott, *Double Concerto for Piano and Harpsichord*
Castelnuovo-Tedesco, Mario, *The Merchant of Venice* (opera)
Chávez, Carlos, *Symphony No. 6*
Dahl, Ingolf, *Sinfonietta*
Dello Joio, Norman, *Blue Moon* (opera)
Einem, Gottfried von, *Philharmonic Symphony*
Gerhard, Roberto, *Symphony No. 3*
Ginastera, Alberto, *Concerto No. 1 for Piano and Orchestra*
Haieff, Alexei, *Symphony No. 3*
Hanson, Howard, *Bold Island Suite* (orchestra)
Henze, Hans Werner, *Elegie für Junge Liebende* (opera)
Hovhaness, Alan, *Symphony No. 9, "Choral"*
Kodály, Zoltán, *Symphony in C*
Ligeti, György, *Atmospheres for Orchestra*
Lutoslawski, Witold, *Jeux Vénitiens* (orchestra)
Moore, Douglas, *The Wings of the Dove* (opera)
Penderecki, Krzystof, *Fluorescences* (orchestra)
                     Dimensions of Time and Silence
Piston, Walter, *Symphonic Prelude*
Pizzetti, Ildebrando, *Il Calzare d'Argento* (opera)
Poulenc, Francis, *Concerto for Oboe and Orchestra*
Schuller, Gunther, *Contrasts for Orchestra*
Shchedrin, Rodion, *Not Love Alone* (opera)
Shostakovich, Dmitri, *Symphony No. 12*
Stravinsky, Igor, *The Flood* (TV ballet)
                 A Sermon, a Narrative and a Prayer
Takemitsu, Toru, *Ki No Kyoku*
Tippett, Michael, *King Priam* (opera)
Varèse, Edgard, *Nocturnal* (unfinished)
Walton, William, *Gloria* (chorus)
Ward, Robert, *The Crucible* (opera)
Yardumian, Richard, *Symphony No. 1*

1962

World Events:

In the U.S., John Glenn becomes the first American to go into orbit in space; other space exploits includes the launching of *Mariner II* to Venus and the first *Telstar* satellite; Russian troops and missiles in Cuba cause a confrontation between the U.S. and Russia; *U-2* pilot Gary Powers is returned in exchange for Soviet spy Rudolf Abel; the Century 21 Exposition opens in Seattle. Internationally, U Thant is elected as Secretary-General of the United Nations; Cuba is expelled from the Organization of American States; Georges Pompidou becomes French Premier; China invades India; Pakistan adopts a new Constitution; the drug thalidomide is found to cause birth defects in unborn children; accused Nazi Adolf Eichmann tried and executed by the Israelis.

Cultural Highlights:

Pulitzers: Drama, Frank Loesser and Abe Burrows (*How to Succeed in Business Without Really Trying*); Fiction, Edwin O'Connor (*The Edge of Sadness*); Poetry, Alan Dugan (*Poems*). American author John Steinbeck receives the Nobel Prize for Literature; the Paul Mellon Foundation for British Art is founded in London; Fluxus is founded in Germany in opposition to traditional art. Deaths in the literary field include American authors e.e. cummings, William Faulkner and poet Robinson Jeffers, British poets Richard Aldington and Wilfred W. Gibson and Spanish novelist Ramón Pérez de Ayala; in the art field, American artists Franz Kline and Morris Louis, French artist Yves Klein, Russian sculptor Antoine Pevsner and Yugoslavian sculptor Ivan Mestrovic. Other highlights include:

Art: Thomas Hart Benton, *The Opening of the West*; Anthony Caro, *Early One Morning*; Chryssa, *Times Square Sky*; Alex Katz, *Washington Crossing the Delaware*; R.B. Kitaj, *Welcome Every Dread*; Yves Klein, *Fire Painting*; Lee Krasner, *Cobalt Night*; James Rosenquist, *Silver Skies*; William Zorach, *Spirit of the Seas*.

Literature: Edward Albee, *Who's Afraid of Virginia Woolf?*; Anthony Burgess, *A Clockwork Orange*; Rachel Carson, *Silent Spring*; Len Deighton, *The Ipcress File*; William Faulkner, *The Reivers*; Katherine Porter, *Ship of Fools*; Alexander Solzhenitsyn, *One Day in the Life of Ivan Denisovich*; John Steinbeck, *Travels with Charley*.

MUSICAL EVENTS

A. Births:

Sep 20 Kathryn Selby (Aust-pn)	Oct 5 Ken Noda (Am-pn)

B. Deaths:

Jan 29 Fritz Kreisler (Am-vn)	Jun 13 Eugene Goosens (Br-cd)
Feb 5 Jacques Ibert (Fr-cm)	Jun 15 Alfred Cortot (Fr-pn-cd)
Feb 18 Bruno Walter (Ger-cd)	Jun 19 Volkmar Andreae (Swi-cm)
Feb 26 Wilhelm Fischer (Aus-mus)	Jul 28 Franz Konwitschny (Ger-cd)
Mar 4 Zdenek Chalabala (Cz-cd)	Aug 23 Irving Fine (Am-cm)
Mar 5 Otakar Jeremiás (Cz-cm-cd)	Oct 20 Florence Wickham (Am-alto)
May 20 Anna Báthy (Hun-sop)	Oct 21 Vanni Marcoux (Fr-bar)
May 24 Cloe Elmo (It-mez)	Dec 8 Kirsten Flagstad (Nor-sop)
May 27 Egon Petri (Ger-pn)	Dec 12 Ilona Steingruber (Aus-sop)
Jun 12 John Ireland (Br-cm)	Dec 31 Hans Rosbaud (Aus-cd)

C. Debuts:

Met ---Erbert Aldridge (ten), Ernest Ansermet (cd), Jan Behr (cd), Umberto Borso (ten), Mariano Caruso (ten), Lilli Chookasian (alto), Régine Crespin (sop), Murray Dickie (ten), Loretta di Franko (sop), Rita Gorr (mez), Richard Hundley (ten), Raina Kabaivanska (sop), Gerda Lammers (sop), Ruth Lansché (sop), Lorin Maazel (cd), John Macurdy (bs), Morley Meredith (bar), Judith Raskin (sop), Vladimir Ruzdale (bar), Nello

Santi (cd), Jeanette Scovotti (sop), Jess Thomas (ten), Hertha Töpper (mez), Anita Välkki (sop), William Walker (bar), William Zakariesen (ten)

U.S. --Mariella Adani, Grace Bumbry (Washington, D.C.), János Ferencsik (tour), Sergio Franchi (N.Y.), Richard Goode (N.Y.), Hans Kaart (Chicago), Gilbert Kalish (N.Y.), Gary Karr (N.Y.), Albert Lance (tour), Wilma Lipp (San Francisco), Edith Peinemann (tour), Ann Schein (N.Y.), Johanna Simon (N.Y.), Tamás Vásary (N.Y.)

Other -Sylvia Anderson (Cologne), Daniel Barenboim (as conductor), Cristina Deutekom (Amsterdam), Helen Donath (Cologne), Peter Frankl (London), Werner Hollweg (Vienna), Gwyneth Jones (Zurich), Matteo Manuguerra (Lyons), Ermanno Mauro (Edmonton), Giorgio Merighi (Spoleto), Edda Moser (Berlin), Simon Preston (London), Margaret Price (Cardiff), Hans Sotin (Essen), Ludovic Spiess (Mantua), Shirley Verrett (Spoleto)

D. New Positions:

Conductors: Antonio de Almeida (Stuttgart SO), Paavo Berglund (Finnish Radio SO), Antal Dorati (BBC SO), Oivin Fjeldstad (Oslo PO), Rafael Frühbeck de Burgos (Madrid SO), Erich Leinsdorf (Boston SO), James Loughran (Bournemouth SO), Zubin Mehta (Los Angeles PO), Kenneth Schermerhorn (New Jersey SO)

Educational: Alberto Ginastera (director, Latin American Center for Advanced Musical Studies), Peter Mennin (president, Juilliard), Gregor Piatigorsky (cello, USC)

Others: William Schuman (President, Lincoln Center, New York)

E. Prizes and Honors:

Prizes: Richard Angas (Ferrier), Vladimir Ashkenazy (Tchaikovsky), Michel Block (Leventritt), Norman Dello Joio (New York Music Critics' Circle), Piero Gamba (Bax), Boris Gutnikov (Tchaikovsky), Yoritsune Matsudaira (Rome), John Ogdon (Tchaikovsky), Michel Plasson (Besançon), Johanna Simon (Anderson), Ralph Votapek (Cliburn), Robert Ward (Pulitzer--*The Crucible*)

Honors: Ross Lee Finney (National Institute), Vernon Handley (Bax Medal), Igor Stravinsky (Musician of the Year, *Musical America*)

F. Biographical Highlights:

Giacomo Aragall receives a scholarship to study in Milan; the Korean Chung family settles in Seattle; Peter Maxwell Davies is granted a fellowship to study with Roger Sessions at Princeton; James DePreist begins his conducting career in Bangkok and the Far East; Placido Domingo takes his family to Israel and joins the Tel Aviv Opera; Mirella Freni makes her La Scala debut; Philip Glass receives his Master's degree from Juilliard; Reri Grist and Renata Scotto makes their Covent Garden debuts; Jerome Hines sings Boris, in Russian, in Moscow with Premier Khrushchev present; Elliott Schwartz receives his Ed.D. from Columbia; Leonard Slatkin enters Indiana University; Igor Stravinsky is allowed to visit Russia after a fifty-year absence; Martti Talvela makes his Bayreuth debut; Benita Valente travels to Germany to gain operatic experience; John Williams makes a concert tour of Russia; Ellen Taafe Zwillich receives a Master's in composition from Florida State University.

G. Institutional Openings:

Performing Groups: John Alldis Choir (London), Group for Contemporary Music (Columbia University), Kenneth Jewell Chorale (Detroit), Minnesota Opera Co. (Minneapolis), Rolling Stones (Rock Group), Heinrich Schütz Chorale (London), Scottish Opera Co. (Glasgow), Talich String Quartet, Tel Aviv String Quartet, Tudor Singers of Montreal, Yomiuri Nippon SO (Tokyo)

Festivals: Eastern Music Festival (North Carolina), Grand Teton Music Festival (Jackson, Wyoming), Lake George Opera Festival (Glenn Falls, N.Y.)

Educational: Interlochen Arts Academy (Michigan), Latin American Center for Advanced Musical Studies (Buenos Aires)

Other: American Harp Society (N.Y.), A-R Editions (New Haven); Alexander Broude, Music Publisher (N.Y.); *Clavier,* Van Cliburn Quadrennial Piano Competition (Dallas), College of Church Musicians (Washington, D.C.), Henry S. Drinker Music Center (Philadelphia); Everest Records, Inc.; Institute for Psychoacoustics and Electronic Music (Ghent), International Conference of Symphony and Opera Musicians (Pennsylvania), Kraushaar Auditorium (Baltimore), Lincoln Center for the Performing Arts (N.Y.), Musical Heritage Society, *Perspectives of New Music,* Rhein-Mosel-Halle (Koblenz), Semanas de Música Religiosa (Cuanca), Théâtre des Arts (Rouen)

H. Musical Literature:

Adorno, Theodor, *Einleitung in die Musiksoziologie*
Craft, Robert, *Expositions and Developments*
Dallin, Leon, *Foundations in Music Theory*
Ewen, David, *Modern Music*
Hopkins, John H., *Carols, Hymns and Songs*
Jacob, Gordon, *Elements of Orchestration*
Newman, Ernest, *The Testament of Music*
Perle, George, *Serial Composition and Atonality*
Schuller, Gunther, *Horn Technique*
Stein, Leon, *Structure and Style*

I. Musical Compositions:

Andriessen, Jurriaan, *Symphony No. 2 for Wind Orchestra*
Barber, Samuel, *Concerto for Piano and Orchestra*
          Andromache's Farewell (soprano and orchestra)
Bassett, Leslie, *Five Movements for Orchestra*
Bazelon, Irwin, *A Short Symphony*
Boulez, Pierre, *Structures II* (two pianos)
Brian, Havergal, *Symphony No. 20*
Britten, Benjamin, *A War Requiem*
Copland, Aaron, *Connotations for Orchestra*
Diamond, David, *Symphony No. 7*
Einem, Gottfried von, *Nachtstücke für Orchester*
Fine, Irving, *Symphony 1962*
Finney, Ross Lee, *Variations for Orchestra*
Floyd, Carlisle, *The Passion of Jonathan Wade* (opera)
Fortner, Wolfgang, *In seinem Garten liebt*
Harris, Roy, *Symphony No. 8*
Henze, Hans Werner, *Symphony No. 5*
Jolivet, André, *Concerto No. 1 for Cello and Orchestra*
Maderna, Bruno, *Concerto for Oboe and Orchestra*
Milhaud, Darius, *Symphony No. 12*
Musgrave, Thea, *Chamber Concerto No. 1*
Nono, Luigi, *Sul Ponte di Hiroshima* (soprano, tenor, orchestra)
Penderecki, Krzystof, *Stabat Mater*
Piston, Walter, *Lincoln Center Festival Overture*
Porter, Quincy, *Symphony No. 2*
Poulenc, Francis, *Sept Répons des Ténèbres* (soprano, chorus, orchestra)
Rorem, Ned, *The Anniversary* (opera)
Schuller, Gunther, *Concerto for Piano and Orchestra*
          Night Music (jazz group)
Schuman, William, *Symphony No. 8*
Shostakovich, Dmitri, *Symphony No. 13, "Babi Yar"*
Stockhausen, Karlheinz, *Momente*
Stravinsky, Igor, *The Dove Descending* (chorus a capella)
Takemitsu, Toru, *Coral Island* (soprano, orchestra)
Xenakis, Iannis, *ST/10* (ten instruments)

1963

World Events:

In the U.S., Lyndon B. Johnson becomes President No. 36 when President Kennedy is assassinated in Dallas, Texas--his assassin, Lee Harvey Oswald is shot and killed in jail by Jack Ruby; a "hot line" telephone is set up between Washington and Moscow; a treaty to ban atmospheric nuclear tests is signed; quasars are discovered in outer space. Internationally, France vetoes Great Britain's entrance into the European Common Market; Conrad Adenauer resigns and Ludwig Erhard becomes Chancellor of West Germany; Malaya, Singapore, Sarawak and Sabah form the Federation of Malaysia; the Organization of African Unity is formed.

Cultural Highlights:

Pulitzers: Fiction, William Faulkner (*The Reivers*); Poetry, William C. Williams (*Pictures from Breughel*). Greek diplomat and poet Georges Seferis receives the Nobel Prize for Literature. Alexander Solzhenitsyn comes under official Soviet censure for his writings; Sonia Delaunay-Terk becomes the first woman to have works exhibited in the Louvre during her lifetime. Deaths in the literary world include American poets Robert Frost, Theodore Roethke and William C. Williams, French poet Jean Cocteau and author Paul Reboux and British author Aldous Huxley; in the art field, French artists Georges Braque and Jacques Villon, British sculptor Frank Dobson and American artist William Baziotes. Other highlights include:

Art: Milton Avery, *Two Figures by the Sea*; Alexander Calder, *Under the White Sickle Moon*; Red Grooms, *Coney Island*; Roy Lichtenstein, *Whaam*; Richard Lippold, *Orpheus and Apollo*; Richard Pousette-Dart, *Sky Presence, Circle*; Edward Ruscha, *Standard Station*; George Segal, *Cinema*; Miroslav Sutej, *Bombardment of the Optic Nerve II*.

Literature: Jacques Cousteau, *The Living Sea*; Daphne du Maurier, *The Birds*; John Le Carré, *The Spy Who Came In from the Cold*; F. Mowat, *Never Cry Wolf*; Carl Sandburg, *Honey and Salt*; Neil Simon, *Barefoot in the Park*; Morris West, *The Shoes of the Fisherman*; Yevgeny Yevtushenko, *A Precocious Autobiography*.

MUSICAL EVENTS

A. Births:

Jan 2	Tzimon Barto (Am-pn-cd)	May 11	Robert Irvine (Scot-cel)
Jan 20	Timothy Lowe (Br-pn)	Jun 29	Anne-Sophie Mutter (Ger-vn)
Apr 17	Elinor Bennett (Br-hp)		

B. Deaths:

Jan 6	Lina Abarbanell (Ger-sop)	Aug 15	John Powell (Am-cm)
Jan 30	Francis Poulenc Fr-cm)	Aug 17	George Weldon (Br-cd)
Feb 6	Werner Josten (Am-cm)	Aug 20	Mabel Garrison (Am-sop)
Feb 20	Ferenc Fricsay (Hun-cd)	Sep 12	Modest Altschuler (Rus-cd)
Mar 1	John Thompson (Am-pn-ped)	Nov 15	Fritz Reiner (Hun-cd)
Mar 3	Erich Hertzmann (Ger-mus)	Nov 26	Amelita Galli-Curci (It-sop)
Mar 6	Mihály Székely (Hun-bs)	Nov 29	Ernesto Lecuona (Cuba-pn)
Mar 28	Alec Templeton (Br-pn)	Dec 5	Karl A. Hartmann (Ger-cm)
Mar 30	Alexander Gauk (Rus-cd-cm)	Dec 11	Anthony Collins (Br-cd)
Apr 9	Benno Moiseiwitsch (Br-pn)	Dec 15	Willibald Gurlitt (Ger-mus)
May 28	Vissarion Shebalin (Rus-cm)	Dec 28	Paul Hindemith (Ger-cm)

C. Debuts:

Met ---Franz Allers (cd), Marcia Baldwin (mez), Joy Clements (sop), Anton Diakov (bs), Justino Díaz (bs), Emil Filip (ten), Arthur Graham (ten), Maria Gray (sop), Joan Grillo (mez), Shirley Love (mez), Virginia MacWatters (sop), Luisa Malagrida (sop), Nicoletta Panni (sop), Robert Patterson (bar), Christopher Russell (bar), Arturo Sergi (ten), Léopold Simoneau (ten), Kenneth Smith (bs), Neyde Thomaz (sop), Richard Verreau

(ten)

U.S. --Peter van der Bilt (San Francisco), Judith Blegen (Philadelphia), Alfred Brendel (N.Y.), Michael Devlin (New Orleans), Stephen Kates (N.Y.), Jerome Lowenthal, Danica Mastilovic, John Ogdon (N.Y.), Itzhak Perlman (N.Y.), Hans Schmidt-Isserstedt, Joel Shapiro, Tatiana Troyanos (N.Y.), André Watts (N.Y.), John Williams (tour)

Other -Eduardo and Sergio Abreu (Rio de Janeiro), Giacomo Aragall (Milan), Arkady Aronov (Leningrad), Vladimir Atlantov (Kirov), Stuart Burrows (Cardiff), Joan Carden (London), Ulrik Cold (Copenhagen), Charles Dutoit (Bern), Birgit Finnila (Göteborg), Artur Korn (Cologne), John Lill (London), Berit Lindholm (Stockholm), Yuri Mazurok (Moscow), Yevgeni Nesterenko (Leningrad), Lucia Popp (Bratislava), Roger Soyer (Paris), Nancy Tatum (Saarbrücken), Mitsuko Uchida (Vienna)

D. New Positions:

Conductors: Eleazar de Carvalho (St. Louis SO), Christoph von Dohnányi (Kassel Opera), Sixten Ehrling (Detroit SO), Charles Groves (Liverpool SO), Josef Krips (San Francisco SO), Jean Martinon (Chicago SO), Horst Stein (Mannheim Opera), Werner Torkanowsky (New Orleans PO)

Educational: William Bergsma (music chairman, University of Washington), Russell Sherman (piano, University of Arizona), Eleanor Steber (voice, Cleveland Institute)

Others: Douglas Guest (music director, Westminster Abbey), Jean Guillou (organ, St. Eustache, Paris), Eric Salzman (music critic, New York Herald Tribune), Hugo Weisgall (president, American Music Center)

E. Prizes and Honors:

Prizes: Claudio Abbado (Mitropoulos), Samuel Barber (Pulitzer--*Piano Concerto*), Eliahu Inbal (Cantelli), Zdenek Kosler (Mitropoulos), Ezra Laderman (Prix de Rome), Michael Roll (Leeds), Mstislav Rostropovich (Lenin)

Honors: Elliott Carter (American Academy), James Dixon (Mahler), Joonas Kokkonen (Finnish Academy), Ernst Krenek (Austrian), Erich Leinsdorf (Musician of the Year, *Musical America*)

F. Biographical Highlights:

Vladimir Ashkenazy decides to stay in the West; Benjamin Britten visits Russia; Lili Chookasian makes her Bayreuth debut; Andrew Davis enters Kings College, Cambridge; Hans Werner Henze visits the U.S. for the premiere of his Fifth Symphony; Christopher Keene enters the University of California at Berkeley to study history; Radu Lupu is given a scholarship to Moscow Conservatory; Charles Mackerras makes his Covent Garden conducting debut; Mario del Monaco suffers injuries in a car accident; Zara Nelsova marries pianist Grant Johannesen; Margaret Price makes her Covent Garden debut; William Primrose suffers a heart attack; Samuel Ramey accepted for the Chorus of Central City Opera; Steve Reich receives an M.A. from Mills College; Maxim Shostakovich becomes assistant conductor of the Moscow SO; Karlheinz Stockhausen founds his Cologne Courses for New Music; Richard Stolzman enters Indiana University as a voice major; Tatiana Troyanos graduates from Juilliard.

G. Institutional Openings:

Performing Groups: Composer's String Quartet (New England Conservatory), Ensemble Moderne de Paris, Gabrieli Ensemble (London), High Tor Opera Co. (N.Y.), Israel Woodwind Quintet (Jerusalem), Japan Women's SO, London Opera Centre, Music of Today (Czechoslovakia), Phoenix Lyric Opera Theater, Pittsburgh Madrigal Singers, Purcell Consort of Voices (London), Sonatori di Praga (Brno), Suburban Opera Society (Pennsylvania), Swingle Singers (Paris), Tulsa Youth SO

Festivals: Cabrillo Music Festival (California), English Bach Festival (Oxford)

Educational: Harlem School of the Arts (N.Y.), International Institute for Comparative Studies and Documentation (W. Berlin), Yehudi Menuhin School of Music (England)

Other: Buffalo Center of the Creative and Performing Arts, Clowes Memorial Hall (Indianapolis), Finnish Music Information Center, Friends of French Opera (N.Y.), Jewish Liturgical Music Society of America, Leeds Piano Competition, Museum of Musical Instruments (Jerusalem), National Association of Organ Teachers, Seesaw Music Corporation (N.Y.), Swedish Institute for National Concerts (Stockholm)

H. Musical Literature:
Boulez, Pierre, *Penser la musique aujourd'hui*
Copland, Aaron, *Copland on Music*
Craft, Robert, *Dialogues and a Diary*
Demuth, Norman, *French Opera: Its Development...*
Donington, Robert, *Interpretation of Early Music*
MacKay, G.F., *Creative Orchestration*
Mitchell, Donald, *The Language of Modern Music*
Newman, William, *The Sonata in the Classic Era*
Schonberg, Harold, *The Great Pianists*
Xenakis, Iannis, *Musiques Formelles*

I. Musical Compositions:
Andriessen, Jurriaan, *Symphonies No. 3 and 4*
Argento, Dominick, *The Masque of Angels* (opera)
Bassett, Leslie, *Variations for Orchestra*
Bazelon, Irwin, *Symphony No. 3*
Bernstein, Leonard, *Symphony No. 3, "Kaddish"*
Binkerd, Gordon, *Symphony No. 4*
Brian, Havergal, *Symphony No. 21*
Brown, Earle, *Available Forms II* (orchestra)
Castelnuovo-Tedesco, Mario, *The Song of Songs* (oratorio)
Crumb, George, *Night Music I* (soprano, piano, percussion)
Finney, Ross Lee, *Still Are New Worlds*
Floyd, Carlisle, *The Sojourner and Mollie Sinclair* (opera)
Ginastera, Alberto, *Concerto for Violin and Orchestra*
Guanieri, Camargo, *Symphony No. 4*
Harris, Roy, *Symphony No. 9, "Polytonal"*
Hindemith, Paul, *Mass* (chorus a capella)
Hovhaness, Alan, *Symphonies No. 15, 16 and 17*
Kabalevsky, Dmitri, *Requiem*
Kay, Ulysses, *Fantasy Variations for Orchestra*
Kirchner, Leon, *Concerto No. 2 for Piano and Orchestra*
Lees, Benjamin, *Concerto for Oboe and Orchestra*
Malipiero, Gian F., *Concerto No. 2 for Violin and Orchestra*
Mennin, Peter, *Symphony No. 7*
Menotti, Gian Carlo, *The Last Savage* (opera)
Milhaud, Darius, *Pacem in Terris* (chorus and orchestra)
Sessions, Roger, *Psalm 140* (soprano and orchestra)
Siegmeister, Elie, *The Plough and the Stars* (opera)
Stockhausen, Karlheinz, *Plus-Minus*
Stravinsky, Igor, *Abraham and Isaac*
                        Elegy for John F. Kennedy
Tippett, Michael, *Concerto for Orchestra*
Walton, William, *Variations on a Theme of Hindemith* (orchestra)
Wuorinen, Charles, *Chamber Concerto*
Xenakis, Iannis, *Strategie* (2 orchestras, 2 conductors)

1964

World Events:
In the U.S., Lyndon Baines Johnson is elected for his first full term as President; the Civil Rights Act of 1964 is passed; the Twenty Fourth Amendment abolishes the southern poll tax; the spaceprobe *Mariner IV* is launched toward Mars; the Verranzano Narrows Bridge opens in New York; the New York World's Fair opens; the Surgeon-General's report links tobacco smoking to cancer and other diseases; General Douglas MacArthur dies. Internationally, Nikita Khrushchev is ousted from office by Aleksei Kosygin and Leonid Brezhnev who take over control in Russia; Harold Wilson becomes British Prime Minister; China explodes its first nuclear bomb; Prime Minister Nehru of India dies; Pope Paul VI becomes the first pope to leave Italian soil in 150 years as he visits the Holy Land.

Cultural Highlights:
Pulitzers: Poetry, Louis Simpson (*At the End of the Open Road*). Jean Paul Sartre refuses to accept a Nobel Prize for political and ideological reasons; novelist C.P. Snow receives a baronet; the Gallery of Modern Art opens in New York. Deaths in the literary world include Irish dramatist Sean O'Casey and poet Brendan Behan, American novelist Flannery O'Connor, Canadian poet Edwin Pratt and British poet Edith Sitwell; in the art field, Russian sculptor Alexander Archipenko, Italian artist Giorgio Morandi and American artist Stuart Davis. Other highlights include:

Art: Joseph Albers, *Reclining Figure* (Lincoln Center); Fernand Botero, *Apples*; Johann Hofmann, *The Man with Yellow Pants*; R.B. Kitaj, *The Ohio Gang*; Henry Moore, *Departing in Yellow*; Pablo Picasso, *Girl in Sling Chair*; Michelangelo Pistoletto, *Pax Vobiscum*; George Rickey, *Two Lines Temporal I*; Frank Stella, *The Green Girl*.

Literature: Edward Albee, *Tiny Alice*; Saul Bellow, *Herzog*; John Cheever, *The Wapshot Scandal*; Ernest Hemingway, *A Moveable Feast*; Richard Hofstadter, *Anti-Intellectualism in American Life*; Arthur Miller, *After the Fall*; Eugene O'Neill, *More Stately Mansions*; Harold Pinter, *The Homecoming*; Leon Uris, *Armageddon*.

MUSICAL EVENTS

A. Births:
May 29 Riccardo Gorrara (It-gui)	Jul 21 Stephen D. Clarke (Br-cd)

B. Deaths:
Jan 2 Ludwig Hoffmann (Ger-bs)	Sep 21 Leo Schrade (Ger-mus)
Jan 7 Colin McPhee (Can-cm)	Oct 1 Ernst Toch (Ger-cm)
Jan 22 Marc Blitzstein (Am-cm)	Oct 4 Set Svanholm (Swe-ten)
Feb 8 Vincenzo Bellezza (It-cd)	Oct 10 Heinrich Neuhaus (Rus-pn)
Feb 9 Samuel Chotzinoff (Am-cri)	Oct 15 Antoine Cherbuliez (Swi-mus)
Mar 29 Willem Andriessen (Hol-cm)	Oct 15 Cole Porter (Am-pop)
May 28 John F. Williamson (Am-cd)	Oct 31 George Wedge (Am-org-ed)
Jun 9 Louis Gruenberg (Am-cm)	Nov 6 George Dickinson (Am-m.ed)
Jul 1 Pierre Monteux (Fr-cd)	Nov 11 Edward Steuermann (Pol-pn)
Aug 19 Antoine Auda (Fr-mus)	Nov 16 Albert H. Malotte (Am-org-cm)
Sep 18 Clive Bell (Br-cri)	Nov 20 John Tasker Howard (Am-au)

C. Debuts:
Met ---Luigi Alva (ten), Gabriel Bacquier (bar), Leonard Bernstein (cd), Nedda Casei (mez), Mary Costa (sop), William Dooley (bar), Elfego Esparza (bs), Geraint Evans (bar), Agostino Ferrin (bs), Luis Forero (bs), Franco Ghitti (ten), Robert Goodloe (bar), Igor Gorin (bar), Donald Gramm (bs), Nicolae Herlea (bar), Robert LaMarchina (cd), Michael Langdon (bs), Lynn Owen (sop), George Prêtre (cd), Elisabeth Schwarzkopf (sop), David Ward (bs)

U.S. --Pierre Boulez (N.Y.), Alfred Brendel (N.Y.), Charles Castleman (N.Y.), Marie Collier

(San Francisco), Fiorenza Cossotto (Chicago), Monica Gaylord (N.Y.), Mindru Katz (Washington, D.C.), Wilhelm Kempff (N.Y.), Pilar Lorengar (San Francisco), Yo Yo Ma, Giorgio Merighi (Houston), Mady Mesplé, Ivan Moravec (Cleveland), John Owings, William Powers, Wolfgang Sawallisch (tour), Rita Shane (Chattanooga), Josef Suk (Cleveland)

Other -Betty Allen (Buenos Aires), Josephine Barstow (London), Aldo Ceccato (Milan), Ileana Cotrubas (Bucharest), Ryland Davis (Cardiff), Ann Howard (London), Roberta Knie (Hagen), Giorgio Lamberti (Rome), Valerie Masterson (Salzburg), Yvonne Minton (London), Elena Obraztsova (Moscow), Michala Petri (Copenhagen), Ruggero Raimondi (Spoleto), Elena Souliotis (Naples), Richard Van Allen (Glyndebourne), Michelangelo Veltri (Buenos Aires), Edo de Waart (Amsterdam)

D. New Positions:

Conductors: Yuri Ahronovich (Moscow Radio SO), Karsten Andersen (Bergen SO), Dean Dixon (Sydney SO), Christoph von Dohnányi (Cologne Radio SO), Lukas Foss (Buffalo SO), Vladimir Golschman (Denver SO), Walter Hendl (Eastman-Rochester SO), István Kertész (Cologne Opera), Carlos Kleiber (Zurich Opera), Paul Kletzki (Bern SO), George Lynn (Westminster Choir), Peter Maag (Vienna Volksoper), Brian Priestman (Edmondton SO)

Educational: Thurston Dart (professor, London University), Kent Kennan (professor, University of Texas), Gunther Schuller (composition, Yale)

E. Prizes and Honors:

Prizes: Pierre Amoyal (Paganini), Dalia Atlas (Mitropoulos), Agnes Baltsa (Enescu), Peter Maxwell Davies (Koussevitsky), James DePreist (Mitropoulos), Jean Jacques Kantorow (Paganini), Bernhard Kontarsky (Mendelssohn), Witold Lutoslawski (Koussevitsky), Evgeny Mogilevsky (Queen Elisabeth), Elizabeth Mosher (Naumberg), Itzhak Perlman (Leventritt), Michael Ponti (Busoni), Paula Robison (Munich), Grigory Sokolov (Tchaikovsky), Ludovic Spiess (Toulouse), José Van Dam (Geneva)

Honors: Benjamin Britten (Musician of the Year, *Musical America*)

F. Biographical Highlights:

John Cage is invited to Hawaii for a series of lectures; James DePreist goes to Europe to begin a freelance conducting career; Leon Fleisher begins to note arm and finger problems in his right hand; Glenn Gould gives up all concertizing and settles down to recording only; Cyprien Katsaris enters Paris Conservatory; Christopher Keene organizes an opera company on Berkeley campus and neglects his history studies; James Levine becomes an assistant to George Szell in Cleveland; Cornell MacNeil makes his Covent Garden debut; Evelyn Mandac leaves the Phillippines for the U.S.; Eduardo Mata begins music study at Tanglewood; David Oistrakh suffers his first heart attack; Rita Orlandi-Malaspina and Galina Vishnevskaya make their La Scala debuts; Murray Perahia graduates from Mannes with a conducting degree; Giuseppe Sinopoli enrolls in medicine in the University of Padua; Nicolas Slonimsky is retired from the University of California; Richard Stolzman enters Yale; Alexander Tcherepnin leaves Chicago for New York; David del Tredici receives his Master's degree from Princeton; Shirley Verrett marries her second husband, artist Lou LoMonaco; Ellen Taafe Zwillich moves to New York.

G. Institutional Openings:

Performing Groups: Adelaide Wind Quintet (Australia), Collegium Aureum (Germany), Consortium Antiquum (Antwerp), Ensemble Nipponia (Tokyo), Guarneri String Quartet, (Marlboro), Jerusalem Chamber Orchestra; Monteverdi Choir of London; Netherlands Opera Co. (Amsterdam), Seattle Opera Association, Youth Orchestra of Los Angeles

Festivals: Meadow Brook Festival (Rochester, Michigan)

Educational: Bowdoin College Music Press (Brunswick, Maine), Canberra Conservatory of Music (Australia), Chilean Academy of Fine Arts (Santiago), Educazione Musicale

(Italy), Jewish Music Research Center (Hebrew University), Società Italiana de Musicologia, Richard Strauss Institute (Munich)

Other: Blaisdell Memorial Center (Honolulu), Dorothy Chandler Pavilion (Los Angeles), *Chigiana Rassegna Annuale de Studi Musicologie* (Italy), Country Music Foundation (Nashville), Faber and Faber, Music Publishers (London), *Revista di Studi Crociani* (Italy)

H. Musical Literature:

Creston, Paul, *Principles of Rhythm*
Dickinson, George S., *Handbook of Style in Music*
Duckles, Vincent, *Music Reference and Research Materials*
Henze, Hans Werner, *Essays*
Hiller, Lejaren, *Informationstheorie und Computermusik*
Klemperer, Otto, *Minor Recollections*
Krenek, Ernst, *Komponist und Hören*
Lowens, Irving, *Music and Musicians in Early America*
Read, Gardner, *Music Notation*
Reed, H.O./Harder, P., *Basic Contrapuntal Techniques*

I. Musical Compositions:

Babbitt, Milton, *Philomel* (voice and magnetic tape)
Blackwood, Easley, *Concerto for Clarinet and Orchestra*
Blitzstein, Marc, *Sacco and Vanzetti* (unfinished opera)
Bock, Jerry, *Fiddler on the Roof* (musical)
Boulez, Pierre, *Figures* (orchestra)
        Double Prisms
Brian, Havergal, *Concerto for Orchestra*
Britten, Benjamin, *Symphony for Violin, Cello and Orchestra*
Brown, Earle, *From Here* (20 musicians, 4 optional choirs)
Chávez, Carlos, *Resonancias for Orchestra*
Copland, Aaron, *Music for a Great City* (symphonic suite)
Davidovsky, Mario, *Synchronism No. 2*
Erb, Donald, *Symphony of Overtures*
Fine, Vivian, *The Song of Persephone* (solo viola)
Finney, Ross Lee, *Symphony No. 3*
Flanagan, William, *Narrative for Orchestra*
Harris, Roy, *Epilogue to Profiles in Courage* (orchestra)
Kabalevsky, Dmitri, *Concerto No. 2 for Cello and Orchestra*
Lutoslawski, Witold, *String Quartet*
Malipiero, Gian F., *Symphony No. 8, "Sinfonia Brevis"*
Mennin, Peter, *Canto for Orchestra*
Miyoshi, Akira, *Concerto for Orchestra*
Persichetti, Vincent, *Concerto for Piano and Orchestra*
Porter, Quincy, *Symphony No. 2*
Sessions, Roger, *Symphony No. 5*
        Montezuma (opera)
Shostakovich, Dmitri, *String Quartets No. 9 and 10*
        The Execution of Stepan Razin
Still, Robert, *Symphony No. 4*
Stockhausen, Karlheinz, *Mikrophonie I*
Stravinsky, Igor, *Orchestra Variations*
Takemitsu, Toru, *Textures* (piano and orchestra)
Toch, Ernst, *Symphony No. 5, "Jephta"*
Wolpe, Stefan, *Symphony No. 1*
Xenakis, Iannis, *Eonta* (piano, brass)
        Hiketides (women's choir, percussion ensemble)
Yardumian, Richard, *Symphony No. 2, "Psalms"*

1965

World Events:
In the U.S., *Gemini* flights 3 and 4 produce the first American "space walk"; riots occur in the Watts sector of Los Angeles causing great damage; the Department of Housing and Urban Development (HUD) is founded; Medicare and Medicaid for the aged is passed by Congress; the Voting Rights Bill and the New Immigration Act are passed. Internationally, Russian cosmonaut A. Leonev, becomes the first man to "space walk"; North Vietnam is bombed by U.S. planes in retaliation for communists attacks in the south; revolution in the Dominican Republic is quelled by U.S. marines; India and Pakistan war over Kashmir; a Soviet probe lands on Venus; the death penalty is abolished in England.

Cultural Highlights:
Pulitzers: Drama, Frank Gilroy (*The Subject Was Roses*); Fiction, Shirley Ann Grau (*The Keepers of the House*); Poetry, John Berryman (*77 Dream Songs*). The Nobel Prize for Literature goes to the Russian author Mikhail Sholokhov. Deaths include former British Prime Minister, author and artist Winston Churchill, British novelist W. Somerset Maugham, American novelists Thomas B. Costain, T.S. Eliot and Thomas Stribling, American artist Milton Avery and sculptor David Smith and Hungarian artist Zoltan Kemény. Other highlights include:

Art: Salvador Dali, *Bust of Dante*; Lucio Fontana, *Spatial Concept*; Alberto Giacometti, *Caroline*; Edward Kienholz, *Visions of Sugarplums*; Barnett Newman, *Here II*; Pablo Picasso, *Self-Portrait*; Larry Rivers, *Jim Dine Storm Window*; Ben Shahn, *Farewell to New York*; David Smith, *Cubi XXVII*; Andrew Wyeth, *Weather Side*.

Literature: John Berryman, *77 Dream Songs*; Truman Capote, *In Cold Blood*; Alex Haley, *Hotel*; Norman Mailer, *An American Dream*; F. Marcus, *The Killing of Sister George*; Robin Moore, *The Green Berets*; Arthur Schlesinger, Jr., *A Thousand Days*; Irving Shaw, *Voices of a Summer Day*; Neil Simon, *The Odd Couple*.

MUSICAL EVENTS

A. Births:

Jul 8   Andrea Lucchesini (It-pn)   Ofra Harnoy (Is-cel)
Aug 24 Matthias Fletzberger (Aus-pn)

B. Deaths:

Jan 14	Jeanette MacDonald (Am-sop)	Sep 4 Albert Schweitzer (Ger-org)
Jan 15	Daniza Ilitsch (Yug-sop)	Sep 9 Julián Carrillo (Mex-cm)
Feb 15	Nat "King" Cole (Am-pop)	Sep 12 Willem van Hoogstraten (Hol-cd)
Feb 25	Heinz Unger (Ger-cd)	Sep 25 Nikolai Sokoloff (Rus-cd)
Mar 9	Anthon van der Horst (Hol-cm)	Oct 25 Hans Knappertsbusch (Ger-cd)
Mar 9	Henry Drinker, Jr. (Am-mus)	Nov 6 Edgar Varèse (Fr-cm)
Mar 25	Georgio F. Ghedini (It-cm)	Nov 11 Sigmund Spaeth (Am-mus)
Apr 26	Aaron Avshalomov (Rus-cm)	Nov 25 Myra Hess (Br-pn)
Apr 26	Michael Bohnen (Ger-bs)	Nov 27 Carl Parrish (Am-mus)
Jun 3	Herbert Janssen (Ger-bar)	Dec 10 Henry Cowell (Am-cm)
Jun 9	Fritz Soot (Ger-ten)	Dec 16 Tito Schipa (It-ten)
Aug 25	Daniel Fryklund (Swe-mus)	Dec 29 Kosack Yamada (Jp-cd-cm)

C. Debuts:
Met ---Patricia Berlin (mez), Gene Boucher (bar), Beverly Bower (sop), Grace Bumbry (mez), Montserrat Caballé (sop), Elena Cernei (mez), Mirella Freni (sop), Nicholai Ghiaurov (bs), Nicola Ghiuselev (bs), Joshua Hecht (bs), Zubin Mehta (cd), Raymond Michalski (bs), Sherrill Milnes (bar), Costas Paskalis (bar), Helga Pilarczyk (sop), Bruno Prevedi (ten), Gianni Raimondi (ten), John Reardon (bar), Renata Scotto (sop), Gérard Souzay (bar), Felicia Weathers (sop)

U.S. --Sergiu Comissiona (Philadelphia), Placido Domingo (N.Y.), Peter Frankl (Dallas), Margherita Guglielmi, Sergiu Luca (Philadelphia), Tamara Milashkina, Robert Preston (N.Y.), Jacqueline du Pré (N.Y.), James de Preist (N.Y.), Kenneth Riegel (Santa Fe), Malcolm Smith (N.Y.), Harry Theyard

Other -Sheila Armstrong (London), Helge Brilioth (as tenor), Maria Chiara (Venice), Paul Esswood (London), Simon Estes (Berlin), René Kollo (Braunschweig), Teresa Kubiak (Lodz), Caterina Ligendza (Linz), Veriano Luchetti (Wexford), Benjamin Luxon (London), Mischa Maisky (Leningrad), Jane Marsh (Spoleto), Thomas Pinschof (Vienna), Gwenneth Pryor (London), Trudeliese Schmidt (Saarbrücken), Maxim Shostakovich (Moscow), Dieter Weller (Bremerhaven)

D. New Positions:

Conductors: Gianandrea Gavazzeni (La Scala), Lászlo Halász (Rochester SO), István Kertész (London SO), James Loughran (BBC Scottish SO), Lorin Maazel (Berlin Opera), Igor Markevitch (Madrid Radio SO), Seiji Ozawa (Toronto SO), Michel Plasson (Metz Opera), Leif Segerstam (Finnish National Opera), Evgeny Svetlanov (USSR State SO), Silvio Varviso (Stockholm Opera)

Educational: George Crumb (composer-in-residence, University of Pennsylvania), Gottfried von Einem (composition, Vienna Hochschule), Elisabeth Grümmer (voice, Berlin Hochschule), André Jolivet (composition, Paris Conservatory), Ralph Kirkpatrick (harpsichord, Yale), Eduardo Mata (music chairman, University of Mexico)

Other: Herbert Graf (director, Geneva Opera)

E. Prizes and Honors:

Prizes: Stephen Albert (Prix de Rome), Martha Argerich (Chopin), Edward Auer (Chopin), Jacob Avshalomov (Ditson), Simon Estes (Munich), Lamberto Gardelli (Toscanini), Tong Il Han (Leventritt), Zdenek Macal (Besançon), Ben Weber (Thorne)

Honors: Benjamin Britten (Order of Merit), Barbara Hepworth (Dame of the British Empire), Vladimir Horowitz (Musician of the Year, *Musical America*), Byron Janis (Legion of Honor), Edgard Varèse (MacDowell Medal)

F. Biographical Highlights:

Claudio Arrau makes a concert tour of Japan; Benjamin Britten makes his second trip to Russia; Placido Domingo leaves Israel for the U.S. and joins the New York City Opera; Philip Glass collaborates with Ravi Shankar on a film score; Hans Haacke marries American Linda Snyder and moves to the U.S.; James King makes his Bayreuth debut; Gidon Kremer enters Tchaikovsky State Conservatory in Moscow; Teresa Kubiak graduates from Lodz Academy of Music; Erich Kunzel becomes Assistant to Max Rudolf in Cincinnati; Bruno Maderna is invited to Boston by Sarah Caldwell to conduct his opera; Yvonne Minton makes her Covent Garden debut; Luciano Pavarotti tours Australia with Sutherland's Opera Co.; Ferruccio Tagliavini retires from the opera stage; Martti Talvela makes his Vienna debut; Randall Thompson retires from teaching; Michael Tippett makes his first visit to the U.S.; Iannis Xenakis becomes a citizen of France; Ellen Taafe Zwillich joins the American SO under Stokowski.

G. Institutional Openings:

Performing Groups: Boston Symphony Chamber Players, Edinburgh Festival Chorus, Fresk String Quartet (Stockholm), Greater Miami SO (Florida PO), Israel Chamber Ensemble, Los Angeles Master Chorale and Sinfonia, Melos String Quartet (Stuttgart), Omaha Regional Ballet Co., Orford String Quartet (Quebec), Phoenix Opera Co. (Arizona), Spanish Radio and Television SO (Madrid), Tokyo Metropolitan SO, Vienna Capella Academica

Festivals: Bratislava Festival (Yugoslavia), Festival Estival de Paris

Educational: North Carolina School of the Arts (Winston-Salem), School for the Discovery and Advancement of New Serial Techniques (Los Angeles)

Other: *The Bulletin* (American Composers' Alliance), Concours International de Montreal, National Foundation on the Arts and Humanities (Washington, D.C.), Netherlands Opera Foundation, Prix Clara Haskil (Switzerland), Pro Musicis Foundation (Paris), Queensbury Festival Auditorium, Rochester Music Publishers, Société de Musique Contemporaine du Québec

H. Musical Literature:

Bamberger, Carl, *The Conductor's Art*
Cohn, Arthur, *Twentieth Century Music in Western Europe*
Gál, Hans, *The Musician's World: Great Composers in Their Letters*
Georgiades, Thrasybulos, *Das Musikalische Theater*
Janecek, Karel, *The Basis of Modern Harmony*
Lang, Paul Henry, *Contemporary Music in Europe*
Merrill, Robert, *Once More, From the Beginning*
Pauly, Reinhard, *Music in the Classical Period*
Seay, Albert, *Music in the Medieval World*
Siegmeister, Elie, *Harmony and Melody*

I. Musical Compositions:

Babbitt, Milton, *Relata I for Orchestra*
Bazelon, Irwin, *Symphony No. 4*
Beeson, Jack, *Lizzie Borden* (opera)
Bernstein, Leonard, *Chichester Psalms* (chorus and orchestra)
Bergsma, William, *Concerto for Violin and Orchestra*
Blacher, Boris, *Tristan and Isolde* (ballet)
Blackwood, Easley, *Symphony No. 3*
Boulez, Pierre, *Éclat* (15 instruments)
Brian, Havergal, *Symphonies No. 22, 23 and 24*
Carter, Elliott, *Concerto for Piano and Orchestra*
Chávez, Carlos, *Concerto No. 2 for Violin and Orchestra*
Crumb, George, *Madrigals, Books I and II*
         Eleven Echoes of Autumn
Davidovsky, Mario, *Synchronism No. 3*
Farberman, Harold, *Concerto for Alto Saxophone and Orchestra*
Fine, Vivian, *Concertino for Piano and Percussion*
Françaix, Jean, *La Princesse de Clèves* (opera)
Gerhard, Roberto, *Concerto for Orchestra*
Harris, Roy, *Symphony No. 10, "Abraham Lincoln"*
Hovhaness, Alan, *Ukiyo--Floating World* (symphonic poem)
Kay, Hersey, *L'Inconnue* (ballet)
Klebe, Giselher, *Jakobowsky und der Oberst* (opera)
Lees, Benjamin, *Concerto for String Quartet and Orchestra*
Leigh, Mitch, *Man of La Mancha* (musical)
Ligeti, György, *Requiem*
Lutoslawski, Witold, *Paroles Tissées*
Martinon, Jean, *Symphony No. 4, "Altitudes"*
         Concerto for Cello and Orchestra
Mimaroglu, Ilhan, *Agony* (tape)
Miyoshi, Akira, *Concerto for Violin and Orchestra*
Piston, Walter, *Symphony No. 8*
Schuller, Gunther, *Symphony No. 1*
Shchedrin, Rodion, *Symphony No. 2*
Stockhausen, Karlheinz, *Stop*
         Mikrophonie II
Stravinsky, Igor, *Introitus: T.S. Eliot*
Subotnik, Morton, *Play!*
Thompson, Randall, *The Passion According to St. Luke* (oratorio)

1966

World Events:

In the U.S., President Johnson makes a tour of the Far East; Robert C. Weaver becomes the first black to be appointed to a cabinet position; *Gemini 8* achieves the first space docking; *Surveyor I* lands on the moon; the Department of Transportation is made into a cabinet post; race riots occur in many cities as the Ku Klux Klan is reorganized. Internationally, President De Gaulle orders NATO out of France; the Soviets land *Luna 9* on the moon; Turkish earthquake kills about 2500 people; Indira Gandhi becomes Prime Minister of India; the "Cultural Revolution" begins in China; Barbados and Guyana are given independence.

Cultural Highlights:

Pulitzers: Fiction, Katherine Anne Porter (*Collected Stories*); Poetry, Richard Eberhart (*Selected Poems*). The Nobel Prize for Literature is shared by Israeli author Shmuel Yosef Agnon and German poet and dramatist Nelly Sachs. The Yale Center for British Art is opened in New Haven; the Whitney Museum of American Art opens in New York. The literary world loses American authors George Chamberlain, Anne Nichols, Kathleen Norris and William Zorach, British novelist C.S. Forester and the French poet and chief theorist of surrealism, André Breton; deaths in the field of art include Finnish sculptor Wäinö Aaltonen, French poet and artist Jean (Hans) Arp, Italian artist Carlo Carrá, Swiss artist Alberto Giacometti, German artist Hans Hoffman, American sculptors Malvina Hoffman, Paul Manship and Frederick Sievers and French artist Tristan Klingsor. Other highlights include:

Art: Fernando Botero, *Our Lady of New York*; Alexander Calder, *Chef d'Orchestre* (mobile); Marc Chagall, *Le Triomphe de la Musique*; Chryssa, *Gates to Times Square*; Salvador Dali, *Tuna Fishing*; Ellsworth Kelly, *White Angel*; Henry Moore, *Three Red Lines*; Lucas Samaras, *Mirrored Room*; Andy Warhol, *Campbell's Soup*.

Literature: Edward Albee, *A Delicate Balance*; John Barth, *Giles Goat-boy*; Abe Burrows, *Cactus Flower*; Graham Greene, *The Comedians*; Bernard Malamud, *The Fixer*; William Manchester, *The Death of a President*; Anne Sexton, *Live or Die*; Jacqueline Susann, *The Valley of the Dolls*; Yevgeny Yevtushenko, *Bratskyaya Station*.

MUSICAL EVENTS

B. Deaths:

Jan 9	Noah Greenberg (Am-cd-mus)	Jul 3	Deems Taylor (Am-cm-au)
Jan 14	Charles van den Borren	Aug 15	Jan Kiepura (Pol-ten)
	(Bel-mus)	Aug 31	Armanda Machabey (Fr-mus)
Feb 13	Marguerite Long (Fr-pn-ped)	Sep 17	Fritz Wunderlich (Ger-ten)
Mar 14	Dennis Noble (Br-bar)	Sep 19	Otto Kinkeldey (Am-mus)
Mar 30	Jelly d'Arányi (Hun-vn)	Sep 22	Friedrich Gennrich (Ger-mus)
Apr 18	Joseph Maddy (Am-m.ed)	Oct 16	Wieland Wagner (Ger-imp)
May 5	Florence MacBeth (Am-sop)	Nov 12	Quincy Porter (Am-cm)
May 8	Glen Haydon (Am-mus)	Nov 13	Mario Chamlee (Am-ten)
May 21	Marya Freund (Pol-sop)	Nov 28	Vittoria Giannini (It-cm)
Jun 12	Hermann Scherchen (Ger-cd)	Dec 9	Yuri Shaporin (Rus-cm)
Jun 24	Alexander Piragov (Rus-bs)		

C. Debuts:

Met ---Karan Armstrong (sop), Gaetano Bardini (ten), Walter Berry (bar), Richard Bonynge (cd), Placido Domingo (ten), Loren Driscoll (ten), Ludmila Dvoráková (sop), Ella Eure (mez), Lamberto Gardelli (cd), Reri Grist (sop), James King (ten), Alfredo Kraus (ten), Alain Lombard (cd), Pilar Lorengar (sop), Helen McIlhenny (sop), Francesco Molinari-Pradelli (cd), Pekka Nuotio (ten), Tycho Parly (ten), Ruza Pospinov (mez), Francesca Roberto (sop), Beverly Sills (sop), Thomas Stewart (bar), Patricia Welting (sop), Virginia Zeani (sop)

U.S. --Janet Baker (N.Y.), Phyllis Bryn-Julson (Boston), June Card (Boston), Gianfranco Cecchele, Misha Dichter (Berkshire), John Duykers (Seattle), Christiane Eda-Pierre (Chicago), Oscar Ghiglia (N.Y.), Elisabeth Grümmer (N.Y.), Richard Kness (St.Louis), Evelyn Lear, Olivera Miljakovic, Magda Olivero (Dallas), Luciano Pavarotti (Miami), Murray Perahia (N.Y.), Margherita Rinaldi

Other -David A. Ahern (Sydney), Michel Béroff (Paris), Nicholas Braithwaite (London), Lorna Haywood (London), Michail Heise (Mannheim), Anne Howells (Cardiff), Christian Du Plessis (Johannesburg), Maxim Shostakovich (as conductor), Walter Weller (as conductor)

D. New Positions:

Conductors: Sergiu Comissiona (Göteborg SO), Antal Dorati (Stockholm SO), Charles Dutoit (Bern SO), Günther Herbig (East Berlin SO), Carlos Kleiber (Stuttgart Opera), Charles Mackerras (Hamburg Opera), Eduardo Mata (Mexico City PO), Michel Plasson (Théâtre du Capitole, Toulouse), Jerzy Semkov (Danish Opera), Edo de Waart (Netherlands Wind Ensemble)

Educational: Lili Kraus (artist-in-residence, TCU), Olivier Messiaen (composition, Paris Conservatory), Roger Sessions (Bloch professor, Berkeley), Italo Tajo (voice, Cincinnati Conservatory)

E. Prizes and Honors:

Prizes: Vladimir Atlantov, Edward Auer & Jane Marsh (Tchaikovsky), Leslie Bassett (Pulitzer--*Variations for Orchestra*), Michele Campanella (Casella), Sylvia Carduff (Mitropoulos), Lawrence Foster & Mauricio Kagel (Koussevitsky), Radu Lupu (Cliburn), Garrick Ohlsson (Busoni), Rafael Orozco (Leeds), Krzystof Penderecki (Westphalia), Paula Robison (Geneva)

Honors: Yehudi Menuhin (Musician of the Year, *Musical America*), Michael Tippett (knighted)

F. Biographical Highlights:

Elly Ameling makes her London debut; Luciano Berio separates from his wife, Cathy Berberian; Peter Maxwell Davies becomes composer-in-residence at the University of Adelaide; Mischa Dichter, Simon Estes and Stephen Kates win Silver Medals in the Tchaikovsky Competition; Philip Glass studies percussion playing in India; Dylana Jenson receives violin lessons from Jascha Heifetz; Ernst Krenek moves to Palm Springs, California; Erich Kunzel takes the Cincinnati SO on a Far East concert tour; Spiro Malas makes his Covent Garden debut; Zinka Milanov gives her farewell performance at the Met; James Morris enters Peabody; Luciano Pavarotti makes his La Scala debut; Lucia Popp debuts at Covent Garden; Dmitri Shostakovich discovers his serious heart ailment; Giulietta Simionato retires from the stage to marry Dr. Cesare Frugoni; Stanislaw Skrowaczewski becomes an American citizen; Leonard Slatkin receives his Bachelor's degree; Karlheinz Stockhausen visits Japan; Oliver Strunk retires from Princeton and moves to Italy; Robert Suderburg receives his Ph.D. from the University of Pennsylvania; Shirley Verrett makes her La Scala debut; Edo de Waart becomes assistant to Haitink at the Amsterdam Concertgebouw; Alexis Weissenberg returns to the concert stage after a ten-year hiatus.

G. Institutional Openings:

Performing Groups: Arkansas SO (Little Rock), Classical PO of Stuttgart, Gabrieli String Quartet (London), London Symphony Chorus, Music Group of London, Orchestre de Paris, Ulster SO (Ireland)

Festivals: Brno International Music Festival, Daytona Beach Festival, Saratoga Festival of the Performing Arts

Educational: American Society of University Composers (N.Y.), Mexican Academy of the Arts, Organ & Piano Teacher's Association

Other: Affiliate Artists, Inc. (N.Y.); Bahia Composers' Group (Brazil), Buchla Associates (Berkely), Casagrande International Piano Competition (Italy), Deutsche Gesellschaft für Musik des Orients, La Grand Écurie et la Chambre du Roy (Paris), Groupe d'Étude et de Realisation Musicales, International Alban Berg Society (Vienna), International Bach Institute, Jesse H. Jones Hall for the Performing Arts (Houston), Bureau de Musique (Paris), Musica Eletronica Viva (Rome), New Metropolitan Opera House (Lincoln Center), New York Consortium for New Music, Rotterdam Concert Hall, Albert Schweitzer Friendship House (Great Barrington, Massachusetts), Würzburger Stadttheater, Yamaha Foundation.

H. Musical Literature:

Austin, William, *Music in the Twentieth Century*
Boulez, Pierre, *Relevés d'apprenti*
Chase, Gilbert, *Music in Latin-America*
    The Composer Speaks
Horsley, Imogene, *The Fugue*
Krenek, Ernst, *Exploring Music*
Lieberman, Maurice, *Creative Counterpoint*
Ulehla, Ludmila, *Contemporary Harmony*
Verrall, John, *Fugue and Invention in Theory & Practice*
Walker, Alan, *An Anatomy of Musical Criticism*

I. Musical Compositions:

Barber, Samuel, *Anthony and Cleopatra* (opera)
Bazelon, Irwin, *Symphony No. 5*
Bennett, Richard R., *Symphony No. 1*
Berio, Luciano, *Sequence IV for Piano*
    Sequence V for Trombone
Brant, Henry, *Hieroglyphics*
Brian, Havergal, *Symphonies No. 25, 26 and 27*
Britten, Benjamin, *The Burning Fiery Furnace* (vocal church parable)
Erb, Donald, *Concerto for Solo Percussionist and Orchestra*
Floyd, Carlisle, *Markheim* (opera)
Harrison, Lou, *Symphony in G*
Henze, Hans Werner, *Muses of Sicily* (boy's choir, percussion)
Imbrie, Andrew, *Symphony No. 1*
Kabalevsky, Dmitri, *The Motherland* (cantata)
Khachaturian, Aram, *Suite No. 4 for Orchestra*
Lees, Benjamin, *Concerto No. 2 for Piano and Orchestra*
Ligeti, György, *Concerto for Cello and Orchestra*
Malipiero, Gian F., *Concerto No. 6 for Piano and Orchestra, "Delle Machine"*
Martin, Frank, *Concerto for Cello and Orchestra*
Moore, Douglas, *Carrie Nation* (opera)
Musgrave, Thea, *Nocturne and Arias* (orchestra)
Penderecki, Krystoff, *Passion According to St. Luke* (soloists, choruses, orchestra)
Rorem, Ned, *Sun* (orchestra)
Schuller, Gunther, *The Visitation* (opera)
Schuman, William, *The Witch of Endor* (ballet)
Sessions, Roger, *Symphony No. 6*
Shostakovich, Dmitri, *Concerto No. 2 for Cello and Orchestra*
    String Quartet No. 11
Stockhausen, Karlheinz, *Adieu* (wind quartet)
Stravinsky, Igor, *Requiem Canticles* (vocal quartet, chorus, orchestra)
Takemitsu, Toru, *Dorian Horizon* (seventeen string instruments)
Tippett, Michael, *The Vision of St. Augustine* (baritone, chorus, orchestra)
Van Vactor, David, *Sinfonia Breve*
Walton, William, *Missa Brevis* (double chorus, organ)

1967

World Events:

In the U.S., President Johnson meets with Soviet Premier Aleksei Kosygin in New Jersey; Thurgood Marshall becomes the first black Supreme Court Justice; the Twenty Fifth Ammendment on Vice-Presidential appointment is ratified; Puerto Rico votes to remain a U.S. Commonwealth member; more race riots develop with Detroit alone sustaining a loss of over $200,000,000 and over 5000 left homeless; protests mount against involvement in Vietnam. Internationally, Egypt blockades Israeli ports and Israel begins the "Six-Day War" against her neighboring Arab states; a military coup establishes a military dictatorship in Greece; Communist troops quell liberalization in Czechoslovakia; Pulsars are discovered in outer space.

Cultural Highlights:

Pulitzers: Drama, Edward Albee (*A Delicate Balance*); Fiction, Bernard Malamud (*The Fixer*); Poetry, Anne Sexton (*Live or Die*). The Nobel Prize for Literature goes to Guatamalan author Miquel Angel Asturias; the Ridiculous Theatrical Co. is founded in New York. Deaths in the art world include American artists Charles Burchfield and Edward Hopper, French sculptor Henri-Georges Adam and Belgian artist René Magritte; the literary world loses American authors Margaret Barnes, Martin Flavin, Carson McCullers, Dorothy Parker, dramatist Elmer L. Rice and poet and author Carl Sandburg as well as French novelist André Maurois and British poet John E. Masefield. Other highlights include:

Art: Karel Appel, *Personnage*; Fernando Botero, *The Presidential Family*; Anthony Caro, *Deep Body Blue*; Marc Chagall, *The Blue Village*; Robert Delaunay, *Rhythme Couleur, No. 1541*; Herbert Ferber, *Environmental Sculpture*; Barnett Newman, *Broken Obelisk*; Matthew Smith, *Cigarette*; Frank Stella, *Singerli II*.

Literature: Christopher Isherwood, *Meeting by the River;* Peter Marshall, *Christy*; R. Massie, *Nicholas and Alexandra*; D. Morris, *The Naked Ape*; Chaim Potok, *The Chosen*; Irwin Shaw, *The Man in the Glass Booth*; William Styron, *The Confessions of Nat Turner*; Leon Uris, *Topaz*; Irving Wallace, *The Plot*; Thornton Wilder, *The Eighth Day*.

MUSICAL EVENTS

A. Births:

Joshua Bell (Am-vn)

B. Deaths:

Jan 4	Mary Garden (Scot-sop)	Aug 14	Hans J. Moser (Ger-mus)
Jan 31	Geoffery O'Hara (Am-pop)	Oct 3	Malcolm Sargent (Br-cd)
Feb 2	Fabien Sevitsky (Rus-cd)	Nov 9	Tomáz Alcaide (Por-ten)
Feb 24	Franz Waxman (Am-cd-cm)	Nov 23	Otto E. Deutsch (Aus-mus)
Mar 6	Nelson Eddy (Am-bar)	Dec 2	Emmanuel Bay (Rus-pn)
Mar 6	Zoltán Kodály (Hun-cm)	Dec 11	Victor de Sabata (It-cd)
Mar 11	Geraldine Farrar (Am-sop)	Dec 13	Valeriya Barsova (Rus-sop)
Apr 5	Mischa Elman (Rus-vn)	Dec 13	Adolphe Borchard (Fr-pn)
Jun 3	André Cluytens (Fr-cd)	Dec 19	Carmen Melis (It-sop)
Jun 21	Emanuel List (Aus-bs)	Dec 24	Karl Ristenpart (Ger-cd)
Jul 26	Matthijs Vermeulen (Hol-cm)	Dec 29	Paul Whiteman (Am-pop)
Aug 8	Jaromir Weinberger (Boh-cm)		

C. Débuts:

Met ---Bruno Amaducci (cd), Teresa Berganza (mez), Collette Boky (sop), Phyllis Brill (sop), Marie Collier (sop), Colin Davis (cd), Cristina Deutekom (sop), Peter Glossop (bar), Elisabeth Grümmer (sop), Gundula Janowitz (sop), Herbert von Karajan (cd), Tom Krause (bar), Josef Krips (cd), Evelyn Lear (sop), Jeannette Pilou (sop), Paul Plishka (bs), Lucia Popp (sop), Karl Ridderbusch (bs), Peter Schreier (ten)

U.S. --Stuart Burrows (San Francisco), Guy Chauvet (San Francisco), Myung-Wha Chung (San Francisco), Joseph Kalichstein (N.Y.), James Morris (Baltimore), John Nelson (N.Y.), Erna Spoorenberg (N.Y.), José Van Dam (Santa Fe)

Other -Arleen Augér (Vienna), James Bowman (Oxford), Noel A. Davies (Kent), Leslie Howard (Melbourne), Elizabeth Howells (London), Václav Hudecek (London), Neil Jenkins (London), Horst Laubenthal (Würzburg), Silvia Marcovici (The Hague), Riccardo Muti (Milan), Leo Nucci (Spoleto), Anna Tomowa-Sintow (Leipzig), Christopher Van Kampen (Bournemouth), Roger Vignoles (London), Anna Wesolowska (Lodz)

D. New Positions:

Conductors: Sergiu Comissiona (Gothenburg SO), Colin Davis (BBC SO), Charles Dutoit (Zurich Radio SO), Bernard Haitink (London PO), Thor Johnson (Nashville SO), Rudolph Kempe (Munich PO), Paul Kletzki (Orchestre de la Suisse Romande), Jorge Mester (Louisville SO), André Previn (Houston SO), Robert Shaw (Atlanta SO), Edo de Waart (Rotterdam PO)

Educational: Maurice André (trumpet, Paris Conservatory), Gunther Schuller (President, New England Conservatory), Russell Sherman (piano, New England Conservatory)

Others: Henry Pleasants (music critic, London International Herald-Tribune), Stanley Sadie (editor, Musical Times)

E. Prizes and Honors:

Prizes: Edward Auer (Long-Thibaud), Igor Buketoff (Ditson), Kyung-Wha Chung (Leventritt), Leon Kirchner (Pulitzer--*String Quartet III*), Radu Lupu (Enescu), Riccardo Muti (Cantelli), Jacques Rouvier (Viotti)

Honors: Olivier Messiaen (French Institute), Nathan Milstein (Legion of Honor), William Walton (Order of Merit)

F. Biographical Highlights:

Arleen Augér wins a voice contest enabling her to go to Vienna where she auditions for the Vienna Opera and is accepted; Peter Maxwell Davies returns to England and founds the Pierrot Players; Andrew Davis given a grant to study conducting in Rome; Placido Domingo makes his Vienna Opera debut; Peter Frankl becomes a British citizen; Philip Glass returns to U.S. following his visit to India; Horacio Gutiérrez becomes a naturalized American citizen; Byron Janis discovers Chopin's lost Waltz in G-flat; Berit Lindholm debuts at Bayreuth; Donald McIntyre debuts at both Covent Garden and Bayreuth; Gerald Moore gives his farewell recital; James Morris joins the Baltimore Civic Opera Co.; Constantin Silvestri becomes a British citizen; Richard Stolzman begins work on a doctorate; H.H. Stuckenschmidt retires from teaching; Robert Suderburg receives a Rockefeller grant; Alexander Tcherepnin becomes the second emigré composer to be invited back to the Soviet Union; Kiri Te Kanawa marries an Australian mining engineer, Desmond Park; Lester Trimble becomes composer-in-residence at the New York PO; Shirley Verrett makes her Covent Garden debut.

G. Institutional Openings:

Performing Groups: Arizona Chamber Orchestra (Tucson), Augusta Opera (Georgia), Barcelona City Orchestra (Spain), Early Music Consort of London, The Fires of London, Opera Orchestra of New York, Pierrot Players (London), Edward Tarr Brass Ensemble, Western Opera Theater (San Francisco)

Festivals: Brighton Music Festival (England), Indiana State University Contemporary Music Festival, Lincoln Center Summer Festival (N.Y.), Savonlinna Opera Festival (Finland), Verdi Festival (Rhode Island)

Educational: Australian Journal of Music Education, Center for Chinese Folk Music Research (Taiwan), Groupe de Recherches Théâtrales et Musicologiques; Mark Educational Recordings, Inc.; *Zeitschrift für Musiktheorie*

Other: American Liszt Society (Baltimore), Claudio Arrau Fund for Young Musicians, Atlantic City Auditorium, British Music Information Centre (London), Hellenic Group of Contemporary Music (Athens), Houston Harpsichord Society, Place des Arts (Montreal), Merriweather Post Pavilion of Music (Maryland), Purcell Room and Queen Elizabeth Hall (London), Reconnaissance des Musiques Modernes (Belgium), Sonda (electronic instrument), *Source*, Deems Taylor Awards (ASCAP)

H. Musical Literature:

Apel, Willi, *History of Organ and Clavier Music*
Aprahamian, Felix, *Essays on Music*
Craft, Robert, *Themes and Episodes*
Demus, Jörg, *Abenteuer der Interpretation*
Frankenstein, Alfred, *Modern Guide to Symphonic Music*
Hanson, Peter S., *Introduction to Twentieth Century Music*
Read, Gardner, *Twentieth Century Notation*
Schwartz/Childs, *Contemporary Composers on Contemporary Music*
Thomson, Virgil, *Music Reviewed*
Yates, Peter, *Twentieth Century Music*

I. Musical Compositions:

Adler, Samuel, *Symphony No. 4, "Geometrics"*
Amram, David, *King Lear Variations*
Ashley, Robert, *She Was a Visitor* (tape)
Badings, Henk, *Concerto for Harp and Winds*
Berio, Luciano, *Sequence VI* (viola)
Blackwood, Easley, *Concerto for Violin and Orchestra*
Brian, Havergal, *Symphonies No. 28, 29 and 30*
Britten, Benjamin, *Suite No. 2 for Solo Cello*
Brown, Earle, *Event: Synergy II* (chamber orchestra)
Chávez, Carlos, *Elatio for Orchestra*
Copland, Aaron, *Inscape* (orchestra)
Crumb, George, *Echoes of Time and the River* (orchestra)
Feldman, Morton, *Chorus and Instruments II*
Foss, Lukas, *Baroque Variations* (orchestra)
                 Concerto for Cello and Orchestra
Françaix, Jean, *Concerto for Flute and Orchestra*
Gerhard, Roberto, *Symphony No. 4, "New York"*
Ginastera, Alberto, *Bomarzo* (opera)
Hanson, Howard, *De Natalis* (orchestra)
Henze, Hans Werner, *Moralities* (scenic cantatas after Aesop)
                 Concerto for Double Bass and Orchestra
Hovhaness, Alan, *The Holy City* (orchestra)
Kokkonen, Joonas, *Symphony No. 3*
Lutoslawski, Witold, *Symphony No. 2*
Malipiero, Gian F., *Symphony No. 10, "Atropo"*
Musgrave, Thea, *Concerto for Orchestra*
Penderecki, Krzystof, *Dies Irae* (Auschwitz Oratorio)
Piston, Walter, *Concerto for Clarinet and Orchestra*
Schuller, Gunther, *Triplum for Orchestra*
Sessions, Roger, *Symphony No. 7*
Shostakovich, Dmitri, *Concerto No. 2 for Violin and Orchestra*
                 October (symphonic poem)
Stockhausen, Karlheinz, *Mixtur*
Subotnick, Morton, *Silver Apples of the Moon* (tape)
Takemitsu, Toru, *Green, November Steps II* (orchestra)
Walton, William, *The Bear* (opera)
Xenakis, Iannis, *Nuits*

1968

World Events:
In the U.S., Richard M. Nixon is elected as President No. 37; during the campaign, Presidential candidate Robert Kennedy is assassinated in Los Angeles while Martin Luther King is assassinated in Memphis; Apollo 8 puts the first men in orbit around the moon; direct airline service opens between the U.S. and Russia; the *U.S.S. Pueblo* is seized by the North Koreans. Internationally, Korean Peace Talks are held in Paris; Russia and her allies invade Czechoslovakia to crush the rise of democracy; the Caribbean Free Trade Area is formed; the Gibraltar-Spanish border is closed by Spain; Catholics and Protestants begin fighting in Northern Ireland; the Olympic Games are held in Mexico City.

Cultural Highlights:
Pulitzers: Fiction, William Styron (*The Confessions of Nat Turner*); Poetry, Anthony Hecht (*The Hard Hours*). Japanese writer Yasunari Kawabata receives the Nobel Prize for Literature. Deaths in the field of art include Italian artist Lucio Fontana and French artist Marcel Duchamp; in the field of literature, American novelists Edna Ferber, Conrad Richter and John Steinbeck, Czech novelist Max Brod, Italian poet and author Salvatore Quasimodo and Russian poet Alexander Yashin. Other highlights include:

Art: Willem de Kooning, *Two Figures in a Landscape*; Alex Katz, *Ada with a Superb Lily*; Lee Krasner, *Green Fuse*; Henry Moore, *Totem Head*; Robert Motherwell, *Open*; Louise Nevelson, *Transparent Sculpture IV*; George Rickey, *Unstable Cube*; Eero Saarinen, *The Gateway Arch* (St. Louis); Pierre Soulages, *Painting, May 9, 1968*.

Literature: Louis Auchincloss, *A World of Profit*; John Barth, *Lost in the Funhouse*; Gwendolyn Brooks, *In the Mecca*; Alex Haley, *Airport*; Norman Mailer, *The Armies of the Night*; Arthur Miller, *The Price*; Howard Sackler, *The Great White Hope*; Neil Simon, *Plaza Suite*; Alexander Solzhenitsyn, *The First Circle*; John Updike, *The Music School*; Gore Vidal, *Myra Breckinridge*; James D. Watson, *The Double Helix*.

MUSICAL EVENTS

B. Deaths:

Jan 9	Louis Aubert (Fr-cm)	May 24	Bernard Rogers (Am-cm)
Jan 11	Mariano Stabile (It-bar)	Jun 14	Karl-Birger Blomdahl (Swe-cm)
Jan 29	Frank Black (Am-cd)	Jul 7	Leo Sowerby (Am-org)
Feb 2	Tullio Serafin (It-cd)	Jul 20	Joseph Keilberth (Ger-cd)
Feb 13	Ildebrando Pizzetti (It-cm)	Aug 8	Fritz Stiedry (Aus-cd)
Feb 16	Victor Belaiev (Rus-mus)	Aug 31	Percy C. Hull (Br-org)
Feb 16	Healy Willan (Can-cm	Sep 6	Anny Konetzni (Aus-sop)
Mar 16	Mario Castelnuovo-Tedesco	Oct 12	Tauno Hannikainen (Fin-cd)
	(It-cm)	Nov 6	Guillaume Landré (Hol-cm)
Mar 31	Elly Ney (Ger-pn)	Nov 6	Charles Munch (Fr-cd)
Apr 21	Norman Demuth (Br-cm)	Nov 27	Hans F. Redlich (Aus-mus)
Apr 27	Alexander Borovsky (Rus-pn)	Dec 14	Margarete Klose (Ger-alto)
May 16	Florence Austral (Aust-sop)		

C. Débuts:

Met ---Claudio Abbado (cd), Giacomo Aragall (ten), Fiorenza Cossotto (mez), Placido Domingo (ten), Ann Florio (sop), Donald Grobe (ten), Hildegard Hillebrecht (sop), Mario Lippert (sop), Rod MacWherter (ten), Edda Moser (sop), Luciano Pavarotti (ten), Gerhard Stolze (ten), Martti Talvela (bs), Josephine Veasey (mez), Shirley Verrett (mez), Teresa Zylis-Gara (sop)

U.S. --Elly Ameling (N.Y.), Kyung-Wha Chung (N.Y.), Maria Ewing (Cleveland), Elizabeth Harwood (N.Y.), Werner Hollweg (N.Y.), Jean-Jacques Kantorow (N.Y.), Aram Khacha-turian (Washington, D.C., as conductor), Evelyn Mandac (Mobile, Alabama), Maurizio

Pollini (N.Y.), Margaret Price (San Francisco), Jerzy Semkov (Boston), Anja Silja (Chicago), Roger Soyer (Miami), Ludovic Spiess

Other -David Atherton (London), Agnes Baltsa (Frankfurt), Paul C. Crossley (tour), Edita Gruberová (Bratislava), Håkan Hagegård (Stockholm), Aage Haugland (Oslo), Gwynne Howell (London), Okko Kamu (Helsinki), Eva Marton (Budapest), Lajos Miller (Budapest), Trevor Pinnock (London), Rosalind Plowright (London), Stephen Preston (London), Eva Randová (Prague), Mstislav Rostropovich (Moscow, as conductor)

D. New Positions:

Conductors: Igor Buketoff (St. Paul Opera), Luciano Chailly (La Scala), Christoph von Dohnányi (Frankfurt Opera), Jean Fournet (Rotterdam PO), Lamberto Gardelli (Berne SO), Henry Lewis (New Jersey SO), Igor Markevitch (Monte Carlo Opera), Jean Martinon (French National SO), Václav Neumann (Czech PO), Michel Plasson (Toulouse SO), André Previn (London SO), Kenneth Schermerhorn (Milwaukee SO), Leif Segerstam (Swedish Royal Opera), Walter Susskind (St. Louis SO), Bryden Thomson (BBC PO)

Educational: Richard Franko Goldman (director, Peabody Institute), Jean Papineau-Couture (Dean of Music, Quebec Conservatory), Bernard Rands (experimental music, York University)

E. Prizes and Honors:

Prizes: Edward Auer (Queen Elisabeth), George Crumb (Pulitzer--*Echoes of Time and the River*), Miriam Fries (Paganini), François Huybrechts (Mitropoulos), Jean Kars (Messiaen), William Mathias (Bax), Jorge Mester (Naumberg), Jessye Norman (Munich), Garrick Ohlsson (Montreal), John Owings (Liszt), Vladimir Selivochin (Busoni), Michael Tilson Thomas (Koussevitsky)

Honors: Wyn Morris (Mahler Medal), Ben Nicholson (Order of Merit), Birgit Nilsson (Musician of the Year, *Musical America*), Krzystof Penderecki (Prix d'Italie), Roger Sessions (MacDowell Medal), Leopold Stokowski (Golden Baton)

F. Biographical Highlights:

Richard Cassilly makes his Covent Garden debut; Myung-Whun Chung arrives in New York and enters Mannes College; Alberto Ginastera visits in the U.S.; Hans Werner Henze's radical socialist music causes a scandal in Hamburg; Arpad Joó emigrates to the U.S.; Christopher Keene becomes assistant to Schippers in Spoleto; James King and Peter Schreier makes their La Scala debuts; Katia and Marielle Labèque take top prize at the Paris Conservatory; George London retires from active singing; James Morris transfers to Philadelphia Academy to study with Moscona; Jessye Norman receives her Master's degree and moves to Munich; Samuel Ramey graduates from Wichita State and tours with the Grass Roots Opera Co.; Andras Schiff enters Liszt Academy in Budapest; William Schuman suffers a mild heart attack and resigns his Lincoln Center post; Peter Serkin takes a long break from music and travels widely; Roger Sessions gives the Norton Lectures at Harvard; Maxim Shostakovich makes his Western conducting debut in London; Leonard Slatkin becomes assistant to Susskind in St. Louis.

G. Institutional Openings:

Performing Groups: Budapest Chamber Ensemble, Cleveland String Quartet, Connecticut String Quartet, Philip Glass Ensemble (N.Y.), Houston Civic SO, Liverpool Lieder Circle, London Sinfonietta, Montevideo Orchestra, Pro Cantione Antiqua (London), Saar Radio Chamber Orchestra, Scottish Baroque Ensemble (Edinburgh)

Festivals: Blossom Music Festival and Music Center (Ohio), Helsinki Music Festival

Educational: Centre International de Recherches Musicales (Paris), National Association of Jazz Educators (MENC)

Other: Atlanta Memorial Arts Center, Garden State Arts Center (New Jersey), International Electronic Music Competition, John F. Kennedy Theater (Fort Worth), Melchior Heldentenor Foundation, Montevideo International Piano Competition, National Arts

Centre (Ottawa), People to People Music Committee (Takoma Park), Powell Hall (St. Louis), San Antonio Theater for the Performing Arts, Santa Fe Opera House, Society of Black Composers, Virtuosi per Musica di Pianoforte (Czechoslovakia)

H. Musical Literature:

Boult, Adrian, *Handbook on...Conducting*
Cone, Edward, *Musical Form and Musical Performance*
Goldovsky, Boris, *Bringing Opera to Life*
Hines, Jerome, *This Is My Story, This Is My Song*
Kerman, Joseph, *A History of Art and Music*
Kohs, Ellis B., *Musical Form*
Lomax, Alan, *Folk Song Style and Culture*
Palisca, Claude, *Baroque Music*
Rorem, Ned, *Music and People*
Stuckenschmidt, H.H., *Twentieth Century Music*

I. Musical Compositions:

Amram, David, *Twelfth Night* (opera)
Arnold, Malcolm, *Symphony No. 6*
Babbitt, Milton, *Relata II* (orchestra)
Bennett, Richard R., *Symphony No. 2*
Berio, Luciano, *Sinfonia*
Blackwood, Easley, *Concerto for Flute and Orchestra*
Brian, Havergal, *Symphonies No. 31 and 32*
Creston, Paul, *Concerto for Two Pianos and Orchestra*
Crumb, George, Songs, *Drones and Refrains of Death*
Dallapiccola, Luigi, *Odysseus* (opera)
Davies, Peter M., *Taverner* (opera)
Egge, Klaus, *Symphony No. 4*
Feldman, Morton, *Vertical Thoughts II*
Ginastera, Alberto, *Concerto for Cello and Orchestra*
Hanson, Howard, *Symphony No. 6*
Harris, Roy, *Symphonies No. 11 and 12*
Henze, Hans Werner, *Concerto No. 2 for Piano and Orchestra*
          The Raft of the "Medusa" (oratorio)
Hovhaness, Alan, *Symphony No. 20*
Husa, Karel, *Music for Prague* (orchestra)
Lutoslawski, Witold, *Livre Pour Orchestre*
Malipiero, Gian F., *Concerto for Flute and Orchestra*
Menotti, Gian Carlo, *Help! Help! the Globolinks* (opera)
Penderecki, Krzystof, *String Quartet No. 2*
          Capriccio for Solo Cello
Reed, H. Owen, *The Turning Mind* (orchestra)
Rochberg, George, *Symphony No. 3*
Schuller, Gunther, *Concerto for Double Bass and Orchestra*
Sessions, Roger, *Symphony No. 8*
Shchedrin, Rodion, *Chimes* (orchestra)
Shostakovich, Dmitri, *String Quartet No. 12*
Stockhausen, Karlheinz, *Kurzwellen*
          Aus den Sieben Tagen
Subotnik, Morton, *The Wild Bull* (synthesizer)
Thomson, Virgil, *Lord Byron* (opera)
Walton, William, *Capriccio Burlesco* (orchestra)
Weisgall, Hugo, *Nine Rivers from Jordan* (opera)
Xenakis, Iannis, *Nomos Gamma*

1969

World Events:

In the U.S.,the *Apollo 11* flight puts the first men on the moon, Neil Armstrong and Edwin Aldrin; *Apollo 12* follows; General of the Armies and former President Dwight D. Eisenhower dies; the My Lai massacre in Vietnam is blamed on American troops--the U.S. begins a troop pullout in Vietnam; Yale University admits its first women students; Strategic Arms Limitations Talks (SALT) begins between representatives of the U.S. and Russia. Internationally, Charles de Gaulle resigns and Georges Pompidou is elected as French President; Golda Meir becomes Prime Minister of Israel; Willy Brandt becomes Chancellor of West Germany; the supersonic airliner, Concorde, is given its first trial flight; Yasir Arafat becomes the leader of the Palestine Liberation Organization.

Cultural Highlights:

Pulitzers: Drama, Howard Sackler (*The Great White Hope*); Fiction, N. Scott Momaday (*House Made of Dawn*); Poetry, George Oppen (*Of Being Numerous*). Samuel Beckett receives the Nobel Prize for Literature, Daphne du Maurier is made a Dame of the British Empire, poet John Betjeman is knighted and poet Sacheverell Sitwell is granted a baronet. Deaths in the art world include German architect Walter Gropius and artist Otto Dix, American artist Louis Bouché and Lithuanian artist Ben Shahn; deaths in the literary field include American novelist Jack Kerouac, British poet and novelist Osbert Sitwell and Polish poet Kazimierz Wierzynski. Other highlights include:

Art: Louise Bourgeois, *Cumul I*; Willem de Kooning, *Seated Woman*; Jim Dine, *Name Painting*; Dan Flavin, *Three` Sets of Tangented Arcs...*; Friberg, *Washington's Prayer at Valley Forge*; Ellsworth Kelly, *Thirteen Panels: Spectrum V*; Robert Rauschenberg, *Banner*; George Rickey, *Two Rectangles Gyratory*; Frank Stella, *River of Ponds II*.

Literature: John Cheever, *Bullet Park*; Michael Crichton, *The Andromeda Strain*; John Fowles, *The French Lieutenant's Woman*; Vladimir Nabokov, *Ada*; Lawrence J. Peter, *The Peter Principle*; Mario Puzo, *The Godfather*; Philip Roth, *Portnoy's Complaint*; John Updike, *Couples*; Kurt Vonnegut, *Slaughterhouse Five*.

MUSICAL EVENTS

A. Births:

Aug 30 Dimitrios Sgouros (Gr-pn)

B. Deaths:

Jan 4	Arthur Loesser (Am-pn)	Jul 8	Gladys Swarthout (Am-mez)
Jan 11	John Brownlee (Am-bar)	Jul 25	Heinrich Bessler (Ger-mus)
Jan 17	Vernon Duke (Rus-cm)	Jul 25	Douglas Moore (Am-cm)
Jan 27	Hanns Jelinek (Aus-cm)	Aug 6	Theodore Adorno (Ger-cri)
Feb 2	Giovanni Martinelli (It-ten)	Aug 11	Karl H. Wörner (Ger-mus)
Feb 20	Ernest Ansermet (Swi-cd)	Aug 31	William Flanagan (Am-cm)
Feb 23	Constantin Silvestri (Rom-cd)	Sep 13	Thomas Burke (Br-ten)
Apr 29	Julius Katchen (Am-pn)	Nov 18	Léon Jongen (Bel-pn)
May 17	Maria Olczewska (Ger-mez)	Dec 8	Higini Anglès (Sp-mus)
May 30	Carl Hartmann (Ger-ten)	Dec 24	Clarence Adler (Am-pn)
Jun 2	Reginald Jacques (Br-cd)	Dec 31	Salvatore Baccaloni (It-bs)
Jul 5	Wilhelm Backhaus (Am-pn)		

C. Débuts:

Met ---Theo Adam (bs), Elizabeth Anguish (sop), Richard Best (bs), Renato Bruson (bar), Carlo Franci (cd), Enrico di Giuseppe (ten), Edmond Karlsrud (bs), Pedro Lavirgen (ten), Octaviano Naghiu (ten), Rita Orlandi-Malaspina (sop)

U.S. --Arleen Augér (N.Y.), Aldo Ceccato (Chicago), Christoph von Dohnányi (Chicago), Carole Farley (N.Y.), Nelson Freire (N.Y.), Miriam Fried (N.Y.), Ani Kavafian (N.Y.), Patricia Kern (Dallas), Walter Klien (tour), Peter Lagger (San Francisco), Johanna Meier

(N.Y.), Carol Neblett (N.Y.), Nathaniel Rosen (Los Angeles), Pinchas Zukerman (N.Y.)

Other -Claes Ahnsjö (Stockholm), Thomas Allen (Cardiff), Francisco Araiza (Mexico City), Alice Artzt (London), Carlo Bini (Naples), Carrel A. Curry (Perth), Thomas Igloi (London), Gustav Kuhn (Salzburg), Jesús Lopez-Cobos (Prague), Jessye Norman (Berlin), Michala Petri (Copenhagen), Katia Ricciarelli (Mantua), Michael Rippon (London), Pascal Rogé (Paris), Matti Salminen (Helsinki), Sylvia Sebastiani (Rome)

D. New Positions:

Conductors: Sergiu Comissiona (Baltimore SO), Louis Frémaux (City of Birmingham SO), Michael Gielen (Belgian National SO), Milan Horvat (Austrian Radio SO), Marek Janowski (Hamburg Opera), Ferdinand Leitner (Zurich Opera), Neville Marriner (Los Angeles Chamber Orchestra), Riccardo Muti (Florence Maggio Musicale), Václav Neumann (Stuttgart Opera), Georg Solti (Chicago SO), William Steinberg (Boston SO)

Educational: Jorge Bolet (piano, Indiana University), Luciano Chailly (composition, Milan Conservatory), Mauricio Kagel (director, Institute of New Music, Cologne)

E. Prizes and Honors:

Prizes: Karel Husa (Pulitzer--*String Quartet No. 3*), Joseph Kalichstein (Leventritt), Okko Kamu (Karajan), Gidon Kremer (Paganini), Jesús Lopez-Cobos (Besançon), Radu Lupu (Leeds), Ursula Oppens (Busoni), Christina Ortiz (Cliburn), Kun-Woo Paik (Busoni), Vladimir Spivakov (Montreal), Lubov Timofeeva (Long-Thibaud)

Honors: Ulysses Kay (honorary doctorate, Arizona University), Peter Maag (Toscanini Medal)

F. Biographical Highlights:

John Adams graduates from Harvard; Vladimir Ashkenazy and his family move to Iceland; Leonard Bernstein is appointed Laureate Conductor of the New York PO; Jorge Bolet leaves Europe to begin teaching at Indiana University; Patricia Brooks, Jess Thomas and Tatiana Troyanos make their Covent Garden debuts; Placido Domingo makes his La Scala debut; Carlo Maria Giulini becomes Principle Guest Conductor of the Chicago SO; Hans Werner Henze spends a year teaching and doing research in Cuba; Lorin Maazel marries pianist Israela Margalit; Bruno Maderna makes his second visit to the U.S.; Howard Mitchell retires after 20 years conducting the National SO; Nadja Salerno-Sonnenberg is brought to the U.S. for further violin study; Joseph Schwantner transfers to Ball State University; José Serebrier marries soprano Carole Farley; Maria Stader retires from the concert stage; Michael Tilson Thomas becomes assistant to Steinberg in Boston; Ransom Wilson enters Juilliard; Ellen Taafe Zwillich marries Joseph Zwillich.

G. Institutional Openings:

Performing Groups: Austrian Broadcast SO, Chamber Music Society of Lincoln Center (N.Y.), Dance Theater of Harlem (N.Y.), Janus Chorale of New York, Kent Opera Co. (Ohio), Light Opera of Manhattan, London Consort of Musicke, Los Angeles Chamber Orchestra, National Arts Centre Orchestra (Ottawa), Opéra de Lyon (France), Purcell String Quartet (Vancouver), Tokyo String Quartet, Vermeer String Quartet

Festivals: Dublin Festival of Twentieth Century Music, New England Bach Festival, Newport Music Festival (Rhode Island)

Educational: International Society for Jazz Research (Graz), National Opera Institute (Washington, D.C.), Scottish Music Archive (Glasgow)

Other: Asian Music Forum (UNESCO), Belwin-Mills Corporation (by merger), Century II Concert Hall (Wichita), Cultural Center of the Philippines, Danish Society for Music Therapy, Dresden Palace of Culture, Karajan Foundation (Berlin), Lyons Concert Hall (York), Milwaukee Performing Arts Center, Nederlands Congresgebouw (The Hague)

H. Musical Literature:

Backus, John, *The Acoustical Foundations of Music*
Berry, Walter, *Eighteenth Century...Counterpoint*
Cage, John, *Notations*
Craft, Robert, *Retrospections and Conclusions*
Hitchcock, H. Wiley, *Music in the United States*
Howes, Frank, *Folk Music of Britain and Beyond*
Longyear, Rey, *Nineteenth Century Romanticism in Music*
Molnár, Antal, *The World of the Composer*
Newman, William, *The Sonata since Beethoven*
Reed, H.O./Leach, J., *Scoring for Percussion*

I. Musical Compositions:

Barber, Samuel, *Despite and Still* (song cycle)
Bassett, Leslie, *Colloquy for Orchestra*
Berio, Luciano, *Sequenza VII* (oboe)
          Opera (opera)
Blacher, Boris, *200,000 Thaler* (opera)
Brown, Earle, *Syntagm III*
Cage, John, *HPSCHD* (multi-media event with L. Hiller)
Carter, Elliott, *Concerto for Orchestra*
Charpentier, Jacques, *Symphony No. 3, "Shiva Nataraja"*
Chávez, Carlos, *Discovery* (orchestra)
          Fuego Olimpico Suite (orchestra)
Colgrass, Michael, *New People* (song cycle)
Creston, Paul, *The Northwest* (chorus and orchestra)
Crumb, George, *Madrigals, Books III and IV*
          Night of the Four Moons
Davies, Peter M., *Eight Songs for a Mad King*
Del Tredici, David, *Lobster-Quadrille* (ballet)
Egge, Klaus, *Symphony No. 5*
Egk, Werner, *Casanova in London* (ballet)
Erb, Donald, *The Seventh Trumpet* (orchestra)
Foss, Lukas, *Geod* (orchestra)
Harris, Roy, *Symphony No. 13*
Henze, Hans Werner, *Versuch über Schweine*
          Symphony No. 6
Hétu, Pierre, *Concerto for Piano and Orchestra*
Kabalevsky, Dmitri, *Sisters* (opera)
Kirchner, Leon, *Music for Orchestra*
Maderna, Bruno, *Concerto for Violin and Orchestra*
Messiaen, Olivier, *Meditations sur le Mystère de la Sainte-Trinité* (organ)
Mennin, Peter, *The Pied Piper of Hamelin* (cantata)
Musgrave, Thea, *Beauty and the Beast* (ballet)
Penderecki, Krzystof, *The Devils of Loudon* (opera)
Quintanar, Hector, *Sideral II* (orchestra)
Schuman, William, *Symphony No. 9, "Le Fosse Ardeatine"*
Searle, Humphrey, *Hamlet* (opera)
Shostakovich, Dmitri, *Symphony No. 14*
Stockhausen, Karlheinz, *Fresco* (4 orchestral groups)
Takemitsu, Toru, *Asterism* (piano and orchestra)
Wuorinen, Charles, *Time's Encomium*
Xenakis, Iannis, *Anaktoria*
          Kraanerg (ballet)
          Synaphai (piano and orchestra)

1970

World Events:
The U.S. Census shows a population of 203,810,000, only a 1.2% increase; the Omnibus Crime Control Act is passed by Congress; student riots take place on Kent State University campus; AMTRAK is formed by congressional action; the Post Office Department is replaced by the Postal Service; Kenneth Gibson becomes the first black mayor of a major city, Newark, New Jersey. Internationally, Martial Law is invoked in Quebec following terrorist attacks; President Nassar dies and Anwar Sadat becomes President of Egypt; the Aswan Dam on the Nile is finished; Edward Heath becomes British Prime Minister; former French President Charles de Gaulle dies; Japan and China both put satellites into orbit; the Soviet spacecraft *Venera 7* sends data back from an extremely hot Venusian surface.

Cultural Highlights:
Pulitzers: Drama, Charles Gordone (*No Place to Be Somebody*); Fiction, Jean Stafford (*Collected Stories*); Poetry, Richard Howard (*Untitled Subjects*). The Nobel Prize for Literature goes to Alexander Solzhenitsyn while Noel Coward is knighted and dramatist Eugène Ionesco is admitted to the French Academy. Deaths include American artist Barnett Newman, Russian artist Mark Rothko and German artist Erich Heckel; in the literary field, American novelist John Dos Passos, French novelist François Mauriac, German novelist Erich Remarque and poet Nelly Sachs, British novelist E.M. Forster and Polish author Shmuel Yosef Agnon. Other highlights include:

Art: Ilya Bolotowsky, *Elongated Diamond*; Fernando Botero, *The Coffee Break;* Richard Estes, *Escalator*; Red Grooms, *The Discount Store*; Edward Hicks, *Fugue Rothschild*; Ellsworth Kelly, *Blue/Green*; Edward Kienholz, *Roxy's*; Henry Moore, *Square Form with Cut*; Mark Rothko, *Black on Grey;* Andrew Wyeth, *Indian Summer*.

Literature: *The New English Bible: Old Testament*; Simone de Beauvoir, *The Coming of Age*; Saul Bellow, *Mr. Sammler's Planet*; James Dickey, *Deliverance;* William Saroyan, *Days of Life and Death*; Erich Segal, *Love Story*; Irwin Shaw, *Rich Man, Poor Man*; Alvin Toffler, *Future Shock*; Leon Uris, *QB VII*.

MUSICAL EVENTS

B. Deaths:

Jan 5	Roberto Gerhard (Sp-cm)	Jul 29	Jonel Perlea (Cz-cd)
Jan 25	Jane Bathori (Fr-sop)	Jul 30	George Szell (Hun-cd)
Feb 12	André Souris (Bel-mus)	Aug 7	Ingolf Dahl (Ger-cm)
Feb 19	Edmund Burke (Can-bs)	Aug 10	Bernd Zimmerman (Ger-cm)
Feb 19	Pavel Ludikar (Aus-bs)	Aug 22	Richard Donovan (Am-cm)
Feb 20	Marta Krásová (Cz-sop)	Oct 4	George F. McKay (Am-cm)
Feb 20	Albert Wolff (Fr-cd)	Oct 13	Julia Culp (Hol-sop)
Feb 26	Ethel Leginska (Br-pn)	Oct 22	Pauline Donalda (Br-sop)
Mar 5	Werner Danckert (Ger-mus)	Oct 22	Samson François (Fr-pn)
Apr 10	Michel Piastro (Rus-vn-cd)	Dec 23	Mimi Benzell (Am-sop)
Apr 12	Kerstin Thorborg (Swe-sop)	Dec 31	Cyril Scott (Br-cm)
Apr 30	Hall Johnson (Am-cd)		Saul Caston (Am-cd)
May 15	Hans Engel (Ger-mus)		Kathryn Meisle (Am-alto)
Jul 28	John Barbirolli (Br-cd)		

C. Débuts:
Met ---Serge Baudo (cd), Judith Blegen (sop), Helge Brilioth (ten), Nico Castel (ten), Dominic Cossa (bar), Gilda Cruz-Romo (sop), Andrij Dobriansky (bs), Marilyn Horne (mez), Jean Kraft (mez), Leopold Ludwig (cd), Hermann Marcus (bs), Edith Mathis (sop), Ruggero Raimondi (bs), Gail Robinson (sop), Elinor Ross (sop), Ursula Schröder-Feinen (sop), Stanislaw Skrowaczewski (cd), Frederica von Stade (mez), Franco Tagliavini (ten), Ivo Vinco (bs), Carol Wilcox (sop)

U.S. --Viorica Cortez (Chicago), Ryland Davies (San Francisco), Brigitte Fassbaender (San Francisco), Alexander Gibson (Detroit), Daniel Heifetz (N.Y.), Carolyne James (St. Paul), Antonin Kubalek (N.Y.), Benno Kusche, Susanne Marsee (N.Y.), Yvonne Minton (Chicago), Garrick Ohlsson (N.Y.), Neva Pilgrim (N.Y.), Carol Rosenberger (N.Y.), Richard Stilwell (N.Y.), Pauline Tinsley (N.Y.), Alan Titus (Washington, D.C.), Helen Watts (N.Y.), Ruth Welting (N.Y.)

Other -Daniel Adni (London), Eduardo Alvares (Linz), Anne-Marie Antoine (Anvers), Gabriela Benacková (Prague), Norma Burrowes (Glyndebourne), Teresa Cahil (Glyndebourne), José Carreras (Barcelona), Andrew Davis (London), Edith Guillaume (Jutland), Michael Halász (Gelsenkirchen), Jorma Hynninen (Helsinki), Zoltán Kocsis (Budapest), Lucia Valentini (Mantua), Robert R. Woodward (London)

D. New Positions:

Conductors: Karel Ancerl (Toronto So), Anshel Brusilow (Dallas SO), Antal Dorati (National SO), Piero Gamba (Winnipeg SO), Charles Mackerras (Sadler's Wells), Kurt Masur (Leipzig Gewandhaus), Eduardo Mata (Phoenix SO), Lovro von Matacic (Zagreb PO), Seiji Ozawa (San Francisco SO), Brian Priestman (Denver SO), Thomas Schippers (Cincinnati SO)

Educational: Henri Dutilleux (composition, Paris Conservatory), Peter Fricker (music chairman, University of California), Joseph Schwantner (composition, Eastman), Richard Stolzman (California Institute of the Arts)

Others: Robert Collinge (President, Opera America), Simon Preston (organ, Oxford)

E. Prizes and Honors:

Prizes: Dmitri Alexeev (Enescu), Pierre Amoyal (Enescu), Ralph Kirshbaum (Tchaikovsky), Vladimir Krainev (Tchaikovsky), Gidon Kremer (Tchaikovsky), Yevgeni Nesterenko (Tchaikovsky), Elena Obraztsova (Tchaikovsky), Garrick Ohlsson (Chopin), Katia Ricciarelli (Parma), Gunther Schuller (Ditson), Charles Wuorinen (Pulitzer--*Time's Ecomium*)

Honors: Beverly Sills (Musician of the Year, *Musical America*)

F. Biographical Highlights:

Emanuel Ax becomes a U.S. citizen and graduates from Columbia with a degree in French; Agnes Baltsa makes her Vienna Opera debut; Semyon Bychkov enters Leningrad Conservatory; Richard Cassilly and Adriana Maliponte make their La Scala debuts; Clamma Dale graduates from Juilliard; Alberto Ginastera moves to Europe; Horacio Gutiérrez and Vladimir Spivakov win Silver Medals in the Tchaikovsky Competition; Christopher Keene debuts at the New York City Opera; István Kertész is voted in by the members of the Cleveland Orchestra as conductor but the board hires Lorin Maazel; Mischa Maisky is arrested and imprisoned in Russia; Thea Musgrave accepts an invitation to teach a term at the University of California in Santa Barbara; Allan Pettersson spends nine months in a Stockholm Hospital; André Previn marries his third wife, actress Mia Farrow; Steve Reich goes to Africa to study native drumming; Martti Talvela makes his Covent Garden debut; Mitsuko Uchida places second in the Chopin Competition.

G. Institutional Openings:

Performing Groups: Bangkok Opera (Thailand), William Byrd Singers (Manchester), Cincinnati Ballet Co., Detroit Symphony Youth Orchestra, Grupo de Acción Instrumental de Buenos Aires, Jeunesses Musicales World Orchestra (Montreal), The King's Singers (London), Liverpool Sinfonia, Manhattan String Quartet, New Irish Chamber Orchestra (Dublin), L'Opéra de Quebec, Opera Rara (London), Philharmonia Chorale (Cleveland), Tanglewood Festival Chorus (Massachusetts), Welsh Philharmonia (Cardiff)

Festivals: International Electro-Acoustic Music Festival (Bourges, France), Kuhmo Chamber Music Festival (Finland), Nottingham Festival (England)

Educational: Centre de Recherches Musicales de Wallonie (Belgium), Rijksmusiekacademie

(Antwerp), Saratoga-Potsdam Choral Institute (Crane School)

Other: ARP Instruments (Maine), *The Canada Music Book, Composium, Music Cataloguing Bulletin,* Norwegian Cultural Council Prize, Opera America, Puget Music Publications (Seattle), *Quanta* (Mexico)

H. Musical Literature:

Bliss, Arthur, *As I Remember*
Creston, Paul, *Creative Harmony*
Frankenstein, Alfred, *Modern Guide to Symphonic Music*
Helm, Everett, *Composer, Performer, Public: A Study in Communication*
Honegger, Marc, *Dictionnaire de la Musique I*
Landon, H.C. Robbins, *Essays on the Viennese Classical Style*
Persichetti, Vincent, *Twentieth Century Orchestral Music*
Rorem, Ned, *Critical Affairs: A Composer's Journal*
Schonberg, Harold, *Lives of the Great Composers*
Sessions, Roger, *Questions about Music*

I. Musical Compositions:

Bazelon, Irwin, *Symphony No. 6*
Blacher, Boris, *Concerto for Trumpet and Orchestra*
Bliss, Arthur, *Concerto for Cello and Orchestra*
Boulez, Pierre, *Multiples* (orchestra)
Britten, Benjamin, *Owen Wingrave* (opera)
Chávez, Carlos, *Clio* (symphonic ode)
Crumb, George, *Black Angels*
   Ancient Voices of Children
Dello Joio, Norman, *Evocations* (chorus and orchestra)
Druckman, Jacob, *Orison*
Dutilleux, Henri, *Concerto for Cello and Orchestra*
Feldman, Morton, *Madam Press Died Last Week at 90* (orchestra)
Floyd, Carlisle, *Of Mice and Men* (opera)
Foss, Lukas, *MAP* (5 instruments)
Françaix, Jean, *Concerto for Violin and Orchestra*
Henze, Hans Werner, *El Cimarrón* (baritone, flute, guitar, percussion)
Hovhaness, Alan, *And God Created Great Whales*
Imbrie, Andrew, *Symphony No. 3*
Lutoslawski, Witold, *Concerto for Cello and Orchestra*
Malipiero, Gian F., *Symphony No. 11, "Dalla Cornamuse"*
Mennin, Peter, *Sinfonia for Large Orchestra*
Menotti, Gian Carlo, *Triple Concerto*
Messiaen, Olivier, *La Transfiguration* (oratorio)
Penderecki, Krzystoff, *Kosmogonia*
Persichetti, Vincent, *Creation* (oratorio)
Pinkham, Daniel, *Concerto for Organ and Orchestra*
Rorem, Ned, *Piano Concerto in Seven Movements*
Schuman, William, *In Praise of Shahn* (orchestra)
Sessions, Roger, *Rhapsody for Orchestra*
   When Lilacs Last in the Dooryard Bloom'd
Shostakovich, Dmitri, *String Quartet No. 13*
Siegmeister, Elie, *Symphony No. 4*
Stockhausen, Karlheinz, *Beethausen, Opus 1970, von Stockhoven*
Subotnick, Morton, *Sidewinder*
Tippett, Michael, *The Knot Garden* (opera)
Wuorinen, Charles, *Ringing Changes for Percussion*

1971

World Events:

In the U.S., the Twenty Sixth Ammendment lowers the voting age to 18; the Pentagon Papers are published and Daniel Ellsberg is indicted; *Mariner 9* orbits Mars; the U.S. blockades North Vietnam; the U.S. Table Tennis Team become the first Americans to enter China since the 1950's; cigarette advertisements are banned from T.V. Internationally, a bloody Civil War separates Bangladesh (East Pakistan) from West Pakistan; the island of Taiwan (Republic of China) is expelled from the United Nations and Communist China is admitted; Idi Amin, in a bloody coup, seizes power in Uganda; the African Congo changes its name to Zaire; the Soviets land two space probes on Mars; an entire tribe of Stone Age people is discovered in the Phillipines.

Cultural Highlights:

Pulitzers: Drama, Paul Zindel (*The Effect of Gamma Rays on Man-in-the-Moon Marigolds*); Poetry, William S. Merwin (*The Carrier of Ladders*). The Nobel Prize for Literature goes to Chilean poet Pablo Neruda; John Betjeman is named British Poet Laureate; Russian-born sculptor Naum Gabo and playwright Terence Rattigan are knighted; the Walker Art Center opens in Minneapolis. Deaths include American humorist and poet Ogden Nash and Greek politician and poet George Seferis. Other highlights include:

Art: Fernando Botero, *The Military Junta*; Roy Lichtenstein, *Mirror No. 3*: Malcolm Morley, *Los Angeles Yellow Pages*; Louise Nevelson, *Night Presence IV*; George Rickey, *Ten Rotors, Ten Cubes, Variation II*; Jack Tworkov, *Partitions*; Vuillard Vicente, *Afternoon*; Tom Wesselmann, *Big Brown Nude*; Andrew Wyeth, *The Kuerners*.

Literature: *The Living Bible, Paraphrased*; James P. Donleavy, *The Onion Eaters*; Edward Forster, *Maurice*; John W. Gardner, *Grendel;* Bernard Malamud, *The Tenants*; Walker Percy, *Love in the Ruins;* Harold Robbins, *The Betsy*; Alexander Solzhenitsyn, *August, 1914*; John Updike, *Rabbit Redux*; Yevgeny Yevtushenko, *Stolen Apples*.

MUSICAL EVENTS

B. Deaths:

Jan 8	Paul Nettl (Am-mus)	Jun 16	George Copeland (Am-pn)
Jan 18	Warwick Braithwaite (Br-cd)	Jun 24	Hans Mersmann (Ger-mus)
Feb 21	Adolph Weiss (Am-bar-cm)	Jun 25	Mignon Nevada (Fr-sop)
Mar 6	Thurston Dart (Br-mus)	Jul 2	Bernhard Paumgartner (Aus-mus)
Mar 17	Piero Coppola (It-cd)	Jul 6	Louis Armstrong (Am-pop)
Mar 24	Margarethe Arndt-Ober	Jul 24	Alan Rawsthorne (Br-cm)
	(Ger-alto)	Jul 25	Leroy Robertson (Am-cm)
Mar 31	Karl L. King (Am-band)	Aug 6	Fausto Cleva (It-cd)
Apr 6	Igor Stravinsky (Rus-cm)	Oct 21	Herbert Weinstock (Am-mus)
Apr 17	Pierre Luboshutz (Rus-pn)	Oct 24	Phillip Wylie (Am-cm)
May 19	Bernard Wagenaar (Hol-cm)	Oct 24	Carl Ruggles (Am-cm)
May 30	Marcel Dupré (Fr-org)	Dec 19	André d'Arker (Bel-ten)

C. Débuts:

Met ---Jeannine Altmeyer (sop), Klara Barlow (sop), Stuart Burrows (ten), Frank Coffey (bs), Viorica Cortez (mez), Gerd Feldhoff (bar), Lorraine Keane (mez), Christopher Keene (cd), Tom Krause (bar), Benno Kusche (bar), James Levine (cd), Catarina Ligendza (sop), Adriana Maliponte (sop), Matteo Manuguerra (bar), James Morris (bs), Joyce Olson (mez), Gabor Otvös (cd), John Pritchard (cd), Ludovic Spiess (ten), Michelangelo Veltri (cd)

U.S. --James Atherton (San Francisco), Agnes Baltsa (Houston), Joan Carden (Houston), Helga Dernesch (Dallas), Helen Donath (San Francisco), Michael Gielen (N.Y.), James Kreger (N.Y.), Teresa Kubiak (Chicago), Cristina Ortiz (N.Y.), Hans Sotin (Chicago),

Eugenia Zukerman (N.Y.), Pinchas Zukermann (N.Y., as conductor)

Other -Hildegard Behrens (Osnabrück), Myung-Whun Chung (Seoul), Robert Cohen (London), Alexandra Hunt (Milan), John Mills (London), Felicity Palmer (Kent), Anne Shasby (Moscow), Howard Shelley (London), Robert Tear (London), Sarah Walker (Glyndebourne)

D. New Positions:

Conductors: Claudio Abbado (Vienna Opera), Pierre Boulez (New York PO), Henryk Czyz (Düsseldorf SO), Colin Davis (Covent Garden), Lukas Foss (Brooklyn PO), Lawrence Foster (Houston SO), Donald Johanos (Pittsburgh SO), Okko Kamu (Finnish Radio SO), Christopher Keene (New York City Opera), James Loughran (Halle Orchestra), Wolfgang Sawallisch (Bavarian Opera), Michael Tilson Thomas (Buffalo PO)

Educational: John Adams (composition, San Francisco Conservatory), Ivan Davis (piano, Indiana University), Henri Pousseur (composition, Liège Conservatory), Eleanor Steber (voice, Juilliard)

Others: George London (director, National Opera Institute)

E. Prizes and Honors:

Prizes: Maurice Abravanel (Ditson), Myung-Wha Chung (Geneva), Mario Davidovsky (Pulitzer--*Synchronisms No. 6*), Yuri Egorov (Thibaud), Vladimir Feltsman (Long-Thibaud), Miriam Fried (Queen Elisabeth), Mayumi Fujikawa (Vieuxtemps), Thomas Igloi (Casals), Ani Kavafian (Naumberg), Kun-Woo Paik (Naumberg), Pascal Rogé (Long-Thibaud), Harold C. Schonberg (Pulitzer for Music Criticism), Robert Suderberg (Naumberg)

Honors: Rudolf Bing (knighted), Geraint Evans (knighted), Ingrid Haebler (Mozart Medal), William Schuman (MacDowell Medal), William Grant Still (honorary doctorate, University of Arkansas), Michael Tilson Thomas (Musician of the Year, *Musical America*)

F. Biographical Highlights:

Kathleen Battle graduates from the University of Cincinnati Conservatory of Music and begins teaching grade school; Myung-Wha Chung becomes a naturalized American citizen; James DePreist is called back to the U.S. to be associate conductor of the National SO; Alberto Ginastera marries his second wife, cellist Aurora Nátola; Lynn Harrell leaves the Cleveland SO after six years and begins his solo career as a cellist; Margaret Harris, conducting the Chicago SO, becomes the first black woman to lead a major orchestra; Eduardo Mata becomes Principle Guest Conductor of the Phoenix SO; Darius Milhaud resigns from his teaching at Mills College due to severity of his arthritis; Thea Musgrave marries American violist Peter Mark; Jan Peerce moves over to Broadway to appear in *Fiddler on the Roof*; Nadja Salerno-Sonnenberg, age 10, performs at children's concert with the Philadelphia Orchestra; Giuseppe Sinopoli receives a diploma in psychiatry and medicine from the University of Padua and begins a short practice; Georg Solti takes the Chicago SO on a European tour; Isaac Stern's film about his visit to China, *From Mao to Mozart*, wins an Academy Award; Klaus Tennstedt, having his passport stamped with the wrong stamp by a Russian official, chooses to stay in the West; Charles Wuorinen is denied tenure at Columbia University after seven years of teaching.

G. Institutional Openings:

Performing Groups: Annapolis Brass Quintet, Arizona Opera Co. (Phoenix), Concord String Quartet (N.Y.), Empire Brass Quintet (Berkshire), Houston Pops Orchestra, Michigan Opera Theater, National Arts Centre Festival Opera (Ottawa), New Prague Trio, Opera/South (Jackson, Mississippi), Orquesta Sinfonica del Estado del Mexico, Philadelphia Singers, Speculum Musicae (N.Y.), Vancouver Chamber Choir

Festivals: Banff Festival of the Arts, Chamber Music Northwest Summer Festival (Portland, Oregon)

Educational: Institute for Studies in American Music (N.Y.), Wolf Trap Farm for the

Performing Arts (Vienna, Virginia)

Other: Adlam-Burnett, Keyboard Maker (London); American Musical Instrument Society (N.Y.), Jerusalem Theater, John F. Kennedy Center for the Performing Arts (Washington, D.C.), *Komponist und Musikerzieher, Mitteilungsblatt der Internationalen Bruckner-Gesellschaft*, Power Center for the Performing Arts (University of Michigan), Repertoire International d'Iconographie Musicale

H. Musical Literature:
Adorno, Theodor, *Gesammelte Schriften I*
Ewen, David, *New Encyclopedia of the Opera*
Hába, Alois, *Mein Weg zur Viertel- und Sechsteltonmusik*
Lang, Paul H., *Critic at the Opera*
Molnár, Antal, *Practical Music Aesthetics*
Myers, Rollo, *Modern French Music*
Southern, Eileen, *The Music of Black Americans*
         Readings in Black American Music
Thomson, Virgil, *American Music since 1910*
Westrup, Jack A., *Musical Interpretation*

I. Musical Compositions:
Adler, Samuel, *Concerto for Orchestra*
Akutagawa, Yasushi, *Rhapsody for Orchestra*
Argento, Dominick, *Letters from Composers* (voice and guitar)
Barber, Samuel, *The Lovers* (cantata)
Berio, Luciano, *Memory* (electronic piano and harpsichord)
Bernstein, Leonard, *Mass* (theater piece)
Blacher, Boris, *Concerto for Clarinet and Orchestra*
Britten, Benjamin, *Canticle No. 4, "Journey of the Magi"*
Carter, Elliott, *String Quartet No. 3*
Creston, Paul, *Thanatopsis* (orchestra)
Crumb, George, *Lux Aeterna*
Druckman, Jacob, *Synapse* (tape)
Einem, Gottfried von, *Bruckner Dialogue*
         Der Besuch der Alten Dame (opera)
Feldman, Morton, *Chorus and Orchestra I*
Ginastera, Alberto, *Beatrix Cenci* (opera)
Hamilton, Iain, *Amphion* (violin and orchestra)
Henze, Hans Werner, *The Tedious Way to the Apartment of Natasha Ungeheuer* (opera)
         Concerto No. 2 for Violin and Orchestra
Hoiby, Lee, *Summer and Smoke* (opera)
Holmboe, Vagn, *Symphony No. 10*
Maderna, Bruno, *Juilliard Serenade*
Mayer, William, *Octagon* (piano and orchestra)
Menotti, Gian Carlo, *The Most Important Man* (opera)
Musgrave, Thea, *Concerto for Horn and Orchestra*
Penderecki, Krzystof, *De Natura Sonoris II* (orchestra)
         Utrenja (soloists, chorus and orchestra)
Persichetti, Vincent, *Symphony No. 9, "Janiculum"*
Reed, H. Owen, *The Touch of the Earth*
Rubbra, Edmund, *Symphony No. 8*
Sessions, Roger, *Concerto for Violin, Cello and Orchestra*
Shostakovich, *Symphony No. 15, Opus 141*
Stockhausen, Karlheinz, *Sternklang*
Stout, Alan, *Symphony No. 4*
Takemitsu, Toru, *Winter* (orchestra)
Williamson, Malcolm, *The Stone Wall* (opera)

1972

World Events:
In the U.S., Richard M. Nixon is re-elected as President and makes a succesful visit to Red China; the Watergate affair begins with the arrest of five men for breaking into the Democratic headquarters in the Watergate Hotel in Washington, D.C.; Selective Service comes to an end; the Supreme Court rules out the death penalty; Georgia governor George Wallace is shot while campaigning for President, and permanently crippled in an assassination attempt. Internationally, Great Britain and Denmark are admitted to the European Common Market; Ceylon changes its name to Sri Lanka; Arab terrorists take hostages at the Munich Olympic Games and 13 Israelis die in the rescue attempt; the Winter Olympics take place in Sapporo, Japan; separate earthquakes kill 5000 people in Iran and 12,000 in Nicaragua.

Cultural Highlights:
Pulitzers: Fiction, Wallace Stegner (*Angle of Repose*); Poetry, James Wright (*Collected Poems*). The Nobel Prize for Literature goes to the German author Heinrich Boll; the Marc Chagall Museum opens in Nice. Deaths include American author Mark Van Doren and poets Marianne Moore, Kenneth Patchen and Ezra Pound, French poet and novelist Jules Romain, Italian author Dino Buzzati and American artist John Berryman. Other highlights include:

Art: Ilya Bolotowsky, *Diamond with Yellow and Orange*; Fernando Botero, *Fruit Basket*; Chryssa, *Automat*; Willem de Kooning, *Clam Digger*; David Hockney, *Panama Hat*; Alex Katz, *Face of a Poet*; Lee Krasner, *Rising Green*; Roy Lichtenstein, *Still Life with Goldfish*; Georgia O'Keeffe, *Black Rock, Blue Sky*; Andrew Wyeth, *Black Water*.

Literature: Louis Auchincloss, *I Come as a Thief*; W.H. Auden, *Epistle to a Godson*; Michael Crichton, *The Terminal Man*; John W. Gardner, *The Sunlight Dialogues*; James Herriot, *All Creatures Great and Small*; Harold Pinter, *Old Times*; Chaim Potok, *My Name Is Asher Lev*; Irving Wallace, *The Ward*; Eudora Welty, *The Optimist's Daughter*.

MUSICAL EVENTS

B. Deaths:

Jan 19	Michael Rabin (Am-vn)		Jul 18	Goeran Gentele (Swe-imp)
Jan 20	Jean Casadesus (Fr-pn)		Jul 22	Hugo Kauder (Aus-cm-the)
Jan 30	Karel Jirák (Cz-cm-cd)		Jul 27	Helen Traubel (Am-sop)
Jan 31	Howard Barlow (Am-cd)		Aug 2	Rudolf Ganz (Swi-pn-ed)
Mar 1	Victor Babin (Rus-pn)		Aug 14	Oscar Levant (Am-pn)
Mar 1	Vladimir Golschman (Fr-cd)		Aug 28	René Leibowitz (Fr-cm-the)
Mar 2	Erna Sack (Ger-sop)		Sep 19	Robert Casadesus (Fr-pn)
Apr 3	Ferde Grofé (Am-cm-arr)		Sep 29	Richard Crooks (Am-ten)
Apr 4	Stefan Wolpe (Am-cm)		Nov 12	Rudolf Friml (Cz-cm)
Jun 21	Seth Bingham (Am-cm-ed)		Nov 28	Havergal Brian (Br-cm)
Jul 9	Robert Weede (Am-bar)		Nov 30	Hans E. Apostel (Ger-cm)
Jul 10	Jean Madeira (Am-alto)			

C. Débuts:
Met ---Peter Adler (ten), Atsuko Azuma (sop), Christoph von Dohnányi (cd), Giovanni Gibin (ten), Rita Hunter (sop), Gwyneth Jones (sop), Kazimierz Kord (cd) Henry Lewis (cd), Peter Maag (cd), Charles Mackerras (cd), Barry McDaniel (bar), Johanna Meier (sop), Gustav Neidlinger (bar), Betsy Norden (sop), Louis Quilico (bar), Anja Silja (sop), Monica Sinclair (mez), Hans Sotin (bs), Roger Soyer (bs), Ragnar Ulfung (ten), Elizabeth Vaughan (sop), Christine Weidinger (sop)

U.S. --José Carreras (N.Y.), Anne Howells (Chicago), Hana Janku, Jesús Lopez-Cobos (San Francisco), James Loughran (N.Y.), Radu Lupu (Cleveland), Zdenek Macal (Chicago), Catherine Malfitano (N.Y.), Michael Ponti (N.Y.), Riccardo Muti (Philadelphia), Katia

Ricciarelli (Chicago), Paul Schenly (Cleveland), Jocelyne Taillon, Sandra Walker (San Francisco), Carol Wincenc

Other -Pierre Amoyal (Paris), Lawrence Amundrud (Saskatoon), Peter Barcza (Canada), Kathleen Battle (Spoleto), Paavo Berglund (Bournemouth), Angela East (London), Nina Fomina (Moscow), Peter Hofmann (Lübeck), Graham Johnson (London), Christopher Kite (London), Stefka Mineva (Bulgaria), Michael Murray (Holland), Katherine Pring (London), Caspar Richter (Berlin), Sylvia Sass (Budapest), Andras Schiff (Budapest), Julian Lloyd Webber (London)

D. New Positions:

Conductors: Gerd Albrecht (Berlin Opera), Jiri Belohlávek (State PO, Brno), Paavo Berglund (Bournemouth SO), Peter Eros (San Diego SO), Peter Maag (Parma Opera), Lorin Maazel (Cleveland Orchestra), Horst Stein (Hamburg Opera), Klaus Tennstedt (Kiel Opera), Kari Tikka (Finnish Radio SO), Silvio Varviso (Stuttgart Opera), Akeo Watanabe (Tokyo Metro SO)

Educational: Yehudi Menuhin (President, Trinity College of Music), Krzystof Penderecki (Rector, Krakow Conservatory)

Others: Schuyler Chapin (general manager, Met), Michael Gielen (music director, Netherlands Opera), Edward Water (Music, Library of Congress)

E. Prizes and Honors:

Prizes: Valery Afanassiev (Brussels), Arnaldo Cohen (Busoni), Luigi Dallapiccola (Honegger), Robert Davidovici (Naumberg), Jacob Druckman (Pulitzer--*Windows*), Eugene Fodor (Paganini), Barbara Hendricks (Paris), Alexander Lazarev (Karajan), Krzystof Penderecki (Charpentier), Murray Perahia (Leeds), Edith Tremblay (Paris)

Honors: Gerald Abraham (Royal Academy), Paavo Berglund (Finnish State Prize), Pierre Boulez (Musician of the Year, *Musical America*), Margaret Hillis (honorary doctorate, Indiana University), Georg Solti (knighted)

F. Biographical Highlights:

Roberta Alexander takes up permanent residence in the Netherlands; Luciano Berio leaves the U.S. to return to Italy; Joseph Brodsky leaves Russia by state invitation; Renato Bruson and Kurt Moll make their La Scala debuts; Maria Chiara marries bass Antonio Cassinelli; James Conlon, a senior at Juilliard, is called upon to substitute conduct for Thomas Schippers; Colin Davis becomes Principle Guest Conductor of the Boston SO; Susan Dunn enters an Arkansas College to study English; Donald Grobe makes his Covent Garden debut; Irene Gubrud passes the Met auditions but is denied a role because of her paralysis; Jascha Heifetz retires from active concert life; Milton Katims takes the Seattle SO on a concert tour of Alaska; Otto Klemperer retires from the conducting podium; Henry Lewis becomes the first black to conduct at the Met; Cho-Liang Lin goes to Australia to the Sydney Conservatory to study; Samuel Ramey is a finalist in the Met auditions; Simon Rattle studies conducting with Boulez; Gerard Schwarz joins the New York PO as trumpeter; Peter Sculthorpe is composer-in-residence at Yale for a year; Alexander Toradze enters Moscow Conservatory; Egon Wellesz suffers a stroke; Ellen Taafe Zwillich enters Juilliard.

G. Institutional Openings:

Performing Groups: Éder String Quartet (Budapest), Hartford Chorale, Manchester Camerata, New York Lyric Opera Co., Orpheus (New York Chamber Orchestra), Sequoia String Quartet, Tucson Opera Co., West Virginia Opera Theater (Charleston), Whitewater Opera Co. (Richmond, Indiana)

Festivals: Des Moines Metro Festival, Sitka Summer Music Festival (Alaska)

Educational: Conservatorio Nacional de Música (Venezuela), Musical Arts Center (Indiana University), Royal Northern College of Music, Manchester (by amalgamation).

Other: Affiliate Artists' Exxon/Arts Endowment Conductors Program (N.Y.), Arnold

Bernhard Arts-Humanities Center (Bridgeport, Connecticut), Chrysler Hall (Norfolk), Concours Gèza Anda (Switzerland), Patricia Corbett Pavilion (University of Cincinnati), Maurice Gusman Philharmonic Hall (Miami), Kunsthumaniora (Antwerp), Aston Magna Foundation for Music (Massachusetts), Music Federation of New Zealand, New Music Distribution Service (N.Y.), Symphony Hall (Phoenix), Wiener Urtext Editions

H. Musical Literature:

Bing, Rudolph, *5000 Nights at the Opera*
Boulez, Pierre, *Werkstatt-Texte*
Chasins, Abram, *Music at the Crossroads*
Craft, Robert, *Stravinsky: Chronicle of a Friendship*
Downes, Edward O., *Perspectives in Musicology*
Hutcheson, Jere, *Musical Form and Analysis*
Kondrashin, Kyrill, *The Art of Conducting*
Menuhin, Yehudi, *Theme and Variations*
Schaeffer, Pierre, *Machines à Communiquer*
Schwarz, Boris, *Music and Musical Life in Soviet Russia*

I. Musical Compositions:

Argento, Dominick, *A Ring of Time* (orchestra)
Birtwistle, Harrison, *The Triumph of Time* (orchestra)
Bliss, Arthur, *Metamorphic Variations*
Briccetti, Thomas, *Overture, The Fountain of Youth*
Brown, Earle, *Time Spans* (orchestra)
Creston, Paul, *Ceremonial* (percussion)
Crumb, George, *Makrokosmos I* (piano)
Del Tredici, David, *Vintage Alice*
Druckman, Jacob, *Windows* (orchestra)
Eaton, John, *Ajax* (baritone and orchestra)
Feldman, Morton, *Voices and Instruments I*
            Chorus and Orchestra II
Finney, Ross Lee, *Symphony No. 4*
Foss, Lukas, *Cave of the Winds*
Hamilton, Iain, *Aurora* (orchestra)
Henze, Hans Werner, *Heliogabalus Imperator* (orchestra)
Hovhaness, Alan, *Symphony No. 23, "Ani"*
Jolivet, André, *Concerto for Violin and Orchestra*
Lees, Benjamin, *The Trumpet of the Swan*
Ligeti, György, *Kylwiria* (opera)
            Double Concerto for Flute, Oboe and Orchestra
Lutoslawski, Witold, *Preludes and Fugues* (13 solo strings)
Martin, Frank, *Requiem*
Nono, Luigi, *Concerto No. 1 for Piano and Orchestra*
Panufnik, Andrzej, *Concerto for Violin and Orchestra*
Pasatieri, Thomas, *The Trial of Mary Lincoln* (TV opera)
Penderecki, Krzystof, *Concerto for Cello and Orchestra*
            Partita
Reed, H. Owen, *For the Unfortunate* (band)
Rochberg, George, *String Quartet No. 3*
Rorem, Ned, *Night Music* (violin and piano)
Sessions, Roger, *Concertino*
Shchedrin, Rodion, *Anna Karenina* (ballet)
Siegmeister, Elie, *Six Songs of Innocence* (on Blake)
Stockhausen, Karlheinz, *Trans* (orchestra)
Tippett, Michael, *Symphony No. 3*
Xenakis, Iannis, *Eridanos*

1973

World Events:

In the U.S., Vice-President Spiro Agnew resigns after being convicted of Income Tax evasion and Gerald R. Ford becomes Vice-President; former President Lyndon B. Johnson dies; the Watergate Trial is held and seven of the participants are given jail sentences; the House studies possible impeachment for President Nixon; Indians seize Wounded Knee, South Dakota, in a grievance issue. Internationally, the Arab countries attack Israel but are repulsed--a peace conference opens in Geneva; an Arab oil embargo causes an energy crisis in the West; Juan Perón returns to Argentina and is re-elected as President; an anti-Marxist coup in Chile overthrows the Allende government; East and West Germany formally establish relations.

Cultural Highlights:

Pulitzers: Drama, Jason Miller (*That Championship Season*); Fiction, Eudora Welty (*The Optimist's Daughter*); Poetry, Maxine W. Kumin (*Up Country*). Australian writer Patrick White receives the Nobel Prize for Literature and Leon Golub is taken into the American Academy. Deaths in the literary field include British writer W.H. Auden, dramatist Noel Coward and novelist J.R.R. Tolkien, Chilean poet Pablo Neruda, Irish novelist Elizabeth Bowen and American novelist Pearl S. Buck and author Arna Bontemps; deaths in the art field include Spanish artist Pablo Picasso, Danish artist Asger Jorn, Lithuanian-born sculptor Jacques Lipschitz and American sculptor Joseph Cornell and artist Philip Evergood. Other highlights include:

Art: Balthus, *The Card Players*; Thomas Hart Benton, *County Politics*; Ilya Bolotowsky, *Variation in Red Diamond*; Jim Dine, *The Art of Painting*; Alex Katz, *Swimmer No. 3;* Lee Krasner, *Peacock;* Malcolm Morley, *Picadilly Circus*; George Segal, *Abraham's Sacrifice of Isaac*; Frank Stella, *Kozangrodek III*; Ernest Trova, *Profile Cantol*.

Literature: Alan Ayckbourn, *The Norman Conquests*; John Cheever, *The World of Apples*; Allen Ginsberg, *The Fall of America*; James Herriot, *All Things Bright and Beautiful*; Bernard Malamud, *Rembrandt's Hat*; Iris Murdock, *The Black Prince*; Alexander Solzhenitsyn, *The Gulag Archipelago*; Thornton Wilder, *Theophilus North*.

MUSICAL EVENTS

B. Deaths:

Feb 19	Joseph Szigeti (Hun-vn)	Jul 3	Karel Ancerl (Cz-cd)
Mar 5	Paul Kletzki (Pol-cd)	Jul 6	Otto Klemperer (Ger-cd)
Mar 18	Lauritz Melchior (Den-ten)	Jul 12	Alexander Mossolov (Rus-cm)
Apr 2	Jascha Horenstein (Rus-cd)	Aug 1	Gian F. Malipiero (It-cm)
Apr 17	István Kertész (Hun-cd)	Aug 17	Jean Barraqué (Fr-cm)
May 6	Ernest MacMillan (Can-cm)	Oct 22	Pablo Casals (Sp-cel-cd)
May 9	Owen Brannigan (Br-bs)	Nov 13	Bruno Maderna (It-cm-cd)
May 9	Mark E. Wessel (Am-cm)	Nov 18	Alois Hába (Cz-cm)
May 10	Guido Gatti (It-mus)	Nov 23	Jennie Tourel (Am-sop)
May 28	Hans Schmidt-Isserstedt	Nov 26	Edith Mason (Am-sop)
	(Ger-cd)	Dec 12	Edith Farnadi (Aus-pn)
Jun 13	Alvin Etler (Am-cm)	Dec 30	Henri Busser (Fr-cm-cd)
Jun 18	Fritz Mahler (Aus-cd)		

C. Débuts:

Met ---Douglas Ahlstedt (ten), Arthur Apy (ten), Cecil Baker (ten), Glen Bater (bs), Lenus Carlson (bar), Richard Cassilly (ten), Carlo Cossutta (ten), Clamma Dale (sop), Sixten Ehrling (cd), Elvira Green (mez), Barbara Hendricks (sop), Marina Krilovici (sop), Rafael Kubelik (cd), Teresa Kubiak (sop), Mady Mesplé (sop), Yvonne Minton (mez), John Nelson (cd), Kenneth Riegel (ten), Leif Segerstam (cd), Rita Shane (sop), Huguette Tourangeau (mez), Benita Valente (sop), Ingvar Wixell (bs), Richard Woitach (cd)

U.S. --Sheila Armstrong (N.Y.), Emmanuel Ax (N.Y.), Jean-Philippe Collard (San Francisco), Kenneth Cooper (N.Y.), Ileana Cotrubas (Chicago), Barbara Daniels (Palm Beach), Sylvia Geszty (N.Y.), Dylana Jenson (N.Y.), Christopher Keene (Rochester), Gyula Kiss, Shlomo Mintz (N.Y.), Joan Morris (N.Y.), Jessye Norman (Boston), Elmar Oliveira (N.Y.), Felicity Palmer (Houston), Anthony and Joseph Paratore (N.Y.), Samuel Ramey (N.Y.), Alberto Remedios (San Francisco), Ingrid Steger, Peter Strummer, Linda Zoghby (Chicago)

Other -Paul Arden-Griffith (London), Barbara Dix (London), Peter Dvorsky (Bratislava), Adam Fischer (Budapest), Herbert Gietzen (Hanover), Anthony Johnson (Glyndebourne), Alexander Lazarev (Moscow), Evelyn Mandac (Salzburg), Janis Martin (London), Judith Nelson (Paris), Marios Papadopoulos (London), Michael Ponder (London), Susanna Ross (Glyndebourne), Julian Smith (Cardiff), Elizabeth Speiser (Glyndebourne), Oana Velcovici (Bucharest)

D. New Positions:

Conductors: Richard Armstrong (Welsh Opera), Aldo Ceccato (Detroit SO), Rafael Kubelik (Met), Raymond Leppard (Northern SO), James Levine (Met), Seiji Ozawa (Boston SO), Max Rudolf (Dallas SO), Lawrence Smith (Portland SO), Edo de Waart (Rotterdam PO)

Educational: György Ligeti (composition, Hamburg Hochschule), Igor Markevich (Accademia di Santa Cecilia, Rome)

Others: Gilbert Amy (music advisor, ORTF), Erhard Karkoschka (director, Studio for Electronic Music, Stuttgart), Rolf Liebermann (director, Paris Opera)

E. Prizes and Honors:

Prizes: Elliott Carter (Pulitzer-*String Quartet III*), Richard Goode (Haskil), Barbara Hendricks (Naumberg), Zoltán Kocsis (Liszt), Joonas Kokkonen (Sibelius), Edmund LeRoy (Naumberg), Leo Nucci (Viotti), Dezsö Ránki (Liszt), James Tocco (Munich), Vladimir Viardo (Cliburn), Susan D. Wyner (Naumberg)

Honors: George Balanchine (Musician of the Year--*Musical America*), Charles Groves (knighted), Arthur Grumiaux (baronet), Peter Maag (Verdi Medal), Dmitri Shostakovich (honorary doctorate, Northwestern U.), John Philip Sousa (Hall of Fame for Great Americans)

F. Biographical Highlights:

Mathieu Ahlersmeyer retires from the stage; Yefim Bronfman emigrates to Israel with his family; Myung-Whun Chung becomes a naturalized American citizen; Jean Coulthard retires from teaching at the University of British Columbia; Håkan Hagegård makes his first appearance outside Sweden at the Glyndebourne Festival; Ani Kavafian makes her European debut in Paris; Kyrill Kondrashin resigns his position as conductor of the Moscow PO but continues teaching at the Conservatory; George London debuts in Seattle as stage director; Ervin Nyiregyházi makes his second debut with the San Francisco SO after a long self-retirement; Eugene Ormandy takes the Philadelphia Orchestra to China on a cultural exchange visit; Steve Reich begins the study of Far Eastern music cultures; Gerard Schwarz, at Aspen, is called at the last minute to substitute for an ailing Eleazar de Carvalho; Peter Serkin, returning to an active musical life, forms the chamber group Tashi; Judith Somogi debuts as a conductor at the Met; Frederica von Stade marries photographer Peter Elkus and also makes her Paris Opera debut; Anna Tomowa-Sintow is championed by Karajan who picks her for the premiere of a new Orff opera; José Van Dam makes his Covent Garden debut; Ransom Wilson graduates from Juilliard.

G. Institutional Openings:

Performing Groups: Academy of Ancient Music (London), Albuquerque Opera Theater, Arkansas Opera Theater (Little Rock), Cleveland Opera Theater, English Consort (London), Hartford Chamber Orchestra, Kronos String Quartet, Mirecourt Trio (Iowa), Swingle Singers II (Paris), Taverner Choir (Oxford)

Festivals: Festival Internacional Cervantino (Mexico), Santa Fe Chamber Music Festival

Educational: Staatliche Hochschule für Musik und Darstellende Kunst (Stuttgart)

Other: Donizetti Society of London, Roy Harris Archive (C.S.U., Los Angeles), Vatroslav Lisinski Concert Auditorium (Zagreb), Minnesota Composers Forum, Music Board of the Australian Council for the Arts (Sydney), New Orleans Theater of the Performing Arts, Sydney Opera House, Teatro Regio II (Turin)

H. Musical Literature:

Cage, John, *Writings '67 - '72*
Donington, Robert, *A Performer's Guide to Baroque Music*
Duerksen, George, *Teaching Instrumental Music*
Forte, Allen, *The Structure of Atonal Music*
Harding, Rosamond, *The Piano-Forte*
Jacobs, Arthur, *A Short History of Western Music*
Karpeles, Maud, *Introduction to English Folk Song*
Sargeant, Winthrop, *Divas: Impressions of Today's Sopranos*
Schwartz, Elliot, *Electronic Music: A Listener's Guide*
Stevenson, Robert, *Foundations of New World Opera*

I. Musical Compositions:

Arnold, Malcolm, *Symphony No. 7*
Bassett, Leslie, *The Jade Garden* (voice and piano)
Bennett, Richard R., *Concerto for Viola and Orchestra*
       Concerto for Orchestra
Bergsma, William, *Murder of Comrade Sharik* (opera)
Berio, Luciano, *Concerto for Two Pianos and Orchestra*
Britten, Benjamin, *Death in Venice* (opera)
Charpentier, Jacques, *Symphony No. 4, "Brasil"*
Crumb, George, *Makrokosmos II* (piano)
Davies, Peter M., *Litany: Runes from a House of the Dead*
Del Tredici, David, *Adventures Underground*
Egk, Werner, *Moria* (orchestra)
Feldman, Morton, *String Quartet and Orchestra*
Ginastera, Alberto, *Concerto No. 2 for Piano and Orchestra*
Henze, Hans Werner, *Tristan* (piano, tape, orchestra)
Hovhaness, Alan, *Symphonies No. 24 and 25*
Lees, Benjamin, *Collage* (string quartet, winds, percussion)
Levy, Martin David, *Masada* (secular oratorio)
Ligeti, György, *Clocks and Clouds* (women's choir, orchestra)
Mennin, Peter, *Symphony No. 8*
Miyoshi, Akira, *Ouverture de Fête*
Musgrave, Thea, *The Voice of Ariadne* (opera)
       Concerto for Violin and Orchestra
Orff, Carl, *The Vigil* (opera)
       Rota (chorus and orchestra)
Panufnik, Andrzej, *Sinfonia Concertante* (flute, harp, strings)
Penderecki, Krzystof, *Symphony No. 1*
       Song of Solomon (chorus, dancers, chamber orchestra)
Rubbra, Edmund, *Symphony No. 9, "Resurrection"*
Schuman, William, *Concerto on Old English Rounds*
Shostakovich, Dmitri, *String Quartet No. 14*
Takemitsu, Toru, *Autumn* (Japanese instruments and orchestra)
Williamson, Malcolm, *Ode to Music* (choruses, orchestra)
Zwillich, Ellen Taafe, *Symposium for Orchestra*

1974

World Events:
In the U.S., Richard Nixon, under the threat of impeachment, becomes the first president to resign and Gerald Ford becomes the first President who was never elected as Vice-President; President Ford gives a full pardon to Nixon in the first month of his office; all price and wage controls are ended; gasoline shortages plague the country because of Arab oil embargo; former UMW president Tony Boyle is convicted of murder. Internationally, the OPEC countries finally lift the oil embargo against the West; Willy Brandt resigns and Helmut Schmidt becomes Chancellor of West Germany; Yitzhak Rabin becomes Prime Minister of Israel; Haile Selassie is deposed in Ethiopia and a pro-communist government set up; Juan Peron dies and his wife Isabel seeks to run Argentina in his place.

Cultural Highlights:
Pulitzer: Poetry, Robert Lowell (*The Dolphin*). The Nobel Prize for Literature goes jointly to Swedish writers Eyvind Johnson and Harry E. Martinson; the Joseph H. Hirschorn Museum opens in Washington, D.C. and the Smart Gallery in Chicago. Deaths include British author H.E. Bates, American novelist Jacqueline Susann and author Margaret Leech, Swedish author Pär Lagerkvist, American artist Adolph Gottlieb and Russian-born artist Moses Soyer. Other highlights include:

Art: Robert Arneson, *The Palace at 9 A.M.*; Alexander Calder, *Universe*; Helen Frankenthaler, *Rapunzel*; Duane Hanson, *Repairman*; R.B. Kitaj, *Autumn of Central Paris*; William Morris, *Off the Pedestal*; Richard Pousette-Dart, *Radiance No. 6, Lavender*; George Rickey, *2 Open Rectangles Eccentric*.

Literature: James Baldwin, *If Beale Street Could Talk*; Donald Barthelme, *Guilty Pleasures*; Peter Benchley, *Jaws*; Carl Bernstein, *All the President's Men*; John Fowles, *The Ebony Tower*; John LeCarré, *Tinker, Tailor, Soldier, Spy;* James Michener, *Centennial*; Cornelius Ryan, *A Bridge Too Far*; Irving Wallace, *The Fan Club*.

MUSICAL EVENTS

B. Deaths:

Feb 15	Kurt Atterberg (Swe-cm)	Sep 14	Roger Bourdin (Fr-bar)
Mar 5	Sol Hurok (Rus-imp)	Oct 5	Ebe Stignani (It-sop)
Mar 28	Dino Ciani (It-pn)	Oct 8	Dom Anselm Hughes (Br-mus)
Apr 23	Günther Hausswald (Ger-mus)	Oct 12	Josef Krips (Aus-cd)
May 10	Herbert Elwell (Am-cri-cm)	Oct 24	David Oistrakh (Rus-vn)
May 14	Hipolito Lazaro (Sp-ten)	Nov 3	Marguerite Namara (Am-sop)
May 24	"Duke" Ellington (Am-pop)	Nov 9	Egon Wellesz (Aus-cm-mus)
Jun 14	Knud Jeppesen (Den-mus-the)	Nov 21	Frank Martin (Swi-cm)
Jun 20	Marc Pincherle (Fr-mus)	Dec 6	John Williams (Am-pn-ped)
Jun 22	Darius Milhaud (Fr-cm)	Dec 15	Karin Branzell (Swi-alto)
Sep 3	Harry Partch (Am-cm)	Dec 20	André Jolivet (Fr-cm)
Sep 5	Wolfgang Windgassen (Ger-ten)	Dec 26	Knudage Riisager (Den-cm)
Sep 6	John Challis (Am-hps.m)		

C. Débuts:
Met ---Steuart Bedford (cd), José Carreras (ten), Brigitte Fassbaender (mez), Jon Garrison (ten), Manfred Jungwirth (bs), Berit Lindholm (sop), Linda Mays (sop), Paolo Montarsolo (bs), Peter Pears (ten), Marius Rintzler (bar), Bengt Rundgren (bs), John Shirley-Quirk (bar), Nancy Tatum (sop), Harry Theyard (ten), Kun Yul Yoo (ten)

U.S. --Maurice André (tour), Riccardo Chailly (Chicago), Andrew Davis (N.Y.), Pablo Elvira (tour), Sheri Greenawald (N.Y.), Barbara Hendricks (San Francisco), Ava June (San Francisco), Ermanno Mauro (San Diego), Mstislav Rostropovich (N.Y.), Peter Schreier (San Francisco), André-Michel Schub (N.Y.), Klaus Tennstedt (Boston), Anna

Tomowa-Sintow (San Francisco)

Other -Yefim Bronfman (Israel), Sigmund S. Cowan (Lucca), Manfred Jung (Dortmund), Emma Kirkby (London), Ann Murray (Glasgow)

D. New Positions:
Conductors: Sixten Ehrling (Göteborg SO), Leon Fleisher (Baltimore SO), Rafael Frühbeck de Burgos (Montreal SO), Eliahu Inbal (Frankfurt Radio SO), Jean Martinon (The Hague SO), Riccardo Muti (New Philharmonic Orchestra), Willem van Otterloo (Düsseldorf SO), Maurice Peress (Kansas City PO), David Zinman (Rochester PO)

Educational: John Alexander (voice, Cincinnati Conservatory), Robert Moevs (music chair, Rutgers University)

E. Prizes and Honors:
Prizes: Richard Atamian (Naumberg), Emanuel Ax (Rubinstein), Robert Benz (Busoni), Christian Blackshaw (Casella), Lynn Chang (Paganini), Andrei Gavrilov (Tchaikovsky), Barbara Gorzynska (Zagreb), Edith Kraft (Naumberg), Donald Martino (Pulitzer-- *Notturno*), Jane Nelson (Viotti), André-Michel Schub (Naumberg), Edo de Waart (Mitropoulos)

Honors: Lennox Berkeley (knighted), Sarah Caldwell (Musician of the Year, *Musical America*), Joan Hammond (Dame of the British Empire), Walter Piston (MacDowell Medal), Roger Sessions (Special Pulitzer), Hans Stuckenschmidt (Berlin Academy)

F. Biographical Highlights:
Christian Badea moves to the U.S. and enrolls in Juilliard; Yefim Bronfman receives a scholarship to study in Israel; Myung Whun Chung and Eugene Fodor both win Silver Medals in the Tchaikovsky competition; Colin Davis becomes Principle Guest Conductor of the London PO; Carlos Kleiber makes his conducting debuts at both Bayreuth and Covent Garden; Gidon Kremer has his traveling ban lifted by the Soviet government opening the way for concertizing in the West; Jamie and Ruth Laredo are divorced after 14 years of marriage; John Macurdy and Paul Plishka make their La Scala debuts; Eduardo Mata, subbing for an ailing Previn, makes a successful London SO debut; Jessye Norman moves to Europe and takes up residency in London; Ashley Putnam receives her B.M. degree in voice from the University of Michigan; Mstislav Rostropovich and Galina Vishnevskaya leave Russia and settle in the U.S.; Leonard Slatkin becomes Principle Guest Conductor of the Minnesota SO; Georg Solti takes the Chicago SO on a second European tour; Shirley Verrett sings a dual role in Berlioz' *Les Troyen* when Christa Ludwig falls ill; Pinchas Zukerman makes his conducting debut in London.

G. Institutional Openings:
Performing Groups: American String Quartet (Juilliard), Atlanta Youth Orchestra, Audubon String Quartet (New York), Tandy Beal and Company (California Dance Group), Cleveland Ballet, Opera Guild of Miami, Orchestre de l'Ille-de-France (Paris), Reykjavik Chamber Ensemble (Iceland), Scottish Chamber Orchester (Edinburgh)

Festivals: Artpark Festival (Lewiston, N.Y.)

Educational: Schoenberg Institute (Los Angeles)

Other: Ambassador Auditorium (Los Angeles), American Society for Jewish Music (N.Y.), Birmingham Concert Hall (Alabama), Centre for American Music (London), Centre Lyrique de Wallonie (Belgium), Meet the Composer Program (N.Y.), Musician's International Mutual Aid Fund, New Music for Young Ensembles (N.Y.), Orchestra Hall (Minneapolis), Artur Rubinstein International Piano Master Competition (Israel), Swedish Arts Council (Stockholm)

H. Musical Literature:

Bloch, Ernest, *Zur Philosophie der Musik*
Cone, Edward T., *The Composer's Voice*
Craft, Robert, *Prejudices in Disguise*
Haase, Hans, *Aufsätze zur harmonikalen Natur-philosophie*
Headington, Christopher, *History of Western Music, Bodley Head*
Nyman, Michael, *Experimental Music: Cage and Beyond*
Strunk, Oliver, *Essays on Music in the Western World*
Vinton, John, *Dictionary of Contemporary Music*
Zimmermann, Bernd, *Intervall und Zeit*

I. Musical Compositions:

Adler, Samuel, *The Disappointment* (opera)
Argento, Domenick, *From the Diary of Virginia Woolf* (voice and piano)
Berio, Luciano, *Points on the Curve to Find...*
Bernstein, Leonard, *The Dybbuk* (ballet)
Boulez, Pierre, *Expolsante-Fixe*
Brant, Henry, *An American Requiem* (chorus)
Britten, Benjamin, *English Folk Song Suite*
Crumb, George, *Makrokosmos III* (amplified pianos and percussion)
Davies, Peter M., *Miss Donnithorne's Maggot* (soprano and orchestra)
              Dark Angels (soprano and guitar)
Davidovsky, Mario, *Synchronism VII*
Dorati, Antal, *Concerto for Piano and Orchestra*
Druckman, Jacob, *Lamia* (soprano and orchestra)
Feldman, Morton, *Instruments I*
              Voice and Instruments II
Finney, Ross Lee, *Concerto for Saxophone and Orchestra*
Hamilton, Iain, *The Catiline Conspiracy* (opera)
Harris, Roy, *Symphony No. 14*
Huston, Scott, *A Game of Circles* (clarinet, piano, celesta)
Lazarof, Henri, *Chamber Concerto No. 3* (12 soloists)
Lees, Benjamin, *Etudes for Piano and Orchestra*
Ligeti, György, *San Francisco Polyphony* (orchestra)
Messiaen, Olivier, *Des Canyons aux Étoiles*
Musgrave, Thea, *Space Play* (for 9 instruments)
Penderecki, Krzystof, *Magnificat* (bass, choruses and orchestra)
Rochberg, George, *Imago Mundi* (orchestra)
Rosenberg, Hilding, *Symphony No. 8, "In Candidum"*
Shostakovich, Dmitri, *String Quartet No. 15*
              6 Songs by Marina Tsvetayeva
Siegmeister, Elie, *A Cycle of Cities*
              Concerto for Piano and Orchestra
Starer, Robert, *Concerto No. 3 for Piano and Orchestra*
Stockhausen, Karlheinz, *Herbstmusik*
Suderberg, Robert, *Piano Concerto, "Within the Mirror of Time"*
Walton, William, *Magnificat* (chorus and orchestra)
Weisgall, Hugo, *Fancies and Inventions*
Wernick, Richard, *Songs of Remembrance*
Wuorinen, Charles, *Concerto No. 2 for Amplified Piano and Orchestra*
Xenakis, Iannis, *Cendrées* (chorus and orchestra)
              Erikhthon (piano and orchestra)
Zwillich, Ellen Taafe, *String Quartet*

1975

World Events:
In the U.S., the Big Three of Watergate fame are given prison terms; the U.S. ship, *Mayaguez*, is seized by the Cambodians and rescued by U.S. Marines; two attempts are made on the President's life in California; Union official Jimmy Hoffa mysteriously disappears and is believed murdered; all U.S. troops and civilians are hurriedly evacuated from Vietnam. Internationally, the Communists take over all of Vietnam, Cambodia and Laos; Russian cosmonauts make a joint link-up with a U.S. spacecraft in orbit; the Sinai Accord is signed by Israel and Egypt; the Helsinki Accord is signed by both the Western and Communist Bloc countries; the Suez Canal is reopened after 8 years; the European Space Agency is founded.

Cultural Highlights:
Pulitzers: Drama, Edward Albee (*Seascape*); Fiction, Michael Shaara (*The Killer Angels*); Poetry, Gary Snyder (*Turtle Island*). Italian author Eugenio Montale receives the Nobel Prize for Literature and British author P.G. Wodehouse is knighted; the Brotherhood of Ruralists is formed in England. Deaths in literature and art include American artists Thomas Hart Benton and James Chapin, British artists Michael Ayrton and sculptress Barbara Hepworth, American novelist Thornton Wilder and French poet Alexis Léger. Other highlights include:

Art: Richard Estes, *Central Savings*; Phillip Guston, *Head and Bottle*; Jasper Johns, *Weeping Woman*; Alex Katz, *Six Women*; Willem de Kooning, *Whose Name Was Writ in Water*; Sol Lewitt, *Four-Part Modular Cube*; Catherine Murphy, *Self-Portrait with Pansy*; Frank Stella, *Jardin Botanica I*; Ernest Trova, *Three Walking Poets*.

Literature: Alan Ayckbourn, *Absurd Person Singular*; Saul Bellow, *Humboldt's Gift*; Gwendolyn Brooks, *Beckonings*; Arthur Hailey, *The Moneychangers*; Ted Hughes, *Cave Birds*; Judith Rossner, *Looking for Mister Goodbar*; John Updike, *A Month of Sundays*; Irving Wallace, *The People's Almanac*; Joseph Wambaugh, *The Choirboys*.

MUSICAL EVENTS

B. Deaths:

Jan 3	Milton Cross (Am-au)	Jun 4	Frida Leider (Ger-sop)
Jan 8	Richard Tucker (Am-ten)	Jun 27	Robert Stolz (Aus-cm)
Jan 11	Max Lorenz (Ger-ten)	Jul 2	Benno Rabinof (Am-vn)
Jan 16	Thor Johnson (Am-cd)	Jul 4	Gilda Dalla Rizza (It-sop)
Jan 20	Franz André (Bel-cd)	Jul 18	Federico Ghisi (It-mus-cm)
Jan 30	Boris Blacher (Ger-cm)	Aug 2	Muir Mathieson (Br-cd)
Feb 16	Norman Treigle (Am-bs)	Aug 9	Dmitri Shostakovich (Rus-cm)
Feb 19	Luigi Dallapiccola (It-cm)	Aug 16	Fritz Bose (Ger-mus)
Feb 24	Marcel Grandjany (Fr-hp)	Aug 31	Geneviève Thibault (Fr-mus)
Mar 27	Arthur Bliss (Br-cm)	Sep 10	Hans Swarowsky (Aus-cd)
Apr 4	Joseph Bentonelli (Am-ten)	Sep 17	Kresimir Baranovic (Yug-cd)
Apr 14	Jean Morel (Fr-cd)	Sep 17	Nicola Moscona (Gr-bs)
Apr 19	Aksel Schiotz (Den-ten)	Nov 22	Friedrich Blume (Ger-mus)
May 2	Conchita Badia (Sp-sop)	Dec 14	Rosa Pauly (Hun-sop)
May 18	Leroy Anderson (Am-pop)	Dec 24	Bernard Hermann (Am-arr)

C. Débuts:
Met ---Ryland Davies (ten), Elena Doria (sop), Carole Farley (sop), Andrew Foldi (bs), Maureen Forrester (alto), Richard Fredericks (bar), Elizabeth Harwood (sop), Heinrich Hollreiser (cd), Anne Howells (mez), Evelyn Mandac (sop), Danica Mastilovic (sop), Donald McIntyre (bar), Leona Mitchell (sop), Magda Olivero (sop), Giuseppe Patané (cd), Katia Ricciarelli (sop), Richard Stilwell (bar), José Van Dam (bs).

U.S. --Norman Bailey (N.Y.), John Brecknock (Houston), John Cheek, Zdzislawa Donat

(San Francisco), Peter Gougaloff (San Francisco), Roberta Knie (Dallas), René Kollo (Washington, D.C.), Robert Lloyd (San Francisco), Yuri Mazurok (tour), Robin McCabe (N.Y.), Robleto Merolla, Yevgeni Nesterenko (N.Y.), Elena Obraztsova (Bolshoi tour), Brenda Roberts (San Francisco), Gianna Rolandi (N.Y.), Vladimir Spivakov (N.Y.)

Other -Elizabeth Altman (London), Yefim Bronfman (Israel), Ivan Fischer (Budapest), Philip F. Fowke (London), Siegfried Jerusalem (Stuttgart), Yvonne D. Kenny (London), James Lancelot (London), Felicity Ann Lott (London), Margaret Marshall (London), Rosalind Plowright (Glyndebourne), Simon Rattle (London), Tamara Smirnova (Gorky)

D. New Positions:

Conductors: Yuri Ahronovich (Cologne PO), Gerd Albrecht (Zurich Tonhalle), Paavo Berglund (Helsinki PO), Andrew Davis (Toronto SO), Charles Dutoit (Göteborg SO), Milan Horvat (Zagreb Radio SO), Okko Kamu (Oslo PO), Christopher Keene (Syracuse SO), Eduardo Mata (Phoenix SO), Jerzy Semkov (St. Louis SO), Kari Tikka (Stockholm Opera)

Educational: Charles Castleman (violin, Eastman), Ian Hobson (piano, University of Illinois), Bernard Rands (composition, U. of California, San Diego), Risë Stevens (President, Mannes College of Music)

Others: Anthony Bliss (director, Met), Ulrik Cold (director, Royal Theater, Copenhagen), John Crosby (President, Opera America), Donald Hunt (organ, Worcester Cathedral), George London (general director, Opera Society of Washington)

E. Prizes and Honors:

Prizes: Dmitri Alexeev (Leeds), Dominick Argento (Pulitzer--*From the Diary of Virginia Woolf*), Dickran Atamian (Naumberg), Victoria Bond (Herbert), Michel Dalberto (Haskil), Clamma Dale (Naumberg), Peter Dvorsky (Geneva), Lynn Harrell (Fisher), Elmar Oliveira (Naumberg), Murray Perahia (Fisher), Ivo Petric (Wieniawski), Joy Simpson (Naumberg), Jeffrey Swann (Ciani), Krystian Zimerman (Chopin)

Honors: Arne Nordheim (Swedish Royal Academy), Eugene Ormandy (Musician of the Year, *Musical America*), Malcolm Williamson (Master of the Queen's Music)

F. Biographical Highlights:

Jeannine Altmeyer, Kurt Moll and Frederica von Stade make their Covent Garden debuts; Arleen Augér, José Carreras and Veriano Luchetti make their La Scala debuts; Victoria Bond receives her Masters from USC; Semyon Bychkov and his wife leave Leningrad and arrive in the U.S.; Paul Creston retires from teaching and moves to San Diego; Clamma Dale receives a Masters degree from Juilliard; Yuri Egorov, at the Queen Elisabeth Competitions, is persuaded not to defect; James Galway leaves the Berlin PO after 6 years and embarks on a solo career; Herbert von Karajan undergoes spinal disc surgery; Dorothy Kirsten gives her farewell Met performance; Zoltán Kocsis graduates from Liszt Conservatory in Budapest; Cho-Liang Lin leaves Australia to study at Juilliard in New York; Christopher Parkening begins a 10-year "vacation" from concertizing; Ashley Putnam receives her Masters from University of Michigan; Bernard Rands leaves York University and decides to settle in California; Gerard Schwarz resigns his position with the New York PO to concentrate on conducting; Elizabeth Schwarzkopf makes her farewell tour of the U.S.; Calvin Simmons becomes assistant to Zubin Mehta in Los Angeles; Bernd Weikl makes his Bayreuth debut; Ellen Taafe Zwillich becomes the first woman to receive a doctorate in composition from Juilliard.

G. Institutional Openings:

Performing Groups: Classic Opera of Miami, Glimmerglass Opera Co. (Cooperstown, N.Y.), Bruno Maderna Ensemble (Venice), Minot Opera Association (North Dakota), New York New Music Ensemble (Juilliard), Pennsylvania Opera Theater (Philadelphia), Pittsburgh New Music Ensemble, San Diego Opera Co., Takács String Quartet (Hungary), Thouvenel String Quartet, Twentieth Century Consort (Washington, D.C.), Virginia Opera Association (Norfolk), Youngstown Opera Co. (Ohio).

Festivals: Cullowhee Music Festival (North Carolina)

Other: Badisches Staatstheater (Karlsruhe), Robert Casadesus International Piano Competition (Paris), Dino Ciani Prize (Milan), Avery Fisher Prize (N.Y.), Kirsten Flagstad International Society (Oslo), Hartford Civic Center, International League of Women Composers (N.Y.), Thor Johnson Living Tribute Fund (North Carolina), New World Records (Milwaukee), Sonneck Society (Washington, D.C.), Richard Tucker Music Foundation

H. Musical Literature:

Benjamin/Horvat/Nelson, *Techniques and Materials of Tonal Music*
Bennett, Robert R., *Instrumentally Speaking*
Cacavas, John, *Music Arranging and Orchestration*
Delone, Richard, *Aspects of Twentieth Century Music*
Ferguson, Howard, *Keyboard Interpretation*
Nathan, Hans, *William Billings*
Read, Gardner, *Style and Orchestration*
Schaeffer, Boguslaw, *Introduction to Contemporary Composition*
Smith-Brindle, Reginald, *The New Music*
Westergaard, Peter, *An Introduction to Tonal Theory*

I. Musical Compositions:

Adler, Samuel, *Symphony No. 5, "We Are the Echoes"*
Badings, Henk, *American Folk Song Suite* (english horn and strings)
Bassett, Leslie, *Echoes from an Invisible World* (orchestra)
Bennett, Richard R., *Concerto for Violin and Orchestra*
Bolcom, William, *Open House* (song cycle)
Brown, Earle, *Cross Sections and Color Fields* (orchestra)
Carter, Elliott, *A Mirror on Which to Dwell* (song cycle)
Charpentier, Jacques, *Concerto No. 5 for Saxophone and Orchestra*
           Concerto No. 6 for Oboe and Strings
           Concerto No. 7 for Trumpet and Strings
Corigliano, John, *Concerto for Oboe and Orchestra*
Davies, Peter M., *A Stone Litany* (soprano and orchestra)
Del Tredici, David, *In Wonderland*
Feldman, Morton, *Piano and Orchestra Instruments II*
Français, Jean, *Cassazione for 3 Orchestras*
Harrison, Lou, *Elegiac Symphony*
Hovhaness, Alan, *Symphonies No. 26 and 27*
Kokkonen, Joonas, *The Last Temptation* (opera)
Lo Presti, Ronald, *Requiem* (chorus and orchestra)
Lutoslawski, Witold, *Les Espace du Sommeil* (baritone and orchestra)
Musgrave, Thea, *Orfeo II*
Nono, Luigi, *Concerto No.2 for Piano and Orchestra*
Norgård, Per, *Symphony No. 3*
Panufnik, Andrzej, *Symphony for Spheres*
Rochberg, George, *Concerto for Violin and Orchestra*
           Symphony No. 3
Rorem, Ned, *Air Music* (orchestra)
Rubbra, Edmund, *Chamber Symphony*
Salzman, Eric, *The Conjurer* (multimedia event)
Schuman, William, *Symphony No. 10, "American Muse"*
Shostakovich, Dmitri, *The Dreamers* (ballet)
Siegmeister, Elie, *Shadows and Light* (orchestra)
           Symphony No. 5, "Visions of Time"
Van Vactor, David, *Symphony No. 5*

1976

World Events:

In the U.S., Jimmy Carter is elected as President No. 39 while Bicentennial Celebrations take place all over the country; *Viking 1* and *2* make soft landings on Mars and begin sending back information on a cold, windy and lifeless planet; *Pioneer 10* passes through Saturn's rings on its way to outerspace; Conrail is formed to control the bankrupt railroads of the Northeast; a breakout of "Legionnaire's Disease" at a Philadelphia convention baffles scientists. Internationally, both Mao Tse-tung and Chou En-lai die in China--the "Gang of Four" seeks to grab power but are unsuccessful and Hua Kuo-feng becomes Premier; great Chinese earthquake leaves 655,000 dead; Civil War breaks out in Lebanon between Christians and Moslems; a military junta seizes power in Argentina; the Winter Olympics take place in Innsbruck, Austria.

Cultural Highlights:

Pulitzers: Drama, Michael Bennett, James Kirkwood, Nicholas Dante, Marvin Hamlisch, Edward Kleban (*A Chorus Line*); Fiction, Saul Bellow (*Humboldt's Gift*); Poetry, John Ashbery (*Self-Portrait in a Convex Mirror*). American author Saul Bellow is also recipient of the Nobel Prize for Literature; the Adolph Gottlieb Foundation is founded; Hugh Casson becomes President of the Royal Academy of Arts in London. Deaths in the art and literary fields include German artists Josef Albers and Max Ernst, American artist Alexander Calder and British novelist Agatha Christie. Other highlights include:

Art: Gifford Beal, *Industry*; Christo, *Running Fence*; Chryssa, *Rhythms*; Jim Dine, *So Many Different Colors*; Mark di Suvero, *For Handel*; Jasper Johns, *End Papers*; Ron B. Kitaj, *If Not, Not*; Malcolm Morley, *Age of Catastrophe*; Ernest Trova, *Abstract Variation*; Andrew Wyeth, *Sea Boots*.

Literature: Peter Benchley, *The Deep*; Carl Bernstein, *The Final Days*; John Gardner, *October Light;* Colleen McCullough, *The Thorn Birds*; Ntozake Shange, *For Colored Girls...*; Neil Simon, *California Suite*; Paul Theroux, *The Family Arsenal*; Leon Uris, *Trinity*; Gore Vidal, *1876*; Irving Wallace, *The R Document*.

MUSICAL EVENTS

B. Deaths:

Jan 23	Paul Robeson (Am-bar)	Oct 1 Maud Karpeles (Br-mus)
Feb 13	Lily Pons (Fr-sop)	Oct 17 Nikolai Lopatnikoff (Rus-cm)
Mar 1	Jean Martinon (Fr-cd-cm)	Oct 18 Janine Micheau (Fr-sop)
Apr 26	Alexander Brailowsky (Rus-pn)	Oct 21 Joseph Müller-Blattau (Ger-mus)
May 11	Rudolf Kempe (Ger-cd)	Oct 26 Deryck Cooke (Br-mus)
May 26	Maggie Teyte (Br-sop)	Nov 3 Dean Dixon (Am-cd)
May 30	Hugo Rignold (Br-cd)	Nov 9 Rosina Lhevinne (Rus-pn)
Jun 6	Elisabeth Rethberg (Ger-sop)	Nov 12 Walter Piston (Am-cm)
Jun 14	Géza Anda (Hun-pn)	Nov 18 Alfred Jerger (Cz-bar)
Jun 24	Samuel Dushkin (Pol-vn)	Nov 27 Victor Alessandro (Am-cd)
Aug 6	Gregor Piatigorsky (Rus-cel)	Dec 4 Benjamin Britten (Br-cm)
Aug 22	Gina Bachauer (Gr-pn)	Dec 9 Nino Martini (It-ten)
Aug 26	Lotte Lehmann (Ger-sop)	Dec 12 Francesco Merli (It-ten)
Sep 30	Louis Fourestier (Fr-cd)	Dec 31 Roland Hayes (Am-ten)

C. Débuts:

Met ---Norman Bailey (bar), Hildegard Behrens (sop), Sarah Caldwell (cd), Gianfranco Cecchele (ten), James Conlon (cd), Stafford Dean (bs), Simon Estes (bs), Maria Ewing (sop), Gianandrea Gavazzeni (ten), René Kollo (ten), Eva Marton (sop), Elena Obraztsova (mez), Alberto Remedios (ten), Ellen Shade (sop), Alan Titus (bar), Tatiana Troyanos (mez), Ruth Welting (sop)

U.S. --John Aler (N.Y.), Dmitri Alexeev (Chicago), Lazar Berman (N.Y.), Yefim Bronfman (Philadelphia), Claudio Desderi (Washington, D.C.), Eliot Fisk (N.Y.), Patricia Johnson

(Dallas), Matti Kastu (San Francisco), Andreas Klein (N.Y.), Ashley Putnam (Virginia), Kathryn Selby (N.Y.), Jane Shaulis (N.Y.), Richard Stolzman (N.Y.)

Other -Andrei Gavrilov (London), Mikael Melbye (Copenhagen), Ilona Tokody (Budapest), Penelope Walker (London)

D. New Positions:
Conductors: Christian Badea (National SO), Daniel Barenboim (Orchestre de Paris), Milton Katims (University of Houston SO), Lorin Maazel (London PO), Zubin Mehta (New York PO), John Nelson (Indianapolis SO), James de Preist (Quebec SO), Gerard Schwarz (YSO, New York)

Educational: Gustav Meier (opera, U. of Michigan), Aulis Sallinen (Finnish State Art Professor), Bernard Rands (University of California, San Diego)

Others: Richard Bonynge (music director, Australian Opera), Milton Katims (artistic director, U. of Houston), James Levine (music director, Met), William Noll (artistic director, Atlanta Lyric Opera), Egon Seefehlner (general manager, Vienna Opera)

E. Prizes and Honors:
Prizes: Roberto Cappello (Busoni), Terence Judd (Liszt), Ani Kavafian (Fisher), Elena Obraztsova (Lenin), Ursula Oppens (Fisher), Sandro de Palma (Casella), Ned Rorem (Pulitzer--*Air Music*), Antonio Suarez (Verdi)

Honors: Dominick Argento (honorary doctorate, York College), Janet Baker (Dame of the British Empire), Benjamin Britten (knighted), William Dawson (Alabama Hall of Fame), Arthur Fiedler (Medal of Freedom and Gold Baton), Scott Joplin (Special Pulitzer), George London (honorary doctorate, Cleveland Institute), Yehudi Menuhin (honorary doctorate, Sorbonne), Thomas Pynchon (Howells Medal), Artur Rubinstein (Medal of Freedom and Musician of the Year, *Musical America*)

F. Biographical Highlights:
Maurice Abravanel undergoes open-heart surgery; Yefim Bronfman emigrates to the U.S.; Renato Bruson, Lenus Carlson, Justino Díaz and Sylvia Sass make their Covent Garden debuts; Teresa Cahil makes her La Scala debut; Sergiu Comissiona and his wife become naturalized American citizens; Glenn Dicterow becomes concertmaster of the Los Angeles PO; Susan Dunn graduates from college and enters Indiana University for further music study; Yuri Egorov defects to the West; Tito Gobbi retires from the opera stage; Horacio Gutiérrez becomes an American citizen; Horst Hiestermann defects to the West; Peter Hofmann makes his Bayreuth debut; Antonio Meneses takes second prize in cello in Rio de Janeiro; Carol Neblett makes her Vienna Opera debut; Steve Reich studies Hebrew ritual for a year; Artur Rubinstein retires from public recital life because of blindness; Claire Watson retires from concert life.

G. Institutional Openings:
Performing Groups: American Composer's Orchestra (N.Y.), An die Musik (New York Chamber Ensemble), Ariel Ensemble, Atlanta Lyric Opera Co., Austin Civic Wind Ensemble (Texas), Denver Early Music Consort, Emerson String Quartet (Juilliard), Bohuslav Martinu Trio (Holland), Philadelphia Opera Theater, Tallis Scholars (London), Utah Opera Co. (Salt Lake City)

Educational: American Institute for Verdi Studies (N.Y.), Instituto Superior de Arte (Cuba), *Journal of the Arnold Schoenberg Institute*

Other: American Women Composers (McLean, Virginia), Australia Music Center (Sydney), Gina Bachauer International Piano Competition, Sacred Music Society of America (N.Y.), Scottdale Center for the Arts (Phoenix), Eleanor Steber Foundation (N.Y.)

H. Musical Literature:
Benjamin, Thomas, *Modal Counterpoint*
Bernstein, Leonard, *The Unanswered Question*

Berry, Wallace, *Structural Functions in Music*
Brendel, Alfred, *Musical Thoughts and Afterthoughts*
Craft, Robert, *Current Convictions*
Downes, Edward, *New York Philharmonic Guide to the Symphony*
Kohs, Ellis, *Musical Form*
Kraft, Leo, *Gradus: An Integrated Approach to Harmony, Counterpoint and Analysis*
Serly, Tibor, *Modus Lascivus: The Road to Enharmonicism*
Stuckenschmidt, H.H., *Music from 1925 to 1975*

I. Musical Compositions:

Argento, Dominick, *The Voyage of Edgar Allen Poe* (opera)
Berio, Luciano, *Concerto for Cello and Orchestra*
Blackwood, Easley, *Symphoy No. 4*
Brant, Henry, *Spatial Concerto* (voices and piano)
Carter, Elliott, *Symphony for Three Orchestras*
Colgrass, Michael, *Letters from Mozart* (piano and orchestra)
        Concertmasters
Davies, Peter M., *The Martyrdom of St. Magnus* (opera)
        Symphony
Del Tredici, David, *Annotated Alice*
        Final Alice
Diamond, David, *Concerto No. 3 for Violin and Orchestra*
Druckman, Jacob, *Mirage* (orchestra)
Einem, Gottfried von, *Kabale und Liebe* (opera)
Erb, Donald, *Concerto for Cello and Orchestra*
Finney, Ross Lee, *Concerto No. 2 for Violin and Orchestra*
Glass, Philip, *Einstein on the Beach* (opera)
Gould, Morton, *Symphony of Spirituals*
Henze, Hans Werner, *We Come to the River* (opera)
Holmboe, Vagn, *Concerto for Tuba and Orchestra*
        Concerto for Flute and Orchestra
Hovhaness, Alan, *Symphonies No. 28, 29, 30 and 31*
        Concerto for Violin and Orchestra
Imbrie, Andrew, *Angle of Repose* (opera)
Lees, Benjamin, *Passacaglia for Orchestra*
        Concerto for Woodwind Quintet and Orchestra
Lutoslawski, Witold, *Mi-parti*
Mayuzumi, Toshiro, *Kinkakuji* (opera)
Menotti, Gian Carlo, *The Hero* (opera)
        Symphony No. 1, "The Halcyon"
Pasatieri, Thomas, *Inez de Castro* (opera)
Rochberg, George, *Symphony No. 4*
Schat, Peter, *Houdini Symphony* (a circus opera)
Schuller, Gunther, *Concerto for Violin and Orchestra*
Shchedrin, Rodion, *Concerto No. 3 for Piano and Orchestra*
Siegmeister, Elie, *Double Concerto for Violin, Piano and Orchestra*
        Night of the Moonspell (opera)
Stockhausen, Karlheinz, *Sirius*
Tavener, John, *A Gentle Spirit* (opera)
Weisgall, Hugo, *The Hundred Nights* (opera)
Wernick, Richard, *Visions of Terror and Wonder*
Wuorinen, Charles, *Percussion Symphony*
Xenakis, Iannis, *Epei*

1977

World Events:

In the U.S., President Carter pardons all Vietnam draft evaders; James Schlesinger becomes head of the newly created Department of Energy; the winter months cause a severe energy crisis for much of the nation; the Panama Canal Treaty providing for eventual Panama Canal ownership by Panama is signed; U.S. territorial waters are extended to 200 miles off the coasts; the space shuttle *Enterprise* is tested. Internationally, Menachem Begin becomes Prime Minister of Israel and begins meetings with Anwar Sadat of Egypt to establish peace between the two nations; Leonid Brezhnev ousts Podgorny to become sole head of Russia; the military seizes power in Thailand and begins border warfare with Cambodia; Indira Gandhi is defeated by M.R. Desai who becomes Prime Minister of India.

Cultural Highlights:

Pulitzers: Drama, Michael Cristofer (*The Shadow Box*); Poetry, James Merrill (*Divine Comedies*). Spanish poet Vicente Aleixandre receives the Nobel Prize for Literature; J.B. Priestley receives the Order of Merit; the Centre National d'Art et de Culture Georges Pompidou opens in Paris; the British Art Center at Yale opens its doors. Deaths include Russian artist Naum Gabo and British artist John Nash, American authors James M. Cain and MacKinlay Kantor and poet Robert Lowell, British poet Thomas Blackburn and Russian novelist Vladimir Nabokov. Other highlights include:

Art: Robert Bechtle, *Stucco Wall*; Fernando Botero, *Pedro on a Horse*; Marc Chagall, *American Windows*; Erté, *Beauty and the Beast*; R.B. Kitaj, *The Orientalist*; Malcolm Morley, *Day of the Locust*; Claes Oldenberg, *Batcolumn*; Ernest Trova, *Falling Man*.

Literature: Louis Auchincloss, Dark Lady; John Cheever, *Falconer*; John Fowles, *Daniel Martin*; James Herriot, *All Things Wise and Wonderful*; Robert Lowell, *Day by Day*; Erich Segal, *Oliver's Story*; Irwin Shaw, *Beggarman, Thief*; Paul Theroux, *Consul's File*.

MUSICAL EVENTS

A. Births:

Stefan Milenkovic (Yug-vn)

B. Deaths:

Jan 2	Erroll Garner (Am-pop)	Aug 7	Jacob Kwalwasser (Am-m.ed)
Jan 4	John Vincent (Am-cm-the)	Sep 7	Gustave Reese (Am-mus)
Feb 7	Sidney Foster (Am-pn)	Sep 13	Leopold Stokowski (Am-cd)
Feb 18	Alessandro Ziliani (It-ten)	Sep 15	Grete Stückgold (Ger-sop)
Mar 10	E. Power Biggs (Br-org)	Sep 16	Maria Callas (Gr-sop)
Mar 15	Thrasybulos Georgiades	Sep 21	Kurt Adler (Am-pn-cd)
	(Gr-mus)	Sep 29	Alexander Tcherepnin (Rus-cm)
Mar 24	Saburo Moroi (Jp-cm)	Oct 14	Bing Crosby (Am-pop)
Mar 29	Fritz Ollendorf (Ger-bs)	Nov 5	Guy Lombardo (Can-pop)
Apr 4	Eugéne Zador (Hun-cm)	Nov 15	Richard Addinsel (Br-cm)
May 16	E. van Remoortel (Bel-cd)	Nov 21	Paul Schöffler (Ger-bar)
Jun 13	Carmela Ponselle (Am-sop)	Dec 16	Thomas Schippers (Am-cd)
Jul 17	Witold Malcuzynski (Pol-pn)	Dec 22	Johann W. David (Aus-cm)

C. Débuts:

Met ---James Atherton (ten), Carmen Balthrop (sop), Josephine Barstow (Sop), Kathleen Battle (sop), Claudine Carlson (mez), Guy Chauvet (ten), John Cheek (bs), Maria Chiara (sop), Ileana Cotrubas (sop), Peter Dvorsky (ten), Edita Gruberová (sop), Heather Harper (sop), Isola Jones (mez), Elena Mauti-Nunziata (sop), Giorgio Merighi (ten), Florence Quivar (mez), Sylvia Sass (sop), Neil Shicoff (ten), Bernd Weikl (bar)

U.S. --Margarita Castro-Alberty (N.Y.), Maria Chiara (Chicago), Kristine Ciesinski (N.Y.), Cynthia Clarey (N.Y.), David Duesing, Jonathan Green (N.Y.), Steven de Groote, Håkan

Hagegård (Seattle), Sylvia Ho (N.Y.), Gwynne Howell (Chicago), Carlos Kleiber (Chicago), Gidon Kremer, Yuri Mazurok (San Francisco), Franz Nentwig (San Francisco), Mariana Nicolesco (N.Y.), Ken Noda (N.Y.), Maria Parazzini (San Francisco), Patricia Payne (San Francisco), Hanna Schwarz (San Francisco), Alexander Toradze (N.Y.), Jacques Trussel (N.Y.), Carol Vaness (San Francisco), Sarah Walker (Chicago), Oxana Yablonskaya (El Paso)

Other -Sharon Isbin (London), Nigel P. Kennedy (London), André Nikolsky (Moscow), Dimitrios Sgouros (Piraeus, Greece), James Tocco (Vienna)

D. New Positions:

Conductors: Claudio Abbado (La Scala), Gary Bertini (Jerusalem SO), Christoph von Dohnányi (Hamburg Opera), Antal Dorati (Detroit SO), Charles Dutoit (Montreal SO), Michael Gielen (Frankfurt Opera), Günther Herbig (East Berlin SO), Arpád Joó (Calgary SO), Kazimierz Kord (Warsaw PO), Eduardo Mata (Dallas SO), Simon Rattle (BBC Scottish SO), Mstislav Rostropovich (National SO), Leif Segerstam (Finnish Radio SO), Leonard Slatkin (New Orleans PO), Judith Somogi (Utica SO), Bryden Thomson (Ulster Orchestra), Edo de Waart (San Francisco SO), Walter Weller (Liverpool PO), Antoni Wit (Polish Radio SO)

Educational: Elliott W. Galkin (director, Peabody), Margaret Harshaw (voice, Philadelphia Academy of Vocal Arts), Grant Johannesen (director, Cleveland Institute), Zinka Milanov (voice, Curtis), James Tocco (Indiana University)

Others: Edward Corn (manager, Opera Co. of Philadelphia), Elliot W. Galkin (director, Peabody), Lofti Mansouri (general director, Canadian Opera), Niels Möller (manager, Danish Royal Opera), Ragnar Ulfung (artistic director, Göteborg Opera)

E. Prizes and Honors:

Prizes: Steven de Groote (Cliburn), Antonio Meneses (Munich), Aprile Millo (Caballé), Ivo Petric (Ljubljana), Nathaniel Rosen (Naumberg), André-Michel Schub (Fisher), Richard Stolzman (Fisher), Richard Wernick (Pulitzer--*Visions of Terror and Wonder*)

Honors: Antonio de Almeida (Legion of Honor), Clifford Curzon (knighted), Placido Domingo (Musician of the Year, *Musical America*), James Galway (Order of the British Empire), Alexander Gibson (knighted), Peter Hall (knighted), Dorothy Kirsten (Order of Merit), Virgil Thomson (MacDowell Medal), David Willcocks (knighted)

F. Biographical Highlights:

John Alexander undergoes two heart by-pass operations; Victoria Bond becomes the first woman to receive a doctorate in conducting from Juilliard; Colin Davis becomes the first British conductor to perform at Bayreuth; Yuri Egorov asks for asylum from the Dutch; Barbara Hendricks meets and marries her manager-husband, Martin Engstrom; Peter Hofmann, following a motorcycle accident, spends 8 months in the hospital; Jeffrey Kahane graduates from San Francisco Conservatory; Vitaly Komar and Alexander Melamid emigrate to Israel; Eva Marton and Matti Salminen make their Bayreuth debuts; Riccardo Muti named as Principle Guest Conductor of the Philadelphia Orchestra; Anne-Sophie Mutter is personally invited by Karajan to play with the Berlin PO; Yevgeni Nesterenko and Tatiana Troyanos make their La Scala debuts; Ervin Nyiregyházi's new recordings bring back a revival of interest in his playing; Andrzej Panufnik's works are taken from the banned list and played once again in Poland; Thomas Schippers, made Conductor Emeritus of the Cincinnati SO, learns of his lung cancer; Gunther Schuller resigns as President of New England Conservatory; Dmitri Sitkovetsky emigrates to the U.S.; Dang Thai Son leaves Hanoi for further music study in Moscow; Alexander Toradze wins the Silver Medal in the Cliburn Competition; Peter Zazofsky, with his Bronze Medal, is the first Westerner to win at the Wieniawski competition in 15 years.

G. Institutional Openings:

Performing Groups: Austin Civic Orchestra (Texas), Chamber Music America (N.Y.),

Chestnut Brass Company, Cincinnati Pops Orchestra, George Coates Performance Works (San Francisco), Kalichstein-Laredo-Robinson Trio, Los Angeles Piano Quartet, Ninety Second Street Y Chamber Orchestra (N.Y.), Opera for Youth (Sarasota, Florida), Opera Theater of St. Louis, Schoenberg (Columbia) String Quartet, Sofia Festival Sinfonietta, Soviet Emigré Orchestra (N.Y.), Tremont String Quartet (N.Y.)

Festivals: Colorado Music Festival (Boulder), St. Magnus Festival (Orkney Islands, Scotland); Spoleto, U.S.A. Festival (Charleston, South Carolina)

Educational: Institut de Recherche et de Coordination Acoustique/Musique (IRCAM, Paris), *Musicologica Austriaca*

Other: American Artists International Foundation, Association of Concert Bands (Allentown, Pennsylvania), Association of Professional Vocal Ensembles (Chicago), Cumberland County Civic Center (Portland, Maine), International Arnold Schoenberg Piano Concours (Netherlands), Muzyka Centrum Artistic Society (Krakow), Sydney International Piano Competition (Australia), Teatro Nacional (Guatamala City)

H. Musical Literature:

Bakst, James, *A History of Russian Soviet Music*
Béhaque, Gerard, *Music in Latin America*
Cope, David, *New Music Composition*
Merrill, Robert, *Between Acts*
Perle, George, *Twelve-Tone Tonality*
Smither, Howard, *A History of the Oratorio*
Strunk, Oliver, *Essays on Music in the Byzantine World*
Ultan, Lloyd, *Music Theory: Problems and Practice in the Middle Ages and Renaissance*

I. Musical Compositions:

Berio, Luciano, *Concerto for Piano and Orchestra*
Colgrass, Michael, *Déjà Vu* (4 percussionists and orchestra)
          Theater of the Universe (voice, chorus and orchestra)
Corigliano, John, *Concerto for Clarinet and Orchestra*
Crumb, George, *Star Child*
Davies, Peter M., *A Mirror of Whitening Light* (orchestra)
Druckman, Jacob, *Chiaroscuro* (orchestra)
Einem, Gottfried von, *Wiener Symphonie*
Fine, Vivian, *Woman in the Garden* (opera)
Finney, Ross Lee, *Concerto for Strings*
Foss, Lukas, *American Cantata*
Gutchë, Gene, *Perseus and Andromeda XX* (orchestra)
Hanson, Howard, *Symphony No. 7, "A Sea Symphony"*
Harbison, John, *Full Moon in March* (opera)
Imbrie, Andrew, *Concerto for Flute and Orchestra*
Lees, Benjamin, *Concerto for Viola and Orchestra*
Martino, Donald, *Triple Concerto for Clarinet, Bass Clarinet and Contrabass Clarinet*
Musgrave, Thea, *Mary, Queen of Scots* (opera)
Panufnik, Andrzej, *Sinfonia Mistica*
Paulus, Stephen, *The Village Singer* (opera)
Penderecki, Krzystoff, *Concerto for Violin and Orchestra*
          De Profundis
Ran, Shulamit, *Concerto for Piano and Orchestra*
Schuller, Gunther, *Concerto No. 2 for Horns and Orchestra*
Shchedrin, Rodion, *Dead Souls* (opera)
Stockhausen, Karlheinz, *Sirius*
Takemitsu, Toru, *A Flock Descends into the Pentagonal Garden*
Tavener, John, *Thérèse* (opera)
Tippett, Michael, *Symphony No. 4*
          The Ice Break (opera)
Williamson, Malcolm, *Symphony No. 4*

1978

World Events:
The United States establishes official diplomatic relations with Communist China; Camp David, Maryland, becomes the site of Mideast Peace talks between Menachim Begin of Israel and Anwar Sadat of Egypt; the Panama Canal Treaty is ratified by Congress; mandatory retirement age is pushed up to 70; First-Class Postage goes up to 15 cents; the first successful Trans-Atlantic balloon crossing is made. Internationally, the Soviets conduct four successful *Soyuz* missions each docking with an orbiting space station; the terrorist organization "Red Brigade" kidnaps and murders Aldo Moro, former Italian Premier; riots break out in Iran against the Shah; Civil War breaks out in Yeman; a military coup overthrows the government of Afghanistan; Pieter Botha becomes Prime Minister of South Africa.

Cultural Highlights:
Pulitzers: Drama, Donald L. Colburn (*The Gin Game*); Fiction, James Alan McPherson (*Elbow Room*); Poetry, Howard Nemerov (*Collected Poems*). Yiddish poet Isaac Bashevis Singer receives the Nobel Prize for Literature. Deaths include American artists Edwin Dickinson, Abraham Rattner and Norman Rockwell, Italian artist Giorgio de Chirico, American novelist Faith Baldwin, poet Louis Zukofsky, author James Cozzens and historian Bruce Catton. Other highlights include:

Art: Robert Arneson, *Splat*; Jack Beal, *Prudence, Avarice, Lust, Justice, Anger*; Patrick Caulfield, *Still Life--Spring Fashion*; Jim Dine, *Self-Portrait with Cigar*; Richard Estes, *Downtown*; Roy Lichtenstein, *Self-Portrait*; Malcolm Morley, *Ultimate Anxiety*; Susan Rothenberg, *The Smoker*; Jeffrey Shaw, *Moonlight Goose*; Frank Stella, *Harewa*.

Literature: *The Bible: New International Version*; Louis Auchincloss, *The Country Cousin*; John Gardner, *On Moral Fiction*; John Irving, *The World According to Garp*; James Michener, *Chesapeake*; Czeslaw Milosz, *Bells in Winter*; Chaim Potok, *Wanderings: History of the Jews*; Isaac B. Singer, *Shosha*; Herman Wouk, *War and Remembrance*.

MUSICAL EVENTS

B. Deaths:

Jan 10	Don Gillis (Am-cm)	May 26	Tamara Karasavina (Rus-bal)
Jan 14	Robert Heger (Ger-cd)	Jul 4	Nino Verchi (It-cd)
Jan 30	Mindru Katz (Rom-pn)	Jul 28	Willem von Otterlo (Hol-cd)
Feb 14	Jindrich Rohan (Cz-cd)	Aug 1	Rudolf Kolisch (Am-vn)
Apr 6	Nicholas Nabokov (Rus-cm)	Aug 2	Carlos Chávez (Mex-cd-cm)
Apr 29	Giacomo Vaghi (It-bs)	Aug 20	Ivan Jirko (Cz-cm)
May 1	Aram Khachaturian (Rus-cm)	Oct 5	Jose Luccioni (Fr-ten)
May 12	Alois Pernerstorfer (Aus-bs)	Oct 8	Tibor Serly (Hun-cd-cm
May 14	Alexander Kipnis (Rus-bs)	Oct 25	Herbert Alsen (Ger-bs)
May 17	William Steinberg (Ger-cd)	Dec 3	William Grant Still (Am-cm)
May 18	Václav Dobiás (Cz-cm)	Dec 24	Raymond Michalski (Am-bs)

C. Debuts:

Met ---John Aler (ten), Karan Armstrong (sop), Arleen Augér (sop), Kathleen Battle (sop), Carlo Bini (ten), John Brecknock (ten), Frederick Burchinal (bar), Ariel Bybee (mez), Patricia Craig (sop), Alan Crofoot (ten), Michael Devlin (bar), Håkan Hagegård (bar), Richard Knies (ten), Luis Lima (ten), Carol Malone (sop), Ermanno Mauro (ten), Yuri Mazurok (bar), Kurt Moll (bs), Mariana Nicolesco (sop), Siegmund Nimsgern (bar), Ashley Putnam (sop), Nicola Rescigno (cd), Calvin Simmons (cd), Anna Tomowa-Sintow (sop), Jena Van Ree (ten), Julia Varady (sop)

U.S. --June Anderson (N.Y.), David Atherton (San Francisco), Arleen Augér (Oregon), Lynn Chang, Katherine Ciesinski (Charleston), Yuri Egorov (N.Y.), Jeffrey Kahane (San Francisco), Ida Kavafian (N.Y.), Emma Kirkby (tour), Katia and Marielle Labèque (Los Angeles), Sandro de Palma (N.Y.), Mario Renaudo (Philadelphia), Andras Schiff (N.Y.),

Luciana Serra (Charleston), Henk Smit (Detroit), Gregory Lee Stapp (Philadelphia), Nunzio Todisco (San Francisco), Carol Vaness (San Francisco), Krystian Zimerman (tour), Marilyn Zschau (N.Y.)

Other -Marianne Häggander (Stockholm), Marie McLaughlin (London), Anne-Sophie Mutter (Berlin)

D. New Positions:

Conductors: Carlo Maria Giulini (Los Angeles PO), Erich Leinsdorf (Radio SO of West Berlin), Kent Nagano (Berkeley SO), Brian Priestman (Miami SO), Gerard Schwarz (Los Angeles Chamber Orchestra), Calvin Simmons (Oakland SO), Klaus Tennstedt (North German Radio SO)

Educational: Eugene Conley (voice, North Texas State), Andrew Foldi (voice, Cleveland Institute), Nell Rankin (voice head, Philadelphia Academy of Arts)

Others: Ezra Laderman (director, music, National Endowment for the Arts)

E. Prizes and Honors:

Prizes: Dalia Atlas (Villa Lobos), Boris Bloch (Busoni), Carter Brey (Munich), Michael Colgrass (Pulitzer--*Déjà Vu*), Michel Dalberto (Leeds), Arthur Greene (Bachauer), André Leplante (Tchaikovsky), Yo Yo Ma (Fisher), Elmar Oliveira (Tchaikovsky), Vincent Persichetti (Friedheim--*Concerto for English Horn and Orchestra*),   Mikhail Pletnev (Tchaikovsky), Nathaniel Rosen (Tchaikovsky), Carol Wincenc (Naumberg)

Honors: Marian Anderson (Kennedy Center), Victoria de los Angeles (Premio Nacional de Arte, Spain), Isobel Baillie (Dame of the British Empire), Aaron Copland (Golden Baton), Dietrich Fischer-Dieskau (honorary doctorate, Oxford), Bernard Haitink (knighted), Herbert von Karajan (honorary doctorate, Oxford), Alicia de Larrocha (Musician of the Year, *Musical America*), Charles Mackerras (Janácek Medal), Peter Pears (knighted), Richard Rodgers (Kennedy Center), Artur Rubinstein (Kennedy Center)

F. Biographical Highlights:

Yefim Bronfman enters Juilliard; Riccardo Chailly makes his conducting debut at La Scala; Barbara Daniels makes her Covent Garden debut; Bella Davidovich, given permission to leave Russia, emigrates to the U.S.; Sergei Edelmann leaves Russia with his family and ends up in Rome for six months; Simon Estes, as Wagner's Dutchman, becomes the first black to sing a lead role at Bayreuth; James Galway makes his first American tour--also suffers two broken legs and broken arm when struck by a motor-cycle in Lucerne; Dylana Jenson, with a Silver Medal in the Tchaikovsky Competition, becomes the first woman to win a prize in Moscow; Kyrill Kondrashin and Ekaterina Novitskaya defect to the West; Yoel Levi becomes assistant to Lorin Maazel in Cleveland; Eva Marton and Sylvia Sass make their La Scala debuts; Shlomo Mintz graduates from Juilliard; Mstislav Rostropovich and Galina Vishnevskaya are stripped of their Russian citizenship; Andras Schiff takes a concert tour of Japan; Neil Shicoff marries soprano Judith Haddon; Georg Solti, on the Chicago SO's third European tour, visits Budapest for the first time in 39 years.

G. Institutional Openings:

Performing Groups: Chanticleer (San Francisco Male Chorus), Four Corners Opera Association (Farmington, New Mexico), Honolulu Symphony Chorus, Idaho Falls Opera Theater, The Mozartean Players (N.Y.), National Opera Studio (London), New Pittsburgh Chamber Orchestra, Opera Go Round (by Scottish Opera), Opera North Co. (Leeds), Pittsburgh Chamber Opera Theater, Quink (Dutch a capella ensemble), Wachovia Little Symphony (Senior Citizens)

Festivals: Dresden Opera Festival

Other: Community Artist Residency Training (CART), Cultural Arts Council of Houston, Denver Center for the Performing Arts, Friedheim Awards (Kennedy Center), Noah Greenberg Award (N.Y.), Grieg Hall (Bergen), *Inter-American Music Review*

H. Musical Literature:

Bevan, Clifford, *The Tuba Family*
Caldwell, John, *Medieval Music*
Cole, Hugo, *The Changing Face of Music*
Eisler, Paul, ed., *World Chronology of Music* (6 vols.)
Geiringer, Karl, *Instruments in the History of Western Music*
Harris, Ernest, *Music Education: A Guide to Information Sources*
Holland, James, *Percussion*
Hoppin, Richard, *Medieval Music*
Robinson, Ray, *Choral Music*
Serly, Tibor, *The Rhetoric of Melody*

I. Musical Compositions:

Barber, Samuel, *Essay No. 3 for Orchestra*
Bennett, Richard R., *Concerto for Doublebass and Orchestra*
Berio, Luciano, *Encore* (orchestra)
Blackwood, Easley, *Symphony No. 5*
Boulez, Pierre, *Notations* (orchestra)
Davies, Peter M., *Salome* (ballet)
Druckman, Jacob, *Concerto for Viola and Orchestra*
Dutilleux, Henri, *Timbres, espace, mouvement* (orchestra)
            Concerto for Viola and Orchestra
Feldman, Morton, *Why Patterns* (instrumental ensemble)
Ferneyhough, Brian, *La Terre est un Homme* (orchestra)
Foss, Lukas, *Brass Quintet*
Françaix, Jean, *Clarinet Quintet*
Gruber, H.K., *Frankenstein* (speaker and orchestra)
Hamilton, Iain, *Anna Karenina* (opera)
Harbison, John, *Concerto for Piano and Orchestra*
Harris, Roy, *Symphony No. 1*
Kraft, William, *Andirivieni* (tuba and orchestra)
Laderman, Ezra, *Concerto for Violin and Orchestra*
Lazarof, Henri, *Chamber Symphony*
Ligeti, György, *The Grand Macabre* (opera)
McCabe, John, *Symphony No. 3, "Hommages"*
Menotti, Gian Carlo, *The Trial of the Gypsy* (opera)
Panufnik, Andrzej, *Metasymphonie* (organ and orchestra)
Penderecki, Krzystoff, *Paradise Lost* (opera)
Perle, George, *13 Dickenson Songs*
Read, Gardner, *Concerto for Piano and Orchestra*
Reich, Steve, *Music for a Large Ensemble*
Reimann, Aribert, *Lear* (opera)
Sallinen, Aulis, *The Red Line* (opera)
            Dies Irae (soloists, chorus, orchestra)
Salzman, Eric, *Noah* (spectacle)
Schat, Peter, *Symphony*
Schnittke, Alfred, *Concerto No. 3 for Violin and Orchestra*
Schwantner, Joseph, *Aftertones of Infinity* (orchestra)
Schuler, Gunther, *Deai* (2 orchestras)
Sessions, Roger, *Symphony No. 9*
Siegmeister, Elie, *Concerto for Violin and Orchestra*
Tavener, John, *Liturgy of St. John Chrysostom* (choir)
Williamson, Malcolm, *Mass of Christ, the King*
Wuorinen, Charles, *Two-Part Symphony*

1979

World Events:
In the U.S., the inflation rate hits a record high of 13%; a nuclear reactor accident causing a near meltdown at Three Mile Island in Pennsylvania almost causes a panic. In Iran, the Iranians storm the U.S. embassy and take 50 Americans hostage--the Shah flees Iran and goes to the U.S. but is met with a violent political uproar causing his departure to Panama--the Ayatollah Khomeini takes over as political and spiritual leader, proclaiming an Islamic Republic--all Iranian assets and oil imports are suspended in the U.S.; Margaret Thatcher becomes England's first woman Prime Minister; Egypt and Israel sign a historic peace treaty; Russian troops invade Afghanistan and Vietnamese troops invade Cambodia causing thousands to flee to Thailand.

Cultural Highlights:
Pulitzers: Drama, Sam Shepherd (*Buried Child*); Fiction, John Cheever (*The Stories of John Cheever*); Poetry, Robert Penn Warren (*Now and Then: Poems 1976-1978*). The Nobel Prize for Literature goes to Greek author Odysseus Elytis while Salvador Dali is inducted into the French Academy. Deaths include Italian sculptor Pietro Lazzari and Russian artist Sonya Delauney, American authors James T. Farrell and S.J. Perelman, poet Elizabeth Bishop, British authors Nicholas Monsarrat and Jean Rhys and Russian author Konstantin Simonov. Other highlights include:

Art: Fernando Botero, *Still Life in Front of a Window*; Joseph Beuys, *Aus Berlin*; Louise Bourgeois, *Partial Recall*; Sandro Chia, *In Strange and Gloomy Waters*; Mark Di Suvero, *She*; Jim Dine, *Our Dreams Still Point North*; Philip Guston, *Entrance*; Henry Moore, *Upright Motive No. 9*; Malcolm Morley, *Christmas Tree*.

Literature: Peter Benchley, *The Island*; C. Lasch, *The Culture of Narcissism*; John Le Carré, *Smiley's People*; Norman Mailer, *The Executioner's Song*; Bernard Malamud, *Dubin's Lives*; Neil Simon, *They're Playing Our Song*; Isaac B. Singer, *Old Love*; William Styron, *Sophie's Choice*; John Updike, *Too Far to Go*.

MUSICAL EVENTS

B. Deaths:

Jan 8	Chester Watson (Am-bs)	Jun 28	Paul Dessau (Ger-cm)
Jan 13	Marjorie Lawrence (Aust-sop)	Jul 16	Alfred Deller (Br-c.ten)
Mar 5	Alan Crofoot (Am-ten)	Jul 23	Mathieu Ahlersmeyer (Ger-bar)
Mar 7	Guiomar Novaës (Bra-pn)	Aug 25	Stan Kenton (Am-pop)
Mar 11	Gerhard Stolze (Ger-ten)	Oct 1	Roy Harris (Am-cm)
Mar 16	Leonide Massine (Rus-bal)	Oct 7	Pierre Bernac (Fr-bar)
Mar 17	Giacomo Lauri-Volpi (It-ten)	Oct 10	Paul Paray (Fr-cd)
Apr 16	Maria Caniglia (It-sop)	Oct 14	Arthur Mendel (Am-mus)
May 9	Ben Weber (Am-cm)	Oct 22	Nadia Boulanger (Fr-m.ed)
May 14	Thomas Scherman (Ger-cd)	Oct 26	Germaine Lubin (Fr-sop)
Jun 9	Alexander Sved (Hun-bar)	Dec 30	Richard Rodgers (Am-pop)

C. Débuts:
Met ---Bruna Baglioni (mez), Agnes Baltsa (mez), Brenda Boozer (mez), Norma Burrowes (sop), Giuliano Ciannella (ten), Philip Creech (ten), Mariella Devia (sop), Dale Duesing (bar), Pablo Elvira (bar), Timothy Jenkins (ten), Makvala Kasrashvili (sop), Dimitri Kavrakos (bs), Catherine Malfitano (sop), Seth McCoy (ten), Julia Migenes-Johnson (sop), Maria Luisa Nave (mez), Carol Neblett (sop), Yevgeni Nesterenko (bs), Florence Quivar (mez), Gianna Rolandi (sop), Harald Stamm (bs)

U.S. --Benito di Bella (San Francisco), Gabriela Benacková (N.Y.), Livia Budai (San Francisco), Myung-Whun Chung (Los Angeles), Robert Cohen (tour), Bella Davidovich (N.Y.), Sharon Isbin (N.Y.), Cyprien Katsaris (Detroit), Kathleen Kuhlmann (Chicago), Kevin Langan (New Jersey), Ann Murray (N.Y.), Iolanta Omilian (Dallas), Carlos Paita (Houston), Christof Perick (San Francisco), Yordi Ramiro (San Francisco), Simon Rattle (Los Angeles), Emily Rawlins (San Francisco), Leslie Richards (San Diego), Evelyn de la Rosa (San Francisco), Anny Schlemm (San Francisco), Stefania Toczyska (San Francisco)

Other -Augustin Dumay (Paris), John Edward Holmquist (London), Joko Kubo (Japan)

D. New Positions:

Conductors: Claudio Abbado (London SO), Philippe Entremont (New Orleans SO), Choo Hoey (Singapore SO), François Huybrechts (San Antonio SO), Okko Kamu (Helsinki SO), Christopher Keene (Long Island PO), Kyrill Kondrashin (Amsterdam Concertgebouw), James Loughran (Bamberg SO), Neville Marriner (Minnesota SO), Riccardo Muti (Philharmonia Orchestra), Simon Rattle (San Francisco and Toronto SO's), Leonard Slatkin (St. Louis SO), Bryden Thomson (BBC Welsh SO), Walter Weller (Royal PO), David Zinman (Rotterdam PO)

Others: Mark Elder (music director, English National Opera)

E. Prizes and Honors:

Prizes: Emanuel Ax (Fisher), Ronald Braunstein (Karajan), Robert Briggs (Steber), Sergiu Comissiona (Ditson), Jay M. Gottlieb (Boulanger), Panayis Lyras (Bachauer), Peter Orth (Naumberg), George Rochberg (Friedheim--*String Quartet No. 4*), Joseph Schwantner (Pulitzer--*Aftertones of Infinity*), Dmitri Sitkovetsky (Kreisler), Diana Soviero (Tucker), Catherine Steiert (Busoni), Geraldine Walther (Primrose), Steven A. Williams (Baltimore), Peter Zazofsky (Montreal)

Honors: Richard Armstrong (Janácek Medal), Aaron Copland (Kennedy Center), Peter Maxwell Davies (honorary doctorate, Edinburgh University), Charles Mackerras (knighted), Leona Mitchell (honorary doctorate, Oklahoma City University), Eugene Ormandy (Golden Baton), Leontyne Price (honorary doctorate, Columbia), Rudolf Serkin (Musician of the Year, *Musical America*), Georg Solti (honorary doctorate, Harvard), Joan Sutherland (Dame of the British Empire)

F. Biographical Highlights:

Claudio Abbado becomes a U.S. citizen; Maurice Abravanel, on his doctor's orders, resigns his Utah SO post; Jeannine Altmeyer and Karan Armstrong make their Bayreuth debuts; Willi Boskovsky suffers a mild heart attack; James Conlon takes over the Cincinnati May Festival; Christoph von Dohnányi secretly marries Anja Silja after 10 years of living together; Antal Dorati takes the Detroit SO on its first international tour; Sergei Edelmann moves to New York from Italy; Vladimir Feltsman, applying for immigration to Israel, is ostracized from all public performance by the Soviets; Leon Fleisher loses control of his right hand and undergoes surgery and therapy; Alexander Goudunov defects to the West; Gary Graffman suffers right hand problems and retires from performance; Wynton Marsalis goes to Juilliard; Birgit Nilsson settles her tax dispute with the IRS and gives her first U.S. performance in 5 years; Eugene Ormandy announces his pending retirement; Seiji Ozawa takes the Boston SO on a tour of China; Kenneth Riegel, Ellen Shade and Kiri Te Kanawa make their La Scala debuts; Julius Rudel steps down after 30 years with the New York City Opera; Andras Schiff leaves Hungary for the West; Isaac Stern invited by the Chinese to advise on implementing a successful music program.

G. Institutional Openings:

Performing Groups: Boston PO, Commedia dell'Opera (Berkeley Opera), Jupiter Symphony (N.Y.), Long Island PO, Opera Midwest (Evanston, Illinois), Orchestra of the Twentieth Century (N.Y.), Singapore SO, Texas Chamber Orchestra (Houston), Tulsa Little SO (Oklahoma Sinphonia), Youth Symphony of the U.S.

Festivals: Buxton Festival (Derbyshire, England), New Music American Festival (Various Locations), Soviet Emigré Music Festival (N.Y.)

Other: Atlantic Center for the Arts (Florida), Ralph R. Bailey Concert Hall (Fort Lauderdale), Berwald Hall (Stockholm), Bowling Green Musical Arts Center (Ohio), Northeastern Records (Boston), Salt Lake City Symphony Hall, Eleanor Steber Musical Foundation Vocal Competition (N.Y.), Leopold Stokowski Conducting Prize, Terrace Theater (Washington, D.C.)

H. Musical Literature:

Benjamin, Thomas, *The Craft of Modal Counterpoint*
Blackwood, Alan, *Encyclopedia of Music*
Block/Neuls-Bates, *Women in American Music*
Brings, Allen, et al, *A New Approach to Keyboard Music*
Kirby, F.E., *Music in the Classic Period*
MacClintock, Carol, *Reading in the History of Music Performance*
Owen, Barbara, *The Organ in New England*
Schaeffer, Boguslaw, *History of Music, Styles and Authors*
Temperley, Nicholas, *Music of the English Parish Church*

I. Musical Compositions:

Argento, Dominick, *Miss Havisham's Fire* (opera)
Arnold, Malcolm, *Symphony No. 8*
Bazelon, Irwin, *Junctures* (orchestra)
Bernstein, Leonard, *Song Fest*
Brant, Henry, *Spatial Concerto* (piano and orchestra)
Crumb, George, *Makrokosmos IV, "Celestial Mechanics"*
Davies, Peter M., *The Lighthouse* (opera)
              Solstice of Light (tenor, chorus and orchestra)
Druckman, Jacob, *Aureole* (orchestra)
Feldman, Morton, *Violin and Orchestra*
Françaix, Jean, *Concerto No. 2 for Violin and Orchestra*
Fricker, Peter R. *Laudi Concertati* (organ and orchestra)
Halffter, Cristóbal, *Concerto for Violin and Orchestra*
Harbison, John, *Full Moon in March* (opera)
Hoiby, Lee, *Concerto No. 2 for Piano and Orchestra*
Hovhaness, Alan, *Concerto for Guitar and Orchestra*
              Symphony No. 36
Kim, Earl, *Concerto for Violin and Orchestra*
Knussen, Oliver, *Symphony No. 3*
              The Rajah's Diamond (opera)
Laderman, Ezra, *Concerto No. 1 for Piano and Orchestra*
Lutoslawski, Witold, *Novelette* (orchestra)
McCabe, John, *The Shadow of Light* (orchestra)
Musgrave, Thea, *A Christmas Carol* (opera)
Nordheim, Arne, *The Tempest* (ballet)
Panufnik, Andrzej, *Concerto Festivo*
Pasatieri, Thomas, *Three Sisters* (opera)
Penderecki, Krzystof, *Te Deum*
Reich, Steve, *Variations for Winds, Strings and Keyboard*
Rorem, Ned, *Nantucket Songs*
Rubbra, Edmund, *Symphony No. 11*
Sallinen, Aulis, *Symphony No. 4*
Schaeffer, Boguslaw, *Concerto for Doublebass and Orchestra*
              Symphony No. 10, "Maah"
Schnittke, Alfred, *Symphony No. 2, "St. Florian"*
Steptoe, Roger, *King of Macedon* (opera)
Stockhausen, Karlheinz, *Michaels Jugend - Michaels Heimkehr*
Tavener, John, *Palintropos* (piano and orchestra)
Tippett, Michael, *Concerto for String Trio and Orchestra*
Williamson, Malcolm, *Fanfarade* (orchestra)

1980

World Events:
At the request of President Carter, the U.S. Olympic Committee votes to boycott the Summer Olympics in Moscow; in the U.S., Ronald Reagan is elected as President No. 40; a rescue mission for the hostages in Iran fails; ABSCAM operations expose several prominent government officials; race riots occur in Miami; Mt. St. Helens in Washington State explodes in a violent eruption; the Winter Olympics take place in Lake Placid, New York. Internationally, Polish workers form an independent union, Solidarity; Soviet Cosmonauts set a new record for time in space, 185 days; gold prices reach a new high of $835 an ounce; Rhodesia becomes the independent state of Zimbabwe; Iraq begins a war with Iran; Quebec voters reject the idea of a separate French state.

Cultural Highlights:
Pulitzers: Drama, Lanford Wilson (*Talley's Folly*); Fiction, Norman Mailer (*The Executioner's Song*); Poetry, Donald Justice (*Selected Poems*). The Polish-born author Czeslaw Milosz receives the Nobel Prize for Literature; Marguerite Yourcenar is taken into the French Academy. The American Book Awards are set up, the D.H. Lawrence Festival begins in Taos, New Mexico and the Metropolitan Museum of Art in New York opens its American Wing. Deaths include American poets Muriel Rukeyser and James Wright and authors Marc Connelly, Mary O'Hara, Henry Miller and Katherine A. Porter, American artists Alexander Brook and Philip Guston, British artist Graham Sutherland, Italian sculptor Marino Marini, Austrian artist Oskar Kokoschka and French philosopher Jean Paul Sartre. Other highlights include:

Art: Enzo Cucchi, *Fish on the Back of the Adriatic Sea*; Mark di Suvero, *Keepers of the Flame*; Richard Diebenkorn, *Ocean Park No. 122*; David Hockney, *Mulholland Drive*; Roy Lichtenstein, *Forest Scene*; Vettor Pisani, *Oedipus and the Sphinx*; Kenneth Price, *De Chirico's Bathhouse*; Andrew Wyeth, *Day Dream (Helga)*.

Literature: John Ciardi, *A Browser's Dictionary*; William Golding, *Rites of Passage*; Judith Krantz, *Princess Daisy*; Vladimir Nabokov, *Lectures on Literature*; Robert Penn Warren, *Being There: Poetry 1977-1980*; Earl Welty, *Collected Stories*.

MUSICAL EVENTS

B. Deaths:

Jan 13	André Kostelanetz (Rus-cd)		May 17	Ernst Wiemann (Ger-bs)
Jan 21	Elvira de Hidalgo (Sp-sop)		Jun 7	Richard Bonelli (Am-bar)
Feb 24	Oliver Strunk (Am-mus)		Jun 20	Allan Pettersson (Swe-cm)
Mar 18	Jessica Dragonette (Am-sop)		Jun 28	José Iturbi (Sp-pn-cd)
Mar 25	Walter Susskind (Cz-cd)		Jul	Cecil Burleigh (Am-cm)
Mar 28	Hans Nissen (Ger-bar)		Jul 28	Otakar Kraus (Cz-bar)
Apr 20	Hilde Konetzni (Am-sop)		Aug 26	Miliza Korjus (Pol-sop)
May	Adele Kern (Ger-sop)		Sep 22	Lawrence Foster (Am-cel)
May 1	John Jacob Niles (Am-folk)		Oct 1	Lina Pagliughi (Am-sop)
May 1	Willi Reich (Swi-mus)		Oct 25	Virgil Fox (Am-org)
May 17	Maria Kurenko (Rus-sop)		Dec 25	Mario Filippeschi (It-ten)

C. Debuts:
Met ---Thomas Booth (ten), Frederick Burchinal (bar), Geraldine Decker (sop), Christiane Eda-Pierre (sop), Aage Haugland (bs), Peter Hofmann (ten), Siegfried Jerusalem (ten), Manfred Jung (ten), Eugene Kohn (cd), Margaret Marshall (sop), Franz Mazura (bar), Franz Nentwig (bar), Leo Nucci (bar), Patricia Payne (mez), Lucy Peacock (sop), Evelyn Petros (sop), David Rendall (ten), Galina Savova (sop), Brian Schexnayder (bar), Edward Sooter (ten), Jocelyne Taillon (alto), Jeffrey Tate (cd), Domenico Trimarchi (bs)

U.S. --Barbara Carter, Ulrik Cold (San Francisco), Luigi DeCorato (Newark), Pascal Devoyon, Martine Dupuy (N.Y.), Richard Estes (N.Y.), Jorma Hynninen (N.Y.), Manfred

Jung (Tulsa), Cecile Licad (Tanglewood), Louis Lortie (Seattle), Valerie Masterson (San Francisco), Lajos Miller (Houston), Aprile Millo (Salt Lake City), Uwe Mund (San Francisco), Leigh Munroe (N.Y.), Bent Norup (Portland, Oregon), William Parker (N.Y.), Dano Raffanti (Dallas), Wolfgang Rennert (San Francisco), Mikhail Svetlev (Washington, D.C.), Benjamin Verdery (N.Y.), Raili Viljakainen (N.Y.)

Other -Sally Ann Bottomley (Birmingham, England), David Edward Francis (Cheltenham), Sergiu Schwartz (London)

D. New Positions:

Conductors: David Atherton (San Diego SO and Royal Liverpool PO), Semyon Bychkov (Grand Rapids SO), Sergiu Comissiona (Houston SO), Dennis R. Davies (Stuttgart Opera), Akira Endo (Louisville Orchestra), Lukas Foss (Milwaukee SO), Michael Gielen (Cincinnati SO), Varujan Kojian (Utah SO), Zdenek Kosler (Prague National Theater), Simon Rattle (City of Birmingham SO), Lawrence Smith (San Antonio SO), Hans Vonk (The Hague SO), Walter Weller (Royal PO), John Williams (Boston Pops), Pinchas Zukerman (St. Paul Chamber Orchestra)

Educational: Ezio Flagello (Philadelphia Academy of Vocal Arts), Bernard Lefort (director, Paris Opera), Roger Guy Steptoe (composition and harmony, Royal Academy), Virginia Zeani (voice, Indiana University)

Others: Mikhail Baryshnikov (director, American Ballet Theater), Marta Istomin (artistic director, Kennedy Center), John Mauceri (music director, Washington Opera), Thomas Pasatieri (Atlanta Civic Opera), Wolfgang Sawallisch (director, Munich Staatstheater)

E. Prizes and Honors:

Prizes: Gregory Allen (Rubinstein), Thai Son Dang (Chopin), Jonathan Del Mar (Malko), David Del Tredici (Pulitzer--*In Memory of a Summer Day*), Richard Goode (Fisher), Barbara Gorzynska (Flesch), Irene Gubrud (Naumburg), John Harbison (Friedheim--*Piano Concerto*), Richard Leech (Caruso), Barry McCauley (Tucker), Michael Morgan (Swarowsky), Viktoria Mullova (Sibelius), Edward Newman (Casadesus), Arne Nordheim (Prix Italia), Jan Opalach (Naumberg), Ivo Pogorelich (Montreal), Lucy Shelton (Naumberg), Jean-Yves Thibaudet (Tokyo)

Honors: Samuel Barber (MacDowell Medal), Leonard Bernstein (Kennedy Center), Colin Davis (knighted), Zubin Mehta (Musician of the Year, *Musical America*), Leontyne Price (Kennedy Center), Beverly Sills (Gold Baton)

F. Biographical Highlights:

Iona Brown takes the Academy of St. Martin-in-the-Fields on its first U.S. tour; Glenn Dicterow becomes concertmaster of the New York PO; Simon Estes marries Yvonne Baer; Bernard Haitink marries for the second time; Ian Hobson takes second prize in the Rubinstein competition; François Huybrechts quits his post as conductor of the San Antonio SO; Neeme Järvi leaves Russia and emigrates to the U.S.; Kazimierz Kord becomes the Principle Guest Conductor of the Cincinnati SO; Kathleen Kuhlmann makes her La Scala debut; Yoel Levi becomes the resident conductor of the Cleveland SO; Eugene Ormandy officially resigns as conductor of the Philadelphia Orchestra; Rosalind Plowright and Arlene Saunders make their Covent Garden debuts; Ivo Pogorelich makes a great hit at the Warsaw Chopin competition, but loses first place causing two judges, including Martha Argerich, to resign in protest--Ivo soon marries his teacher, Alice Kezeradze; Peter Serkin gives up playing with Tashi.

G. Institutional Openings:

Performing Groups: Ax-Kim-Ma Trio, Chamber Music Plus (Hartford), Chamber Opera Theater of New York, Cleveland Chamber Symphony, English String Orchestra (Worcester, England), Las Vegas SO, Los Angeles Opera Repertory Theater, Opéra de Montreal, Res Musica (Maryland Contemporary Music Organization), San Jose Community Opera Theater (Opera San Jose), Solisti New York

Festivals: Connecticut Harp Festival, Lyons Berlioz Festival (France)

Other: Conducting Institute (South Carolina), Danish Music Information Center, Louise M. Davies Symphony Hall (San Francisco), De Vos Hall for the Performing Arts (Grand Rapids), Charles Ives Center for American Music (Connecticut), Kitchenor Centre in the Square (Ontario), Oscar Mayer Auditorium and Madison Civic Center (Wisconsin), Tata Theater of the National Center for the Performing Arts (Bombay, India), Young Artists Development Program (Met)

H. Musical Literature:

Blatter, Alfred, *Instrumentation/Orchestration*
Hodges, Donald A., *Handbook of Music Psychology*
Jablonski, Edward, *Encyclopedia of American Music*
Mach, Elyse, *Great Pianists Speak for Themselves*
Rahn, John, *Basic Atonal Theory*
Reed/Sidnell, *Materials of Music Composition*
Sadie, Stanley, *The New Groves Dictionary of Music and Musicians*

I. Musical Compositions:

Bazelon, Irwin, *Symphony No. 7*
Berkeley, Lennox, *Magnificat*
Carter, Elliott, *Night Fantasies* (piano)
Del Tredici, David, *In Memory of a Summer Day*
Druckman, Jakob, *Prism* (orchestra)
Eaton, John, *The Cry of Clytaemnestra* (opera)
Feldman, Morton, *The Turfan Fragments* (orchestra)
Francaix, Jean, *Concerto for Bassoon and Orchestra*
Ginastera, Alberto, *Concerto No. 2 for Violin and Orchestra*
　　　　　　　Iubilum: Celebración Sinfonica
Glass, Philip, *Satyagraha* (opera)
Harbison, John, *Concerto No. 2 for Piano and Orchestra*
　　　　　　Concerto for Violin and Orchestra
Hoiby, Lee, *Something New for the Zoo* (opera buffa)
Knussen, Oliver, *Where the Wild Things Are* (fantasy opera)
Laderman, Ezra, *Symphony No. 4*
　　　　　　Summer Solstice (orchestra)
Lees, Benjamin, *Mobiles* (orchestra)
Leighton, Kenneth, *Columba* (opera)
Lutoslawski, Witold, *Concerto for Oboe, Harp and Chamber Orchestra*
Mennin, Peter, *Sinfonia Capricciosa*
Oliveros, Pauline, *Gone with the Wind*
Panufnik, Andrzej, *Concertino for Timpani, Percussion and Strings*
Pasatieri, Thomas, *The Student from Salamanca* (opera)
Penderecki, Krzystoff, *Symphony No. 2, "Christmas"*
Perle, George, *A Short Symphony*
Rorem, Ned, *Santa Fe Songs* (song cycle)
Schuller, Gunther, *Concerto for Trumpet and Orchestra*
Schwantner, Joseph, *Through Interior Works*
Stockhausen, Karlheinz, *Donnerstag* (opera)
Tavener, John, *Akhmatova: Requiem*
Ward, Robert, *Sonic Structures*
Williamson, Malcolm, *Symphony No. 5, "Aquerò"*

1981

World Events:
In the U.S., the U.S. hostages are released by Iran on President Reagan's inauguration day; the President is shot by would-be assassin, John Hinckley, Jr.; the Space Shuttle Columbia makes a safe return after orbiting the earth for 2 days; Federal Air Controllers on a nationwide strike are dismissed by the new President; Sandra O'Connor becomes the first woman Supreme Court Justice. Internationally, General Wojciech Jaruzelski becomes Polish Prime Minister and friction builds between the Solidarity Union and the government; Israel annexes the Golan Heights; Anwar Sadat of Egypt is assassinated and Hosni Mubarek is elected President; fighting breaks out between rebels and government troops in El Salvador.

Cultural Highlights:
Pulitzers: Drama, Beth Henley (*Crimes of the Heart*); Fiction, John Kennedy Toole (*A Confederacy of Dunces*); Poetry, James Schuyler (*The Morning of the Poem*). The Nobel Prize for Literature goes to Bulgarian-born author Elias Cenetti; the Neue Pinakothek (Art Museum) opens in Munich. Deaths include American artist Theodore Roszak, Russian artist Ilya Bolotowsky and Hungarian architect Marcel Breuer; in the literary field, Americans Nelson Algren, Will Durant, Paul Green, Anita Loos and William Saroyan, Britishers Enid Bagnold and Pamela Johnson and Scottish novelist A.J. Cronin. Other highlights include:

Art: Jack Beal, *The Painting Lesson*; Sandro Chia, *The Water Bearer*; Greg Constantine, *Artists' Licenses*; Rainer Fetting, *Man in Shower*; Willem de Kooning, *Pirate*; Jane Freilicher, *Landscape, July, 1981*; Anselm Kiefer, *Landscape with Wing*; Malcolm Morley, *Underneath the Lemon Tree*; A.R. Penck, *OA TE MI 1*; Wayne Thiebaud, *Apartment Hill*.

Literature: J. Abbott, *In the Belly of the Beast*; Saul Bellow, *The Dean's Daughter*; Taylor Caldwell, *Answer as a Man*; John Irving, *Hotel New Hampshire*; Colleen McCullough, *An Indecent Obsession*; Sylvia Plath, *Collected Poems*; Chaim Potok, *The Book of Lights*; John Updike, *Rabbit is Rich*; Joseph Wambaugh, *The Glitter Dome*.

MUSICAL EVENTS

B. Deaths:

Jan 19	Iva Pacetti (It-sop)	Aug 18	Robert R. Bennett (Am-arr)
Jan 23	Samuel Barber (Am-cm)	Sep 3	Mafalda Favero (It-sop)
Feb 15	Dezsö Ernster (Hun-bs)	Sep 14	Sydney Rayner (Am-ten)
Feb 16	Karl Richter (Ger-cd)	Oct	Boyd Neel (Can-cd)
Feb 26	Howard Hanson (Am-cd)	Oct 17	David Guion (Am-cm)
Mar 8	Kyrill Kondrashin (Rus-cd)	Nov 11	Giuseppe Zampieri (It-ten)
May 25	Rosa Ponselle (Am-sop)	Nov 27	Lotte Lenya (Aus-sop)
Jun 1	Jan Z. Bartos (Cz-cm)	Dec 2	Hershy Kay (Am-arr-cm)
Jun 22	Alfred Frankenstein (Am-cri)	Dec 10	Sylvia Marlowe (Br-hps)
Jul 3	John McCormack (Am-ten)	Dec 21	Eugene Conley (Am-ten)
Aug 5	Reginald Kell (Am-cl)	Dec 27	Hoagy Carmichael (Am-pop)
Aug 14	Karl Böhm (Aus-cd)		Augusta Oltrabella (It-sop)

C. Debuts:
Met ---Thomas Allen (bar), Rockwell Blake (ten), Gwendolyn Bradley (sop), Sesto Bruscantini (bar), Miquel Cortez (ten), David Cumberland (bar), Andrew Davis (cd), Stephen Dickson (bar), Zdzislawa Donat (sop), Birgit Finnila (alto), David Kuebler (ten), Dano Raffanti (ten), Eva Randová (mez), Matti Salminen (bs), Spas Wenkoff, Heinz Zednik (ten)

U.S. --Gerd Albrecht (San Francisco), Joshua Bell (Philadelphia), Giovanni Cassolla (San Diego), Janis Eckhart (N.Y.), Simon Estes (Tulsa), Linda Gray (Dallas), Irene Gubrud (St. Paul), Denés Gulyás (N.Y.), Laura Hamilton, Hei-Kyung Hong (Charleston), Gottfried

Hornik (San Francisco), Marek Janowski (Chicago), Gustav Kuhn (Chicago), Elisabeth Leonskaja (Los Angeles), Ivo Pogorelich (N.Y.), Wolfgang Probst (Dallas), Michael Rudy, Caryl Thomas (N.Y.), Jeffrey Thomas (Charleston), Daniel Versano

Other -Barry Douglas (London), Benjamin Frith (London), John Gough (London)

D. New Positions:

Conductors: Jiri Belohlávek (Czech PO), Nicholas Braithwaite (Göteborg Opera), Philippe Entremont (New Orleans PO), Christoph Eschenbach (Zurich Tonhalle SO), Jesús Lopez-Cobos (Berlin Opera), Charles Mackerras (Sydney SO), Neville Marriner (Stuttgart Radio SO)

Educational: Marcia Baldwin (voice, Cleveland Institute), Eileen Farrell (voice, Hartt), Andrew Foldi (chairman, Opera Department, Cleveland Institute), Jan Peerce (voice, Mannes)

Others: Anthony Bliss (general manager, Met), Ardis Krainik (general manager, Chicago Lyric Opera), Simon Preston (organ, Westminster Abbey), Risë Stevens (director, Met Auditions)

E. Prizes and Honors:

Prizes: Philippe Bianconi (Casadesus), Colin Carr (Piatigorski and Naumberg), Michael Charry (Ditson), Cecilia Gasdia (Callas), Ian Hobson (Leeds), Timothy Jenkins (Melchior), Gary Lakes (Melchior), Cecile Licad (Leventritt), Dan Locklair (Friedheim), Wolfgang Manz (Mendelssohn), Marvis Martin (Ferrier), Viktoria Mullova (Sibelius), Gundaris Poné (Trieste), J. Patrick Raftery (Tucker), Nadja Salerno-Sonnenberg (Naumberg), André-Michel Schub (Cliburn), Joseph Schwantner (Friedheim)

Honors: Norman Bailey (Royal Academy), Leonard Bernstein and Jack Tworkov (American Academy), Karl Böhm (posthumous Mozart Medal), Aaron Copland (honorary doctorate, Queens), Phyllis Curtin (honorary doctorate, Yale), Leontyne Price (honorary doctorate, Harvard), Rudolf Serkin (Kennedy Center)

F. Biographical Highlights:

Karan Armstrong makes her Covent Garden debut; Vladimir Ashkenazy becomes Principle Guest Conductor of the Philharmonia Orchestra; Christian Badea becomes a U.S. citizen; Carter Brey, in Paris, wins third prize and special commendation from Rostropovich; Sarah Caldwell takes the Boston Opera to China; Antal Dorati, resigning as conductor of the Detroit SO, is made Conductor Laureate; Ofra Harnoy tours Canada on a grant from the Jeunesses Musicales; Hans Werner Henze makes a second American tour; Günther Herbig becomes Principle Guest Conductor of the BBC Northern PO; Johanna Meier becomes the first native-born American to sing Isolde at Bayreuth; Simon Rattle becomes Principle Guest Conductor of the Los Angeles PO; Santiago Rodriguez wins a Silver Medal in the Cliburn Competition; Maxim Shostakovich and his son defect to the West and settle in the U.S.; Beverly Sills visits China.

G. Institutional Openings:

Performing Groups: Alexander String Quartet (N.Y.), Austin Symphonic Band, Chamber Orchestra of Europe, Greensboro Opera Co. (North Carolina), New Baroque Soloists, Opera St. Paul, Rosamonde String Quartet, St. Michael's Sinfonia (Oxford), Sinfonia San Francisco, Tallahassee SO

Festivals: Corfu Festival, Helsinki Biennial Festival of Contemporary Music, International Festival of the Art Song (Milwaukee), Lockenhaus Music Festival (Austria), U.S.S.R. International Music Festival

Educational: San Diego Opera Institute

Other: Baird Music Hall (State University of New York, Buffalo), Composers in Red Sneakers (Boston), Conductor's Institute (West Virginia), Fazioli Piano Co. (Sacile, Italy); Friends of the Gamelan, Inc. (Chicago); Music at La Gesse Foundation (France), National Congress on Women in Music (Los Angeles), National Foundation for Advancement in the Arts, Luciano Pavarotti International Voice Competition, Rostropovich International Cello Competition (Paris), Tureck Bach Institute

H. Musical Literature:
The Opera Libretto Library (Avenel Books)
Agay, Dénes, *Teaching Piano* (2 volumes)
Del Mar, Norman, *The Anatomy of the Orchestra*
Griffiths, Paul, *Modern Music: The Avant Garde...*
Krummel, D.W., et al, *Resources of American Music History*
Routley, Erik, *The Music of the Christian Hymns*
Schonberg, Harold, *Facing the Music*
Winn, James, *Unsuspected Eloquence*

I. Musical Compositions:
Amram, David, *Concerto for Violin and Orchestra*
Argento, Domenick, *Fire Variations* (orchestra)
            Miss Havisham's Wedding Night (opera)
Berio, Luciano, *Accordo* (four wind groups)
Boulez, Pierre, *Répons* (ensemble and electronics)
Cage, John, *Thirty Pieces for Five Orchestras*
Crumb, George, *Apparitions*
Davies, Peter Maxwell, *Symphony No. 2*
Del Tredici, David, *All in the Golden Afternoon*
Erb, Donald, *Concerto for Keyboards and Orchestra*
Floyd, Carlisle, *Willie Stark* (opera)
Gould, Morton, *Burchfield Gallery* (orchestra)
Harbison, John, *Symphony No. 1*
Hovhaness, Alan, *Revelations of St. Paul* (oratorio)
Husa, Karel, *The Trojan Women* (ballet)
Kokkonen, Joonas, *Requiem*
Kubelik, Raphael, *Orphikon: Symphony in 3 Movements*
Laderman, Ezra, *Concerto for String Quartet and Orchestra*
Mennin, Peter, *Symphony No. 9*
            Concerto for Flute and Orchestra
Musgrave, Thea, *Peripateia* (orchestra)
Norgard, Per, *Symphony No. 4*
Panufnik, Andrzej, *Sinfonia Votiva*
Pasatieri, Thomas, *The Confidence Man* (opera)
Paulus, Stephen, *The Postman Always Rings Twice* (opera)
Reich, Steve, *Tehilim*
Reimann, Aribert, *Lear* (opera)
Starer, Robert, *Concerto for Violin and Orchestra*
Steptoe, Roger Guy, *Sinfonia Concertante*
Stockhausen, Karlheinz, *Jubilee*
Tower, Joan, *Sequoia* (orchestra)
Wuorinen, Charles, *The Celestial Spheres*
Zwillich, Ellen Taafe, *Three Movements for Orchestra*
            Passages

1982

World Events:

In the U.S., the Equal Rights Ammendment fails in a ratification attempt; the President announces his "New Federalism" program; the recession deepens, especially in the north; John Hinckley, Reagan's would-be assassin, found not guilty by reason of insanity; poisoning by deliberately tainted Tylenol occurs in Chicago. Internationally, Martial Law is declared in Poland after demonstrations and the Solidarity Union is outlawed; Polish Solidarity leader Lech Walesa freed after 11 months' imprisonment; Helmut Kohl replaces Helmut Schmidt as Chancellor of West Germany; Great Britain and Argentina go to war over the Falkland Islands; Leonid Brezhnev dies and Yuri Andropov becomes top Soviet leader; Deng Xiaoping becomes top man in Communist China.

Cultural Highlights:

Pulitzers: Drama, Charles Fuller (*A Soldier's Play*); Fiction, John Updike (*Rabbit is Rich*); Poetry, Sylvia Plath (*Collected Poems*). The Columbian-born Mexican author Gabriel García Márquez is the recipient of the Nobel Prize for Literature. The Salvador Dali Museum opens in St. Petersburg, Florida and the Canberra National Gallery of Art opens in Australia. Deaths include British artists Ben Nicholson and Allan Gwynne-Jones and Polish-born artist Jack Tworkov, American authors John Cheever, John Gardner, Granville Hicks, Archibald MacLeish, Ayn Rand and Howard Sackler, poet Horace Gregory, French poet Louis Aragon, Russian poet Marya Zaturenska and New Zealand-born novelist Ngaio Marsh. Other highlights include:

Art: Jennifer Bartlett, *Up the Creek*; Ilya Borofsky, *Running Man (Berlin Wall)*; Francesco Clemente, *Fourteen Stations*; Enzo Cucci, *The Mad Painter*; Jasper Johns, *Perilous Night*; Markus Lüpertz, *Orpheus in Hell*; Nam June Paik, *The Moon is the Oldest T.V. Set*; Robert Rauschenberg, *Dirt Shrine: South*; Julian Schnabel, *Nighttime Rhonda*.

Literature: Saul Bellow, *The Dean's December*; William Golding, *A Moving Target*; Maxine Kumin, *Our Ground Time Here Will Be Brief*; Robert Ludlum, *The Parsifal Mosiac*; Larry McMurtry, *Cadillac Jack*; James Michener, *Space*; Paul Theroux, *The Mosquito Coast*.

MUSICAL EVENTS

B. Deaths:

Feb 17	Thelonious Monk (Am-pop)	Jul 10	Maria Jeritza (Aus-sop)
Mar 1	Charlie Spivak (Am-pop)	Aug 6	Hans Heinz (Aus-ten)
Mar 24	Igor Gorin (Rus-bar)	Aug 12	Oliviero de Fabritiis (It-cd)
Mar 29	Carl Orff (Ger-cm)	Aug 21	Calvin Simmons (Am-cd)
Apr 9	Wilfrid Pelletier (Can-cd)	Sep 1	Clifford Curzon (Br-pn)
May 1	William Primrose (Scot-vla)	Sep 15	Christian Ferras (Fr-vn)
May 12	Humphrey Searle (Br-cm-mus)	Oct 4	Glenn Gould (Can-pn)
May 26	Nanny Larsen-Todsen (Swe-sop)	Oct 23	Mario del Monaco (It-ten)
Jul 6	Frederick Jagel (Am-ten)	Dec 20	Artur Rubinstein (Rus-pn)

C. Débuts:

Met ---Margarita Castro-Alberty (sop), Riccardo Chailly (cd), Barbara Conrad (mez), Simon Estes (bar), Kay Griffel (sop), Anton Guadagno (cd), Angeles Gulin (sop), Bernard Haitink (cd), Julia Hamari (mez), Vernon Hartman (bar), Emily Hastings, Marvis Martin (sop), Corneliu Murgu (ten), Adelaide Negri (sop), J. Patrick Raftery (bar), Olivia Stapp (sop), Linda Zoghby (sop)

U.S. --Francisco Araiza (San Francisco), Christian Badea (N.Y.), Aldo Bertolo (Dallas), Hermann Brecht (San Francisco), Young-ae Cho (Cleveland), Ghena Dimitrova (Dallas), Barry Douglas (N.Y.), Susan Dunn (Peoria), Michael Gurt, Nikki Li Hartliep (San Francisco), Nina Lelchuck, Andrew Litton (San Diego), Nicola Martinucci (San Francisco), Jan Opalach (N.Y.), Michala Petri (N.Y.), Rosalind Plowright (Philadelphia), Ewa Podles (Newport), Cynthia Raim, Donato Renzetti (N.Y.), Nadja Salerno-Sonnenberg

(N.Y.), Marga Schiml (Dallas), Sergiu Schwartz (N.Y.), Dimitri Sgouros (N.Y.), Peter Zazofsky (Philadelphia), Dolores Ziegler (Seattle)

Other -Stephen Hough (London), Michael Morgan (Vienna)

D. New Positions:

Conductors: Yuri Ahronovich (Stockholm PO), Neeme Järvi (Göthenburg SO), Andrew Litton (BBC SO), Lorin Maazel (Vienna Opera), Judith Somogi (Frankfurt Opera)

Educational: Seth McCoy (voice, Eastman)

Others: John Adams (composer-in-residence, San Francisco SO), Edward Corn (general manager, Minnesota Opera), Donald Erb (President, American Music Center), John Harbison (composer-in-residence, Pittsburgh SO), Terence A. McEwen (general manager, San Francisco Opera), William Noll (general director, Providence Opera)

E. Prizes and Honors:

Prizes: Martin Bernheimer (Pulitzer, music criticism), Colin Carr (Naumberg), Hung-Kuan Chen (Busoni), Kaaren Erickson (Munich), Michael Gurt (Bachauer), Horacio Gutiérrez (Fisher), Joyce Guyer (Steber), C. William Harwood (Stokowski), Alexander Markov (Paganini), Mihaela Martin (Indianapolis), Antonio Meneses and Viktoria Mullova (Tchaikovsky), Cecily Nall (Steber), Jessye Norman (Dixon), Russell Patterson (Ditson), Gundaris Poné (Friedheim), Roger Sessions (Pulitzer--*Concerto for Orchestra*)

Honors: Milton Babbitt (Special Pulitzer), Benny Goodman and Eugene Ormandy (Kennedy Center), Marilyn Horne (Rossini Medal), Zubin Mehta (honorary doctorate, Princeton), Birgit Nilsson (honorary doctorates, Michigan State University and Manhattan School of Music), Jessie Norman (Musician of the Year, *Musical America*), Krystoff Penderecki (Grand Medal, Paris), Itzhak Perlman (honorary doctorate, University of South Carolina), Kiri Te Kanawa (Dame of the British Empire)

F. Biographical Highlights:

Claudio Abbado appointed Principle Guest Conductor of the Chicago SO; Thomas Allen and Brenda Boozer both debut at the Paris Opera; Janet Baker gives her farewell opera performance; Victoria Bond makes her European conducting debut in Dublin; Riccardo Chailly becomes Principle Guest Conductor of the London PO; Stefka Evstatieva, Cecilia Gasdia and Aprile Millo make their La Scala debuts; Leon Fleisher, after 17 years of self-imposed exile, re-debuts with a two-handed repertoire; Philip Glass renounces the "establishment" and begins minimalist experimentation; Barbara Hendricks, Kathleen Kuhlman and Samuel Ramey all debut at Covent Garden; Jerome Hines earns a doctorate in engineering from Stevens Institute of Technology; Lili Kraus retires from the concert stage; Katia and Marielle Labèque make their first U.S. tour; James Levine debuts at Bayreuth with Parsifal; Jan Peerce suffers a stroke; Margherita Rinaldi and Josephine Veasey announce their retirement from the opera stage; Gerard Schwarz becomes musical advisor to the Mostly Mozart Festival.

G. Institutional Openings:

Performing Groups: Back Bay Brass Quintet (Boston), Baton Rouge Opera Co., Cathedral SO (New Jersey), Choral Arts Society of Philadelphia, Contemporary Chamber Orchestra of London, Icelandic Opera Co., Opera Colorado (Denver), Opera Company of the Philippines (Boston)

Festivals: Music Festival of Arkansas (Fayetteville), New World Festival of the Arts (Miami), San Antonio Festival, Sandpoint Music Festival (Idaho)

Educational: Villa Pace (Maryland Opera Museum sponsored by the Rosa Ponselle Foundation)

Other: Artistic Ambassador Program (U.S. Information Agency), Association for Classical Music (N.Y.), Austin Performing Arts Center (Texas), Barbican Centre for Arts and Conferences (London), Council for Young Musicians (Czechoslovakia), Great Plains Chamber Music Institute (Emporia, Kansas), Hult Center for the Performing Arts

(Eugene, Oregon), International Federation of Choral Music (IFCM), Terence Judd International Piano Award, Los Angeles Philharmonic Institute, Joseph Meyerhoff Symphony Hall (Baltimore), Opera Factory (London), Orpheum Theater (reopening, New Orleans), Peoria Civic Center Theater (Illinois), Pikes Peak Center (Colorado Springs), Royal Concert Hall (Nottingham, England), Roy Thompson Hall (Toronto), Wharton Center for the Performing Arts (Michigan State University)

H. Musical Literature:

Adler, Samuel, *The Study of Orchestration*
Burton, Stephen, *Orchestration*
Cooke, Deryck, *Vindications: Essays on Romantic Music*
Deutsch, Diana, ed., *The Psychology of Music*
Ewen, David, *American Composers: A Biographical Dictionary*
Henze, Hans Werner, *Music and Politics*
Irwin, Phyllis A., *Music Fundamentals*
Merriman, Margaret, *A New Look at 16th Century Counterpoint*
Rastall, Richard, *The Notation of Western Music*
Rosenstiel, Leonie, ed., *The Schirmer History of Music*

I. Musical Compositions:

Balada, Leonardo, *Concerto for Violin and Orchestra*
Berio, Luciano, *La Vera Stória* (opera)
Brant, Henry, *Inside Track* (piano and orchestra)
Brown, Earle, *Sounder Rounds* (orchestra)
Carter, Elliott, *In Sleep, In Thunder*
Colgrass, Michael, *Concerto for Two Pianos and Orchestra*
Corigliano, John, *Three Halllucinations* (orchestra)
               Pied Piper Fantasy
Creston, Paul, *Symphony No. 6, "Organ"*
Crumb, George, *Gnomic Variations* (piano)
Del Tredici, David, *Quaint Events* (soprano and orchestra)
Glass, Philip, *The Photographer* (opera)
Hamilton, Iain, *St. Mark Passion*
La Montaine, John, *Symphonic Variations, Opus 50*
Lees, Benjamin, *Concerto for Piano, Cello and Orchestra*
Lutoslawski, Witold, *Symphony No. 3*
McCabe, John, *Concerto for Orchestra*
Menotti, Gian Carlo, *A Bride for Pluto* (children's opera)
Nordheim, Arne, *Concerto for Cello and Orchestra*
Paulus, Stephen, *Translucent Landscapes* (orchestra)
Penderecki, Krzystoff, *Concerto No. 2 for Cello and Orchestra*
Picker, Tobias, *Symphony*
Rorem, Ned, *After Long Silence* (song cycle)
Sallinen, Aulis, *Shadows* (orchestra)
Schnittke, Alfred, *Concerto No. 4 for Violin and Orchestra*
               The History of Dr. Johann Faust (cantata)
Ward, Robert, *Minutes to Midnight* (opera)

1983

World Events:
In the U.S., the Missouri town of Times Beach is threatened by buried waste containing toxic chemical, Dioxin; U.S. forces, aided by other Caribbean forces, invade Grenada and overthrow the Marxist regime; Anne Gorsuch Burford is forced to resign as head of the Environmental Protection Agency; Sally Ride, in *Challenger*, becomes the first American woman in space; Barney Clark is the first man to be given an artificial heart; the Federal Government forces American Telephone and Telegraph to break up into smaller companies. Internationally, Yuri Andropov consolidates his position as Soviet head; Russians shoot down a Korean airliner over Russian held waters; the Russians break off arms talks with the West; the U.S. begins deploying missiles in Europe; Menachem Begin resigns as Israeli Prime Minister; AIDS becomes the scare disease of the year.

Cultural Highlights:
Pulitzers: Drama, Marsha Norman (*'Night, Mother*); Fiction, Alice Walker (*The Color Purple*) becomes the first black woman to receive a Pulitzer for Fiction; Poetry, Galway Kinnell (*Selected Poems*). The Nobel Prize for Literature goes to British novelist William Golding. The Getty Center for the History of Art and the Humanities is founded in Santa Monica, the Museum of Contemporary Art opens in Mönchengladbach, the Portland Museum of Art opens in Oregon, the High Museum of Art opens in Atlanta and the Glasgow Art Museum opens its doors. Deaths include British art historian Kenneth Clark, American artist Ivan Albright and Spanish artist Joan Miró, British actor Ralph Richardson, Spanish poet José Gutierrez, British authors Richard Llewellyn, Mary Renault and Rebecca West, American sculptor Richard Stankiewicz and author Tennessee Williams. Other highlights include:

Art: Will Barnet, *Dawn*; Ilya Borofsky, *Molecule Man and Briefcase*; Sandro Chia, *Young Man with Red Arm*; Christo, *Surrounded Islands*; Greg Constantine, *Van Gogh Visits New York*; Al Held, *Mantegna's Edge*; Jasper Johns, *Racing Thoughts*; Malcolm Morley, *Day Fishing at Heraklion*; Richard Tuttle, *Monkey's Recovery*.

Literature: R. Carver, *Cathedral*; Laura Hobson, *Laura Z.: A Life*; Erica Jong, *Ordinary Miracles*; Norman Mailer, *Ancient Evenings*; Larry McMurtry, *The Desert Rose*; James Michener, *Poland*; William Least, *Heat Moon, Blue Highways*; August Wilson, *Fences*.

MUSICAL EVENTS

B. Deaths:

Jan 7	Edith Coates (Br-mez)	Jun 2	Donald Gramm (Am-bar)
Feb 8	Charles Kullman (Am-ten)	Jun 10	Nadia Reisenberg (Rus-pn)
Feb 8	Alfred Wallenstein (Am-cd)	Jun 13	Carl F.W. Ludwig (Am-pub)
Feb 12	Eubie Blake (Am-pop)	Jun 17	Peter Mennin (Am-cm)
Feb 17	Tancredi Pasero (It-bs)	Jun 25	Alberto Ginastera (Arg-cm)
Feb 23	Adrian Boult (Br-cd)	Jun 26	Ruth Miller (Am-sop)
Mar 6	Cathy Berberian (Am-sop)	Jul 4	Klaus Adam (Am-cel-cm)
Mar 7	Igor Markevitch (Rus-cd)	Jul 10	Bruna Castagna (It-mez)
Mar 8	William Walton (Br-cm)	Jul 10	Werner Egk (Ger-cm)
Apr 18	William Horne (Am-ten)	Sep 25	Paul Jacobs (Am-pn-hps)
Apr 30	George Balanchine (Rus-bal)	Sep 25	Peter Van der Bilt (Hol-bar)
May 4	Nino Sanzogno (It-cd)	Dec 7	Germaine Tailleferre (Fr-cm)
May 16	Vina Bovy (Bel-sop)	Dec 27	Fidela Campina (Sp-sop)

C. Débuts:
Met ---Roberta Alexander (sop), Francisco Araiza (ten), Silvano Carroli (bar), Terry Cook (bar), Barbara Daniels (sop), Enrico Fissore (bs), Ingrid Kremling (sop), Jessye Norman (sop), Anthony Raffell (bs), Klaus Tennstedt (cd), Jane White (sop), Gösta Winbergh (ten)

U.S. --Jeannine Altmeyer, Gabriele Bellini (N.Y.), Evelyn Brunner (Baltimore), Elizabeth Connell (N.Y.), Lella Cuberli (N.Y.), Alberto Cupido (San Francisco), Christian DuPlessis (Ft. Worth), Kaaren Erickson, Stefka Evstatieva (Philadelphia), Mechthild Gessendorf (Tulsa), Reiner Goldberg (N.Y.), Joyce Guyer (N.Y.), John LaPierre (St. Louis), Eunice Lee (Pittsburgh), Alexander Markov, Barbara Martin (N.Y.), Mihaela Martin, Mikael Melbye (Santa Fe), Nelly Miricioiu (San Francisco), Cheryl Ann Parrish (San Francisco), Vladimir Popov (Portland), Tibère Raffalli (San Francisco), Stephen Robinson (N.Y.), Shauna Rolston, Robert Schunk (Chicago), Giuseppe Sinopoli (N.Y.), Ilona Tokody (San Francisco), John Tomlinson (San Francisco), Kumiko Yoshii (Charleston)

Other -Andrea Lucchesini (Milan), Jard van Nes (Amsterdam), Helen Willis (London)

D. New Positions:

Conductors: Christian Badea (Columbus SO), Richard Buckley (Oakland SO), Sarah Caldwell (New Opera Co., Israel), Riccardo Chailly (Berlin Radio SO), James Conlon (Rotterdam PO), Colin Davis (Bavarian Radio SO), John Eliot Gardiner (Opèra de Lyon), Marek Janowski (Royal Liverpool PO), Kenneth Schermerhorn (Nashville SO), Joseph Silverstein (Utah SO), Giuseppe Sinopoli (Philharmonia Orchestra), Klaus Tennstedt (London PO)

Educational: Colin Carr (New England Conservatory), Phyllis Curtin (dean, School for the Arts, Boston University), Martin Katz (University of Michigan), Jaime Laredo (St. Louis Conservatory

E. Prizes and Honors:

Prizes: Youngshin An (Casadesus),Maria Bachmann (Kreisler), Larry Bell (Prix de Rome), Hung-Kuan Chen (Rubinstein), Susan Dunn (Tucker), Stephen Hough (Naumberg), Jeffrey Kahane (Rubinstein), Andrea Lucchesini (Ciani), Robert McDonald (Busoni), Elmar Oliveira (Fisher), Krystoff Penderecki (Sibelius), Cornelius Sullivan (Melchior), Frederick Tristan (Goncourt), Ellen Taafe Zwillich (Pulitzer--*Three Movements for Orchestra*)

Honors: Elliott Carter (MacDowell Medal), Van Cliburn (Schweitzer), Colin Davis (Shakespeare), Gwendolyn Killebrew (honorary doctorate, Temple), Sherrill Milnes (Order of Merit), Nathan Milstein (Commander, Legion of Honor and Musician of the Year, *Musical America*), John Pritchard (knighted), Frederica von Stade (honorary doctorate, Mannes), Virgil Thomson (Kennedy Center)

F. Biographical Highlights:

Jeannine Altmeyer, Hildegard Behrens and Brigitte Fassbaender all make their Bayreuth debuts; Gabrielle Bellini makes her Covent Garden debut; Elliott Carter becomes the first American to receive an honorary doctorate from Cambridge; Barbara Conrad makes her Vienna Opera debut; Ghena Dimitrova, Erie Mills, Rosalind Plowright and Madelyn Renée make their La Scala debuts; Charles Dutoit become Principle Guest Conductor of the Minnesota Orchestra; Peter Hofmann undergoes a tonsilectomy; Raymond Leppard appointed Principle Guest Conductor of the St. Louis SO; conductor Vakhtang Jordania defects to the West; Viktoria Mullova defects to the West by taking a taxi across the Finnish-Swedish border; George Rochberg retires from the University of Pennsylvania to devote full time to composing; Esa-Pekka Salonen makes his debut outside Finland with the Philharmonia Orchestra; Alan Titus makes his Paris Opera debut; Alexander Toradze, on tour in Spain, defects to the West; Josephine Veasey retires from the stage; Dolores Ziegler makes both her La Scala and Paris Opera debuts; Ellen Taafe Zwillich becomes the first woman to win a Pulitzer for composition.

G. Institutional Openings:

Performing Groups: Dae Woo Chorale (Korea), Franciscan String Quartet, Harmonia Opera (N.Y.), Indiana Opera Theater, New Opera Co. of Israel, Shanghai String Quartet

Festivals: Bridgehampton Chamber Music Festival (N.Y.), Connecticut Early Music Festival, Southeastern Music Center Summer Festival (Georgia)

Educational: Musica Camerit (Hebrew Art School)

Other: *American Music*, Caravan of Dreams (Fort Worth, Texas), Teresa Carreño Arts Center (Caracas), Derngate Centre for the Performing Arts (Northhampton), Finger Lakes Performing Arts Center (Rochester), Harborfront Dance Theater (Toronto), Indianapolis Quadrennial International Violin Competition, Erich Korngold Society (Scotland), Lahti Performing Arts Center (Finland), Alexander Tcherepnin Society (N.Y.), The Yard (dance colony, Massachusetts)

H. Musical Literature:

Arnold, David, ed., *New Oxford Companion to Music*
Ballantine, Christopher, *Twentieth Century Symphony*
Duncan/Ochse, *Fundamentals of Music Theory*
Lerdahl/Jackendorff, *A Generative Theory of Tonal Music*
Levy, Alan H., *Musical Nationalism*
Matheopoulos, Helena, *Maestro: Encounters with Conductors...*
Rahn, John, *A Theory for All Music*
Rasponi, Lanfranco, *The Last Prima Donnas*
Schwarz, Boris, *Great Masters of the Violin*

I. Musical Compositions:

Argento, Dominick, *The Andrée Expedition* (song cycle)
       Letters of Elizabeth Browning (song cycle)
Bazelon, Irwin, *Concerto for Piano and Orchestra*
Birtwistle, Harrison, *Yan Tan Tethera* (TV opera)
Brant, Henry, *Desert Forest* (orchestras)
Erb, Donald, *Prismatic Variations* (orchestra)
Fine, Vivian, *Drama for Orchestra*
Hall, Charles J., *A Celebration Overture*
Hamilton, Iain, *Lancelot* (opera)
Harbison, John, *Ulysses Bow* (ballet)
Henze, Hans Werner, *The English Cat* (opera)
Husa, Karel, *Symphony No. 2, "Reflections"*
Kubik, Gail, *Concerto for Piano and Orchestra*
Laderman, Ezra, *Symphonies No. 5 and 6*
       A Mass for Cain
Lees, Benjamin, *Concerto for Brass Choir and Orchestra*
Lutoslawski, Witold, *Chain I* (orchestra)
McCabe, John, *Concerto for Orchestra*
Menotti, Gian Carlo, *Concerto for Doublebass and Orchestra*
Messiaen, Olivier, *St. Francis of Assissi* (opera)
Pasatieri, Thomas, *Maria Elena* (opera)
Paulus, Stephen, *Concerto for Orchestra*
Rands, Bernard, *Canti del Sole* (tenor and orchestra)
Reich, Steve, *The Desert Music*
Rochberg, George, *Concerto for Oboe and Orchestra*
Siegmeister, Elie, *Concerto for Violin and Orchestra*
Tal, Josef, *The Tower* (opera)
Tippett, Michael, *The Mask of Time* (oratorio)
Wuorinen, Charles, *Concerto No. 3 for Piano and Orchestra*

1984

World Events:
In the U.S., Ronald Reagan is re-elected as President and visits China; Geraldine Ferrar becomes the first woman to run for Vice-President on the Democratic ticket and Jesse Jackson becomes the first black to run for President; the shuttle Challenger succeeds in retrieving a satellite for repairs in space; the Louisiana Exposition opens in New Orleans and the Summer Olympics are held in Los Angeles. Internationally, Yuri Andropov dies and is succeeded by Constantin Chernenko as Russian head; Russia and its satellites boycott the Los Angeles olympics; Indira Gandhi of India is assassinated by her own guard; Margaret Thatcher escapes an assassination attempt; Pierre Trudeau resigns as Canadian Prime Minister and is replaced by M. Brian Mulroney; José Napoleon Duarte is elected President of El Salvador.

Cultural Highlights:
Pulitzers: Drama, David Mamet (*Glengarry Glen Ross*); Fiction, William Kennedy (*Ironweed*); Poetry, Mary Oliver (*American Primitive*). The Nobel Prize for Literature goes to the Czeck writer Jaroslav Seifert, Ted Hughes is made British Poet Laureate and Al Held is inducted into the American Academy. New museums include the Dallas Museum of Art, the Brussels Modern Art Museum and the New State Gallery in Stuttgart. Deaths include the Spanish poets Vicente Alexandre and Jorge Guillen, British authors Elizabeth Goudge and J.B. Priestley, poet John Betjeman, Irish author Liam O'Flaherty and American writers Lillian Hellman, Truman Capote and Irwin Shaw as well as Russian author Mikhail Sholokhov and American artist Peter Hurd. Other highlights include:

Art: Eric Fischl, *Cargo Cults*; Leon Golub, *Mercenaries V*; Robert Longo, *Cindy*; Malcolm Morley, *Farewell to Crete*; Robert Motherwell, *The Marriage*; Nam June Paik, *BSO and Beyond*; Julian Schnabel, *King of the Wood*; Frank Stella, *Abercrombie's Curtain*.

Literature: Joan Didion, *Democracy*; Alison Lurie, *Foreign Affairs*; J. MacInerney, *Bright Lights, Big City*; Norman Mailer, *Tough Guys Don't Dance*; P. Powell, *Edisto*; Muriel Spark, *The Only Problem*; John Updike, *The Witches of Eastwick*; Gore Vidal, *Lincoln*; Yevgeny Yevtushenko, *Wild Berries*.

MUSICAL EVENTS

B. Deaths:

Jan 7	Anna Case (Am-sop)	Jul 20	Gail Kubik (Am-cm)
Jan 15	Paul Ben-Haim (Is-cm)	Jul 28	Valter Poole (Am-cd)
Jan 21	Kari Nurmela (Fin-bar)	Jul 29	Fred Waring (Am-cd)
Feb 2	Margherita Perras (Gr-sop)	Aug 1	Fernando Previtali (It-cd)
Feb 20	Fikret Amirov (Azer-cm)	Aug 11	Alfred Knopf (Am-pub)
Feb 22	Giovanni Manurita (It-ten)	Sep 7	George Posell (Am-cd)
Mar 6	Pierre Cochereau (Fr-org)	Sep 23	Barbara Troxell (Am-sop)
Mar 15	Tito Gobbi (It-bar)	Oct 17	Georges Thill (Fr-ten)
Apr 13	Ralph Kirkpatrick (Am-hps)	Nov 16	Leonard Rose (Am-cel)
Apr 21	Ania Dorfmann (Rus-pn)	Dec 10	Fernando Corena (It-bs)
Apr 26	"Count" Basie (Am-pop)	Dec 15	Jan Peerce (Am-ten)
Jun 16	Meredith Willson (Am-cd)	Dec 21	Judith Raskin (Am-sop)
Jul 8	Reginald Stewart (Am-cd)		Imogen Holst (Br-mus-cd)
Jul 9	Randall Thompson (Am-cm)		

C. Débuts:
Met ---Cleopatra Ciurca (mez), Imogen Cooper (sop), Brent Ellis (bar), Hei-Kyung Hong (sop), Jorma Hynninen (bar), Marek Janowski (cd), Artur Korn (bs), Aprile Millo (sop), Ann Murray (mez), Dennis O'Neill (ten), Ewa Podles (mez), Vladimir Popov (ten), Samuel Ramey (bar), Dawn Upshaw (sop), Carol Vaness (sop), Ute Vinzing (sop)

U.S. --Sergiu Celibadache (N.Y.), Alessandro Corbelli (Philadelphia), Rubin Dominguez (Cincinnati), Sergei Edelmann (Chicago), Mark Elder (N.Y.), David Freeman (Houston), Christopher Hogwood (Chicago), Stephen Hough (N.Y.), Lorraine Hunt, Kristian Johannsson (Columbus), Elizabeth Knighton (N.Y.), Richard Leech (N.Y.), Mischa Lefkowitz (N.Y.), Frank Lopardo (St. Louis), Andrea Lucchesini (Newport), Jirina Markova (N.Y.), Marie McLaughlin (Washington, D.C.), Hermann Michael (Seattle), Emile Naoumoff, Daniel Oren (Houston), Helmut Pampuch (San Francisco), Jon Kimura Parker (N.Y.), Terry Reid (Seattle), Cynthia Rose, Esa-Pekka Salonen (Los Angeles), Cheryl Studer (Chicago), Viviane Thomas (N.Y.), Donna Wissinger

Other -Alteouise DeVaughn (Trieste), Joseph Evans (Geneva), Claudette Peterson (Geneva)

D. New Positions:

Conductors: Christoph von Dohnányi (Cleveland SO), Neeme Järvi (Scottish National SO), Peter Maag (Berne SO), John Mauceri (American SO), Jorge Mester (Pasadena SO), Daniel Oren (San Carlo), Kenneth Schermerhorn (Hong Kong PO), Gerard Schwarz (Seattle SO), Stanislaw Skrowaczewski (Hallé SO), Edo de Waart (Netherlands Opera)

Educational: Anna Moffo (voice, New York University)

Others: Tito Capobianco (director, Pittsburgh Opera), Bruce Crawford (general manager, Met), Ivan Fischer (music director, Kent Opera), Peter Hall (artistic director, Glyndebourne), Eric Salzman (editor, Musical Quarterly)

E. Prizes and Honors:

Prizes: David Buechner (Bachauer), Jonathan Del Mar (Leeds), Mark Doss (London), Cindy Halgrimson (Steber), David Hamilton (Steber), Kenneth Jean (Stokowski), Louis Lortie (Busoni), Tod Machover (Koussevitzky), Jon Kimura Parker (Leeds), Bernard Rands (Pulitzer--*Canti del Sole*), Roger Roloff (Tucker), Patrick Waroblewski (Ponselle)

Honors: Claudio Arrau (Legion of Honor), Antal Dorati (knighted), Lukas Foss (American Academy), James Levine (Musician of the Year, *Musical America*), Berit Maria Lindholm (Swedish Academy), Gian Carlo Menotti and Isaac Stern (Kennedy Center), Sherrill Milnes (Order of Merit), Danny Newman (Gold Baton), William Schwann (Peabody Medal)

F. Biographical Highlights:

Renato Bruson, Vincent Cole and Jessye Norman make their Paris Opera debuts; Phyllis Curtin retires from public performance; Bella Davidovich receives American citizenship; Placido Domingo debuts as a conductor at the Met; Heather Harper retires from the opera stage; Grant Johannesen resigns as President of the Cleveland Institute; Lorin Maazel resigns from the Vienna Opera in a storm of controversy; James Morris and Dolores Ziegler make their Vienna Opera debuts; Eugene Ormandy cancels all conducting engagements after suffering a January heart attack; Gunther Schuller resigns as artistic director of the Berkshire Music Center; Graziella Sciutti makes her debut a stage manager at the Met; Judith Somogi becomes the first woman conductor at La Scala; Ilona Tokody makes her Covent Garden debut; Carol Vaness makes both her Vienna Opera debut and a Met debut.

G. Institutional Openings:

Performing Groups: Carmina String Quartet, Concordia (New York Chamber Orchestra), New Orchestra of Boston, North Beach Grand Opera (Opera Nova), Renaissance City Chamber Players (Detroit)

Festivals: Castello Svevo International Festival (Sicily), Havana International Festival of Contemporary Music, International Festival of the Americas (University of Miami)

Other: Braun Music Center (Stanford), Filene Center (Wolf Trap Farm), Grawemeyer Award (University of Louisville), Kentucky Center for the Arts (Louisville), Miami Center for the Fine Arts, *Opus*, Riverbend Music Center (Cincinnati)

H. Musical Literature:

Brass Anthology (Instrumentalist)
Percussion Anthology (Instrumentalist)
Burbank, Richard, *Twentieth Century Music*
Goldovsky, Boris, *Good Afternoon, Ladies and Gentlemen*
Harder, Paul, *Music Manuscript Technique*
Kostka/Payne, *Tonal Harmony*
Pantinga, Leon, *Romantic Music*
Rochberg, George, *The Aesthetics of Survival*
Sadie, Stanley, *The New Grove Dictionary of Musical Instruments*

I. Musical Compositions:

Argento, Dominick, *Casanova's Homecoming* (opera)
Ashley, Robert, *Atalanta Strategy* (opera)
Balada, Leonardo, *Zapata!* (opera)
Berio, Luciano, *Voci* (viola and orchestra)
Bolcom, William, *Songs of Innocence and Experience*
        Concerto for Violin and Orchestra
Brant, Henry, *Western Springs* (double chorus and orchestra)
Crumb, George, *A Haunted Landscape* (orchestra)
Davies, Dennis R., *Symphony No. 3*
Erb, Donald, *Concerto for Contrabass and Orchestra*
Feldman, Morton, *Concerto for Violin and Orchestra*
Finney, Ross Lee, *Weep, Torn Land* (opera)
Glass, Philip, *Akhnaton* (opera)
Harbison, John, *Symphony No. 1*
        Ulysses Raft (ballet)
Henze, Hans Werner, *Symphony No. 7*
Laderman, Ezra, *Symphony No. 7*
Machover, Tod, *Nature's Breath* (chamber orchestra)
Mayer, William, *A Death in the Family* (opera)
Oliver, Stephen, *Beauty and the Beast* (opera)
Pasatieri, Thomas, *Mass*
Penderecki, Krystoff, *Koenig Ubu* (opera)
Reimann, Aribert, *Gespenstersonate* (opera)
Rorem, Ned, *An American Oratorio*
        Concerto for Violin and Orchestra
Sallinen, Aulis, *The King Goes Forth to France* (opera)
Schnittke, Alfred, *Symphony No. 4*
Schuller, Gunther, *Concerto for Saxophone and Orchestra*
Stockhausen, Karlheinz, *Samstag aus Licht* (opera)
Takemitsu, Toru, *Star Isle* (orchestra)
Ward, Robert, *Concerto for Saxophone and Orchestra*
Webber, Andrew Lloyd, *Requiem*
Wuorinen, Charles, *Movers and Shakers*

1985

World Events:
In the U.S., President Reagan undergoes cancer surgery and meets with Premier Gorbachev in Geneva; the Gramm-Rudman bill to end the Federal deficit is passed by Congress; General Electric buys out RCA Corporation; E.F. Hutton, one of the largest brokerage houses, pleads guilty to fraud and account manipulation. Internationally, Mikhail Gorbachev becomes Russian leader on the death of Konstantin Chernenko; terrorists hijack the Italian cruise ship *Achille Lauro* on the high seas; terrorists in Rome and Vienna airports kill civilians planning to fly El Al airlines; the African famine intensifies; an earthquake in Mexico City takes 20,000 lives and a volcano eruption in Colombia claims 25,000 lives; Iran and Iraq begin bombing civilian targets in each others' countries.

Cultural Highlights:
Pulitzers: Drama, Stephen Sondheim and James Lapine (*Sunday in the Park with George*); Fiction, Alison Lurie, (*Foreign Affairs*); Poetry, Carolyn Kizer (*Yin*). The Nobel Prize for Literature goes to French author Claude Simon. The Pollock-Krasner Foundation for art and artists is founded. Deaths include Mexican sculptor José Rivera, Russian artist Marc Chagall, French artist Jean Dubuffet and American artist Eric Sloane; the literary world loses Americans Robert Fitzgerald, Helen Macinnes and E.B. White, Italian author Italo Calvino and British writers Robert Graves and Philip Larkin. Other highlights include:

Art: Eric Fischl, *Manhattoes*; Alex Katz, *The Green Cap*; Anselm Kiefer, *Midgard*; Leon Kossoff, *A Street in Willesden*; Hans Haacke, *MetroMobilitan*; Martin Puryear, *The Spell*; Terry Winters, *Dystopia*; Andrew Wyeth, *Refuge (Helga)*.

Literature: Ann Beattie, *Love Always*; Edgar L. Doctorow, *World's Fair*; John Fowles, *A Maggot*; Garrison Keillor, *Lake Wobegon Days*; Ursula Leguin, *Always Coming Home*; James Michener, *Texas*; Anne Tyler, *The Accidental Tourist*; Charles Yeager, *Yeager*.

MUSICAL EVENTS

B. Deaths:

Feb 22	Efrem Zimbalist (Am-vn)	Sep 13	Dane Rudhyar (Fr-cm-au)
Mar 1	Eugene List (Am-pn)	Sep 23	Coe Glade (Am-mez)
Mar 12	Eugene Ormandy (Hun-cd)	Oct 3	Mischa Schneider (Rus-cel)
Mar 16	Roger Sessions (Am-cm)	Oct 6	Nelson Riddle (Am-pop)
Mar 24	George London (Am-bar)	Oct 14	Emil Gilels (Rus-pn)
Jul 16	Wayne King (Am-pop)	Oct 17	Joseph Rosenstock (Pol-cd)
Aug 15	Richard Yardumian (Am-cm)	Oct 23	Viorica Ursuleac (Rom-sop)
Aug 24	Paul Creston (Am-cm)	Dec 22	Richard P. Condie (Am-cd)
Sep 11	William Alwyn (Br-cm)	Dec 28	David Ewen (Am-mus)

C. Débuts:
Met ---Gregg Baker (bar), June Card (sop), Elizabeth Connell (sop), Helga Dernesch (mez), Kaaren Erickson (sop), George Fortune (bar), Denés Gulyás (ten), Marianne Häggander (sop), Gwynne Howell (bs), Stefka Mineva (mez), Václav Naumann (cd), García Navarro (cd), Wieslaw Ochman (ten), Christof Perick (cd), Margaret Price (sop), Giuseppe Sinopoli (cd), Giuseppe Taddei (bar), Marilyn Zschau (sop)

U.S. --David Arnold (N.Y.), Leland Chen (tour), Alteouise DeVaughn (Virginia), Jenny Drivala (Houston), José Feghali, Cecilia Gasdia (Philadelphia), Andrei Gavrilov (N.Y.), Karen Hutchinson, Fiamma Izzo d'Amico (Houston), Michael Lipman (Pittsburgh), Waltraud Meier (Dallas), Suzanne Murphy (N.Y.), János Nagy, Wolfgang Neumann (Dallas), Liang Ning (San Francisco), Ekaterina Novitskaya, Michael Pabst (Philadelphia), David Pittsinger (Hartford), Flora Rafanelli (Chicago), Irina Tseitlin, Mitsuko Uchida (Chicago), Dawn Upshaw (N.Y.), Rian de Waal, Dolora Zajick (San

Francisco)

Other -James Anderson (Nancy), Carla Basto (Avignon), Myrna Bismark (Warsaw), Adrian Goss (London), Makiko Kawahito (Tokyo), Adriana Vanelli (Hamburg), Neil Wilson (Stuttgart)

D. New Positions:

Conductors: Matthias Bamert (Scottish National Opera), Herbert Blomstedt (San Francisco SO), Semyon Bychkov (Buffalo PO), Philippe Entremont (Denver SO), Günther Herbig (Detroit SO), Jean-Jacques Kantorow (Auvergne Chamber Orchestra), Jeffrey Tate (Covent Garden), David Zinman (Baltimore SO)

Educational: Martina Arroyo (voice, Louisiana State University), David Cerone (president, Cleveland Institute of Music)

Others: Leon Fleisher (artistic director, Tanglewood), John Harbison (composer-in-residence, Los Angeles PO), Leonard Slatkin (president, Association for Classical Music), Joan Tower (composer-in-residence, St. Louis SO)

E. Prizes and Honors:

Prizes: Stephen Albert (Pulitzer--*Symphony, River Run*), Mark Beudert (Pavarotti), Stanislav Bunin (Chopin), David Diamond (Schuman), Jo Ann Falletta (Stokowski), José Feghali (Cliburn), Maria Giordano (Pavarotti), Marc-André Hamelin (Carnegie), Nai-Yuan Hu (Queen Elisabeth), Daijin Kim (Casadesus), Witold Lutoslawski (Grawemeyer--*Symphony No. 3*), Aprile Millo (Tucker), Christopher Trakas and Dawn Upshaw (Naumberg)

Honors: Reginald Goodall (knighted), Neville Marriner (knighted), Yehudi Menuhin (Legion of Honor), Leontyne Price (National Medal of Arts), Mstislav Rostropovich (Schweitzer), William Schuman (Special Pulitzer and Gold Baton), Beverly Sills (Kennedy Center), John Williams (honorary doctorate, New England Conservatory)

F. Biographical Highlights:

Roberta Alexander makes her Vienna Opera debut; June Anderson makes a show-stopping debut at the Paris Opera; Richard Bales retires as music Director of the National Gallery of Art; Kathleen Battle, Chris Merritt and Kenneth Riegel make their Covent Garden debuts; Wolfgang Brendel and Giuseppe Sinopoli make their Bayreuth debuts; Semyon Bychkov, with Karajan's approval, becomes the first conductor to take the Berlin PO on tour; Maria Chiara, Susan Dunn and Håkan Hagegård make their La Scala debuts; Steven DeGroote is almost killed in an airplane crash; Christopher Hogwood takes the Academy of Ancient Music on its first American tour; Milton Katims goes to China to give viola master classes at Shanghai Conservatory; Evelyn Lear and Leontyne Price give their farewell performances at the Met; Leona Mitchell makes her Vienna Opera debut; Esa-Pekka Salonen becomes Principle Guest Conductor of the Philharmonia Orchestra; Rudolf Serkin celebrates his 50th year as a performer in a Carnegie Hall recital; Kyoko Takezawa enter Juilliard to study violin with Dorothy Delay.

G. Institutional Openings:

Performing Groups: Atlantic Brass Quintet (Boston), Lark String Quartet (St. Paul), Lyric Opera Theater of Baton Rouge, Merrimack Lyric Opera (Lowell, Massachusetts), Pacific Chamber Orchestra (Seattle), Virtuosi della Rosa (Portland, Oregon)

Festivals: Festa Musicale Stiana (Florence), Pensacola Chamber Music Festival (Florida), Sedona Chamber Music Festival (Arizona)

Educational: Foundation for the Advancement of Education in Music (Reston, Virginia)

Other: American Music Week, Boston Early Music Festival Orchestra; Composer's Guild, Inc. (N.Y.); Glenn Gould Memorial Foundation (Canada), Lyric Theater Center (Houston), Darius Milhaud Archive (Mills College), Newport Classic Recordings (Providence), Ordway Music Theater (St. Paul), Queensland Performing Arts Complex (Brisbane,

Australia), Fritz Reiner Center for Contemporary Music (Columbia University), Seaver/NEA Conductors Award (by Affiliate Artists)

H. Musical Literature:

Butterworth, Neil, *Dictionary of American Composers*
Christiansen, R., *Prima Donna: A History*
Gauldin, Robert, *A Practical Approach to Sixteenth-Century Counterpoint*
Greene, David M., *Greene's Biographical Encyclopedia of Composers*
Griffiths, Paul, *The String Quartet, A History*
Hasse, John E., *Ragtime: It's History, Composers and Music*
Jacobson, Robert, *Magnificence--Onstage at the Met*
Roads, Curtis, ed., *Composers and the Computer*
Sloboda, John A., *The Musical Mind*

I. Musical Compositions:

Adams, John, *Harmonielehre* (orchestra)
Adler, Samuel, *The Lady Remembers* (Statue of Liberty Suite)
Albert, Stephen, *Concerto for Violin and Orchestra, "In Concordium"*
Babbitt, Milton, *Concerto for Piano and Orchestra*
Brant, Henry, *Desert Forest*
Carter, Elliott, *Penthode* (5 instrumental quartets)
Davidovsky, Mario, *Divertimento for Cello and Orchestra*
Davis, Anthony, *X* (opera)
Del Tredici, David, *March to Tonality* (orchestra)
Diamond, David, *Symphony No. 9*
            Concerto for Flute and Orchestra
Dorati, Antal, *Querela Pacis, Symphony in One Movement*
Dutilleux, Henri, *Concerto for Violin and Orchestra*
Eaton, John, *The Tempest* (opera)
Erb, Donald, *The Dream Time*
Harbison, John, *String Quartet*
Imbrie, Andrew, *Requiem*
Kirchner, Leon, *Belshazzar* (opera)
Laderman, Ezra, *Symphony No. 6*
            Concerto for Flute and Orchestra
Larsen, Libby, *Symphony: Water Music*
Lees, Benjamin, *Symphony No. 4, "Memorial Candles"*
Musgrave, Thea, *Harriet, the Woman Called Moses* (opera)
Paulus, Stephen, *The Woodlanders* (opera)
Reich, Steve, *Three Movements for Orchestra*
Rochberg, George, *Symphony No. 5*
Sallinen, Aulis, *Symphony No. 5*
Schuller, Gunther, *Concerto for Orchestra III, "Farbenspiel"*
Schwantner, Joseph, *A Sudden Rainbow* (orchestra)
Shchedrin, Rodion, *The Seagull*
Wernick, Richard, *Concerto for Violin and Orchestra*
Zimmermann, Udo, *Die Weisse Rose* (opera)
Zwillich, Ellen Taafe, *Symphony No. 2*

1986

World Events:
In the U.S., the space shuttle *Challenger* blows up after liftoff, killing the entire crew; White House scandal over Iranian aid surfaces; U.S. bombs Libya for bombing a West Berlin disco; Ivan Boesky is barred from Wall Street in another business scandal; Congress passes a new income tax reform law; Reagan and Gorbachev meet in a dismal Iceland meeting and fail to agree on arms limitations; Statue of Liberty Centennial celebration in New York. Internationally, a Haitian revolution forces Jean-Claude Duvalier to flee to Europe; a revolution in the Phillipines causes Ferdinand Marcos to flee to Hawaii while Corazon Aquino becomes President; Russia suffers a major nuclear accident at Chernobyl and endangers most of Europe with fall-out; terrorist attacks continue in Paris, Pakistan and Turkey.

Cultural Highlights:
Pulitzers: Fiction, Larry McMurtry (*Lonesome Dove*); Poetry, Henry Taylor (*The Flying Change*). The Nobel Prize for Literature goes to Nigerian author Wole Soyinka; Robert Penn Warren is named Poet Laureate of the U.S. Deaths in the art field include American artist Georgia O'Keeffe and sculptors Seymour Lipton and Reuben Nakian, German sculptor Joseph Beuys and British sculptor Henry Moore; death in the literary field include Americans John Ciardi, Laura Z. Hobson, John D. MacDonald, Bernard Malamud, Helen Santmyer and Theodore White, French philosopher Simone de Beauvoir and author Jean Gênet and British writers John Braine and Christopher Isherwood. Other highlights include:

Art: Romare Bearden, *Evening of the Blue Snake*; Greg Constantine, *Picasso Visits Chicago*; Helms, *Night Window*; David Hockney, *Pearblossom Hwy., April, 1986*; Anselm Kiefer, *Iron Path*; Jeff Koon, *Rabbit* (Stainless Steel); Robert Longo, *All You Zombies*; David Salle, *Footmen*.

Literature: Richard Condon, *Prizzi's Family*; Ernest Hemingway, *The Garden of Eden* (posth.); Ruth Jhabvala, *Out of India*; Robert Ludlum, *The Bourne Supremacy*; G. Marquez, *The Story of a Shipwrecked Sailor*; Robert Schuller, *The Be-Happy Attitudes*; Peter Taylor, *A Summons to Memphis*; Alex Waugh, *Brideshead Benighted*.

MUSICAL EVENTS

B. Deaths:

Jan 6	Frank Miller (Am-cel-cd)	Jun 16	Maurice Duruflé (Fr-org)
Jan 8	Pierre Fournier (Fr-cel)	Jun 23	Patricia Welting (Am-sop)
Feb 13	Edmund Rubbra (Br-cm)	Jun 29	Dusolina Giannini (Am-sop)
Feb 15	Galliano Masini (It-ten)	Jul 16	Claire Watson (Br-sop)
Feb 18	Francisco Mignone (Br-cm)	Aug 13	Caterina Jarboro (Am-sop)
Feb 18	Václav Smetácek (Cz-cd)	Aug 15	Winthrop Sargent (Am-cri)
Feb 26	G. von Milinkovic (Cz-mez)	Sep 9	Magda Tagliaferro (Bra-pn)
Mar 25	George Cehanovsky (Am-bar)	Oct 16	Arthur Grumiaux (Bel-pn)
Apr 1	Donald Grobe (Am-ten)	Nov 6	Elisabeth Grümmer (Ger-sop)
Apr 3	Peter Pears (Br-ten)	Nov 6	Lili Kraus (Hun-pn)
Jun 13	Benny Goodman (Am-pop-cl)	Nov 13	Rudolf Schock (Ger-ten)
Jun 14	Alan Jay Lerner (Am-lib-pop)	Nov 22	Robert Whitney (Am-cd)

C. Débuts:
Met ---Rosario Andrade (sop), Christian Badea (cd), Gabriela Benacková (sop), Sylvain Cambreling (cd), Joyce Castle (mez), Myung-Whun Chung (cd), Salvatore Fisichella (ten), Cecilia Gasdia (sop), Mechthild Gessendorf (sop), Gail Gilmore (mez), Thomas Hampson (bar), Kathryn Harries (sop), Gottfried Hornik (bar), Taro Ichihara (ten), Gary Lakes (ten), Barry McCauley (ten), Marie McLaughlin (sop), Marita Napier (sop), Stanford Olson (ten), Madelyn Renée, Leslie Richards (mez), Bruno Sebatian (ten), Maria Slatinaru (sop), Sheila Smith (mez), Sarah Walker (mez), Yoko Watanabe (sop)

U.S. --Tzimon Barto (N.Y.), Harolyn Blackwell (Chicago), Paata Burchuladze (Philadelphia), Mariana Cioromila (Houston), Helena Doese (Houston), Mark Doss (N.Y.), François-René Duchable (N.Y.), Jean Glennon, József Gregor (Houston), Eric Halfvarson (St. Louis), Della Jones, Kaludi Kaludov (Houston), Felicity Lott (N.Y.), Christine Meadows (Portland), Alan Oke (Boston), Juliana Osinchuk (N.Y.), Vyacheslav Polosov (Chicago), Gino Quilico (San Francisco), Thomas Sanderling, Konstantin Sfiris (San Francisco), Eduard Tumagian (Pittsburgh)

D. New Positions:

Conductors: Claudio Abbado (Vienna Opera), Zuohuang Chen (Central PO, Beijing), Philippe Entremont (Denver SO), Michael Gielen (Baden-Baden Radio SO), Vernon Hadley (Ulster SO), Bernard Haitink (Covent Garden), Christopher Hogwood (Boston Handel and Haydn Society), Marek Janowski (Gürzenich Orchestra, Cologne), Jesús Lopez-Cobos (Cincinnati SO), Lorin Maazel (Pittsburgh SO), Zdenek Macal (Milwaukee SO), André Previn (Los Angeles PO), Maxim Shostakovich (New Orleans SO), Edo de Waart (Minnesota SO), Hugh Wolff (New Jersey SO), David Zinman (Baltimore SO)

Educational: Robert Fitzpatrick (dean, Curtis Institute), Leon Fleisher (piano, Curtis Institute)

Others: Earle Brown (President, American Music Center), Bruce Crawford (general manager, Met), Morton Gould (President, ASCAP), Ezra Laderman (President, National Music Council), John Pritchard (music director, San Francisco Opera)

E. Prizes and Honors:

Prizes: Paata Burchuladze (Pavarotti), Alec Chien (Bachauer), Barbara Custer (Steber), Andrés Díaz (Naumberg), Barry Douglas (Tchaikovsky), Benjamin Frith (Busoni), Arthur Greene (Kapell), Mark Hester (Graz), Barbara Kilduff (Munich), György Ligeti (Grawemeyer), Grant Llewellyn (Leeds), Stanford Olson (Steber), George Perle (Pulitzer- *Wind Quintet IV*), Derek Ragin (Munich), Bernard Rands (Friedheim), Richard Stolzman (Fisher), Kyoko Takezawa (Indianapolis), Natalya Terasova (Tchaikovsky), Richard Wernick (Friedheim), Dolora Zajick (Tucker)

Honors: Marian Anderson (Medal of Arts), Morton Gould (American Academy), Gwyneth Jones (Dame of the British Empire), Itzhak Perlman (Medal of Liberty), Leontyne Price (honorary doctorate, Mannes), Janos Solyom (Swedish Medal of Honor), Ann Maria Stancyzk (Liszt Medal), Isaac Stern (Musician of the Year, *Musical America*)

F. Biographical Highlights:

June Anderson, Jenny Drivala, Simon Estes, Linda Roark-Strummer and Neil Schicoff all make their La Scala debuts; Leonard Bernstein sues G. Schirmer Co. with a breach-of-contract suit; Catharine Comet becomes the first woman to be conductor of a fully professional orchestra in Grand Rapids; Barry Douglas becomes first Westerner to win the Tchaikovsky competition since 1958; Simon Estes and Ashley Putnam make their Covent Garden debuts; Vladimir Horowitz returns to his native Russia with a triumphant concert tour; Christopher Keene announces his retirement from the New York City Opera; Evelyn Lear gives her farewell Met performance; Vyacheslav Polosov defects to the West; Kenneth Schermerhorn takes the Hong Kong PO on a tour of China; Renata Scotto takes up stage directing at the Met; Joseph Silverstein takes the Utah SO on a tour of both Berlins, the first American orchestra to do both; Giuseppe Sinopoli takes the Philharmonia Orchestra of London on a tour of the U.S.; Leonard Slatkin takes the St. Louis SO on a Far East concert tour; Cheryl Studer makes her Paris Opera debut; Julian Lloyd Webber discovers Arthur Sullivan's lost Cello Concerto, which is reconstructed by David Mackie; Patricia Welting and her two daughters are found shot to death.

G. Institutional Openings:

Performing Groups: Austin Lyric Opera (Texas), Boston Composers Orchestra, Cleveland Orchestra's Youth Orchestra, Illinois Chamber Orchestra, Innisfree Festival Opera, Los

Angeles Music Center Opera, Manchester Sinfonietta (England), Miami City Ballet, Opera Northern Ireland, Washington Guitar Quintet

Festivals: Mackinac Island Music Festival (Michigan), Nakamichi Baroque Music Festival (UCLA), Omaha Festival of Contemporary Music, Schleswig-Holstein Festival

Educational: Hong Kong Academy for the Performing Arts

Other: American Berlin Opera Foundation, Beijing Concert Hall (China), Beijing International Youth Violin Competition, Czech Music Society of St. Louis, The Dance Place (Washington, D.C.), Richard Gaddes Fund for Young Singers (St. Louis Opera), Great Woods Center for the Performing Arts (Massachusetts), Het Muziektheater (Amsterdam), International Ermanno Wolf-Ferrari Society, National Museum of Dance (Saratoga Springs), Orange County Performing Arts Center (Segerstrom Hall, California), Paul Sacher Foundation (Basel)

H. Musical Literature:
Brindle, Reginald Smith, *Musical Composition*
Craven, Robert R., *Symphony Orchestras of the U.S.*
Griffiths, Paul, *The Thames and Hudson Encyclopedia of 20th Century Music*
Hitchcock/Sadie, *New Grove Dictionary of American Music*
Matheopoulos, Helena, *Divo: Great Tenors, Baritones and Basses Discuss Their Roles*
Peyser, Joan, ed., *The Orchestra: Origins and Transformations*
Randel, Don M., ed., *New Harvard Dictionary of Music*
Rosenberg, Neil, *Bluegrass: A History*
Slonimsky, Nicolas, *Supplement to Music Since 1900*

I. Musical Compositions:
Adams, John, *The Chairman Dances* (opera)
Bernstein, Leonard, *Jubilee Games* (orchestra)
Bose, Hans-Jürgen von, *The Sorrows of Young Werther* (opera)
Carter, Elliott, *String Quartet No. 4*
Davies, Peter M., *Concerto for Violin and Orchestra*
Del Tredici, David, *Child Alice*
Druckman, Jacob, *Athanor* (orchestra)
Feldman, Morton, *Coptic Light*
Foss, Lukas, *Renaissance Concerto for Flute and Orchestra*
Hall, Charles J., *Psalmic Symphony for A Capella Chorus*
Harbison, John, *The Flight into Egypt*
Henze, Hans Werner, *Concerto for Guitar and Orchestra*
Husa, Karel, *Concerto for Orchestra*
Laderman, Ezra, *Pentimento* (orchestra)
Larsen, Libby, *Coming Forth into Day* (oratorio)
Menotti, Gian Carlo, *Goya* (opera)
Messiaen, Olivier, *Livre du Saint Sacrement* (organ)
Panufnik, Andrzej, *Concerto for Bassoon and Orchestra*
Pasatieri, Thomas, *The Three Sisters* (opera)
Penderecki, Krystoff, *The Black Mask* (opera)
Reimann, Aribert, *Troades* (opera)
Sallinen, Aulis, *Symphony No. 5, "Washington Mosaics"*
Schuman, William, *On Freedom's Ground* (cantata)
Skrowaczewski, Stanislaw, *Concerto for Orchestra*
Tower, Joan, *Concerto for Piano and Orchestra*
          Silver Ladders (orchestra)
Trimble, Lester, *Symphony No. 3, "Tricentennial"*
Wuorinen, Charles, *Concerto No. 3 for Piano and Orchestra*
Zwillich, Ellen Taafe, *Concerto for Piano and Orchestra*

1987

World Events:

In the U.S., the first trillion-dollar budget is proposed by President Reagan; relations with Panama become strained; Texaco, Inc., is forced to file for bankruptcy; Wall Street Crash in October ruins many investors; sex scandals end the Presidential quest of Senator Hart and cause the fall of PTL Tele-evangelists, Jim and Tammy Bakker; Chrysler Corporation buys out American Motors; Constitution Bicentennial celebrations held around the country. Internationally, Gorbachev announces a new Soviet position of "Glasnost" (openness); a truce is called in Afghanistan, but not kept; Deng Xiaoping steps down in China and Zhao Ziyang is elected General Secretary; a new constitution is drafted in the Phillipines.

Cultural Highlights:

Pulitzers: Drama, August Wilson (*Fences*); Fiction, Peter Taylor (*A Summons to Memphis*); Poetry, Rita Dove (*Thomas and Beulah*). Russian-born author Joseph Brodsky receives the Nobel Prize for Literature, Richard Wilbur is named Poet Laureate of the U.S. and Robert Penn Warren is given the National Medal of Arts. *Irises* by Vincent van Gough sold for a record $54 million; The Terra Museum of American Art opens in Chicago and the Georgia O'Keeffe Foundation and J. Paul Getty Trust are set up. The art world loses Leon Berkowitz, Peter Fingesten, André Masson and Raphael Soyer; deaths in the literary field include Jean Anouilh, James Baldwin, Erskine Caldwell, Alistair MacLean and Marguerite Yourcenar. Other highlights include:

Art: Jennifer Bartlett, *Fence*; Susan Crile, *The Seer*; Eric Fischl, *The Evacuation of Saigon*; Nancy Graves, *Spanse*; Charles Hewitt, *Promised Land*; Yvonne Jacquette, *Times Square (Overview)*; Jasper Johns, *The Seasons*; Anselm Kiefer, *Osiris and Isis*; Mark Kostabi, *Dress for Success*; Fabrizzio Plessi, *Roma*; John Raimondi, *Dance of the Cranes*

Literature: Allan Bloom, *The Closing of the American Mind*; Mary Gordon, *Temporary Shelter*; Garrison Keillor, *Leaving Home*; Judith Krantz, *I'll Take Manhattan*; Tony Morrison, *Beloved*; Tip O'Neill, *Man of the House*; Oliver Sacks, *The Man Who Mistook His Wife for a Hat*; Sidney Sheldon, *Windmills of the Gods*; Wallace Stegner, *Crossing to Savety.*

MUSICAL EVENTS

B. Deaths:

Feb 16	Dmitri Kabalevsky (Rus-cm)	Jul 4	Paul Fromm (Am-pat)
Mar 13	Gerald Moore (Br-pn)	Jul 22	Natalie Hinderas (Am-pn)
Mar 25	Joy Simpson (Am-sop)	Aug 14	Vincent Persichetti (Am-cm)
Mar 26	Eugen Jochum (Aus-cd)	Sep 3	Morton Feldman (Am-cm)
Mar 28	Maria von Trapp (Aus-voc)	Sep 22	Norman Luboff (Am-cd)
Apr 2	Buddy Rich (Am-pop)	Oct 19	Jacqueline du Pré (Br-cel)
Apr 12	Ervin Nyiregyházi (Hun-pn)	Oct 29	Woody Herman (Am-pop)
Apr 20	Anthony Tudor (Br-bal)	Nov	Charles Holland (Am-ten)
Jun 2	Sammy Kaye (Am-pop)	Nov 19	Clara Petrella (It-sop)
Jun 2	Andrés Segovia (Sp-gui)	Nov 20	James Atherton (Am-ten)
Jun 21	Abram Chasins (Am-pn-au)	Dec 6	Izler Solomon (Am-cd)
Jun 26	Henk Badings (Hol-cm)	Dec 10	Jascha Heifetz (Rus-vn)
Jun 30	Federico Mompou (Sp-cm)		

C. Débuts:

Met ---Simone Alaimo (bs), Mark Baker (ten), Gweneth Bear (alto), Bruno Beccaria (ten), Harolyn Blackwell (sop), Angela-Maria Blasi (sop), Barbara Bonney (sop), Livia Budai (mez), Paata Burchuladze (bs), Harry Dworchak (bs), Hermann Eckhoff (bar), Jean Fournet (cd), Sonya Ghayarian (sop), Ann Gjevang (sop), Franco de Grandis (bs), Jerry Hadley (ten), Horst Hiestermann (ten), Barbara Kilduff (sop), Gregory Kunde (ten),

Mario Luperi (bs), Alessandra Marc (sop), Waltraud Meier (mez), Alexandrina Milcheva (mez), Erie Mills (sop), Diana Montague (mez), Mi Hae Park (sop), Jan-Hendrik Rootering (bs), Neil Rosenheim (ten)

U.S. --Martin André (Seattle), Spiros Argiris (Charleston), Maria Bachmann (N.Y.), Etelka Csavlek (San Francisco), Michel Dalberto, Francesco Ellero d'Artegna (Chicago), Vladimir Feltsman (D.C.), Alain Fondary (San Francisco), Natalia Gutman (tour), Frederick Kalt (Eugene, Oregon), Nigel Kennedy (tour), Mario Malagnini (N.Y.), Stefan Milenkovic (Newport), Jard van Nes (Minneapolis), Antonio Ordoñez (Dallas), Maria Radicheva (N.Y.), Gustavo Romero (N.Y.), Paul Shaw (N.Y.), Clive Swansbourne, Kyoko Takezawa , Natalia Troitskaya, Mara Zampieri (San Francisco)

Other -Roy Stevens (Alessandria)

D. New Positions:

Conductors: Theo Alcantara (Pittsburgh Opera), Sergiu Comissiona (New York City Opera), Dennis Russell Davies (Bonn SO), Joan Dornemann (Minnesota Opera), Bernard Haitink (Covent Garden), Raymond Leppard (Indianapolis SO), Gilbert Levine (Cracow PO), Charles Mackerras (Welsh National Opera), John Mauceri (Scottish Opera), Riccardo Muti (La Scala), Joseph Silverstein (Chataugua SO), Geoffrey Simon (Albany SO)

Educational: Simon Estes (voice, Juilliard), Lynn Harrell (cello, LSC)

Others: Spiros Argiris (music director, Spoleto, U.S.A.), John Corigliano (composer-in-residence, Chicago SO), Lee Goldstein (composer-in-residence, Chicago Lyric Opera)

E. Prizes and Honors:

Prizes: Dmitri Berlinski (Montreal), Harrison Birtwistle (Grawemeyer--*The Mask of Orpheus*), William Curry (Stokowski), Dennis Russell Davies (Ditson), Mark Doss (London), Harry Dworchak (Tucker), Efrain Guigui (Ditson), John Harbison (Pulitzer--*The Flight into Egypt*), Gwyneth Jones (Shakespeare), Susan Patterson (Puccini), Artur Pizarro (da Motta), Bernard Rands and Richard Wernick (Friedheim), Catherine Stolz (Steber), David Allen Wehr (O'Shea), Qian Zhou (Thibaud)

Honors: Marian Anderson (honorary doctorate, University of Connecticut), Victoria de los Angeles (honorary Doctorate, all Spanish Universities), Leonard Bernstein (Schweitzer and MacDowell Medal), Peter Maxwell Davies (knighted), Barbara Kolb (Friedheim), Jessye Norman (honorary doctorate, Harvard), André Previn (ASCAP Golden Award), Mstislav Rostropovich (Musician of the Year, *Musical America*), Bidú Sayao (Order of Merit), William Schuman (National Medal of Arts)

F. Biographical Highlights:

Phyllis Curtin gives voice masterclasses in Beijing Conservatory; Maria Ewing severs ties with James Levine and the Met over differences in performance; Vladimir Feltsman is allowed to perform publicly after 8 years of virtual house arrest and is given an exit visa besides; Alexander Goudonov becomes a naturalized American citizen; Karen Huffstadt makes her Vienna debut; Stephen Kates gives concerts and classes in Russia; Lorin Maazel takes the Pittsburgh SO on a concert tour of China; Julia Migenes makes her Covent Garden debut; James Morris makes his Covent Garden debut and marries Susan Quittmeyer; John Nelson takes the Indianapolis SO on its first European tour; Richard M. Nixon is assigned a seat in the French Academy; Felicity Palmer makes her La Scala debut; Alexander Simionescu shares the Montreal Prize with Catherine Cho; the Toscanini Legacy (scores, letters, notebooks, etc.) is donated to the music library at Lincoln Center.

G. Institutional Openings:

Performing Groups: International Youth Philharmonic (Czechoslovakia), New World Symphony (Miami)

Festivals: Mendocino Music Festival (California), Mozart in Monterey, SoundCelebration (Louisville)

Other: Foundation for Musical Performance (N.Y.), Glimmerglass Opera House (Cooperstown, N.Y.), Glenn Gould Prize (Canada), International New Music Composer's Group (N.Y.), Kammermusiksaal (Berlin), National Museum of Women in the Arts (Washington, D.C.), National Theater (Taipei, Taiwan), Opera/Music Theater Institute (New Jersey), Pacific Contemporary Music Center, Tampa Performing Arts Complex, Gus S. Wortham Theater Center (Houston)

H. Musical Literature:

Babbitt, Milton, *Words about Music*
Del Mar, Norman, *A Companion to the Orchestra*
Dunsby, J./Whittall, A., *Music Analysis in Theory and Practice*
Heussenstamm, George, *The Norton Manual of Music Notation*
Lewin, David, *Generalized Musical Intervals and Transformations*
Page, Christopher, *Voices and Instruments of the Middle Ages*
Winsor, Phil, *Computer-Assisted Music Composition*
Zinn, M./Hogenson, R., *Basics of Music*

I. Musical Compositions:

Adams, John, *Nixon in China* (opera)
Baley, Virko, *Concerto for Violin and Orchestra*
Bolcom, William, *Symphony No. 4*
          Twelve New Etudes for Piano
Cage, John, *Europeras 1 and 2*
Erb, Donald, *Concerto for Brass Section and Orchestra*
Glass, Philip, *Concerto for Violin and Orchestra*
          The Light (orchestra)
Guarnieri, Adriano, *Trionfo della Notte* (opera)
Husa, Karel, *Concerto for Trumpet and Orchestra*
Paulus, Stephen, *Concerto for Violin and Orchestra*
Previn, André, *Concerto for Piano and Orchestra*
Rands, Bernard, *Hiraeth* (cello and orchestra)
Reich, Steve, *The Four Sections* (orchestra)
Schelle, Michael, *Concerto for 2 Pianos and Orchestra*
Schuller, Gunther, *String Quartet No. 3*
Schwantner, Joseph, *Toward Light* (orchestra)
Testi, Flavio, *Riccardo III* (opera)
Tower, Joan, *Piano Concerto and Orchestra*

1988

World Events:
   In the U.S., George Bush is elected as President No. 41; Shuttle *Discovery*   puts the U.S. back in the space program after 2½ year delay; President Reagan visits Moscow and Gorbachev vists the U.S. in December; severe drought weakens the midwest region; Jimmie Swaggert falls in another televangelist sex scandal; several Reagan aides are indicted on various ethics charges; a major tobacco company is held liable for lung cancer in a habitual smoker. Internationally, Panama strongman Manuel Noriega is indicted by U.S. courts for drug smuggling; Iraq uses poison gas against Iran; a cease fire and talks begin to end the Irag-Iran War; truce in Nicaragua between Contras and Sandinistas; Russia signs an agreement to pull out of Afghanistan; an Iranian airliner is shot down by a U.S. Naval vessel; great Armenian earthquake kills thousands of people; terrible monsoon floods in southeast Asia.

Cultural Highlights:
   Pulitzers: Drama, Alfred Uhry (*Driving Miss Daisy*); Fiction, Toni Morrison (*Beloved*); Poetry, William Meredith (*Partial Accounts: New and Selected Poems*). Egyptian novelist Naquib Mahfouz is awarded the Nobel Prize in Literature; the magazine, *Modern Painters*, begins publication; the Liverpool Branch of the Tate Gallery opens; the Pollack-Krasner Museum opens on Long Island; the new National Galley of Canada opens in Monteal; the Andy Warhol Foundation for the Visual Arts is founded; the Minneapolis Sculpture Gardens open; the Los Angeles Pavilion for Japanese Art opens and Nahan Galleries opens in Japan. Howard Nemerov is named American Poet Laureate, Saul Bellow is given the National Medal of Arts and William Golding is knighted. Deaths include American artists Romare Bearden, Isobel Bishop, Stanley Hayter and Charles Pollack, Russian-born sculptress Louise Nevelson, American novelist Max Schulman, British poet Sachaverell Sitwell, poet Miguel Piñero, French author René Char and South African author Alan Paton. Other highlights include:

   Art: Howard Buchwald, *Sight Unseen*; Charles Greeley, *Nude Descending Spiral*; Tom Lynch, *Sunday Drivers, Paris*; Merrill Mahaffey, *Heart of the Mountain*; Brice Marsden, *1* (Grey); Jules Olitski, *Gold Blaze*; Mark di Suvero, *Symbiosis* (Stuttgart).

   Literature: Peter Carey, *Oscar and Lucinda*; Dominick Dunne, *People Like Us*; Loup Durand, *Daddy*; Thomas Flanagan, *The Tenants of Time*; Lee Iacocca, *Straight Talk;* Paul Kennedy, *The Rise and Fall of the Great Powers*; Joe McGinniss, *Blind Faith*; Roxanne Pulitzer, *The Prize Pulitzer*; Danielle Steel, *Zoya*; John Updike, *S*.

MUSICAL EVENTS

B. Deaths:

Jan 12	Bruno Prevedi (Rus-cd)	Apr 29	Irving Kolodin (Am-cri)
Jan 21	Eugene Mravinsky (Rus-cd)	Apr 30	James McCracken (Am-ten)
Feb 9	Kurt Herbert Adler (Am-cd)	Jun 22	Howard Mitchell (Am-cd)
Feb 14	Frederick Loewe (Aus-pop)	Jun 27	Heinz Rehfuss (Ger-bar)
Feb 22	Afro Poll (It-bar)	Jul 18	José Braga Santos (Por-cm)
Feb 22	Solomon (Br-pn)	Jul 22	John Carter (Am-ten)
Mar 3	Henryk Szeryng (Pol-vn)	Aug	Jens Peter Larsen (Den-mus)
Mar 12	Gianna Pederzini (It-mez)	Oct 15	K.S. Sorabji (Br-cm)
Mar 25	Robert Joffrey (Am-bal)	Nov 13	Antal Dorati (Hun-cd)
Mar 28	Judith Somogi (Am-cd)	Nov 21	Raymond Lewenthal (Am-pn)
Apr 15	Yuri Egorov (Rus-pn)	Nov 24	Irmgard Seefried (Aus-sop)
Apr 16	John Reardon (Am-bar)		Jean-Pierre Ponelle (Fr-dir)

C. Débuts:
   Met ---Katherine Ciesinski (sop), Martine Dupuy (mez), Mark Elder (cd), Alain Fondary (bar), Jeffrey Gall (c.ten), Ronald Hamilton (ten), Anthony Johnson (ten), Linda Kelm (sop), Carlos Kleiber (cd), Elizabeth Knighton (sop), Toni Kramer (ten), Jean-Philippe

Lafont (bar), Veriano Luchetti (ten), Nicola Martinucci (ten), Marilyn Mims (sop), Silvia Mosca (Sop), Wolfgang Neumann (ten), Timothy Nobel (bar), Anne Sofie von Otter (mez), Susan Quittmeyer (mez), Alberto Rinaldi (bar), Heinrich Schiff (N.Y.), Hanna Schwarz (mez), Stefania Toczyska (mez), Margaret Jane Wray (sop), Dolora Zajick (mez)

U.S. --Bruno Aprea (Columbus), Bruce Brubaker (N.Y.), Elizabeth Campbell (tour), Hung-Kuan Chen, Christopher Costanza (N.Y.), Semyon Fridman (N.Y.), Hai-jing Fu (Philadelphia), John David de Haan (San Francisco), Andreas Haefliger (N.Y.), Matt Haimovitz (N.Y.), Pamela Hinchman (Pittsburgh), Keith Ikaia-Purdy (Boise), Lynda Keith (Wolftrap), Klaus König (Houston), Jiri Kout (Los Angeles), Frank Lopardo (Chicago), Angelo Marenzi (Portland, OR), Jeanne Piland (Houston), Mikhail Pletnev (Newport), Peter Seiffert (Philadelphia), Ory Shihor, David Wehr (N.Y.), Annalisa Winberg (Philadelphia)

D. New Positions:

Conductors: Semyon Bychkov (Orchestre de Paris), Philippe Entremont (Denver SO), Christoph Eschenbach (Houston SO), Yoel Levi (Atlanta SO), Andrew Litton (Bournemouth SO), Lorin Maazel (Pittsburgh SO), Zdenek Macal (San Antonio SO), Michael Palmer (New Haven SO)

Educational: Richard E. Adams (dean, Manhattan School of Music), Jeffrey Kahane (piano, Eastman)

Others: James de Blasis (artistic director, Cincinnati Opera), Donald Erb (composer-in-residence, St. Louis SO), Stephen Paulus (composer-in-residence, Atlanta SO), Greg Steinke (chairman, Society of Composers, Inc.), David del Tredici (composer-in-residence, New York PO)

E. Prizes and Honors:

Prizes: Avner Arad (Koussevitsky), William Bolcom (Pulitzer--*12 New Etudes for Piano*), Chris Delane and Richard M. Lewis (Corbett-Treigle), Ben Heppner (Nilsson), Leonidas Kavakos (Naumburg), Lafayette String Quartet (Fischoff), Richard Leech (Tucker), Louise Mendius (Steber), André Watts (Fisher), David Allen Wehr (O'Shea), Kong Xiangdong (Bachauer), Eva Zseller (Tokyo & Cusumano)

Honors: Harrison Birtwistle (knighted), Max Rudolf (Theodore Thomas Award); Rudolf Serkin (National Medal of Arts), Robert Shaw (Golden Baton), Georg Solti (Musician of the Year, *Musical America*), Francis Thorne (American Academy), Honorary Doctorates-- Milton Babbitt (Northwestern), Lukas Foss (Curtis), George Rochberg (Curtis), Alexander Schneider (Kennedy Center), William Schuman (Yale), Leonard Slatkin (Juilliard)

F. Biographical Highlights:

José Carreras returns to the stage in Barcelona after a year of battling leukemia; Stuart Challender takes the Sydney (Australia) SO on a concert tour of the U.S.; Barry Cooper reconstructs a movement of Beethoven's "Tenth"; Peter Maxwell Davies takes the Scottish Chamber Orchestra on a tour of the U.S.; Vladimir Horowitz donates his collection of papers and recordings to Yale University; Marie McLaughlin and Deborah Polaski make their La Scala debuts; Eduardo Mata is named Principle Guest Conductor of the Pittsburgh SO; Zubin Mehta announces his retirement from the New York PO as of 1991; Simon Rattle takes the City of Birmingham SO on a tour of the U.S.; Robert Shaw takes the Atlanta SO and Chorus on a European tour; Beverly Sills announces her plans for retirement from the New York City Opera, effective January, 1989; Peter Trussel makes his Covent Garden debut; Ruben Vartanyan defects from the Bolshoi Ballet orchestra while touring in Bolivia.

G. Institutional Openings:

Performing Groups: Amadeus Trio (Amsterdam), D'Oyly Carte Opera (rebirth), Paris PO

Festivals: New York International Festival of the Arts

Educational: New World School of the Arts (Miami)

Other: Marian Anderson Awards for American Singers, Benedum Center (Pittsburgh),

James McCracken Memorial Fund for Young Tenors (N.Y.), World Cello Congress (Maryland)

H. Musical Literature:

Cook, Gary, *Teaching Percussion*
Gauldin, Robert, *A Practical Approach to Eighteenth-Century Counterpoint*
Kramer, Jonathan, *Listen to the Music*
Leppart, R./McClary, S., *Music and Society*
Lester, Joel, *Analytic Approaches to Twentieth-Century Music*
Rorem, Ned, *Settling the Score: Essays on Music*
Sadie, Stanley, ed., *The Norton/Grove Concise Encyclopedia of Music*
Spencer/Temko, *A Practical Approach to the Study of Form in Music*
Stevens, John, *Words and Music in the Middle Ages*
Watkins, Glenn, *Soundings: Music in the Twentieth Century*

I. Musical Compositions:

Adams, John, *Fearful Symmetries*
Albert, Stephen, *Anthems and Processionals* (orchestra)
Argento, Dominick, *Te Deum*
　　　　　　　The Aspern Papers (opera)
Del Tredici, David, *Tattoo* (orchestra)
Glass, Philip, *The Making of the Representative for Planet 8* (opera)
　　　　　　1000 Airplanes on the Roof (opera)
Kagel, Mauricio, *Tanz-Schul* (opera)
Kreisberg, Matthias, *Chronosymphonies*
Lloyd, George, *Symphony No. 7*
Locklair, Dan, *Creation's Seeing Order* (orchestra)
Mennin, Peter, *Flute Concerto*
Neikrug, Marc, *Los Alamos* (opera)
Paulus, Stephen, *Concerto for Violin and Orchestra*
Reise, Jay, *Rasputin* (opera)
Rodriguez, Robert, *A Colorful Symphony*
Rorem, Ned, *Goodbye, My Fancy* (soloists, chorus, orchestra)
Rouse, Christopher, *Symphony No. 1*
Schnittke, Alfred, *Violin Concerto no. 4*
Schuller, Gunther, *Concerto for Flute and Orchestra*
Shifrin, Lalo, *Songs of the Aztecs* (orchestra)
Stockhausen, Karlheinz, *Montag aus Licht* (opera)
Trojahn, Manfred, *Variations for Orchestra*
Zwillich, Ellen T., *Symbolon* (orchestra)

General Musical Index

A

Abarbanell, Lina- 1963b
Abbado, Claudio- 1933a, 1958e, 1960c, 1963e,
    1968c, 1971d, 1977d, 1979df, 1982f, 1986d
Abbey Theater- 1904g
Abel, Jenny- 1942a
Abendroth, Irene- 1932b
Abert, Hermann- 1927b
Abott, Bessie- 1906c
Abraham, Gerald- 1904a, 1933h, 1935h, 1936h,
    1938h, 1961e, 1972e
Abramowitz, Jonathan- 1947a
Abrányi, Kornél- 1900h, 1903b
Abravanel, Maurice- 1903a, 1933f, 1936c,
    1948d, 1961e, 1971e, 1976f, 1979f
Abreu, Eduardo- 1949a, 1963c
Abreu, Sergio- 1948a, 1963c
Academia de Musica Euterpe- 1934g
Academia Granados- 1901g
Academic Choral Society- 1953g
Academy of Ancient Music- 1973g
Academy of St. Martin-in-the-Fields- 1959g
Academy of Vocal Arts- 1935g
Accademia dei Dilettanti di Musica- 1928g
Accademia Monteverdiana- 1961g
Accardo, Salvatore- 1941a, 1956e, 1958e
Achucarro, Joaquín- 1950c
Ackté, Aïno- 1904c, 1944b
Acosta, Adolovni- 1946a
Adachi, Motohiko- 1940a
Adám, Jenö- 1957e(p & h)
Adam, Klaus- 1983b
Adam, Mariella- 1934a
Adam, Theo- 1926a, 1949c, 1969c
Adams, Charles- 1900b
Adams, Horst- 1937a
Adams, John- 1947a, 1969f, 1971d, 1982d,
    1985i, 1986i, 1987i, 1988i
Adams, Richard E.- 1988d
Adams, Suzanne- 1953b
Adani, Mariella- 1962c
Addinsell, Richard- 1942i, 1977b
Adelaide:
    A. Festival of Arts- 1960g
    A. Singers- 1936g
    A. Wind Quintet- 1964g
Adesi Chorus- 1924g
Adison, Adele- 1925a, 1948c
Adlam-Burnett, Keyboard Maker- 1971g
Adler, Clarence- 1914c, 1969b
Adler, F. Charles- 1959b

Adler, Guido- 1911h, 1941b
Adler, Kurt- 1905a, 1938d, 1943d, 1951c,
    1953di, 1977b
Adler, Kurt Herbert- 1988b
Adler, Peter- 1959d, 1972c
Adler, Richard- 1955i
Adler, Samuel- 1928a, 1957i, 1959i, 1960i,
    1967i, 1969b, 1971i, 1974i, 1975i, 1982h,
    1985i
Adni, Daniel- 1951a, 1970c
Adorno, Theodor- 1956h, 1959h, 1962h, 1969b,
    1971h
Aeolian American Corporation- 1932g
Aeolian Chamber Players- 1961g
Aeolian Hall (London), 1904g
Aeolian String Quartet- 1927g
Afanassiev, Valery- 1972e
Affiliate Artists' Exxon/Arts Endowment
    Conductors Program- 1972g
Affiliate Artists, Inc.- 1966g
Affré, Agustarello- 1911c
African Music- 1952g
Agay, Dénes- 1911a, 1981h
Agostini, Giuseppe- 1951b
Agrupación Coral Nuestra Señora de la
    ' Almudena- 1959g
Agrupación Nueva Música- 1944g
Aguirre, Julián- 1924b
Ahern, David- 1947a, 1966c
Ahlersmeyer, Mathieu- 1929c, 1973f, 1979b
Ahlstedt, Douglas- 1945a, 1973c
Ahnsjö, Claes- 1942a, 1969c
Ahrend & Burmzema, Organ Builders- 1954g
Ahrens, Joseph- 1934d
Ahronovich, Yuri- 1932a, 1964d, 1975d, 1982d
Aibel, Howard- 1959e
Aimaro, Lina- 1939c
Aitken, Robert- 1939a
Aitken, Webster- 1929c, 1935c
Ajemian, Anahid- 1946e
Akiyama, Kazuyoski- 1941a
Akutagawa, Yasushi- 1925a
Alaimo, Simone- 1987c
Alain, Jehan- 1911a, 1927f, 1936e, 1940b
Alain, Marie Claire- 1926a, 1936c, 1944f,
    1950c
Alarie, Pierrette- 1921a, 1940c, 1945c
Alaska Festival of Music- 1956g
Albanese, Licia- 1913a, 1934c, 1940c, 1945f
Albani, Emma- 1925e, 1930b
Albéniz, Isaac- 1909bi
Alberghetti, Anna- 1936a
Albert, Eugène d'- 1932b

American Musical Instrument Society- 1971g
American Musicological Society- 1934g
American Opera Society- 1951g
American Orchestral Society- 1920g
American Organist- 1918g
American Piano Co.- 1908g
American Prix de Rome- 1905g
American Recorder Society- 1939g
American School Band Directors' Association-
    1953g
American Society for Jewish Music- 1974g
American Society of Ancient Instruments-
    1929g
American Society of Composers, Authors and
    Publishers- 1914g
American Society of University Composers-
    1966g
American String Quartet- 1974g
American String Teachers Association- 1946g
American SO- 1915g
American Symphony Orchestra League- 1942g
American Wind SO- 1960g
American Women Composers- 1976g
Amici della Musica- 1914g
Amigos de Musica- 1939g
Amirkhanian, Charles- 1945a
Amirov, Fikret- 1922a, 1984b
Amoyal, Pierre- 1949a, 1964e, 1970e, 1972c
Amparán, Belén- 1956c
Amram, David- 1930a, 1967i, 1968i, 1981i
Amsterdam Chamber Orchestra- 1957g
Amundrud, Lawrence- 1954a, 1972c
Amy, Gilbert- 1936a, 1973d
An, Youngshin- 1983e
An die Musik- 1976g
Ancerl, Karel- 1908a, 1950d, 1970d, 1973b
Anchorage:
    A. Civic Opera- 1955g
    A. SO- 1946g
Ancona, Mario- 1931b
Anda, Géza- 1921a, 1955c, 1976b
Anday, Rosette- 1920c
Anders, Peter- 1931c
Anderson, Anton- 1926b
Anderson, Arthur- 1929h, 1932c
Anderson, James- 1985c
Anderson, June- 1978c, 1985f, 1986f
Anderson, Karsten- 1964d
Anderson, Laurie- 1947a
Anderson, Leroy- 1908a, 1950i, 1975b
Anderson, Marian- 1902a, 1925c, 1955cf,
    1978e, 1986e, 1987e
Anderson, Marian, Awards for American
    Singers- 1988g
Anderson, Sybil- 1903b
Anderson, Sylvia- 1962c
Andrade, Rosario- 1986c
André, Franz- 1952e

André, Martin- 1987c
André, Maurice- 1933a, 1954c, 1955e, 1967d,
    1974c, 1975b
Andreae, Volkmar- 1906d, 1962b
Andrée, Elfrida- 1929b
Andrésen, Ivar- 1919c, 1930c, 1940b
Andreva, Stella- 1937c
The Andrews Sisters Trio- 1932g
Andriessen, Hendrik- 1926d, 1937di, 1946i,
    1949d, 1952d, 1954i
Andriessen, Jurriaan- 1925a, 1962i, 1963i
Andriessen, Louis- 1939a
Andriessen, Willem- 1964b
Angas, Richard- 1942a, 1962e
Angeles, Victoria de Los- 1923a, 1947e, 1944c,
    1950c, 1951c, 1978e, 1987e
Angelici, Martha- 1938c
Angelis, Nazarena de- 1909c
Angelo, Gianna d'- 1961c
Angelo, Louis d'- 1917c
Angermüller, Rudolph- 1940a
Anglès, Higini- 1969b
Anguish, Elizabeth- 1969c
Anievas, Augustin- 1934a, 1952c, 1961e
Anitua, Fanny- 1913c
Annapolis Brass Quintet- 1971g
Anrooy, Peter van- 1954b
Ansbach Bach Festival- 1948g
Anselmi, Giuseppe- 1929b
Ansermet, Ernest- 1915d, 1916c, 1918d, 1943h,
    1948h, 1961h, 1962c, 1969b
Ansorge, Conrad- 1930b
Ansseau, Fernand- 1913c, 1923c
Anthes, George- 1902c
Antheil, George- 1900a, 1926i, 1930i, 1933i,
    1937i, 1942i, 1943i, 1945hi, 1949i, 1959b
Antoine, Anne-Marie- 1944a, 1970c
Anthologie Sonore- 1934g
Anthony, Charles- 1929a, 1954c
Anthony, Grace- 1921c
Antoine, Josephine- 1936c
Antonicek, Theophil- 1937a
Antonicelli, Giuseppe- 1947c
Antoniou, Theodore- 1935a
Antwerp:
    A. PO- 1955g
    Collegium Musicum Antwerpiense- 1938g
Apel, Willi- 1932h, 1934h, 1942h, 1944h, 1946h,
    1947h, 1957h, 1967h
Apostel, Hans E.- 1972b
Appel, Toby- 1952a
Appia, Edmond- 1952e, 1961b
Aprahamian, Felix- 1967h
Aprea, Bruno- 1988c
Apthorp, William- 1901h
Apy, Arthur- 1973c
A-R Editions- 1962g
Aragall, Giacomo- 1939a, 1962f, 1963c, 1968c

Busoni, Ferruccio- 1901f, 1904i, 1907h, 1912i,
    1913dei, 1916i, 1916i, 1917i, 1920i, 1922fi,
    1924bi
Busoni International Piano Competition- 1949g
Busse, Barry- 1946a
Busser, Henri- 1938e, 1973b
Bussotti, Sylvano- 1931a
Bustini, Alessandro- 1904h
Butt, Clara- 1920e, 1936b
Butterworth, Arthur- 1923a
Butterworth, George- 1913i
Butterworth, Georges- 1915a
Butterworth, Neil- 1985h
Buxton Festival- 1979g
Bybee, Ariel- 1978c
Bychkov, Semyon- 1952a, 1970f, 1975f, 1980d,
    1985df, 1988d
Byrd, William, Singers- 1970g
Byrum, Rose- 1956c
Byström, Oscar- 1909b

C

Caballé, Monserrat- 1933a, 1954c, 1965c
Cabilli, Giuseppina- 1948b
Cabrillo Music Festival- 1963g
Cacavas, John- 1975h
Cadman, Charles- 1902d, 1903f, 1906i, 1908di,
    1909fi, 1910i, 1913i, 1914i, 1915i, 1917fi,
    1918i, 1921i, 1922i, 1924fi, 1925i, 1928i,
    1933i, 1937i, 1939i, 1942i, 1944i, 1945i,
    1946b
Cage, John- 1912a, 1930f, 1933f, 1934f, 1937f,
    1942f, 1951i, 1952i, 1953i, 1958i, 1961h,
    1964f, 1969hi, 1973h, 1981i, 1987i
Cahier, Mme. Charles- 1904c
Cahiers de la Quinzaine- 1900g
Cahil, Teresa M.- 1944a, 1970c, 1976f
Calder, Alexander- 1926f
Caldwell, John- 1978h
Caldwell, Sara- 1965(f), 1974e, 1976c, 1981f,
    1983d
Cali Conservatory and School of the Fine
    Arts- 1933g
California Institute of the Arts- 1961g
Call, Lucy Lee- 1904c
Callas, Maria- 1923a, 1947c, 1954c, 1956c,
    1977b
Callaway, Paul- 1909a, 1939d
Calvé, Emma- 1942b
Calvocoressi, Michel- 1907h, 1923h, 1927h,
    1936h, 1944b
Camanini, Cleofonte- 1913d
Cambreling, Sylvain- 1986c
Cambridge Summer School of Music- 1946g
Cambridge Theater- 1930g
Camerata Singers- 1960g
Cammaerts, Émile- 1908f

Campanari, Giuseppe- 1927b
Campanella, Michele- 1947a, 1966e
Campanini, Cleofonte- 1910d, 1919b
Campbell, Elizabeth- 1988c
Campina, Fidela- 1913c, 1983b
Campo, Conrado del- 1953b
Campora, Giuseppe- 1924a, 1950c, 1955c
The Canada Music Book- 1970g
Canadian Academy of Music- 1911g
Canadian Broadcasting Co. SO- 1952g
Canadian League of Composers- 1951g
Canadian Music Centre- 1959g
Canadian Opera Co.- 1950g
Canadian Performing Rights Society- 1925g
Canberra Conservatory of Music- 1964g
Caniglia, Maria- 1905a, 1930c, 1938c, 1979b
Canin, Stuart- 1959e
Canteloube, Maria J. -1957b
Cantelli, Guido- 1920a, 1949c, 1956b
Canto- 1919g
Caovocoressi, Michel-
Cape Town SO- 1914g
Capecchi, Renato- 1923a, 1949c, 1951c
Capellen, George- 1903h, 1906h
Capet String Quartet II- 1903g; III- 1910g
Caplet, André- 1901e
Capobianco, Tito- 1984d
Cappuccilli, Piero- 1929a, 1957c, 1960c
Caramoor Festival- 1946g
Caravan of Dreams- 1983g
Card, June- 1942a, 1966c, 1985c
Carden, Joan- 1963c, 1971c, 1977c
Cardenas, Sergio- 1951a
Cardew, Cornelius- 1936a
Cardiff:
    C. Municipal Choir- 1942g
    C. (Herbert Ware) SO- 1918g
Carduff, Sylvia- 1966e
Carelli, Gabor- 1915a, 1951c
Carina, Maria- 1917c
Carlson, Claudine- 1977c
Carlson, Jane- 1947e
Carlson, Lenus J.- 1945a, 1973c, 1976f
Carlstedt, Jan- 1926a
Carlton, Jean- 1944e
Carlyle, Joan- 1931a
Carmichael, Hoagy- 1981b
Carmina String Quartet- 1984g
Carmirelle, Pina- 1914a
Carmirelle String Quartet- 1954g
Carnegie, Andrew- 1919b
Carner, Mosco- 1942h, 1944h
Carosio, Margherita- 1908a
Carner, Mosco- 1904a
Carpenter, John Alden- 1906f, 1913i, 1914i,
    1917i, 1918e, 1919i, 1921e, 1922i, 1926i,
    1928i, 1931i, 1933ei, 1937i, 1940i, 1941i,
    1942e, 1943i, 1945ei, 1948i, 1951b

D

G

International Bruckner Society- 1929g
International Composers Guild- 1921g
International Conference of Symphony and
    Opera Musicians- 1962g
International Congress of Strings- 1959g
International Electro-Acoustic Music Festival-
    1970g
International Electronic Music Competition-
    1968g
International Ermanno Wolf-Ferrari Society-
    1986g
International Federation of Choral Music-
    1982g
International Festival of the Americas- 1984g
International Festival of the Art Song- 1981g
International Folk Music Council- 1947g
International Frédéric Chopin Piano
    Competition- 1927g
International Gustav Mahler Society- 1955g
International Harp Contest- 1959g
International Institute for Comparative Studies
    and Documentation- 1963g
International League of Women Composers-
    1975g
International Library for African Music- 1953g
International Liszt Piano Competition- 1933g
International Music Center- 1961g
International Music Co.- 1941g
International Music Council- 1949g
International New Music Composer's Group-
    1987g
International Rostrum of Composers
    (UNESCO)- 1954g
International Society for Contemporary Music-
    1922g
International Society for Jazz Research- 1969g
International Society for Music Education-
    1953g
International Society for Musicology- 1927g
International Society of Organ Builders- 1957g
International Youth PO- 1987g
Internationale Arbeitsgemeinschaft für
    Hymnologie- 1959g
Internationales Musiker-Brief-Archiv- 1945g
Intimate Opera Co.- 1930g
Intimate Opera Group- 1957g
Ippolitov-Ivanov, Mikhail- 1900i, 1905d, 1934h,
    1935b
Ireland, John- 1904d, 1921i, 1913i, 1927f,
    1962b
Irish Folksong Society- 1904g
Irish Orchestra of London- 1911g
Irvine, Robert- 1963a
Irving, Robert- 1913a
Isaacson, - 1959h
Isador, Michael- 1951c
Isbin, Sharon- 1956a, 1977c, 1979c
Isherwood, Christopher- 1946f

Ishikawa, Shizuka- 1954a
Israel:
    I. Academy of Music- 1945g
    I. Chamber Ensemble- 1965g
    I. Chamber Orchestra- 1960g
    I. National Opera- 1947g
    I. Opera Co.- 1923g
    I. (Palestine) PO- 1936g
    I. String Quartet- 1939g
    I. Woodwind Quintet- 1963g
    New Opera Co. of I.- 1983g
Israeli Music Publications- 1949g
Istel, Edgar- 1948b
Istomin, Eugene- 1925a, 1943ce
Istomin, Marta- 1980d
Iturbi, José- 1928c, 1929cf, 1936d, 1980b
Ivanov, Mikhail M.- 1910h, 1927b
Ives, Burl- 1909a, 1948h, 1958h
Ives, Charles- 1900d, 1901i, 1902i, 1904i,
    1905i, 1906i, 1907i, 1908fi, 1909fi, 1910i,
    1911fi, 1912fi, 1913i, 1914i, 1915i, 1916i,
    1918f, 1924i, 1934f, 1947e, 1954b
Ives, Charles, Center for American Music-
    1980g
Ives and Myrick Insurance Co.- 1907g, 1909f
Ivey, Jean E.- 1923a
Ivogün, Maria- 1913c, 1922c, 1926c
Iwaki, Hiroyuki- 1956c
Izzo d'Amico, Fiamma- 1985c

J

Jablonski, Edward- 1980h
Jacchia, Agide- 1932b
Jachimecki, Zdzislaw- 1919h, 1953b
Jackendorff, R.- 1983h
Jackson, Carl A.- 1958a
Jackson, George- 1933h
Jacksonville College of Music- 1926g
Jacob, Gordon- 1931h, 1944h
Jacobi, Frederick- 1952b
Jacobo, Clara- 1928c
Jacobs, Arthur- 1973b
Jacobs, Max, String Quartet- 1912g
Jacobs, Paul- 1951c, 1983b
Jacobson, Robert- 1985h
Jacobsthal, Gustav- 1912b
Jacoby, Josephine- 1903c, 1948b
Jacon, Gordon- 1962h
Jacques, Janet E.- 1943a
Jacques, Reginald- 1969b
Jaques-Dalcroze, Emile- 1922h, 1950b
Jadassohn, Solomon- 1902b
Jadlowker, Herman- 1910c
Jagel, Frederik- 1924c, 1927c, 1982b
Jalas, Jussi- 1908a, 1945d
James, Carolyne- 1945a, 1970c
James, Harry, Band- 1939g

Menotti, Tatiana- 1931c
Menter, Sophie- 1918b
Menuhin, Hephzibah- 1920a, 1928c
Menuhin, Jeremy- 1951a
Menuhin, Yehudi- 1916a, 1926c, 1966e, 1972d, 1976e, 1985e
Menuhin, Yehudi, School of Music- 1963g
Meo, Cléontine de- 1927c
Mercer, Ruby- 1934e, 1937c
Der Mercur- 1909g
Mercure Musicale- 1905g
Meredith, Morley- 1962c
Merighi, Giorgio- 1962c, 1964c, 1977c
Merikanto, Aarre- 1951d
Merikanto, Oskar- 1911d
Merlet, Dominique- 1957e
Merli, Francesco- 1932c, 1976b
Mermaid Theater- 1951g
Merö(-Irion), Yolanda- 1902c, 1909c
Merolla, Robleto- 1975c
Merrill, Robert- 1917a, 1944c, 1945c, 1965h, 1977h
Merrimack Lyric Opera- 1985g
Merriman, Margaret- 1982h
Merriman, Nan- 1920a, 1940c, 1955c
Merritt, Chris- 1985f
Mersmann, Hans- 1971b
Mesplé, Mady- 1931a, 1953c, 1964c, 1973c
Messager, André- 1927e, 1929b
Messiaen, Olivier- 1908a, 1930di, 1933i, 1935i, 1936i, 1940f, 1941di, 1943i, 1944hi, 1948i, 1950(f), 1951i, 1952(f), 1953i, 1954(f), 1958i, 1960i, 1966d, 1967e, 1969i, 1970i, 1974i, 1983i, 1986i
Messner, Joseph- 1922d
Mester, Jorge- 1935a, 1955c, 1967d, 1968e, 1984d
Metallov, Vassili- 1926b
Metcalf, Frank- 1917h, 1928h, 1945b
Metropolitan Opera Auditions- 1936g
Metropolitan Opera Broadcasts- 1931g
Metropolitan Opera Guild- 1935g
Metropolitan Opera Studio- 1960g
Metternich, Josef- 1945c, 1953c
Metzger-Lattermann, Ottilie- 1922c
Meulen, Henk van der- 1955a
Mexican Academy of the Arts- 1966g
Mexican SO- 1928g
Meyer, Kerstin- 1952c, 1960c
Meyerhoff, Joseph, Symphony Hall- 1982g
M'Guckin, Barton- 1917b
Miami:
    Classic Opera of M.- 1975g
    Greater M. SO- 1965g
    M. Center for the Fine Arts- 1984g
    M. City Ballet- 1986g
    Opera Guild of M.- 1974g
Miami Beach SO- 1953g

Miaskovsky, Nicolai- 1906f, 1908i, 1911i, 1914i, 1918i, 1923i, 1926(f), 1927i, 1932i, 1933i, 1934i, 1940i, 1941i, 1943i, 1946i, 1950b
Michael, Hermann- 1984c
Michaelis, Ruth- 1933c
Michaels, Timothy C.- 1951a
Michalski, Raymond- 1933a, 1958c, 1965c, 1978b
Micheau, Janine- 1914a, 1933c, 1938c, 1976b
Michelangeli, Arturo- 1920a
Michigan:
    M. Opera Theater- 1971g
    M. State University School of Music- 1927g
Midwest National Band and Orchestra Clinic- 1947g
Mielke, Antonia- 1907b
Migenes(-Johnson), Julia- 1979c, 1987f
Mignone, Francisco- 1986b
Mikhailova, Maria- 1943b
Milan:
    M. Studio di Fonologia Musicale- 1955g
    Opera da Camera di M.o- 1957g
Milanov, Zinka- 1906a, 1927c, 1937c, 1966f, 1977d
Milashkina, Tamara- 1965c
Milburn, Ellsworth- 1938a
Milcheva, Alexandrina- 1987c
Mildenburg, Anna von- 1947b
Milenkovic, Stefan- 1977a, 1987c
Milhaud, Darius- 1913i, 1916fi, 1918fi, 1920i, 1921i, 1922fi, 1923i, 1924i, 1926i, 1927i, 1928i, 1929i, 1930i, 1936i, 1937i, 1938i, 1940fi, 1941i, 1942i, 1943i, 1944i, 1946i, 1948i, 1949i, 1950i, 1954i, 1957i, 1958i, 1962i, 1963i, 1971f, 1974b
Milhaud, Darius, Archive- 1985g
Milinkovic, Georgina von- 1937c, 1986b
Miljakovic, Olivera- 1966c
Miller, Dayton- 1916h, 1935h
Miller, Dolores- 1943d
Miller, Foster- 1932e
Miller, Frank- 1986b
Miller, Glenn- 1944b
Miller, Lajos- 1968c, 1980c
Miller, Mildred- 1951c
Miller, Ruth- 1917c, 1983b
Milles, Carl- 1945f
Millo, Aprile- 1958a, 1977e, 1980c, 1982f, 1984c, 1985e
Mills, Erie- 1983f, 1987c
Mills, John- 1947a, 1971c
Mills Music, Inc.- 1928g
Milnes, Sherrill- 1935a, 1965c, 1983e, 1984e
Miloradovich, Milo- 1932e
Milstein, Nathan- 1904a, 1920c, 1925f, 1929c, 1942f, 1967e, 1983e

Milwaukee:
    M. Civic Orchestra- 1921g
    M. Opera Co.- 1932g
    M. Performing Arts Center- 1969g
    M. SO- 1958g
Mimaroglu, Ilhan- 1926a, 1965i
Mims, Marilyn- 1988c
Mineva, Stefka- 1972c, 1985c
Minghetti, Angelo- 1922c
Minghini-Cattaneo, Irene- 1918c
Minkus, Alois- 1917b
Minneapolis:
    M. Auditorium- 1905g
    M. SO- 1903g
Minnesota:
    M. Composer's Forum- 1973g
    M. Opera Co.- 1962g
    University of M. Music Dept.- 1902g
Minot Opera Association- 1975g
Minton, Yvonne- 1938a, 1961e, 1964c, 1965f,
    1970c, 1973c
Mintz, Shlomo- 1957a, 1973c, 1978f
Mirecourt Trio- 1973g
Miriam, Alice- 1920c
Miricioiu, Nelly- 1983c
Mischakoff, Mischa- 1912c
Missiano, Eduardo- 1908c
Mississippi Opera Association- 1945g
Mitchell, Donald- 1963h
Mitchell, Howard- 1911a, 1949d, 1969f, 1988b
Mitchell, Leona- 1949a, 1975c, 1979e, 1985f
Mitropoulos, Dmitri- 1937c, 1946f, 1950d,
    1954c, 1960b
Mitsukuri, Shukichi- 1921b
Mitteilungsblatt der Internationalen Bruckner-
    Gesellschaft- 1971g
Miura, Tamaki- 1915c
Miyoshi, Akira- 1933a, 1960i, 1964i, 1973i
Mlynarski, Emil- 1904d
Mobile:
    M. Opera Guild- 1946g
Mocquereau, André- 1930b
Modern Jazz Quartet- 1952g
Modern Music Masters Society- 1952g
Moderne Music- 1923g
Mödl, Martha- 1912a, 1942c, 1957c
Moeran, Ernest J.- 1950b
Moevs, Robert- 1974d
Moffo, Anna- 1934a, 1955c, 1957c, 1959c,
    1984d
Mogilevsky, Evgeny- 1964e
Moiseiwitsch, Benno- 1908c, 1963b
Moldenhauer, Hans- 1906a, 1938f
Molinari, Bernardino- 1928c, 1952b
Molinari-Predelli, Francesco- 1966c
Moll, Kurt- 1938a, 1972f, 1975f, 1978c
Moll, Marquita- 1954c
Molleda, José Muñoz- 1934e

Mollenhauer, Gustav- 1914b
Mollica, Giulio- 1958c
Möllner, Niels- 1977d
Molnár, Antal- 1914h, 1925h, 1926h, 1929h,
    1930h, 1936h, 1940h, 1948h, 1969h, 1971h
Mompou, Federico- 1987b
Monaco, Mario del- 1915a, 1939c, 1950c,
    1963f, 1982b
Monk, Edwin- 1900b
Monk, Meredith- 1943a
Monk, Thelonious- 1982b
Monmart, Berthe- 1924a, 1951c
Montague, Diana- 1987c
Montarsolo, Paolo- 1956c, 1957c, 1974c
Monte, Toti dal- 1924c
Monteux, Pierre- 1911d, 1916f, 1917cd, 1924df,
    1929d, 1936df, 1942f, 1961d, 1964b
Montemezzi, Italo- 1941c
Montesanto, Luigi- 1909c, 1918c
Monteverdi Choir of London- 1964g
Montevideo:
    M. International Piano Competition-
        1968g
    M. Municipal SO- 1959g
    M. Orchestra- 1968g
    M. SO- 1931g
Monti, Augusto- 1922c
Monti, Nicola- 1940c
Montreal:
    Concours International de M.- 1965g
    Les Festivals de M.- 1936g
    Opéra de Montreal- 1981g
    Opera Guild of M.- 1942g
    Tudor Singers of M.- 1962g
Moog, Robert- 1934a
Moog, R.A., Co.- 1954g
Moore, Agnes- 1925c
Moore, Douglas- 1926i, 1928i, 1930i, 1931i,
    1935i, 1937i, 1939i, 1940d, 1941i, 1942h,
    1947i, 1948i, 1951i, 1956i, 1958i, 1961i,
    1966i, 1969b
Moore, Gerald- 1943h, 1967f, 1987b
Moore, Grace- 1901a, 1928c, 1947b
Moos, Paul- 1902h
Morales, Melesio- 1908b
Moran, Katherine- 1903c
Moran, Robert L.- 1937a
Moran-Olden, Fannie- 1905b
Moranzoni, Roberto- 1917c
Moravec, Ivan- 1930a, 1946c, 1964c
Moravian Music Foundation- 1956g
Moravian PO- 1951g
Moravian String Quartet- 1923g
Moréas, Jean- 1910b
Morel, Jean- 1903a, 1956c, 1975b
Morel, Marisa- 1938c
Morell, Barry- 1958c
Morelli, Carlo- 1922c, 1932c, 1935c

T

T. SO- 1947g
T. Youth SO- 1963g
Tumagian, Eduard- 1986c
Tuminia, Josephine- 1941c
Tureck, Rosalyn- 1914a, 1935c, 1958f
Tureck Bach Institute- 1981g
Turina, Joaquin- 1905f, 1912i, 1913f, 1914f,
    1916i, 1917i, 1920i, 1923i, 1929i, 1930d,
    1931i, 1946h, 1949b
Turner, Claramae- 1946c
Turner, Eva- 1916c, 1924f, 1929c
Turok, Paul- 1929a
Turp, André- 1950c
Twentieth Century Consort- 1975g
Tworkov, Jack- 1913f, 1981e
Tyers, John- 1952c
Tyl, Noel- 1936a
Tynes, Margaret- 1959c
Tyroler, Willi- 1911c

U

Uchida, Mitsuko- 1948a, 1963c, 1970f, 1985c
Uhde, Hermann- 1936c, 1955c
Uhl, Fritz- 1952c
Ulehla, Ludmila- 1966h
Ulfung, Ragnar- 1972c, 1977d
Ulms Conservatory of Music- 1921g
Ulrich, Homer- 1906a, 1948h, 1949h, 1952h
Ulster SO- 1966g
Ultan, Lloyd- 1977h
Unger, Heinz- 1965b
Unger, Max- 1959b
Uninski, Alexandre- 1932e
Universal Edition- 1901g
University of Arizona School of Music- 1934g
University of Louisville School of Music-
    1932g
University of Minnesota Music Dept.- 1902g
Uppman, Theodor- 1941c, 1953c
Upshaw, Dawn- 1984c, 1985ce
Upton, William T.- 1961b
Urlus, Jacques- 1913c
Ursprung, Otto- 1960b
Ursuleac, Viorica- 1922c, 1985b
Ussachevsky, Vladimir- 1911a, 1931f, 1935f,
    1936f, 1954i
USSR International Music Festival- 1981g
USSR State Choir- 1942g
USSR State SO- 1936g
Utah:
    U. Chorale- 1950g
    U. Opera Co.- 1976g
Uzunov, Dimiter- 1958c

V

Vaghi, Giacomo- 1901a, 1946c, 1978b

Vail, Edith- 1904c
Vajda, Frederick- 1925c
Valasek, Erno- 1941e
Valdengo, Giuseppe- 1936c, 1946c, 1947c
Valen, Fartein- 1906c, 1909f, 1916f, 1927f,
    1932f, 1935e, 1952b
Valencia Municipal Orchestra- 1943g
Valente, Benita- 1939a, 1950f, 1959f, 1960f,
    1962f, 1973c
Valentin, Erich- 1906b
Valentin de Carvalho, Music Publisher- 1914g
Valentini, Lucia- 1948a, 1970c
Valentino, Frank- 1930c, 1940c
Välki, Anita- 1962c
Valleria, Alwina- 1925b
Valletti, Cesare- 1921a, 1922a, 1947c, 1953c
Vallin, Ninon- 1934c
Valverde, Joaquin- 1910b
Van Allen, Richard- 1964c
Van Dam, José- 1961c, 1964e, 1967c, 1973f,
    1975c
Van den Borren, Charles- 1912h
Van der Bilt, Peter- 1983b
Van Dyck, Ernest- 1923b
Van Dyck, Rosina- 1908c
Van Kampen, Christopher- 1967c
Van Niessen-Stone, Matja- 1908c
Van Ree, Jena- 1978c
Van Rooy, Anton- 1903f
Van Vactor, David- 1906a, 1959i, 1966i, 1975i
Van Vulpen Brothers, Organ Builders- 1940g
Vancouver (B.C.):
    V. Chamber Choir- 1971g
    V. International Festival- 1958g
    V. Opera Association- 1961g
    V. Opera Co.- 1959g
    V. SO- 1931g
Vander Cook College of Music- 1909g
Vanelli, Adriana- 1985c
Vaness, Carol- 1952a, 1977c, 1978c, 1984cf
Vanguard Recording Society- 1949g
Vanni, Helen- 1956c
Vannuccini, Luigi- 1911b
Vanzo, Alain- 1954c
Varady, Julia- 1941a, 1978c
Varèse, Edgard- 1900g, 1903f, 1905f, 1907f,
    1910i, 1913f, 1915f, 1917c, 1922i,
    1923(f)i, 1924i, 1926i, 1927i, 1928f,
    1930(f), 1931i, 1934i, 1936i, 1937i, 1938f,
    1954i, 1957f, 1958i, 1961i, 1965be
Varga, Tibór- 1931c
Varnay, Astrid- 1918a, 1920f, 1941c, 1948f,
    1951f
Vartanyan, Ruben- 1988f
Vartenissian, Shakeh- 1954c
Varviso, Silvio- 1924a, 1944c, 1959c, 1961c,
    1965d, 1972d
Vásary, Tamás- 1962c

W

About the Compiler

CHARLES J. HALL is Professor of Music Theory and Composition and teacher of graduate Music History at Andrews University, Berrien Springs, Michigan. He has several publications to his credit and is a radio personality and prize-winning composer. His compositions have been performed by the Houston and Indianapolis Orchestras.